A REVELATION OF JESUS CHRIST

A Commentary on the Book of Revelation

A REVELATION OF JESUS CHRIST

BY J. B. SMITH

Author of Greek-English Concordance

EDITED BY J. OTIS YODER

*Professor of New Testament Language and Literature at
Eastern Mennonite College*

INTRODUCTION BY MERRILL C. TENNEY

Dean of Wheaton College Graduate School

HERALD PRESS, SCOTTDALE, PA.

A Commentary on the Book of Revelation
A REVELATION OF JESUS CHRIST

Copyright © 1961 by Mennonite Publishing House, Scottdale, Pa. 15683
Library of Congress Catalog Card Number: 61-7091
International Standard Book Number: 0-8361-1478-7
Printed in the United States

Fourth Printing, 1971

PREFACE

In many respects this commentary is more than simply another book. It represents a lifetime of studying and lecturing on the Book of Revelation by the late J. B. Smith. For many years he was in demand within his Christian fellowship to speak on this great book. One of his cherished hopes was to see the results of his labors sent forth in a commentary for the common man. This being his aim, studied effort was made to avoid the language of the scholar, yet at the same time Smith wanted to employ all the tools of Bible study.

The Book of Revelation contains a considerable number of textual variants. These, it will be observed, affected the author's interpretation. In his effort to ascertain the proper reading, he consulted the standard critical works as shown by the study, *Kings and Priests*, in the Appendices. While he usually accepted the received text as the reading, it was not always so, and when he deviated it was not without reasons. It may be noted that he placed rather strong emphasis on the intrinsic evidence, seeking to evaluate the manuscript evidence along with it to arrive at his conclusion.

At the time of his death the manuscript was in the custody of Herald Press, who secured the services of the late John L. Stauffer, of Harrisonburg, Virginia, to guide the typist in the first draft and to check the Scripture citations. Later the editor was selected to continue the work of preparing the manuscript for the publisher. It was with a sense of inadequacy yet challenge that the work was undertaken. Although it was necessary at times to rearrange materials, it is hoped that the commentary truly will be the author's work and that those who heard him lecture and now read the book may feel certain that although he is dead, yet he speaks.

Among the books Smith most often referred to in his study of Revelation the following may be listed: R. H. Charles, D. Litt., D.D., *A Critical and Exegetical Commentary on the Revelation of St. John*, Charles Scribner's Sons, New York, 1920 (2 vols.); Henry Barclay Swete, D.D., F.B.A., *The Apocalypse of St. John*, Macmillan and Company, Limited, London, 1911; Victorinus, the earliest of the writers on the Book of Revelation found in Vol. VII of *The Ante-Nicene Fathers*, edited by the Reverend Alexander Roberts, D.D., and James Donaldson, LL.D., the Christian Literature Company, Buffalo, 1886. Smith was very conscientious in letting the Bible be its own commentary; consequently there are frequent references to other prophetic books, viz., Daniel, Ezekiel, and Jeremiah, and to such passages as the Olivet Discourse of the Synoptic Gospels, I Thessalonians 4, II Thessalonians 2, *et al.* This relating of the various prophecies to the Book of Revelation is indeed a valuable feature of the commentary.

No doubt the most difficult part of the work of editing came at the point where it was necessary to place oneself into the thought framework of the author and make certain that what Smith wanted to say was being said. A few rather large gaps were filled in by the editor and indicated by brackets thus: [J. O. Y.]. In only one major section of the book was it found expedient to present a differing

v

interpretation. As indicated in the commentary, this was done, in fairness to Bible students of the same basic eschatological persuasion as the author.

The editor wishes to express his appreciation to the Herald Press for the opportunity of helping to bring this work to the reading public. His special thanks go to Ellrose D. Zook, Executive Editor of Herald Press, for his continuing encouragement, suggestions, and patience; to the late John L. Stauffer and to John L. Horst, the editor's counseling committee; to Merrill C. Tenney, Dean of the Graduate School, Wheaton College, Wheaton, Illinois, for reading the entire manuscript, for offering a number of helpful suggestions, and for writing the Introduction; to Mrs. Sanford (Merna Brenneman) Shank for the final typing of the manuscript; to his wife, Isabelle K. Yoder, for the painstaking reading of the manuscript for grammatical corrections; and to the friends who sustained a keen interest in the work.

It is to be deeply regretted that "Bro. J. B.," as he was affectionately called by his friends, could not live to see the printing of his lifetime work. It is hoped that the readers will remember that the author did not have opportunity to read the manuscript in its final form. Whatever blessing and inspiration students of the prophetic Word receive through the use of this commentary should be attributed to the prayerful study of the author. Any criticism of arrangement should fall to the editor and publisher.

The volume is sent forth, therefore, with a prayer that Jesus Christ, the "Alpha and Omega, the beginning and the end, the first and the last," will be pleased in these last days to use this book to inspire renewed hope in His soon return. No doubt the author would wish all who read to join him in praying with the seer, "Even so, come, Lord Jesus."

J. Otis Yoder

Homestead Hill
Harrisonburg, Virginia
August 24, 1960

VI

INTRODUCTION

The world outlook today for Christian believers is both alarming and hopeful. The disturbing conflict of a militant atheistic communism with the democratic traditions and at least partly Christian ideals of the free world, the rise of missionary activity in Buddhism and Islam that threatens to invade the Christian nations, and the growing ecclesiastical power of the church of Rome are some of the disquieting symptoms of the present hour. Christians are beginning to realize that the currents of history are changing. The social prestige and the political superiority which they have enjoyed in the past century are vanishing. They are finding themselves to be a minority group, hated by the world in general, and threatened with persecution, if, indeed, they are not enduring it already. Evangelical Christianity has been smothered in Spain, would not be tolerated in the Soviet Union were it not for political reasons, and is so hard pressed in China that some Chinese Christians have inquired if the great tribulation has already begun. Not since Constantine ended the imperial persecution of Christianity has the future seemed so threatening to the church of God.

For situations like this, the Book of Revelation has a definite message. It was written to churches of the first century to offer them a stimulus to repent of their sins, and to endure the trials that would beset them prior to the coming of the Lord. To churches menaced by persecution, weakened by corruption, and plagued by heresy the Lord spoke His message of encouragement: "Behold, I come quickly; and my reward is with me, to give every man according as his work shall be" (Revelation 22:12).

Although nearly nineteen centuries have passed since the seer of Patmos committed these words to paper and ink, they are still relevant to Christian thinking. Perhaps they apply even better to our period than to his because we are nearer the fulfillment of the coming of the Lord than was he. Many of the symbols seem more nearly literal as we enter the space age in which concepts like the mountain cast into the sea, the drying up of the Euphrates, and other bits of imagery are far less improbable than they used to be. We are beginning to realize that history is running on schedule, and that only God knows what the outcome will be. For our encouragement He has lifted part of the veil that we may go forward with Him confidently. Revelation is a directive which He has given to a pilgrim church in order that it may know what to expect from the world at large, and that it may not lose courage in the struggle with evil.

This commentary is an attempt to make plain the meaning of Revelation. With commendable reserve Dr. Smith has restricted himself largely to interpretation by other passages of Scripture which are related to Revelation by actual quotation or by striking parallelism. His painstaking studies of vocabulary and of related ideas make the book valuable to the earnest student of the Bible.

Dr. Smith is a futurist and a premillenarian, holding that all of the Book of Revelation beginning with the fourth chapter relates to the future period of judgment known as "the great tribulation," which will be followed by the personal return of Christ and by the establishment of His kingdom. In this regard he is in a

vii

long line of renowned commentators, including Seiss, Gaebelein, Ottman, and others.

The distinguishing feature of this commentary is its use of Biblical statistics and comparisons. The uses of important terms in the Revelation are cataloged, and their interpretation is derived from their context. The appendices contain some extensive studies of individual topics, correlating information not easily obtainable elsewhere.

Dr. Smith follows a literal interpretation except where avowed symbolism demands a different procedure. He has sought to make his exposition consistent in method and in results. His use of Greek is apt, and shows a careful investigation of the underlying vocabulary of the Greek text.

This commentary will probably be the mainstay of premillennial exposition for some years to come. It contains few novelties, though there are in it some fresh insights into the meaning of the Apocalypse. It is regrettable that the writer did not live to see his work completed, but, like the martyrs of the Apocalypse, "[his] works do follow . . . [him]."

Merrill C. Tenney

CONTENTS

Preface   v
Introduction   vii

INTRODUCTION   1

    The Name of the Book   1
    The Nature of the Book   3
    The Purpose of the Book   5
    The Scope of the Book   6
    The Importance of the Book   9
    The Interpretation of the Book   12
    The Occasion of the Book   29
    The Outline of the Book   30

PART I—THE PROLOGUE (1:1-8)
    The Preface (1-3)   32
    The Salutation (4, 5a)   38
    The Doxology (5b, 6)   41
    The Prophetic Forecast (7)   43
    The Divine Declaration (8)   45

PART II—THE THINGS WHICH THOU HAST SEEN (1:9-20)
    (The Apostle's Vision)
    The Antecedents of the Vision (9-12a)   48
    The Vision (12-16)   52
    The Effects of the Vision (17, 18)   54
    The Inspired Outline (19)   56
    The Interpretation of the Vision (20)   57

PART III—THE THINGS WHICH ARE (2:1-3:21)
    (The Messages to the Seven Churches)
    Introduction   61
    The Message to the Church at Ephesus (2:1-7) 62
        The Annunciation   62
        The Presentation   63
        The Declaration   63
        The Approbation   63

The Reprobation 64
The Exhortation 64
The Remuneration 65
The Message to the Church at Smyrna (2:8-11) 65
The Annunciation 65
The Presentation 66
The Declaration 66
The Approbation 68
The Reprobation 68
The Exhortation 68
The Remuneration 69
The Message to the Church at Pergamos (2:12-17) 70
The Annunciation 70
The Presentation 71
The Declaration 72
The Approbation 72
The Reprobation 72
The Exhortation 73
The Remuneration 74
The Message to the Church at Thyatira (2:18-29) 74
The Annunciation 74
The Presentation 75
The Declaration 76
The First Approbation 76
The Reprobation 77
The Second Approbation 78
The First Exhortation 78
The Remuneration 79
The Second Exhortation 81
The Message to the Church at Sardis (3:1-6) 81
The Annunciation 81
The Presentation 81
The Declaration 82
The First Reprobation 82
The First Exhortation 82
The Approbation 84
The Remuneration 84
The Second Exhortation 85
The Message to the Church at Philadelphia (3:7-13) 85
The Annunciation 85
The Presentation 86
The Declaration 86

x

The Approbation   86
The First Remuneration   87
The First Exhortation   89
The Second Remuneration   90
The Second Exhortation   91
The Message to the Church at Laodicea (3:14-22)   91
The Annunciation   91
The Presentation   92
The Declaration   92
The Approbation   92
The Reprobation   92
The Exhortation   93
The Remuneration   95

PART IV—THE THINGS WHICH SHALL BE HEREAFTER
(4:1–22:5, Events Following the Church Age)
1. The Church in Glory (4, 5)   101
The Open Door (4:1)   101
The Throne-Sitters (4:2-11)   102
The Sealed Book (5:1)   111
The Strong Angel (5:2-5)   111
The Lamb in the Midst of the Throne (5:6-10)   113
The Universal Praise to the Lamb (5:11-14)   116
2. The Tribulation (6:1–16:21)   120
The Seal Judgments (6:1–8:1)   120
The Lamb Opens the Seals (6:1)   120
The First Seal (6:2)   121
The Second Seal (6:3, 4)   121
The Third Seal (6:5, 6)   122
The Fourth Seal (6:7, 8)   123
The Fifth Seal (6:9-11)   123
The Sixth Seal (6:12-14)   125
The Episode of Sealing 144,000 of the Tribes of Israel (7:1-8)   127
The Episode of the Great Multitude (7:9-17)   133
The Seventh Seal (8:1)   136
The Trumpet Judgments (8:2–14:20)   137
The Seven Angels (8:2-6)   137
The First Trumpet (8:7)   139
The Second Trumpet (8:8, 9)   139
The Third Trumpet (8:10, 11)   139
The Fourth Trumpet (8:12)   140

The Angel Flying Through Midheaven (8:13) 140
The Fifth Trumpet (9:1-12) 141
The Sixth Trumpet (9:13-21) 146
The Episode of the Strong Angel and the Little
 Opened Book (10:1-11) 147
The Episode of Measuring the Temple (11:1, 2) 163
The Episode of the Two Witnesses (11:3-14) 168
The Seventh Trumpet (11:15-19) 176
The Episode of the Two Wonders and the War of
 Angels (12:1-17) 181
The Episode of the Beast Out of the Sea (13:1-10) 192
The Episode of the Beast Out of the Earth (13:11-18) 202
The Episode of the Lamb with the 144,000 on
 Mt. Zion (14:1-5) 208
The Angel Announcing the Everlasting Gospel
 (14:6, 7) 211
The Angel Announcing the Doom of Babylon (14:8) 214
The Angel Announcing the Doom of the Beast-
 Worshipers (14:9-13) 215
The Harvest of the Earth (14:14-20) 219
The Vial Judgments (15, 16) 222
The Prelude (15:1—16:1) 222
The First Vial (16:2) 228
The Second Vial (16:3) 229
The Third Vial (16:4-7) 230
The Fourth Vial (16:8, 9) 231
The Fifth Vial (16:10, 11) 232
The Sixth Vial (16:12) 233
The Episode of the Unclean Spirits (16:13-16) 234
The Seventh Vial (16:17-21) 236
3. Babylon, the Great (17:1—19:6) 240
The Mystery of the Woman and the Scarlet-colored
 Beast (17:1-18) 240
The Fall of Babylon (18:1-8) 249
The Three Lamentations of Men (18:9-19) 251
The Final Dirge of the Angel (18:20-24) 255
The Four Alleluias of the Saints (19:1-6) 257
4. The Marriage of the Lamb (19:7-10) 261
5. The Battle of Armageddon (19:11-21) 263
6. The Millennium (20:1-15) 268
The Binding of Satan (1-3) 268
The Reign with Christ (4-6) 270

xii

The Deception of the Nations (7-9)   274
The Doom of the Devil (10)   277
The Final Judgment (11-15)   278
7. The Great Finale (21:1-8)   281
8. The Holy Jerusalem (21:9—22:5)   286

PART V—THE EPILOGUE (22:6-21)   301

Appendices
1. Word Study of Revelation 6—19   309
2. Comparisons of I Thessalonians 4:13-18; Revelation 19:11-21; John 14:1-3   311
3. Visions of the Apocalypse Listed   313
4. The Seven Spirits Which Are Before the Throne   314
5. The Lord's Day   319
6. Death and Hades   324
7. The Ministry of Angels   326
8. As a Thief   328
9. To Blot Out of the Book of Life   329
10. From That Hour   331
11. Kings and Priests   334
12. The Glorified Groups of the Tribulation   339
13. The Holy City   340
14. The Two Witnesses   342
15. The Man Child   346
16. The Fall of Satan   349
17. The Preservation of Israel   351
18. The Tribulation   355
19. The Beast Out of the Earth   358
20. The Resurrection from the Dead   360
21. On Nonconformity   361
22. "Son" Applied to Christ   363

Bibliography   364

INTRODUCTION

In order to enable the reader to approach the study of this book in the most advantageous manner, careful attention needs to be paid to the following particulars: the name, the nature, the purpose, the scope, the importance, the interpretation, and the outline of the book.

I. *The Name of the Book.* It should be remembered that the titles of the books of the Bible are not a part of the sacred record. They were placed there by the editors of the various versions and editions. What is meant by the common title in the King James Version, "The Revelation of St. John the Divine," is that John was the human author or writer of the book. Not only is John's own testimony given on this point (1:9-11; 22:8), but the command for him to write occurs as often as twelve times. However, were the apostle living today he would doubtless not approve of the title in its entirety.

The real title of the book appears in the opening phrase, "A Revelation of Jesus Christ"—so the Greek. The absence of the definite article "the" is significant, for its presence would imply that reference is made to a previous revelation, whereas the absence of the article signifies that the book consists of a separate and distinct revelation. The word *revelation* means an unveiling or unfolding of things not previously known and which otherwise could not be known. And so the Apostle Paul explains: "By revelation he made known unto me the mystery . . . which in other ages was not made known unto the sons of men, as it is now revealed unto his holy apostles and prophets" (Ephesians 3:3, 5). It is noteworthy, too, that the word *mystery* occurs four times in the Book of Revelation and in each case explanation is made of what previously had not been known. 1:20; 10:7; 17:5, 7. The Greek word *apocalypsis* occurs eleven times in this sense. Luke 2:32; Romans 16:25; I Corinthians 14:6, 26; II Corinthians 12:1, 7; Galatians 1:12; 2:2; Ephesians 1:17; 3:3; Revelation 1:1. The word *revelation (apocalypsis)* is also used in reference to a future event when Jesus Christ will be revealed from heaven at which time every eye shall see Him. It is used seven times in this sense. Romans 2:5; 8:19; I Corinthians 1:7; II Thessalonians 1:7; I Peter 1:7, 13; 4:13.

Coming now to the consideration of the full title, "A Revelation of Jesus Christ," it appears, upon internal evidence, that the term may signify either (1) that the book reveals things about Jesus Christ not made known before, or (2) that the book tells about a future event, known as the Revelation of Jesus Christ, or (3) that Jesus Christ reveals or makes known the things recorded in the book. There is truth in each of the foregoing propositions.

The book does reveal things *about* Jesus Christ: what He is, as seen in the names applied to Him, and what He does.

What He is. There are certain names not previously applied to Him and which add new significance or emphasis pertaining to His nature, character, or

1

office: faithful witness (1:5); prince of the kings of the earth (1:5); Alpha (1:11); Omega (1:11); the first (1:11); the last (1:11); the living one (Greek) (1:18); the Amen (3:14); the . . . true witness (3:14); Lion of the tribe of Juda (5:5); Root of David (5:5); King of nations (Greek) (15:3); offspring of David (22:16); bright and morning star (22:16).

There are other names applied to Him before but which reappear with a new emphasis.

The Son of man. The reappearance of this name is highly significant. In the Gospels it is applied to our Lord 84 times, 21 of which are related to His second coming. The title all but disappears in the later Scriptures, occurring only once in the Acts where it is used by Stephen, the first Christian martyr (Acts 7:56), and only once again in all the intervening books in a quotation from the Psalms (Hebrews 2:6). The title occurs twice in this book. 1:13; 14:14. In both cases the use of the title is in connection with our Lord in His capacity as judge. This accords with what the Father says concerning the Son—He has committed all judgment to the Son because He is the Son of man. John 5:21, 27.

The Lamb. This term has been sparingly applied to our Lord in previous Scriptures: in type (Exodus 12:1-13); in prophecy by way of simile (Isaiah 53:6); metaphorically by John the Baptist when introducing Him to the multitude at the Jordan River (John 1:29); and then again by way of simile by the Apostle Peter in reference to His atoning work (I Peter 1:19). In the Revelation, however, the title is applied to Him 28 times. This frequency of the title *Lamb* in the last book of the Bible distinguishes it from all others, for lamb is the title of sacrifice and atonement. As such He verily was foreordained before the foundation of the world, yet in Revelation universal praise is accorded to Him forever and ever. He is the all-sufficient Saviour, "the Lamb of God, which taketh away the sin of the world."

What He does. He shows His servants things which must shortly come to pass. 1:1. He commands John to write what he sees in a book and to send it unto the seven churches which are in Asia. 1:11. He dictates to John the messages to the seven churches. Chapters 2, 3. He summons the seer to come up hither (i.e., to heaven) in order that He might show him things which must be hereafter. 4:1. He takes a book sealed with seven seals out of the hand of Him that sits on the throne. 5:1, 7. As Lamb, He stands in the midst of the throne. 5:6. He opens (one by one) the seals of the book. 6:1-17; 8:1. As Lamb, He stands on Mt. Zion. 14:1. As Son of man, He reaps the harvest of the earth. 14:14-16. He appears on a white horse with a sharp sword to smite the nations. 19:11 ff. He warns against adding to or taking from the words of this prophecy. 22:18, 19. He announces His speedy return. 22:7, 12, 20.

Thus clearly the book reveals new truth about Jesus Christ. The book also reveals a future event known as "The Revelation of Jesus Christ," by which is meant His personal revelation from heaven "in great power and glory."

There are numerous previous allusions to this great event both in the Old and New Testament Scriptures. For the present purpose two passages in the New Testament will be cited. The first (Matthew 24:29, 30) gives precisely the *time* of this revelation: *"Immediately after the tribulation of those days* shall the sun be darkened, and the moon shall not give her light, and the stars shall fall from heaven, and the powers of the heavens shall be shaken: and *then shall appear the sign of the Son of man in heaven:* and *then shall all the tribes of the earth mourn, and they shall see the Son of man coming in the clouds of heaven with power and great glory."* (Italics mine.) These are the words of the Lord Himself. Observe that His second coming is preceded by the tribulation period; that all the tribes of the earth shall mourn when they see Him coming. In the second passage (II Thessalonians 1:7, 8) the Apostle Paul uses the term, *the revelation of Jesus Christ:* "When the Lord Jesus shall be revealed from heaven [Greek: at the revelation of the Lord Jesus from heaven] with his mighty angels, in flaming fire taking vengeance on them that know not God, and that obey not the gospel of our Lord Jesus Christ." This is plainly a different phase of the Lord's coming described in Paul's previous letter (I Thessalonians 4:13-18) where the meeting of the Lord in the air is explained. Further studies will show that this meeting in the air takes place *before* the tribulation, while that in the second epistle quoted above (like the passage from Matthew's Gospel) refers to His coming *after* the tribulation and is described as the Revelation of the Lord Jesus from heaven. Besides these, note carefully two passages in Revelation.

"Behold, he cometh with clouds; and every eye shall see him, and they also which pierced him: and all kindreds of the earth shall wail because of him" (Revelation 1:7). This is a direct allusion to the passage in Matthew 24:30 spoken by the Lord, for the clause "all kindreds of the earth shall wail" is precisely identical (in the Greek) with that in Matthew, "all the tribes of the earth shall mourn."

The other passage is Revelation 19:11-21 and is too long to quote here. Suffice it to say that this is the only detailed description of the coming of the Lord from heaven in all the Bible, and that this coming occurs immediately after the tribulation period (described in chapters 6–18); furthermore that the Lord here comes from heaven with His saints; and finally that He comes to "smite the nations." Here, then, is an actual description of *the revelation of Jesus Christ* from heaven. Therefore, the book *does* record that future event.

Jesus Christ reveals the things written in the book. This is plainly declared in the first verse: "A Revelation of Jesus Christ, *which God gave unto him,* to shew unto his servants." This revelation has reference to the contents of the entire book. This being true, it follows that since the things *about* Jesus Christ, as well as the revelation *of* Jesus Christ from heaven, are a part of the book, the former includes the latter two.

The conclusion therefore is that the sense of the phrase given in the first proposition is the one that is primarily intended, namely, that by "A Revelation of Jesus Christ" is meant primarily that Jesus Christ reveals or shows to His servants the things written in this book [which things have to do with His character, conduct, and coming.—J. O. Y.].

II. *The Nature of the Book.* It is pre-eminently a book of prophecy. [By "prophecy" Smith meant prediction, and not "edification, and exhortation, and comfort" (I Corinthians 14:3).—J. O. Y.] It is so designated five times—once in the first chapter and four times in the last: "the words of this prophecy" (1:3), "the sayings [words] of the prophecy of this book" (22:7, 10, 18), "the words of the book of this prophecy" (22:19). Observe, too, that the book comes from the Lord God of the holy prophets. Thus John is brought into the succession of the great prophetic order through whom the sure word of prophecy came to men.

It is significant also that this is the only book in all the Scriptures that is expressly called a book of prophecy. Not only is it meant that the element of prophecy predominates in a general way, but the very words are declared to be words of prophecy. Hence, barring the introduction and conclusion, it must be of a prophetic character throughout in every part. To take away from the words of the book is to take away from "the words of the book of this prophecy." This point should be kept carefully in mind, for there are those who fail to recognize this point when they come to chapters 2 and 3.

That predictive prophecy is intended is evident from the fact that the opening verse refers to its contents as "things which must shortly come to pass." And again when the book closes, all that has been said is declared to be "things which must shortly be done" [Greek: come to pass] (22:6).

The prophetic character is further emphasized by the following considerations: in the frequency of its quotations from the Old Testament prophets, notably Isaiah, Jeremiah, Ezekiel, and Daniel; it contains over 400 quotations or allusions, of which over 50 are from the Book of Daniel; it deals with the same great prophetic themes and events regarding the future program of God as do the Old Testament prophets—the great tribulation; the beast or Antichrist; God's judgments upon Israel; God's judgments upon the nations; the great day of the Lord; the coming of the Lord; the future reign; the future glory.

It deals likewise with the great prophetic themes of the New Testament Scriptures: the apostasy of the church; the signs of His coming; the church in glory; the great tribulation; the Antichrist; the coming in great power and glory; the future reign; the ultimate glory.

In a special sense the book is a supplement to that of Daniel. Daniel was a man greatly beloved; so John was the disciple whom Jesus loved. To each was given a vision of things to come. Both were at the time in exile—the former in an alien country among the captives of Judah, the latter on the isle of Patmos "for [because of] the word of God, and for the testimony of Jesus Christ." Daniel is informed of a time of trouble such as never was. John devotes thirteen chapters to a description of this awful period. Daniel with eagerness makes request, "O my Lord, what shall be the end of these things?" He is informed, "The words are closed up and sealed till the time [season] of the end." John was commanded to write what he sees. 1:11. In 5:1 ff. he sees a book closed up and sealed, whereas in 6:1 ff. he sees the Lamb opening the sealed book.

It is significant that in the opening verses of Revelation there occurs the declaration, "the time [season] is at hand." After the church period has run its course (chapters 2 and 3) and the church is seen in glory (chapters 4 and 5), the sealed book is opened and the seals loosed by One who is worthy. Following this is a record of a series of judgments or plagues, answering to the "time of trouble"

(Daniel 12:1), culminating in the coming of the Lord in triumph taking vengeance upon His enemies.

The two seers continue to see eye to eye, for both declare that after the last world kingdom is destroyed, the kingdom of the Son of man will be established and He will reign with His saints upon the earth or, as Daniel says, "under the whole heaven."

There are yet synthesis, synchronism, symmetry, and symphony to consider in the nature of Revelation. By *synthesis* is meant that all the prophetic portions of the Old Testament and the New dealing with God's future program are here brought together in a connected whole—not one word which God has uttered will fall to the ground. By *synchronism* is meant an orderly arrangement of future events in chronological sequence. By *symmetry* is meant the harmonious arrangement of the prophetic program in all its parts, each having its proper place like the members of a body and thus constituting a symmetrical whole. By *symphony* is meant that there is no clash or disorder or discordant note when all the parts of the prophetic word are thus brought together.

III. *The Purpose of the Book.* The purpose of the book is clearly expressed in the first verse which declares that God gave it to Jesus Christ in order that He (Jesus) might show it unto His servants.

It is a matter both of interest and encouragement to the reader as he begins the study to call to mind a number of Scripture passages which stress the fact that God desires to show His word to His servants either directly or through His chosen vessels. A few follow: in the patriarchal period (Genesis 32:10); at the giving of the law (Deuteronomy 5:5); in the days of Samuel (I Samuel 9:27); in the time of David (Psalm 25:14); in the days of the later prophets—to Jeremiah (Jeremiah 33:3), to Daniel while in prayer that he might "understand the . . . [truth]" (Daniel 9:23); in the time of Jesus—at the close of His earthly ministry He declared, "He [the Spirit of truth] shall glorify me: for he shall receive of mine, and shall shew it unto you. . . . He will shew you things to come" (John 16:13, 14). (There is a probable allusion here to the Book of Revelation.)

But in no place in all the Bible is this desire of God to *shew* so strongly emphasized as in the Book of Revelation. The word occurs in seven passages and is used in introducing visions of special importance:

"Come up hither, and I will *shew* thee things which must be hereafter [lit. after these things]" (4:1).

"Come hither; I will *shew* unto thee the judgment of the great whore that sitteth upon many waters" (17:1).

"Come hither, I will *shew* thee the bride, the Lamb's wife" (21:9).

"And he carried me away in the spirit to a great and high mountain, and *shewed* me that great city, the holy Jerusalem, descending out of heaven from God" (21:10).

"And he *shewed* me a pure river of water of life, clear as crystal, proceeding out of the throne of God and of the Lamb" (22:1).

"The Lord God of the holy prophets sent his angel to *shew* unto his servants the things which must shortly be done [*come to pass* as in 1:1]" (22:6).

"And when I had heard and seen, I fell down to worship before the feet of the angel which *shewed* me these things" (22:8). While most of the passages tell about showing things to John, they are not intended for him only, but for all the servants of God. This is plainly declared in the first passage (1:1) and it is repeated by way of emphasis in 22:6. May the reader be as anxious to *know* as He is to *shew* the words of this prophecy.

IV. *The Scope of the Book.* By this is meant the range of materials contained in the book. This is briefly expressed in the opening verse as "things which must shortly come to pass." The same declaration is repeated in the closing chapter (22:6) after the "things" of the book have been presented in orderly fashion from beginning to end. In short, here is a detailed outline of the future program of God from the days of John on to the conclusion of the present order. It is not meant that all the things spoken of by prophets and apostles yet awaiting fulfillment are repeated here in detail. If that were the case, such repetition would not be revelation at all, for revelation implies making known that which was not previously revealed. It is true, however, that the things revealed in previous Scriptures concerning unfulfilled prophecies are clearly implied here. To note a few examples:

The rapture of the church. This subject has received due consideration by Jesus in such passages as Matthew 24:40, 41 and John 14:1-3, and by the Apostle Paul in I Corinthians 15:51-53 and I Thessalonians 4:13-17. Hence it is not repeated here, but that it is implied is clear from the fact that a group of redeemed ones come out of every kindred and tongue and tribe and nation and are seen in heaven seated on thrones (chapters 4 and 5) which, as will be seen, can represent none other than the church in a glorified state. Objection has been taken to the use of the term *rapture* on the ground that there is no Scriptural basis for it. The fact is that it is derived from the Latin *raptum* (see the Vulgate, I Thessalonians 4:17), and means to seize or snatch away.

The regathering of Israel. There are scores of passages in the Old Testament and several in the New which tell of the final regathering of Israel and their dwelling again in their own land, yet not a word is mentioned concerning that event in this entire book. However, their regathering is implied in chapter 7 by the sealing of 144,000 Israelites.

The future temple with its furniture. The prophets make special mention of a future temple as does also the Lord in His Olivet discourse. Both tell of the abomination of desolation standing in the holy place. Nothing is said about the building of the temple, yet in the tenth chapter, not only is the temple mentioned but the altar and the outer court as well.

The judgment of the nations. This is given in graphic outline in Matthew 25:31-46 and will take place "when the Son of man shall come in his glory, and all the holy angels with him." This important event is entirely omitted in the Revelation.

Coming now to those that are mentioned, note the following:

A vision of the Son of man is seen in the midst of the churches. 1:12-18.

The seven churches of Asia (chapters 2 and 3) present a prophetic forecast of church history from the days of John on to the close of the church age. Since the book purports to tell of the things which must shortly come to pass, it is unthinkable that the seer would pass over the entire church age without giving us an epitome of church history. Moreover, since the words of the book are declared to be words of prophecy, the words of chapters 2 and 3 necessarily must be words of prophecy. Accordingly, the conditions prevailing in the seven churches are prophetic or anticipative, in the order mentioned, of universal church conditions from the days of John on to the close of the church age. It should be recognized, too, that the present age is the Laodicean age, for that church alone of all the seven depicts in clear outline the conditions of apostasy prevailing in Christendom today.

Next is *the vision of the church in glory*. Chapters 4 and 5. In all the chapters following there is no mention again of the church until after the prophetic program has reached its end (22:5), whereupon in the hortatory portion of the epilogue the church is once more mentioned (22:16); thus showing that while the entire book is *for* the church, only a small portion is *about* the church.

In chapters 4 and 5 the evidence is sufficiently clear that the church, declared to be kings and priests (1:6), is in a glorified state (4:4; 5:10). In the succeeding chapters she is seen a number of times in that condition, whereas chapter 19 records the marriage supper of the Lamb. This is followed by the church coming with Christ out of heaven when He appears (after the tribulation) in power and great glory. Clearly, since the church follows Christ out of heaven, she must have been taken up into heaven before this time. Chapters 4 and 5 may be considered as descriptive of the throne sitters and the crown wearers.

In chapter 6 is found *the opening of the sealed book by Christ as the Lamb*. He does not open it until after the redeemed and glorified church proclaims His worthiness to do so. 5:9, 10. The opening of the sealed book brings the first series of judgments upon the earth. The chapter may be remembered as that of the *seal* judgments.

In chapter 7 mention is made of two groups—the first part tells of 144,000 Israelites who are sealed in order that they might be exempt from the torment of a coming plague, while the latter part of the chapter tells about a second glorified group which comes out of the great tribulation. Chapter 7 may be designated as comprising *the sealed Israelites* and *the robe wearers*.

Chapters 8 and 9 describe *the trumpet judgments*. During the sixth judgment alone one third of mankind perish.

Chapter 10 describes *a little book which the seer is requested to eat*. The message of the book is to the effect that he must prophesy again before many peoples and nations and tongues and kings.

In chapters 11 to 13 certain time notes appear, indicating the *middle of the tribulation period*. The Gentiles (nations) will tread underfoot the holy city (Jerusalem) forty-two months. 11:2. Two witnesses are mentioned who, after 1,260 days, having finished their testimony, are killed by the beast (the final Antichrist), who emerges out of the bottomless pit at this time. The witnesses ascend to heaven. Men who are eyewitnesses fear and glorify God at the sight, while the host of the redeemed (apparently the two glorified groups before mentioned), in consquence of this event, anticipate the final triumph of righteousness upon earth as they jubilantly proclaim, "The kingdoms of this world are become the kingdoms of our Lord, and of his Christ."

Chapter 12 attests likewise *the beginning of the final triumph.* The angel Gabriel in conflict with Satan casts him and his angels upon the earth. 12:9. Dwellers in heaven rejoice. And no wonder, for if one of God's creatures is mightier than Satan and his angels, there can be no question about the final issue when the Lord Himself comes into conflict with the forces of evil.

In contrast with the rejoicing in the heavens, woe is announced as coming upon the earth, for the devil is come down, having great wrath. Having failed in his war in heaven, Satan now determines to win the conflict upon earth. This is the third woe. 12:12.

For this purpose (as chapter 13 shows) he associates with himself two infernal agents, *the beast out of the sea and the beast out of the earth.* The former represents the political system of the world and the latter, the apostate and corrupt religious system, later called the false prophet. 19:20. These three, the dragon (Satan, 20:2), the beast, and the false prophet, constitute a diabolical trinity demanding universal homage and worship. Satan energizes both the beast and the false prophet with his own power. The latter makes an image of the beast; whereupon an edict goes forth that all men worship the image on pain of death.

Chapter 14. *First is the episode of the 144,000,* evidently identical with those of chapter 7. Then follows *a series of angel-messengers* announcing the everlasting Gospel, the fall of Babylon, and the judgment of those who worship the beast. The Son of man with a sharp sickle appears to reap the earth's wicked. *The time of the divine judgment* has come!

Chapter 15. This chapter introduces *the vial judgments,* which are the last and most intense of the three series.

Chapter 16. *The outpouring of the vials* occurs in this chapter. Some point needs to be made of the similarity of the first four to the trumpet judgments. Warning is given in the words, "I come as a thief." Reference is made again to the fall of Babylon. The vision of the three unclean spirits as frogs leaping from the mouths of the dragon, the beast, and the false prophet is seen.

Chapter 17. *The judgment of Babylon,* designated as the great whore, is shown as drawing near. The particulars of the vision of the woman and the seven-headed, ten-horned beast are explained.

Chapter 18. *The fall of Babylon is revealed.* The cause, severity, and totality of the judgment are shown. Kings, merchants, and shipmasters lament her downfall.

Chapter 19. *The marriage supper of the Lamb* is announced. Three glorified groups rejoice over the destruction of Babylon and acclaim God as just and true. Heaven is seen opened and the White Horse Rider emerges to take vengeance on His enemies. The battle with the beast and kings of the earth is described.

Chapter 20. *The triumph of Christ is unveiled.* Herein is contained the binding of Satan, the first resurrection, the millennial reign of Christ, the doom of Gog and Magog and of Satan, and the great white throne judgment and the doom of the wicked.

Chapter 21. *The new heaven and new earth* are created. The holy city comes down from God out of heaven. Three promises are given to the faithful. The doom of the wicked is reiterated and the holy Jerusalem described.

Chapter 22. The river of the water of life and the tree of life are seen. The curse is removed. *The final state* and fixed reward are revealed. The longing for the return of Christ pulsates from the heart of the seer, and the church, and the Spirit.

[Due to the fact that the scope of chapters 18—22 was not included by the author, chapters 14—17 were condensed from the notes and 18—22 written for completeness.—J. O. Y.]

V. *The Importance of the Book. The inspirational emphasis.* No other book in the Bible is so strongly supported as to its divine inspiration. The entire Godhead is engaged in its deliverance to man—God gave it to Christ, Christ revealed it, the Spirit spoke to the churches, and it came to man through the medium of an angel. We may say, therefore, the book is from God, of Christ, by the Spirit, through an angel, unto John, for His servants. Or to confine ourselves to the opening verses (1-3), God thought it, Christ showed it, an angel brought it, John wrote it.

The place in the canon. Were it not for this book, the Bible would end with Jude. There would be no word of hope for the Jew, or the nations. The church of God would be pictured as having in her fellowship "certain men [who] crept in unawares . . . turning the grace of our God into lasciviousness, and denying the only Lord God, and our Lord Jesus Christ" (Jude 4). What a sad outlook were Jude the last word from heaven! Let us thank God for the Book of Revelation, for it closes the sacred volume in a manner consistent with the dignity and honor of its divine Author and in complete harmony with His eternal purpose.

The time of its deliverance to man. The book was written near the close of the first century. Jesus had returned to heaven some 60 years previous. This fact would show that the contents of the book must be of tremendous importance. Surely anyone who has neglected its contents or advised others to let it alone has not duly considered its divine source nor the remarkable manner of its deliverance to man.

The promise of blessing. This is the only book of the Bible which distinctly promises a blessing upon those who faithfully peruse its contents. The words are, "Blessed is he that readeth, and they that hear the words of this prophecy, and keep those things which are written therein" (1:3). Thus the promise appears in the opening of the book, apparently to encourage the believer to read the entire book in the hope of enjoying the blessing promised. The clause that follows, *for the time is at hand,* expresses the motive in the study of the book. The thought is, hear the words and keep the things written therein that you may be ready when the *time* comes.

Observe, too, the promise of blessing is repeated at the close of the book— "Blessed is he that keepeth the sayings [words] of the prophecy of this book" (22:7). This promise is prefaced by the words, "Behold, I come quickly." From these words it may be inferred that the *time* referred to in the former passage is the imminent coming of the Lord. *Keeping* (i.e., cherishing or meditating upon) alone is repeated in the latter passage, indicating that the keeping is more important than merely reading and hearing. In other words, reading and hearing should be with a view to keeping.

It is noteworthy, too, that whereas the book contains seven beatitudes, two of these tell of the importance of keeping the words of the book.

The inviolability. The contents of the book are not to be tampered with in any way, but they are to be regarded as sacred and of supreme importance. It is declared in a twofold manner near the very close of the book, "If any man shall add unto these things, God shall add unto him the plagues that are written in this book." Also, "If any man shall take away from the words of the book of this prophecy, God shall take away his part out of the book of life" (22:18, 19). Just as there is a double blessing pronounced upon the one that takes a right attitude toward the book, so a double curse is pronounced upon the one that takes a wrong attitude toward it.

One need not write another chapter to add to its contents, nor Jehoiakim-like cut away bit by bit with a penknife, to take away from it. One may take away by sheer neglect or, as some have done, advise others to "let it alone." Or one may add to the book either by rationalizing or by spiritualizing. In the former case, matters of miracle or revelation are made to conform to the dictates of unsanctified reason, while in the latter, imagination runs loose and the plain literal sense of language becomes a prey to the whims and meanderings of a fanciful brain.

One should look long enough at these words of warning to recognize the terrible implications of adding to the words. The punishment of this one is that God will add to him the plagues written in this book. Now it is clear that these plagues will be inflicted during the tribulation period. So the inference is that the curse applies directly to those who will not be ready when the Lord comes. Those who add to the words will remain here and suffer the plagues of the tribulation period.

There is a warning against taking away from the words. The punishment of this one is that God will take away his part out of the book of life. This shows that he has been a saved man. What will happen to one whose name is not found in the book of life? The word is plain—"Whosoever was not found written in the book of life was cast into the lake of fire" (20:15). Remember—the writer does not say these things; he is merely calling attention to what God says in the words of the book. A great commentator has called these verses an interpolation: i.e., he takes these very words from the book. May God have mercy!

The prophetic character. The book is important because it is a book of prophecy. The Bible consists of more prophetical books than of any other kind. In the English Old Testament there are 17; the Hebrew Bible listed 21 as prophetical. To these must be added the Book of Revelation, besides the portions in books of the New Testament not listed as prophetic.

Various witnesses to the importance of prophecy will help to amplify this fact.

The testimony of one of the books not listed as prophetic: "Believe his prophets, so shall ye prosper" (II Chronicles 20:20).

The testimony of Christ. He severely rebuked certain disciples who betrayed their ignorance and neglect of the words of prophecy. His words are, "O fools, and slow of heart to believe all that the prophets have spoken" (Luke 24:25). And again, "All things must be fulfilled, which were written in the law of Moses, and in the prophets, and in the psalms, concerning me" (Luke 24:44). The Old Testament was divided into the three portions indicated; so this shows plainly that the entire Old Testament was regarded as prophetic by our Lord.

The testimony of the Apostle Paul. In his defense before Felix he declared, "So worship I the God of my fathers, believing all things which are written in the law and in the prophets" (Acts 24:14). It is significant that in his first writing (I Thessalonians 5:20) he makes the admonition, "Despise not prophesyings" [Greek—the same word as in Revelation 22:18, 19].

The testimony of Peter. In referring to the "word of prophecy" he declares, "Whereunto ye do well that ye take heed in your hearts as unto a light that shineth in a dark place, until the day dawn, and the day star arise" (II Peter 1:19). (Note —"in your hearts" occurs at the end of the verse in the KJV, but we have inserted it here for the sake of emphasis; it really modifies "take heed.")

The testimony of the angel Gabriel. Daniel the prophet had understood by the books that the captivity of his people (Israel) was to continue 70 years. Daniel 9:1, 2. He then gave himself to prayer and confession that he might know God's plan and purpose regarding the future of his people. God immediately sent Gabriel to inform Daniel on this matter. So Gabriel testified, "O Daniel, I am now come forth to give thee skill and understanding. At the beginning of thy supplications the commandment came forth, and I am come to shew thee; for thou art greatly beloved: therefore understand the matter, and consider the vision" (9:22, 23). The angel then proceeds to show Daniel the duration of the future of his people. In a later vision the angel again appears and declares: "Now I am come to make thee understand what shall befall thy people in the latter days . . ." (10:14). He addresses him as "O Daniel, a man greatly beloved" (10:11), "O man greatly beloved" (10:19). Two times these striking words are applied to Daniel, and observe the *time* of this remarkable address—it was when he was seeking to know things pertaining to the future of his people. No such words of endearment are to be found elsewhere in Holy Writ. Here, then, is God's own estimate of a man interested in things to come. There are those who take the position that we need not concern ourselves regarding things to come—just so we are faithful in our present tasks, the future will take care of itself. It is certainly a reflection upon the wisdom of Him who gave this book to hold the view that prophetic truth has no practical value, since He stresses the importance of this book as He does no other.

This is a dark period of the world's history. Evil in all its forms is increasing. Problems, political and religious, are bewildering the greatest thinkers of the day. Fortunately God has not left men to seek light and guidance from the guesses and prognostications of the wise men of the times. The Book of Revelation purports to contain a record of things to come. In it is a preview of the closing events of the world's history. It was written by the unerring hand of divine inspiration. Not one word shall fall to the ground. It warns not only of coming catastrophes, but it inspires the believer with hope in prospect of coming glories.

Because of its intrinsic worth, men in olden times searched and inquired about, and angels desired to look into, the things written beforehand pertaining to the first coming of Christ. Truly men should not fail in their partnership with angels to be similarly searching and inquiring about the things of His second coming [which for the Christian is also of intrinsic worth.—J. O. Y.].

The only consistent attitude for every believer to take is to recognize its importance since God, Christ, the Spirit, the angel, and John regard it as important.

VI. *The Interpretation of the Book.* Several fundamental rules apply to the interpretation of the whole body of Scripture. (These will be followed by several suggestions applying in particular to the Book of Revelation.)

Faith. Says the apostle: "Through faith we understand that the worlds were framed by the word of God . . ." (Hebrews 11:3). In other words, we understand how God made all things by believing the creation story as written in the first book of the Bible. Similarly we understand things to come by believing what is written in the last book of the Bible. Just as men who have relied upon reason to understand how all things came into being have failed in their conclusions, so have those failed to understand the last book of the Bible who, instead of believing the things that are written, have relied on the process of reason or the vagaries of spiritualization. "Through faith we understand." Regarding things material "seeing is believing," but as pertaining to spiritual things, believing is seeing. This was the order Jesus gave—Believe and ye shall see. John 1:50; 11:40; 20:29. And Paul—"Believe and know the truth" (I Timothy 4:3). The unbelieving reversed this order: "What sign shewest thou then, that we may see, and believe" (John 6:30)? "Descend now from the cross, that we may see and believe" (Mark 15:32). So did doubting Thomas. John 20:29a. Too much cannot be made of this point. Someone says, "I don't understand the book." A more important matter is, Do you believe it? If the question be asked, "How can I believe it?" the answer is, "Read it." "Faith cometh by hearing and hearing by the word of God" (Romans 10:17). "God says it, I believe it, that settles it" should be the attitude of every child of God. Read the book and faith will come, and with it understanding.

Prayer. This is another important key to Bible knowledge. Two passages will suffice. "Open thou mine eyes, that I may behold wondrous things out of thy law" (Psalm 119:18). "Call unto me, and I will answer thee, and shew thee great and mighty things, which thou knowest not" (Jeremiah 33:3). The former passage stresses the desire to know; the latter, God's willingness to show. The Book of Revelation is a book of great things. The word "great" occurs 84 times. Mention is made of 35 different great things. Great voices are heard 20 times. There are also mighty things in the book—the word "mighty" occurs seven times. (Greek.) The promise for Jeremiah has therefore a special fitness in the study of the Book of Revelation, for we all appear to be conscious that here there are great and mighty things which we know not. We may be certain, however, that if we read, and hear, and keep the things written in this book, He will show us the great and mighty things written therein. Prayer is one of the important keys that opens the treasury of truth. The average person who approaches the book by faith and prayer is on a better way to understand the book than the scholar who substitutes reason for faith and self-sufficiency for prayer. In such a case the saying is true, "A saint on his knees sees farther than a philosopher on his tiptoes." [Better yet is the man trained in mind as a scholar, plus the experience in heart of honest faith in God.—J. O. Y.]

A third fundamental rule of interpretation must not go unheeded—*the guidance of the Holy Spirit*. It is the Spirit that speaks unto the churches. He alone who moved men to write the Scriptures can move men to rightly interpret and understand the book. The promises are precious: ". . . when he, the Spirit of truth, is come, he will guide you into all truth . . . he will shew you things to come" (John 16:13). ". . . the anointing which ye have received of him abideth in you . . . the same anointing teacheth you of [concerning] all things" (I John 2:27). ". . . we have received . . . the spirit which is of God; that we might know the things that are freely given to us of God" (I Corinthians 2:12).

A fourth key is *application*. Someone has said, "Salvation comes by faith, but a knowledge of the Word by works." It appears appropriate that the word "works" occurs 22 times in the book, once for each chapter.

The law of first mention may be added as a fifth. The first mention of a word in Scripture is always highly important to its proper interpretation. The meaning of a word can usually be determined by its use in the first mention. By way of illustration we cite the first mention of seven words.

God. Genesis 1:1. The word means the powerful One. This is seen in that He created the heaven and the earth.

Sanctify. Genesis 2:3. God sanctified the seventh day; that is, He set it apart for a sacred use. This idea of "set apart" is seen in the word "sanctify" in all its uses throughout Scripture.

Grace. Genesis 6:8. "But Noah found grace in the eyes of the Lord." A remarkable illustration of grace, seeing that in the preceding verse the Lord said, "I will destroy man whom I have created."

Believe. Genesis 15:6. "He [Abram] believed in the Lord; and he counted it to him for righteousness." A most notable example of faith when we recall that this was said of him after he was told that his seed would be as the stars of heaven, although he was now childless and nearly one hundred years old.

Mercy. Genesis 19:19. It was Lot who declared, "Thou hast magnified thy mercy." A remarkable exhibition of the Lord's mercy. He had pitched his tent toward Sodom and made his habitation in that corrupt and now doomed city. In spite of his failings the Lord delivered him. No wonder he declared, "Thou hast magnified thy mercy." After all, the Lord knew that Lot's righteous soul was vexed at the wickedness of the city.

Love. Genesis. 22:2. The Lord gave orders to Abraham: "Take now thy son, thine only son Isaac, whom thou lovest . . . and offer him . . . [as] a burnt offering." The point here is in the words, "thine only son Isaac, whom thou lovest . . . and offer him . . . [as] a burnt offering." Abraham's love for Isaac, his only son, is typical of God's love for His only begotten Son, and so was the offering typical. In the offering of his son, Abraham's love was not diminished, but rather heightened, for his son. It would mean death, but he accounted that "God was able to raise him up, even from the dead," "whence also he received him in a figure." This accords with Abraham's testimony to the young men: "I and the lad will . . . come again to you" (Genesis 22:5).

Praise. Genesis 29:35. "Now will I [Leah] praise the Lord: therefore she called his name Judah." The word "praise" (Hebrew: Judah) means literally "give thanks." Leah had six sons, but only once did she thus express her thankfulness. Judah is the progenitor of Christ; hence the title occurring in our book, "the Lion of the tribe of Juda" (Revelation 5:5).

We herewith submit the testimonies of three great Bible scholars on the importance of first mention: "The first occurrence of a word, or an expression, or an utterance is the key to its subsequent usage and meaning; or at least a guide as to the essential point connected with it."[1] "I find in Scripture a principle of interpretation which I believe, if conscientiously adopted, will serve as an unfailing guide as to the mind of God as contained therein: The first mention of a thing, the very first words of any subject of which the Holy Spirit is going to treat are the keystone of the whole matter."[2] "The only unfailing method of interpreting Scripture is the structural method. Where do you first hear of any matter, and where the end of it? Then compare the beginning and the end, in order to get a firm grasp of the general character of all that intervenes."[3]

The principle of first mention is accordingly one of the most important factors in the correct interpretation of our book. As the reader begins the study of the book, he will at the very first find words and phrases which have occurred in previous Scriptures. Attention has already been called to the use of the first phrase, "the Revelation of Jesus Christ." It was found that it is used in three different senses and that its use in the book makes it clear in what sense it is to be understood in the opening verse. The use of the word "shew" has also been illustrated by pertinent passages beginning with the first mention. Genesis 32:10.

The phrase, "things which must shortly come to pass" (verse 1), occurs elsewhere (in whole or in part) seven times. The word "shortly" can likewise only be understood by its use in previous Scriptures. The same is true of the phrase, "the time is at hand," in verse 3. To the careful student two questions will at once present themselves: What particular time is meant? What is to be understood by the term "at hand"? The meaning of words is determined by their use. It is vitally important therefore to discover their first use and then proceed to examine all the uses in succeeding passages. To the extent this is faithfully done, to that extent will one have a full understanding of the word or phrase in question. The law of first mention does not only apply to the Bible as a whole, but is especially applicable to the contents of the Book of Revelation in itself. No matter where he reads, the student will at every turn meet with words or phrases that have been mentioned previously in the book. If the meaning of these is not clear, the reader should turn back to the place where the language is first used and then continue with subsequent uses until he gets to the passage before him. Such examination and meditation will always be illuminating.

The law of full mention. By this is meant that all the passages of a given word or subject must be carefully considered in the course of interpretation. Only when this work has been carefully done, may the interpreter be sure of his conclusions, for the omission of only one important passage may result in serious error.

Again, when it is found that one word is the equivalent of another, all passages thus related should likewise be considered. For instance, in the study of the living creatures (beasts of chapter 4), when it is observed that the living creatures are identical with the cherubim or the cherubim are identical with the living creatures (Ezekiel 10:15, 20), all the passages mentioned containing the word *cherubim* should be duly considered in all its occurrences.

The law of antecedent mention. This applies in particular to prophetic events in the distant future. To illustrate: Let us note that prophecy is merely history written in advance. History is nothing more than the sum total of the succession of events. They are so related that any given event is the result of preceding causes and the cause of succeeding effects. No good historian would undertake to describe any important event in history without first relating the causes leading up to it. Similarly, when a prophet foretells a future event, he either assumes a knowledge of foregoing events or, as is frequently the case, prefaces the distant disclosure by related events leading up to it. For example: When Daniel is about to tell Nebuchadnezzar what shall be in the latter days (2:28) and what should come to pass hereafter (2:29), he begins with Nebuchadnezzar himself. "Thou, O king, art a king of kings. . . . Thou art this head of gold" (2:37, 38). Thus he continues with the three remaining Gentile world kingdoms. Following this he declares that the "God of heaven [will] set up a kingdom, which shall never be destroyed . . . but it shall break in pieces and consume all these kingdoms," and then concludes: "the great God hath made known to the king what shall come to pass hereafter [literally, after these things, that is, after the world kingdoms have run their course]" (Daniel 2:44, 45).

Another illustration of the law of antecedent or intervening mention is found in Daniel 10:14 ff. Here Gabriel informs Daniel, "I am come to make thee understand what shall befall thy people [Daniel 9:20] in the latter days." He then proceeds (Daniel 11:1 ff.) by showing Daniel that three kings shall yet arise in Persia; then follows with a brief survey of events up to the time of the end, including the "time of trouble," at which time Daniel's people ("every one that shall be found written in the book") shall be delivered. Daniel 12:1.

In Revelation 1:7 there is an instance which may be designated "the law of antecedent or prophetic mention" in which a future event is spoken of as already at hand. In prophetic literature the chief purpose appears to be to inspire encouragement and hope in the faithful and warn the wayward and wicked with a view to repentance and amendment of life. As is frequently the case, present conditions have a vital relationship to the far-off event and, as already mentioned, intervening events lead up to the latter through a series of causes and effects in which each effect becomes the cause of succeeding effects until the end of the chain is reached. Now let us apply the law of antecedent mention to the leading events recorded in the Book of Revelation. The prophetic event named is the coming of the Lord in the clouds. What are the events leading up to it?

First is a description of the church age. The existence of the church is itself the effect or result of Israel's failure—Israel was cut off and the Gentiles were grafted in. Revelation 1, cf. Romans 11.

The history of the church leads up to her apostasy (Revelation 2, 3), at which time the faithful few will be caught up to be with the Lord. Revelation 4, 5. As a result of this, the great tribulation will follow, which will be the time of Jacob's trouble as well as the time of judgment upon the nations. Revelation 6.

The result will be that a great multitude of the nations will learn righteousness and come out of the great tribulation having washed their robes and made them white in the blood of the Lamb. Revelation 7. Besides these a remnant of Israel will be saved—the first fruits unto God and to the Lamb. Revelation 14.

When judgments fail to bring the guilty to repentance, *the Lord will come with clouds*, at which time He will destroy the obdurate and impenitent among the nations (Revelation 19), after which the "rest of the nations" and "all Israel will be saved" and worship the Lord at Jerusalem. Revelation 20—22.

The literal interpretation. The discussion in regard to this matter must necessarily be brief and confined principally to the subject matter of Revelation.

An important rule of interpretation is that *what is literal must explain the figurative and never should the figurative be used to explain the literal.* Faith believes what is literal and understands what is figurative if elsewhere explained, either expressly or by implication, but the interpretation that is necessarily based only upon reason is in all probability erroneous. There are those who go to profane authors for the interpretation of symbols. On this point Archbishop Trench remarks: ". . . this book moves exclusively within the circle of sacred, that is, Jewish imagery and symbols; nor is the explanation of its symbols in any case to be sought beyond this circle."[4]

"In cases where the context does not immediately explain the symbols employed, a safe method of interpreting them is this. Ascertain what other parts of Scripture which are not symbolic reveal respecting the subjects in question. Then seek to express in Scripture-symbols the truths thus ascertained. If we find the symbols we so select, to be similar to those which the passage we are considering employs, we need feel no hesitancy as to the interpretation."[5]

To illustrate: "I . . . have the keys of hell and of death" (1:18). What is meant by the keys? We turn to Matthew 16:19: "I will give unto thee the keys of the kingdom of heaven." The context shows that by the keys, Jesus meant authority.

Since so much importance is attached to the *words* contained therein, it would appear that they should be interpreted in their plain literal sense unless, or in case, evidence in the book itself appears to the contrary. We may be certain that we are not left to guesses as though we had here a catena of riddles. Again, if the words as they occur are not to be tampered with, no one will need fear that it will not be safe for a teacher to give the words to men as he finds them written in the book, and the student need not hesitate to believe them in the form God has given them. In the interpretation of symbolism and figurative language as well as in any portion of the Scripture one may well observe that it is best to take the literal sense, where it will stand, remembering that the farthest from it will likely be the worst. A recent statement is, "If the literal sense makes good sense, seek no other sense." And it may be added, every other sense is usually nonsense. It is generally the case that if words do not mean what they say, no one can say what they mean.

On the other hand, the Bible contains warning against bald literalism. The apostle in his Gospel quotes the saying of Jesus: "The words that I speak unto you, they are spirit, and they are life" (John 6:63). Paul declares, "The letter killeth, but the spirit giveth life" (II Corinthians 3:6). But it is a significant fact that neither in this book of prophecy nor in any other prophetic utterance throughout the Scriptures is there any such warning or precaution. This being the case, it appears conclusive that prophecy is to be fulfilled literally. It is a well-known fact and is generally admitted that prophecies which have been fulfilled have been fulfilled literally. That is, their fulfillment has had an objective reality perceptible to the physical senses and especially to the eye. The prophets themselves were seers. They saw the future as though it were present. And those who live when the fulfillment comes will "see" what the prophets saw beforehand. For example, the signs that will precede the second coming will be seen by those then living—". . . when ye see these things come to pass, know ye that the kingdom of God is nigh at hand" (Luke 21:31). "And when ye shall see Jerusalem compassed with armies, then know that the desolation thereof is nigh" (Luke 21:20). And when the Lord comes men will *see* Him. ". . . It doth not yet appear what we shall be: but . . . when he shall appear, we [the believers] shall be like him; for we shall see him as he is" (I John 3:2). ". . . then shall all the tribes of the earth mourn, and they [the wicked] shall see the Son of man coming in the clouds of heaven with power and great glory" (Matthew 24:30).

More than one half of Revelation is descriptive of the tribulation period, at which time judgments or plagues come upon the inhabitants of the earth. These have a striking resemblance to the ten plagues of Egypt as well as to the four sore judgments of Ezekiel. Ezekiel 14:21. Now these plagues appeared as natural phenomena; they had an objective reality, for they were perceived by the senses. For instance, the Egyptian plagues were discernible by one or the other of the five senses—they were either seen, heard, felt, tasted, or at least on two occasions smelled, for both the river and the heaps of frogs stank. They were entirely literal. So doubtless the plagues that are yet to come upon the earth will be literal as well. They certainly will be felt—for example, ". . . they should be tormented five months. . . . And in those days shall men seek death, and shall not find it . . ." (Revelation 9:5, 6); ". . . and they gnawed their tongues for pain" (Revelation 16:10). In the first series of judgments (plagues), Revelation 6, we have the three judgments of Jeremiah and Ezekiel: sword (red horse), famine (black horse), and pestilence; and death (pale horse) is added, thus making them identical (so the Greek) with the four sore judgments of Ezekiel. (Jeremiah and Ezekiel mention the three judgments 14 and 7 times respectively.)

If the judgments are literal, why should the glories not be literal likewise? They take place on the same theater of action. The prophet Daniel plainly says that "the stone . . . filled the whole earth" (Daniel 2:35), whereas in the interpretation (verse 44) this is said to mean that "the God of heaven [will] set up a kingdom, which . . . [will] consume all these [earthly] kingdoms" while in Daniel 7:27 the kingdom is described as being "under the whole heaven." Note, too, Isaiah says (Isaiah 26:9) that when the judgments of the Lord are *upon the earth*, the *inhabitants of the world* will learn righteousness. And, in conformity with this prediction, out of the heart of the tribulation period comes the announcement, "The kingdoms of this world are become the kingdoms of our Lord, and of his Christ" (Revelation 11:15). Both the judgments and the glories that will follow will doubtless have a literal objective fulfillment on the earth as these Scriptures plainly declare. So one may safely and wisely conclude with the proposition that just as truly as inspired predictions already fulfilled have had a literal fulfillment, so those not yet fulfilled will likewise have a literal fulfillment.

The interpretation of symbols. Fortunately, and no doubt purposefully, many symbols of this book are interpreted in the book itself. Note the following list:

(1) The seven stars (1:16) are seven angels (1:20).

(2) The seven candlesticks (1:13) are seven churches (1:20).

(3) The morning star (2:28) is Jesus (22:16).

(4) The city of my God (3:12) is the new Jerusalem (of 21:2).

(5) The seven lamps of fire are the seven spirits of God (4:5).

(6) The seven eyes are the seven spirits of God (5:6).

(7) The odors proceeding from the golden vials are the prayers of the saints (5:8).

(8) The star [fallen] (9:1) is the angel of the bottomless pit (9:11).

(9) The great city (11:8) is Jerusalem (11:8).

(10) Sodom is Jerusalem (11:8).

(11) Egypt is Jerusalem (11:8).

(12) The stars of heaven (12:4) are the angels of Satan (12:9).

(13) The male child (12:5) is Christ (19:15).

(14) The great dragon is Satan (12:9).

(15) The old serpent is Satan (12:9).

(16) The devil is Satan (12:9).

(17) Time, times, and half a time (12:14) are 1,260 days (12:6).

(18) The beast out of the earth (13:11 ff.) is the false prophet (19:20).

(19) The woman is that great city which ruleth (present tense) over the kings the earth, therefore Rome (17:18).

(20) The woman sits on seven hills, therefore Rome (17:5).

(21) The woman is Babylon the Great, thus Rome (17:18).

(22) The waters (17:1) are peoples and multitudes and nations and tongues (17:15).

(23) The seven heads are (geographically) seven mountains (17:9).

(24) The seven heads are (politically) seven kings (17:10).

(25) The beast is the eighth king (17:11).

(26) The ten horns are ten (contemporaneous) kings (17:12).

(27) The Lamb is Lord of lords (17:14).
(28) The Lamb is King of kings (17:14).
(29) The great city is Babylon (18:10).
(30) The Lamb's wife (19:7) is the holy Jerusalem (21:9, 10).
(31) The fine linen is the righteousness of the saints (19:8).
(32) The white horse Rider is called Faithful (19:11).
(33) The white horse Rider is called True (19:11).
(34) The white horse Rider is called Word of God (19:13).
(35) The white horse Rider is the King of kings (19:16).
(36) The white horse Rider is the Lord of lords (19:16).
(37) The white horse Rider (19:16) is the Lamb (17:14).
(38) Those that sit on thrones and those beheaded and those refusing to worship the beast are the first resurrection (20:4, 5).
(39) The lake of fire is the second death (20:14).
(40) The bride is the Lamb's wife (21:9).
(41) The bride (21:9) is the great city (21:9, 10).
(42) The bride (21:9) is the holy Jerusalem (21:9, 10).
(43) The Lord God Almighty and the Lamb are the temple of the city (21:22).
(44) The Lamb is the light of the city (21:23).
(45) Jesus is the root of David (22:16).
(46) Jesus is the offspring of David (22:16).

From this list one observes that many of the symbols of the book are explained. There are other symbols whose use and meaning are explained in the light of other Scriptures. For instance, Lamb is a symbolic word, but no one would think of a quadruped when he meets with the word here. So also with the symbol, 'the Lion of the tribe of Juda." This is understood because Christ came from that tribe and more especially because in his dying blessing Jacob spoke of Judah as a lion's whelp. Genesis 49:9. Similarly one should deal with the other symbols that occur. Therefore the conclusion may be drawn that symbols occurring in the book are either explained in the text or may be understood from their use in previous Scriptures. The inference follows that *whatever is not thus explained is to be taken as literal.*

Possibly the symbolism descriptive of the Son of man (Revelation 1:13-16) presents the greatest difficulty. The consideration of this will be left until the passage in its contextual relations is taken up.

In this connection, attention should be given to an important matter regarding the explanation of symbols given in the inspired record. When the divine Author explains a symbol, the explanation is to be taken as final and decisive. In other words, one should avoid reinterpreting our Lord's own interpretation. Sufficient care has not been exercised in this matter, for in some cases commentators have proceeded as though the Lord had explained one symbol by another. To cite a few examples from our text:

The first explanation of a symbol occurs in 1:20—the seven stars are the angels of the seven churches. Here star is the symbol and angel the explanation of the symbol, just as in the next clause, candlestick is the symbol and church the explanation. Some have taken the liberty to interpret the Lord's own interpretation. In other words, they take it that He explained one symbol by another and so they proceed by declaring that the angels are the pastors of the churches in the face of the fact that pastors are never spoken of as angels anywhere in the Scriptures. The Lord made a similar interpretation in His earthly career in His interpretation of a symbol in the parable of the tares and the wheat when He explained that the reapers are the angels. No one would think of reinterpreting the word "angels" and declare, "the reapers are the pastors."

Another case in point is found in 17:9, 10, "The seven heads are seven mountains. . . . And they [Greek] are seven kings." A well-known commentator takes "mountains" to be symbolic here. That is, he explains one symbol by another and then interprets it as signifying "kingdom." In the next clause he says the word "king" means kingdom. And so he thinks apparently his figuring is correct because he got the same answer! The fact is, the seven heads have a twofold meaning: They represent seven mountains and they represent seven kings.

A word should be said on the question, What is the purpose of symbolic language? Why did the Lord not "declare unto us plainly"? The answer is no doubt to be found in Jesus' explanation of the purpose of parables (Matthew 13:10, 15; Mark 4:11, 12; Luke 8:10); namely, that His disciples might understand but that those "without" might be kept in ignorance respecting the future program of God. Undoubtedly it is according to God's will and purpose that, while His own followers are led to greater light from the use of the word of prophecy, those who refuse to own Him as their personal Saviour remain in ignorance regarding God's future program.

The forms of comparison. Two words of comparison are "like" and "as." Comparison is a method frequently employed in the book for the purpose of making truth plain. Things unfamiliar are compared with things familiar in order to bring out the meaning. The two words are at times used interchangeably, but since this is generally not the case they will be treated separately.

Like (Greek: *homoios*). This word is used almost entirely to express likeness in external form or appearance. It occurs 22 times here, 21 times in the Gospels, and only 4 times elsewhere in the New Testament. The great Teacher used it almost exclusively in His teaching in the parables. (See Matthew 13; Luke 6 and 13.) It is really teaching by object lessons—making the unfamiliar known by a comparison with the familiar. And since Jesus reveals the things written in this book, it becomes a matter of profound interest to learn that the use of the word is confined almost exclusively to Him. Examples are as follows:

"I saw . . . one *like* unto a [Greek] Son of man" (1:12, 13).

"His feet *like* unto fine brass" (1:15).

"A sea of glass *like* unto crystal" (4:6).

"The shapes of the locusts were *like* unto horses" (9:7).

"The city was pure gold, *like* unto clear glass" (21:18).

As (Greek: *hos*). This word, although used at times in the same relation as "like," is frequently employed to express similarity in action, conduct, quality, etc.

It occurs 65 times in Revelation, which is far above the average elsewhere in the New Testament. Moreover, it is used here almost exclusively to denote comparison, whereas it is used far more frequently in other senses elsewhere. The value of this method of clarifying truth by our Lord cannot be too highly appreciated and it goes a long way toward making various parts of the book intelligible and profitable to the reader. The following examples will serve to show the importance and value of comparison in the interpretation of Scripture:

"I . . . heard behind me a great voice, *as* of a trumpet (1:10).

"I fell at his feet *as* dead" (1:17).

"*As* the vessels of a potter shall they be broken" (2:27).

"I will come on thee *as* a thief" (3:3).

"To him that overcometh will I grant to sit with me in my throne, even *as* I also overcame" (3:21).

The forms of contrast. The use of "another." There are two words in the Greek language for the English "other" or "another"—*allos* and *heteros*. The former denotes simply one more, one in addition. The latter signifies another in kind, one different. Both occur frequently in the New Testament—*allos* 160 times, *heteros* 97 times. *Allos* needs no explanation; however, a few examples of *heteros* to illustrate its use follow:

"Art thou he that should come, or do we look for another [*heteros*]" (Matthew 11:3)? The question was as to whether they were to look for one different from Jesus.

"After that he appeared in another form unto two of them" (Mark 16:12). This shows that the body of Jesus had undergone a notable change in His resurrection.

"One shall be taken, and the other shall be left" (Luke 17:34). Here, as often, the use of the words suggests difference in character.

"And there were also two other [that is] malefactors" (Luke 23:32). Thus Jesus is distinguished, as to His character, from the two others crucified with Him.

Two notable passages, the one by the Apostle Peter, the other by Paul, contain both words. They are of special interest because they illustrate in a striking manner the distinction in the words. "Neither is there salvation in any other [*allos*]: for there is none other [*heteros*] name under heaven given among men, whereby we must be saved" (Acts 4:12). The thought of *allos* is, there is no other person but Jesus in whom there is salvation; while *heteros* implies that were one to do so, he would of necessity be different in character. "I marvel that ye are so soon removed from him that called you into the grace of Christ unto another [*heteros*] gospel; which is not another [*allos*]" (Galatians 1:6, 7). The apostle marveled that the Galatians had been led away by hearing a Gospel different in kind from what he had preached. A *heteros* Gospel is really no Gospel at all.

It is remarkable that John, the human author of Revelation, while he uses *allos* 18 times, does not once use *heteros*. In fact, he uses it only once in all his writing, namely, in John 19:37. He had been quoting a passage from the Psalms and then proceeds to quote another (*heteros*) Scripture, not from the Psalms division this time but from the prophets. If it be asked why he almost entirely omitted using this word, the answer is clear—he had no occasion to use it. In other words, he used other modes of expression when differences existed in what he wished to explain. Anyone reading his Gospel never is perplexed at what he meant. One should suspect the same when he reads Revelation.

All this is necessary to correct, if possible, what may be called an unwarranted handling of certain verses in our book containing the word "another." For since the word *heteros* does not occur here, "another" should never be understood as applying to one different in kind. Out of the 18 occurrences of the word *allos*, ten are used as modifying angel. Some writers interpret the word "angel" in three different senses: first, as a celestial being (1:1); second, as pastors of churches (1:20); and third, as referring to Jesus Christ (8:3; 10:1; 21:1). If John meant that an angel could mean either a celestial creature or a pastor of a church, there would have been reasons over and over for the use of *heteros* with angel and not merely *allos*. And the need of this word would be all the more important because of the close proximity of the word "angel."

Note the following examples: In chapter 1 an angel is correctly taken to mean a heavenly messenger, but in the same chapter (verse 20) angel is said to mean pastor or bishop of a church. In 3:1 angel is taken to mean the pastor of the church, while in verse 5 the word signifies a heavenly messenger. In 8:2 angels mean celestial creatures, while in the next verse "another" angel is taken to mean Christ. Here surely one should expect *heteros* as one different in kind from the preceding verse, but it is *allos* as always throughout the book. In 10:1 another mighty angel is taken to mean Jesus Christ, while in verse 7 it means an ordinary angel. Much stress has been laid on the word "mighty," but the same word *ischuros* occurs in 5:2 where it cannot refer to Jesus Christ, for He is at the time standing in the midst of the throne. Neither is it probable that in verse 11 of this chapter Jesus is speaking to John seeing He Himself said that He would send His angel to speak to John the things that are to come to pass.

In the comments further reasons will be given on the meaning and use of the word "angel." These points are mentioned here because a vital principle of interpretation is at stake. Where the same word is said to have different meanings without the use of any qualifying word such as would be available as well as necessary, there is not only unjustifiable license in the handling of God's Word, but hopeless confusion on the part of the interpreter as well as with those who look to such guides for instruction and illumination.

The marks of identification. These are hints or "catchwords" occurring throughout the book which serve as a clue to the understanding of a given text, by what has been said before. Note a few examples:

Kings and priests—this earmark occurs three times. In 1:5c, 6, the members of the church declare themselves as having been made kings and priests unto God (cf. I Peter 2:9, "Ye are . . . a royal priesthood"). In 5:10 the kings and priests are in heaven where they declare, "We shall reign on the earth." By this it is understood that the church is in glory before the tribulation begins. Chapter 6. In 20:6 one reads, "They [of the first resurrection] shall be priests of God and of Christ, and shall reign [be kings] with him a thousand years."

White robes. In 6:11 one learns that "white robes" were given to those who in verse 9 were slain for the word of God and for the testimony which they held. Now the only other place in all the Scriptures where a group is spoken of as wearing white robes (*stolai*) occurs in Revelation 7:9, 13, 14. Hence the reference there is plainly to this verse. In answer to the question, "What are these which are arrayed in white robes? and whence came they?" one of the elders tells John, "These are they which came out of the [Greek] great tribulation, and have washed their robes, and made them white in the blood of the Lamb." Here the earmark identifies the groups in chapters 6 and 7.

A book closed up and sealed. Mention is made of this book in chapters 5 and 6. There is only one other Scripture in which mention is made of such a book, namely, in Daniel 12:4, 9. The prophet is told that the book is "closed up and sealed till the time of the end." In Revelation 5:1-4, the book is in the right hand of God still closed and sealed. However, in verse 7 Christ as the Lamb takes the book out of His hand and after the elders (kings and priests) declare Him worthy, He proceeds (chapter 6) to open the seals. Evidently "the time of the end" begins at this place.

The two witnesses. 11:3-6. There has been a great deal of confusion as to who is meant by the two witnesses. The answer must be found by the hints (verse 6) that God Himself has put into the passage for the purpose of identification. "These have power to shut heaven, that it rain not in the days of their prophecy: and have power over waters to turn them to blood, and to smite the earth with all plagues, as often as they will." There should be no question or argument as to who is intended since in the whole Biblical record only two are mentioned as having the power to do the things named. Elijah only had power to shut up heaven that it did not rain. I Kings 17:1; James 5:17. Moses only had power to turn water into blood (Exodus 7:20), and to smite the earth with plagues (Exodus 7—11). The earmarks decide the matter of interpretation.

The great city of chapter 11. It is said: "Their dead bodies [of the two witnesses] shall lie in the street of the great city, which spiritually is called Sodom and Egypt" (verse 8). Reading this far only would naturally lead to the conclusion that the reference is to Babylon (Rome). However, the earmark following, "where also our Lord was crucified," clearly decides the matter—the great city here is Jerusalem.

If the Lord's own earmarks were carefully observed and *believed* as they occur, much of the confusion and discord resulting from the misunderstanding of the book would be avoided.

Prophetic passages. These are such as speak of future events as though they already had taken place. They are frequent in other portions of prophetic literature; e.g., "Unto us a child is born, unto us a son is given" (Isaiah 9:6).

"He was wounded for our transgressions, he was bruised for our iniquities: the chastisement of our peace was upon him; and with his stripes we are healed" (Isaiah 53:5). In these passages Isaiah speaks of events some 700 years in the future as though they had already occurred. The prophet, of course, in each case, saw the vision before he wrote it down and this may account for the form of language employed. A good example is the announcement on separate occasions of the fall of Babylon previous to its occurrence:

In 14:8 an angel declares, "Babylon is fallen, is fallen."

In 16:19 under the seventh vial the statement occurs, "Great Babylon came in remembrance before God, to give unto her the cup of the wine of the fierceness of his wrath."

Again in 18:2 occur the words, "Babylon the great is fallen, is fallen"; however, in verse 8 of the same chapter her doom is still spoken of as future: "Therefore shall her plagues come in one day, death, and mourning, and famine; and she shall be utterly burned with fire: for strong is the Lord God who judgeth her."

It is not until verse 9 of chapter 18 that her doom has befallen her, for "the kings of the earth . . . shall . . . lament for her, when they shall see the smoke of her burning."

Important phrases—"I saw," "I heard," and "after these things." "I saw." This phrase in its various forms and relations is found a number of times in the prophecies of Ezekiel and Daniel, but beyond question John is the greatest seer in the Scriptures both as to the nature and the number of things that he saw. The entire book is spoken of in the preface as "all things that he saw" (1:2). The word occurs over 60 times in the book as applying to John, 44 of which refer to separate and distinct visions. Each "I saw" is to be taken and considered by itself. In other words, the "things" following each occurrence of the term have an organic inner relation and therefore should be thought of as a unit of revelation. It is true, there are groups of visions likewise which are organically related, such as those coming under the seals, trumpets, and vials, but the series will only be understood to the extent that the individual visions are clearly apprehended. The entire book will become one's true possession only to the extent that the smaller portions have been mastered.

It will be observed that the visions vary greatly in the extent of their subject matter. This is all according to divine arrangement and it becomes the part of the reader to carefully observe this arrangement if he expects the best results from his study. Space will not permit to make an exhaustive study of the various forms and interrelations of these visions, but as an aid further attention should be given to the following observations:

A vision may cover one or more chapters. This is true of the first vision: "I saw seven golden candlesticks; and in the midst of the seven candlesticks one like unto the Son of man" (1:12b, 13a). The student will observe that the words, "when I saw him" (verse 17), and "Write the things which thou hast seen" (verse 19), do not refer to new vision but that both allude to the one afore-mentioned. Neither will there be found another occurrence in either of chapters 2 and 3. It is not until chapter 4 that a new vision is introduced. (It should be said here that *I saw, I looked, I beheld* are the same in the Greek.) It will be obvious in the study of this portion that the entire section from 1:12 to the end of chapter 3 constitutes an organic whole and that the various parts are vitally related to each other. This much may be said here—the Son of man is Christ in the capacity of judge (of John 5:22, 27) while in chapters 2 and 3 judgment evidently begins at the house of God

(I Peter 4:17), for the Son of man draws the line of cleavage between good and evil in the churches, approving the one and reproving the other.

Another vision of many details begins in chapter 10 where "I saw" occurs. There is no additional use of the term until chapter 13. It is true that other things come into view here besides the "mighty angel." But it is with the appearance of the angel that a new series of events and personages are introduced. That chapters 10 to 12 belong together is apparent from the time notes—42 months; 1,260 days; time, times, and half a time—occurring there. These are of equal duration, and indicate that this is the middle of the tribulation period. Chapter 13 belongs to the same time period because the same time note appears there. However, the coming of the beast is such an outstanding event that it is introduced as a separate vision. 13:1.

Visions may be brief, covering but one verse. An instance of this is found in chapter 5. In the first verse the vision reveals a sealed book in the hand of Him that sat on the throne. In the next verse another vision reveals a strong angel proclaiming with a loud voice, "Who is worthy to open the book, and to loose the seals thereof?" Each verse, therefore, should be carefully pondered by itself, because each is fraught with matters of distinct importance. This meditation and reflection will prepare the student to appreciate what is further revealed.

"I saw" is accompanied by "behold" or "lo" (same in Greek) in eleven passages. Though exactly identical in Greek, the English translation appears in the following forms:

"I looked, and, behold" (4:1; 6:8; 14:14; 15:5).

"I beheld, and, lo" (5:6; 6:5, 12; 7:9).

"I saw, and behold" (6:2; 19:11).

"I looked, and, lo" (14:1).

The reader should note carefully that these all should be translated "I saw, and behold." The Greek word for "behold" is identical with that translated "see." By this the seer calls particular attention to the matter he now proposes to show.

In a similar manner, "I heard" needs to be noted. A total of 28 occurrences can be listed. In each case close attention should be given to what follows. [Thus the seer has use of the eye gate and the ear gate to receive the Revelation.— J. O. Y.]

"After these things." The Greek formula consists of two words: *meta* (after) *tauta* (these), i.e., after these. But since the last word is neuter, it is properly rendered *after these things*. The expression occurs scores of times in the Old Testament and 35 times in the New Testament. In a few cases the singular is used and occasionally when the original is plural. However, there appears to be no essential difference in their use.

The phrase is so simple and easily understood by its familiar and constant use in all ages and places that it almost appears foolish to offer a definition or explanation. A child understands what the words mean. Yet some men apparently fail to observe their meaning. The predicament is that when one goes to define in this case, the definition is harder to understand than what he undertakes to define. The term in narrative is used as a hallmark or catchword denoting that what has just been given, precedes in order of time what follows. In other words, the phrase denotes subsequence, temporal succession, chronological sequence, and thus serves as a connecting link or transition between what has been mentioned and what is to follow in order of time. For instance, when the Apostle John, in his Gospel, in narrating the ministry of Jesus, says, "After these things came Jesus and his disciples into the land of Judaea" (3:22), or again, "After these things Jesus went over the sea of Galilee" (6:1), no one would dispute the fact that this is temporal succession. That is, what he had just written preceded in order of time what he was now about to write. The same order of sequence must obtain when the term occurs in prophetic literature, for, as noted before, prophecy as used in this book (namely, things to come) is really history written in advance.

The phrase "after these things" occurs ten times in Revelation: five times in conjunction with "I saw"; once it is joined with "I heard" (19:1); four times without being thus joined (1:19; 4:1b; 9:12; 20:3). Sometimes "after these things" is joined with "I saw"; i.e., "after these things I saw." In such cases it may denote order of vision merely and does not necessarily mean that the order of fulfillment follows that of the preceding vision. The content will usually decide which is intended. If, however, as is the case in four passages (1:19; 4:1b; 9:12; 20:3), *the phrase is not joined in this way, it can only mean succession in time.* In 4:1 the phrase occurs in each of the ways mentioned: *"After these things I saw* (Greek) and, behold, a door was opened in heaven: and the first voice which I heard was as it were of a trumpet talking with me; which said, Come up hither, and I will shew thee things which must be *after these things"* (Greek). Observe that in the opening of the verse the phrase is joined with "I saw" and hence may or may not denote succession in time, but in the last case it stands alone and of necessity means that the things that will now be shown the seer must be "after these things," that is, they must follow in order of time those mentioned in the preceding chapters.

However, just as a writer of history who presents facts in true chronological sequence may find it necessary to go back to previous events in order to make intelligible things he is about to relate, so John in a few cases goes back to events of the past to connect them with the future which he is about to describe.

Law of recurrence. This has been defined by Dr. James M. Gray as ". . . that peculiarity of the Holy Spirit as an author by which He gives first the outlines of a subject, and then recurs to it again for the purpose of adding details."[6]

The law is well illustrated in the first two chapters of Genesis. Moses first gives an orderly symmetrical account of the six days of the creative week in the first chapter. In chapter 2 he adds details pertaining to the work of the fifth and sixth days by saying how God made every fowl of the air (verse 19) and how God made the cattle, man and woman (verses 7, 19, 21, 22), besides giving many other details. There is evidently a wise purpose in this arrangement of materials of the story of creation. If the details mentioned in chapter 2 had been included in the last two days' record of chapter 1, it would have lacked the beauty, symmetry, and simplicity which now characterize it.

The first three verses of chapter 2 belong to chapter 1. The week really is not complete without the Sabbath day. Note that the first verse of chapter 2 says:

"Thus the heavens and the earth were finished, and all the host of them." Consequently the details mentioned in chapter 2 concerning the creation of the fowls, of every beast of the field as well as of the man and the woman all fall into the time period covered by chapter 1. This law of literary arrangement has special merit when a series of events are in contemplation such as the creation story.

Now in the Book of Revelation there are a number of instances where the law of recurrence is employed. In the three series of judgments, namely, the seven seals, the seven trumpets, and the seven vials, there is a remarkable similarity of arrangement to that of the first two chapters of Genesis.

The fifth seal (6:9-11) mentions martyrs "slain for the word of God, and for the testimony which they held." "And white robes were given unto every one of them." Little would be known about these if this were all that is recorded of them. In the next chapter, however, the question is raised: "What are these which are arrayed in white robes? and whence came they?" The reply was given: "These are they which came out of [the] great tribulation, and have washed their robes, and made them white in the blood of the Lamb."

In 10:7 it is stated distinctly that when the seventh trumpet shall begin to sound, the mystery of God would be finished. When the seventh trumpet sounds, the declaration follows: "And the nations were angry, and thy wrath is come, and the time of the dead, that they should be judged, and that thou shouldest give reward unto thy servants the prophets, and to the saints, and them that fear thy name, small and great; and shouldest destroy them which destroy the earth" (Revelation 11:18).

This indeed reads as though the end had come. But the following chapter shows that the reference is to events taking place in the middle of the tribulation period just as those mentioned earlier in chapter 11. This plainly shows that proceeding from chapter to chapter does not mean that there is necessarily a going forward in the course of time.

When the seventh vial is poured out (16:17), a great voice comes out of the temple of heaven from the throne, saying, "It is done." In this connection comes the declaration, "Great Babylon came in remembrance before God, to give unto her the cup of the wine of the fierceness of his wrath" (verse 19).

But chapters 17 and 18 go back in time and mention events leading up to the fall and then repeat that event in the latter part of chapter 18 with many graphic details. Here again is an illustration of the law of recurrence, for the close of these chapters is still occupied with events belonging to the seventh vial, for all these must necessarily precede in order of time the divine dictum, "It is done."

The use of the definite article "the." There is a well-known rule in the usage of language that at the first mention of a person or object the article may be omitted but that in subsequent mention, the article is used for the purpose of maintaining identity. The careful observance of this principle is an important matter in the correct interpretation of Scripture and especially in our book where examples of this usage are frequent and on the whole maintained. A few exceptions occur, as when the identity of an object is asserted in some other way. A few examples from chapters 4 and 5 follow:

In chapter 4:2, a throne set in heaven is mentioned. After this when the same throne is mentioned, it is always the throne. That is, the one mentioned in chapter 4:2. However, in chapter 20:11 *a* white throne is seen. This shift shows conclusively that the white throne, chapter 20, is not the same as the one mentioned in chapter 4.

Verse 4 of chapter 4 mentions the four and twenty elders. In every subsequent case where they are mentioned, it is always *the* twenty-four elders.

Similarly in verse 6, "round about the throne were four beasts," thereafter always *the* four beasts.

Chapter 5 speaks of a book sealed with seven seals. After that, it is always *the* book. (See verses 2, 3, 4, 5, 7, 9 following.)

In 5:6 one reads, "in the midst of the elders, stood *a* Lamb." There are altogether 28 uses of this word as referring to Christ the Redeemer and in every subsequent occurrence it is always *the* Lamb. However, in chapter 13:11 the same word occurs *without* the article. Of the beast coming up out of the earth it is said, "And he had two horns like *a* lamb." The definite article does not occur, for this is altogether a different lamb.

The reader will note the importance of observing carefully the use or absence of the definite article in the pursuit of a correct interpretation of the book.

Use of words. A book of Scripture is known by its vocabulary. It gives the book its complexion. Just as the face shows the man, so the words used show the book. They give the book its individuality as well as its peculiarity. Just as some men have outstanding personalities that one will always remember and be able to distinguish from others, so with the books of the Bible. There are certain ones that, if they are read once, there will be no difficulty in distinguishing them from the rest. The Book of Revelation is one of these books. There is no book in all literature so strikingly dramatic as this. Scenes shift from earth to heaven in rapid succession. The glories of heaven are set in sharp contrast with the sufferings of earth. But it is the magnitude of performance which stirs the imagination to its depths. For innumerable hosts of the redeemed and multiplied millions of angels unite in the praises of heaven, while the sword, famine, and pestilence destroy dwellers upon the earth to the extent that "there will be few men left." In short, the description of conditions in this book appears as a halfway station between the present age and the final state of things in the eternal destinies of heaven and hell.

The Bible speaks of ages past, of the present age, the age to come, ages to come, and ages of ages. All who have any degree of familiarity with the Scriptures recognize that God has dealt in different ways with the human family in times past. But no one who reflects upon the Book of Revelation can fail to realize that in no period of the world's history has there been so great a difference in the state of things on earth as there is between the present church age and that described from chapter 6 to the end of chapter 19. It appears, therefore, that if there ever was a reason for speaking of different ages or dispensations, surely the conditions described in these chapters would seem to be that reason, and that chapters 6–19 belong to a different dispensation from the present. A listing of 27 words of distinct character occurring in chapters 6–19 inclusive will show how valid this proposition is.⁷ What a misfit most of these words would be in a supplement either to the Gospel of John or to the Epistle of Paul to the Romans!

The Bible student will recognize, if he examines the list, that nowhere in Holy Writ are these words or a similar list brought together within the brief compass of 14 chapters (6—19). It is noteworthy that with the exception of two (God and blood) none of these words occur so frequently in any one section of the Bible. Moreover, the two excepted are used almost entirely in a different relation. For instance, while previous New Testament passages emphasize the love and righteousness of God as freely bestowed upon the believer, here the wrath and judgments of God coming upon the wicked and unbelieving are stressed. And whereas the Book of Hebrews frequently mentions blood, the reference is most often to its atoning merits. Here it is mostly used in connection with judgment and martyrdom.

The test of comparison. Sometimes events which some consider identical are seen to differ upon careful examination of the words used to describe each. As an example, compare the coming of the Lord as described in I Thessalonians 4:13-18 and Revelation 19:11-21 familiarly known as the rapture and the revelation.⁸ If the two accounts describe the same event, one must expect a similarity of the words describing each. In any case, if the records describe the same event, there can be no contradictions in the personnel or in the acts described.

It would be difficult if not impossible to find elsewhere any two important passages of Scripture that are so diverse in the words employed and so opposite in their implications. It appears as though this dissimilarity was providentially directed in order to safeguard the reader from error and confusion in their interpretation.

The comparison of the words of these two passages will convince all open-minded readers that they describe different events. True interpretation must be based upon the written word, not on reason, speculation, or imagination. Further study will make it equally clear that the former event will take place previous to the tribulation period, the latter immediately after that period. It is the writer's firm conviction that unless the reader believes and accepts this distinction he will never arrive at a correct interpretation and understanding of the Book of Revelation.

It is most instructive to make another comparison. This time compare John 14:1-3 and I Thessalonians 4:13-18. The words, sequence, persons all agree so that there can be no doubt that both passages describe the same event. But John 14 and Revelation 19 have no more similarity than do I Thessalonians 4:13-18 and Revelation 19.⁸

VII. *The Occasion of the Book.* This is plainly stated in Revelation 1:9—John "was in the isle that is called Patmos, for the word of God, and for the testimony of Jesus Christ."

The seer was banished here by the Emperor Domitian because of (Greek) the Word of God and because of the testimony which he held. Although this is not the meaning of the text, it may nevertheless be inferred that he was banished to this lonely isle for the Word of God. In other words, under God's providence the banishment occurred in order that he might receive the Word of God as revealed in this book. He, like Paul when in prison at Rome and Bunyan in Bedford jail, might have concluded that the days of usefulness were over. But solitude in each case proved to be "the audience chamber of God." From the Bedford jail came the immortal *Pilgrim's Progress;* from the Mamertine Prison came some of the most priceless treasures in the possession of the Christian Church. The apostle spoke truly and wiser than he knew when he declared, "the things which happened unto me have fallen out rather unto the furtherance of the gospel." As a free man he might still have spoken here and there to comparatively small groups for a few years, but in the epistles which had their birth behind prison walls he speaks to the church universal for all time.

But apparently none of the sons of men were honored as was the disciple whom Jesus loved. It is true, Paul was once caught up into heaven and saw things unlawful to be uttered. II Corinthians 12:1-4. John was not only called up into heaven, but while there he saw the glory of God, he saw Jesus face to face, he saw the cherubim, the glorified saints, the myriads of angels, the new Jerusalem, and the city foursquare, "having the glory of God." Besides this, he heard the songs of the redeemed, the adoration of the heavenly hosts, and the hallelujahs of the great multitude, with the final climax, "the Lord God omnipotent reigneth." What an inestimable loss the church would have sustained were it not for this revelation that was given to the apostle during his banishment to this solitary spot of earth! The prophetic word has ever had its birth "in a dark place." "The people that walked in darkness have seen a great light" (Isaiah 9:2), even as prophecy itself is a light for those in a dark place. II Peter 1:19.

VIII. *The Outline of the Book.* It is indeed a matter of encouragement and satisfaction to the reader that the divine Author has provided him with an outline of its contents. It is found in 1:19 and consists of three parts:

1. Write the things which thou hast seen,
2. And the things which are,
3. And the things which shall be hereafter.

Since this verse will soon come up for consideration in the comments, further remarks will be postponed until then. However, note them carefully because they are of utmost importance to the proper understanding of the book.

---

1. Bullinger, p. 304.
2. Pierson, p. 41. (Quoted from B. W. Newton.)
3. *Ibid.*, p. 94. (Quoted from B. W. Newton.)
4. Trench, p. 133.
5. Newton, pp. 376, 377.
6. Gray, p. 9.
7. See Appendix, p. 309, "Word Study of Rev. 6—19."
8. See Appendix, p. 311, "Comparisons of I Thess. 4:13-18; Rev. 19:11-21; John 14:1-3."

1

PART I
THE PROLOGUE
1:1-8

THE PROLOGUE

The Book of Revelation, like the Gospel by the same author, opens with a prologue and closes with an epilogue. The prologue consists of eight verses; the epilogue, of sixteen. In the prologue we have the following subdivisions:

The Preface, verses 1-3.
The Salutation, verses 4, 5a.
The Doxology, verses 5b, 6.
The Prophetic Announcement, verse 7.
The Divine Declaration, verse 8.

The Preface (1-3)

Verse 1. *The Revelation of Jesus Christ, which God gave unto him, to shew unto his servants things which must shortly come to pass; and he sent and signified it by his angel unto his servant John.*

The Revelation of Jesus Christ. As far as the language is concerned three interpretations need to be examined: a revealing or making known of things about Christ not revealed before; a revelation of Christ Himself, that is, of a future event at which time He is revealed from heaven (II Thessalonians 1:7); a revelation by Jesus Christ, that is, He reveals the things written in the book. The context makes it clear that the last interpretation is the sense intended. However, this does not exclude the other two, for the book makes things known about Christ not revealed before, and it also gives a description of the future revelation of Christ (19:11 ff.), at which time every eye shall see Him. 1:7. (For details see Introduction, *The Name of the Book.*)

The Greek has no definite article; so "A Revelation of Jesus Christ" should be read. *The* Revelation would imply that reference is made to a previous revelation. Without the article, the meaning is—here is a unique and distinct revelation. Since by revelation as here employed is meant a revealing of what was not made known before (Ephesians 3:3-5), the phrase at once invests the book with a freshness and interest all its own.

As noted in the Introduction, the real title of the book is "A Revelation of Jesus Christ." What is meant by "The Revelation of John" in the title is that the apostle was the human writer.

Which God gave unto him. The question naturally arises, Why should it have been necessary for God to give this revelation to Jesus Christ? Was He not Himself God and did He not know all things? In reply, note the following observations: When Jesus was on earth He Himself declared with reference to His second coming (concerning which this book treats) that "of that day and that hour knoweth no man, no, not the angels which are in heaven, neither the Son, but the Father"

33

(Mark 13:32). Even after His resurrection, in answer to the disciples' question, "Lord, wilt thou at this time restore again the kingdom to Israel?" His reply was, "It is not for you to know the times or the seasons, which the Father hath put in his own power" (Acts 1:6, 7). It is significant also that Jesus disclaimed the words He spoke throughout His earthly ministry. In at least seven passages the Lord expressed Himself: "I have not spoken of [Greek: 'from'] myself; but the Father which sent me, he gave me a commandment, what I should say, and what I should speak." (See John 3:34; 7:16; 8:28, 40; 12:49; 14:10, 24.) In His high priestly prayer He testifies, "I have given unto them the words which thou gavest me" (John 17:8). It is indeed remarkable that after Jesus was in heaven with the Father for approximately sixty years, He, notwithstanding, speaks of this revelation as that *which God gave unto him.*

To shew unto his servants. These words declare God's purpose in giving this revelation to Jesus Christ; namely, that He (Jesus) might show it to His servants. No one who truly ponders this divine purpose can be indifferent toward the contents of the book. It is not merely intended for a select few, but for all His servants. This passage shows plainly that by a revelation of Jesus Christ one is to understand primarily that Jesus Christ shows or reveals its contents.

Things which must shortly come to pass. These words occur (with slight variation) four times in the Book of Daniel (2:28, 29a, 29b, 45), and three times in Revelation (1:1; 4:1; 22:6). The word *must* denotes necessity and certainty. We note an interesting variation in the language employed in Daniel and in Revelation. In the former, mention is made of things which must come to pass "in the latter days." Undoubtedly the reference is to the same things referred to in Revelation as *things which must shortly come to pass.* The Greek *en tachei* is translated "shortly" and "quickly" (22:6, 7). It occurs elsewhere in the New Testament five times. Luke 18:8; Acts 12:7; 22:18; 25:4; Romans 16:20. Its first use (Luke 18:8) serves as a good example of its true sense: "And shall not God avenge his own elect, which cry day and night unto him, though he bear long with them? I tell you that he will avenge them speedily [quickly]." The meaning appears to be that when the time of vengeance comes, there will be no delay in its execution. And so, also, with reference to the things which must come to pass. Their fulfillment is certain, but the time of fulfillment may appear to be distant. Since the time is uncertain, expectancy and vigilance are essential attitudes on the part of believers.

Another form of the same original word (*tachus*), uniformly translated *quickly*, occurs seven times. 2:5, 16; 3:11; 11:14; 22:7, 12, 20. The third and last three of these pertain to the second coming of Christ, three of them in the form of an appeal and warning, "Behold, I come quickly," and the last with the special emphasis, "Surely I come quickly." This last and most urgent appeal occurs in next to the last verse in the book. It is the one event the fulfillment of which above all others we are now expecting.

He sent and signified it. The antecedent of He is Jesus Christ. It is He who showed the contents of the book. Some have taken the word *signified* as though it meant to show by signs. The usage of the word elsewhere (John 12:33; 18:32; 21:19; Acts 11:28; 25:27) does not warrant such a meaning. In each case the sense is to signify by word and not by symbol. Note also that in three of these passages the words are by John.

By his angel. The reference is apparently to a particular angel. One cannot speak with certainty on this point, but it was probably Gabriel, who may be called the informing angel.

The probability is based on several considerations:

Gabriel is the angel who is particularly mentioned as showing Daniel a large portion of the things written in that book, to which Revelation stands related as a supplement. Daniel 8:16; 9:2, 21, 22.

He was the angel sent from God to Mary to announce that she should bring forth a son and call His name Jesus. Luke 1:26-31.

He was probably the angel announcing the good tidings of great joy. Luke 2:10; cf. verse 21.

Unto his servant John. The name "John" occurs five times—three times in this chapter (verses 1, 4, 9) and twice in the last two, in which he adds his own imprimatur, "I John" (21:2; 22:8). We believe the writer was none other than John, the apostle, the author of the Gospel and three epistles, on the following grounds:

As noted above, the structure of the book bears a marked resemblance to that of the Gospel of John, each opening with a prologue and closing with an epilogue.

The opening chapters of each exhibit a striking similarity in that they each mention as many as eighteen titles of our Lord. No such massing together of divine titles within the same compass is approximated anywhere else in the Holy Scriptures.

The books of Daniel and Revelation are closely related in subject matter, the latter being both a complement and supplement of the former.[1] Daniel is the greatly beloved of the Old Testament (9:23; 10:11, 19); John, the disciple whom Jesus loved in the New (John 13:23; 19:26; 21:7, 20). It is fitting, therefore, that the Lord would vouchsafe to John as He did to Daniel a vision of things to come.

It was the prevailing opinion among the early church fathers, for Justin Martyr, Irenaeus, Tertullian, Hippolytus, Origen, Methodius, and Victorinus unite in ascribing the authorship of Revelation to John, the apostle.

There are two objections which have been made against the Johannine authorship:

John refers to himself as servant, not as apostle. The argument is invalid, for the Apostle Paul (Romans 1:1) and Peter (II Peter 1:1), likewise, refer to themselves as servants.

The chief objection pertains to the difference in style and diction apparent in the Gospel and Revelation. This difference may readily be accounted for by the fact that the Revelation abounds with allusions to the Old Testament, while in the Gospel they are very rare. In a total of 404 verses there are approximately 300 such references. It has been well said that although the apostle wrote in Greek, he thought in Hebrew. Thus to a degree the language employed is an adaptation of Hebrew idioms and modes of expression. It must be remembered, too, that the words he employed were strictly not his own, for they are "a Revelation of Jesus Christ, which God gave unto him."

Verse 2. *Who bare record of the word of God, and of the testimony of Jesus Christ, and of all things that he saw.*

Bare record (*martureo*) occurs three times: once here in the prologue, and twice in the epilogue, where it is more accurately translated "testify." Hence the thought is, *who testified the word of God*. The human, angelic, and divine agencies in the deliverance of this book are clearly seen in the three passages: "John testified the word of God" (as above); "I Jesus have sent mine angel [the same as His angel above] to testify unto you these things in the churches" (22:16); "He [Jesus] which testifieth these things saith, Surely I come quickly" (22:20).

The word of God. It is the word of God because God is the ultimate source of the book. He gave it to Jesus Christ.

The testimony of Jesus Christ. The word for testimony (*marturia*) occurs nine times, seven of which refer to the testimony or witness of Jesus Christ because He showed it to His servants by revealing the words comprising it. The combined expression, word of God and testimony of Jesus Christ, occurs four times in Revelation (1:2, 9; 6:9; 20:4) and three additional passages (12:11, 17; 14:12) are somewhat similar. [It is the noun of the verb "bare record."—J. O. Y.]

And of all things that he saw. *And* has the sense of "even" or "that is to say." *All things John saw* is the equivalent of "the word of God and the testimony of Jesus Christ." The reference is to the visions contained in the book, of which there are forty-four.[2]

Verse 3. *Blessed is he that readeth, and they that hear the words of this prophecy, and keep those things which are written therein: for the time is at hand.*

Blessed. This is the first of seven beatitudes. 1:3; 14:3; 16:15; 19:9; 20:6; 22:7, 14.

He that readeth, and they that hear. Observe that in the first clause the subject *he* is in the singular number—(lit.) "blessed is the one that readeth." The allusion is to the reader in the congregation whose duty it was to read a portion of the Word of God in the presence of the assembled congregation. There was need of this because not everybody had a copy of the Scriptures. The reader was blessed for reading, the hearer for hearing. Since Bibles were scarce, there doubtless were some good hearers in that day.

The words of this prophecy. This phrase shows plainly that the entire book is to be regarded as having a prophetic sense. (See Introduction, *The Nature of the Book*.)

And keep those things which are written therein. A double blessing is pronounced upon those who keep the things written in the book—once here, and again in the epilogue. 22:7. *Keep* has the twofold sense of treasuring in the heart and obeying it in life and practice. All the "beatitude" passages should be read in succession to observe the promised blessing in the various conditions indicated. The reader will note that it is highly significant that the promise of blessing is repeated alone in reference to "those who keep the words of this prophecy."

For the time is at hand. *For* has a causal sense in this place, indicating that those who keep the "words of this prophecy" are blessed because this will assure readiness for the time when it comes. Again there is a parallel passage in the epilogue. 22:10. Though the words occur in a different aspect, they have a similar import. The passage reads, "Seal not the sayings [words] of the prophecy of this book: for [because] the time is at hand." The purpose of the passage is manifest— the book is to be kept open for the perusal of all in order that they may be ready for the time when it comes.

The time. The Greek word *kairos* denotes a season or period, and not merely a point in time. In other words, *kairos* has a durative, not a punctiliar, sense. This is seen in such expressions as "the time of harvest"; "the time of figs"; and "the sufferings of this present time." The definite article *the* points to a particular "time" mentioned before, with which the reader is supposed to be familiar. As is so frequently the case in Revelation, the reference is undoubtedly to the Book of Daniel where we find the phrase, "the time of the end," occurring five times. 8:17; 11:35, 40; 12:4, 9. Counting the passage in 22:10, we have seven occurrences of the word "time" in Revelation, which apparently are to be understood as expressing the same period as that with which Daniel deals. It will be seen later that the time here alluded to begins with the events of chapter 6 and continues on through chapter 19.

At hand. The term in its verbal and adjectival form is variously translated; e.g., "at hand," "is at hand," "near," "nigh," "is nigh," and "approach."

It is used with respect to both time and place and in either case it denotes proximity or nearness. In this text it is plainly used in respect to the nearness in time of predicted events, just as "shortly" (verse 1) denotes imminence. The term is used by John the Baptist, Jesus, Paul, James, Peter, and John in their various end-time phraseology; e.g., "the kingdom of heaven," "the day of the Lord," "the coming of the Lord," "the end of all things," and "the time" are all spoken of as "at hand." Things fulfilled within a day or two, e.g., "My time" and "the hour" (Matthew 26:18, 45), as well as the signs preceding His second coming (Matthew 24:33; Luke 21:28), are spoken of as "at hand."

Why this emphasis with respect to the imminence of events which the Lord knew would not be fulfilled for centuries to come? To this there may be several answers:

"One day is with the Lord as a thousand years, and a thousand years as one day" (II Peter 3:8; cf. Psalm 90:4). In other words, a day "with the Lord" (or in His sight) is as 365,000 days with man and vice versa. This is literally the case with Him who inhabits eternity.

The duration of man's life is brief and fleeting. It is but as yesterday when it is gone (Psalm 90:4), as the grass that perishes (I Peter 1:24), and as the grass of the field (Psalm 103:15).

It would seem that, in accordance with Scripture language, the church age is a timeless period, and is not considered directly in predictive Scriptures. It is seen in the fact that prophecies referring to both the first and the second coming of Christ follow each other in the closest possible proximity; e.g., "Unto us a son is given [first coming]: and the government shall be upon his shoulder [second coming] (Isaiah 9:6); "the acceptable year of the Lord [first coming], and the day of vengeance of our God [second coming]" (Isaiah 61:2); "the sufferings of Christ [first coming], and the glories [Greek] that should follow [second coming]" (I Peter 1:11).

Doubtless, exercise of constant vigilance occasioned by the uncertainty of the time of the Lord's coming has had, and still has, a salutary effect upon the believer. While he continues cherishing the hope of seeing Christ as He is, this very hope is purifying him, "even as he is pure" (I John 3:3).

The Salutation (4, 5a)

Verse 4. *John to the seven churches which are in Asia: Grace be unto you, and peace, from him which is, and which was, and which is to come; and from the seven Spirits which are before his throne.*

The seven churches which are in Asia. Three times reference is made to the seven churches which are in Asia. Their names are mentioned in verse 11 below. Note, however, in the epilogue (22:16) that the book is intended not merely for the seven churches in Asia, but for the church universal.

Grace be unto you, and peace. Grace was the usual Greek salutation, peace the Hebrew. Each word occurs only once more—grace in 22:21, peace in 6:4, where the red horse rider is said to "take peace from the earth."

From him which is, and which was, and which is to come. This phrase with slight variations occurs five times. 1:4, 8; 4:8; 11:17; 16:5. It expresses the eternal existence of the great "I AM" who inhabits eternity, and who is "the same yesterday, and today, and for ever." To the same effect are the two-part phrases: "Alpha and Omega," "the beginning and the ending," "the first and the last."

The seven Spirits which are before his throne. There are two prevalent interpretations of these words:

They signify the Holy Spirit in His sevenfold perfections or energies. Briefly stated, the arguments run as follows: Isaiah 11:2 presents a sevenfold description of the Spirit as related to Christ: "And the spirit of the Lord shall rest upon him, the spirit of wisdom and understanding, the spirit of counsel and might, the spirit of knowledge and of the fear of the Lord." As one can note, there are seven expressions regarding the Spirit, yet it should be pointed out that these are bestowals of the Spirit rather than perfections, for they do not include some of the most outstanding of His attributes, such as holiness, truth, life, and glory.

They signify seven special angels, presumably seven archangels. Other instances of the number seven in connection with angels occur in Revelation 1:20; 8:2, 6; and 15:1. Both angels and spirits are incorporeal creatures. Furthermore, "Are they [the angels] not all ministering spirits, sent forth to minister for them who shall be heirs of salvation" (Hebrews 1:14)? Angels, therefore, are ministering spirits sent forth.

The seven spirits of God are *before his throne*, which implies inferiority, subordination, and the like, and since no member of the Godhead ever occupies this position in the heavenly relationship they cannot signify the Holy Spirit.

Finally, the idea of sending forth angels with relation to end-time events occurs in Matthew 13:41: "The Son of man shall send forth his angels." This sending forth of the angels is said to occur in the "time of harvest," or the end of the world (Greek: *age*), which time is identical with the tribulation period. Revelation 6—18. In Revelation 14 a voice from heaven is heard and six angels come into view in addition to the "Son of man" with a sharp sickle, "for the harvest of the earth is ripe." Evidently the angelic ministry of chapter 14 is the fulfillment of the prophecy in Matthew 13:41. This sending forth calls to mind once more the Hebrews 1:14 passage where the verb "sent forth" is used in the perfect participial form and could easily signify that in the past they had been sent forth to minister to those who should be heirs of salvation and they are, during the tribulation period also, being sent forth to execute the judgment of God upon unrepentant men. It seems conclusive that the Holy Spirit cannot be intended by the seven spirits because there is no evidence here, nor in the entire Scripture, that He will be sent a second time during the tribulation period.[3]

Verse 5a. *And from Jesus Christ, who is the faithful witness, and the first begotten of the dead, and the prince of the kings of the earth.*

The faithful witness—as prophet in the past. God the Father gave Him as a witness to the people. Isaiah 55:4. Jesus Himself declared: "To this end was I born, and for this cause came I into the world, that I should bear witness unto the truth" (John 18:37). In Revelation 3:14 He refers to Himself as the faithful and true witness. John calls Him the faithful witness. 1:5.

The first begotten of [Greek: *from*] *the dead*—His present work as priest. Resurrection from the dead and exaltation by the right hand of God entitled Christ to the position of priest forever after the order of Melchisedec. Hebrews 7:16, 17, 24, 25; 9:12; 10:12.

For the use of the Greek word *prototokos* (translated "first born" and "first begotten") see Romans 8:29; Colossians 1:15, 18; Hebrews 6.

First begotten denotes, simply, priority in this case. Christ is "the firstborn of every creature [all creation]: for [because] by him were all things created . . . and he is before all things" (Colossians 1:15-17). This shows plainly that Christ Himself is no creature. If He were, He would have had to create Himself. He would have had to exist before He was created, which involves an absurdity and impossibility.

The term, *first begotten from the dead* (Greek), is well explained by Acts 26:23: "He should be the first that should rise from the dead [lit. the first from the resurrection of the dead]." It is true that certain individuals both of the Old Testament and the New Testament period rose from the dead. But all these had been raised by divine power; moreover, they died again.

The figurative term "firstfruits" which the Apostle Paul applies to the resurrection has a similar connotation: "But now is Christ risen from the dead, and become the firstfruits of them that slept" (I Corinthians 15:20). The thought again is, simply, that of precedence or priority. The apostle further explains: "But every man in his own order: Christ the firstfruits; afterward they that are Christ's at his coming. Then [Greek: *afterward*] cometh the end" (I Corinthians 15:23, 24). The period between the resurrection of Christ and them that are Christ's, represented by the first "afterward," is already over 1900 years. The period between the resurrection of them that are Christ's, or "the dead in Christ," and the end, when "the rest of the dead" will be raised, will be one thousand years. Revelation 20:5, 6.

The dead (Greek: *nekros*) should be carefully distinguished from death (*thanatos*). The former occurs always in the masculine plural and has reference to the dead people, that is, those who, for the time being, remain in their graves. The resurrection of Christ was a resurrection from the dead (people). The apostles were persecuted, not because they preached the resurrection "of" the dead (which the "men of Israel" also allow—Acts 24:15), but because they preached the resurrection "from" the dead. Acts 4:2. They indicated that Jesus Christ's resurrection was prior to and distinct from all others.

The resurrection of the dead in Christ is also spoken of as a resurrection "from" the dead. The wicked are not raised until "afterward," that is, "at the end," when the thousand years are finished. The importance of the distinction between the resurrection "of" the dead (which is true of all men) and the resurrection "from" the dead is seen in that the latter phraseology is applied 34 times to the resurrection of Christ and 14 times to that of believers. The resurrection of the wicked is not included in Paul's discussion in I Corinthians 15. This is indicated by what is said of those raised; e.g., "It [the body] is sown in dishonour; it is raised in glory" (I Corinthians 15:43). This cannot be true of the wicked dead. These wicked dead will not join in the rapturous exclamation: "O death, where is thy sting? . . . But thanks be to God, which giveth us the victory through our Lord Jesus Christ" (I Corinthians 15:55, 57).

The prince [ruler] of the kings of the earth—His future office of king. The title is applied to Christ in various aspects: Prince of Peace (Isaiah 9:6); God gave Him to be a witness and a leader (Hebrew: Prince) (Isaiah 55:4); "Prince of princes" (Daniel 8:25; cf. Revelation 1:5); "Prince of life" (Acts 3:15); "a Prince and a Saviour" (Acts 5:31); "out of thee shall come a Governor, that shall rule my people Israel" (Matthew 2:6).

On the side of evil and opposed to Him is Satan, the prince of demons (Matthew 9:34; 12:24; Mark 3:22; Luke 11:15), prince of this world (John 12:31; 14:30; 16:11), and prince of the power of the air (Ephesians 2:2).

Jesus is ruler of the kings of the earth de jure (by right). He, evidently, is not yet this de facto (in reality). When He was on earth, "the kings of the earth set themselves, and the rulers . . . [took] counsel together, against . . . [him]" (Psalm 2:2; Acts 4:26) and "killed the Prince of life" (Acts 3:15). In this day we see "not yet all things put under him" (Hebrews 2:8). In what were once known as Christian nations, rulers have arisen who would bow the Lord out of the universe. No ruler upon earth has given His name a place in the legal document governing the nation. The principles of the Sermon on the Mount have not been applied in the administration of civil law.

Before Jesus Christ will be ruler de facto, He shall "strike through kings in the day of his wrath" (Psalm 110:5). It is at Armageddon (near Jerusalem) that the kings will meet their Waterloo. Following this, those that are "left of all the nations which came against Jerusalem shall even go up from year to year to worship the

King" (Zechariah 14:16). Not until then will all kings "fall down before him: all nations shall serve him" (Psalm 72:11), and "the Lord shall be king over all the earth" (Zechariah 14:9).

The Doxology (5b, 6)

Verses 5b, 6. *Unto him that loved us, and washed us from our sins in his own blood, and hath made us kings and priests unto God and his Father; to him be glory and dominion for ever and ever. Amen.*

Unto him that loved us. There is no warrant for changing the past tense for the present. The internal evidence is wholly against the change. Jesus loved before He redeemed; e.g., "who loved me, and gave himself for me" (Galatians 2:20). In no case where love and redemption are mentioned together do we find the order reversed [which argues for the past tense (Greek: aorist)—J. O. Y.]. Barring a few authorities, now known to be untrustworthy, upon whom the Westcott-Hort edition and the Revisers leaned heavily, the weight of evidence in favor of the change is negligible. The early commentators Oecumenius, Andreas, and Arethas likewise have the ordinary reading. It is significant that the apostle of love strikes, in this first doxology, the keynote of love which is the master emotion indwelling and engaging the heart of Deity.

And washed us from our sins in his own blood. The Westcott-Hort text reads *loosed* for *washed.* The Greek word for the former is *luo,* for the latter *louo*—the variation consisting in the omission of a single letter "o." Probably the same scribe who changed the past tense of the verb "love" into the present in the preceding clause is also responsible for the change here. At any rate, the authorities for changes in both cases are much the same. Not only is the preponderance of external evidence in favor of the common reading, but the internal evidence in the latter instance points decidedly to the same conclusions. For instance, the word *luo* is never used in a redemptive sense in the New Testament Scriptures. We also observe that John never speaks of redemption in a judicial sense, such as the word "loosed" implies. On the other hand, he mentions Jesus' love for His disciples and His declaration that they were "washed" and "[made] clean every whit" in close proximity. John 13:1, 10.

The death of Christ is both the manifestation and the proof of love; therefore this and the preceding clause stand related to each other as cause and effect. For example: "God commendeth his love toward us, in that, while we were yet sinners, Christ died for us" (Romans 5:8); "Who loved me, and gave himself for me" (Galatians 2:20); "Hereby know we the love [Greek], because he laid down his life for us" (I John 3:16). The unprecedented emphasis upon the sacrificial character of Christ's death in the following chapters appears in the fact that the title "Lamb" is ascribed to Him 28 times. The crescendo of praise attains the highest pitch when every creature acclaims, "Blessing, and honour, and glory, and power . . . . [to] the Lamb for ever and ever" (5:13).

And hath made us kings and priests unto God and his Father. This passage, like the one pertaining to Jesus Christ mentioned above, has likewise a *de jure* implication; for the believer's kingship (while it is his by right) is not yet a reality. That it refers to the church is plain from Peter's declaration, "ye are . . . a royal priesthood [a kingly priesthood]" (I Peter 2:9). We note a marked similarity between 1:5b, 6a and 5:9b, 10: "for thou wast slain, and hast redeemed us to God by thy blood out of every kindred, and tongue, and people, and nation; and hast made us unto our God kings and priests: and we shall reign on the earth." Here, however, the church (kings and priests) is on earth; there, "before the Lamb" in heaven. Note also that even in the latter passage, the reign on earth has not yet been realized, for they themselves declare, "we shall reign on the earth."

Believers are made kings and priests *unto God and his Father*. (Note that "and" here has the sense of "even.") Evidently this means more than the mere bearing of an honorary title. It means service rendered to Him in the sense implied by the term. Bible readers will recall that this is not the first mention pertaining to the church in the capacity of rulership. We have Jesus' words to His disciples in this respect: ". . . in the regeneration when the Son of man shall sit in the throne of his glory, ye also shall sit upon twelve thrones, judging the twelve tribes of Israel" (Matthew 19:28); and "I appoint [lit. *give*] unto you a kingdom, as my Father hath appointed unto me; that ye may eat and drink at my table in my kingdom, and sit on thrones judging the twelve tribes of Israel" (Luke 22:29, 30). Paul declares: "Do ye not know that the saints shall judge the world? . . . Know ye not that we shall judge angels" (I Corinthians 6:2, 3)? Note the future tense in each instance. This is also implied in the phrase, "in the regeneration," signifying as it does the new order of things. The service implied by the word "priests" doubtless includes a ministry of intercession. Our Lord Himself will be "a priest upon his throne" (Zechariah 6:13).

To him be glory and dominion. There is apparently an allusion here to Daniel 7:14: "And there was given him dominion, and glory, and a kingdom, that all people, nations, and languages, should serve him: his dominion is an everlasting dominion, which shall not pass away." *Glory* pertains to the exalted spiritual state of our Lord; *dominion* to His absolute sovereignty. The glory man lost in the beginning through sin is now ascribed to the Son of man.

For ever and ever. This durative term corresponds in meaning with the closing words of the passage quoted above from Daniel, viz., "everlasting," and "which shall not pass away." It occurs seven times in the epistles (Galatians 1:5; Philippians 4:20; I Timothy 1:17; II Timothy 4:18; Hebrews 13:21; I Peter 4:11; 5:11) —three times in relation to the Father, four times in relation to Christ. It occurs fourteen times in Revelation—ten times in reference to God and Christ, once each to: reign of saints, the eternal torment of Babylon, the image worshipers, the devil, the beast, and the false prophet.

Amen. This is the common Hebrew word of confirmation as when one confirms the words of another, hence usually with the sense of "so be it!" "truly!" "verily!" It is derived from the word "believe"; hence it means "regard as true." It is used as a noun in Isaiah 65:16 in the phrase, "the God of truth [Hebrew: Amen]." The word is similarly applied to Christ in 3:14, where He is designated "the Amen" (the truth). Compare this with John 14:6, where Jesus' own testimony is, "I am . . . the truth."

The Prophetic Forecast (7)

Verse 7. *Behold, he cometh with clouds; and every eye shall see him, and they also which pierced him: and all kindreds of the earth shall wail because of him. Even so, Amen.*

Behold he cometh with clouds. This is the first call to *behold* which with its variant "lo" occurs thirty times in the book. "Behold" or "lo" is the imperative form of the verb to "see" or "look." In Revelation it is always used in what is known as the middle voice, which gives it the sense, "look for yourself," i.e., for your own interest or benefit.

We have here an example of the law of antecedent mention. (See Introduction.) In this law a distant event is spoken of as taking place in the present time. When the future event refers to the second coming of our Lord, the purpose of the previous mention is to inspire the faithful with courage and hope, and to warn the wayward and wicked to repentance and amendment of life. After the announcement is made, events follow each other, beginning with the present, in the order of chronological sequence until the distant event (His coming with clouds) is reached. Since these events compose almost the entire contents of Revelation, this may well be regarded as the key verse.

His coming with clouds is mentioned once in the Old Testament (Daniel 7:14) and seven times in the New Testament (Matthew 24:30; 26:64; Mark 13:26; 14:62; Luke 21:27; Revelation 1:7; 14:14). That this aspect of His coming takes place after the tribulation period is plainly seen in the parallel passage from the Olivet discourse recorded by Matthew. "Immediately after the tribulation of those days shall the sun be darkened, and the moon shall not give her light, and the stars shall fall from heaven, and the powers of the heavens shall be shaken: and then shall appear the sign of the Son of man in heaven: and then shall all the tribes of the earth mourn, and they shall see the Son of man coming in the clouds of heaven with power and great glory" (Matthew 24:29, 30).

And every eye shall see him. This corresponds with Matthew's statement, "and they [all the tribes of the earth] shall see the Son of man coming in the clouds of heaven with power and great glory" (Matthew 24:30). (See also Mark 13:26; Luke 21:27.) This clause is in sharp contrast with Hebrews 9:28: "Unto them that look for him shall he appear [be seen] the second time." The word "appear" is the same as that used, by the evangelists, in reference to the appearances of Christ after His resurrection. Matthew 28:7, 10; Mark 16:7; Luke 24:34. See also Paul's testimony in I Corinthians 15:5-8: "he was seen of Cephas, . . . after that, he was seen of above five hundred brethren at once; . . . he was seen of James. . . . And last of all he was seen of me also." In each of these terms "was seen of" means "appeared to." Plainly in His appearances Jesus was not seen by the world. Compare also His appearing to Saul and the direct statement, "the men which journeyed with him stood speechless, hearing a voice, but seeing no man [Greek: *one*]" (Acts 9:7). And so it will be when the Lord appears to them that look for Him—

the rest may hear a voice, but they will see no one. Further studies will show that the church will be in heaven (chapters 4, 5) before the tribulation. The coming alluded to in the phrase, "and every eye shall see him," is described in detail in 19:11 ff. It is immediately after the tribulation, a description of which closes with chapter 18.

And they also which pierced him. The phrase is in part a quotation from Zechariah 12:10, which reads: "And I will pour upon the house of David, and upon the inhabitants of Jerusalem, the spirit of grace and of supplications: and they shall look upon me whom they have pierced, and they shall mourn for him, as one mourneth for his only son." The reference is plainly to Israel, and the time is, as the preceding verse shows, when God will "seek to destroy all the nations that come against Jerusalem." An account of the fulfillment is given in Revelation 19. The Apostle Peter plainly charged the Jews with the guilt of the death of Christ. "Ye men of Israel, hear these words; Jesus of Nazareth . . . . ye have taken, and by wicked hands have crucified and slain" (Acts 2:22, 23); and again, Ye men of Israel "denied the Holy One and the Just . . . and killed the Prince of life" (Acts 3:14, 15).

And all kindreds of the earth shall wail because of him. In the Greek of Matthew 24:30, precisely the same words are used except that in Revelation 1:7 the significant words *because of him* are added. More literally we would translate *shall wail over him,* thus stressing the intensity of the wail. Compare Revelation 18:9, where the kings of the earth "lament" (Greek: *wail*) over Babylon. Note the contrast in 18:20 where those in heaven are commanded to "rejoice over her." The identity of this passage with that in Matthew again proves conclusively that the coming alluded to takes place "immediately after the tribulation" (Matthew 24:29). The recognition of this fact should once for all correct two prevailing errors: that the world will grow better before His coming as held by postmillennialists, and that the tribulation referred to is already past. It is plain that no past tribulation can be intended from the fact that the Lord did not come "immediately" after any tribulation of the past.

Some have erroneously held the view that the word "tribes" refers always to Israel. This view is untenable from the following considerations: The same words appear in the Septuagint translation of Genesis 12:3: "In thee shall all families [tribes] of the earth be blessed." The tribes here evidently include all the people on earth, not only the descendants of Abram; hence the reference cannot be restricted to Israel. In Zechariah 14:17 "all the families (Greek: *tribes*) of the earth" is the equivalent of "every one that is left of all the nations" (Zechariah 14:16). Hence "tribes" refers to "nations," not to Israel. See also the following verse: "And if the family [tribe] of Egypt go not up . . ." (Zechariah 14:18). The word *tribes* occurs five times in Revelation as one of four groups comprising the world population—"kindreds [tribes], tongues, people, and nations" (5:9; 7:9; 11:9; 13:7; 14:6). Similarly, in the world groups mentioned in Genesis 10:5, 20, 31, the Greek word for families is the same as that translated kindred (tribe) here.

Even so, Amen. The identical words (*nai, Amen*) occur again in 22:20. In each case they are in response to the declaration of the Lord's second coming. The first is the Greek; the second, the Hebrew word of affirmation. In a time like this the reader ought to join in this double affirmation, "Yes, yes, come, Lord Jesus!"

The Divine Declaration (8)

Verse 8. *I am Alpha and Omega, the beginning and the ending, saith the Lord, which is, and which was, and which is to come, the Almighty.*

I am Alpha and Omega. Alpha is the first and Omega the last letter in the Greek alphabet. In the received text only the letters "A" and "O" are given. The same couplet of titles appears again in 1:11 and in later chapters twice. 21:6; 22:13.

The beginning and the ending. These words are explanatory of the former two. They are repeated in 21:6 and in 22:13. Terminology of similar meaning occurs elsewhere. The phrase, "the first and the last," occurs three times in Isaiah. 41:4; 44:6; 48:12. In Isaiah 43:10 we have an interesting variant: "before me there was no God formed, neither shall there be after me." In Revelation the same double expression occurs. 1:11, 17; 2:8. The last two are followed by interesting explanatory statements: "I am he that liveth, and was dead" (1:18), and "which was dead, and is alive" (2:8).

Which is, and which was, and which is to come. This threefold expression occurs elsewhere (1:8; 4:8; 11:17) and in abbreviated form (16:5). The terminology is a close equivalent of that mentioned in Hebrews 13:8: "the same yesterday, and to day, and for ever." Both the twofold and the threefold terms are extensions of the revelation of His name, which God gave to Moses: "I AM THAT I AM," or the more simple form: "I AM" (Exodus 3:14).

The Almighty. The Greek word occurs nine times in Revelation. It is translated "omnipotent" once. 19:6. It occurs only once before in the New Testament. II Corinthians 6:18. The word, however, denotes more than omnipotence; it has the sense of universal rulership.

A question remains: Who is the speaker in verse 8? Since the phrase, "which is, and which was, and which is to come," is applied to God in verse 4, it is natural to conclude that God is the speaker here. There are, however, a number of reasons why this is not the correct view: (1) Since God gave this revelation to Christ that He (Christ) might show it to His servants (1:1), it would seem unlikely that He would add words of His own directly from heaven; (2) since the phrase, "which is, and which was, and which is to come," has already been applied to God (1:4), there appears to be no good reason why there should be a repetition of this statement, if the reference is to God the Father; (3) we have seen (1:7) that the prophetic announcement pertaining to the coming of Jesus Christ is followed by the double affirmation, "Even so, Amen." This verse therefore appears to be a response of Jesus to this affirmation.

That the remaining titles of 1:7 are applied to Jesus Christ will appear from an examination of passages where they occur: I "heard behind me a great voice, as of a trumpet, saying, I am Alpha and Omega, the first and the last. . . . And I turned to see the voice that spake with me. And being turned, I saw . . one like unto the Son of man" (1:10-13). The speaker here is Christ, "the Son of man."

"And he laid his right hand upon me, saying unto me, Fear not; I am the first and the last: I am he that liveth, and was dead" (1:17, 18). Here again the speaker is Christ, for He refers to His own death and resurrection.

"Behold, I come quickly. . . . I am Alpha and Omega, the beginning and the end, the first and the last" (22:12, 13). As in 1:8, the divine titles appear after the mention of His coming.

"There were great voices in heaven, saying, The kingdoms of this world are become the kingdoms of our Lord, and of his Christ; and he shall reign for ever and ever. And the four and twenty elders, which sat before God on their seats [thrones], fell upon their faces, and worshipped God, saying, We give thee thanks, O Lord God Almighty, which art, and wast, and art to come; because thou hast taken to thee thy great power, and hast reigned" (11:15-17). The reign (11:17) plainly refers to that of Christ (11:15). It could not refer to God the Father because He never relinquished His reign and hence it could not be said of Him that He has taken it again.

There is, however, one passage (21:6, 7) in which the titles are applied to God. It is to be noted, however, that the setting is in the new heaven and new earth, at which time Jesus will have delivered up the kingdom to the Father that God may be all and in all. I Corinthians 15:24-28.

It is noteworthy that the early church fathers who quoted this verse uniformly hold the view that Christ is the speaker, e.g., ". . . the Word is called the Alpha and the Omega, of whom alone the end becomes beginning, and ends again at the original beginning without any break."[4] Hippolytus, after citing Romans 9:5, "Who is over all, God blessed for ever," continues, "For to this effect John also has said, 'Which is, and which was, and which is to come, the Almighty.' And well has he named Christ the Almighty. For in this he has said only what Christ testifies of Himself."[5] And so Origen, after quoting Revelation 1:8, remarks: "For who else was 'He which is to come' than Christ? And as no one ought to be offended, seeing God is the Father, that the Saviour is also God; so also, since the Father is called omnipotent, no one ought to be offended that the Son of God is also called omnipotent. For in this way will that saying be true which He utters to the Father, 'All Mine are Thine, and Thine are Mine.'"[6]

FOOTNOTES, PART I

1. See Introduction.

2. See Appendix, p. 313, "Visions of the Apocalypse Listed."

3. See Appendix, p. 314, "The Seven Spirits Which Are Before the Throne."

4. Clement of Alexandria, "The Stromata," Bk. IV, Chap. XXV, *The Ante-Nicene Fathers,* Vol. II, p. 438, col. b.

5. Hippolytus, "Against the Heresy of One Noetus," Sec. 6, *op. cit.,* Vol. V, p. 225, col. b.

6. Origen, "De Principiis," Bk. I, Chap. II, Sec. 10, *op. cit.,* Vol. IV, p. 250, col. b.

2

PART II
THE THINGS WHICH THOU HAST SEEN
(THE APOSTLE'S VISION)
1:9-20

THE THINGS WHICH THOU HAST SEEN

Antecedents of the Vision (9-12a)

Verse 9. *I John, who also am your brother, and companion in tribulation, and in the kingdom and patience of Jesus Christ, was in the isle that is called Patmos, for the word of God, and for the testimony of Jesus Christ.*

I John occurs in 21:2 and 22:8. The name of the apostle occurs elsewhere only in 1:1 and 1:4 above.

Brother. The word expresses both endearment, equality, and fellowship. *Your* is plural and includes the entire membership of the "seven churches which are in Asia" (1:4).

Companion. The word means literally "sharer" or "partaker" and shows that not only he but the brethren to whom he was writing were undergoing tribulation at the time of his writing, probably about A.D. 96. Stephen and James, the brother of John, as well as Paul and Peter had already suffered martyrdom.

In tribulation. John was a copartner not only in the tribulation incident to the child of God, but also in that related to the kingdom and patience of Jesus Christ. Tribulation precedes entrance into the kingdom. This is in accord with Paul's admonition to the early churches: "we must through many tribulations [Greek] enter into the kingdom of God" (Acts 14:22). We are assured also that "tribulation worketh patience" and patience is one of the rounds in the ladder reaching to the abundant entrance of the everlasting kingdom.

The early church fathers furnish us with valuable corroborative information regarding John's exile.

According to Hippolytus, "John . . . was banished by Domitian the king to the isle of Patmos, in which also he wrote his Gospel and saw the apocalyptic vision."[1]

". . . the Apostle John was first plunged, unhurt, into boiling oil, and thence remitted to his island-exile."[2]

". . . listen to a tale, which is not a tale but a narrative, handed down and committed to the custody of memory, about the Apostle John. For when, on the tyrant's [Domitian's] death, he returned to Ephesus from the isle of Patmos, he went away, being invited, to the contiguous territories of the nations, here to appoint bishops, there to set in order whole Churches, there to ordain such as were marked out by the Spirit."[3]

For the word of God, and for the testimony of Jesus Christ. John was banished to Patmos because of the Word of God and because of the testimony of Jesus Christ. The Greek preposition (*dia*, accusative) has the same sense here as in 6:9 and 20:4. In other words, his exile was not in order that he might receive the Word of God, etc., but because of his active service in promulgating the Word of God and because he bore testimony concerning Jesus Christ. The Lord, however,

49

overruled his banishment so that it might serve as a most appropriate occasion for revealing to him the Word and testimony as we have it in this book.

Verse 10. *I was in the Spirit on the Lord's day, and heard behind me a great voice, as of a trumpet.*

Was. This means literally "became," hence the sense of "came to be." The language employed is repeated in 4:2, "hence I came to be in the Spirit."

In the Spirit. The expression occurs again in 4:2; 17:3; 21:10; the two latter having a lengthened form—"he carried me away in the spirit." Similar terms occur in Ezekiel, where the prophet testifies, "the spirit entered into me" (2:2); "took me up" or "lifted me up" (3:12, 14; 8:3; 11:1, 24; 43:5); and "carried me out" (37:1).

Compare further the following passages in the New Testament: "He fell into a trance, and saw heaven opened" (Acts 10:10, 11); "I was in the city of Joppa praying: and in a trance I saw a vision" (Acts 11:5); "While I prayed in the temple, I was in a trance; and saw him . . ." (Acts 22:17, 18).

The word "trance" (Greek: ecstasy) means to stand outside one's self. It will be noticed that where Ezekiel and John say "in the Spirit," the passages in Acts use the word "trance," for in both cases visions follow. Hence, *in the Spirit* signifies to be in a trance or state of spiritual ecstasy.

On the Lord's day. Two views prevail regarding the meaning of these words. The term refers to, (1) the Christian Sabbath; (2) the future day of the Lord spoken of by the prophets of the Old Testament and apostles of the New. It may be noted in passing that both views could be correct, since it might be possible that John came to be in the Spirit on a certain Sunday and that at the same time he had a vision of things pertaining to the future day of the Lord. Since the first day of the week is commonly thought of as being the Lord's day, it is easy for a commentator to convey the idea that such is the case here and pass on as though no other view merited consideration. Frequently it happens that the easiest interpretation is not the correct one. [By a careful study of the use of the terms "the Lord's day" and "the day of the Lord" as found in the entire Scriptures, Smith came to the conclusion that the expression here in the Book of Revelation can only mean the future day of the Lord. That is to say, the day when the Lord takes over the affairs in the world of men. Since the book under study, by all odds, is a prophetic book, the term "the Lord's day" should be taken in its prophetic meaning, which as stated above is to be understood as "the day of the Lord."[4]—J. O. Y.]

Heard behind me a great voice. "I heard" occurs 28 times and "I saw" 44 times. The two verbs occur in close proximity—five times "heard and saw," and five times "saw and heard."

The voice John heard was *behind* him. Why the word *behind?* See the probable answer in verse 12. He mentions this same voice again in 4:1. Note that he did not hear a second voice at that juncture, for he says, "the first voice as of a trumpet which I heard." This supports the view that when John came to be in the Spirit he saw things from the point of view of the Lord's day which will not begin until after the close of the church age.

The word *great* (*megas*) occurs 82 times and "great men" (*megistanes*) twice. *Great voice* (sometimes translated *loud*) occurs 20 times. Nowhere in the Bible do we find so many great things in the same compass. We may say then that the Book of Revelation is the "great" book of the Bible.

As of a trumpet. As stated before, frequent mention is made of trumpets in connection with the future Lord's day. But in no instance do we find the word used in connection with our Sunday. [The voice *as of a trumpet* was meant to catch and to hold the seer's attention.—J. O. Y.]

Verse 11. *Saying, I am Alpha and Omega, the first and the last: and, What thou seest, write in a book, and send it unto the seven churches which are in Asia; unto Ephesus, and unto Smyrna, and unto Pergamos, and unto Thyatira, and unto Sardis, and unto Philadelphia, and unto Laodicea.*

I am Alpha and Omega. That the titles, *Alpha and Omega*, the first and the last, are those of Christ, is plain from verse 17. The great voice then is that of Christ. He is therefore also the one who says, "Come up hither" (4:1). Hence, the voice John heard perhaps is to be identified with the shout of the Lord. I Thessalonians 4:16.

What thou seest, write in a book. What thou seest corresponds with "all things that he [John] saw" (1:2). Compare 22:8. In other words, it includes the entire contents of the book. This is the first of twelve commands, *write.* That the writing followed immediately after seeing the vision, appears from 10:4, where John is bidden not to write.

And send it unto the seven churches which are in Asia. Several reasons may be given why these churches are mentioned in particular. The seven churches were the nearest to Patmos, the place where John wrote the book. Ephesus was situated about fifty miles northeast of Patmos. John at the time of his banishment was one of the elders of the church at Ephesus. According to Clement of Alexandria, ". . . the Apostle John . . . on the tyrant's [Domitian's] death, . . . returned to Ephesus from the isle of Patmos, he went away, being invited, to the contiguous territories of the nations, here to appoint bishops, there to set in order whole Churches, there to ordain such as were marked out by the Spirit."[5] This shows that the apostle's first concern was for the welfare of the churches in this vicinity. Another reason for sending the "book" first to these churches was undoubtedly that they were chosen by divine appointment as representative and typical of the church universal. It is plain that they were not chosen because of their superior spiritual attainment or their popularity; for only one besides Ephesus (Laodicea) is so much as mentioned in the other Scriptures.

Their names are indicative of their character. "Smyrna lay 40 miles north of Ephesus, Pergamum 40 north of Smyrna, Thyatira 45 S.E. of Pergamum, Sardis 30 nearly due S. of Thyatira, Philadelphia 30 E.S.E. of Sardis, and Laodicea 40 S.E. of Philadelphia."[6] (See map of Ramsay.)

In examining Ramsay's map, *Letters to the Seven Churches,* we observe that the distance between Ephesus and Smyrna is at least ten miles less than between Smyrna and Pergamos, so that it is more nearly correct to say that the distances are thirty-five and forty-five respectively. In order to get a mental picture of their relative location, one should think of an irregular inverted capital V, in which the line from Ephesus through Smyrna to Pergamos is almost perpendicular south to north while the line from Pergamos through Thyatira and Philadelphia to Laodicea extends somewhat irregularly in a southeasterly direction. Laodicea is almost directly east of Ephesus, a distance of about ninety miles.

The Vision (12b-16)

Verse 12. *And I turned to see the voice that spake with me. And being turned, I saw seven golden candlesticks.*

By the figure of metonymy, *voice* is here used instead of Him who spoke, namely, the Lord.

John turned to see the voice "behind" him. Verse 19. The mentioning of this unusual gesture has apparently seemed too trivial a matter to attract the attention of commentators. However, we know that "no word from God . . . [is] void of power" (Luke 1:37, RV). This double allusion, "the voice behind," and the sequel, *I turned to see*, cannot be without significance. The following points are given as probable and suggestive interpretations: As to his body, John is on the isle of Patmos; as to his spirit, he is in the future Lord's day. As yet he has had no vision, but he hears a voice "behind him." He turns his body to see the voice and the One that spoke with him. Having turned, he saw seven golden candlesticks. The seven candlesticks are the seven churches in Asia. Verse 20. The seven churches in Asia are to the east of Patmos; consequently before he turned, he was facing westward. This posture of facing westward may be accounted for by the fact that the first actor in the day of the Lord comes from Rome. (Compare Daniel 9:26, 27.) The voice comes from behind, i.e., from the one who stands in the midst of the churches.

According to the law of intervening mention, since the things pertaining to the church (1-5) precede those of the day of the Lord, John is bidden to write them first. He writes of her history on earth (2, 3), and of her glorified state in heaven (4, 5). The things of the Lord's day, i.e., the judgments of the Lord, begin with the opening of chapter 6.

Verse 13. *And in the midst of the seven candlesticks one like unto the Son of man, clothed with a garment down to the foot, and girt about the paps with a golden girdle.*

In the midst describes our Lord's position in respect to the church. Observe: "Where two or three are gathered together in my name, there am I in the midst of them" (Matthew 18:20). Here He is seen in the midst of the candlesticks (churches). In 2:1 He walks "in the midst of the seven golden candlesticks." In 5:6 He is seen in the midst of the elders (the glorified church).

Christian people upon assembling who pray, "Lord, come into our midst," apparently fail to recognize that He is already there. A more consistent prayer would be, "Lord, make us worthy of Thy presence."

This is the first mention of the *Son of man* in Revelation. It occurs only once more, viz., in 14:14. The term alludes to the humanity of our Lord. It is the term Jesus used most frequently in reference to Himself. Even when others declare

Him to be the Son of God, He immediately speaks of Himself as the *Son of man*. Matthew 16:16, 27; 26:63, 64.

The title *Son of man* occurs 84 times in the Gospels, 21 of which refer to His second coming. In Revelation 14:14 it is again used in connection with that event. It is also the term employed in relation to His capacity as judge. This is brought out clearly by John in his Gospel: "The Father judgeth no man, but hath committed all judgment unto the Son," and "hath given him authority to execute judgment also, because he is the Son of man" (John 5:22, 27). The world will be judged by *a* (Greek) "man whom he hath ordained" (Acts 17:31).

Apparently the title *Son of man* is here introduced in reference to Jesus because the passage is introductory to chapters 2 and 3. This is evident from the fact that the varied imagery applied to Him is employed in these chapters in the presentation of Himself to the individual churches where He passes judgment on them. This preliminary judgment of men in the flesh is in accord with a statement of the Apostle Peter when he says "For the time is come that judgment must begin at the house of God" (I Peter 4:17). No code of ethics is comparable to this. The *Son of man* Himself draws the line of cleavage between right and wrong, approving the right and condemning the wrong. We may be certain that He will employ the same standards and criteria of judgment at the judgment seat of Christ. The words He speaks here will judge men in that day. In the description following, the language employed is plainly figurative. That He is eminently qualified to judge is seen not only because, as human, He "was in all points tempted like as we are" (Hebrews 4:15), and thus can sympathize with man, but as divine, He is possessed of all the major attributes belonging to deity. An attempt will be made to point out various attributes of the Son of man in light of the symbolism of numerous Scripture passages. Before proceeding with the terms employed in the present verse, note the remaining verses pertaining to the symbolism.

Verse 14. *His head and his hairs were white like wool, as white as snow; and his eyes were as a flame of fire.*

Verse 15. *And his feet like unto fine brass, as if they burned in a furnace: and his voice as the sound of many waters.*

Verse 16. *And he had in his right hand seven stars: and out of his mouth went a sharp twoedged sword: and his countenance was as the sun shineth in his strength.*

Attributes of the Son of Man as Suggested by the Symbolism
in Verses 13-16

1. In the midst of the seven candlesticks: love and familiarity.
2. Clothed with a garment down to the foot: righteousness and dignity.
3. Girt about the paps with a golden girdle: compassion and virility.
4. His head and his hairs . . . white like wool, as white as snow: eternity and wisdom.
5. His eyes . . . as a flame of fire: omniscience and scrutiny.
6. His feet like unto fine brass, as if they burned in a furnace: judgment and purity.
7. His voice as the sound of many waters: grandeur and dignity.

8. And he had in his right hand seven stars: omnipotence and authority.
9. Out of his mouth went a sharp twoedged sword: truth and severity.
10. His countenance . . . as the sun shineth in his strength: holiness and glory.

The Effects of the Vision (17, 18)

Verse 17. *And when I saw him, I fell at his feet as dead. And he laid his right hand upon me, saying unto me, Fear not; I am the first and the last.*

And when I saw him. This is not to be regarded as a separate vision; the allusion is to verse 12 and the details described in 13-16.

I fell at his feet as dead. The writers of the Bible record numerous examples of similar prostrations of holy men of God at the appearance of heavenly messengers among which are the following: Abraham (Genesis 17:3), Gideon (Judges 6:22, 23), Manoah (Judges 13:20), Job (Job 42:5, 6), Isaiah (Isaiah 6:5), Ezekiel (Ezekiel 1:28; 3:23; 43:3; 44:4), Daniel (Daniel 8:17; 10:8, 9, 15-17), the three disciples (Matthew 17:6), Zacharias (Luke 1:12), and Peter (Luke 5:8).

He laid his right hand upon me. This was not only an expression of power but undoubtedly also one of love and compassion toward "the disciple whom Jesus loved."

Fear not. Much confusion prevails as to the number of occurrences in the Scriptures of these comforting and assuring words. From one source we are told there is a separate mention for each day of the year! On the other hand, unless variant translations, i.e., "be not afraid" and "dread not," are included, the total will not be secured. The original expression occurs 93 times in the Old Testament and 24 times in the New, or a total of 117 times.

The words are most frequently those of God, of Christ, or of angels to men. From these sources they came to Abram, Hagar, Isaac, Jacob, Moses, Joshua, Gideon, Elijah, Isaiah, Jeremiah, Ezekiel, Daniel, Zerubbabel, Joshua (the high priest), and Israel as a nation. They came also in New Testament times to Joseph, the twelve disciples, the three (Peter, James, and John), the women at the grave, the ruler of the synagogue, Mary, the shepherds, Peter, Jairus, Paul, and John.

This is apparently the tenth time John heard these words coming from the lips of the Master. The nearest approach to the present occasion was when he and Peter and James were with Him in the holy mount at which time they fell on their faces and were sore afraid. Matthew 17:6.

I am the first and the last. The repetition of this attribute which implies eternal existence was peculiarly fitting upon this occasion. Similar words of encouragement continue in the verse following.

Verse 18. *I am he that liveth, and was dead; and, behold, I am alive for evermore, Amen; and have the keys of hell and of death.*

To get the full force of the words they must be taken in connection with the preceding words of the Son of man. A literal translation would read: *Fear not; I am the first and the last, and the living [One], and I came to be dead and behold! living I am, unto the ages of the ages.*

No words could be more invigorating than these to the apostle who, although he was not dead (as was his Master), yet he was "as dead." Undoubtedly as he heard the words, *behold, living I am*, he recalled his own previous testimony regarding his Master: "In him was life"; "whosoever believeth in him should not perish, but have everlasting life," as well as the words of Jesus: "I am the way, the truth, and the life"; "I am the bread of life"; "I am come that they might have life, and that they might have it more abundantly"; "I am the resurrection, and the life: he that believeth in me, though he were dead, yet shall he live," and "whosoever liveth and believeth in me shall never die."

This is the second of fourteen occurrences of the phrase, "unto the ages of the ages." (See verse 6 above.)

Amen. This is the third of ten occurrences. (See verses 6, 7 above.) While the word is used as a confirmation of the truth spoken, it is also used as applying directly to Christ who, Himself, is the truth. 3:14; cf. John 14:6. Since in its next occurrence it is prefixed by the definite article, it is probable that we should understand it here as a title of Christ.

And have the keys of hell and of death. Key is a symbolic word denoting authority. This is seen by its use in Matthew 16:19. To Peter were given the keys of the kingdom of heaven, signifying that to him was given authority to bind or to loose. [Providing, of course, that that which he bound or loosed had already been bound or loosed in heaven, as the Greek tense and syntax would indicate. Authority over death and hell was most conclusively demonstrated by the death and resurrection of the Master, ". . . because it was not possible that he should be holden of it" (Acts 2:24b).—J. O. Y.][7]

Just as verses 1-3 are introductory to the entire book, so the Patmos vision is introductory to chapters 2 and 3.

The names of the seven churches (1:11) recur with details in chapters 2 and 3.

The vision proper begins with the distinctive earmark, "I saw" (1:12), which does not occur again until 4:1. This shows that all the intervening materials constitute a single vision and that the several parts are organically related.

The description of the Son of man as given in verses 12-18, with slight allusions to verses 4 and 5, recurs in part in the presentation of Himself to the individual churches:

to Ephesus (2:1 with 1:13, 16),
to Smyrna (2:8 with 1:18),
to Pergamos (2:12 with 1:16),
to Thyatira (2:18 with 1:14, 15),
to Sardis (3:1 with 1:4, 16),
to Philadelphia (3:7 with 1:18),
and to Laodicea (3:14 with 1:5, 18).

For details, see the address to each church. As for the meaning of the symbols, candlesticks and stars, see verse 20 below.

The Inspired Outline (19)

Verse 19. *Write the things which thou hast seen, and the things which are, and the things which shall be hereafter.*

The things which thou hast seen. The reference is plainly to John's vision of the Son of man in the midst of the seven golden candlesticks as described in 1:12-18. These verses are implied because they are introductory to the vision as well as to the contents of the entire book. The first part of the outline pertains therefore to the contents of chapter one.

And the things which are. The things *which are* have already been mentioned twice. 1:4, 11. That the seven churches in Asia are intended is further evidenced by the fact that following the things *thou hast seen* (chapter 1), chapters 2 and 3 are a detailed description of the seven churches in the order of occurrence as in 1:11, including the condition prevailing in each. Observe that after these two chapters, no further mention is made of the seven churches. Indeed the word "church" does not appear again except once in the last chapter, where the reference is to the church universal. Clearly therefore by the second division of the outline, *the things which are,* is meant the description of the seven churches as contained in chapters 2 and 3.

And the things which shall be hereafter. (Lit., the things which are about to come to pass after these things.) *Hereafter* is an unfortunate translation, for it might lead to the mistaken idea that the reference is to future existence. The Greek phrase *meta tauta* means *after these things.* It occurs frequently in narrative prose —some 70 times in the Old Testament and 35 in the New. Ten of these New Testament references occur in Revelation. The phrase denotes succession—a passing from what is now past to that which is to follow. When, however, the phrase is accompanied by "I saw," the reference may be simply to order of vision and not necessarily to order in time. When it occurs alone, however, as in the present instance, it invariably denotes succession in time.

Consequently, *after these things* must necessarily refer to things that will follow, in order of time, the conditions prevailing in the seven churches as described in these chapters. And since the conditions prevailing in these seven churches are anticipative and descriptive of universal church conditions from the time of John to the end of the church age, it necessarily follows that from chapter 4 on, there is given a record of things which shall be after the church age has run its course.

[This is not to say that the messages to the seven churches had no significance for the churches of Asia. The conditions described were conditions in those churches, but they were chosen for their prophetic forecast.—J. O. Y.]

This is further confirmed by the fact that this third division of the outline is repeated, with emphasis, in the first verse of chapter 4: "Come up hither, and I will shew thee things which must be after these things." Note the change from "shall be" to "must be." The things of chapter 4 and following must be after the things of chapters 2 and 3, which pertain to the church age. That this included the remaining chapters of Revelation is plain from the fact that the third clause of 1:19 concludes the things concerning which John was commanded to write.

To summarize what is intended by the three divisions of the outline of the book as given in 1:19—Write: *the things which thou hast seen*, i.e., seven golden candlesticks and in their midst one like unto the Son of man having in His right hand seven stars; *and the things which are*, i.e., the description of the seven churches which are in Asia (chapters 2 and 3); *and the things which shall be after these things*, i.e., after the church age has run its course (chapters 4—22).

The Interpretation of the Vision (20)

Verse 20. *The mystery of the seven stars which thou sawest in my right hand, and the seven golden candlesticks. The seven stars are the angels of the seven churches: and the seven candlesticks which thou sawest are the seven churches.*

Mystery. Something previously unknown and unknowable by finite minds but now revealed. Cf. Ephesians 3:3-5. The mystery here pertains to the seven stars and the seven golden candlesticks. The revelation of the mystery immediately follows. The stars signify angels; the candlesticks, churches. There are two opposing views of interpretation. One school of thought holds that by *angels*, celestial beings are intended; the other, that the reference is to the bishops or pastors of the churches. That angels in the literal sense are intended, appears from the following discussion.

Consider the meaning, use, and translation of the original word for angel. The Hebrew word is *malak;* the Greek, *anggelos*, from which comes the English *angel*. The word means "messenger," that is, one sent forth. It is applied alike to human and to celestial beings.

However, the Lord's own interpretation would indicate that literal angels are intended. *The seven stars are the angels of the seven churches.* This interpretation must be taken as final, for the Lord never interpreted one symbol by the use of another. When He said, upon a previous occasion, "the reapers are the angels" (Matthew 13:39), He meant "angels" in the literal sense as the context shows. To reinterpret His interpretation given in Revelation 1:20 as some do by adding, "and the angels are bishops," is both presumptuous and hazardous.

If stars are angels and angels are bishops, the middle term doubtless would have been omitted, and it would be a direct statement, "the seven stars are the bishops of the seven churches." The conclusion is preposterous, and only a few church officials would welcome such a concept.

A rapid survey of the extensive ministry of angels both in the Old and New Testament Scriptures[8] would show that it is altogether consistent and essential that this ministry be recognized and portrayed in the complete manner described throughout the section of the book (chapters 2 and 3) which deals in particular with the church age.

In the Book of Revelation angels have a superintending control over the elements or realms, e.g., the four angels holding (in check) the four winds of the earth (7:1), the angel of the bottomless pit (9:11), an angel having the power over fire (14:18), an angel of the waters (16:5). If there are angels of winds, an angel in charge of fire, an angel of the waters, and an angel of the bottomless pit, it should appear but fitting and appropriate that angels should have a similar charge with respect to the churches. [Condensed from extended notes.–J. O. Y.]

Why the message in each case was addressed to the angel deserves further consideration. It should be remembered that while the messages are addressed to the angels, they are intended primarily for the churches. This is plain from the hortatory declaration in each case: "He that hath an ear, let him hear what the Spirit saith unto the churches." Moreover, the praise or the blame is meant for the church, not the angel. The view that the angels are charged with guilt or lauded with praise in accordance with the conditions prevailing in the church is without foundation. No one would think of charging God with guilt because man fell into sin. Why then should angels be thus charged?

Since angels exercise a certain superintendence over the churches, it appears but reasonable and fitting that they be addressed. How could they perform their functions without being acquainted with the prevailing conditions?

Angels have a keen interest in the word of prophecy: "Searching what, or what manner of time the Spirit of Christ . . . did signify, when it testified beforehand the sufferings of Christ, and the glories [Greek] that should follow. . . . Which things the angels desire to look into" (I Peter 1:11, 12).

Angels learn from the revelation in God's Word. This is implied in the following words: "Unto me, who am less than the least of all saints, is this grace given, that I should preach among the Gentiles the unsearchable riches of Christ; and to make all [Greek does not have 'men'; so angels are included] see what is the fellowship of the mystery, which from the beginning of the world hath been hid in God, who created all things by Jesus Christ: to the intent that now unto the principalities and powers in heavenly places [i.e., to angels] might be known by the church the manifold wisdom of God" (Ephesians 3:8-10).

The angel who signifies this book to John (1:1) expressly testifies that he keeps the words (Greek) of the prophecy of this book (22:7). Plainly, therefore, he must be interested in its contents.

These reasons should be sufficient to show that the *angels* addressed are to be understood in a literal sense.

FOOTNOTES, PART II

1. Hippolytus, "On the Twelve Apostles," *The Ante-Nicene Fathers*, Vol. V, p. 255, col. a.

2. Tertullian, "Prescription Against Heretics," Chap. XXXVI, *op. cit.*, Vol. III, p. 260, col. b.

3. Clement of Alexandria, "Who Is the Rich Man That Shall Be Saved?" Chap. XLII, *op. cit.*, Vol. II, p. 603, col. a.

4. See Appendix, p. 319, "The Lord's Day."

5. Clement of Alexandria, *op. cit.*

6. Charles, Vol. I, p. 25.

7. See Appendix, p. 324, "Death and Hades."

8. See Appendix, p. 326, "The Ministry of Angels."

3

PART III
THE THINGS WHICH ARE
(THE MESSAGES TO THE SEVEN CHURCHES)
2:1–3:21

THE THINGS WHICH ARE

Introduction

Before proceeding with the comments, note the following particulars:

The churches named are selected not because of their prominence in the days of the apostles (only two—Ephesus and Laodicea—are previously mentioned in the Bible) but because of their representative character. In these messages, the Spirit of God speaks not only to the individual churches named, but to the church universal, the exhortation to each being uniformly, "He that hath an ear, let him hear what the Spirit saith unto the churches." Note also in 2:23 the phrase, "all the churches shall know. . . ."

The seven churches are typical and prophetic in the sense that conditions prevailing in the order of mention anticipate universal church conditions from the time of John on to the close of church history.

That these seven churches have this typical and prophetic character is manifest by the following observations:

Chapters 2 and 3 constitute a part of "the words of this prophecy" (1:3; cf. 22:18). Of necessity, therefore, these two chapters have a prophetic sense.

The number seven as usual suggests completeness, for no other churches are mentioned in the book. Moreover, chapters 4 and 5 which follow tell of "things which must be hereafter" (4:1), i.e., of things following those mentioned in chapters 2 and 3. Undoubtedly there is some truth in the view that the various conditions prevailing in these seven churches are typical of universal church conditions in any given period of the entire church age, but this is only the case in a very limited sense. If the view were wholly correct, then church history would have to be uniform throughout which, as anyone familiar with it knows, is far from being true to fact. On the other hand, the varying conditions represented in these seven churches in order of their succession fit uniquely into the checkered history of the church universal from start to finish.

Ephesus pictures the early decline of vital Christianity at the close of the first century, in this, that she had left her first love.

Smyrna covers the period of martyrdom prevailing during the first three centuries familiarly known as the ten general church persecutions.

Pergamos prefigures the union of church and state under Constantine including the development of priestcraft and moral corruption.

Thyatira portrays the domination of the Roman hierarchy, when a corrupt spiritual leadership under the guise of a lewd woman "knew the depths of Satan."

Sardis points to the days of the Reformation at which time "a few names . . . which . . . [had] not defiled their garments," again brought a saving message to a benighted Christendom and a needy world.

61

Philadelphia speaks of a period of orthodoxy and evangelism inaugurated by such leaders as Wesley and Whitefield, at which time all the nations of the world presented "open doors" for the reception of the Gospel.

Laodicea stages the end-time apostasy in language precisely the same as that employed concerning the last days by Jesus and the apostles Paul, James, Peter, John, and Jude.

The Message to the Church at Ephesus (2:1-7)

The Annunciation

Verse 1a. *Unto the angel of the church of Ephesus write.*

That *angel* in the plain literal sense is intended see 1:20. The definite article "the" shows that there was but a single angel at or over each church. This fact is in direct opposition to the view that by the angel a presiding church official (bishop or elder) is intended, for when Paul came to Miletus, he sent to Ephesus and called for the "elders" of the church. Acts 20:17. In addressing them, he remarked: "Take heed therefore unto yourselves, and to all the flock, over the which the Holy Ghost hath made you overseers [Greek: bishops]" (Acts 20:28). It is contrary to Scripture as well as to early church history to hold the view that a single bishop was in charge of a congregation of believers as early as the last decade of the first century. [Reference seems to be made therefore to the angel as a ministering spirit, not as an overseeing elder.—J. O. Y.]

The city of Ephesus was located some fifty miles northeast of Patmos and was nearest to John geographically. The Ephesian church was also nearest to his heart, for he was a resident there at the time of his exile and, as noted before, he returned to this place "after the death of the tyrant" (Domitian). (See page 48.) Ephesus was the citadel of idolatry in this region. In it was located the temple of the great goddess Diana (Acts 19:27), one of the seven wonders of the world. Ephesus was also the mother church of these parts. After establishing the church (Acts 19:1-8), the Apostle Paul, for the space of two years, disputed daily in the school of Tyrannus, after which, upon the eve of a great revival, believers made a great bonfire of books of magical arts valued at 50,000 pieces of silver. Here, too, Paul met the elders of the church, warning them that after his departure "grievous wolves [would] enter . . . not sparing the flock" and declaring that "by the space of three years I ceased not to warn every one night and day with tears" (Acts 20:29, 31). Paul's letter to the church at Ephesus, written but a few years later, shows that his labors at this place were abundantly rewarded, for he speaks of them as being "blessed . . . with all spiritual blessings in heavenly places in Christ" (Ephesians 1:3).

As is frequently the case, Biblical names have a meaning of vital importance in correct interpretation. Thus Ephesus comes from a word meaning "let go" or "allow," hence "declension" or "relaxation." This church of high privilege and attainment, due to her lack of vigilance, soon fell from her lofty estate, and apparently as a judgment upon her unfaithfulness and defection, her place is now described as "a mere desolation, altogether waste and without inhabitant." [W. M.

Ramsay, *The Letters to the Seven Churches*, referred to Ephesus as the city of change, which seems to have been reflected in the church.—J. O. Y.]

The Presentation

Verse 1b. *These things saith he that holdeth the seven stars in his right hand, who walketh in the midst of the seven golden candlesticks.*

Notice the similarity of these words to a portion of the symbolism applied to the Son of man in chapter 1. (Cf. verses 12, 13, 16.) In his presentation to the several churches addressed, the symbolism selected in each case corresponds precisely with the condition prevailing in the particular church. In this case, however, a strengthened form of the symbolism is employed. For instance, in 1:16 the Son of man is said to be "having" the seven stars "in his right hand"; here He *holds them fast* (Greek). In 1:13 He is in the midst of the seven candlesticks; here He *walks* in their midst. This increased emphasis is apparently due to the greater responsibility of the angels in view of the perilous circumstances and decadent tendencies of the church of Ephesus when John wrote.

The Declaration

Verse 2a. *I know.*

Judgment now begins at the house of God. I Peter 4:17. Call to mind again that "the Father judgeth no man [as John declares in his Gospel], but hath committed all judgment unto the Son, because he is the Son of man" (John 5:22, 27). As observed before, the title "Son of man" indicates His competency to judge, for, as man, He knows what is in man, because He was "in all points tempted like as we are" (Hebrews 4:15). Hence, also, He appears as the "merciful and faithful high priest" (Hebrews 2:17), and as God (indicated by the imagery employed 1:14-16), He is competent to judge, "for in him dwelleth all the fulness of the Godhead bodily" (Colossians 2:9).

The Approbation

Verses 2, 3, 6. *I know thy works, and thy labour, and thy patience, and how thou canst not bear them which are evil: and thou hast tried them which say they are apostles, and are not, and hast found them liars: and hast borne, and hast patience, and for my name's sake hast laboured, and hast not fainted. . . . But this thou hast, that thou hatest the deeds of the Nicolaitanes, which I also hate.*

It is significant that in passing judgment upon the churches, the Son of man begins with the things He approves and apparently enlarges upon them, for He approves more (on the whole) than He condemns. In this, as in every other excellence, He is our perfect and needful example.

The Son of man commends them for a number of virtues: *Works* are mentioned first and then *labour* and *patience*. The two latter are repeated, but in the reverse order. The church apparently was keenly averse to the encroachment of evil workers and false pretenders and it hated those whom the Son of man hates.

What impresses one most, however, is not the good things that are mentioned, but the better things that are not mentioned. Faith, hope, and love are sadly missing. Contrast this church with the Thessalonians: Ephesus had works, but not work of faith; labor, but not labor of love; patience, but not patience of hope. I Thessalonians 1:3. Indeed, they had "left" the greatest of these. I Corinthians 13:13. It is not too much to say that a church may have all the virtues mentioned and yet be devoid of spiritual life.

Who are the Nicolaitanes? Possibly the best answer is that which is based on the literal sense of the word: *Nikao* means to conquer, and *laos*, people; from which comes the English word "laity," hence "laity-conquerors." Apparently the prediction of Paul, given by inspiration, was being fulfilled at this time.

To this class probably belonged Diotrephes, "who loveth to have the preeminence," of whom John himself wrote in his last epistle. III John 9. A good name for the Nicolaitanes would therefore be *Diotrephesians*. They were leaders in the church who posed as lords over God's heritage. Doubtless here are the beginnings of priestcraft, a system which later developed into the Roman hierarchy. It appears they were permitted to remain in the church, for we find that in the period covered by the church in Pergamos, their deeds had developed into a doctrine. Revelation 2:15.

The Reprobation

Verses 4, 5. *Nevertheless I have somewhat against thee, because thou hast left thy first love. Remember therefore from whence thou art fallen, and repent, and do the first works; or else I will come unto thee quickly, and will remove thy candlestick out of his place, except thou repent.*

The word *somewhat* would appear to mitigate the judgment pronounced against the church. The word, however, is in italics, showing that it is not in the original. The sense is, *But I have this against thee, that thou hast left thy first love.* The charge is not (as it is frequently quoted), *thou hast "lost" thy first love*, as though it had been by accident, but *thou hast "left" thy first love*, a responsible, if not a willful, act. Hence the divine rejoinder, *repent, and do the first works*, by which is probably meant the work of faith. For "repentance from dead works" and "faith toward God" are named as the first or foundation principles of the doctrine of Christ. Hebrews 6:1. Without these, it is impossible to please God.

The threat follows. There must be repentance first and last (the order is repeated, verse 5) without delay, for unless this is forthcoming, He will come to the church in judgment and remove her candlestick, that is, she would cease to be a witness for Him. The present solitude and barrenness of the place speaks as with a thousand tongues that this has actually happened.

The Exhortation

Verse 7a. *He that hath an ear, let him hear what the Spirit saith unto the churches.*

The words of exhortation are uniform in the letters of the seven churches. A similar exhortation in an abbreviated form occurs in 13:9: "If any man have an ear, let him hear." The latter clause is omitted, implying that the church at that time is no longer on earth.

The words imply that while the letter is addressed to the angel, it is meant for the churches. (See 1:20.)

The Remuneration

Verse 7b. *To him that overcometh will I give to eat of the tree of life, which is in the midst of the paradise of God.*

The thought of overcoming is most prominent in the writings of John. The verbal form is used 24 times and occurs only four times in the rest of the New Testament. The passages are distributed as follows: once in his Gospel (16:33); six times in his first epistle (2:13, 14; 4:4; 5:4, 5), and 17 times in Revelation, variously applied: to Christ (3:21b; 5:5; 17:14), to the Antichrist (6:2; 11:7; 13:7), to the believer (2:7, 11, 17, 26; 3:5, 12, 21a; 12:11; 15:2; 21:7).

To overcome in John's writings does not mean immunity from death as might be the case in physical warfare. For instance, in 12:11 a group of martyrs is mentioned: "And they overcame him [Satan] by the blood of the Lamb, and by the word of their testimony; and they loved not their lives unto the death." In 15:2 John sees "them that had gotten the victory over [lit., them that overcame] the beast, and over his image, and over his mark, and over the number of his name, stand on the sea of glass, having the harps of God." Plainly these had died as martyrs. The same is true of Christ, for He said, "I lay down my life" (John 10:17), and again "as I also overcame" (Revelation 3:21).

The promise to eat of the tree of life points back to Genesis 2:9; 3:22, and forward to Revelation 22:2, 14. Sin barred man from access to the tree; overcoming sin restores his right to eat of the tree and thus "live forever."

The Message to the Church at Smyrna (2:8-11)

The Annunciation

Verse 8a. *And unto the angel of the church in Smyrna write.*

The word *Smyrna* means bitter, and this accords with the severe persecutions endured by the Christians at that place. Smyrna was the most important seaport of the whole country and is situated about 35 miles north of Ephesus. Because of its beautiful location, its orderly arrangement, and its gradual elevation to a lofty summit, the city was variously designated as "the First City," "the Beauty of Asia," or "the City of Life and Strength." Due to its popularity, a heathen temple was erected here in honor of Tiberias, the Roman emperor, whom the heathen worshiped as God. Apostate Jews were numerous in the city, and they were among the chief agitators in the persecutions raging there. Its present population is approximately 320,000,[1] about three fourths of whom profess the Christian faith. It is interesting to note that this church, in spite of repeated and severe persecutions, is today the only one of the seven in a prosperous condition, the rest being either entirely extinct or in a low state of existence.

The church in its prophetic character is typical of the period of general persecutions by the heathen world from the time of the apostles on to the year A.D. 313, when the Roman emperor, Constantine, himself having espoused the Christian faith, issued a decree making Christianity a lawful religion. In A.D. 323 he went still further and made it the religion of the state.

The Presentation

Verse 8b. *These things saith the first and the last, which was dead, and is alive.*

Here the allusion is to 1:18a: "I am he that liveth, and was dead; and, behold, I am alive for evermore." Again, Jesus presents Himself in a manner befitting the condition of the church addressed. Here it is for encouragement, because He Himself was dead and now is alive; in other words, there is life after death for those who are His. John could undoubtedly recall similar words of assurance from Jesus while He was still with His disciples and as recorded in his Gospel: "I am the resurrection, and the life: he that believeth in me, though he were dead, yet shall he live: and whosoever liveth and believeth in me shall never die" (John 11:25, 26). Again, ". . . because I live, ye shall live also" (John 14:19).

The Declaration

Verses 9, 10b. *I know thy works, and tribulation, and poverty . . . and . . . the blasphemy of them which say they are Jews, and are not, but are the synagogue of Satan. . . . Behold, the devil shall cast some of you into prison, that ye may be tried; and ye shall have tribulation ten days.* (Passages containing neither praise nor blame in regard to the church addressed will be included under *The Declaration* in each case.)

Works. Some texts omit *works,* but others of high authority retain the word. The internal evidence is in favor of its retention, for it is certain that Jesus recognized whatever activity there might have been in each church. He even speaks of the works of a dead church. 3:1. Moreover, in five of the churches addressed, we have the uniform reading: "I know thy works."

Tribulation and poverty. The same apostle recorded similar words of Jesus in his Gospel: "In the world ye shall have tribulation"; but he could also recall the reassuring words following: ". . . be of good cheer; I have overcome the world" (John 16:33). John, while writing this letter, was with them a "companion in tribulation" (1:9). The word *tribulation* occurs elsewhere in 2:22 and 7:14, where, however, mention is made of a "great tribulation."

Their poverty was probably due to the spoiling of goods which usually follows in the wake of persecution.

That those *which say they are Jews, and are not* took a prominent part in the persecution of Christians is evident from the account of the martyrdom of Polycarp. They united their voices with the heathen in the first outcry of hate against the martyr as being "the father of the Christians, and the overthrower of our gods, he who has been teaching many not to sacrifice, or to worship the gods." In the preparation of the funeral pile, ". . . the multitudes immediately gathering together wood and fagots out of the shops and baths; the Jews especially, according to custom, eagerly assisting them in it," the record reads. Concerning the day of martyrdom, we are told, "the day being that of the great Sabbath." Seeing the body of

Polycarp was not being consumed by the fire, the Jews urgently requested the governor not to give it to the Christians for burial "lest . . . forsaking Him that was crucified, they begin to worship this one. . . . The centurion then, seeing the strife excited by the Jews, placed the body in the midst of the fire, and consumed it."[2] Although the martyrdom of Polycarp occurred about half a century after this message came to the Smyrneans, the blasphemy and hypocrisy of certain Jews as well as their domination by Satan as given in the text accords precisely with their characterization at the later date.

The devil shall cast. The Lord graciously forewarns concerning the trial that was about to come upon them. While man is the instrument, Satan is the instigator, and the Lord the permitter of the trial. The tribulation which He allowed to come upon the church apparently was intended to be both corrective and purgative as was that of Job. He, too, was tried by Satan under God's permission. Holy Writ furnishes no instance of faithfulness and endurance under test more noble than that of Job. Hear his words of grim determination and unswerving loyalty: "Though he slay me, yet will I trust in him" (Job 13:15), and again, "when he hath tried me, I shall come forth as gold" (Job 23:10).

Tribulation ten days. The tribulation, while it was severe, was nevertheless brief, as the phrase *ten days* implies. Apparently the Smyrneans quickly learned the lesson and secured the "profit" intended by the chastening rod, whereupon Satan's hand of affliction was stayed and the tribulation ceased.

The *ten days* probably have also a symbolic sense, for they appear to allude to the ten general persecutions of the early Christian Church which all historians recognize and which ended with the decrees of Constantine already referred to. The spiritual declension of Ephesus which characterized the first church period was apparently checked by the persecutions which the Lord permitted to come upon the church during the second period.

History records that in spite of (or perhaps because of) the bitter persecution which raged during this period, it was the most prosperous in the spread of Christianity that the world has ever witnessed. It was during this period that the now familiar slogan arose: "the blood of the martyrs is the seed of the church." In proof of this early rapid growth of Christianity the testimonies of three witnesses living during this period are cited:

"Christians are scattered through all the cities of the world. . . . The Christians, though subjected day by day to punishment, increase the more in number. . . . Do you not see that the more of them are punished, the greater becomes the number of the rest?"[3]

"There is not one single race of men, whether barbarians, or Greeks, or whatever they may be called, nomads, or vagrants, or herdsmen living in tents, among whom prayers and giving of thanks are not offered through the name of the crucified Jesus."[4]

"The word of our Teacher remained not in Judea alone, as philosophy did in Greece; but was diffused over the whole world, over every nation, and village, and town, bringing already over to the truth whole houses, and each individual of those who heard it . . . and not a few of the philosophers themselves."[5]

Probably no uninspired words more heartening and consoling ever fell from human lips than those of Cyprian, a church father who lived in the days of the Decian persecution (A.D. 250) and himself a martyr. As if by premonition he declared: "In persecutions, earth is shut up, but heaven is opened; Antichrist is threatening, but Christ is protecting; death is brought in, but immortality follows; the world is taken away from him that is slain, but paradise is set forth to him restored; the life of time is extinguished, but the life of eternity is realized."[6]

The Approbation

Verse 9. *But thou art rich.*

Here we have indeed "multum in parvo" (much in little). Moreover, in the Greek, *rich* is emphatic by position, viz., *rich art thou.* Do not forget that the Son of man, He who knew what is in man, for He Himself was man, and who Himself was God (as is attested by the major divine attributes ascribed to Him, 1:13 ff.), is the speaker and judge.

The word *rich* is set over against *poverty* and follows it. *I know thy poverty, but rich art thou* (Greek). They were poor in this world's goods, but rich toward God—they had laid up treasures in heaven.

The church in Smyrna appears in marked contrast with Laodicea. The Lord judged the Smyrneans and said, *rich art thou;* the Laodiceans appraised themselves and said, "rich am I" (Greek). The Lord, however, refuses to let their verdict stand. He looks at the heart and declares not only the desperate poverty of Laodicea, but what is worse, they "know not" that they are wretched and miserable and poor and naked and blind.

The Reprobation

Only the churches at Smyrna and Philadelphia are without a word of blame or disapproval. The supreme Judge apparently gives the church at Smyrna the highest grade among the seven.

The Exhortation

Verse 10a. *Fear none of those things which thou shalt suffer.* (Lit., *Fear not what you are about to suffer.*)

This is the last of twenty-five "Fear not's" occurring in the New Testament. Many are words of comfort from heaven. The only other occurrence in Revelation has been noted. 1:17. Eight are addressed to six individuals: Joseph (Matthew 1:20), Jairus (Mark 5:36; Luke 8:50), Zacharias (Luke 1:13), Mary (Luke 1:30), Paul (Acts 18:9; 27:24), John (Revelation 1:17).

Verse 10b. *Be thou faithful unto death.*

The phrase *unto death* occurs elsewhere in two places: "I [Paul] persecuted this way unto the death" (Acts 22:4). "They loved not their lives unto the death" (Revelation 12:11). In each case the article is omitted in the Greek. The thought is degree rather than duration; that is, as the parallel phrases indicate, be faithful to the extent that you will die for your faith, not merely until you die.

Out of the many unknown, unheralded, and uncrowned of this period who were thus *faithful unto death*, a few notable names are preserved in the writings of the church fathers.

Ignatius, bishop of Antioch, reputed to be the little child which Jesus set in the midst of the disciples, because of his testimony concerning Jesus Christ was banished to Rome by the Emperor Trajan. There he was thrown into the amphitheater to be devoured by the wild beasts for the entertainment of the spectators. This was about the year A.D. 110, during the third general persecution.

Polycarp's notable dying testimony always bears repeating. When his persecutors endeavored to persuade him to swear by the fortune of Caesar and to reproach Christ, he openly declared: "Eighty and six years have I served Him, and He never did me any injury: how then can I blaspheme my King and my Saviour?"[7]

Justin Martyr, the foremost apologist and historian of the early church, likewise suffered martyrdom at Rome, probably the year after Polycarp, about A.D. 166.

These persecutions were due to two principal causes: (1) The secluded meetings of the early Christians and their refusal to join in the worship of the heathen aroused suspicion; consequently Christians were slanderously charged with incest and other abominations. (2) Terrible floods, famines, pestilences prevailing at this time were charged to the alleged impiety of the Christians.

The great Latin father, Tertullian, when about twenty years of age, having been educated at Rome, apparently witnessed these martyrdoms, for later he bears the significant testimony: "If the Tiber has overflowed its banks, if the Nile has remained in its bed, if the sky has been still, or the earth been in commotion, if death has made its devastations, or famine its afflictions, your cry immediately is, 'This is the fault of the Christians!' "[8]

Verse 11a. *He that hath an ear, let him hear what the Spirit saith unto the churches.* (See verse 7.)

The Remuneration

Verse 10b. *I will give thee a crown of life.*

Again compare the appropriateness of the presentation, "which was dead, and is alive," to conditions prevailing in the church, *Be thou faithful unto death, and I will give thee a crown of life,* for death and life are set in contrast in both.

Of all creatures, men and angels, only to the church are crowns promised. Not in all the Scriptures do we find crowns promised to Israel. Neither do angels (including cherubim and seraphim) wear crowns. Observe this point, because it is most important in the matter of distinguishing various groups mentioned in chapter 4.

Five variant terms are employed in describing crowns promised to believers in the church age. There is an incorruptible crown. I Corinthians 9:25. This crown is promised to the one who strives for the mastery in things which have abiding spiritual values. It is mentioned in contrast with the corruptible crown obtained by the winner in earthly games. A crown of rejoicing is the reward of the soul winner. "For what is our hope, or joy, or crown of rejoicing? Are not even ye in the presence of our Lord Jesus Christ at his coming" (I Thessalonians 2:19)'

A crown of righteousness (II Timothy 4:8) is promised to him who keeps the faith. A crown of life (James 1:12 and Revelation 2:10) is to be the reward of the one faithful under trial or unto death. A crown of glory (I Peter 5:4) is to be given to undershepherds who "feed the flock of God."

Those only who constitute or represent the glorified church (Revelation 4:4) have the high distinction of having on their heads, like the Son of man (14:14), crowns of gold.

Verse 11b. *He that overcometh shall not be hurt of the second death.*

These promises are only for the overcomer. Failure to be an overcomer means to be an *undergoer*. While faith is the victory that overcometh (I John 5:4), note it does not say that faith will bring victory, but it *is* the victory, i.e., the one having faith (in Christ) has, or is in possession of, the victory.

Like the promise to the Ephesians, Revelation 2:7 goes back to Genesis 2:9, which also ties in with the Book of Genesis. 2:17; 3:22. In the former case there is a declaration of immunity to, and in the second, of escape from, the consequences of sin.

The promise plainly points forward also to Revelation 20:6: "Blessed and holy is he that hath part in the first resurrection: on such the second death hath no power." Since the clause, *shall not be hurt of the second death,* is identical in meaning with "on such the second death hath no power," we are to understand that the one who overcomes is he that hath part in the first resurrection. What the term *second death* signifies is twice declared in later passages: to be cast into the lake of fire (20:14); to have one's part in the lake of fire (21:8). In each case it is said this is "the second death." The security of the overcomer is doubly sure, for the Greek uses the double negative. *He that overcometh shall in no case be hurt of the second death.*

The Message to the Church at Pergamos (2:12-17)

The Annunciation

Verse 12a. *And to the angel of the church in Pergamos write.*

Pergamos, an inland city, was situated about 45 miles north of Smyrna and 75 miles north of Ephesus, on a lofty crag between two rivers. The first part of the name evidently arose from its high altitude, and was derived from "pergos," meaning a tower. The same root is seen in the German, "berg," a mountain, preserved in its modern name, Bergama. The latter part of the word is generally understood to come from the root, "gam," one "g" being elided in the formation of the compound, Perg-gam. "Gam" signifies to unite; hence "gamos" equals marriage. There are two ideas in the word "Pergamos"—one of "elevation" and the other, "marriage" or "union." Both these ideas fit precisely into the description of the church.

The details connected with the conversion (?) of Constantine are familiar to students of history. As the story goes, the emperor was in conflict with rivals for the imperial throne. One night he had a dream in which a cross appeared in the sky emblazoned with the words, *in hoc signo vince* (in this sign conquer). Constantine promptly followed the suggestion from the dream, united, it is said, with the church, and immediately became an "active member." Persecutions ceased and he made Christianity the religion of the state. Consequent to his prestige as civil head of the empire he virtually became also the religious head. Owing to doctrinal controversies prevailing in the church, he convened the first oecumenical conference at Nicea, Bithynia, with a view to a settlement of the issues involved, which dealt chiefly with the nature of the person of Christ. Three hundred and eighteen bishops were in attendance and approximately five times as many of the laity. As the emperor walked in the aisle arrayed in his royal paraphernalia, the vast assembly rose en masse and cheered him with hand clapping to the echo. He was accorded the honor of moderator of the meeting. It was a high day for Christendom, but also for the world. One is reminded of the words of one greater than Constantine: " . . . that which is highly esteemed among men is abomination in the sight of God" (Luke 16:15b). Another doctrine which might have been considered with profit at the meeting is the new birth. That the emperor himself had hazy views on this basic doctrine is evidenced by the fact that he deferred his baptism until the day of his death under the delusion that the waters of baptism purge the sins of the soul. Consequently he desired to have his sins all in before receiving baptism.

The church of Pergamos as a whole had suffered a serious relapse. This is evident from the evils she condoned within her ranks. The church prophetic lost her pilgrim character by her elevation to a state religion; her position as a called-out body, by her union or marriage to the state, political system.

Pergamos was a great pagan center and seat of worship. The first heathen temple in Asia was erected here in honor of Augustus Caesar, the Roman emperor who reigned when Jesus was born in Bethlehem of Judea.

The Presentation

Verse 12b. *These things saith he which hath the sharp sword with two edges.*
The imagery is taken from 1:16. The conditions prevailing at Pergamos are the occasion for the manner in which the Son of man presents Himself.

The sword stands for retributive justice. This is especially the case where it is accompanied by the qualifying word *sharp*. When Christ finally is revealed from heaven (chapter 19), He comes with a *sharp sword*, "that with it he should smite the nations." The Word of God is also described as the "sword of the Spirit" (Ephesians 6:17), and again it is said to be "sharper than any twoedged sword, piercing even to the dividing asunder" (Hebrews 4:12). Thus the sword stands for division. This is plainly indicated by Jesus' own words as given in two passages: "Think not that I am come to send peace on earth: I came not to send peace, but a sword" (Matthew 10:34). "Suppose ye that I am come to give peace on earth? I tell you, Nay; but rather division" (Luke 12:51).

When the persecuting forces of the world sought to destroy the church, she flourished all the more both numerically and spiritually. In the church at Pergamos, persecution is barely mentioned. She seems to court the friendship of the world, for she condones evil workers, and she is threatened with swift judgment.

The Declaration

Verse 13a. *I know thy works, and where thou dwellest, even where Satan's seat is.*

The church at Pergamos dwelt in the midst of a perilous environment. Satan dwelt there and his throne was there. Apparently his tactics are different than at the church of Smyrna. There he appeared as a roaring lion seeking whom he might devour; here, as an angel of light to deceive and seduce.

The original word for *dwell* occurs 15 times in Revelation and always in an evil sense. *Satan's seat* appears to allude to the heathen temple erected at Pergamos in honor of the Roman emperor, Augustus, in which he was deified and worshiped. According to reliable historical testimony, this form of worship is directly traceable to the Baal worship of the Scriptures and had its origin in the former Babylon, where it was introduced as a parody on the true worship of Jehovah. Its original founder was Nimrod, the mighty hunter.

The Approbation

Verse 13b. *And thou holdest fast my name, and hast not denied my faith, even in those days wherein Antipas was my faithful martyr, who was slain among you, where Satan dwelleth.*

In spite of her evil environment, the church at Pergamos still receives a measure of commendation, for she holds fast the name of Christ and has not denied the faith. In other words, she continued professedly orthodox.

Antipas is a noted example of faithfulness "unto death." He apparently dwelt adjacent to where Satan dwelt, that is, near his throne. The word *martyr* is in the Greek *witness*. The Lord speaks of Antipas as *my faithful witness*. Such he was, in proof of which he made the supreme sacrifice. Van Braght informs us that "some of the ancient writers maintain that he was enclosed in a red-hot brazen ox, and thus burned alive with great pain, yet in steadfastness."[9]

The Reprobation

Verse 14. *I have a few things against thee, because thou hast there them that hold the doctrine of Balaam, who taught Balac to cast a stumblingblock before the children of Israel, to eat things sacrificed unto idols, and to commit fornication.*

It is always perilous for a church to be located in an evil environment, but the greater peril at Pergamos was her condoning evil among her own membership.

Balaam was a hireling prophet in the employ of Balak, king of Moab. The narrative shows plainly that for the sake of gain, Balaam purposed to carry out the will of Balak, which was to curse Israel. Not succeeding in this, he contrived to corrupt Israel by casting before them a stumbling block (Greek: *a snare*). Through the intrigue of Balaam, Israel was beguiled into participation with unholy festivities with the Baal worshipers and this was followed by illict relations with the daughters of Moab. Satan repeats at Pergamos the tactics he employed in Old Testament days. God's people always fall under His displeasure when they pursue a course of compromise with evil workers. They will ultimately come to defeat and spiritual ruin.

Verse 15. *So hast thou also them that hold the doctrine of the Nicolaitanes, which thing I hate.*

Mention is made of this same group in the church at Ephesus. However, a notable difference is evident in the attitude of the church toward these evildoers. There the reference is to their deeds; here, deeds have become doctrine. There, like Christ, the church hated their deeds; here, while Christ is said to hate their doctrine, the church has them as members even though they hold fast (Greek) their pernicious doctrine.

Viewing now the church at Pergamos in a typical or prophetic sense, observe that the prevailing conditions, both the moral corruption of the Balaamites and the ambitions of the Nicolaitanes, are a notable forecast of conditions prevailing in the major portion of Christendom during the centuries immediately following the period of general persecutions forecast by the church at Smyrna. An example is the rise and development of the papacy. A brief outline from its beginnings up to the sixth century will point out this fact.

In the New Testament, mention is made of a twofold ministry—elders (or bishops) and deacons; or perhaps better, elder was the office and bishop (Greek), overseer, was the work.

In the second century, bishops began to be regarded as officers distinct from and superior to the presbyters or elders.

In the so-called writings of Ignatius, bishops were to be honored as God, and nothing was to be done without the bishop.

The bishop of Rome was spoken of by some as being the successor of Peter and sitting in his chair.

In the third century, by way of endearment, Cyprian was spoken of as papa [which is the English for the Latin word, father—J. O. Y.].

In the fourth century, the bishops of important cities such as Rome, Antioch, and Alexandria were called metropolitanes and archbishops and held the distinction of being bishops over bishops.

Leo I claimed the bishops of Rome were successors of Peter, the first pope.

In the fifth century, the emperor, Valentinian III, issued a law by which the Roman bishop was declared the supreme head of the western church.

The Exhortation

Verse 16. *Repent; or else I will come unto thee quickly, and will fight against them with the sword of my mouth.*

Repent here means that the church is to cease her fellowship with the "unfruitful works of darkness" by putting away the two classes of evildoers—the Balaamites and the Nicolaitanes. Failure to do so would result in a twofold judgment:

I will come unto thee (i.e., in judgment). The reference is to the faithful of whom he says (verse 13), "Thou holdest fast my name, and hast not denied my faith."

And will fight against them [the two groups of evildoers] *with the sword of my mouth.* The implication is that these latter, even though they are held as members, would be held among those who will be judged at His appearing "after the tribulation," for it is then that "out of his mouth goeth a sharp sword" (Revelation 19:15).

Verse 17a. *He that hath an ear, let him hear what the Spirit saith unto the churches.* (See verse 7.)

The Remuneration

Verse 17b. *To him that overcometh will I give to eat of the hidden manna, and will give him a white stone, and in the stone a new name written, which no man knoweth saving he that receiveth it.*

There are three promises by way of reward:

The hidden manna. To eat of the hidden manna is apparently set in contrast with "to eat . . . things . . . offered to idols." Those who ate of the latter perished in the wilderness; those who eat of the former live forever. *Hidden* implies preciousness. The church at Pergamos was located in an evil environment. Many were doubtless led astray, but the overcomer was encouraged with this precious promise of the hidden manna. As much as to say, "I have a special blessing for you: I will not make it public now, but you will be in full enjoyment of it hereafter."

A white stone. The allusion, like that of the hidden manna, apparently pertains to God's people during the wilderness journey. It is not probable that the white stone symbol is taken from pagan sources, and especially so at this place where the Son of man warns against worldly relations on the part of His people. The white stone promised to the overcomer may allude to the stones in the garment of the high priest and perhaps to the Urim signifying "light." White stands for purity in contrast to the pollution of the Balaam worshipers.

A new name. It is folly to seek to interpret what *no man knows.* We do well in this case to remember that ". . . secret things belong unto the Lord our God: but those things which are revealed belong unto us and to our children for ever . . ." (Deuteronomy 29:29). However, the *new name* is probably identical with "my new name" of Revelation 3:12. Reference is made to a secret name in Revelation 19:12, ". . . a name written, that no man knew, but he himself."

The Message to the Church at Thyatira (2:18-29)

The Annunciation

Verse 18a. *And unto the angel of the church in Thyatira write.*

Thyatira was situated about 35 miles southeast of Pergamos in a rich and fertile valley and was noted for its numerous trade guilds. The inscriptions, according to Ramsay, mention the following: "wool workers, linen workers, makers of outer garments, dyers, leather workers, tanners, potters, bakers, slave dealers, and bronze smiths."[10] Lydia, a seller of purple, was a native of this city. Acts 16:14. Her house in Philippi was about 200 miles from Thyatira.

Again we find that the name agrees with the nature of the church under consideration. The word *Thyatira* plainly comes from *thuos* (sacrifice) and *ateires* (unweary), hence unweary of sacrifices. That this points unmistakably to Rome, in the prophetic picture, further study will abundantly verify. Note a few finger points in this direction.

In our study of the church at Pergamos, we have already observed that conditions there are symbolic of universal church conditions up to approximately A.D. 500, when Rome came to be regarded not only as the imperial city in a political sense but also as the metropolis (mother city) of the religious world. This is simply a matter of plain historic fact. The literal sense of the name, "unweary of sacrifice," points to the multiplicity of religious rites and ceremonies characteristic of Rome. The typical significance indicated fits precisely into the long period of pretensions and ambitions of Rome toward supremacy and triumph after more than a millennium of varying struggle and success.

Two outstanding evils, sacrilege and fornication, designated in the Pergamos period, characterize also the Thyatirian period in an aggravated form.

The greater severity indicated in the "presentation" suggests a deeper dye of sin and guilt. To Pergamos (as we have seen) Christ appears as the One having the "sharp sword with two edges"; to Thyatira, as the "Son of God, who hath his eyes like unto a flame of fire, and his feet are like fine brass."

In Thyatira a woman (Jezebel) is the prominent figure. A woman in Scripture symbolizes a religious system; e.g., in the Old Testament, Israel is spoken of as the wife of Jehovah; He as her husband. Isaiah 54:1, 5; Jeremiah 31:32. In the New Testament, the true church is the bride or wife of Christ. Ephesians 5:23, 32; Revelation 19:7; 21:9. The mother of harlots is Rome. The corrupt Protestant churches, which came out of Rome, are her daughters.

Observe, too, that the sins of the woman, Jezebel, are similar to those of the great harlot (Revelation 17:1-6); hence the conditions prevailing in Thyatira reappear in Rome and her daughters in the latter days.

The Presentation

Verse 18b. *These things saith the Son of God, who hath his eyes like unto a flame of fire, and his feet are like fine brass.*

The title *Son of God*[11] is significant, for it occurs only here in the entire book. It denotes the deity of our Lord in contrast with His humanity, where the term "Son of man" is used. Revelation 1:13; 14:14.

The question naturally rises: Why should the title *Son of God* be employed in this presentation of Himself to the church at Thyatira rather than that of "Son of man" as in 1:13? Since the manner of presentation is conditioned upon the state of the church addressed, this must be the case here. In other words, in view of the low moral and spiritual condition of the church, it is most important that in His presentation there be no doubt that He possesses all the attributes of Deity; of omniscience, so that there can be no question that He absolutely knows the conditions as they actually are; of omnipotence, enabling Him to execute judgment commensurate with the depths of Satan into which many had fallen; of holiness, setting off their guilt in the presence of His utter abhorrence of their deeds; of righteousness, vindicating the necessity for Him to punish the guilty.

Aside from this, His mercy and love are also in evidence, because He first speaks in particular of the good works still in evidence and in the closing words He makes most assuring promises to the overcomer.

The sins of Rome which characterize Thyatira may well have included the view that Clement (the bishop when John wrote) is the successor of Peter, the alleged foundation upon whom the church was built. The title "Son of man" would have furnished no formidable persuasion to correct their error. On the other hand, "Son of God" should have reminded them that Peter is no true foundation, and that they, like Peter, should acknowledge Christ as the Son of the living God (Matthew 16:16-19), and as the only true foundation (I Corinthians 3:11).

The Declaration

Verse 19a. *I know thy works.*

It has been observed that in His address to the church at Thyatira, our Lord enlarges upon their good works more than He does upon those of Smyrna and Philadelphia against whom He offers no word of correction. Truly He judges righteous judgment. How different is He in this than many who are called by His name. How often all the good is forgotten in an individual when some evil report gets under way concerning him. We would do well to follow the Master's method in judging. In many cases, if all the good qualities in an individual were considered first, there would be little occasion or inclination to dwell on the lesser.

The First Approbation

Verse 19. *I know thy works, and charity, and service, and faith, and thy patience, and thy works; and the last to be more than the first.*

As already noticed, much is made of commendable things at Thyatira. Only one church (Ephesus) exceeds her in this respect. Two fundamentals are present here—love and faith—which are strangely wanting at Ephesus.

The order of words here indicated should likewise be observed, for works and love and service precede faith, which plainly is contrary to normal Christian experience. Moreover, we have works first and last, and *the last . . . more than the first.* That the *last* refers to *works* for its antecedent is probable because it is in the plural and neuter, thus agreeing with *works* in gender and number. This superemphasis on works may well point to Rome, for her religion is known to abound in works. Some of her "saints" are said to have works to spare—the so-called works of supererogation—which it is alleged may be set to the account of others whose works may not be sufficient to assure deliverance from purgatory! Before proceeding to the dark picture following, keep in mind the good "the Spirit saith" unto Thyatira. Moreover, it must be admitted that Rome, whom she symbolizes, is at least reverent and expresses love and holy regard for the sacred. These qualities are frequently sadly lacking among others who profess His name.

The Reprobation

Verse 20. *Notwithstanding I have a few things against thee, because thou sufferest that woman Jezebel, which calleth herself a prophetess, to teach and to seduce my servants to commit fornication, and to eat things sacrificed unto idols.*

Most texts omit *few things* as in 2:14. The thought then is: *I have (this) against thee that thou sufferest.* . . .

The immoralities of Jezebel were similar to those of her namesake of the Old Testament. II Kings 9:22, 32.

Some texts insert "thy"; hence, *thy woman* [wife] *Jezebel.* The context, however, is against its inclusion, for even if by the angel a local bishop were intended, it is altogether improbable that Jezebel was the bishop's wife, and to conceive of her as an angel's wife is plainly abhorrent.

Prophetess was a self-styled title which alone suggests insincerity and arrogance.

For a woman to teach the art of fornication and idolatry is rightfully designated *the depths of Satan,* because the archfiend himself is capable of no more hideous vice. There may be a prophetic forecast of the Dark Ages (near A.D. 1000) known as the Period of Pornocracy when popes were the playthings of vile women, one of whom posed hypocritically as a man in a man's clothing. It should be observed that Jezebel had the audacity to teach some of the very things forbidden by the council at Jerusalem. Acts 16:29.

Verse 21. *And I gave her space to repent of her fornication; and she repented not.*

Repent has its literal significance here, that is, to "change one's mind." That Rome will not change her mind is evident from the fact that she is characterized by the inspired writer as "the great harlot" at the time when she is finally destroyed. Revelation 17:1, 16.

Verse 22. *Behold, I will cast her into a bed, and them that commit adultery with her into great tribulation, except they repent of their deeds.*

The *bed* alludes to the nature of her most heinous and abominable sin. Those who commit fornication with her will apparently include all nations, people, and multitudes. Kings, merchants, and shipmasters receive special mention. Revelation 18:9-19. The bed also refers symbolically to "great tribulation." The reference is undoubtedly to the period preceding the coming of the Lord in power and great glory and described in chapters 6—18. *Great tribulation* is anarthrous here, probably due to its first mention in the book, for in 7:14 it appears in the Greek with the article.

The additional words, *except they repent of their deeds,* are an illustration of the long-suffering of God waiting for any possible signs of repentance after the threat of grim retribution.

Verse 23. *And I will kill her children with death; and all the churches shall know that I am he which searcheth the reins and hearts: and I will give unto every one of you according to your works.*

What is said of Thyatira has long since come to pass; for all her children (the membership of succeeding generations) have long since passed from the stage of action. It is significant that the very site of the church has long been obliterated and nothing remains but a melancholy and solitary waste.

All the churches may come into possession of this knowledge through travelers who have been on the scene and reported their findings in this respect. Their knowledge will be twofold. The Lord searcheth the reins and hearts. The phrase occurs six times in the Old Testament alternating "hearts and reins, reins and hearts" three times each (Psalm 7:9; 26:2; 73:21; and Jeremiah 11:20; 17:10; 20:12), and here—a total of seven times. "The reins are the seat of the emotions just as the heart is the seat of the thoughts and feelings."[12]

The clause, I will give unto every one of you according to your works, is repeated (with slight variations) in 18:6; 20:12, 13; 22:12, and it occurs in the entire Bible some 40 times. Note especially the stern reminder as the book draws to a close.

The Second Approbation

Verse 24. But unto you I say, and unto the rest in Thyatira, as many as have not this doctrine, and which have not known the depths of Satan, as they speak; I will put upon you none other burden.

You is plural here, showing clearly that the message is not directed to the "angel." See other occurrences of the plural pronoun you in 2:10, 13, 23, and of plural verbs: "have" (2:10, 24, 25); "hold fast" (2:25); know (2:24); try (2:10). All of which shows as Ramsay says: " . . . he addresses the angel, but really he writes to the church. . . ."[13]

And has the sense of "even" because "you" refers to the "rest" in Thyatira who do not have the doctrine or teaching of the woman, Jezebel. The initial but shows that these are set in contrast to those who had been seduced by the prophetess, and who knew the depths of Satan. The latter (as Wesley said of Methodists who did not fulfill all righteousness) will have the hottest place in hell. Their speaking about it appears to imply that they gloated in their fiendish attainments.

The last clause evidently alludes to the decision of the council of Jerusalem, for it includes two of the restrictions and mentions burden. However, it was sufficient that the rest refrain from the two evils. The burden of abstaining from blood and things strangled was not imposed upon them.

The First Exhortation

Verse 25. But that which ye have already hold fast till I come.

The plural ye is used, showing that members in particular are to heed the exhortation.

Hold fast is the word used in verse 13. Here it is in the plural; in the former in the singular, although in a collective sense. The faithful in Thyatira are exhorted to hold fast the truth as the unorthodox in Pergamos were holding fast to error.

The exhortation is hold fast till I come. This shows plainly that the message to Thyatira is not intended merely for the local congregation at Thyatira, for it implies that she will continue in some sense until the coming of Christ. We have already noted that the local church in Asia Minor has long since passed from the scene of action and that its very site is now a solitary waste. However, conditions prevailing in Thyatira in the days when John penned these lines still continue upon the earth, and the sure word of prophecy plainly indicates that they will continue till the time of the tribulation, and that the antitype of Thyatira will be ". . . that great city, which reigneth over the kings of the earth" (Revelation 17:18). All of which goes to show that the conditions prevailing in these seven churches are to be understood as being typical because they present a forecast of universal church conditions from the time of John on until the end of the church age, or until Jesus Christ returns. [Some discrepancy may be noted between what is said here and what the author set forth in the earlier outline. However, it must be remembered that not every condition which the individual church symbolized ceased to exist with the end of the general period. This is clearly the case with the Thyatiran period, for the Roman problem exists today in some places as intense as it ever did.—J. O. Y.]

The Remuneration

Verse 26. *And he that overcometh, and keepeth my works unto the end, to him will I give power over the nations.*

The present participle occurs in each of the promises to the seven churches. This denotes continued action. The Greek has the definite article—"the" (one) overcoming. The thought then is, the one who continues to overcome, not merely an act of the past, but a continuing experience.

The definite article and the participial form occur likewise in the second clause; hence we have the one overcoming and the one keeping my works. The second definite article with the participle indicates that *kai* (Greek for *and*) has the sense of *even.* Hence we may render freely, *he who overcomes, even he who keeps my works,* i.e., *who does the works I command.* It is implied therefore that an overcomer is one who obeys God's commandments.

End refers to the end of one's life; hence the promises following are only to such as continue faithful to the end.

The Greek word translated *power* is *exousia,* signifying *authority.* To the overcomer is given the right to exercise authority over the nations. Thus the authority of the overcomer is not inherent, but delegated. The centurion said, "Go," not because of his own authority, but because he was under the authority of the emperor. Matthew 8:9.

The entire last clause alludes to Psalm 2:8, where the Lord (the Father) addresses the Son: "Ask of me, and I shall give thee the nations [Hebrew] for thine inheritance, and the uttermost parts of the earth for thy possession." What God gave to Christ in this prophecy, He (Christ) now promises to the overcomer.

Verse 27. *And he shall rule them with a rod of iron; as the vessels of a potter shall they be broken to shivers: even as I received of my Father.*

It has been observed that of the 404 verses in Revelation, over 300 allude to the Old Testament; however, the present verse is one of the few which occur almost verbatim. The reference is plainly to Psalm 2:9, "Thou shalt break them with a rod of iron; thou shalt dash them in pieces like a potter's vessel." Revelation 2:27 also points forward to chapter 19:15, ". . . out of his mouth goeth a sharp sword, that with it he should smite the nations: and he shall rule them with a rod of iron"; thus indicating when this ruling of the nations will take place, viz., after He has smitten them with the sharp sword at His coming with the armies of heaven. He will, of course, rule only those who are left of the nations. Isaiah 45:20; Zechariah 14:16.

The word for *rule* means literally *to shepherdize*. The same word is used in the Greek of Psalm 2:9 and also in Revelation 19:15. That the word is used in connection with a rod should present no difficulty, for Psalm 23:4 reminds us that a shepherd bears a rod as well as a staff—the former to correct, the latter to protect. In the case before us, the nations evidently need the rod of correction, seeing they have set themselves against the Lord and against His anointed.

[It should be pointed out that *hrabdos* (Greek for *rod*) is used also in the sense of the scepter of a ruler (cf. Hebrews 1:8 and Psalm 45:6, 7), and in this right Jesus Christ surely will exercise Himself. The Hebrew word *shephet* lying behind the Greek *hrabdos* and the English *scepter* clearly sustains this idea.— J. O. Y.]

The breaking to shivers as a potter's vessel has special reference to the wicked whom He will destroy with the brightness of His coming. II Thessalonians 1:7-9; Revelation 19:17-21.

The last clause, *even as I received of my Father,* evidently refers to the decree mentioned in Psalm 2:7. Jesus refers to a similar decree in vindication of His dealing with the nations. (See Psalm 110:1, 2, where the Lord [Father] speaks to David's Lord [the Son] before He [the Son] rules in the midst of His enemies.)

It may be asked, When will this ruling of saints over the nations take place? In reply, note: not during the present lifetime, because it will be after "the end" (of life); not after the end of time, because then all things will be subjected to God alone (I Corinthians 15:28); not in heaven, because there are no nations in heaven, much less will anyone be broken into shivers in that celestial abode; not in hell, because there will be no saints there.

The only time left for this reigning over the nations is between the departure of the saints and the final appearance of a new heaven and earth. The only place must be on earth, the only sphere which saints and nations alike inhabit. Moreover, this accords with numerous Scripture passages.

"And the kingdom and dominion, and the greatness of the kingdom under the whole heaven, shall be given to the people of the saints of the most High" (Daniel 7:27). (Note: "under the whole heaven.")

". . . Judgment was given to the saints of the most High; and the time came that the saints possessed the kingdom" (Daniel 7:22).

"And I appoint unto you a kingdom, as my Father hath appointed unto me; that ye may eat and drink at my table in my kingdom, and sit on thrones judging the twelve tribes of Israel" (Luke 22:29, 30).

"Do ye not know that the saints shall judge the world" (I Corinthians 6:2)?

"And hast made us unto our God kings and priests: and we shall reign on the earth" (Revelation 5:10).

As for the duration of the reign, the inspired author writes, ". . . they shall be priests of God and of Christ, and shall reign [be kings] with him a thousand years" (Revelation 20:6).

Verse 28. *And I will give him the morning star.*

Him has reference to the overcomer. The speaker, Jesus Himself, is the morning star. (See 22:16.) In II Peter 1:19, He is designated "the day star"—the Greek word *phosphoros* means "light bearer." It already has been observed that the symbol "stars" is applied to angels generally. The term *star* is first applied to Christ in Numbers 24:17. However, the general term is employed in Job (an earlier book), chapter 38:7, in reference to angels.

The Second Exhortation

Verse 29. *He that hath an ear, let him hear what the Spirit saith unto the churches.* (See verse 7.)

Commentators usually call attention to the reversal of the remuneration and the exhortation at this point.

The Message to the Church at Sardis (3:1-6)

The Annunciation

Verse 1a. *And unto the angel of the church in Sardis write.*

Sardis, the capital of Lydia, was located 30 miles south of Thyatira. The Acropolis on which the city was built was well defended. Its capture by Cyrus, king of Greece, when Croesus, of fabulous wealth, was king, has often been related. As the story goes, a slave divulged a secret path up the heights on the side which was considered impregnable, and consequently was undefended. Cyrus with his army, like "a thief in the night," silently made his way up the Acropolis and led Croesus with his army captive before they had time to draw up a battle line.

According to Ramsay, "Sardis today is a wilderness of ruins and thorns, pastures and wild flowers, where the only habitations are a few huts of Yuruk nomads."[14] [Excavations of old Sardis are currently in progress.—J. O. Y.]

The Hebrew word *sarid,* meaning "the rest or remnant," is the probable source of Sardis. The suggestion of Rudolf Stier (author of the notable work, "The Words of the Lord Jesus," and coeditor of a valuable Bible polyglot) implies a Sanskrit derivation signifying "newborn" or "renewed."[15] "The rest" fits the description, "the things that remain," literally "the rest," and is so rendered in verse 24; "the remnant" is suitable to the prophetic aspect because a few names, while their works were not perfect, after all restored the faith-way of salvation.

The Presentation

Verse 1b. *These things saith he that hath the seven Spirits of God, and the seven stars.*

The fallacy of the view which regards the seven spirits of God as the Holy

Spirit and the seven stars (that is, the seven angels—1:20) as seven bishops appears evident from the use and association in this place, for then the passage paraphrased would read, "These things saith He that has the Holy Spirit and the seven bishops." No human being is worthy of so high a distinction. The error of such an interpretation is further shown by the following considerations:

The Bible nowhere speaks of God "having" (in His power or possession) the Holy Spirit, for He Himself is God.

The Holy Spirit is never said to stand before the throne as do the seven angels. Revelation 1:4.

Dr. Charles remarks, ". . . the conjunction of the πνεύματα [spirits] and the ἀστέρες [stars] in iii.1 suggests that they are to some extent kindred conceptions. . . . In i.20 the ἑπτὰ ἀστέρες [seven stars] are definitely stated to be the ἄγγελοι τῶν ἑπτὰ ἐκκλησιῶν [angels of the seven churches], and Christ is said to hold these ἀστέρες, ι.ε. ἄγγελοι [stars, i.e., angels] in His right hand, i.16: that is, to have supreme authority over them. Hence in iii.1 the seven πνεύματα [spirits] of God and the seven ἄγγελοι [angels] of the churches are conjoined, as apparently kindred conceptions."[16] This is all according to our interpretation in chapter 1.

And (Greek: *kai*) has here again the sense of *even;* hence the thought: *He that has the seven angels, even* [or, that is to say] *the seven stars,* thus alluding to 1:20b.

The Declaration

Verse 1c. *I know thy works.*

Contrary to the usual order of procedure, the Son of man in judging Sardis begins with words of censure.

The First Reprobation

Verse 1d. *Thou hast a name that thou livest, and art dead.*

There was a semblance of life but it lacked reality. Sardis apparently was reputed as being a "live church"—there was much activity, but He who does not look on the outward appearance but on the heart declares, *Thou . . . art dead.* Prophetically, this was the condition of Christendom just preceding the Reformation.

Again the usual order is set aside (probably due to the abnormal condition of the church).

The First Exhortation

Verse 2. *Be watchful, and strengthen the things which remain, that are ready to die: for I have not found thy works perfect before God.*

Be watchful. They are exhorted to look into their real condition. There is possibly an allusion to the calamity which had befallen the city when through lack of vigilance it was taken by the enemy under cover of darkness at a point where the inhabitants supposed vigilance was not required.

The word *strengthen* occurs only here in Revelation. In the Pauline writings (always rendered "stablish" or "establish") it occurs six times. Romans 1:11;

16:25; I Thessalonians 3:2, 13; II Thessalonians 2:17; 3:3. James uses it once: "stablish your hearts" (James 5:8). It is used by Christ of Peter, "when thou art converted, strengthen thy brethren" (Luke 22:32), and by Peter two times (I Peter 5:10; II Peter 1:12).

The things which remain. The words are the same in the original as "the rest" in 2:24, except that in this case, the Greek is in the neuter gender, while in 2:24 it is masculine or neuter. The language employed may therefore include lawful principles, activities, institutions, as well as individuals. Included among the latter are undoubtedly the "few names" mentioned in 3:4.

Viewing our passage in a prophetic sense, there may be a purposeful allusion to "the rest" in Thyatira, for they apparently constitute the nucleus of the few faithful ones in the Thyatira region.

"The rest" in both instances evidently consist of a minority, but the words are not restricted to this usage. (Cf. 9:20; 20:5.)

Ready to die. The word *ready* is not in the Greek, and since the verb (*mello*) is in the imperfect tense, Tregelles renders correctly, "that were about to die." The meaning is evidently that the rest would soon have died, but now since the exhortation has been given to strengthen them, there is the prospect of a renewed vitality.

I have not found thy works perfect before God. The reason for this decadence is next declared. While the works of many in Sardis gave them a name before men, before God they were sadly deficient—they lacked not in quantity but in quality. They were not full or complete in the sight of God.

Verse 3. *Remember therefore how thou hast received and heard, and hold fast, and repent. If therefore thou shalt not watch, I will come on thee as a thief.*

We have already noticed the similarity of the presentation between the churches at Sardis and Ephesus. The exhortation to *remember* is likewise peculiar to both. To Ephesus, the exhortation is: "Remember therefore from whence thou art fallen, and repent, and do the first works"; to Sardis, *Remember therefore how thou hast received and heard* ["since first you knew the Lord"], *and hold fast, and repent.*

The present verse, which speaks of a renewal, a coming back to *how thou hast received and heard,* accords very favorably with the Sanskrit derivation suggested by Dr. Stier, viz., that of renewal. The Sardis period which synchronizes with that of the Reformation is like a new start, a return to basics such as Ephesus enjoyed before she left her first love. The Reformation (imperfect as it was) is not to be sought in the "dead" portion of the church, but in the few names which had not defiled their garments.

The salutary effect of reflection upon one's first experience of salvation is frequently recognized in Scripture; e.g., "As ye have therefore received Christ Jesus the Lord, so walk ye in him" (Colossians 2:6). "Call to remembrance the former days, in which, after ye were illuminated, ye endured a great fight of afflictions" (Hebrews 10:32). ". . . if we hold the beginning of our confidence stedfast unto the end" (Hebrews 3:14). "Ye did run well; who did hinder you that ye should not obey the truth" (Galatians 5:7)?

As a thief. Cyrus came upon Sardis "as a thief in the night" and conquered the city before the inhabitants had time "to put on their boots" simply because there was no watching at the right time and place. So it will be finally in a spiritual sense. Only those that watch and pray will be accounted worthy to escape the awful things that are to come upon the earth. Luke 21:36. The rest will enter the great tribulation—only to them will Christ come as a thief.[17]

The Approbation

Verse 4. *Thou hast a few names even in Sardis which have not defiled their garments.*

The few names are included in the things that remain, and the reference is probably to the reformers, for while their works were not perfect before God, they nevertheless preached the way of salvation by faith.

There were Wycliffe in England, John Huss in Bohemia, Martin Luther in Germany, Menno Simons in Holland, John Knox in Scotland, John Calvin in France, and Ulrich Zwingli in Switzerland. This cock-crowing period foretells the coming of a better day.

A *few names* had not defiled their garments. There is apparently a contrast intended with the prevailing sin at Thyatira—these have kept themselves pure. (Cf. 14:4.) Garments also have a symbolic sense, denoting righteousness; hence we have the phraseology in Scripture as:

garments of salvation (Psalm 132:16; Isaiah 61:10),
clothed with righteousness (Job 29:14; Psalm 132:9; Isaiah 59:17; Ephesians 6:14; Revelation 19:11, 14),
robe of righteousness (Isaiah 61:10).

The righteousness of the self-righteous is spoken of as filthy rags. Isaiah 64:6.

The Remuneration

Verse 4b. . . . *and they shall walk with me in white: for they are worthy.*

White denotes spotless purity. The uses in the Bible describe various relations and personalities:

of the raiment of Christ on the mount of transfiguration (Matthew 17:2; Mark 9:3; Luke 9:29),
of the raiment of angels (Matthew 28:3; Mark 16:5; Revelation 15:6),
of the apparel of two men (males)—probably Moses and Elias, at the ascension of Christ (Acts 1:10),
of the apparel of the glorified church (Revelation 19:8, 14).

It is true of all who avail themselves of the redemption that is in Christ: "Though . . . [their] sins be as scarlet, they shall be as white as snow" (Isaiah 1:18); "wash me, and I shall be whiter than snow" (Psalm 51:7).

The wise man's exhortation is to be heeded: "Let thy garments be always white" (Ecclesiastes 9:8).

The word of prophecy is heartening: "Many shall be purified, and made white" (Daniel 12:10).

Were it not that the Lord is the speaker here, some might challenge the assertion: *for they are worthy.* Worthy for what? Let *Him* answer: *worthy to walk with me in white.* One should think grace could go no further. But there are other promises of like import equally gracious:

"Where I am, there shall also my servant be" (John 12:26).

"They shall see his face" (Revelation 22:4).

"We shall be like him" (I John 3:2).

"So shall we ever be with the Lord" (I Thessalonians 4:17).

"Sit with me in my throne" (Revelation 3:21).

"Appear with him in glory" (Colossians 3:4).

"Reign with him" (II Timothy 2:12; Revelation 5:10; 20:6; 22:5).

Verse 5. *He that overcometh, the same shall be clothed in white raiment; and I will not blot out his name out of the book of life, but I will confess his name before my Father, and before his angels.*

Of all creatures, only the glorified church is spoken of as wearing *white raiment* (Greek: *himation*). It is mentioned only here and in 3:18 and 4:4. In both cases the elders are spoken of as seated on thrones clothed in white raiment. This is one of the marks of identification between the church on earth (chapters 2 and 3) and in glory (chapters 4 and 5).

The overcomer is given the divine assurance that his name will not be blotted out of the book of life. That such a blotting out is possible and implied is apparent from a number of Scripture passages: Exodus 32:33; Psalm 69:25-28; Deuteronomy 9:14; 25:19; 29:20.[18]

On the other hand, Revelation 3:5 emphasizes the personality of the overcomer by the mention of *his name.* The individualization here evidently alludes to the "few names" in Sardis mentioned above.

It will be observed, too, that the terms *before* (in the presence of) the Father and *before* the angels of God are combined. Why does He (the Son) confess before the Father and the *angels?* Why not before the Holy Spirit instead of before the angels, so as to make the Trinity complete? The answer is: This pertains to the church age, at which time the Holy Spirit is not in heaven but upon the earth convicting men of sin and indwelling the believer. For the same reason as already noted, the seven spirits of God (1:4; 3:1) refer not to the Holy Spirit but to seven angels, and when He comes again, He will come in His own glory and in His Father's and of the holy angels (not in the glory of the Holy Spirit). Luke 9:26.

The Second Exhortation

Verse 6. *He that hath an ear, let him hear what the Spirit saith unto the churches.* (See 2:7.)

The Message to the Church at Philadelphia (3:7-13)

The Annunciation

Verse 7a. *And to the angel of the church in Philadelphia write.*

Philadelphia is located about 25 miles southeast of Sardis. The name means brotherly love, and the city was named after King Attalus III, who received this title because of his unselfish devotion to his brother Eumenes at the risk of his own interest and reputation. The city was liable to severe earthquakes. These were so numerous that many of the inhabitants had their dwelling places outside the city limits.

According to Swete, "The modern city has a resident bishop, five churches, and about 1,000 Christian inhabitants."[19] It is significant that the two churches, Smyrna and Philadelphia, against whom the Son of man prefers no blame, are the only ones of the seven where Christian churches have survived.

The Presentation

Verse 7b. *These things saith he that is holy, he that is true, he that hath the key of David, he that openeth, and no man shutteth; and shutteth, and no man openeth.*

The attributes, *holy* and *true*, occur together only here and in 6:10 where they are apparently ascribed to God. Thus Christ presents Himself as possessed with the attributes of deity. Compare 1:8, where the fullest declaration of His deity is couched in the briefest compass in Holy Writ.

True is joined with righteous three times—15:3 (just equals righteous); 16:7; 19:2; with faithful, four times—3:14; 19:11; 21:5; 22:6.

The word *key* is used as a symbol of authority in Scripture in the same sense as it is used today. By giving a man a key we give him the right or authority to open and shut whatever the key was designed to fit. *The key of David* and words following are taken practically verbatim from Isaiah 22:22. As authority was given to God's servant Eliakim, over David's house, so now Christ in His own right has authority to open and to shut. Where He opens or shuts, no one (Greek), whether of men or of demons, is able to shut or open.

The Declaration

Verse 8a. *I know thy works.* (See 2:2.)

The Approbation

Verse 8b. *Behold, I have set before thee an open door, and no man can shut it; for thou hast a little strength, and hast kept my word, and hast not denied my name.*

Behold occurs four times in the message to Philadelphia (verses 8, 9a, 9b, 11) and only three times in the other six churches (2:10, 22; 3:20). Each occurrence should be carefully noted, for the word is given to arrest attention. Remember, it is the middle voice of the verb "see," which gives it the meaning, "see for yourself," i.e., "see or look for your own interest or benefit."

The important fact there declared is stated in the words following (lit.): *I have given before thee an open door, and no one can shut it.* What Ramsay says in this place is undoubtedly true: "It is not stated explicitly that Philadelphia used this opportunity that had been given it; but that is clearly implied in the context. The door had been opened for the Philadelphian church by Him who does nothing in vain: He did this because the opportunity would be used."[20]

The *little strength* is not an indication of spiritual infirmity, but of fewness in number, because of the commendable things mentioned in the verses following.

To keep the Word means more than holding it as a possession and safeguarding it. It means obeying from the heart as well. Romans 6:17. It is used in this sense seven times in Revelation (1:3; 3:8, 10; 12:17; 14:12; 22:7, 9), and some twenty times elsewhere in the New Testament. Negatively, they did not deny His name, that is, they did not bring reproach upon the Christian name, which they professed, by inconsistent living. They were not only of "this way"; they also walked in it.

Verse 9. *Behold, I will make them of the synagogue of Satan, which say they are Jews, and are not, but do lie; behold, I will make them to come and worship before thy feet, and to know that I have loved thee.*

The word *behold* is introduced twice in this verse by way of encouragement to the faithful with the consciousness that the Lord in due time will reward them for their patience, for He will make their enemies come and worship at their feet. In this way they will acknowledge their own error and at the same time testify to the faithfulness of those whom they persecuted, which is probably here an allusion to the future, at which time the apostles who represent the church universal will "sit on thrones judging the twelve tribes of Israel" (Luke 22:30).

As in the message to Smyrna, the "are-not" Jews are designated the synagogue of Satan because of their malicious character. It is significant that the two churches against whom the Lord prefers no blame suffer persecution.

This is the only place in these two chapters in which Jesus expresses His personal love for a church except as implied for a minority in 3:19. Moreover, *I*, being expressed separately, is emphatic: *I have loved thee.* This particular statement would appear to put the church at Philadelphia in the highest place of honor among the seven.

The First Remuneration

Verse 10. *Because thou hast kept the word of my patience, I also will keep thee from the hour of temptation, which shall come upon all the world, to try them that dwell upon the earth.*

The reference here is to the patience of Christ as in 1:9. Compare also II Thessalonians 3:5 where the literal rendering is: "The Lord direct you . . . into the patience of Christ." The believers at Philadelphia followed the example and teaching of Christ who likewise endured the contradiction of sinners (Hebrews 12:3), and they had the mind of Christ who was obedient unto death, even the death of the cross. Philippians 2:5, 8; Hebrews 12:2.

Now this, as Trench observes,[21] follows the benign law of recompense— *because thou hast kept . . . I also will keep thee from the hour of temptation.* The words just quoted call for careful consideration due to the fact that an erroneous interpretation at this time will disqualify the student from arriving at a true view of what is to follow in succeeding chapters. Suffice it to say that two prominent but conflicting views are held regarding this passage. Continuing our heads as above, we will take up the crucial words of the passage in hand.

88   A REVELATION OF JESUS CHRIST

The assuring pledge is most emphatic (lit.): Also *I you* will keep. This is again the emphatic *I* of the Lord. *You*, too, is emphatic by position. This double emphasis, "I have loved thee" (verse 9) and *Also I thee will keep*, in such close proximity, is probably unsurpassed in Scripture as expressing the boundless affection and good will of Christ for His people.

We next consider the word *temptation* (Greek: *peirasmos*, meaning trial). The word occurs in Luke 8:13 in the parable of the sower. In the parallel passages of Matthew 13:21; Mark 4:17 we have "tribulation" or "persecution"; hence *temptation* is used as the equivalent of both of these. Again in Revelation 2:10 we have the word "tribulation," a different word, and also the verbal form *peirazo, try*—the latter being uniform with the word "try" in the verse under study. Obviously, therefore, the hour of trial may be equated with the time of tribulation yet to come. Thus Dr. Hatch, after quoting 3:10, remarks: ". . . with evident reference to the tribulations which are prophesied later on in the book."[22]

"Hour" is John's favorite word for a time period whether long or short. It is somewhat synonymous with season, a word usually employed by the Synoptists, except that it frequently occurs in an ominous sense.

Since the tribulation will immediately precede the coming of the Lord in great power and glory (Matthew 24:29, 30), and since the group of believers to whom John was writing have long since passed away, it is evident that Philadelphia, as well as the other churches, is representative of the church universal.

Now comes the crucial question: What is meant by the passage, *I . . . will keep thee from the hour of temptation?* What parallel passages, if any, throw light upon these words? In reply, note that commentators have a well-beaten track to John 17:15 and to nowhere else. The charge that commentators follow one another as sheep is well sustained in this case. The passage referred to reads, "I pray not that thou shouldest take them out of the world, but that thou shouldest keep them from the evil [lit., the evil one]." The point of comparison is, of course, in the expression "keep from" (Greek: *tereo ek*), which is common to both. It is claimed that just as Jesus prayed that God would keep the disciples immune from the snares of the evil one, so He Himself would keep the faithful secure and unharmed in the midst of the judgments and plagues of the tribulation period.

There are, however, serious objections to such a view. The points of similarity are too slender to warrant such sweeping and far-reaching deductions. As a matter of fact, the differences between the two passages outweigh the resemblances; hence the effort to explain the latter by the former obscures rather than elucidates the meaning.

In the John passage the disciples were already in the midst of evil. Indeed, they were in the midst of evil when they became disciples. In the Revelation, the plagues of the tribulation period were still in the future. In fact, they are still future in our day.

The judgments and plagues of the tribulation should not be regarded as evil or of the evil one, because the Lord sends them in order that "the inhabitants of the world will learn righteousness" (Isaiah 26:9).

It is not true to fact that saints of the tribulation period will be exempt from suffering or martyrdom. Two great groups (6:9-11; 7:9-14; and 14:1-3; 15:1-3), besides individuals and smaller groups of saints (11:7-10; 12:11), will die as martyrs during that period. These are not saints of the church age, for they are repeatedly distinguished from them as further studies will show.

In John, immunity is promised from a person—the evil one; in Revelation, from a time period—the hour of trial which is yet to come. The examination of John 17:15 has shown that it cannot be consistently used as a guide or criterion in the interpretation of this passage. Indeed, the passage fails to shed light on the very place where it is most needed and that is, not merely about being kept from (*tereo ek*), but about being kept from *what*. Here the passages are dissimilar, for the one tells about a personage, and the other about a time period. Before looking elsewhere for light or direction, note the remaining portion of the verse.

The *hour of temptation* or *period of tribulation* is to come upon all the inhabited world and the purpose is to try the earth dwellers. The earth dwellers apparently are a special class of obdurate sinners distinct from the nations of the world. This is the first of the twelve occurrences. The word is in the participial form, denoting their continuance in complacency and obduracy. While the plagues are sent in particular to try them, in no instance do we read of any of them repenting. In this they are like Pharaoh of old who hardened his heart more and more as the judgments continued.

It should be noted in particular that the plagues and judgments incident to the hour of trial are sent to try the earth dwellers, *not the church*, thus implying that the church will be no longer on earth when the tribulation opens.[23]

There are numerous other passages teaching this same truth, i.e., the pretribulational rapture of the church, the most convincing and unmistakable being those appearing in Revelation. See Appendix 18, "The Tribulation."

The First Exhortation

Verse 11. *Behold, I come quickly: hold that fast which thou hast, that no man take thy crown.*

This is the fourth mention of *behold* in the message to Philadelphia and the eighth in the book out of its thirty occurrences. The entire phrase, "*Behold, I come quickly,*" occurs again three times in the closing hortatory section (22:6-21) in which the angel again testifies to the churches (verse 16). The last occurrence significantly appears in an intensified form: "Surely I come quickly" (verse 20). It is noteworthy that neither this nor any other note of imminence pertaining to the second coming of Christ occurs in the entire tribulation section (chapters 6–18) until after the pouring out of the sixth vial (16:15) and just preceding the mention of Armageddon (16:16). From this we learn that "*Behold, I come quickly*" is the appropriate watchword for the church; "Behold, I come as a thief," for the tribulation saints. 16:15. In this connection compare I Thessalonians 5:4: "But ye, brethren, are not in darkness, that that day should overtake you as a thief." In the Greek "ye" is emphatic by its separate mention; "you" by position. In this watchword (Behold, I come quickly), the Spirit speaks to *all* the churches. The implication is that there will be true believers on earth (as represented by the church at Philadelphia) when the Lord comes. These are they that will meet Him in the air and thus escape the hour of trial yet to be.

The word for *hold fast* is *krateo*, which means to hold tenaciously. It is used of Christ holding fast the seven stars (2:1); of the faithful in Pergamos (2:13); of the unfaithful as holding fast the doctrine of Balaam and of the Nicolaitanes (2:13, 14); and of the faithful remnant in Thyatira (2:24, 25). The poet wrote, "He Will Hold Me Fast." Here the point is stressed that the believer is to hold fast as well. The exhortation is, *hold that fast which thou hast.* The things are mentioned above: "Thou hast a little strength" (though few in number); "and hast kept my word"; "and [negatively] hast not denied my name." The second is repeated as the word of my "patience."

The importance of holding fast is shown in that failure to do so will issue in the loss of the crown promised to the faithful. (Cf. 2:10.) The Greek says that *no one* take thy crown, be it man, or Satan who "goes about seeking whom he may devour." Doubtless many, through neglect, or yielding to the tempter, lose their crown. On the contrary, the Apostle Paul, having "kept the faith," was confident of the crown awaiting him. II Timothy 4:8.

It should be noted that only to the church are crowns promised. Not to angels, neither to Israel (from whom the kingdom was taken, Matthew 21:43), nor to the tribulation saints is this honor bestowed. Only kings wear crowns and only the church group are declared to be kings and priests. Moreover, the church is said to judge Israel (Matthew 19:28; Luke 22:30), the world (I Corinthians 6:2), and angels (I Corinthians 6:3).

The Second Remuneration

Verse 12. *Him that overcometh will I make a pillar in the temple of my God, and he shall go no more out: and I will write upon him the name of my God, and the name of the city of my God, which is new Jerusalem, which cometh down out of heaven from my God: and I will write upon him my new name.*

The reference is to the new heaven and new earth described in 21:1-6a "when . . . [Christ] shall have delivered up the kingdom to God . . . that God may be all in all" (I Corinthians 15:24-28). Observe how God alone is mentioned both here and in the later passage. Observe, too, that the mention of the temple of God and the new Jerusalem corresponds to the tabernacle of God and the new Jerusalem in Revelation 21:1-6 and is distinguished from the holy Jerusalem described as a city foursquare in which account (21:9—22:5) the Lamb is mentioned seven times and in which there is *no* temple (21:22). [Except that the Lamb Himself is the temple.—J. O. Y.]

The only part Jesus had in the picture is that He is occupied with putting overcomers upon the honor roll who, in an evil day, keep the word of His patience. This high distinction is compared by Jesus Himself in a fourfold manner:

I will make him *a pillar in the temple of my God, and he shall go no more out.* The word "pillar" is obviously used in a metaphorical sense. It denotes strength. It is possible to be strong in the Lord and in the power of His might in such a time as this, for God has provided a panoply that enables one to stand in an evil day. The word also implies rarity—only three (James, Peter, and John) are mentioned as pillars in the early church. Galatians 2:9.

Temple (Greek: *Naos*) signifies the holy place and most holy.

The overcomer "shall no more go out." This denotes fixity in existence. It has been well said,

> "When we've been there ten thousand years,
> Bright shining as the sun,
> We've no less days to sing God's praise
> Than when we first begun."

And I will write upon him the name of my God. This denotes possession as well as identification. In 14:1 record is given of 144,000 having the Father's name written in their foreheads. These are martyrs who died during the tribulation period. Again in 22:4 we are told His name shall be in their foreheads.

And the name of the city of my God, which is new Jerusalem, which cometh down out of heaven from my God. The identification with 21:1 is unmistakable.

I will write upon him my new name. What is not revealed cannot be known. What the new name is must remain a mystery to man in the flesh. The unknown name is again mentioned in 19:12, where it is definitely stated, "He hath a name written which no man knoweth but he himself."

The Second Exhortation

Verse 13. *He that hath an ear, let him hear what the Spirit saith unto the churches.* (See 2:7.)

The Message to the Church at Laodicea (3:14-22)

The Annunciation

Verse 14a. *And unto the angel of the church of the Laodiceans write.*

Laodicea was situated about 45 miles southeast of Philadelphia, and about 90 miles nearly due east from Ephesus. The name of the city is a compound word derived from *laos* (people) and *dike* (judgment); hence judgment of the people. The literal sense is practically synonymous with the English word "democracy," which signifies the people ruling. In other words, here is democracy in religion. The Laodiceans therefore present a marked contrast with the Nicolaitanes, so prominent in the church at Ephesus and Pergamos, which denotes conquerors of the people in reference to priestcraft, or "lording" it over the people. Both extremes are to be avoided in religious groups, for the one, as the unerring voice of history declares, leads to priestly domination; the other to Laodicean lukewarmness and latitudinarianism so prevalent in more recent years in religious circles.

The city of Laodicea is now utterly desolate and without inhabitants, and the church centuries ago became extinct. It is noteworthy that, as in the case of the first church, the candlestick has long since been removed; in the last church the Lord has long since spued her out of His mouth.

The Presentation

Verse 14b. *These things saith the Amen, the faithful and true witness, the beginning of the creation of God.*

The Amen. The word occurs ten times. Elsewhere it is anarthrous and perhaps is used merely in the sense of a confirmation to the statements preceding. Here, as the article shows, it is used as a title in reference to Him who is eternally true in His nature and being.

The faithful and true witness. (See 1:5; also 19:11, where the same descriptive words occur.) They are probably applied to the Lord by way of contrast to the unfaithful and untrue which are mentioned in each case. As to His being a *true witness,* His own testimony amply indicates (John 5:31; 8:14), and also that of our writer (John 19:35; 21:24).

The beginning of the creation of God. The word *beginning* here denotes not the first of a series but priority; that is, He was before all created things. Compare Colossians 1:15, where He is designated, "the firstborn of every creature," and this is followed by the declaration, "For by him were all things created, that are in heaven, and that are in earth . . . all things were created by him, and for him: and he is before all things" (Colossians 1:16, 17). Plainly, therefore, He is not a creature or the first of creatures, for in that case, He would have had to create Himself.

The Declaration

Verse 15a. *I know thy works.* (See 2:2a.)

The Approbation

There is none except as implied in verse 19a: "As many as I love, I rebuke and chasten," and in verse 20b: "if any man hear my voice, and open the door."

The Reprobation

Verses 15-17. *I know thy works, that thou art neither cold nor hot: I would thou wert cold or hot. So then because thou art lukewarm, and neither cold nor hot, I will spue thee out of my mouth. Because thou sayest, I am rich, and increased with goods, and have need of nothing; and knowest not that thou art wretched, and miserable, and poor, and blind, and naked.*

Neither cold nor hot expresses gross indifferentism. As Ramsay fittingly declares, "The Laodicean church is neither one thing nor another. It is given to compromise. It cannot thoroughly reject the temptations and allurements of the world. And therefore it shall be rejected absolutely and inexorably by Him whose faithfulness and truth [see above] reject all halfheartedness and compromise."[24] (Note, however, that there is an implied remnant.)

He declares, *I will spue thee out of my mouth,* just as one feels disposed to do with insipid lukewarm water. The Greek brings out the idea of *ad nauseam* more realistically, for it says, *I will vomit thee out of my mouth.* This sense of loathsomeness on the part of the faithful and true witness in respect to the condition of the church of the Laodiceans is undoubtedly the saddest and most lamentable appraisal of God's professed people in Holy Writ. And since this church, by its position as last of the seven, symbolizes universal church conditions of the last days, the picture just described must necessarily depict the final apostasy mentioned in II Thessalonians 2:3, just preceding the coming of the Lord. While this forecast of universal church conditions is undoubtedly the most disheartening of all, it is simply a climax of similar utterances of inspired men (including those of the Lord Himself) regarding church conditions of the last days. To this the following passages bear unmistakable testimony: Luke 18:8; Matthew 24:12, 37-39; I Timothy 4:1, 2; II Timothy 3:1-5, 13; James 5:1-3; II Peter 3:3, 4; Jude 17, 18.

In Laodicea conditions are just the reverse of those at Smyrna. The Smyrnean church was poor in the material and rich in the spiritual. Laodicea is rich in the material but poor in the spiritual. The literal rendering of the passage, *I am rich and have gotten riches and have need of nothing*, implies, as both Charles[25] and Swete[26] observe, the boast, "I have gotten riches by my own exertions." Evidently the church shared in the wealth of the city, for it was a prominent trading post, a center of banking and finance, and was noted for its manufacture of "fine, glossy, black and violet garments," and its famous school of medicine. It is significant that in A.D. 60, when the city suffered heavy damage from a destructive earthquake, it declined the offer of aid by the Imperial Government with the reply, "I have grown rich and have need of nothing."

The tragedy lay in the fact that while she gloated over her material wealth, she was unconscious of her spiritual poverty. He who knows (verse 15) makes the solemn analysis, *Thou . . . knowest not that thou art wretched, and miserable, and poor, and blind, and naked.* By way of emphasis, the Greek has the definite article before the first descriptive word: Thou art "the" wretched one. (Romans 7:24 uses the same word for wretched.) *Miserable* appears to be correlative with *wretched.* (See I Corinthians 15:19 for the other occurrence.) The three remaining characteristics, *poor, and blind, and naked,* are without the article, and appear to indicate the source of their wretchedness and misery. The next verse alludes to these latter characteristics and thus confirms this view.

The Exhortation

Verses 18, 19. *I counsel thee to buy of me gold tried in the fire, that thou mayest be rich; and white raiment, that thou mayest be clothed, and that the shame of thy nakedness do not appear; and anoint thine eyes with eyesalve, that thou mayest see. As many as I love, I rebuke and chasten: be zealous therefore, and repent.*

The Counselor (Isaiah 9:6) here gives counsel to buy of Him the true riches. The *gold tried in the fire,* which constitutes true riches, is contrasted with their poverty (verse 17); the *white raiment,* the only sufficient covering for spiritual purity, with their nakedness; the anointing of the eyes, which gives spiritual sight, with their blindness. The only price to be paid for the gold which He provides is to endure suffering for His sake, as is well illustrated by the testimony of Job: "When he hath tried me, I shall come forth as gold" (Job 23:10). And Peter says as much: "The trial of your faith, being much more precious than of gold that perisheth" (I Peter 1:7). The raiment He provides: the garments of salvation (Isaiah

61:10), and to be clothed with His righteousness (Job 29:14). Redemption itself came not "with corruptible things, as silver and gold, . . . but with the precious blood of Christ" (I Peter 1:19). As for eyes that see, all whose eyes He touched were blessed with spiritual sight as well.

One of the chief defects of the church of the Laodiceans was that they did the very things Jesus forbade when He said, "Lay not up for yourselves treasures upon earth, where moth and rust doth corrupt" (Matthew 6:19). Likewise, James charges the rich man with the indictment, "Ye have heaped [lit., laid up] treasure together for the last days" (James 5:3). He also declares, "Your garments are motheaten. Your gold and silver is cankered" (James 5:2, 3).

In no way is the apostasy more evident than in the modern dress of so-called Christians. In few places is there a more gorgeous display of fashionable attire than in nominal Christian congregations. Gold is worn for ornamentation; garments are frequently superfluous so that many dollars of the Lord's money are annually worse than wasted by Christian professors. On the other hand, many wear garments so abbreviated that the shame of their nakedness is barely covered. All this is in direct violation of the New Testament passages on Christian attire. I Timothy 2:9, 10; I Peter 3:3-5.

Eyesalve. Ramsay tells us, "The Laodicean church must also learn that it is blind, but yet not incurably blind. It is suffering from disease, and needs medical treatment. But the physicians of its famous medical school can do nothing for it. The tabloids which they prescribe, and which are now used all over the civilized world, to reduce to powder and smear on the eyes, will be useless for this kind of ophthalmia [eye trouble]."²⁷ The same writer suggests that those who are afflicted with this kind of ophthalmia must go to the author and buy at the price of suffering and steadfastness. What is needed is the anointing of the Spirit of wisdom and understanding to the end that the eyes of the understanding might be enlightened. Ephesians 1:17, 18.

[It is remarkable how well one can see with the physical eye and yet how blind he may be with the spiritual eye. So much depends upon the attitude of the heart. Spiritual eyesight comes by way of believing. One knows, believes, and then understands.—J. O. Y.]

As many as I love. Commentators as a rule agree in declaring that nothing good is mentioned concerning Laodicea. Ramsay goes as far as to say, "It shall be rejected absolutely and inexorably." The words quoted, however, imply a remnant whom the Lord *loved.* It is noteworthy that the word for love here is *phileo,* which denotes the love of friendship, and not *agapao,* the higher type of love, as in 3:9 with reference to Philadelphia. *Phileo* is a universal term of affection of God toward man, of man toward man, and even of brutes, they tell us. *Agapao* had its origin in divine revelation and is not found in heathen writers. God's love for believers at Philadelphia, it should be noted, was not only of a higher order than for those at Laodicea, but it embraced the whole church, while here His affection is expressed only toward a certain portion and that doubtless a small minority—the rest He has abandoned as hopelessly obdurate and impenitent.

I rebuke and chasten. For those whom He rebukes and chastens and calls to repentance there is hope. He chastens "for our profit, that we might be partakers of his holiness" (Hebrews 12:10).

The Remuneration

Verses 20, 21. *Behold, I stand at the door, and knock : if any man hear my voice, and open the door, I will come in to him, and will sup with him, and he with me. To him that overcometh will I grant to sit with me in my throne, even as I also overcame, and am set down with my Father in his throne.*

This is the seventh and last occurrence of the call to *Behold* in the church section. It is one of the most impressive and significant.

I stand at the door, and knock. The *door* is presented in at least four different aspects in the New Testament:

To the sinner Christ Himself is the door. The sinner is invited to enter. The invitation is sufficient; no knocking is required. If he enters, he shall be saved. John 10:9.

Believers are invited to knock (at the door of God's storehouse), with the assurance that it will be opened. Matthew 7:7, 8.

Christ makes His abode or dwelling place in the heart of the believer (John 14:23; 15:5; Ephesians 3:17; Colossians 1:27), and dwells with the body of believers. Due to the worldly and compromising spirit of the Laodicean church, He has taken His place on the outside of *her* door. He is standing outside and knocking. The verbs are in the present tense, implying continuity and prolonged waiting for admittance. The church as a whole having rejected Him, He makes His appeal to the individual: *If any [one] will open the door, I will come in to him*—note the singular number in each case. Next to Calvary this is one of the most pathetic and heart-rending scenes in the entire Bible.

The fourth instance is that of knocking when once the door is shut. An example is found in the parable of the ten virgins. Matthew 25:10. See also Luke 13:24, 25. There should be no period at the close of verse 24, so that the correct reading is, "for many, I say unto you, will seek to enter in, and shall not be able, when once the master of the house is risen up, and hath shut to the door."

I will sup with him, and he himself [by way of emphasis] *with me.* That certain ones opened the door and "let the Saviour in" is indicated by the promises which Jesus makes. One must wonder what kind of table the individual believer has to set for such a distinguished guest, unless it be his sins, his sorrows, his burdens, and his cares. This menu He tasted at the cross. However, what He shares with the believer as He enters his heart, is rather the joy of salvation that has come through His atoning work. The believer will sup with Him to share *His* joys. For the Father has anointed Him with the oil of gladness above His fellows, which means that He is the happiest "fellow" that ever lived. The supping with Him will not be concluded when He enters the heart of the believer. As belonging to the bride of Christ, he will also be present at the marriage supper of the Lamb (Revelation 19:9), and he will have part in the celebration of the Lord's Supper in His kingdom. Luke 22:16, 29, 30.

Consider now the church of the Laodiceans in a representative and prophetic sense. What is to be understood by the position of Christ standing without the door of the church universal in this the last epoch of church history? Plainly He has been rejected by Christendom as a whole and the last apostasy has set in. The church evidently *does not know* that she is wretched, and miserable, and poor, and blind, and naked, for the consciousness of being rich and increased in goods has become her satisfying portion. When one considers the holy character of Christ, it will occasion no surprise that He has taken His stand outside of popular Christianity, for He could not consistently abide in the hearts of the disobedient and world-conformed professors of the Christian religion. For what men do with His words, they do with *Him*. This is clear from such passages as: "Why call ye me, Lord, Lord, and do not the things which I say" (Luke 6:46)? "Whosoever shall be ashamed of me and of my words, of him shall the Son of man be ashamed" (Luke 9:26); "The word that I have spoken, the same shall judge him in the last day" (John 12:48).

Anyone who had reached his maturity at the close of the last century could bear abundant testimony that this is a changed world, as well as a different religious environment. At that time infidels were regarded with horror and alarm by the average Christian. For example, true Christians were shocked to hear that Ingersoll lectured on the "Mistakes of Moses." However, before the noted infidel died, he bore testimony that he had quit lecturing on the mistakes of Moses because preachers and religious instructors in church institutions now do the same work more effectively than he ever did. The fact is, they went much farther in their attacks on the Bible than Ingersoll had, for they not only spoke of the mistakes of Moses but denied the Mosaic authorship of the Pentateuch and claimed this portion of the Scriptures was the patchwork of various authors who likely lived centuries apart. They went farther than this. They spoke of the mistakes of Jesus as well, one of which was His belief that Moses was the author of the entire Pentateuch, for He said so much when He declared, "Moses gave you the law," and when He quoted from the five books as being the words of Moses. Following their claim that the Bible contained mistakes, they declared categorically that it was not divinely inspired and they were quick to seize at the faulty translation of the basic text (compare II Timothy 3:16 as given in the American Revised Version) which declares that "all scripture inspired of God is also profitable," implying that some Scripture is *not* inspired and hence not profitable. With the repudiation of the perfection of Jesus came the denial of His virgin birth, of the absolute truthfulness of His utterances, of His atoning work, of His resurrection from the dead, and of His personal second coming. With such views prevailing in many of the great religious institutions of present-day Christianity, it is no surprise to learn that Jesus is standing outside the door. [As one reads certain passages, he is deeply impressed with the accuracy of the writers of Scripture when they undertake to describe the last days, even the twentieth century. Take, for example, "But there were false prophets also among the people, even as there shall be false teachers among you, who privily shall bring in damnable heresies, even denying the Lord that bought them . . ." (II Peter 2:1).—J. O. Y.]

Since the Laodicean period represents religious conditions during the last days of the church, this would be the place to note some of the various "signs" contained in the Scriptures, descriptive of these days:

The Ecclesiastical Sign. Matthew 24:12; II Thessalonians 2:3; I Timothy 4:1-3; II Timothy 3:5, 8.

The Social Sign. Matthew 24:38, 39; II Timothy 3:2-7; James 5:5.

The Intellectual Sign. Daniel 12:4; II Timothy 3:7.

The Financial Sign. James 5:1-4; Revelation 13:16, 17.

The Moral Sign. II Timothy 3:13.

The Physical Sign. Luke 21:25, 26.

The Political Sign. Matthew 24:6, 7.

The Jewish Sign. Matthew 24:32, 33.

Remember, these signs pertain to the tribulation period, but the trends in that direction are doubtless apparent for some time beforehand. It would be a separate project to give examples in detail of the increasing evidence that the above signs are all in process of fulfillment now. Others are giving themselves diligently and efficiently to this task, and since the present work is intended as a commentary of what has been revealed in this last book of the Bible, detailed descriptions regarding the signs of the times are left for others.

FOOTNOTES, PART III

1. Statistics from 1956 *World Almanac.*
2. "The Martyrdom of Polycarp," *The Ante-Nicene Fathers,* Vol. I, pp. 37-44.
3. "Epistle of Mathetes, a Disciple of the Apostles, to Diognetus," Chaps. VI and VII, *op. cit.,* Vol. I, pp. 27, 28.
4. Justin Martyr, "Dialogue with Trypho," Chap. CXVII, *op. cit.,* Vol. I, p. 258.
5. Clement of Alexandria, "The Stromata," Bk. VI, Chap. XVIII, *op. cit.,* Vol. II, p. 520, col. a.
6. Cyprian, "The Treatises of Cyprian," Treatise XI, Sec. 13, *op. cit.,* Vol. V, p. 507, col. a.
7. "The Martyrdom of Polycarp," *op. cit.,* Vol. I, p. 41, col. a.
8. Tertullian, "Ad Nationes," Chap. VIII, *op. cit.,* Vol. III, p. 117, col. b.
9. Van Braght, p. 96.
10. Ramsay, p. 325.
11. See Appendix, p. 363, " 'Son' Applied to Christ."
12. Delitzsch (Psalm 7:9 [according to Hebrew number, verse 10.—J. O. Y.]
13. Ramsay, p. 70.
14. *Ibid.,* pp. 389, 390.
15. Stier, Vol. 9, p. 165.
16. Charles, Vol. I, pp. 12, 13.
17. See Appendix, p. 328, "As a Thief."
18. See Appendix, p. 329, "To Blot Out of the Book of Life."
19. Swete, p. 53.
20. Ramsay, p. 405.
21. Trench, p. 183.
22. Hatch, p. 73.
23. See Appendix, p. 331, "From That Hour."
24. Ramsay, p. 424.
25. Charles, Vol. I, p. 96.
26. Swete, p. 61.
27. Ramsay, p. 429.

4

PART IV
THE THINGS WHICH SHALL BE HEREAFTER
(EVENTS FOLLOWING THE CHURCH AGE)
4:1—22:7

1. THE CHURCH IN GLORY (4, 5)

The Open Door (4:1)

Verse 1. *After this I looked, and, behold, a door was opened in heaven: and the first voice which I heard was as it were of a trumpet talking with me: which said, Come up hither, and I will shew thee things which must be hereafter.*

I saw. The words, *I saw*, show here is a new and distinct vision. This is the second vision mentioned in the book. The first "I saw" occurs in 1:12. Since all the details of a vision are organically related and there is no recurrence of the phrase previous to this, it shows that all the remaining materials of chapter 1 and all of those of chapters 2 and 3 are part of one organic whole. Here, however, a new vision occurs, and since the phrase does not occur again until 5:1, the entire chapter constitutes one organic whole. Its parts are to be regarded as vitally interrelated. (It should be remembered that the terms, "I saw," "I looked, "I beheld," are identical in Greek and that each alike introduces a new vision.)

After these things (so the Greek). This phrase denotes sequence or a passing from what was mentioned to what follows in order of time. However, when the phrase modifies "I saw," as it does eleven times in the book, the reference may be to the order of vision merely and not necessarily (though usually) to the chronological sequence of events. For instance, as far as the language employed is concerned, the seer may refer merely to his having had a new vision and not necessarily to the fact that the things he is about to mention succeed those already mentioned in order of time.

Behold. This is the tenth occurrence of the watchword "behold." Its meaning, "see for your own benefit," should be kept in mind.

A door . . . opened. Of special interest is the statement that a door is opened up in heaven. Only once again does the seer mention heaven opened: "I saw heaven opened, and behold a white horse; and he that sat upon him was called Faithful and True. . . . And the armies which were in heaven followed him upon white horses, clothed in fine linen, white and clean" (Revelation 19:11, 14). The context explains that those clothed in fine linen clean and white constitute the bride, the Lamb's wife. 19:7; cf. 21:9. In chapter 19, observe therefore that heaven opens when Christ comes with the bride, an important event. In chapter 4, the door opened in heaven is likewise attached to an occasion of high importance.

The first voice. The first voice as of a trumpet evidently is identical with that of 1:10. It is the voice of Jesus. The following, therefore, are His own words.

Come up hither, and I will shew thee things which must be hereafter [Greek: *after these things*]—a plain allusion to 1:19c. So far, while John has been receiving his messages for the churches, he has been on earth. Now he is bidden to come up hither, that is, to heaven. In accordance with chapter 1:1, Jesus now continues to show unto His servant the things written in this book.

Things which must be hereafter. Observe that the term, *meta tauta* (after these things), is used in an absolute sense, that is, without being modified by the expression, "I saw," as above. In other words, the things He is now about to show are subsequent in time to the things of chapters 2 and 3 and correspond with the third division of the outline. 1:19. Hence the seer is about to write of things which will come to pass after the things of the church age have run their course. He utters his words with an emphasis and note of certainty, for they must be after the things he has already mentioned.

The Throne Sitters (4:2-11)

Verse 2. *And immediately I was in the spirit; and, behold, a throne was set in heaven, and one sat on the throne.*

I was in the spirit. The thought is that John was transported in the Spirit through the opened door. That John is now in heaven is evidenced by the personal observations he now makes. Undoubtedly the actions and performances of individuals and groups in heaven as described in the two chapters following those describing the church age are those which follow in order of time.

Behold. The word *behold* serves again as a signal for attention to one of the major particulars of the present vision.

A throne was set in heaven. Throne is anarthrous (without the article), indicating first mention. The word *throne* occurs 45 times in Revelation, and only 15 times in the rest of the New Testament. Revelation, therefore, may well be called the *throne book of the Bible.* The throne was a special one set or placed in heaven ostensibly for the purpose of executing the judgments of the tribulation period following. The word *set* is the same as that used in I Corinthians 3:11: "Other foundation can no man lay than that is *laid*," and in 21:16: "the city *lieth* foursquare." The word denotes fixity, security, durability as contradistinguished from earthly thrones which have been tottering and tumbling in accordance with the prophetic forecast concerning the last days. Ezekiel 21:27; Haggai 2:22; Luke 21:25.

A difference of thrones as well as of administrations should be carefully noted. Before Israel rejected God from reigning over them (I Samuel 8:7), He dwelt between the cherubim and communed with His people from thence. Exodus 25:18, 22; I Samuel 4:4. There is no mention of His having His throne elsewhere during this period.

After God was rejected by Israel, the theocracy ceased, for God withdrew Himself from the earth and henceforth heaven is declared to be the place of His throne. Psalms 11:4; 103:19; Isaiah 66:1; Matthew 5:34; 23:22; Acts 7:49. As far as the record goes, He sat alone on His throne up to and during the earthly ministry of Christ.

After the ascension, at which time Jesus sat down at the right hand of God (Mark 16:19; Hebrews 10:12, 13), and during the entire church period, Jesus will continue His session with the Father, as is evident from His own testimony at the very close of the church age: "I . . . am set down with my Father in his throne" (Revelation 3:21). A most remarkable change now takes place as the remaining portion of the verse indicates, for God is now alone on what appears to be a special throne.

Attention should be called to the fact that in Revelation 20:11 *throne* is again anarthrous, for here the seer testifies, "I saw *a* great white throne." This is therefore a different throne from that previously mentioned. Not only is the word without the article, but it is further distinguished from the afore-mentioned throne by the descriptive terms "great" and "white." (See the notes on Revelation 20.)

One sat on the throne. This is at once a startling statement and full of meaning. The Greek says, (*One*) *sitting on the throne.* The present participle is used to denote continuity. Like throne, the participle is anarthrous, i.e., (One) sitting, not the (one) sitting, thus likewise indicating first mention. Following this it occurs *with* the article six times in chapters 4 and 5 (4:3, 9, 10; 5:1, 7, 13), and five times in succeeding chapters (7:10, 15; 19:4; 21:5; 22:1). It will be observed that in the Authorized Version it is rendered, "He that sat," "Him that sat," or "sitteth," and such like, but in the Greek it is uniformly *the* (one) sitting on the throne, except in 4:2 where the article is absent due to first mention.

Verse 3. And he that sat was to look upon like a jasper and a sardine stone: and there was a rainbow round about the throne, in sight like unto an emerald.

He that sat [Greek: *The (One) sitting*]. As noted before, the definite article points to the previous mention. It would be entirely correct to translate the previous phrase, (One) seated; and this, "He that sat," but it does not show either the use of the definite article or the participial form of the verb "sit."

To look upon. The words *to look upon* are identical in meaning with "in sight." Both are the translation of *orasis*, which is rendered "vision" in 9:17 and Acts 2:17. It is correct, therefore, to read, *He that sat* [was] *in appearance like a jasper and sardine* (or better, sardius).

Jasper and a sardine stone. The jasper is well described in 21:11, where the light of the city "having the glory of God" is said to be "like unto a stone most precious, even like a jasper stone, clear as crystal." The light evidently proceeds from the glory of God. God is therefore likened in appearance to a jasper because of its brilliance or luminosity. The sardius is named after the city of Sardis, where the most beautiful specimens of this variety of stone have been found. It has been described as being almost blood red and again as flesh color. Some have taken God's likeness to a sardius as denoting His atoning work through the redemption that is in Christ Jesus. If this is the correct interpretation, it must be in that He is about to vindicate His redemptive plan by bringing judgment upon those who have refused to accept it. Perhaps it is better to think of this resemblance as denoting His anger as a reaction of His holy nature in view of the prevailing sinfulness of man and in consequence of which He is about to send judgment upon the earth, that "the inhabitants of the world will learn righteousness."

A rainbow round about the throne. The rainbow encircling the throne denotes the faithfulness of God. He has declared that He would render "indignation and wrath, tribulation and anguish, upon every soul of man that doeth evil . . ." (Romans 2:8, 9). His faithfulness requires Him to execute His avowed purpose. The rainbow is in appearance like an emerald. Thayer describes it as "a transparent stone noted especially for its light green color."[1] The rainbow mediates apparently between the brilliant glow of the jasper and the red hue of the sardius, thus in symbol reconciling God's holiness with His retributive justice, and uniting both in the prosecution of the judgments just ahead. It is a rider on a *red* horse that brings the first judgment upon the earth, and a white horse rider clothed with a vesture *dipped in blood* appears at the close of the judgments that follow. This would lend support to the view that the sardius stone symbolizes the wrath of God rather than His work of redemption. The lightnings, thunderings, and voices mentioned in verse 5 likewise support this view.

Verse 4. *And round about the throne were four and twenty seats: and upon the seats I saw four and twenty elders sitting, clothed in white raiment; and they had on their heads crowns of gold.*

Seats. The word is misleading, for the Greek word is in both instances *thronos.* The same word is used as for that upon which God sits; hence it should read "four and twenty thrones." The same correction should be made in 11:16; 13:2; 16:10, where the translation "seats" erroneously occurs. The twenty-four elders are said to be sitting *round about the throne.* The same relative position is ascribed to the rainbow. The chief concern in this connection, however, is—Who are these elders, or whom do they represent? First, why are they called elders? Apparently they are a representative group, as were the elders of the church at the Jerusalem council, who, with the apostles and elders, were the living representatives of the church when they came together "to consider of this matter" (Acts 15:6). It should be noted that during the entire New Testament period there were recognized officials and representatives of the church. Elder was the official title, while bishop (Greek: overseer) was the function. Acts 20:28. Whom these glorified elders represent and why twenty-four are mentioned will be further discussed later. That elder was the official title of the highest functionary official of the church at the beginning appears clear because they are mentioned six times in conjunction with the apostles, whereas the word "bishop," a word signifying function and not office, is never conjoined in this manner.

Observe that four descriptive statements are made concerning the elders; namely, they have golden crowns on their heads, they sit on thrones, they wear white raiment, and their number is twenty-four. Some have taken them to be angels; others as representatives of Israel; and others still as a group representing both Israel and the church. Possibly the best way to proceed with a test as to which is intended is by the process of elimination. They are not angels because angels are never spoken of as sitting on thrones nor as having crowns on their heads. They do not represent Israel because neither thrones nor crowns were ever promised to Israel or groups representing her, either in the Old or New Testament.

There is one passage of Scripture which has been used in maintaining the view that since Israel was spoken of as a kingdom of priests, and since a kingdom implies a king, therefore thrones and crowns are implied likewise. "Now therefore, if ye will obey my voice indeed, and keep my covenant, then ye shall be a peculiar treasure unto me above all people: for all the earth is mine: and ye shall be unto me a kingdom of priests, and an holy nation" (Exodus 19:5, 6).

There is one fatal objection to the argument based on this passage, namely, it overlooks the initial "if." In other words, the promise or covenant here given is conditioned upon obedience. Israel failed to keep the covenant as is evident from her entire history.

To the overcomer of the Laodicean period the promise is given to sit with Christ on His throne. The reference is plainly not to the throne set in heaven because that throne is definitely declared to be the Father's throne. 3:21. The throne of Christ is on the earth. He will sit on the throne of David, which will then be the throne of glory. Isaiah 9:7; Luke 1:32. As for the place, the prophet Jeremiah says, "At that time they shall call Jerusalem the throne of the Lord; and all the nations shall be gathered unto it, to the name of the Lord, to Jerusalem" (Jeremiah 3:17). It is here that the joint session of the twelve apostles with Christ will occur and to which reference is made in Matthew 19:28 and Luke 22:30.

Mention is made of throne sitters in two more passages in Revelation which should be referred to briefly in this connection.

In 11:16 the four and twenty elders which sit before God upon their thrones (Greek) fall upon their faces and worship God. The passage is of interest in this connection because it shows that in the middle of the tribulation they are still seated on their thrones while the awful judgments are continuing on the earth below.

"And I saw thrones, and they sat upon them, and judgment was given unto them" (20:4). Here in a vision after the tribulation is over and after the coming of the Lord "in power and great glory" (19:11 f.), John sees a group sitting upon thrones. That they are identical with the church group is further seen in that "judgment was given unto them." Compare I Corinthians 6:2: "Do ye not know that the saints shall judge the world?"

White raiment. There are only two passages in the Scriptures outside of those in Revelation in which mention is made of white raiment. One is Ecclesiastes 9:8: "Let thy garments be always white." The words are obviously used in a figurative sense, white having reference not to color but to purity as in Psalm 51:7; Isaiah 1:18; Daniel 12:10. Moreover, in Ecclesiastes the words are not related in the sentence as they are here. Nowhere else do we find either men or angels spoken of as wearing *himation leukon (raiment white)*, such as is indicated of the glorified church group, and as is promised to the overcomers of Sardis (3:5), and counseled for purchase to the church of Laodicea (3:18). Jesus only, besides these, is said to have appeared in white raiment. This was at His transfiguration, when His raiment became "white as the light" (Matthew 17:2); "exceeding white as snow" (Mark 9:3); "white and glistering" (Luke 9:29). The Greek word here used means flashing out like lightning. It is interesting to observe that His raiment was like that ascribed to glorified groups of elders.

Remember, thrones and crowns are the possession of kings. However, to rule is not the only ministry belonging to the church; the ministry of intercession (I Timothy 2:1) which implies priesthood belonged to her as well. She is designated a body of kings and priests (1:6), and as a royal (i.e., kingly) priesthood (I Peter 2:9). Finally, the ministry belongs to the church during the thousand years because Revelation 20:6 says they shall be priests of God and of Christ and shall reign with Him 1,000 years. The title "kings and priests" is ascribed to her also in 5:10, when like here she is in a glorified state. Thus her future ministry will be akin to Christ's. It is said He will be a priest on His throne. Zechariah 6:13.

Since priestly ministry belongs to a glorified church, the *white raiment* probably alludes to her priestly function. The priest, as well as the high priest, wore linen garments. Exodus 39:1-28; Leviticus 6:10; 16:4.

Four and twenty. Consider now the number ascribed to the glorified elders. The number twenty-four apparently alludes to the twenty-four courses of the priestly order mentioned in I Chronicles 24. It may be called to mind again that due to their disobedience of the conditional covenant the Lord made with Israel, both her kingly and her priestly functions passed over to the church as expressed in I Peter 2:9: "Ye are . . . a royal priesthood." The "ye" is emphatic (Greek) as if to stress the right of the church to the title in contrast with Israel's forfeiture of it.

This is not to be taken as in opposition to the express statement of Scripture, "And so all Israel shall be saved" (Romans 11:26). The unconditional covenant which the Lord made with Abraham and his seed, "I will bless thee . . . and thou shalt be a blessing . . . and in thee shall all families of the earth be blessed" (Genesis 12:2, 3), will yet be literally fulfilled. This is confirmed by the testimony of "all the prophets." (See especially Isaiah 2:2, 3; Zechariah 8:20-23.) However, due to the defection of Israel, the kingdom was taken from her and given to the church, and the church instead of Israel is now a royal priesthood. Jesus' further word to the church has given her a peculiar prerogative to sit on thrones judging the twelve tribes of Israel. This subordinate position of Israel as compared with the regal and sacerdotal ministry of the church "in the regeneration" and the coming kingdom as well as the uniform position of the twenty-four elders encircling the throne, is in direct opposition to the view that twelve of the throne sitters represent the church and another twelve Israel. It is altogether improbable that Israel would have equal rank with the church in heaven and afterward be judged by the church during the kingdom age.

Probably the most convincing evidence that Israel is not represented among the glorified elders in heaven is that she as a nation will not have turned to the Lord at the time of the rapture. It is contrary to reason and to all the facts of Revelation concerning Israel that those of the Old Testament will be united with the bride of Christ in heaven or that the Israel of the future will be separated from those of the Old Testament and be judged by them. Let it be observed that Israel will remain a separate people, and will not be swallowed up by the church, as some erroneously hold. If such were the case, how could the church judge Israel?

Crowns of gold. Crowns are promised to the church and to her only.

Various titles are applied to crowns given as a reward for various kinds of service. An incorruptible (crown)—the word is implied as in contrast with the corruptible crown mentioned. The Christian life is compared to a race that is run. The Christian, in order to win an incorruptible crown, must run like the one who wins the prize in a race. I Corinthians 9:25. A crown of rejoicing is the reward for the soul winner. Philippians 4:1; I Thessalonians 2:19. A crown of righteousness is the reward for keeping the faith. II Timothy 4:8. A crown of life awaits the one patient under trial (James 1:12), or faithful unto death in times of persecution (Revelation 2:10). A crown of glory is promised to elders who witness to the sufferings of Christ and feed the flock of God. I Peter 5:2. In no case do we find crowns promised to angels or to the faithful of Israel in the past, but only to believers of the church age; hence the view that Israel is represented among the elders finds no support in Scripture and thus it is at best a mere assumption.

Observe that the elders wear golden crowns. Besides them only Christ is said to appear with a golden crown. The place of their mention may be readily recalled by the similarity of the passages—that of the elders being chapter 4:4; and of Jesus, 14:14.

Verse 5. *And out of the throne proceeded lightnings and thunderings and voices: and there were seven lamps of fire burning before the throne, which are the seven Spirits of God.*

The throne. The throne of God is mentioned twice in this verse. If Revelation is the throne book of the Bible, then chapter 4 is the throne chapter. The word occurs fourteen times. Twelve times the reference is to God's throne; twice to the elders'.

An outline of the relative positions of personages or objects connected with the throne will enable one to get a mental picture of it and its environs.

Upon (*epi*) the throne, said of
    God (4:2, 9, 10);
    Elders (4:4b).

Round about (*kuglothen, kuklo*—cf. English word "circle")
    A rainbow (4:3);
    Elders (4:4a);
    Four beasts (4:6c).

Out of or from (*ek*)
    Lightnings, thunders, voices (4:5a).

Before (*enopion*)
    Seven lamps of fire (4:5b);
    A sea of glass (4:6a);
    Elders cast crowns (4:10b).

In the midst (*en meso*)
    Four beasts, i.e., living creatures (4:6b).

Lightnings and thunderings and voices. These are premonitions of the storm of judgment soon to follow. Similar and more severe portents occur at various intervals in the succeeding chapters and in each case judgment follows with increasing intensity. 8:5; 11:19; and 16:18. The reader will observe that such mundane disturbances in later instances serve both as a conclusion to the series of judgments just past and as an introduction to others pending.

Seven lamps of fire. For the seven lamps before the throne we have the angel's own interpretation—they are the seven spirits of God mentioned in 1:4 and 3:1. They are mentioned the last time in 5:6, where they are said to be "sent forth into all the earth." This is an inspired definition of an angel. Hebrews 1:14 records that angels are ministering spirits "sent forth"—the very word (*apostello*) being employed. Observe therefore: as standing before the throne they are seven spirits; as "sent forth" they are seven angels. This accounts for the fact that whereas the phrase "spirits of God" occurs four times up to 5:6, thereafter this phrase does not occur again, but instead we have "*the* seven angels which stood before God" (8:2). Note also the definite article in the latter passage which implies previous mention and confirms the view that the seven spirits and the seven angels are identical. (See 1:4.)

Verse 6. *And before the throne there was a sea of glass like unto crystal: and in the midst of the throne, and round about the throne, were four beasts full of eyes before and behind.*

A sea of glass. This is mentioned again in 15:2. Here it is anarthrous. There the article occurs, showing that the reference at that place is to the same sea. It has the same appearance as *jasper* (verse 3), and is like the city foursquare, which also is like jasper, "clear as crystal" (21:11). Hence, as the passage there shows, it is luminous or effulgent like the glory of God. This radiant light before the throne shows that all the performances occurring there are in harmony with the holy character of God.

Beasts. The word *beast* in Revelation is the translation of three different Greek words:

Dzoon occurs 20 times. Compare the English word "zoology." The translation here employed is unfortunate, for the word means *living one.* The same word occurs twelve times in the first ten chapters of Ezekiel where it is uniformly rendered *living creature.* From its use in Ezekiel it is clear that the living creatures are identical with the cherubim, for in Ezekiel 10:15 the prophet testifies: "The cherubims were lifted up. This is the living creature that I saw by the river of Chebar." And to make this identity doubly sure he adds in 10:20: "This is the living creature that I saw under the God of Israel by the river of Chebar; and I knew that they were the cherubims." "Cherubims," as in the Authorized Version, is a double plural. The singular is cherub [the plural cherubim, without the final "s."—J.O.Y.]. The elders and beasts are mentioned nine times in close conjunction.

Therion occurs 38 times. The word is used once in its ordinary sense of wild beasts as a species of plague (6:8); of the false prophet (13:11); 36 times it is applied to the Antichrist.

Ktenos. Of a domestic animal. 18:13.

Full of eyes before and behind denotes both keen observation and high intelligence. The imagery is taken from Ezekiel 1:18; 10:12.

Verse 7. *And the first beast was like a lion, and the second beast like a calf, and the third beast had a face as a man, and the fourth beast was like a flying eagle.*

The four resemblances are similar to those of the Septuagint version of Ezekiel 1:10. The Hebrew has ox in place of calf. The allusion appears to be to the four heads of the creatures upon earth: to the lion as the head of wild beasts; the ox, of domestic animals; man as the sovereign head of all creatures (Genesis 1:26); and the eagle as the bird of highest wing. In Ezekiel the order of mention— man, lion, ox, eagle—is apparently given in the order of strength and power to subdue, whereas in this text the inspired writer appears to have varied the order.

In the Old Testament, the four living creatures represented God's presence in earthly creation. However, when Christ came, He was the true Emmanuel (God with us). Anyone familiar with the four Gospels recognizes that He represented Himself in a fourfold manner and in order of sequence corresponding to the subject matter of the four Gospels. In Matthew He appears as the Lion of the tribe of Judah; in Mark as the servant of the Lord (corresponding to the ox of sacrifice, 10:45); in Luke He is the Son of man seeking the lost (19:10); and in John He is the eagle that soars on highest wing in His apprehension and exhibition of grace and truth.

Verse 8. *And the four beasts had each of them six wings about him; and they were full of eyes within: and they rest not day and night, saying, Holy, holy, holy, Lord God Almighty, which was, and is, and is to come.*

Six wings. The living creatures have six wings. In Ezekiel (1:6) they have but four. In the number of wings they correspond with the seraphim of Isaiah 6:2, but this does not mean that we should regard the latter as identical with the cherubim. On the other hand, their ministry is quite distinct as far as the record goes, for while that of the cherubim relates itself to the holy character of God, the concern of the seraphim appears to be that of purging men from sin so as to accord them access to a holy God.

Full of eyes. Texts vary on this clause, but evidently what is said here about being full of eyes is an additional characteristic to what is said in verse 6, whether it is understood to mean eyes within merely, that is, under, or both under and outside the wings. The variations in the symbolism expressed here and in Ezekiel may be accounted for by the difference of circumstances apparent on the two occasions.

Rest is a noun in the original and it is emphatic by position, viz., *and rest they have not day and night.* This voluntary and gladsome abstinence from rest is in marked contrast to that of the image worshipers (14:9-11) who have no rest day nor night because "the smoke of their torment ascendeth up for ever and ever."

Holy, holy, holy. This is familiarly designated the *trisagion* (thrice holy) and occurs only here and in Isaiah 6:3. It is one of some thirty heavenly utterances recorded in Revelation. Here the acclamation comes from the cherubim, in Isaiah from the seraphim. There is a probable allusion in each case to the Trinity, i.e., ascription of holiness to the Father, Son, and Spirit. There is another interesting resemblance between the two passages, for "Lord of hosts" of the former corresponds with the words of omnipotence, "Lord God Almighty." The former closes with the omnipresence of His glory; this closes with the triple formula of His eternity.

Verse 9. *And when those beasts give glory and honour and thanks to him that sat on the throne, who liveth for ever and ever.*

When. The Greek for *when* is *hotan*, meaning *whensoever, in case that, so often as.* Thus the adverb used gives to the verb an occasional or periodic sense. This throws light on the action of the living creatures in the preceding verse. The sense is not that there was unbroken continuity in their acclamation of the *trisagion*, but rather that whenever occasion called for it their response is immediate and unfailing.

Glory and honour and thanks. This phrase occurs eight times: 4:9, 11; 5:12, 13; 7:12; 19:1; 21:24, 26.

Thanks (usually rendered thanksgiving or giving of thanks) occurs once again in 7:12. Its use at this place by the living creatures is significant, for in it they give expression to the prospect of final triumph, now that a group of redeemed have appeared in heaven.

The doxology is directed to "the One sitting on the throne" (see verses 2, 3)— the lone throne sitter now that the church age has closed. The participle—the living (One)—is used, thus denoting continued living existence. God is further spoken of as the living God in 7:2, and as the living (One) as here in 4:10; 5:14; 10:6; 15:7. The entire Bible stresses the fact of a living God. His own testimony, "the living God," occurs 32 times. Again He declares, "I live," 24 times; and the testimony of others, "He lives, i.e., the living One," 54 times—a total of 110.

Verse 10. The four and twenty elders fall down before him that sat [Greek: sitteth] *on the throne, and worship him that liveth for ever and ever, and cast their crowns before the throne, saying.*

The four and twenty elders. Note the article at the second mention of the elders, thus pointing back to first mention in verse 4. The four and twenty elders fall down and worship four times: twice alone—here and in 5:14; twice in conjunction with the living creatures (5:8; 19:4). The living creatures in no instance fall down and worship of their own accord. Observe that the twenty-four elders fall down and worship whenever the living creatures give glory and honor and thanks to God; that to say, "Holy, holy, holy, Lord God Almighty," is to give glory and honor to God; and that this ascription of honor and glory could not be continuous because the elders in that case would have to be continually falling, which involves an absurdity.

Him that sat on the throne. This is the third mention of the lone Throne Sitter, lit., the One sitting on the throne.

Worship him that liveth. Worship is really *worth-ship*, that is, ascribing worth to one. It is an attitude rather than an act. One may worship God without uttering a word. Words are not worship. True worship subsists in the attitude of spirit back of the words. The word occurs 24 times in Revelation. The fact that eleven of these are directed toward God, nine to the beast or his image, two to the devil and demons (making eleven to evil powers), and two misdirected to an angel is indicative of the mighty conflict prevailing throughout the book between the powers of good and evil. "Worship God" (19:10; 22:9) is one of the most succinct, meaningful utterances of the entire Scriptures. Its twofold occurrence near the close of the sacred volume is timely and arresting in its implications.

True worship may be defined as a devout attitude of the soul superinduced by a sense of one's own unworthiness in contemplation of the infinite worth of God. Hence worship is said to be at His feet (3:9; 19:10), but the elders, being kings and priests (1:6; 4:4; 5:10), cast their crowns before the throne because that is the source of their royal estate.

Here is the second testimony that the glorified elders wear crowns (cf. 1:6 with verse 4 above); hence that they are kings.

Verse 11. *Thou art worthy, O Lord, to receive glory and honour and power: for thou hast created all things, and for thy pleasure they are and were created.*

Thou art worthy, O Lord. A sense of one's own unworthiness is indeed the first essential of true worship, and the ascription to the Lord as alone possessing worth is the second. Unless the worth of the Lord is sensed by the worshiper, his own unworthiness will not be realized. It will be observed in this, the third heavenly utterance, that adoration by the elders is similar to that of the living creatures with the exception that they ascribe power to the Lord in place of thanksgiving as the living creatures do. This interchange is at first sight perplexing. We should rather expect just the reverse, viz., that the elders would *give thanks* for their salvation and glorification which naturally is the greatest cause for thanksgiving and which does not apply to the living creatures, since they are sinless. On the other hand, since the living creatures were directly interested in creation, we would rather suspect them to ascribe power to the Lord. The only apparent explanation is that each group is interested not primarily in its own state but in that of the other. The living creatures rejoice in the presence of a redeemed group in whom they see the "earnest" of a restored race; the elders rejoice that the hope and prospect of the living creatures is about to be realized, namely, that "the creation [Greek] itself . . . [is to be delivered] from the bondage of corruption into the glorious liberty of the children of God" (Romans 8:21).

The Sealed Book (5:1)

Verse 1. *And I saw in the right hand of him that sat on the throne a book written within and on the backside, sealed with seven seals.*

The present vision consists of but one verse. It should be remembered that each vision comprises a unit and that all its parts constitute an organic whole. When a vision is brief, as here, it implies not only distinctness but outstanding importance calling for separate consideration and reflection.

Right hand. The book upon (Greek) the right hand of God suggests not only its divine source, but supreme authority as pertaining to its subject matter. The hand of God would indicate power to translate it into action.

Him that sat on the throne. The book is upon the right hand "of the [One] sitting on the throne" (Greek). This is the fifth mention of the lone Throne Sitter (see 4:2, 3, 9, 10), thus stressing again the important fact that Jesus, who was still seated with the Father on His throne (3:21), has left His place of intercession at God's right hand, and the time has come for Him to put His enemies under His feet (Psalm 110:1, and its repetitions in the New Testament).

Book written within and on the backside, sealed with seven seals. This denotes fixity, fullness, and security as to its contents.

The Strong Angel (5:2-5)

Verses 2, 3. *And I saw a strong angel proclaiming with a loud voice, Who is worthy to open the book, and to loose the seals thereof? And no man in heaven, nor in earth, neither under the earth, was able to open the book, neither to look thereon.*

A strong angel. The vision opens with three notes of emphasis: a strong angel—only twice more is reference made to a strong angel in the book, viz., 10:1 and 18:21 (Greek). The angel proclaims—not merely says. The word signifies to announce as a herald. *With a loud voice* denotes urgency and great concern. Loud voices are one of the distinguishing features of the book. Moreover, they occur in heaven and generally are heard on the earth. This is in marked contrast with the silence of heaven during the present age and serves as another indubitable proof that the church period has come to a close.

If it be asked, Who is the strong angel making the challenge? the answer is, doubtless, Gabriel, the one who ordered the closing and sealing of the book to Daniel. The name "Gabriel" means "strength of God"; so he is well entitled to be called a strong angel. The chief reason for concluding that the reference is to Gabriel, however, is that he is beyond any other the informing angel. (See Daniel 8:16; 9:22, 23; 10:14, 21; 11:2; Luke 1:13, 14-17, 26 ff., and 35.)

No one (Greek). No man, or angel, or any other creature, was able to open the book, or even look thereon (better, therein—Tregelles).[2]

Verse 4. And I wept much, because no man was found worthy to open and to read the book, neither to look thereon.

I wept much. His disappointment was great, for the word *weep* means more than to shed tears. It is the same word as is used in reference to Jesus when He wept over Jerusalem. Luke 19:41. There is only one other instance where the verb is modified by an adverb of degree—he confesses, "I wept much." Of Peter it is said, he "wept bitterly" (Matthew 26:75).

No man was found worthy. This implies that search had been made but of no avail. No creature was found either able (verse 3) or worthy (verse 4).

Verse 5. And one of the elders saith unto me, Weep not: behold, the Lion of the tribe of Juda, the Root of David, hath prevailed to open the book, and to loose the seven seals thereof.

[*One of the elders.* The reference, no doubt, is to the twenty-four referred to earlier in the book. Evidently they were well informed as to the happenings that bore on the nature of the predictions contained in the book, so that one of them could serve as spokesman.

Weep not. Actually John is told to stop weeping. The demonstrations of heaven are about to take place. It is no time to weep!—J.O.Y.]

The Lion of the tribe of Juda, the Root of David. Observe that Jesus is expressly described as "the Lion," thus pointing out His ability to open the book. Jesus sprang from Juda according to the flesh. Matthew 1:2, 3. He is spoken of as the Lion of the tribe of Judah in an allusion to Genesis 49:8, 9, where Jacob, in telling what shall befall his sons in the latter days, says of Judah: "Thy hand shall be in the neck of thine enemies. . . . Judah is a lion's whelp . . . he couched as a lion, and as an old lion; who shall rouse him up?" He is also called the Root of David because He sprang from David. He is referred to as the offspring of David in Revelation 22:16, which apparently is to be taken as epexegetical of the

Root of David. In Isaiah 11:10 He is described as the root of Jesse, as He is in Romans 15:12. These references take the lineage back a step further.

The Lamb in the Midst of the Throne (5:6-10)

Verse 6. *And I beheld, and, lo, in the midst of the throne and of the four beasts, and in the midst of the elders, stood a Lamb as it had been slain, having seven horns and seven eyes, which are the seven Spirits of God sent forth into all the earth.*

And I beheld. A separate vision here in what appears to be a connected account of the order of events denotes the unique and distinct importance of the further proceedings. These are of such vital significance as to call for careful and separate consideration. The elder had just informed John that the *Lion of the tribe of Juda* overcame to open the book. But when John looks and sees not *the Lion* but a *Lamb,* the inference is that whereas as Lion He is able, as Lamb He is *worthy* to open the book on the ground of the sacrificial character of His death, for He "loved the church and gave himself for it" (Ephesians 5:25).

Stood a Lamb. Observe that the Lamb is "standing" in the midst of the throne. Nowhere in all the succeeding chapters do we read of the Lamb being either at the right hand of God or seated on the throne of God. However, in the last chapter mention is made of the throne of God and of the Lamb. Verses 1, 3.

In the midst of the elders. In 1:13 and 2:1 He is in the midst of the candlesticks, i.e., the churches. Here, after the church is glorified and represented by the elders, we see Him in the midst of the glorified church. Jesus promised to be "in the midst" wherever a group of His disciples are gathered together. Matthew 18:20. It will be a blessed reality even after the church is in glory.

As it had been slain. Christ as Lamb bears the insignia or marks of death (cf. Luke 24:40; John 20:20, 27), even in His glorified state, and at His appearing in glory (Zechariah 12:10); hence He is described "as having been slain" (Greek).

Seven horns and seven eyes. Horns are symbolic of strength and *eyes* of intelligence. These are characteristics of the seven spirits "sent forth into all the earth."

Seven Spirits. There seems to be another direct allusion to Hebrews 1:14. It is noteworthy that this is the last mention of seven spirits. When the angelic ministry begins in chapter 8, mention is made of *the* seven angels which stood before God. The definite article appears to refer back to the seven spirits previously mentioned and thus identifies the seven angels with the seven spirits.

Verse 7. *And he came and took the book out of the right hand of him that sat upon the throne.*

And he came. This expression bears further and decisive testimony that Jesus was no longer at the right hand of the Father, or on His throne. The significance of the procedure is both incomprehensible and indescribable. No movement of equal majesty has ever been staged in all the annals of time. The great God sits on His throne holding in His hand a mysterious book sealed with seven seals. All creation stands aghast in solemn awe when Jesus as a Lamb steps forward to take the book out of the Throne Sitter's hand. Immediately the redeemed and glorified respond with acclamations of praise and worship. These are followed by millions of angels and eventually every creature follows with ascriptions of *blessing, and honour, and glory, and power, . . . [to] him that sitteth upon the throne, and unto the Lamb for ever and ever.*

And took the book. Of course the word *take* used does not carry with it the idea of snatching away or taking by force. On the contrary, it denotes rather to receive or obtain as a possession from another. It is frequently used as a correlative of give; for example, "Ask, and it shall be given you . . . for every one that asketh receiveth" (Matthew 7:7, 8). "Freely ye have received, freely give" (Matthew 10:8). "It is more blessed to give than to receive" (Acts 20:35). Compare the same words used in the phrase, "having received of the Father." II Peter 1:17; Revelation 2:27. Compare also Revelation 10:8-10, where similar language is employed.

It is noteworthy that the sealed book does not come into view until after church history has run its course. It would appear that the revelation God gave to Jesus Christ (1:1) has reference more particularly to the book now coming into view and that God at this time gives it to Jesus Christ in order that He (Jesus) might show it to His servants. Moreover, what the Spirit said to the churches was not contained in the sealed book mentioned in Daniel 12, for the angel says to Daniel expressly that it consists of things which will befall Daniel's people in the latter days.

Verse 8. *And when he had taken the book, the four beasts and four and twenty elders fell down before the Lamb, having every one of them harps, and golden vials full of odours, which are the prayers of saints.*

The four beasts and four and twenty elders. The four beasts (living creatures) again appear with the four and twenty elders and as in 4:10 join them in worship. However, in chapter 4 they both are seen ascribing honor and glory to the One sitting upon the throne, whereas here they unite in the worship of the Lamb. While these two groups are mentioned together nine different times, only once again (19:4) do the living creatures fall down and worship, where they also follow the example of the elders. Their falling down undoubtedly bespeaks the awful solemnity of the occasion.

What follows appears to apply to the elders, only because the grammatical implication favors this view. *Every one* is masculine and agrees with elders, not with beasts, which is neuter, elders probably being put last, not first as in 4:4, 6, for grammatical reasons. Solecisms, that is, instances where dogma overrides grammatical rules, are frequent in Revelation.

Harps are never used by spirit beings, whether living creatures (cherubim) or angels.

The odors (incense) issuing from the vials are explained as the prayers of saints, not of angels. Angels, however, may offer incense "given" to them with the prayers of saints. 8:3.

Neither living creatures nor angels are ever said to *sing*, either in the Old Testament or the New. Job 38:7 might be cited as proof for their doing so, for it reads, "When the morning stars sang together, and all the sons of God shouted for joy." This is an example of parallelism in which the latter clause explains the former—the morning stars are angels; the verb *sing* is explained by the word *shout*. What is more decisive, however, is the fact that the word translated *sing* is a synonym of the word rendered *shout*. It is rendered seven times by the phrase, *make a joyful noise*. Psalms 66:1; 81:1; 95:1, 2; 98:4, 6; 100:1. Note Psalm 65:13, "they shout for joy, they also sing." The word rendered "sing" in the passage from Job is the same as that rendered "shout for joy" in the passage from the Psalms, and here it is clearly distinguished from *shir*, the regular Hebrew verb for sing.

Only the redeemed directly address the Lord—"Thou art worthy." See the same words in 4:11 and compare 11:17, the words "thee" and "thou."

The two following verses can apply only to the elders.

Verses 9, 10. *And they sung a new song, saying, Thou art worthy to take the book, and to open the seals thereof: for thou wast slain, and hast redeemed us to God by thy blood out of every kindred, and tongue, and people, and nation; and hast made us unto our God kings and priests: and we shall reign on the earth.*

A new song. The song was new (Greek: *kainos*) in quality, not new (Greek: *neos*) in respect to time merely. The substance of the song consists of verse 10. What appears to be another new song sung by another group of the redeemed and glorified is mentioned in 14:3. For instance, this is sung by the elders, that by one hundred and forty-four thousand *before the elders;* this is sung in the midst of the throne, that before the throne; this before the Lamb, that apparently before God, the One sitting on the throne. Only the one hundred and forty-four thousand could learn that song. No such exclusiveness is predicated about this song. This is not the first mention of a new song. Mention is made six times of new songs. Psalm 33:3; 96:1; 98:1; 144:9; 149:1; Isaiah 42:10. An examination of these passages will show (according to the Septuagint) that the same word (*kainos*) is employed in each case. The songs all varied as to main theme.

It is a matter of absorbing interest to learn that Victorinus, a bishop of the early church during the latter part of the second century and author of the first commentary on the Book of Revelation, refers to "the Christian people singing a new song." In reference to the characteristics which make this song a "new song" he remarks: "It is a new thing to ascend to heaven with a body [implying the rapture of the church] . . . and to look for a kingdom of unbounded promise [showing that according to his view the glorious kingdom was yet future]."[3]

Thou art worthy. The elders proclaim the worth of the Lamb to open the book and to loose the seals thereof. Great importance attaches to this testimony because it shows that the opening of the book was effected not because of the *ability* of the Lion of the tribe of Judah, but because of the *worth* of the Lamb. It is highly significant that the Lamb does not proceed to open the book until after the glorified group in heaven proclaims His worth to do so, thus indicating that the church is in glory before the seals which introduce the judgment are loosened. It is noteworthy also that in keeping with this testimony the Lamb opens the seals one by one, and thus releases the judgments that are to come upon the earth.

For thou wast slain. . . . The worth of the Lamb to open the seals is grounded on the fact of His redemptive act. *For* has the sense of *because*. The cause is twofold: because He was slain; because He has brought redemption through His blood. The redeemed come out of every kindred and tongue and people and nation. This fourfold terminology, which includes all humanity, occurs as many as seven times in the book. 7:9; 10:11; 11:9; 13:7; 14:6; 17:15. It follows plainly that the elders are not angels because good angels need no redemption, and for wicked angels there is no redemption, seeing they are "reserved in everlasting chains under darkness unto the judgment of the great day" (Jude 6). The reference cannot be to Israel, for she is a single nation, whereas these come out of every kindred and tongue and people and nation. The reference to redemption also excludes the living creatures and further proves that the song is sung by the elders only. This is additional proof that the elders represent the church, for her membership consists of disciples of "all nations" (Matthew 28:19; Acts 10:35; 15:14). It is evident, too, that the elders are a representative group. Twenty-four would come far short of being a sufficient number to come out of every kindred and tongue and people and nation.

Hast made us unto our God kings and priests. These words as well as the former, "Thou . . . hast redeemed us . . . by thy blood," point unmistakably back to 1:5b, 6, "Unto him that loved us, and washed us from our sins in his own blood, and hath made us kings and priests unto God," where the reference is plainly to the church universal as represented by the seven churches of Asia. Observe that in 1:5b and 6 the kings and priests are on earth; in 5:10 they are in heaven. Later, in 20:6, those who have part in the first resurrection "shall be priests of God and of Christ, and shall reign with him a thousand years."[4]

The Universal Praise to the Lamb (5:11-14)

Verses 11, 12. And I beheld, and I heard the voice of many angels round about the throne and the beasts and the elders: and the number of them was ten thousand times ten thousand, and thousands of thousands; saying with a loud voice, Worthy is the Lamb that was slain to receive power, and riches, and wisdom, and strength, and honour, and glory, and blessing.

I beheld, and I heard. The seer was an auditor as well as a spectator. [In this regard John is in the line of the great prophets of the Old Testament. Take either Isaiah, Ezekiel, or Daniel. Read at random and it becomes apparent at once that Revelation came from God to men through both the eye and the ear. In his first epistle John likewise stresses the need to be convinced by way of the eye and the ear when he writes, "That . . . which we have heard, which we have seen with our eyes. . . ." Thus the validity of the vision is vindicated.—J.O.Y.]

The voice of many angels. It might be questioned as to whether the adoration by the angels was occasioned by the introduction of the sealed book or by the song and testimony of the elders or by both. It appears, however, that their response was due chiefly to the testimony of the elders. Angels desire to look into the things that accompany salvation following the preaching of the Gospel. I Peter 1:10-12. By the church is made known unto the principalities and powers in the heavenly places the manifold wisdom of God. Ephesians 3:10. The fact that the testimony came through the ministry of song undoubtedly had a tremendous effect upon the angels, because as far as the Biblical record goes this is the first song ever sung in heaven. Angels never are said to sing. Many people would testify to the beauty and power of song among the redeemed in the church today and especially of the great oratorios like Handel's *The Messiah* sung by trained voices. But these must be increased beyond a hundredfold when the redeemed and glorified out of every kindred and tongue and people and nation join in their praises to the Lamb that was slain. It is also noteworthy that the elders take the initiative in the adoration of the Lamb and thus set the pace for the innumerable throng which follows.

Round about the throne. The fact that the angels are round about the elders should settle the question forever that the elders themselves are *not* angels. Similarly in 7:11 the angels are said to stand round about the elders. Moreover, the latter passage says *all* the angels stood round about the elders. Consequently, if language means anything, elders could not be angels, for they constitute a separate and distinct group.

The number of them. The angels are declared to be an innumerable host, for the Greek term employed denotes an innumerable multitude. Ten thousand (*murias*) is the greatest number expressed by the Greek vocabulary and in itself may denote an unlimited number, but here we have a double plural—ten thousands of ten thousands (lit., *myriads of myriads*). There may be an allusion to Daniel 7:10. However, the former passage manifestly pertains to the last judgment, which is not the case here. Again, in the former case ten thousand is used as an adjective, thus showing that the present number (if possible) exceeds the former. Thousands of thousands is likewise plural. All that can be meant by this adjunct is to impress the reader with the vast magnitude of the numberless host.

Saying with a loud voice, Worthy is the Lamb. Observe that they *say*, not *sing* as did the twenty-four elders. The angels tell about the worth of the Lamb, but they do not directly address the Lamb as do the elders. 4:11; 5:9. The word *receive* is the same as *take* above. Verses 7, 9. This sense of the word is certainly implied in the former passages. The adoration is sevenfold. The words are anarthrous (without the article), thus showing the close relationship of the terms employed. Compare with this the polysyndetic (many and's) acclamation in 7:12. Since the present passage is plainly cumulative and climactic in structure and content, it is hoped that it may carry its own distinct message to the reader.

Verse 13. And every creature which is in heaven, and on the earth, and under the earth, and such as are in the sea, and all that are in them, heard I saying, Blessing, and honour, and glory, and power, be unto him that sitteth upon the throne, and unto the Lamb for ever and ever.

And every creature. The passage is plainly proleptic, for it is evident that the adoration of every creature does not take place at this juncture of God's future program. Here is another illustration of *der Drang nach dem Ende* (the urge or drive toward the end) so common in prophetic literature. Attention already has been called to this forward look in the closing portion of each of the messages to the seven churches, e.g., the tree of life in the message to Ephesus; immunity from the second death to Smyrna; the new name written to Pergamos; the morning star to Thyatira; the white raiment to Sardis; the new Jerusalem to Philadelphia; sitting with Jesus on His throne to Laodicea. In each there is a reference to the end time. In subsequent studies three successive prophetic cycles will be pointed out, each of which carries the seer forward to the close of the present world order.

In heaven, and on the earth . . . in the sea, and all that are in them. That the atoning merits of Christ's death will be as universal as the sin which affected the universe is plainly indicated in Scripture, e.g., Paul in his letter to the Romans declares: "For the earnest expectation of the creature [creation] waiteth for the manifestation of the sons of God. For the creature [creation] was made subject to vanity, not willingly [i.e., not by its own volition], but by reason of him who hath subjected the same in hope, because the creature [creation] itself also shall be delivered from the bondage of corruption into the glorious liberty of the children of God" (Romans 8:19-21). (Compare Colossians 1:20 and Hebrews 2:7, 8. For the time of fulfillment, see I Corinthians 15:24, 25.) That the death of Christ is the ground or basis of the restoration of all things is also implied in Philippians 2:8-11. Note that "every knee should bow" because of His death on the cross. (With this compare Romans 14:11.) The universal adoration expressed in Revelation 5:13, 14 presupposes the fulfillment of the passages cited.

Here too is a theodicy *par excellence,* by which is meant a vindication of God's justice in the creation of man even though He foreknew that a being thus created would fall into sin. By the church is made known unto the principalities and powers in the heavenly places the manifold wisdom of God. Heaven gains immeasurably much through the creation of man including his subsequent redemption according to God's eternal purpose which He purposed before the foundation of the world. Were it not for this, heaven would be minus the adoration of the innumerable multitude of angels and of the ascription of praise ascending from *every creature which is in heaven, and on the earth, and under the earth, and such as are in the sea, and all that are in them, . . . saying, Blessing, and honour, and glory, and power, be unto him that sitteth upon the throne, and unto the Lamb for ever and ever.*

It will be observed that the adoration by the many angels varies from that of every creature. The former is sevenfold, denoting fullness of perfection. The latter is fourfold—four being the earth number. The former begins with power and ends with blessing; the latter reverses the order, for it begins with blessing and ends with power (a synonym of the former word). Honor and glory are conjoined also in 4:9, 11; 19:1; 21:24, 26 (but in the reverse order)—a total of seven times in the book. In the former instance all the words except the first are anarthrous; here each has an article, thus suggesting that all creaturehood ascribes the same quality or degree of the attributes mentioned as do the angels. According to the Greek, the structure of the latter is identical with that of the former in that the object of adoration is emphatic by position, i.e., "Unto the one sitting upon the throne, and unto the Lamb, be the blessing, and the honour, and the glory, and the power." It is the praise of many angels, yea of all, the salvation of all (verse 12), and the testimony of the universal creation (verse 13), bringing to our Lord thanksgiving for the deliverance of men (verses 9, 10) from the destruction of death [which, as we shall see, begins in the succeeding chapter as the tribulation opens with its plagues of destruction. See especially verses 7, 8].

Verse 14. *And the four beasts said, Amen. And the four and twenty elders fell down and worshipped him that liveth for ever and ever.*

For the fourth time *the beasts* (living creatures) and the elders are mentioned conjointly in these two chapters and always in the same order. Remember, the living creatures, as is the case with angels, never are spoken of as sitting on thrones, while the elders are seen sitting (on thrones) round about the throne (4:4), or, as in 11:16, before the throne, save when they fall upon their faces and worship God. The four living creatures respond with an "Amen" to the doxology of the angelic host and to that of the cosmic congregation. As their manner is on important occasions, and apparently with a higher conception of their significance, the four and twenty elders fall down and worship God. The expression "liveth for ever and ever" occurs seven times in the book—once of Christ (1:18—Greek) and six times of God (4:9, 10; 5:14; 10:6; 11:15; 15:7).

2. THE TRIBULATION (6:1—16:21)

It was with considerable regret that the editor found it necessary to write the comments on Revelation 6. For some unknown reason Smith's notes on these verses were mislaid. In his penciled first draft he inserted a line: "I fail to find my comments on chapter 6." In an effort to find these notes the editor spent considerable time going through a collection of notes, clippings, letters, etc., in the J. B. Smith collection in the Eastern Mennonite College Library, which had not yet been classified. But even these yielded no notes on Revelation 6. It therefore became imperative that the editor, for the sake of completeness, write the comments on this section of the book. The task was considerably lessened by the fact that he had access to the books to which Dr. Smith most often referred. His penciled notes in the margins of these books were of inestimable value. Cross references were continually cited, which facilitated the study to a large degree. It is supremely hoped that the notes on this chapter will not be out of harmony with the remainder of the commentary, or with those which the author himself had written.—J. O. Y.

The Seal Judgments (6:1—8:1)

According to the structural outline of the book, chapter 6 initiates the beginning of the tribulation period. This period ostensibly still lies in the future, as related to the church age. A series of visions portray the outpourings of the wrath of God upon unrepentant mankind. After man fails both under the Mosaic law of the Old Testament and the "grace and truth" of the New Testament, God must resort to justice that He might vindicate His holiness. This is of central importance if one is to be able to understand the measure of divine wrath. Nowhere else in Scripture does one meet up with such an ascending intensification of judgment. The Flood of Genesis 6—9 is of small proportions compared to Revelation 6—18. The plagues of Egypt, surely designed by and carried through under God, though in many respects parallel with the last judgments of God, were nonetheless of a lesser extent. In each case where God acts in justice one needs to see the ultimate purpose, viz., a vindication of His holiness. Man's rebellious heart cannot be left to continue in its devising of evil. Otherwise God Himself would admit defeat and would cease to be the Almighty.

The Lamb Opens the Seals (6:1)

Verse 1. *And I saw when the Lamb opened one of the seals, and I heard, as it were the noise of thunder, one of the four beasts saying, Come and see.*

And I saw . . . the Lamb. Bear in mind the vision formula, *I saw.* Reference to 5:5 ff. is no doubt intended by *the Lamb.* It was there the seer was first aware of One worthy to take the book and to open the seals. The Lamb changes His attitude from a docile, yielding spirit to one of activated justice. But so He is pictured by the Old Testament prophets, Isaiah in particular: ". . . and the government shall be upon his shoulder . . . to establish it with judgment and with justice . . ." (Isaiah 9:6, 7).

120

And I heard. Again the revelation is to come by the ear gate as well as the eye gate. The announcement is made by one of the four living creatures. From the subsequent verses of the chapter, one easily concludes that each of the living creatures announces one of the first four seals.

Come and see. This invitation is variously interpreted. Some, notably Swete[5] and Alford,[6] have taken this to be addressed to Christ. To arrive at such an interpretation, the presence of *and see* must be resolved. It is true that here is a textual problem with respect to *and see.* Tregelles omits it. Greisbach has it in the text. Souter[7] lists the following MSS. as having some form of the verb "to see"—Adeph, 046, the Old Latin, the Latin Vulgate, several versions of the Syriac, and the Ethiopic. While these may not be the most outstanding MSS., the intrinsic evidence would seem to support *and see,* for verse 2 begins with *and* (Greek: *kai*), which should be taken as continuative, its most logical usage. If *and see* is not to be read, the *kai* should be taken in an adversative sense, *but.* A contrast must be understood by verse 2, if that be the case. It would seem clear therefore that the *and see* belongs in the text, if not in fact, then in sense.

The First Seal (6:2)

Verse 2. *And I saw, and behold a white horse: and he that sat on him had a bow; and a crown was given unto him: and he went forth conquering, and to conquer.*

A white horse. Only in the Book of Zechariah (1:8; 6:6), besides Revelation, does one read of white horses. However, in Revelation 19:11 mention is made again of a white horse rider. Some have taken these two (6:2 and 19:11) to be identical. That they are not seems abundantly clear by the differences between the two passages. The rider in chapter 6 is unnamed; in chapter 19 He is called "Faithful and True . . . The Word of God . . . King of kings, and Lord of lords." In chapter 6 the rider goes *forth conquering, and to conquer;* in chapter 19 the rider has "a sharp sword, that with it he should smite the nations: and . . . rule them with a rod of iron: and he treadeth the winepress of the fierceness and wrath of Almighty God" (verse 15). The rider in chapter 6 seems to be a lone rider; the one in chapter 19 is followed by the armies of heaven also on white horses. Swete makes a clear statement on the matter: ". . . the two riders have nothing in common beyond the white horse. . . . A vision of the victorious Christ would be inappropriate at the opening of a series which symbolizes bloodshed, famine, and pestilence."[8]

Conquering, and to conquer. Beyond doubt the words are meant to convey the idea of complete mastery, perhaps even a dictatorship. This refers either to the Antichrist himself, or to some conditions leading up to his introduction.

The Second Seal (6:3, 4)

Verses 3, 4. *And when he had opened the second seal, I heard the second beast say, Come and see. And there went out another horse that was red: and power was given to him that sat thereon to take peace from the earth, and that they should kill one another: and there was given unto him a great sword.*

The second seal . . . the second beast. The seer is careful to indicate the proper sequence. Any interpreter ought to give careful attention to this fact.

Another horse that was red. While this horse is similar, as indicated by *another* (Greek: *allos*), he is also different. The color is red, which by what follows is suggestive of war and bloodshed. The rider is given power to take peace from the earth. Anyone who has lived during the twentieth century knows what frustration and bloodshed can come when peace has been taken away even for a brief period of time.

They should kill one another. Men of moral concerns have noted the technological advance which has been made in the face of the moral lag. Could it be possible that man's scientific progress turned loose might well-nigh annihilate the race? From the Scripture one would gather that withal God Himself will yet be the final Judge, and will execute justice of a divine character.

The Third Seal (6:5, 6)

Verses 5, 6. *And when he had opened the third seal, I heard the third beast say, Come and see. And I beheld, and lo a black horse; and he that sat on him had a pair of balances in his hand. And I heard a voice in the midst of the four beasts say, A measure of wheat for a penny, and three measures of barley for a penny! and see thou hurt not the oil and the wine.*

The third seal. Note again the sequence. To be sure, the order cannot be denied as being a most natural order.

A black horse . . . a pair of balances. The color deepens from one to three, no doubt suggesting increased awfulness. The combination, *black horse* and *a pair of balances,* surely would indicate a scarcity or famine. Any student of history remembers well that famine follows war. Men are taken from the pursuits of peace to practice war, and the production of life's necessities lags far behind the needs.

I heard a voice in the midst of the four beasts. The location of the voice would show that it is not the voice of the rider. Neither is it the voice of one of the living creatures. There is One in the midst of the elders, even the Lamb. Revelation 5:6. Consequently the Lamb, the Opener of the seals, makes the solemn announcement of the scarcity of staple foods.

A measure of wheat for a penny. A measure (Greek: *choinix*), "less than our [English] 'quart' . . . as much as would support a man of moderate appetite for a day . . .,"[9] would indicate how carefully the cereal grains are to be measured out. A *penny* (Greek: *denarion*) constituted a day's wages. Cf. Matthew 20:10. Thus in the time when the rider of the black horse goes forth, a workingman's daily wages will buy wheat enough for himself for a day. If he were to purchase barley, he might have enough food for himself and his family! One may well wonder whether the other needs of life will be obtainable at all!

Hurt not the oil and the wine. Does this not show how perverted the scale of values can become? Needs are scarce; luxuries plentiful. It may be that at last men will see that wine does not belong!

According to Charles,[10] history saw something of this kind of situation during Domitian's time. Men had given themselves to the cultivation of vineyards and the making of wine until the emperor ordered half the vineyards in Italy to be cut down and no new ones to be planted so that the cereal grains might be grown. However, the populace prevailed upon their ruler to reverse himself and to impose punishment upon those who had neglected their vineyards. So debauched can man become!

The Fourth Seal (6:7, 8)

Verses 7, 8. *And when he had opened the fourth seal, I heard the voice of the fourth beast say, Come and see. And I looked, and behold a pale horse: and his name that sat on him was Death, and Hell followed with him. And power was given unto them over the fourth part of the earth, to kill with sword, and with hunger, and with death, and with the beasts of the earth.*

The fourth seal . . . the fourth beast. The living creatures do not announce the remaining three seals. Their work in connection with the outpouring of divine wrath seems to be over. In subsequent judgments angels play an important role.

A pale horse. The word *pale* (Greek: *chloros*) should be understood as yellowish-green. (See Thayer.) It is used on occasion in the Scripture in the sense of green. Mark 6:39; Revelation 8:7. One can well imagine a sickly, yellowish-green horse, the last of the awful horsemen. Swete suggests, "The 'pale' is the symbol of terror. . . ."[11]

His name . . . Death. This is the only one of the four that is named. Charles insists that *Death* should be understood as *Pestilence.*[12] However, there seems to be no textual evidence for his arguments. The rider is the personification of death. *Hades,* his inseparable companion, follows him. The seer does not say how *Hades* follows, whether on the same horse, or another, or on foot. One should note the clear inference that *Death* never goes alone, i.e., Death does not end all. Hades companions with death!

Over the fourth part of the earth. This is the first mention in the Book of Revelation of a percentage of earth's inhabitants being killed by divine judgments, though it is not the last. Four means of extermination are to be employed: The sword (war), hunger (famine), death (perhaps by disease), and beasts of the earth. Thus by man's own plotting in war, by the inevitable famine, by the spread of disease through war and famine, and by the ravages of wild beasts God seeks to awaken the consciences of sinful men.

The Fifth Seal (6:9-11)

Verses 9-11. *And when he had opened the fifth seal, I saw under the altar the souls of them that were slain for the word of God, and for the testimony which they held: and they cried with a loud voice, saying, How long, O Lord, holy and true, dost thou not judge and avenge our blood on them that dwell on the earth? And white robes were given unto every one of them; and it was said unto them, that they should rest yet for a little season, until their fellowservants also and their brethren, that should be killed as they were, should be fulfilled.*

The fifth seal. I saw. There is no announcement accompanying the opening of this seal. In silent contemplation John gazes upon the solemn evidence that the

faithful follow their Lord and may even need to be offered for the *word of God,
and for the testimony which they held*. One may well sense with what awe and
holy reverence the seer witnesses this proof of the Master's own words, "If they
have persecuted me, they will also persecute you . . ." (John 15:20).

The altar. Six times in subsequent passages the altar is a part of the scene,
8:3, 5; 9:13; 11:1; 14:18; 16:7. It is not clear whether this is the prototype of the
brazen altar or the golden altar of the tabernacle and temple worship ritual. In
two of the other places (8:3b and 9:13) the noun *altar* is qualified by the adjective
golden. In those cases it would more definitely point to the altar of incense. However, in 6:9 the inference seems to be that this is the altar of sacrifice, for here are
the souls of those who had been slain. Some association may be seen between this
and Paul's entreaty in Romans 12:1, ". . . present your bodies a living sacrifice."

Them that were slain. The word *slain* (Greek: *esphagmenon*) is a perfect
passive participle, which as for the tense stresses the state of these martyrs. In
meaning, it would indicate death by violence. At times it may mean "to butcher."[13]
It is used to describe the Lamb in 5:6. This is further evidence that these followed
the Lamb to the bitter end. On the other hand, the word would indicate that the
executioner had no intent of offering a sacrifice, but rather to rid the world of
undesirables. The common word in the New Testament for sacrificing is the Greek,
prosphero. However, God does not always look at the experiences of men as man
does, so that these who were brutally slain became an offering to God. Charles
points out[14] that martyrs were thought of as sacrifices to God by Judaism, as well
as by Christianity. II Timothy 4:6; Philippians 2:17.

For the word of God, and for the testimony which they held. The turn of interpretation may rest upon the meaning of the word *held*. It is true that the Greek
word *echo* means to have, as to possess, e.g., ". . . have everlasting life" (John
3:16). Yet in the context of the Revelation passage it would seem to have a different meaning. This meaning is not contrary to its usage as a transitive verb. One
would then understand the meaning—to have the word and the testimony as a
badge of allegiance to Christ, i.e., as being a Christian. The imperfect tense could
easily amplify this idea. Literally translated then it would read, *which they were
having*, as an ongoing experience and expression.

The English *for* is the translation of the Greek preposition *dia*, which is used
in a causal sense. It might well be translated *because of*. One would hardly expect
that these were slain simply for possessing a copy of the Bible, though from syntax
this may not be impossible. Rather, it is clear that the reason, or ground, for their
martyrdom was their unyielding loyalty to Jesus Christ, the Lamb, and thus they
suffered a fate like His. Stuart remarks, "That the martyrs were once merely in possession of the word, etc., would not have occasioned their death; it was their *stead-
fast adherence* to it which caused them to be sacrificed on the altar of religion."[15]
(Italics his.)

They cried with a loud voice. The aorist tense of *cried* would show both the
urgency and the finality of their prayer. This is one of the two times in Revelation
that any human beings cry with a *loud voice*. (See 7:9, 10.)

How long? From the blood of righteous Abel on to the end of time men unjustly die for the word of God which they believe. Rightly these call out for justice, for they, even as the Lord, committed themselves "to him that judgeth righteously" (I Peter 2:23).

Holy and true. No doubt these are two of the most outstanding of divine attributes. God's holiness cannot tolerate unholiness, nor His truth, injustice. Basic to equity is a perception of holiness and truth. Both *holy and true* are used in referring to Christ in Revelation 3:7, where He presents Himself to the Philadelphian church. The saints under the altar therefore appeal to the Lord (Greek: *Despotes*) by His holiness and truth to recompense their injustices. If He should refuse, He would be neither holy nor true! It is, consequently, an appeal on the basis of the divine character.

White robes. The word *robes* (Greek: *stole*) is described as "a loose outer garment for men which extended to the feet."[16] In every case *white* refers to purity. One may well associate these *white robes* with the definition of the clean white linen of Revelation 19:8, where it is said to be "the righteousness of saints." It would be clear then that these martyrs were slain "for righteousness' sake" (Matthew 5:10).

It was said unto them. While the speaker is not identified by the nature of the prayer in verse 10, one may easily conclude that the Lord Himself replies.

Rest . . . a little season. The word *season* may not best translate the Greek word *chronos.* Present-day usage would define *season* as an opportune time. The Greek term used is time in a more general sense. The qualification would place a limit on it. In common speech one might say, "Wait a little while." *Rest* does not necessarily imply inactivity.

Until their fellowservants also and their brethren. Some problem may arise out of the double use of the Greek conjunction *kai*—the first translated by *also,* the second by *and.* In certain contexts this usage may be translated by *and . . . even.* This would equate *fellowservants* and *brethren.* However, such a translation becomes difficult in this context. Therefore, *fellowservants* may easily refer to saints in general, while *brethren* would refer to martyrs in particular.[17]

That should be killed . . . should be fulfilled. The first clause in reality carries more definiteness since it is a somewhat regular construction which would indicate an impending event in the immediate future—something about to happen. Literally it would read, *Those being about to be killed.* The second clause suggests a determined number. It needs to be borne in mind, however, that the subjunctive mood in Greek is a mood of potentiality. In fact, the aorist active subjunctive by some grammarians, notably A. T. Robertson,[18] is believed to be closely related to the future active indicative. While the subjunctive is a potential mood, one does not need to feel any uncertainty with regard to the Lord's understanding of the circumstances. He surely completely foreknows who will suffer martyrdom.

The Sixth Seal (6:12-14)

Verses 12-14. *And I beheld when he had opened the sixth seal, and, lo, there was a great earthquake; and the sun became black as sackcloth of hair, and the moon became as blood; and the stars of heaven fell unto the earth, even as a fig tree casteth her untimely figs, when she is shaken of a mighty wind. And the heaven departed as a scroll when it is rolled together; and every mountain and island were moved out of their places.*

The sixth seal. The first six seals follow in what appears to be a short time and in rapid sequence. Whether there is a lapse of time between five and six is not indicated. Neither is it indicated that the sixth seal is the answer to the prayer of the saints under the altar, although this may easily be the case.

A great earthquake. Without doubt this describes an earthquake of greater proportions than any known heretofore. Charles aptly states, "The earthquake here is not to be explained by that in Laodicea in 61, or at Pompeii in 63. It is rather a single great earthquake, which is a precursor of the end of the world."[19]

The descriptions that follow, apocalyptic scholars note, are typical of eschatological scenes. Cf. Amos 8:8; 9:5; Ezekiel 38:19, 20; Joel 2:10, 30, 31; Isaiah 34:4; Matthew 24:29; Mark 13:24, 25; Luke 21:25. In ancient times all such physical disturbances were viewed with alarm as evidences of divine wrath and judgment. At any rate, man learns his utter helplessness in the face of such demonstrations in the universe. That these descriptions surpass all known in history is self-evident. That those living at the time will be terrorized into flight is also self-evident with only brief reflection. And that this is not the final end is abundantly clear by what follows. There will still be caves, mountains, rocks, even though there has been a terrible shaking! The Apostle Peter predicts that the end will take place by a renovation of fire, in which "the heavens shall pass away with a great noise" (II Peter 3:10). John sees the heavens roll up as a scroll, referring to a papyrus scroll so common in his day.

It needs to be noted that each of the heavenly descriptions is in the form of a simile: the sun *as* sackcloth, the moon *as* blood, stars fall *as* winter figs, the heaven rolled *as* a scroll, but every mountain and island was moved! With the mountains and islands there is no figure of speech. One does not need to wonder how such manifestations can be possible, if he remembers that the God of the universe is THE ALMIGHTY. When He begins to deal in divine wrath and judgment, He will employ that which befits His character.

Verses 15-17. *And the kings of the earth, and the great men, and the rich men, and the chief captains, and the mighty men, and every bondman, and every free man, hid themselves in the dens and in the rocks of the mountains; and said to the mountains and rocks, Fall on us, and hide us from the face of him that sitteth on the throne, and from the wrath of the Lamb: for the great day of his wrath is come; and who shall be able to stand?*

Kings . . . great men . . . rich men . . . chief captains . . . mighty men . . . every bondman . . . free man. It is remarkable, indeed, how quickly all strata of society are erased! Let catastrophe strike and all are on the same level. Before the judgment of a righteous God none can claim superiority. All seek the only human concept of safety, the depth of the earth.

Hide us from the face of him that sitteth on the throne, and from the wrath of the Lamb. Those who have ignored or even scoffed at the grace of God shall learn too late that the God who shakes the earth with such a shaking cannot be hidden from in dens and caves! Once again it should be noted that only *One* sits on the throne. The Lamb is in the midst of the elders and is in the process of opening the sealed book. *The wrath of the Lamb* seems to be somewhat of an enigmatic statement. He is now not the Lamb of sacrifice but the Executor of justice upon those who have spurned His overtures of grace. Some of the commentators have seen this enigma and have answered it by alleging that the clause, *and from the wrath of the Lamb*, is an interpolation. Among them are Vischer, Spitta, Weyland, Voelter, and Weiss. However, there seems to be no MSS. evidence for the consideration of a variant reading. The clause is entirely in keeping with the role of the Lamb in the scenes of chapter 6.

The great day of his wrath is come. Beyond question the intent is that which the Old Testament prophets knew to be the day of the Lord. That this is a period of the outpouring of divine judgment is amply proved in the Appendices, *The Lord's Day*, page 319 (which see). Bible believers have always insisted upon the fact that God is both a God of justice and a God of love. While the current age of grace is extended, men incline to forget or minimize God's justice. Yet both justice and love are clearly taught in Holy Writ. Even John 3:16 would indicate this dual aspect of God's dealings with men. If one does not believe, he perishes. Consequently it is not to be thought inconsistent with the character of the Lamb to be an Executor of divine wrath. He Himself told the Pharisees that the Father had committed all judgment to the Son. John 5:22. One cannot conceive of judgment without justice, or of justice without retribution.

The Episode of Sealing 144,000 of the Tribes of Israel (7:1-8)

Before proceeding with the consideration of chapter 7 it is appropriate to call to mind that the tribulation period (chapters 6–18) contains three great series of judgments, namely, the seven seals, the seven trumpets, and the seven vials. It has been observed that chapter 6 gives a description of six seal judgments and that the last of these brings events up to the very threshold of the day of wrath. One should now naturally expect the immediate mention of the seventh seal. Such, however, is not the case; instead, chapter 7 contains two incidents: the sealing of 144,000 of the tribes of Israel; a great multitude of all nations and kindreds and people and tongues. Following these, occurs the opening of the seventh seal.

One finds a similar arrangement in the order of procedure in the two remaining series of judgments. Following the sixth in each series, mention is made of one or more incidents, before the series is concluded. The more common, and probably more suitable, name for these interludes is episode.

As here employed, an episode may be defined as an incident, story, or act inserted within a series of judgments for the purpose of adding details or supplementing matters already related, or in order to introduce or prepare the way for things to come. Thus an episode may be either retrospective (i.e., point back to things previously mentioned) or prospective (i.e., allude to things about to be related).

If it should seem improbable to the reader that an invisible mark will be set upon the 144,000, let him read Ezekiel 9:4 where it is said that the Lord commanded a man with an inkhorn to "set a mark upon the foreheads of the men that sigh and that cry for all the abominations that be done in the midst thereof [Jerusalem]."

This episode is introduced by two visions.

Verse 1. *And after these things I saw four angels standing on the four corners of the earth, holding the four winds of the earth, that the wind should not blow on the earth, nor on the sea, nor on any tree.*

After these things. When the phrase *after these things* accompanies *I saw*, it does not necessarily imply sequence in time, but may denote merely sequence in the order of vision. Such indeed is the case, for the things about to be related will have their fulfillment before the opening of the sixth seal.

Four angels . . . four corners . . . four winds. The prominence of the number four is apparent—four angels, four corners, four winds. Four is the earth number and denotes universality. Note also the threefold repetition of "earth." Instead of four corners men today say four points of the compass. The Biblical writers in using this mode of expression thought no more of the earth as having four corners than men think of a compass as having somewhere four points.

There are angels of winds just as there are angels of churches, of fire, of water, and of wrath. Winds are symbolic of judgment. One reads early in the Scriptures concerning their blasting effect on vegetation. Genesis 41:6, 23, 27. There is a remarkable passage in the Book of Ecclesiasticus in reference to the period of time now under consideration which, while it is not inspired, must nevertheless have been taken from inspired sources, for it is a most graphic description of the Biblical forecasts of this period, in an unusually terse and compact form. The passage reads: "There be winds that are created for vengeance, and in their fury lay on their scourges heavily; in the time of consummation they pour out their strength, and shall appease the wrath of him that made them. Fire, and hail, and famine, and death, all these are created for vengeance; teeth of wild beasts, and scorpions and adders, and a sword punishing the ungodly unto destruction."[20] While this sentence was written centuries before the Book of Revelation, it would be difficult to write a more exact epitome of judgments in progress subsequent to the sounding of the first trumpet.

Verses 2, 3. *And I saw another angel ascending from the east, having the seal of the living God: and he cried with a loud voice to the four angels, to whom it was given to hurt the earth and the sea, saying, Hurt not the earth, neither the sea, nor the trees, till we have sealed the servants of our God in their foreheads.*

Another angel ascending from the east (lit., *from the rising of the sun*). While the east winds bring most devastating judgments (Isaiah 27:8; Ezekiel 17:10; 19:12; Hosea 13:15; Jonah 4:8), the east is also the way of blessing. The Wise Men from the east came to bless the Christ child; the glory of the Lord is to come "from the way of the east"; the morning star rises in the east, whence also the Sun of righteousness will come with healing in His wings; moreover, we love to sing of the meeting at the eastern gate. The four angels are entrusted with the bringing of judgment, the one with the bestowment of blessing.

Hurt not the earth, neither the sea, nor the trees, till we have sealed the servants of our God in their foreheads. The angel from the east is addressing the four till *we*, not I, have sealed the servants of God. So before they let loose the winds of judgment, the angel from the east [cries] *with a loud voice* (thus showing the urgency of the occasion). The implication seems to be that they are to join him in the bestowal of blessing, before they release the winds of judgment.

The word *till* has its ordinary force here. It is implied that after the sealing is done, the judgments are next in order in the divine program and accordingly these come in the next chapter. Those sealed are *the servants of our God.* These do not constitute the church, for they are upon earth while the church is already in glory at this time (chapters 4 and 5) and as such they are never called servants. They may be the "fellowservants" of the previous chapter (6:11), for later the same group is "before the throne of God" (14:3, 5).

They are sealed with *the seal of the living God.* The Scriptures throughout emphasize the great truth that our God is a *living God.* The term occurs 15 times in the Old Testament and at least as many times in the New. It stands opposed to the worship of idols or false gods. It occurs immediately after the giving of the Ten Commandments (Deuteronomy 5:26) with the emphasis on the worship of the only true God. Its last occurrence in the Old Testament has a direct application to this time, for it occurs in connection with the reconciliation of Israel. Hosea 1:10. Apparently these 144,000 will meet the alternative, worship the image of the beast or die. Power will be given to the beast to overcome the saints. They will choose to die, for it is written, "They loved not their lives unto the death."

The reference to the living God seems to imply also that while they will suffer martyrdom they will live beyond death. A parallel passage is found in Revelation 2, where Jesus presents Himself as "alive" while He exhorts the church, "Be thou faithful unto death, and I will give thee a crown of life" (verse 10).

One purpose of the sealing is ostensibly that the servants of God may be exempt from the torment which is to come upon all men not having the seal of God in their foreheads (9:4), but sealing also implies possession and security and service. They belong to God—that is possession; they have the seal of God—that is security; they are servants—that is loyalty and service.

Before giving the list of the sealed, contemplate briefly the significance of the prominence given to Israel. It implies that the church period is over and that the last week of seven years is now running its course. The church age and the times of Israel cannot overlap. Israel was cut off before the church had her origin on the day of Pentecost when the Gentiles were "graffed," and so at the end "the fulness of the Gentiles" will have come in before Israel is "graffed in" again. Not all of Israel yet, for later these are called the "firstfruits unto God" (14:4). It is not until they will look upon Him whom they have pierced, that all Israel [nationally], that is, "those that are left," will be saved.

Verses 4-8. *And I heard the number of them which were sealed: and there were sealed an hundred and forty and four thousand of all the tribes of the children of Israel.*

Of the tribe of Juda were sealed twelve thousand.

Of the tribe of Reuben were sealed twelve thousand.
Of the tribe of Gad were sealed twelve thousand.
Of the tribe of Aser were sealed twelve thousand.
Of the tribe of Nepthalim were sealed twelve thousand.
Of the tribe of Manasses were sealed twelve thousand.
Of the tribe of Simeon were sealed twelve thousand.
Of the tribe of Levi were sealed twelve thousand.
Of the tribe of Issachar were sealed twelve thousand.
Of the tribe of Zabulon were sealed twelve thousand.
Of the tribe of Joseph were sealed twelve thousand.
Of the tribe of Benjamin were sealed twelve thousand.

The versification apparently should have been made, not as it is by triplet, but by pairs of names, i.e.—

Leah's sons	{ Judah { Reuben
Zilpah's sons (Leah's maid)	{ Gad { Asher
Bilhah's sons (Rachel's maid)	{ Naphtali { Manasseh, substitute for Dan
Leah's sons	{ Simeon { Levi
Leah's sons	{ Issachar { Zebulun
Rachel's sons	{ Joseph { Benjamin

There are no fewer than 29 lists of the tribes of Israel throughout the Scriptures, thus showing the prominence accorded them in the sacred page. The first list is found recorded in Genesis 29. However, this does not yet include Benjamin and so the first full list of names occurs in Genesis 35. The order of the names varies in each case except in Numbers 2, 7, and 10. This lack of uniformity and order can only be accounted for on the ground that it is to bear witness that Israel has been "out of tune with the Infinite," for the only place in which there is uniformity in the order of mention is when necessity required it, occurring only in the description of the order of encampment around Sinai.

In the present list the names of Dan and Ephraim are omitted. This omission apparently is due to the fact that these two tribes were notorious for their fickleness and proclivity to idol worship. In His Palestinian covenant the Lord solemnly warned His people that if any "man, or woman, or family, or tribe" turn from the Lord to serve the idols of the nations, He would "blot out his name from under heaven and . . . separate him unto evil out of all the tribes of Israel." (See Deuteronomy 29:18-21.)

The children of Dan were the first of all the tribes of Israel to fall into idolatry.

In less than half a century after this solemn warning they set up a graven image. Judges 18:30. It was in Dan and at Bethel (at the southern boundary of Ephraim) where Jeroboam set up the two calves of gold with the proclamation: "It is too much for you to go up to Jerusalem: behold thy gods, O Israel, which brought thee up out of the land of Egypt" (I Kings 12:28). How complete this abandonment to idol worship had become is obvious from the words of a later prophet: "Ephraim is joined to idols: let him alone" (Hosea 4:17).

It should be remembered in this connection that in the allotment of the land to the tribes of Israel, Joseph received a double portion. This favor was doubtless bestowed upon him because of the great kindness he manifested toward his father and brethren in the land of Egypt. [Or because he was the first-born of Rachel.— J. O. Y.] His two sons, Ephraim and Manasseh, each received an equal portion of territory with the rest of the tribes. In the present list, while the name of Manasseh occurs, Ephraim is omitted and instead Joseph, the father's name, is given. The tribe of Ephraim is obviously represented under the name Joseph, but the name likely is omitted because of the evil report attached to it elsewhere in the Scriptures.

The tribe of Dan is entirely omitted in the list. This should not be construed to signify, however, that it has become extinct at this time, "for the gifts and calling of God are without repentance" (Romans 11:29). The covenant which God made with Abraham was confirmed to Isaac and later to Jacob. Among the provisions of the covenant was the promise, "For all the land which thou seest, to thee will I give it, and to thy seed for ever" (Genesis 13:15). Dan was of the seed of Jacob; hence it is reasonable to expect that he would have his share in the inheritance. Attention has been called to the purpose of this sealing, viz., that those here mentioned may be exempt from the torment that is to come upon those men who have not the seal of God on their foreheads. 9:4. In other words, Dan, because of his sins and defections, must be tried in the furnace of affliction (with the remaining members of all the tribes not sealed), that he might be "purified, and made white." The Scripture expressly declares, "In their affliction [tribulation] they will seek me early" (Hosea 5:15).

There are reasons, however, why one might conclude that Dan had forfeited his right to any part in the covenanted blessings. In addition to his lapse into idolatry on different occasions, one of his offspring was the first to break the third commandment, "Thou shalt not take the name of the Lord thy God in vain." He was the son of Shelomith, the daughter of Dibri, of the tribe of Dan. Of him it was said, "He blasphemed the name of the Lord and cursed." For this he was stoned. Leviticus 24:10-15.

But the darkest, most foreboding factor in the career of Dan occurs in the first Book of Chronicles. There (2:3—9:44) is a record of the genealogical tables of the tribes of Israel. Dan alone is missing. One might suspect the statement somewhere, "Write . . . this man childless." But there is not even that—he is simply ignored in the record and that apparently by divine intention.

But what are the facts as pertaining to the last word concerning Dan in the future and final program of God as revealed in the Scriptures? Revelation 7:5-8 does not contain the last list of the tribes of Israel in God's program. This list speaks of Israel during the tribulation period. This period is definitely described as "the time of Jacob's trouble" (Jeremiah 30:7). The prophet Zechariah, after giving a vivid description of the repentance of Israel during this time "when the judgments of the Lord are upon the earth," goes on to say, "And it shall come to pass, that in all the land, saith the Lord, two parts therein [of Israel] shall be cut off and die; but the third shall be left therein. And I will bring the third part through the fire, and will refine them as silver is refined, and will try them as gold is tried: they shall call on my name, and I will hear them: I will say, It is my people: and they shall say, The Lord is my God" (13:8, 9).

It remained for the prophet Ezekiel to give a detailed account of Israel's future inheritance and blessing in the last nine chapters in his book. 40—48. The last two chapters contain a detailed description of a new and enlarged apportionment of the land of Israel among the twelve tribes. The extent of the land appears to be identical with the original grant as described by the Lord to Abraham in Genesis 15:18, "Unto thy seed have I given this land, from the river of Egypt unto the great river, the river Euphrates." This promise is repeated in Deuteronomy 11:24 and Joshua 1:3, 4, only in the later accounts the boundary is given in the reverse order—from the river Euphrates unto the great sea toward the going down of the sun (Mediterranean). In the Ezekiel account (chapter 47) the eastern boundary is described as reaching unto the east sea. Verse 18. As to what is meant by the "east sea," various views have been expressed. The first part of the chapter tells of a river issuing from the sanctuary: "These waters issue out toward the east country, and go down into the desert, and go into the sea: which being brought forth into the sea, the waters shall be healed. . . . And every thing shall live whither the river cometh" (verses 8, 9). Some have thought the mention of the healing of the waters indicates that the eastern boundary is the Dead Sea. No doubt the allusion here is to the Dead Sea, but the sea here is hardly the same as the east sea in verse 18. Apparently the river flows into and through the Dead Sea (thus healing its waters) and then flows on toward the east country and goes down into the desert and goes into the sea (east sea). The distance from the sanctuary at Jerusalem to the Dead Sea would seem to be entirely too short to allow for the description of a river flowing through the east country, unto the desert, and other details as herewith described. A passage in Joel apparently throws light on the matter: "I will remove far off from you the northern army, and will drive him into a land barren and desolate, with his face toward the east sea, and his hinder part toward the utmost [Mediterranean—see Deuteronomy 34:2] sea . . ." (Joel 2:20). "The northern army [removed] far off . . . into a land barren and desolate" evidently refers to the great desert between the Jordan and the Euphrates River; and the east sea to the Persian Gulf and Indian Ocean into which the Euphrates empties. Only in this way can the land correspond in description with the one promised to Abraham, Isaac, and Jacob. Space will not permit a detailed description of this remarkable future inheritance of God's people. The portions assigned to the several tribes run in parallel strips east and west from the Euphrates River to the

Mediterranean Sea beginning at the north. As each succeeding portion lies farther south, the last-mentioned tracts would begin at the "east sea" and extend to the river of Egypt.

This brings us to the point of chief interest in this Scripture—all the tribes of Israel reappear under the names in the Book of Exodus after Levi had been assigned to the service of the sanctuary, and now prepare for the shock—*Dan heads the list*. The record says first "a portion for Dan"! An eternal testimony that where sin abounds, grace does much more abound.

But that is not all. The closing verses of Ezekiel give us another list of the twelve tribes. Here we have a description of the temple with its twelve gates. Each gate represents a tribe of Israel and the names of the tribes are precisely identical with the first complete list as recorded in Genesis 35. This earthly Jerusalem is evidently a counterpart of the new Jerusalem described in Revelation 21. A fuller description will be given at that place. Only the gates on the east are of concern now. The east is the side toward the morning star, toward the sunrising, and toward the coming of the glory: "And, behold, the glory of the God of Israel came from the way of the east . . . and the earth shined with his glory" (Ezekiel 43:2).

What names will appear upon the three gates on the east? "One gate of Joseph, one gate of Benjamin." This must be because they are the sons of Jacob's beloved wife Rachel. The third is "one gate of Dan." After reading that, one pauses with deep humility. Grace abounding to the chief of sinners! Those who feel they need some of the grace that is yet to be revealed, when they read this, "at the east side . . . one gate of Dan," may thank God and take courage. Since Dan does not appear in the genealogical list of I Chronicles and is omitted in Revelation (tribulation period among the sealed), one might conclude he was doomed to oblivion and extinction, but in Ezekiel he is at the head of the list! ["Grace enough for me!"—J. O. Y.]

The Episode of the Great Multitude (7:9-17)

Verses 9-17. *After this I beheld, and, lo, a great multitude, which no man could number, of all nations, and kindreds, and people, and tongues, stood before the throne, and before the Lamb, clothed with white robes, and palms in their hands; and cried with a loud voice, saying, Salvation to our God which sitteth upon the throne, and unto the Lamb. And all the angels stood round about the throne, and about the elders and the four beasts, and fell before the throne on their faces, and worshipped God, saying, Amen: Blessing, and glory, and wisdom, and thanksgiving, and honour, and power, and might, be unto our God for ever and ever. Amen. And one of the elders answered, saying unto me, What are these which are arrayed in white robes? and whence came they? And I said unto him, Sir, thou knowest. And he said to me, These are they which came out of great tribulation, and have washed their robes, and made them white in the blood of the Lamb. Therefore are they before the throne of God, and serve him day and night in his temple: and he that sitteth on the throne shall dwell among them. They shall hunger no more, neither thirst any more; neither shall the sun light on them, nor any heat. For the Lamb which is in the midst of the throne shall feed them, and shall lead them unto living fountains of waters: and God shall wipe away all tears from their eyes.*

After this. The Greek uses the plural, i.e., *After these things (meta tauta).* The phrase here modifies *I saw* as in verse 1 and hence denotes merely a subsequent vision and not necessarily succession in time. In fact, this vision seems to be retrospective (at least as far as verse 15).

I beheld, and, lo. This is the same in Greek as 6:2: "I saw, and behold." As explained before, behold is in the middle voice and signifies behold for one's own interest or benefit.

Great multitude. In 19:1, the same words are translated *much people.* It is important to remember that these words, *great multitude* and *much people,* are identical because, as further evidence shows, the groups are undoubtedly the same in each case.

No man. Literally this is *no one,* since the word *man* does not occur.

Of all nations, and kindreds, and people, and tongues. The four groups mentioned constitute the world population. Four is the world number. The word *kindred* is the word usually translated *tribe;* hence when these groups are mentioned, Jews are not excluded, for they are frequently referred to under tribe.

The preposition *of* is in the Greek *out of.* This is of course to be understood as modifying *kindreds, people,* and *tongues* as well as nations.

Stood before the throne. This signifies that they are in heaven because they died as martyrs. The word *stood* lends support to the view that the group is in a glorified state. Compare such passages as "stand before the Son of man" (Luke 21:36); "we shall all stand before the judgment seat of Christ" (Romans 14:10); and "I saw as it were a sea of glass mingled with fire: and them that had gotten the victory over the beast . . . stand on the sea of glass, having the harps of God" (Revelation 15:2).

White robes. See below.

Palms in their hands. The palms in their hands denote victory and rejoicing. The word occurs only here and in John 12:13 on the occasion of the triumphal entry.

Loud [or great] *voice.* This occurs 21 times in the book; cried with a loud voice 7 times—in one of these instances (18:2), namely, at the fall of Babylon, an angel cries *mightily* with a loud voice. One should carefully ponder these passages in order to ascertain as far as possible the great importance the words carry.

Salvation. This is ascribed to God in the sense that God is the source of salvation. The ascription of praise goes to the Lamb likewise. Note again that the Lamb no longer sits on the throne.

And worshipped God. As in 5:11, 12, the angels follow the saved group in a sevenfold adoration. The words employed, with one exception (thanksgiving for riches), are identical, although they are arranged in a slightly different manner. It is noteworthy, too, that here the angels fall before the throne on their faces and worship God.

What are these? The elder's query is noteworthy, especially as it appears in the original: *These arrayed in white robes, who are they and whence came they?* As the "Venerable Bede" remarks, "he questions that he may teach." A Greater Teacher on a previous occasion used a similar method to draw the confession of ignorance and consequently the need of instruction from His pupil: "And he [the Lord] said unto me, Son of man, can these bones live" (Ezekiel 37:3)? The answer was, "O Lord God, thou knowest." So here, *Sir, thou knowest* (implying I don't. And with the curiosity now aroused, implying in addition *"you tell me"*). The answer comes forthwith: *These are they which came out of the* [Greek] *great tribulation, and have washed their robes, and made them white in the blood of the Lamb.*

⌐   Here then appears a *second* group of redeemed ones in heaven during the tribulation period. In verse 15 they attribute their happy estate to their appropriation of the merits of the blood of the Lamb. Thus like the church group (the elders of chapters 4 and 5) they ascribe their heavenly bliss to the efficacy of the redemption that is in Christ Jesus.

That they are distinct from the church appears from the following considerations: Those were kept out of the great tribulation (3:10); these came out. Those wear white raiment; these white robes. Those sit on thrones round about the throne; these stand before the throne. Those wear crowns; these are uncrowned. Those have harps and vials; these have palms in their hands. Those sing a new song; these cry with a loud voice. Those are kings and priests and reign with Him; these serve Him day and night.

Furthermore, they are not identical. If they were, John who had previously seen the glorified church group (chapter 4) would have recognized them. The angel would not have inquired of John who they are.

They are distinct from the previous group (the 144,000) as held by a noted recent commentator. Briefly these points may be noted: The previous group consist of Israelites only; these come *out of all nations, kindreds, people, and tongues.* The former consist of a specific number; these of a great multitude which no one was able (Greek) to number. The former are still upon earth in an unglorified state (verse 3; cf. 9:4); these are in a state of glory before the throne of God.

There remains yet one group which has not been compared with the present one. May the white robed multitude be identical with (or at least include) those who were "slain for the word of God, and for the testimony which they held" of chapter 6:9-11?

This is undoubtedly the case, and when all the facts are considered, such a conclusion appears to be inevitable.[21]

⌐   The chapter closes with a prospect of the future glory in the new heaven and new earth when God will tabernacle (cf. 21:3) (Greek) among men and wipe away every tear from their eyes (21:4). It is noteworthy that the description in chapter 21 is followed with the significant phrase, "It is done."

Chapter 5 likewise closes with the triumphant prospect of the future glory. The other chapters dealing with judgment likewise pass on to a description of the end time concerning which again it is said, "It is done" (16:17). Neither the description of the judgments nor of the glories stops where this significant phrase,

"It is done," occurs. In each case what follows is the adding of particulars, in accordance with the law of occurrence, to things previously mentioned.

The Seventh Seal (8:1)

After the episodes in chapter 7 pertaining to the sealing of the 144,000 Israelites, and the great multitude, the seal judgments are now resumed and concluded. As in the opening of the previous seals, so in this case a vision follows, revealing its contents. Verses 2-6.

Some hold the view that the seventh in the first two series of judgments contains the series following, the seventh seal contains the seven trumpets, and the seventh trumpet contains the seven vials. Whatever may be said in favor of such a view, it is misleading in reference to the order of sequence regarding the three great series of judgments—the seals, the trumpets, and the vials.

Further study will show that the three series are not strictly consecutive, but that they move in cycles, each reaching to the end of (or beyond) the tribulation period. However, in the case of the trumpets, they begin later than the seals, and the vials later than the trumpets. [Which means that while they move in cycles and end at the same time, they do not begin at the same time.—J. O. Y.]

A summary of the seals:

The first four seals are plainly successive, introducing the successive judgments at the beginning of the tribulation period. The fifth is subsequent to these since it gives the toll of the slain.

The sixth, however, reveals the signs from heaven, including the parted heavens, the One seated on the throne, and the impending wrath of the Lamb. Cf. Matthew 24:29, 30.

It is clear, therefore, that the seal judgments take the scene up to the end of (and beyond) the tribulation period; consequently, the trumpet judgments, since at least all but the last are confined within the limits of the tribulation period, cannot be placed subsequent to the close of the seal judgments.

Even the seventh seal (while it is opened last in the order of revelation), since it reveals things pertaining to the tribulation, cannot of necessity go beyond the time indicated by the sixth vial. As a matter of fact, it reveals matters taking place in the first half of the tribulation.

Chapter 8 resumes and closes the seal judgments, and after a brief prelude, proceeds with the revelation of four of the seven trumpet judgments.

Verse 1. *And when he had opened the seventh seal, there was silence in heaven about the space of half an hour.*

Remember, the Opener of the seals is the "Lamb" and the title pertains to His redemptive work upon which is grounded His "worth" to open the seals. 5:9.

Silence in heaven. Observe that the silence mentioned is in heaven. Consequently, Scripture passages such as Zephaniah 1:7; Habakkuk 2:20, and Zechariah 2:13, which call for silence on earth, do not apply here. Again there is no call for silence in Revelation 8 as there is in the passages cited. The silence must be accounted for some other way. It is in marked contrast with the loud voice of the great multitude, and what appears as the most extended of all the heavenly utterances recorded in the book by "all the angels." Even the cherubim, of whom it is said "they rest not day and night, saying, Holy, holy, holy, Lord God Almighty," now are silent for *the space of half an hour*. Something unusual, something of tremendous importance, must be about to take place. In the seal judgments human agencies had a large part in the proceedings; under the trumpet judgments heavenly messengers as well as messengers from the bottomless pit, including Satan himself, will have a share in the devastation of things material and in the infliction of torment and punishment with death.

Perhaps the silence is not merely in view of what is to happen immediately, but it may be anticipative of the prolonged conflict and antagonism now to be set in motion between the forces of righteousness and the forces of evil, but which will ultimately, after indescribable travail and pain, issue in the triumph of righteousness and peace in the earth. The following verses describe some of the initial movements in heaven of this great drama.

The Trumpet Judgments (8:2—14:20)

The Seven Angels (8:2-6)

Verses 2-6. *And I saw the seven angels which stood before God; and to them were given seven trumpets. And another angel came and stood at the altar, having a golden censer; and there was given unto him much incense, that he should offer it with the prayers of all saints upon the golden altar which was before the throne. And the smoke of the incense, which came with the prayers of the saints, ascended up before God out of the angel's hand. And the angel took the censer, and filled it with fire of the altar, and cast it into the earth: and there were voices, and thunderings, and lightnings, and an earthquake. And the seven angels which had the seven trumpets prepared themselves to sound.*

And I saw. A new vision begins here. Observe that this vision includes the first four trumpets, for *I saw* (beheld) does not occur again until verse 13. In the seal judgments, the first four are distinguished from the last three in this, that they were introduced by the cherubim, while the last three were announced without their mediation. Here the distinction appears in the fact that the first four are included in one vision, while the last three are included in a separate vision as woe trumpets.

The seven angels which stood before God. The definite article implies previous mention of, and familiarity with, these angels. It is declared that they stood before (in the presence of) God. The word *stood* is used in the perfect tense. The tense is both punctiliar and durative. It expresses the continuance of completed action. If the verb were in the present tense, the reference might only refer to the "presence" angels in their ministries. John refers to angels, which mention was previously made, as standing before the throne and this can only refer to the seven spirits which are first spoken of in 1:4, and referred to later in 3:1; 4:5; 5:6. It is also noteworthy that whereas the seven spirits before the throne are mentioned four times in the previous chapters (1:4; 3:1; 4:5, and 5:6), now with the occurrence of the seven angels, no further mention is made of the seven spirits.

To them were given seven trumpets. Since the execution of all judgment has been committed to the Son (John 5:22, 27), in all probability the Son of man is He who gives the trumpets to the seven angels. The sounding of trumpets (and especially in heaven) is always succeeded by events of outstanding importance. Note the first occurrence at the giving of the law (Exodus 19:16; 20:18) and the last at the rapture of the saints (I Corinthians 15:51, 52; I Thessalonians 4:16). Here, as in Joel the second chapter, they are precursors of divine judgment as the following verses indicate.

The seven spirits are said to be before the throne of God (1:4); the seven angels stand "before God." Observe that the terms, "before the throne" and "before God," are used interchangeably. See, for example, that in verse 3 the golden altar is described as being "before the throne," while in 9:13, "before God."

Stood at the altar. The altar where the angel stands with the golden censer is the brazen altar, the altar of sacrifice. It is here (6:9, 10) the martyrs have been crying with a loud voice, *How long, O Lord, holy and true, wilt thou not judge and avenge our blood upon the earth dwellers?* The angel is familiar with those cries. And not only the angel, but the Lord to whom the prayers for vengeance are directed.

"An altar in heaven is mentioned seven times in the Apocalypse, vi.9, viii.3 (bis),5, ix.13, xiv.18, xvi.7. Most interpreters agree that the two altars—burnt offering and incense—are referred to in our text."[22] Ebrard and Bousset are of the opinion that the altar of burnt offering is referred to in vi.9, viii.3a, 5, xvi.7, and the altar of incense in viii.3b, ix.13.

"Swete, that burnt offering in vi.9 and the latter in viii.3, 5, ix.13, and that there is no determining which is referred to in xiv.18 and xvi.7."[23]

That he should offer. The angel ministering as a priest is not Christ. Christ is no longer at the right hand of God, the place of intercession. He acts now in the capacity of judge, not priest. If He were the angel, there would be no need of giving Him incense, for His prayers alone would avail before the Father, who hears Him always. It is undoubtedly He who orders the proceedings of the angel. He gives him much incense that he might give (Greek) it, or as the Revisers rendered it, *add* it, to *the prayers of all saints upon the golden altar,* i.e., the altar of incense. Prayer to be acceptable must be in the name of Christ. He offered Himself as a sacrifice to God for a sweet-smelling savor. Ephesians 5:2. Thus the incense, representing the atoning merit of Christ's death, renders the prayers effective.

Before the throne. Observe that the golden altar is declared to be "before the throne." In 9:13, where this altar is again mentioned, it is said to be *before God.* The particular mention of the location of this golden altar shows clearly that the altar first mentioned in the present verse is not the golden altar, for if it were, that would have been the place to specify its location.

The angel took the censer. The angel now takes the censer and fills it with fire from the (brazen) altar, that is, the altar of judgment. He casts the fire upon the earth—a token that the prayers which ascended to heaven would be followed by judgments descending upon the earth. Like the hush before the storm, so the silence in heaven is broken.

Voices, and thunderings, and lightnings, and an earthquake. The voices which proceed from intelligent beings are the first to sound the warning note. Thunders are mute rumblings of nature which tell of the approaching storm. Lightnings suggest the rapidity with which they strike the earth. The earth quakes as if to shudder at the outrages of her inhabitants.

[In rewriting the remainder of this chapter, the notes left by Dr. Smith were incorporated wherever it was possible. It is hoped, as in chapter 6, that the tone of the comments will ring true to the whole book.—J. O. Y.]

The First Trumpet (8:7)

Verse 7. *The first angel sounded, and there followed hail and fire mingled with blood, and they were cast upon the earth: and the third part of trees was burnt up, and all green grass was burnt up.*

Now begins this series of judgments upon the earth. Each angel follows in his order. The first trumpet judgment resembles the seventh plague of Egypt (Exodus 9:22 ff.) when hail and fire fell upon the earth and smote every herb and tree in Egypt, except those in the land of Goshen. One need not question the literalness of these judgments if he accepts the plagues of Egypt as literal. The time has come to *hurt . . . the earth . . . the sea . . . the trees.* Cf. Revelation 7:3.

The Second Trumpet (8:8, 9)

Verses 8, 9. *And the second angel sounded, and as it were a great mountain burning with fire was cast into the sea: and the third part of the sea became blood; and the third part of the creatures which were in the sea, and had life, died; and the third part of the ships were destroyed.*

The seer is careful to indicate the figures of speech by the usual *as.* One does not need to seek to explain this as a meteor (though it might be) or by any natural phenomenon, for this is supernatural judgment! How an object like a burning mountain will turn the third part of the sea into blood, cause a third part of marine life to perish, and destroy a third part of the nations' shipping is most difficult to explain from a naturalistic standpoint, but not from a supernaturalistic. In view of the atom bomb, or the hydrogen bomb (1956), who would wish to say that God could not entirely fulfill the judgment described by the second trumpet? Once again one need not have difficulty with this judgment if he accepts as historical the Egyptian plagues, for the second trumpet judgment resembles the first plague. Exodus 7:20-25.

The Third Trumpet (8:10, 11)

Verses 10, 11. *And the third angel sounded, and there fell a great star from heaven, burning as it were a lamp, and it fell upon the third part of the rivers, and upon the fountains of waters; and the name of the star is called Wormwood: and the third part of the waters became wormwood; and many men died of the waters, because they were made bitter.*

Divine judgment rolls on. None can stay it. Now the source of water for man is affected. Wormwood is bitter! To be sure, there is nothing figurative about that!

There is a strange parallel between this and the experience of Israel at Marah. Exodus 15:23-25. If by divine intervention water can be sweetened for human use, is it improbable that by divine intervention water can be made bitter and unfit for human consumption? If the miracle of Marah was literal, the third trumpet judgment is possible.

The Fourth Trumpet (8:12)

Verse 12. *And the fourth angel sounded, and the third part of the sun was smitten, and the third part of the moon, and the third part of the stars; so as the third part of them was darkened, and the day shone not for a third part of it, and the night likewise.*

It is of considerable interest to note the progress—one third of the green trees and grass, one third of marine life and shipping, one third of the waters, and one third of the heavenly bodies. Food is destroyed; distribution is crippled; water supply is limited; production is hampered. In the fourth trumpet judgment the signs in the sun, moon, and stars (Luke 21:25) seem to be foreshadowed. This judgment compares with the ninth Egyptian plague. Exodus 10:21-23. In the case of the Egyptian plague, the darkness could be felt; in the fourth trumpet judgment, only one third of the day and night was affected.

The Angel Flying Through Midheaven (8:13)

Verse 13. *And I beheld, and heard an angel flying through the midst of heaven, saying with a loud voice, Woe, woe, woe, to the inhabiters of the earth by reason of the other voices of the trumpet of the three angels, which are yet to sound!*

An angel flying through the midst of heaven. This is the first of such angels. Although some rather important texts have *eagle* for *angel*, which Westcott and Hort adopted, as did the ASV and the RSV, yet the internal evidence is entirely against *eagle* as the reading. This is of deep significance. When God uses angels to announce the plans of heaven, great events are taking place. Bear in mind the visit of the angel to Abraham before the destruction of Sodom, to Gideon before the routing of the Midianites, to Zacharias before the birth of John the Baptist, to Mary and Joseph before the birth of the Lord Jesus Christ in His incarnation, to the shepherds at the birth of Jesus.

Heaven referred to may be either the atmospheric heaven, if the message is intended for the earth dwellers, and apparently it is, or else the dwelling place of God, if the message is simply an announcement of the divine intent.

Woe, woe, woe. The Greek word is *ouai*, and is an instance of onomatopoeia —the sound indicates the meaning. Thus to get the sound of the proclamation, let the reader slowly and solemnly repeat aloud the words as they are in the Greek text, *Ouai, ouai, ouai* (pronounced ouaye). The sound itself ringing out through heaven would strike terror to the stoutest heart.

The inhabiters of the earth. This clearly fixes the judgments as being upon mankind. There hardly can be any symbolic intention. Rebellious, self-sufficient mankind will thus be brought to task. The self-sufficiency of this rationalistic, naturalistic age may be the preparation for the end-time woes upon the earth dwellers.

By reason of the other voices . . . yet to sound. This is a solemn warning of immediately impending judgments, of which there are three to correspond with the three woes.

Because of the widespread tendency to consider the trumpet judgments from a symbolic or figurative point of view, it is important to stress once more the complete possibility of a literal fulfillment. One needs to be cautious how he regards the miracles in unfulfilled passages of divine *prophecy* lest he undermine his own faith in the miracles of divine *history.* It is well to remember the oft-repeated rule, "When the literal sense makes good sense, seek no other sense." To which one may add, "Any other sense is usually nonsense." It may further be added that some miracles of history do not make even "good sense" from a purely naturalistic point of view. Of central importance is it to take as one's primary postulate: The God of the Universe is the God of Biblical Revelation. When one operates on this premise, he finds answers which defy his pure "good sense" but immeasurably bolster his faith. This is not to say that a believer in literal fulfillment of prophecy lacks "good sense." It is to assert that the literal sense of literal language is the only sound hermeneutical principle on which to proceed, whether the human mind can explain all the details or not.

The Fifth Trumpet (9:1-12)

Verse 1. *And the fifth angel sounded, and I saw a star fall from heaven unto the earth: and to him was given the key of the bottomless pit.*

Star. That a literal *star* is not meant is evident from the part that to him was given the key, that is, the authority (Matthew 16:19; Revelation 1:18), to open the bottomless pit. An intelligent being must be intended. It has been observed that a star is used as a symbol of an angel. 1:20. As early as the days of Job there is a similar use of the word. The Lord in addressing the patriarch speaks of the time "when the morning stars sang together, and all the sons of God shouted for joy" (Job 38:7). This is evidently an example of Hebrew parallelism conveying the idea that "morning stars" are the figurative parallel of the "sons of God," which of necessity denote angels, since the time is antecedent to the creation of man. Note in Revelation 12 that Michael casts out the dragon, also called old serpent, devil, and Satan. Note also that in Revelation 20 the same epithets are applied to the devil; hence the angel there is probably Michael.

The context speaks about locusts from the bottomless pit. Now observe that in verse 11 *they had a king over them, which is the angel of the bottomless pit.* Evidently the one that has rule over the locusts is identical with the one having authority over the bottomless pit. Hence the *star* of verse 1 is a term symbolic of the angel of the bottomless pit, who is none other than Satan, the destroyer, as the language in verse 11 indicates.

Fall. Observe carefully the word *fall.* The word is in the perfect tense, denoting completed action in the past. John did not see the star falling, but he saw it (him) after the fall had occurred. Cf. Luke 10:18 and Revelation 9:1. The cause of the fall of Satan is not given until chapter 12. There it is learned that Michael the archangel fought against Satan and cast him to the earth. Note that it does not say that Satan fought against Michael. The latter took the initiative, evidently to displace him as "prince of the power of the air" (Ephesians 2:2). Two important passages pointing forward to the fall of Satan, "star of light" (Isaiah 14:12-17; Luke 10:18), will be considered in chapter 12 where is recorded the actual description of his fall from heaven.

The key of the bottomless pit. To him was given the key of the pit of the abyss (Greek). Two questions naturally present themselves: Who gave him this authority? Why was it given to him? The answer to the first is: The Lord Jesus Christ, the Son of man Himself, gave him this authority either in person or mediately through an angel. He (the Son of man) has "the keys of death and of Hades" (Revelation 1:18, ASV). "He . . . openeth, and no one [Greek] shutteth; and shutteth, and no one openeth" (3:7). "All authority" (Greek) is given to Him. Matthew 28:18. Plainly therefore Satan does not possess the authority to open the pit *de jure,* i.e., in his own right. It was obviously delegated to him for a specific purpose. The answer to the second question is found in verse 20. There it is said that men worshiped demons. Even after the second woe has come upon them they persist in this awful delusion. After Satan is cast upon the earth, he has "great wrath" (12:12) and the Lord will use even the wrath of Satan to praise Him by releasing demons from the pit. The gods whom men worship become agencies of their own torment. Similarly the gods of Egypt—the Nile, frogs, lice, flies, etc.— were turned into plagues upon their worshipers.

The Greek word *abussos* occurs seven times. 9:1, 2, 11; 11:7; 17:8; 20:1, 3. In the first two instances the English translation is the single word *bottomless,* whereas *pit* is here the translation of the Greek word *phrear,* hence *pit of the abyss.* In the remaining instances *abussos* is translated by the two English words *bottomless pit. Abussos* occurs elsewhere only in Luke 8:31 and Romans 10:7. That it is the abode of demons appears from its use in the Luke passage. The demons besought Him (Jesus) that He would not command them to go out into the *abyss* (Greek). The Romans passage, "Who shall descend into the abyss? (that is, to bring up Christ again from the dead)," implies that He had been, if not in, at least adjacent to the abyss in the interval between His death and resurrection. Cf. Ephesians 4:9—"Now that he ascended, what is it but that he also descended first into the lower parts of the earth?"

Verse 2. And he opened the bottomless pit; and there arose a smoke out of the pit, as the smoke of a great furnace; and the sun and the air were darkened by reason of the smoke of the pit.

He opened the [Greek: pit of the abyss] . . . *pit.* Having obtained the authority, Satan forthwith proceeds to open the pit, knowing that his time is short.

Smoke . . . as the smoke of a great furnace. The two words of comparison, *as (hos)* and *like (homoios),* occur more frequently in this chapter than anywhere else in the Bible, the former ten, and the latter four times. The words do not signify identity but similarity. Moreover, they enable one to form a mental picture of the things described. Smoke ascended out of the pit *as* the smoke of a furnace. The word *smoke* occurs 12 times in Revelation—six times in this chapter. Twice it is used in connection with things holy—the "smoke of the incense" (8:4), and "smoke from the glory of God" (15:8). The other uses relate to judgment, doom, and torment.

The familiar saying, "Where there is smoke there is fire," appears to apply here, e.g., *the smoke of a great furnace* (9:2); *fire and smoke and brimstone* (9:17, 18); *smoke of her burning* (18:9, 18). The clauses, *smoke ascended* [Greek] *out of the pit* (9:2); and *the smoke of their torment ascends* [Greek] *for ever and ever* (19:3), express a marked similarity. "Smoke of their torment" is a terrible conception and suggests that the smoke issues from the sufferings of the doomed. In the example pertaining to the doom of Babylon it is evident there was torment, for the merchants beholding the doom of the city "stand afar off for the fear of her torment, weeping and wailing" (18:15). That there is torment in the pit (abyss) is clear, for the rich man in Hades was in a place of torment; moreover, he testified "I am tormented in this flame" (Luke 16:24b). If then smoke issues from the torment of the doomed, one need not wonder that the sun and the air will be darkened by reason of the smoke accumulating in the pit from the days of Cain unto that future occasion.

Verses 3, 4. *And there came out of the smoke locusts upon the earth: and unto them was given power, as the scorpions of the earth have power. And it was commanded them that they should not hurt the grass of the earth, neither any green thing, neither any tree; but only those men which have not the seal of God in their foreheads.*

This plague reminds one of the eighth plague of Egypt (Exodus 10:12-15) at which time locusts likewise appeared. Judgment accompanies their appearance in each case.

Power, as the scorpions. Power was given to them *as*, that is, resembling, the power of scorpions, but note that they are not likened to locusts but said to be locusts. While their appearance is quite different from ordinary locusts, their lack of resemblance to them is unduly stressed by those who say these do not prey on vegetation while locusts naturally do, for when the plague of locusts came in Egypt, vegetation was the first object of their attack. Exodus 10:15. That the nature of these is exactly similar is evident from a part of verse 4, *And it was commanded them that they should not hurt the grass of the earth, neither any green thing, neither any tree.* These were the very objects devastated by the locusts in Egypt, and the locusts at this time evidently will do likewise, else why should there be need for the prohibition? The chief difference between these locusts and those of Egypt is that these were possessed by demonic spirits and so they were possessed of intelligence. This is plainly implied by the opening clause, "And it was . . . [said to] them." The original word for *said* means to utter words. The clause is exactly the same as in 6:11 in the address to those wearing white robes. That demons could possess locusts should occasion no difficulty when we recall that upon a former occasion they "entered into the swine" (Luke 8:33).

But only those men which have not the seal of God in their foreheads. Recall that in 7:1-3 the angels holding in check the four winds of judgment were commanded: "Hurt not the earth, neither the sea, nor the trees, till we have sealed the servants of our God in their foreheads." Then follows the sealing of the 144,000 Israelites. The purpose of the sealing was evidently for the sake of protection and immunity from suffering already in the first and second trumpets at which time the earth and sea are affected, and now more particularly when suffering was to come upon men. Thus, even as during the plagues in Egypt, God will put a difference between Israel and other men. And for what purpose did God "give this people favour in the . . . [eyes] of the Egyptians"? First, that Israel might know the Lord. Exodus 6:7. In the next place, and chiefly, that "Pharaoh" and the Egyptians might know the Lord and that there is "none like . . . [him] in all the earth." (Cf. Exodus 7:5, 17; 8:10, 22, 23; 9:14, 29; 11:7; 14:4, 18.) Moreover, just as Israel of old was favored and preserved for a testimony in those days, so again will it be with Israel in the days to come. All this accords precisely with the prophetic declaration: ". . . when thy [the Lord's] judgments are in the earth, the inhabitants of the world will learn righteousness" (Isaiah 26:9b).

Verse 5. *And to them it was given that they should not kill them, but that they should be tormented five months: and their torment was as the torment of a scorpion, when he striketh a man.*

The purpose of this torment was apparently remedial as well as punitive, the ultimate object of the infliction of punishment being amendment of life. The five months may allude to the duration of the normal period of life of the locust.

Verse 6. *And in those days shall men seek death, and shall not find it; and shall desire to die, and death shall flee from them.*

Another testimony that this is no longer in the church age, for there is no such restraint now, nor has there been during the Christian centuries. And the nearer history approaches this period, the more suicides there are. In what way this divine restraint will come upon men is not disclosed, but evidently there will be a direct interference by God in the affairs and actions of men, such as has not been before.

Verses 7-10. *And the shapes of the locusts were like unto horses prepared unto battle; and on their heads were as it were crowns like gold, and their faces were as the faces of men. And they had hair as the hair of women, and their teeth were as the teeth of lions. And they had breastplates, as it were breastplates of iron; and the sound of their wings was as the sound of chariots of many horses running to battle. And they had tails like unto scorpions, and there were stings in their tails: and their power was to hurt men five months.*

Like . . . as. These verses abound with the two common words of comparison: *like (homoios)*, three times; *as (hos)*, seven times. The former is uniformly translated by "like" and denotes similarity in form or appearance; the latter is translated by "as" and "as it were," and like *homoios* may express resemblance in form but sometimes in either nature or action. Angels have power to appear in visible forms at will, only, however, in accordance with their mission as directed by an overruling Providence. In Daniel both good and evil spirits are mentioned as functioning in behalf of men. And similarly in Revelation, good angels appear in various forms. So why not the evil? Here they assume the unusual forms indicated. Later they have the appearance of frogs. 16:13.

There can be no doubt but that their outward forms will strike the eye as here described. The detailed resemblances are given in order to enable the reader to visualize their incarnate forms with exactness.

Horses. Their similarity to horses is stressed more since the nominal (noun) form of *homoios (homoiomata)* occurs in the first clause of the description, i.e., their "shapes" or likenesses are *like unto horses prepared unto battle.* Obviously here is an allusion to the prophecy in Joel 2:4, "The appearance of them is as the appearance of horses; and as horsemen, so shall they run." However, the prophecy of Joel is not fulfilled (filled to the full) in this plague, for no exemption to either man or vegetation is made in the former prophecy as is the case in the present instance.

In an effort to visualize their forms, observe that according to the description their form is not erect but prostrate as the locust "in all forms." Observe, too, that the description begins at the head and moves backward, ending with a description of their tails, thus—

on their heads crowns like gold

faces as men

hair as women

teeth as lions

breastplates as of iron

the sound of their wings as the sound of chariots of many horses rushing to battle

tails like scorpions with stings to torment men five months

Thus runs the sevenfold description of the hideous forms in which these demonic spirits incarnate themselves. Their very appearance will, no doubt, strike terror to the stoutest heart. Further comment appears unnecessary. To believe what is written is here as always the best "key of knowledge."

Verse 11. *And they had a king over them, which is the angel of the bottomless pit, whose name in the Hebrew tongue is Abaddon, but in the Greek tongue hath his name Apollyon.*

A king over them. Contrary to ordinary locusts (Proverbs 30:27) these have a king over them. The king is *the angel of the bottomless pit.* This one is undoubtedly the same as the fallen star (verse 1) to whom was given the key of (authority over) the bottomless pit. The very title *king* implies one having authority. Only one had authority over the pit; so the star must be identical with the angel and, as in 1:20, the former is a symbol of the latter.

Abaddon . . . Apollyon. The name of the king is given in two tongues, Hebrew and Greek, so that neither Jew nor Greek can fail to identify him. The Hebrew word *Abaddon* means "destruction" or a place of destruction, equivalent to abyss. Here, however, the word is personified and is applied to him who leads souls to destruction, i.e., to Satan, the destroyer. This is evident from the Greek equivalent *Apollyon,* which is a masculine noun and means destroyer.

It has been shown, therefore, that the star of verse 1 is identical with the king of verse 11. The king is the angel; the angel is the destroyer which, as the Scriptures declare, is Satan, called the prince of demons. Matthew 9:34; 12:24.

Verse 11 shows the devil has not yet given his power to the beast (13:2), but that he is inflicting pain and destruction through evil spirits. He is called *angel of the bottomless pit* because he is the one to whom was given the key, that is, the authority, to open the pit.

Verse 12. *One woe is past; and, behold, there come two woes more hereafter.*

One woe is past. The last three trumpet judgments are called the three woes because of the terrible calamities and suffering they inflict. The period covered by the fifth trumpet or first woe will be at least five months and probably considerably longer, for it is not to be supposed that the infliction imposed continued only a single day.

Hereafter. The word *hereafter* means literally *after these things.* The words show there is progression in time in these judgments. The woes are not simultaneous; the first is *past* before the second begins.

The Sixth Trumpet (9:13-21)

Verses 13, 14. *And the sixth angel sounded, and I heard a voice from the four horns of the golden altar which is before God, saying to the sixth angel which had the trumpet, Loose the four angels which are bound in the great river Euphrates.*

The judgment following the sounding of the sixth trumpet is probably the greatest of all in the pre-advent series because the description covers a greater amount of detail than any other. It includes the rest of this chapter, all of chapter 10, and chapter 11 as far as verse 14. It is only then that *the second woe is past.* The agents employed, demonic, angelic, and human, are the most varied in their nature and function ever brought together under a single judgment. The issues and conclusions of the activities here described are among the most remarkable recorded. Not until the Lord Himself appears as the chief actor are the eventualities more comprehensive, extraordinary, and significant.

I heard a voice from the four horns of the golden altar. The golden altar is mentioned only here and in 8:3. The voice from the four horns of the altar is presumably that of the angel ministering on the previous occasion. The repetition of this ministry apparently signifies that the law of retributive justice as announced by Jesus, "all they that take the sword shall perish with the sword" (Matthew 26:52), and repeated below (13:10), is about to function on the earth with increasing intensity in answer to the prayers of the saints "slain for the word of God, and for the testimony which they held" (6:9, 10).

Loose the four angels. "The angels that sinned" appear to have a different abode from men who die in their sins. Peter writes, "God . . . cast them down to Tartarus [Greek], and delivered them into chains of darkness, to be reserved unto judgment" (II Peter 2:4). And similarly Jude (verse 6), "And the angels which kept not their first estate, but left their own habitation, he hath reserved in everlasting chains under darkness unto the judgment of the great day." On the other hand, "the wicked shall be . . . [cast into Hades], and all the nations that forget God" (Psalm 9:17). And later the Lord Himself declared: "And thou, Capernaum, which art exalted unto heaven, shalt be brought down to Hades [Greek]: for if the mighty works, which have been done in thee, had been done in Sodom, it would have remained until this day" (Matthew 11:23). That the dead of Capernaum are not in the final hell is evident from the following verse: "But I say unto you, That it shall be more tolerable for the land of Sodom in the day of judgment, than for thee." Observe, too, that nothing is said about the wicked in Hades being bound with chains.

In the Revelation text mention is made of four angels *bound* at the Euphrates River. Perhaps Tartarus is in the region of the Euphrates. It is significant that the Euphrates is again mentioned when the sixth vial is poured out and that immediately following the "three unclean spirits like frogs come out of the mouth of the dragon [Satan], and out of the mouth of the beast [Antichrist], and out of the mouth of the false prophet" (16:13). This region therefore appears to be the headquarters of the infernal trinity. It should occasion no surprise that Satan, after his fall from heaven, should make his stronghold in the region of the Euphrates, for it was in these parts that he made his first appearane after the creation of man and caused his fall. The Euphrates had its source in the Garden of Eden, which was the cradle of the human race. Satan, however, is not given the authority to release the demonic forces held in reserve at the Euphrates. It is at the command of the voice from the golden altar to the sixth angel that the infernal spirits get a temporary release. Four of the infernal angels, themselves bound, have been holding the myriads in ward, there being principalities and powers among evil spirits as well as among the good. With the release of the four, all are released for the dread purpose indicated in the following verses.

Verse 15. And the four angels were loosed, which were prepared for an hour, and a day, and a month, and a year, for to slay the third part of men.

Four angels. Though the number four is the earth number and denotes universality, they cannot be identified with any other group, certainly not with the four angels of chapter 7. Those are holy angels and engaged in a work of preserving men, while these are wicked angels devoted to the purpose of destroying men.

Prepared. Though wicked, these angels in the providence of God have been held in readiness for this occasion. The word *prepared* is a perfect passive participle and denotes a state of readiness in the past which continues to the present. God, being sovereign, uses wicked agents to fulfill His purpose. Thus He used Pharaoh, Judas, and others, making the wrath of men to praise Him.

Hour. The definite article, as it is in the Greek, would more sharply define this as a point of time in the providence of God and would signify *the* hour of the day and month and year.

[The remainder of the comments on this chapter are by the editor.—J. O. Y.]

Verse 16. And the number of the army of the horsemen were two hundred thousand thousand: and I heard the number of them.

Two hundred thousand thousand. Let the student write out the figure and he will get 200,000,000. To make it certain that the figure is not misunderstood, the seer adds, *I heard the number.*

Verses 17-19. And thus I saw the horses in the vision, and them that sat on them, having breastplates of fire, and of jacinth, and brimstone: and the heads of the horses were as the heads of lions; and out of their mouths issued fire and smoke and brimstone. By these three was the third part of men killed, by the fire, and by the smoke, and by the brimstone, which issued out of their mouths. For their power is in their mouth, and in their tails: for their tails were like unto serpents, and had heads, and with them they do hurt.

I saw the horses. Note carefully the use of the words of comparison. They were not *like* horses. The only indication of symbolism may be the phrase, *in the vision,* although even this would not require the prophet's description of the horses to be taken as symbolic. By way of comparison one might inquire whether Peter's vision of the sheet contained all manner of beasts or not. Acts 10:9 ff. A vision does not nullify the realness of the objects seen by the viewer. These horses have heads *like* lions and tails *like* serpents—surely most unusual horses. They are hardly the product of crossbreeding! On the contrary, they are demon-possessed, hideous monstrosities. One could wish most keenly never to meet with such monsters of destruction.

The third part of men. Call to mind that 6:8 records the slaying of a fourth part of men. These horsemen are charged with the slaying of a third part—of those left, of course. A little arithmetic would show that one fourth plus one third of three fourths equals one half. So then by the fourth seal and the sixth trumpet one half of the earth's population will be slain.

Verses 20, 21. *And the rest of the men which were not killed by these plagues yet repented not of the works of their hands, that they should not worship devils, and idols of gold, and silver, and brass, and stone, and of wood: which neither can see, nor hear, nor walk: neither repented they of their murders, nor of their sorceries, nor of their fornication, nor of their thefts.*

Yet repented not. The word *repent* here used is the one which etymologically means *to change one's mind.* The residue of men were so hardened in their pernicious ways that they would not change their minds.

The works of their hands . . . worship devil, and idols. Man has repeatedly tried to throw off the yoke of creaturehood. In fact, this seems to be his chief malady. He wishes to be independent of the God who created him. In so doing he binds himself inexorably to destruction by that through which he sought liberation! By *worship devils,* properly demons, one is reminded of the temptations of Jesus in the wilderness. "If thou therefore wilt worship me, all shall be thine," said the devil after having shown Jesus "all the kingdoms of the world in a moment of time" (Luke 4:5, 7). A perversion of the basic worship urge in man can only lead to the worship of the ego, devils (demons), and idols.

Neither repented they of their murders. This would clearly indicate that the perversion of one's religious life must lead to the perversion of one's social life. The acts mentioned in this series are regarded today in every society as vices of the lowest sort. It would appear that when the time comes for the sixth trumpet judgment, men will have become so completely perverted that vices will reign in the place of virtues. Indeed, one finds this an intensification over Paul's description of the pagan world in Romans 1:18-32, where it is said, "God gave them over to a reprobate mind . . ." (verse 28).

The Episode of the Strong Angel and the Little Opened Book (10:1-11)

The present vision is the longest of the entire book. It covers three whole chapters (10, 11, 12). These chapters are closely related and should be considered as an organic whole. The next "I saw" does not occur until chapter 13.

Call to mind that the sixth seal was followed by two episodes (the 144,000 sealed Israelites and the great multitude of robe wearers—chapter 7) before the opening of the seventh seal. 8:1. In the present instance mention is made of three episodes—the strong angel with the little book, the measuring of the temple, and the martyrdom of the two witnesses before the sounding of the seventh trumpet. 11:15. These episodes, however, form a part of the sixth trumpet as is evident from the declaration of 11:14, "The second woe is past." It should be remembered therefore that in giving the details of the sixth trumpet which sounds at 9:13, one should include not merely the ravages of the army of horsemen but the three episodes (10:1—11:14) as well.

It has been noted before that more than one vision may occur under the same judgment (6:1, 2) as well as under the same episode (7:1, 2). This is so because of the distinct importance of each vision. Under the present judgment, mention is made of two visions. 9:1; 10:1.

Recall, too, that following the opening of the seventh seal (8:1) there is a distinct vision of the two angels ministering at the two altars. This ministry pointed back to the prayers of the saints and forward to the judgments following under the trumpets. Following the sounding of the seventh trumpet four entire chapters (12–15), in the form of episodes, intervene before the next series of judgments come upon the earth. Several of these (12:1—13:3) are retrospective and belong in point of time between the fourth and fifth trumpet, while others following are subsequent to the sixth trumpet and introductory to the vial judgments to follow.

Attention should be called to the proleptic character of numerous passages within the chapters following, by which is meant that events of the future are related as though they already had taken place. A striking example of this is at the close of the sixth seal, where occurs the announcement, "the great day of his wrath is come" (6:17). These proleptic statements are all of special importance and they are made either as a threat to the wicked in the way of warning of coming catastrophes or to the righteous by way of hope and fond anticipation.

Chapter 10 is the very heart of Revelation and in point of time is the middle of the tribulation period. It is a matter of interest to note that the seventh trumpet is sounded at the close of the first half of the entire number of chapters. The time notes (42 months—11:2; 1,260 days—11:3; time, times, and half a time—12:14) show that these chapters belong together in point of time and that this is the middle of the tribulation period.

Some striking parallels are noticeable between chapter 10 and chapter 5, for in each mention is made of a mighty angel crying with a loud voice and of a book, the contents of which are of supreme importance. In chapter 5, however, the book was shut up and sealed. In chapter 10 (undoubtedly what remains of the same book) it is open.

In the Introduction, attention was called to the fact that the Book of Revelation may be regarded as a supplement to the Book of Daniel. From chapter 6 on it forms a complement to Daniel, for it completes the unfolding of truth from the "scripture of truth" which began at Daniel 11:2 and continued until Daniel 12:3, at which point Gabriel gave orders to Daniel: "Shut up the words, and seal the book, even to the time of the end." In Revelation 6 the Lamb, who alone was found worthy, proceeded with the opening of six seals. In Revelation 8:1 the last seal was opened. The "scripture of truth" is now an open book and seven angels are in readiness with trumpet sound to herald further revelations of its contents. These are recorded in Revelation 8 and 9. The present chapter is introductory to the remaining revelations which are about to issue from the "scripture of truth."

It is a matter of profound interest to observe that the last chapter of Daniel deals precisely with the period of time now under consideration and that in Revelation 10 several verses are almost an exact parallel to words found in Daniel. Since the passage in Daniel is so important to the proper understanding of Revelation 10:1-7, it will be necessary to make brief comments on the Daniel passage. In order to compare Scripture with Scripture to greatest advantage, the corresponding passages will then be presented in parallel columns.

Comments on Daniel 12:1-6

Verse 1. *And at that time shall Michael stand up, the great prince which standeth for the children of thy people: and there shall be a time of trouble, such as never was since there was a nation even to that same time: and at that time thy people shall be delivered, every one that shall be found written in the book.*

And at that time. The time referred to is the "time of the end" mentioned twice before. Daniel 11:35, 40. It occurs elsewhere in Daniel. 8:17; 12:4, 9. The word for time in the Greek is *kairos*, which denotes season; hence a period, and never a mere point in time. That the term applies to the whole period of tribulation is evident from the preceding chapter, where mention is made of the rival movements of the king of the north and the king of the south as taking place in the *time of the end* (11:40-44) before the king of the north plants the tabernacle of his palace between the seas in the glorious holy mountain. It is evident from other passages (Daniel 9:27; Matthew 24:15; Revelation 13:11 f.) that this occurs in the middle of the tribulation period.

Shall Michael stand up. This prophecy is fulfilled in the twelfth chapter of Revelation where Michael, in contending with Satan, casts him to the ground. This victory over Satan in the air takes place in the middle of the tribulation period as observed above.

And there shall be a time of trouble. The Greek word for trouble is *thlipsis*, which in Matthew 24:21 is translated tribulation. Hence this is merely another name for the tribulation period.

Thy people shall be delivered. These words find their fulfillment in such passages as Matthew 24:16-21; Revelation 7:4-8; 9:4; 12:13-16.

Verse 2. *And many of them that sleep in the dust of the earth shall awake, some to everlasting life, and some to shame and everlasting contempt.*

Many of them . . . awake. The words refer probably to the resurrection of Israel, Daniel's people only; therefore not as later, "all that are in the graves" (John 5:28). This resurrection apparently takes place just after the coming of the Lord with power and great glory when ". . . he shall send his angels with a great sound of a trumpet, and they shall gather together his elect from the four winds, from one end of heaven to the other" (Matthew 24:31). To the same purpose is the passage in Isaiah 27:12, 13, ". . . ye shall be gathered one by one, O ye children of Israel. . . . The great trumpet shall be blown, and they shall come which were ready to perish in the land of Assyria, and the outcasts in the land of Egypt, and shall worship the Lord in the holy mount at Jerusalem." And similarly in Matthew 8:11, ". . . many shall come from the east and west, and shall sit down with Abraham, and Isaac, and Jacob, in the kingdom of heaven." It should be remembered that a resurrection includes both the "dead raised" and "those alive" changed.

Some to everlasting . . . and some . . . contempt. The original says *these* [i.e., the righteous—those written in the book] *to everlasting life; those* [the wicked] *to shame and everlasting contempt.* Later Scriptures reveal that the resurrection of the righteous precedes the resurrection of the wicked and the last one to speak on this point calls the resurrection of the righteous the first resurrection and declares, "the rest of the dead lived not again until the thousand years were finished" (Revelation 20:5).

Verse 3. *And they that be wise shall shine as the brightness of the firmament; and they that turn many to righteousness as the stars for ever and ever.*

They that be wise. The wise are those who have spiritual understanding and, as the original would imply, who impart it to others. Moreover, turning others to righteousness comes alone through the diffusion of spiritual light. The promise of this verse is to those of Daniel's people who turn to the Lord in the tribulation period, many of whom, in Revelation, are "slain for the word of God, and for the testimony which they held."

It is not amiss to observe that the "scripture of truth" does not contain one syllable concerning the church. Gabriel distinctly informs Daniel that the book consists of things that "shall befall . . . [his] people in the latter days" (Daniel 10:14, 21). One feels to rejoice that God has left these heartening promises to the faithful in Israel for the coming "time of trouble." He ought not insist in claiming them for the church while he naively permits Israel to retain the curses.

Verse 4. *But thou, O Daniel, shut up the words, and seal the book, even to the time of the end: many shall run to and fro, and knowledge shall be increased.*

Shut up . . . and seal. Apparently the angel proposed to close his unfolding of the truth with the grand climax regarding the final triumph and glory of the faithful. Yet it appears that Daniel had the "scripture of truth" in his own hands while the angel was showing him its contents, for he was ordered to shut up the words and seal the book. The words of the angel imply that the book would be opened whenever the time of the end comes. The book did open at Revelation 6; therefore the "time of the end" began at that time, and not in the middle of the tribulation period as some have held.

Many shall run to and fro, and knowledge shall be increased. The thought appears to be that many will diligently search the words of prophecy and as a consequence, knowledge of these things will be increased. This is certainly the case now. Let no one be dissuaded from interest in the prophetic Scriptures by the taunt of scoffers: "Where is the promise of his coming" (II Peter 3:4)? It is enough to know that the writer of these words was three times addressed as a man "greatly beloved," and this at the very time that he was praying and searching for light regarding things to come. 9:23; 10:11, 19.

Verses 5, 6. *Then I Daniel looked, and, behold, there stood other two, the one on this side of the bank of the river, and the other on that side of the bank of the river. And one said to the man clothed in linen, which was upon the waters of the river, How long shall it be to the end of these wonders?*

Other two. These were likely angels as was Gabriel who had so far shown Daniel things from the "scripture of truth," for if they were men, they would not be referred to merely as *other two.*

The man clothed in linen, which was upon [or above] *the waters of the river.* This man is mentioned before. 10:4, 5. One learns from the former passage that the river spoken of is the Hiddekel, which was the ancient name of the Tigris. It empties into the Euphrates about 40 miles above its mouth at the Persian Gulf. It is a matter of interest, and probably of high significance, that now, as the time is approaching when the Lord is about to finish transgression, i.e., make an end of sins and bring in everlasting righteousness, the place where sin entered the world comes thus prominently into view.

One said to the man. One (of the other two) now addresses the man clothed in linen, *How long shall it be to the end of these wonders?* This is likely not for his own, but for Daniel's benefit. At any rate, Daniel overhears the conversation and thus receives light on the future that was withheld by Gabriel. The circumstance is altogether peculiar and unique. It is noteworthy that the information thus vouchsafed to Daniel at this time is virtually repeated in Revelation 10 as the verse by verse comparison will indicate.

The *wonders* mentioned in the query probably allude to the plagues or judgments prevailing in the time of trouble. Verse 1. The same word is used in Exodus 3:20 where the Lord declares, "I will stretch out my hand, and smite Egypt with all my wonders"; and again in Exodus 15:11 in the song of praise for deliverance, "Who is like unto thee, O Lord, among the gods? who is like thee, glorious in holiness, fearful in praises, doing wonders?"

From the description given in the following verse and because of his ability to answer the query of verse 6, including the remarkable acts he performs in this connection, the man clothed in linen is evidently an angel of the highest order.

Daniel 12:7-9 reappears (with essential variations) in Revelation 10. It is hoped that the comments on Daniel, which lead up to Revelation 10, will enable the student to understand it better. For convenience of comparison, the passages from Revelation and Daniel will be presented side by side.

The glorious form of the man clothed in linen is given in Daniel 10.

Revelation 10:1	Daniel 10:5, 6
And I saw another mighty angel come down from heaven, clothed with a cloud: and a rainbow was upon his head, and his face was as it were the sun, and his feet as pillars of fire.	*. . . behold a certain man clothed in linen . . . his face [was] as the appearance of lightning, and his eyes as lamps of fire, and his arms and his feet like in colour to polished brass. . . .*

I saw another mighty angel come down from heaven. The word *another* implies that John had seen a mighty angel on a previous occasion. *Another* signifies one not previously mentioned. It is no difficult matter to determine which angel was in the seer's mind, for only once before did he see a strong angel in a vision, namely, in Revelation 5:2. (The same Greek word is translated *strong* and *mighty*.)

Some have taken this angel to be Christ. However, several reasons why this view is erroneous will appear. The angel in chapter 5 plainly is not Christ, for when he presents his challenge, Christ as the Lamb is seen standing in the midst of the elders. And since "the strong angel" of the former chapter is evidently a created celestial being, so must this one be, else he could not be consistently called *another* angel. The angel comes down from heaven. The Bible knows nothing about a coming of Christ from heaven midway in the tribulation period. In the passage from Daniel mention is made of a *man*. It might appear from this that the mighty angel and the man are not identical. It should be noted, however, that the radiance of the man as given by Daniel exceeds that of the mighty angels. But what is more convincing to the probable identity of the two in addition to the similarity in form is that the angel Gabriel is referred to as the *man* Gabriel in the same book. Daniel 9:21.

Clothed with a cloud. The imagery is of necessity symbolical. *Clothed with a cloud* denotes that he is a heavenly messenger; the rainbow, that He who commissioned him would faithfully execute His eternal purpose according to His word; His face as the sun, the reflection of the ineffable glory of the Holy One whom he represents; the feet as pillars of brass, that further judgments are about to be executed upon a sinful and rebellious race.

If the angel of Revelation 5 is Gabriel, this is probably Michael. It would not be pertinent at this place to present all the evidence that points in that direction.

Michael means "who is like God." This indicates that he is not Christ, for it would be misleading to say that Christ is like God merely, for He *is* God. On the other hand, in the appearance of Michael, since he is like God we should suspect a description just as we have in Daniel and in Revelation.

While Gabriel is occupied chiefly in "showing the truth," Michael "stands up" for God's people and contends with and vanquishes His enemies. This is seen in his disputation with the devil regarding the body of Moses (Jude 9) as well as in his victory over Satan in casting him out of heaven (Revelation 12).

Gabriel and Michael are the only archangels mentioned in Scripture; hence the presumption that the two mighty angels who are so prominently mentioned in these two chapters are these two archangels. Gabriel and Michael are seen in intimate collaboration in the Book of Daniel, for Gabriel testifies that Michael helped him in a conflict with the prince of Persia (10:13), and further that he too "stood to confirm and to strengthen him [Michael]" (11:1). That neither Gabriel nor Michael could be Christ appears evident since Christ needed no one to help Him overcome an enemy.

Verses 2, 3. *And he had in his hand a little book open: and he set his right foot upon the sea, and his left foot on the earth, and cried with a loud voice, as when a lion roareth: and when he had cried, seven thunders uttered their voices.*

He had in his [right] *hand.* The right hand denotes authority and power—characteristics commonly ascribed to Michael.

A little book opened (so the Greek). The question naturally arises, Has this book any connection with that of Revelation 5? If so, what relation does it sustain to that book? Observe that the former book was closed and sealed; this book is neither closed nor sealed, but *opened.* Like the verb "fall" in 9:1, *open* is in the perfect tense and implies that it was opened in the past and continues open to the present. Six of the seals of the former book were opened by the Lamb who alone was worthy in chapter 6. The Lamb opened the seventh or the last seal in 8:1. All the seals having been removed, it was now an open book. With the opening of each seal a new revelation issued from its contents.

In chapters 8 and 9 six trumpets uttered their voices, proclaiming judgments in the form of plagues which are to come upon the earth. Plainly these announcements proceeded from further revelations made from the now open book. It seems conclusive therefore that the opened book of chapter 10 is none other than the previously sealed one mentioned in chapter 5. Observe, too, that the former is called book, while this is a little book or booklet (Greek). The implication is one of smaller size. This is due to the removal of the seals and the contents revealed with each removal.

In the comments on Revelation 5 the book "closed and sealed" was identified with the one mentioned in Daniel, and hence identical with the "scripture of truth" (Daniel 10:21), which contains "what shall befall . . . [Daniel's] people [Israel] in the latter days" (10:14). In Daniel 11 the angel Gabriel reveals in part its contents: the conflict of nations affecting Israel in the centuries immediately following (verses 2-35); the rise of a willful king (Antichrist) in the time of the end (verses 36, 40), who overthrows kingdoms, enters the "glorious land" (verse 41), and plants the tabernacle of his palace in the glorious holy mountain (verses 36-45). This conflict of the willful king with other powers occurs in the first half of the time of the end. It is clear that beginning with the latter half, power will be given him over all kindreds and tongues and nations. Revelation 13:7. Moreover, other passages abundantly testify that this planting of his tabernacle in the glorious holy mountain will occur in the middle, not in the end, of the time of the end.

With the first verse of Daniel 12 the revelation concerning the time of the end abruptly comes to a close with two particulars: Michael shall stand up for Daniel's people; his people shall be delivered. Now let it be emphasized that this prophecy dovetails exactly with the portion of Revelation now under consideration, for both these predictions are fulfilled in the present vision—that of Michael in Revelation

12:7-9 and the deliverance of Israel in Revelation 12:14-16. And it is from this point that the concluding revelations proceed from the little book.

It is not necessary that the contents of the little book include *all* the prophecies that follow in the succeeding chapters. Just as there are whole chapters (1–5) in the first part of the book that do not proceed from the "scripture of truth," so there may be portions in the latter half in addition to what is contained therein. One may be certain that the contents of the little book will be fully revealed and that more will be learned about what will befall Israel in the latter days.

And cried with a loud voice, as when a lion roareth. These words denote both urgency and defiance in view of coming conflicts with the powers of evil. This cry of the angel, as when a lion roareth, agrees very well with the supposition that the angel is Michael, for just as a lion is king of the beasts, so Michael is not merely a contender but a vanquisher of his enemies, even of the archenemy. The lionlike roar of the angel signifies that he is about to triumph over his adversary. If the reference is to Michael, he has already cast him to the earth, while in chapter 20 he shuts him up in the bottomless pit. The roar therefore is a signal for the final triumph over the adversary.

Seven thunders uttered their voices. Thunders are harbingers of coming storms. They are doubtless anticipative of the rapidly approaching day when the Lord will rise "to shake terribly the earth." There is probably an allusion here to Psalm 29, where "the God of glory thundereth" and where "the voice of the Lord" is heard seven times in acclamation of His power and majesty.

Verse 4. *And when the seven thunders had uttered their voices, I was about to write: and I heard a voice from heaven saying unto me, Seal up those things which the seven thunders uttered, and write them not.*

Seven thunders had uttered their voices. The voices proceeding from the thunders were more than mere reverberations, for they were expressed in words and hence the utterance of an intelligent personality. Probably they were the voice of the "God of glory."

I was about to write. It can be inferred from this incident that John was in the habit of writing his revelations as they appeared to him. In this case he was forbidden to write. It is folly for anyone to venture a guess as to the content of the words of the seven thunders. Since Christ was universally recognized as having the right or worth to deal with things sealed (5:2-9), He as God is probably the voice which speaks from heaven.

Revelation 10:5, 6a	Daniel 12:7a
And the angel which I saw stand upon the sea and upon the earth lifted up his hand to heaven, and sware by him that liveth for ever and ever, who created heaven, and the things that therein are, and the earth, and the things that therein are, and the sea, and the things which are therein.	*And I heard the man clothed in linen, which was upon the waters of the river, when he held up his right hand and his left hand unto heaven, and sware by him that liveth for ever.*

Both the appeal and the substance of the oath in the two passages further establish the identity of the man clothed in linen and the strong angel. While there are variations in the way of additions and omissions, these can readily be accounted for by the change in circumstances. In the Daniel passage both hands were raised to heaven. In Revelation, one—and (as most texts read) apparently the right one; in the other he held the book.

The oath announces an important prophetic event. Since the time of fulfillment has drawn near, the appeal notably has increased in intensity and solemnity. *Stand upon the sea and upon the earth.* Standing upon the sea and upon the earth is evidently a symbolic gesture, signifying that He who commissioned the angel is the rightful owner and sovereign of sea and land, for He it is who created both, and all things which are therein. This claim to the rightful possession of earth and sea is presumably made at this time in anticipation and defiance of the avowed purpose of Satan to establish an infernal trinity with himself as absolute sovereign, a beast out of the sea as his visible representative, and a beast out of the earth as his prophet. The stage is being set for the really decisive battle of the world.

And sware by him. Here is another testimony that the angel is not Christ, for the appeal implies inferiority on the part of him who makes it. Christ, however, is eternal and Creator of all things; hence He could swear by no greater. Therefore the one making the oath cannot be Christ.

<table>
<tr><td>Revelation 10:6b, 7</td><td>Daniel 12:7b</td></tr>
</table>

Revelation 10:6b, 7	Daniel 12:7b
That there should be time no longer: but in the days of the voice of the seventh angel, when he shall begin to sound, the mystery of God should be finished, as he hath declared to his servants the prophets.	*That it shall be for a time, times, and an half; and when he shall have accomplished to scatter the power of the holy people, all these things shall be finished.*

Each passage should be read as a whole. It is important to keep in mind that this is the middle of the tribulation period and that the time of the end and the tribulation period are synchronous, both beginning and ending together, and that the length of the entire period is seven years.

Both passages are given under oath; hence their fulfillment is certain. The variations are mutually explanatory and their joint consideration is the best possible way of arriving at their meaning and import.

Time shall be no more. Thus begins the oath of the angel. The American Revised Version translates, *There shall be delay no longer.* Many commentators have followed suit. This, however, is interpretation, not translation. The original word *chronos* occurs over 60 times in the Old Testament and over 50 times in the New. This is its second last occurrence and nowhere else has it been translated *delay.* This alone is enough to reject the translation. Sound exegesis does not permit a change of meaning to a word that has been uniformly translated throughout the Scriptures.

The word *delay,* moreover, is misleading; for it implies that there has been delay. "Some men" may charge the Lord with delay or slackness. Matthew 24:48;

II Peter 3:9. Just as the first coming of Christ took place in the fullness of time (Galatians 4:4) and His death came at the appointed "hour," so the things of the end will come on schedule time and at the hour determined in God's fixed and unalterable program. In chapter 9 it was noted that even the four angels bound by the Euphrates are prepared to release the demonic agents which slay one third of men at the appointed hour and day and month and year.

As to the exact form and order of words there should be no difficulty, since five other passages occur in this same book precisely similar to these, except the subject of the sentence. In each there is the negative *no*, the verb *to be*, and the word *eti* translated *more*. Following the order in Greek note:

The sea is no more.—21:1.
The death shall be no more.—21:4.
Pain shall be no more.—21:4.
Curse shall be no more.—22:3.
Night shall be no more.—22:5.

Accordingly, so in this text: *Time shall be no more.*

There is an expletive in each occurrence and the noun, for emphasis, comes first.

The proposed translation *delay* is given, of course, to get rid of a difficulty; namely, that time evidently continues. Some writers, however, merely shift the difficulty to the following verse; others, to the sounding of the seventh trumpet (11:15-19), to which the verse refers. However, time still continues, even there. Indeed in the following chapter, mention is made of "a time, and times, and half a time" and later about a thousand years and even after that a little season (*chronos*). So the difficulty in the interpretation cannot be disposed of consistently by shifting it to the future.

The chronological perspective (by which is meant the point of view taken in the course of time) of the man clothed in linen and the strong angel are precisely identical, for they each speak of the prophetic outlook following the middle of the tribulation period. The man clothed in linen who replies to the query: "How long shall it be to the end of these wonders?" says under oath, "It shall be for a time, times, and an half," that is, three and a half years. The angel who speaks over two thousand years later under similar solemnity declares, *Time shall be no more.* That the former declaration accords with the prophetic picture given by John in the following chapters shows that John's declaration here must be viewed in the light of the declarations alluded to. The only way this is possible is to take the present passage in a proleptic sense, that is, John speaks of the future as though it were already present.

The word *chronos*, time, occurs but four times in the Book of Revelation as follows: The Lord gave the church in Thyatira "space [*chronos*] to repent . . . and she repented not" (2:21). To the souls that were slain under the altar who cried with a loud voice, "How long, O Lord, holy and true, dost thou not judge and avenge our blood on . . . [the earth dwellers]?" the answer was given that "they should rest yet for a little season [*chronos*], until their fellow-servants also and their brethren, that should be killed as they were, should be fulfilled" (6:10, 11). The oath of the angel, *time* [*chronos*] *shall be no more,* may be meant for assurance to these saints that during the days when the seventh trumpet sounds their prayers will be answered. The last occurrence is after the one thousand years when the devil must be loosed a little season (*chronos*). This can only be understood by recognizing that two ends are in view in prophetic literature.

The proleptic view is nothing new in the prophetic literature. Thus spoke Isaiah when he said, "Unto us a child is born, unto us a son is given." And since the record was made after the vision appeared, the future is even spoken of as already past. So the same prophet writes, "He was wounded for our transgressions, he was bruised for our iniquities."

This proleptic element appears also in passages of imminency so numerous in the New Testament, e.g., "The night is far spent, the day is at hand"; "yet a little while [Greek: how little, how little], and he that shall come will come, and will not tarry"; "the time is at hand"; "behold, I come quickly." A notable example occurred in Revelation 6: "The wrath of the Lamb . . . is come," and yet the wrath will not actually come until 19:11-21. More proleptic statements are soon to follow.

Note in the passage from Daniel that the words *accomplish* and *finish* are translations of the same Hebrew word *kalah.* It is variously translated: to make an end, to finish, to accomplish. Its first use is in Genesis 2:1, "Thus the heavens and the earth were finished." The noun is frequently translated full end and utter end. So Daniel 12:7 would read: *and when he shall have made an end of scattering the power of the holy people, all these things shall be finished.*

The subject of the action here described is undoubtedly the willful king of the preceding chapter. As many as 28 acts of his are traceable in that chapter. His last is that of planting the tabernacle of his palace between the seas (Mediterranean and Dead Sea) in the glorious holy mountain. This is otherwise expressed as setting up the abomination of desolation in the holy place. Daniel 9:27; 12:11; Matthew 24:15.

The "holy people" are evidently Israel. They and only they are thus named in the Old Testament Scriptures. Five times they are thus referred to in the Book of Deuteronomy (7:6; 14:2, 21; 26:19; 28:9), the last of which is conditioned upon obedience: "The Lord shall establish thee an holy people unto himself, as he hath sworn unto thee, if thou shalt keep the commandments of the Lord thy God, and walk in his ways."

Shortly after this gracious promise was given, the disobedience came and no more is Israel called an holy people until by way of prediction in the latter days when she will pass through the furnace of affliction. ". . . in their affliction [tribulation] they will seek me early" (Hosea 5:15). "Many shall be purified, and made white, and tried" (Daniel 12:10). They shall again be called "The holy people" (Isaiah 62:12).

The scattering of the holy people will be occasioned by the setting up of the abomination of desolation in the holy place. Our Lord Himself orders this flight to the mountains by those dwelling in Judea (Matthew 24:16), and its fulfillment is seen in Revelation 12:13-15 in the vision now being considered.

When the power of the holy people is thus broken, all these things will be finished. Their extremity will be God's opportunity. Thus sang Moses: "The Lord shall judge his people, and repent himself for his servants, when he seeth that their power is gone, and there is none shut up, or left" (Deuteronomy 32:36).

Along with favor for His people will come vengeance upon those who afflicted her: ". . . he will avenge the blood of his servants, and will render vengeance to his adversaries, and will be merciful unto his land, and to his people" (Deuteronomy 32:43). Thus significantly ends the swan song of Moses. But note more particularly, "[the willful king] shall come to his end, and none shall help him" (Daniel 11:45). He will prosper only "till the indignation be accomplished" (Daniel 11:36); "that determined [the indignation] shall be poured upon the desolate" (Daniel 9:27). The willful king is identical with the beast; hence the words: ". . . the beast was slain, and his body destroyed, and given to the burning flame" (Daniel 7:11).

The corresponding verse in Revelation does not need much comment, for the particulars pointed out will appear in detail in the succeeding chapters.

But in the days of the voice of the seventh angel. The initial word *but* (Greek: *alla*) has probably been the principal reason for giving *chronos* in the preceding verse the sense of *delay*, as though *but* were of necessity an adversative; thus giving the sense, There shall be no longer delay, but (that is, on the other hand) when the seventh angel sounds, the mystery of God will be finished. As stated before, this need not be the interpretation for exegetical reasons.

Dr. A. T. Robertson has shown, by numerous examples, that but (*alla*) is frequently confirmatory, continuative, or climactic. Anyone having an Englishman's Greek Concordance will find that it is translated *yea* 15 times. Luke 24:22; John 16:2; Romans 3:31; I Corinthians 4:3; II Corinthians 7:11 (six times); Galatians 4:17; Philippians 1:18; 2:17; 3:8; James 2:18. See also Luke 12:7; 16:21; 24:21; John 4:23; 8:26; II Corinthians 1:9.

[The editor has done a careful tracing of the use of the Greek *alla* in the Apostolic Fathers, Vols. I and II, and found a number of incidents where the sense is that of *in fact*. This is true especially where the second clause is an intensification of the first. It would appear that this is the case in Revelation 10:7.—J. O. Y.]

So in the present instance, if for *but*, yea, indeed, or that is to say, be understood, the supposed difficulty disappears, for then the sense is confirmatory of the preceding statement, *time shall be no more.* (Compare: Elijah being *about* to come—Matthew 11:14. He has not come yet; hence, shall come.)

When he shall begin to sound. The word *begin* is *mello* in the Greek. It occurs 110 times in the New Testament and is nowhere else translated as here, but usually by *shall* or *should.* The word by itself means "about to," but where used with an infinitive as here, it frequently denotes mere futurity and such is evidently the sense here or else (as Dr. Charles shows) the mystery of God would be finished *before* the angel sounds the trumpet. Hence the meaning is simply, when he shall sound. Cf. 1:19; 2:10; 3:16; 17:8.

The mystery of God should be finished. We may consistently translate the verb *is finished. In the days* denotes an undefined period of time. Either the seventh trumpet sounds at different intervals in time to come or the meaning is that the events included in one sounding cover a considerable period of time.

The Bible makes mention of mysteries in various aspects and relations. In each case, however, a revelation is made of things pertaining to God's great purpose in the world. No effort is made to exploit the secret counsels of God with a view to arouse curiosity or provoke fear. The creature is to be content with the divine dictum: "The secret things belong unto the Lord our God: but those things which are revealed belong unto us and to our children for ever . . ." (Deuteronomy 29:29).

When mention is made of a mystery, it is always in connection with its revelation; hence a mystery has come to mean something now revealed which had not been revealed before, and which could not have been known without such revelation. The mystery of God is a general term, signifying the sum total of all that it has pleased God to reveal to man concerning His counsel and purpose in the world. The seventh trumpet includes all that God purposes still to reveal, by which is meant not that the end has come when the trumpet sounds, but that the revelation of the mystery will then be concluded. *In the days of the voice of the seventh angel* may well signify that his voice may be heard repeatedly in the future unfolding of God's purpose as revealed in the little book.

As he hath declared to his servants the prophets. The original word for declare, *evangelize*, is significant in this connection. Literally it would read, *as he announced the good news to his servants the prophets.* Plainly the reference cannot be to the martyrdom of saints, not even to the judgments upon God's enemies, for God is "not willing that any should perish, but that all should come to repentance" (II Peter 3:9).

What, then, was the good news God announced to the prophets? And to which of the prophets came the good news? Some close their Bible with Jude, which speaks of apostasy and the coming of the Lord in judgment upon the ungodly—a dark picture indeed. Others would have us believe that nations, having learned the folly of war, will finally emerge from the present chaos and then, whether by the promotion of civic righteousness or world evangelism, human society will ultimately merge into the kingdom of righteousness and peace "when the whole wide world will be bound by golden chains about the feet of God." This is wishful thinking, for God did not speak thus to the prophets. Both views are contrary to what the Lord announced to the prophets and what the prophets committed to writing in the Scriptures.

As to the first view, the prophets are not thus minded, for they with one voice declare the final triumph of righteousness in the earth.

As to the second view, it is in error, for all the prophets bear testimony that the final triumph and glory will be preceded by tribulation and judgment, and that the golden age will be ushered in not by human agency but by divine interference: by the removal of the church to meet the Lord in the air; by sending judgments upon the earth through which the inhabitants of the world will learn righteousness; by the revelation of the Lord from heaven in flaming fire taking vengeance upon His enemies; by His session, when He is come, upon His throne, at which time He will judge the world in righteousness "and all the ends of the earth will remember and turn unto the Lord." This is the good news announced to His servants the prophets and this is the good news that comes from heaven when the seventh trumpet sounds. The kingdoms of this world are to become the kingdoms of our Lord and of His Christ. Observe that this news comes out of the heart of the tribulation period and not following an era of social evolution or world evangelism! Thus John's outlook accords with "all the prophets."

Verse 8. *And the voice which I heard from heaven spake unto me again, and said, Go and take the little book which is open in the hand of the angel which standeth upon the sea and upon the earth.*

And the voice. The voice is that of verse 4 which forbade John to write the things which the seven thunders uttered.

The little book . . . upon the sea and upon the earth. The angel still stands upon the sea and upon the earth. John is asked to go to him and take the little book. This shows clearly that John is now upon the earth.[24]

Since the next two verses closely resemble passages from Jeremiah and Ezekiel, as an aid to interpretation we will again present in parallel columns the related passages. Details of parallel passages do not always occur in the same order; those given in Jeremiah and Ezekiel are arranged in the order as given in Revelation.

Revelation 10:9-11	Ezekiel 2:9, 10; 3:1-4, 14	Jeremiah 15:16-18
(A book written within and on the backside. — 5:1.) *And I went unto the angel, and said unto him, Give me the little book. And he said unto me, Take it, and eat it up; and it shall make thy belly bitter, but it shall be in thy mouth sweet as honey. And I took the little book out of the angel's hand, and ate it up.*	*A roll of a book . . . written within and without.* *Moreover he said unto me, Son of man, . . . eat this roll. . . . So I opened my mouth, and he caused me to eat that roll. And he said unto me, . . . cause thy belly to eat. . . . Then did I eat it; and it was in my mouth as honey for sweetness.*	
		Thy words were found, and I did eat them; and thy word was unto me the joy and rejoicing of mine heart. . . .
. . . and as soon as I had eaten it, my belly was bitter.	*. . . I went in bitterness, in the heat of my spirit. . . . And there was written therein lamentations, and mourning, and woe.*	*. . . I sat alone because of thy hand: for thou hast filled me with indignation. Why is my pain perpetual . . . ?*
And he said unto me, Thou must prophesy again before many peoples, and nations, and tongues, and kings.	*And he said unto me, . . . go, get thee unto the house of Israel, and speak with my words unto them.*	

In each case mention is made of a book divinely inspired and miraculously bestowed, which formed the basis of prophetic testimony. The earliest of the books mentioned is that referred to by Jeremiah. His prophetic ministry began in the thirteenth year of Josiah's reign. In the eighteenth year of the same reign, Hilkiah the high priest "found the book of the law." Jeremiah undoubtedly refers to this book when he says, *Thy words were found, and I did eat them.*

The books mentioned in connection with the ministry of Ezekiel and that of John were unique in this that they both were written within and without. The same two prophets were commanded to eat the book. John testifies: *I took the . . . book . . . and ate it up.* He apparently did it voluntarily and without hesitation. Ezekiel, being more reluctant, declares: *I opened my mouth, and he caused me to eat,* i.e., He fed me—the Greek word used here, *psomidso,* means "to feed by putting little bits into the mouth as nurses do children." *Then,* he says, *did I eat it.* Evidently, this is of his own accord.

Note that both Ezekiel and John carry the physiological figure farther than the mere eating, for they speak of the belly (and Ezekiel adds the bowels) as the receptacle of the book. Jeremiah, however, who uttered his prophecy before Ezekiel, makes the figure clear, for he says the heart, which denotes the inner and spiritual nature of man, is the true receptacle of the word. This is similarly illustrated in other passages, e.g., "These words, which I command thee . . . shall be in thine heart" (Deuteronomy 6:6); "Thy word have I hid in mine heart" (Psalm 119:11). Eating God's Word signifies therefore to receive it and hide it in the heart by the act of one's will.

It shall make thy belly bitter, but it shall be in thy mouth sweet as honey. In his announcement to John with reference to the effect of the eating, the angel mentions the bitter before the sweet, probably so that the thought of agreeableness might linger with him and consequently the inducement to eat. The effect, however, was in the reverse order, as is also implied in the angel's statement. In the figure employed this is certainly in the realm of probability, for what is pleasant to the taste may be distressing in the process of digestion. The figure as applying to John may be understood without difficulty, for while he was doubtless delighted with the *fact* of a new revelation from the Lord, he nevertheless was distressed with the *nature* of that revelation. While he doubtless rejoiced in a measure at the revelation of the coming triumph and glory, yet he was saddened and grieved because preceding that glory were to occur the most terrible judgments and martyrdoms of all history.

The reader undoubtedly will share somewhat in this experience of John, for while he appreciates the blessing that comes to those who read, hear, and keep the prophecy of this book, it is nevertheless saddening to contemplate the awful calamities which are yet to come upon the unbelieving inhabitants of the earth.

Ezekiel, like John, testifies, *it was in my mouth as honey for sweetness.* While he does not mention any bitter aftereffect in this connection, he nevertheless declares, *there was written therein lamentations, and mourning, and woe.*

Jeremiah undoubtedly perused the newly found book with great avidity. Without command, as in the case of Ezekiel and John, he declares, *Thy words were found, and I did eat them.* His way of testifying to their sweetness is couched in his testimony, They were "the joy and rejoicing of mine heart"—the "bitterness" comes quickly.

Thou must prophesy again. Each of the three prophets was commissioned to declare the contents of the book to his people.

Jeremiah in one breath declares, *Thy words were . . . the joy and rejoicing of mine heart.* In the next he cries, *I sat alone because of thy hand* [his word of authority]: *for thou hast filled me with indignation.* Apparently Jeremiah reflects on what the book of the law, which he had just eaten, says regarding his people if they disobey. For example, see Leviticus 26:14-43; Deuteronomy 28:15-68. He realizes that he is commissioned to speak with God's words to his people, which includes the judgments and curses in case of disobedience. He is to be the bearer of God's indignation to Israel. He despairs, *Why is my pain perpetual, and my wound incurable, which refuseth to be healed* (15:18)?

To Ezekiel came the commission, *Go, get thee unto the house of Israel, and speak with my words unto them* (3:4). *But the house of Israel will not hearken unto thee; for they will not hearken unto me: for all the house of Israel are impudent and hardhearted* (3:7). *So the spirit lifted me up, and took me away, and I went in bitterness, in the heat of my spirit . . .* (3:14). The bitterness came with the commission to speak the words revealed to the *rebellious house* of Israel.

John apparently anticipated his commission, for the bitterness preceded it. To him comes now the word: *Thou must prophesy again before* [better, *concerning* —Greek: *epi*] *many peoples, and nations, and tongues, and kings* (Revelation 10:11). The word *again* is significant, for it implies that he had already prophesied and moreover that his prophetic messages include the content of the words of the little book.

The Episode of Measuring the Temple (11:1, 2)

Verse 1. *And there was given me a reed like unto a rod: and the angel stood, saying, Rise, and measure the temple of God, and the altar, and them that worship therein.*

A reed like . . . a rod. The reed is a species of cane. It thrives in abundance in the Jordan valley and grows as high as 20 feet. John the Baptist, preaching there, was unlike "a reed shaken with the wind" (Matthew 11:7). Lighter portions were used for writing pens (III John 13); the stronger for walking sticks (hence the word "cane"). Being both light in weight and durable, they served well as measuring rods. Cf. 21:15, 16.

And the angel stood, saying. Some manuscripts omit the words, *and the angel stood,* and most recent editors have done likewise. This, however, leaves the participle, *saying,* without any antecedent, so that some word like angel must be supplied, and since some authorities, such as the Armenian Version and Victorinus, in the earliest commentary on Revelation, contain the passage, there is a strong probability that it is genuine. [Though, as pointed out in 11:3, the message actually comes from either God or Christ.—J. O. Y.]

Rise, and measure the temple of God, and the altar, and them that worship therein. This is one of the few instances where the writer serves as one of the actors in the drama. 1:12; 5:4; 7:14; 10:9, 10; 11:1; 19:10; 22:8. It appears fitting that John, a human worshiper, should be chosen in this capacity when the place where men worship, the means of worship, and the worshipers themselves come thus prominently into view. The measuring is obviously performed in anticipation of the defilement and desolation about to be inflicted upon these sacred environments by the coming Antichrist. It is the Lord's formal claim to His right of ownership of the things measured. It is also a challenge to the effect that even though they may temporarily fall into the hands of the enemy, He will eventually make good the claim of His rightful possessing by the ejection and everlasting destruction of the vile and malicious intruder.

The Greek word used here for temple is *naos,* which includes only two compartments, the holy place and the most holy. The altar is therefore the altar of incense, for the brazen altar stood in the outer court.

The worshipers are undoubtedly pious Israelites and it is probable that they turned to the Lord through the testimony of the two witnesses.

Some have spiritualized the temple, overlooking the fact that a literal temple at Jerusalem during the tribulation period is required by the sure word of prophecy.

The testimony of Daniel: "In the midst of the week [the seven years of tribulation] he shall cause the sacrifice and the oblation to cease, and for the overspreading of abominations he shall make it desolate" (9:27). The mention of sacrifice and oblation presupposes the existence of everything mentioned in Revelation 11:1 —the temple, an altar, and worshipers.

The testimony of Jesus: In the Olivet discourse, He speaks of the abomination of desolation, spoken of by Daniel the prophet as standing in the holy place. Matthew 24:15. The Lord thus endorses the prophecy of Daniel and vouches for the certainty of its fulfillment by His own testimony. That the reference is to the very period of time now being considered is plain, for He declares further, "for then shall be great tribulation" (Matthew 24:21).

The testimony of Paul: In his second letter to the Thessalonians the apostle reveals that the man of sin "sitteth in the temple [*naos*] of God, shewing himself that he is God" (2:4). The time indicated accords precisely with that of Revelation, for this profaning of the temple takes place between "our gathering together unto him" (II Thessalonians 2:1) (an allusion to the rapture—I Thessalonians 4) and the destruction of the man of sin "with the brightness of his coming" (II Thessalonians 2:8).

Verse 2. *But the court which is without the temple leave out, and measure it not; for it is given unto the Gentiles: and the holy city shall they tread under foot forty and two months.*

The court. The court with its "buildings" (Matthew 24:1) surrounded the temple (*naos*). Together they formed the *hieron.* It is unfortunate that one word in English (temple) is used to translate the two Greek words. The Gentiles were permitted to worship in the *hieron,* which included the court. Compare the words of Jesus, "My house shall be called the house of prayer; but ye [the money-changers] have made it a den of thieves" (Matthew 21:13). It is important to observe that Jesus called the *hieron*, "my house." As a matter of fact, neither He nor any of the apostles ever were in the *naos* either before or after His death and resurrection. Indeed, the only person spoken of in the Gospels or Acts as having been in the *naos* is Zacharias while ministering in the priest's office. Luke 1. The only possible exception is Judas when he flung the 30 pieces of silver into the *naos* and then departed and went and hanged himself. Matthew 27:5.

Measure it not. John was commanded not to measure the court but to cast it out, without (so the Greek), for it is given to the Gentiles. The language implies the utter rejection of the court and its purposeful abandonment to the Gentiles. This appears all the more remarkable when one recalls that this is the only part of the *hieron* that Jesus ever entered during His earthly career. Here He was presented as a babe (Luke 2:27); here He sat in the midst of the doctors as a youth (Luke 2:46); here He healed the blind and the lame (Matthew 21:14); and during the last period of His public ministry, in a final effort to win the Jewish leaders, He taught daily in the temple (Matthew 26:55), and preached the Gospel (Luke 20:1). Instead of accepting His doctrine, the scribes and chief priests sought how they might destroy Him. Mark 11:18. In the reaction of Jesus after His final rejection by the Jewish leaders there lies the key to the proper understanding of the opening verses of Revelation 11. He commits Himself decisively and pungently on three points of great significance.

In reference to His people, the Jews, as represented by their leaders, the scribes and Pharisees, His attitude is one of denunciation for their hypocrisy, blindness, and chicanery and a pronouncement upon them of the most terrible woes that ever yet fell upon mortal man. Matthew 23:1-35. He made the positive declaration, "Ye shall not see me henceforth, till ye shall say, Blessed is he that cometh in the name of the Lord" (Matthew 23:39). The allusion is plainly to the testimony of the multitude at the triumphal entry (21:9), yet Jesus will continue until they will receive Him and bear a like testimony at His second coming.

In reference to the temple, immediately after His triumphal entry, He purified it and declared to the money-changers, "My house shall be called the house of prayer; but ye have made it a den of thieves" (Matthew 21:13). Now He declares, ". . . your house is left unto you desolate. For I say unto you, Ye shall not see me henceforth, till ye shall say, Blessed is he that cometh in the name of the Lord" (Matthew 23:38, 39). That temple is to be left desolate until the coming of the Lord in glory.

In reference to the city, Jesus wept over it twice. "And when he was come near, he beheld the city, and wept over it, saying, If thou hadst known, even thou, at least in this thy day, the things which belong unto thy peace! but now they are hid from thine eyes. For the days shall come upon thee, that thine enemies shall cast a trench about thee, and compass thee round, and keep thee in on every side, and shall lay thee even with the ground, and thy children within thee; and they shall not leave in thee one stone upon another; because thou knewest not the time of thy visitation" (Luke 19:41-44). In 21:20-24, Luke gives further particulars about the "desolation" (fulfilled by the Romans in A.D. 70) and then continues:

"And they [inhabitants of Jerusalem] shall fall by the edge of the sword, and shall be led away captive into all nations [the present dispersion]: and Jerusalem shall be trodden down of the Gentiles, until the times of the Gentiles be fulfilled."

"O Jerusalem, Jerusalem, thou that killest the prophets, and stonest them which are sent unto thee, how often would I have gathered thy children together, even as a hen gathereth her chickens under her wings, and ye would not" (Matthew 23:37)!

In the Matthew passage Christ refers to the wickedness and obduracy of the inhabitants of the city; in the Luke passage, to the desolation coming upon the city as a consequence of apostasy.

[This analogy of Scripture should clearly show that Revelation 11 is the fulfillment of the words of Jesus. One can readily see that there is an eschatological goal in the Scripture.—J. O. Y.]

To return to Revelation 11 several questions may be raised: Why was not the temple miraculously preserved from defilement, seeing it was measured in accordance with divine direction? The building of the temple was premature and without divine direction and authorization. It was built with the approval of and in covenant relationship with the Antichrist in the beginning of the seventieth week of Daniel, that is, the beginning of the tribulation period. Cf. Daniel 9:27. The prophet Isaiah with prophetic foresight speaks of this unholy covenant as "a covenant with death, and with hell," and forewarns: "your covenant with death shall be disannulled, and your agreement with hell shall not stand; when the overflowing scourge shall pass through [the destructive forces of the Antichrist], then ye shall be trodden down by it" (Isaiah 28:15a, 18). This is exactly what will take place as depicted in the Book of Revelation.

When the tabernacle in the wilderness and Solomon's temple were finished, the glory of the Lord filled each. This was a visible token of the divine approval and acceptance. When Israel forsook the Lord, the glory of the Lord departed from the temple, as Ezekiel has so vividly and pathetically described. 8:4; 9:3; 10:4, 18, 19; 11:22-24. Since the days of Hosea, Israel has been *Lo-ammi*, i.e., "not my people," and this is sufficient to account for the fact that since that time the glory of the Lord has not filled any of the temples built. Even that of Zerubbabel was not visited by any visible manifestation of God's favor and acceptance; besides, it lacked the ark of the covenant and the cherubim. Accordingly the prophet Haggai raised the question, "Is it not in your eyes in comparison of it [the former temple] as nothing" (Haggai 2:3b)? However, God has repeatedly declared His purpose to dwell in the midst of His people. The dwelling on earth with its holy place and most holy was a copy of the heavenly. Seven times the Scriptures repeat with slight variations the high significance of this earthly house: "And look that thou make . . . [it] after . . . [the] pattern, which was shewed thee in the mount" (Exodus 25:40). The conception and plan is of this sacred enclosure and He will not give His glory to another. Moreover, the Scriptures plainly declare that He will make good His claim: ". . . in the place where it was said unto them [Israel], Ye are not my people, there it shall be said unto them, Ye are the sons of the living God" (Hosea 1:10). This accords with Jesus' words, "Your house is left unto you desolate . . . till ye shall say, Blessed is he that cometh in the name of the Lord" (Matthew 23:38, 39). When Israel turns to the Lord, He will make good His claim to an earthly sanctuary with its holy place and holy of holies.

Note the testimony of Ezekiel. He relates the account of the future restoration of Israel, chapters 36–39, and the outpouring of His Spirit upon them. He goes on to describe the spacious dimensions of the future temple and then he comes to the grand finale: "Behold, the glory of the God of Israel came from the way of the east: and his voice was like a noise of many waters: and the earth shined with his glory. . . . And, behold, the glory of the Lord filled the house" (43:2, 5).

Why was the court cast out and given to the Gentiles? The time of special favor to the Gentiles is past, for "the fulness of the Gentiles . . . [has] come in" at this time, that is, at the end of the church age. The tribulation period is identical with the seventieth week in Daniel and this period has been determined for Daniel's people (Israel). Daniel 9:24.

The Gentiles refused to receive the love of the truth, hence "God shall send them strong delusion, that they should believe *the* lie" (II Thessalonians 2:11) [the Greek text has the definite article—J. O. Y.], by which is meant the lie that Antichrist foists upon his dupes when he deifies himself in the temple of God. "And all that dwell upon the earth shall worship him, whose names are not written in the book of life" (Revelation 13:8).

Given unto the Gentiles. While the judicial blindness has at this time been removed from Israel, they are so wedded to forms and ceremonies that they fail to turn to the Lord until after these have been destroyed. Being no longer a blessing, the Gentiles now become Israel's scourge in God's hands, for He has foretold that only "in their affliction they will seek me early" (Hosea 5:15).

Tread under foot. The treading underfoot is to continue for forty-two months. This is the first time note occurring in the book which shows that this is the middle of the tribulation period. This accords with the sure word of prophecy as uttered by the Lord after His rejection by the Jews: "Jerusalem shall be trodden down by [Greek] the Gentiles, until the times of the Gentiles be fulfilled" (Luke 21:24). (It should be remembered that by Gentiles, the nations are meant.) That the times of the nations continue until the end of the tribulation period is evidenced in the succeeding chapters.

The holy city. Why should Jerusalem be called the *holy city,* seeing it has been "given unto the Gentiles" ever since it was taken by Nebuchadnezzar? II Kings 24; II Chronicles 36. The title occurs ten times in the Bible—five times in the Old Testament (Nehemiah 11:1, 18; Isaiah 48:2; 52:1; Daniel 9:24) and five times in the New (Matthew 4:5; 27:53; Revelation 11:2; 21:2; 22:19). It is significant that all these passages (with the exception of the last two, which refer to the eternal city) allude to the city during its occupation by the Gentiles. Plainly, therefore, the epithet "holy" is not descriptive of the city during "the times of the Gentiles." An examination of the Scriptures which tell of the origin, history, and destiny of the city would make it clear why it is called the *holy* city. It is impossible here to make an exhaustive study of all related passages.[25]

[The Scriptures upon many occasions indicate that objects, places, and persons are declared holy because of their associations with God. Whom or what God chooses He makes holy by His indwelling presence.—J. O. Y.]

The Episode of the Two Witnesses (11:3-14)

Verse 3. *And I will give power unto my two witnesses, and they shall prophesy a thousand two hundred and threescore days, clothed in sackcloth.*

I will give power. The speaker is probably the same as the voice from heaven. Chapter 10:4, 8. Whenever words are quoted as coming directly from the author of the book (either God or Christ) as in this instance, they should always be regarded as of special importance. This mode of communication should not be regarded, however, as being independent of the mediating agency (by His angel) as expressed in 1:1 and 22:6, 16.

The word *power* (as the italics show) is not in the original, but the sequel, *and they shall prophesy,* is evidently a purpose clause. The giving therefore is in reference to the prophesying. The word *power* is seldom used with *give* in the New Testament. One may think of such passages as "all power is given unto me" (Matthew 28:18); they worshiped the dragon which gave power unto the beast (Revelation 13:4, 5); "power was given him over all kindreds" (Revelation 13:7); but in all these cases the original word is *authority.* The thought here may be well expressed in either of the following ways: *I will give authority . . . and they shall prophesy,* or *I will give authority . . . to prophesy,* or *I will commission . . . to prophesy.* The prophesying apparently is to be understood in a predictive sense.

My two witnesses. The Greek has the definite article: *the two witnesses of mine.* This implies that the persons alluded to are familiar to Bible readers. Earmarks of identity will appear presently.

A thousand two hundred and threescore days. The duration of the prophecy is identical with that of the treading underfoot. A prophetic month (of 30 days) is undoubtedly meant; hence 42 months equals 1,260 days. Attention will be given later as to whether or not the witness is to be understood as occurring during the first or the latter half of the tribulation period.

Clothed in sackcloth. The clothing in sackcloth suggests that the witnessing includes the preaching of repentance. Cf. Isaiah 37:1, 2; Daniel 9:3-5.

Verse 4. *These are the two olive trees, and the two candlesticks standing before the God of the earth.*

The two olive trees. The two witnesses are anointed by the Lord as prophets for this particular time. The figure is brought over from Zechariah 4:3. These are explained there as "the two anointed ones" (Zechariah 4:14).

The two candlesticks. The imagery likewise alludes to Zechariah (4:2), although in that instance there was only one candlestick. Candlesticks are light bearers and this was the mission of these two witnesses in this dark period.

Standing before the God of the earth. The reference is to Zechariah 4:14, where the anointed ones are to "stand by the Lord of the whole earth." The textual evidence, including that of the church fathers, is strongly in favor of the reading, *Lord of the earth.*

It is significant that after Israel went into captivity, and the glory of the Lord departed from between the cherubim, and the Lord no longer dwelt in the midst of Israel, the title "God of heaven" occurs so prominently in the books describing that period. It is found fourteen times in Ezra and Nehemiah, five times in Daniel, and once each, "the Lord of heaven" and "the King of heaven," in Daniel. Now when He is about to make good His claim to His rightful sovereignty over the earth as well as over Israel, He again assumes His title as *Lord of the earth.*

Observe again that to stand *before the Lord* denotes service or worship, thus implying inferiority in rank or station. It is never used in reference to Christ or the Holy Spirit. Here it signifies readiness to serve the Lord of the earth.

Verse 5. *And if any man will hurt them, fire proceedeth out of their mouth, and devoureth their enemies: and if any man will hurt them, he must in this manner be killed.*

Any man will [Greek: *any one willeth to*]. As the Greek shows, if anyone merely has the desire to injure the witnesses, he (or any number harboring the evil thought) will be destroyed by fire issuing from their mouth.

The law "of old time," "An eye for an eye, and a tooth for a tooth," is again in vogue even as pertaining to God's witnesses, thus showing clearly that retribution is again based on Jewish law, and that the church age is over. This destroying of the lives of enemies is not merely a prerogative of these human witnesses, for they are divinely commissioned and act with divine order and approval. Contrast this with Jesus' declaration during His earthly career: "The Son of man is not come to destroy men's lives, but to save them" (Luke 9:56).

Must in this manner be killed. That is "by fire." Thus were the enemies of Moses consumed (Numbers 16:35); and later those of Elijah (II Kings 1:10, 12). In the same manner, too, will the beast from the bottomless pit, who kills the two witnesses, meet his doom, for he will be cast alive into the lake of fire. Revelation 19:20.

Verse 6. *These have power to shut heaven, that it rain not in the days of their prophecy: and have power over waters to turn them to blood, and to smite the earth with all plagues, as often as they will.*

These have power (better would be authority) to consume their enemies by fire; to shut up heaven that it rain not; to turn water into blood; to smite the earth with plagues.

Putting these now in the form of questions, even a young pupil in a Sunday school would be able to answer promptly in each case to whom reference is made. Who commanded fire to consume his enemies? Elijah. Who shut up heaven that it did not rain? Elijah. Who turned water into blood? Moses. Who smote the earth with plagues? Moses.

Here are two earmarks pertaining to Elijah and two to Moses. The Scriptures identifying them are: II Kings 1:10, 12 (cf. Luke 9:54); I Kings 17:1; 18:41-45 (cf. James 5:17, 18) for Elijah; and Exodus 7:20; 8:1—12:29 for Moses. All we need, as "children of a larger growth," is the faith of a child to accept these inspired hints of identification at their face value and it will be clear that Moses and Elijah are intended. Furthermore, it is highly significant that the names of Moses and

Elijah are brought together with such prominence in the closing verses of the Old Testament: "Remember ye the law of Moses my servant. . . . Behold, I will send you Elijah the prophet . . ." (Malachi 4:4, 5).

(The reappearance of the two on the Mount of Transfiguration with Christ [Matthew 17:3; Mark 9:4; Luke 9:30], and since they spoke of His decease [*exodus, departure*] which He should accomplish at Jerusalem [Luke 9:31], it is probable that they are the two men who appeared in white apparel on the Mount of Olives when Jesus ascended to heaven. Acts 1:10.)

Commanding of fire upon enemies and shutting up heaven that it rain not apply to Elijah alone, and as far as the record is concerned the turning of water into blood and smiting the earth with plagues apply only to Moses.[26]

Verse 7. And when they shall have finished their testimony, the beast that ascendeth out of the bottomless pit shall make war against them, and shall overcome them, and kill them.

When they shall have finished their testimony. On this clause, Dr. Seiss beautifully remarks, "These witnesses are immortal till their work is done."[27] This is fine rhetoric but poor theology, for immortality does not come to the body until after death. Not until the resurrection will mortality put on immortality. I Corinthians 15:53, 54. What is intended undoubtedly is that these witnesses serving faithfully under the will and purpose of God will live until their work is done.

The beast that ascendeth out of the bottomless pit. This is the first of 36 references to the final Antichrist under the title *beast.* Care should be taken to maintain the distinction between the beast (*therion*) and one or more of the four beasts or living creatures (*dzoon*) of chapter 4:6-9. *Therion* (which signifies a wild beast) is used in 6:8 in a literal sense. As applied to the Antichrist it denotes his beastlike character.

The word, although occurring here for the first time in reference to the Antichrist, has the definite article. In its second occurrence, 13:1, it is anarthrous (without the article). This is a very unusual exception to the rule, but it is highly significant and indicates that the beast rises out of the sea before he comes out of the bottomless pit; in other words, the passage in 13:1 antedates this passage. [This has reference to what Smith believed to be a necessary conclusion to the understanding of the book. He was confident that the recording of the events and predictions was not in a chronological order.—J. O. Y.] In 17:8 mention is made again of the ascending of the beast from the bottomless pit. As this evidently occurs only once, that verse must synchronize with this passage. In chapter 13:3, 14 there is an allusion to the same event, only there the beast is spoken of as having been wounded to death and living again. From 13:5 and 17:10 one may conclude that the beast will continue 42 months after he has come from the bottomless pit. Further consideration of the beast will be left until chapter 13.

And kill them. When are the witnesses slain? In the middle or at the end of the tribulation period? Hippolytus' testimony favors the first half. ". . . when Daniel said, 'I shall make my covenant for one week,' he indicated seven years; and the one half of the week is for the preaching of the prophets, and for the other half of the week . . . Antichrist will reign upon the earth."[28]

"As also it was announced to Daniel: 'And one week shall confirm a covenant with many; and in the midst of the week it shall be that the sacrifice and oblation shall be removed'—that the one week might be shown to be divided into two. The two witnesses, then, shall preach three years and a half; and Antichrist shall make war upon the saints during the rest of the week. . . .'"[29]

The evidence is conclusive that the period of their testimony will be during the first half of this period, as the following particulars indicate: The Prince of the Romans will make a covenant with Israel in the beginning of the period (Daniel 9:26, 27), thus making it possible for Jewish leaders to exercise themselves in their religious activities in Jerusalem. The 144,000 Israelites were providentially protected during the first half of the period and they were not slain until after the beast had come out of the pit. Revelation 7 and 14. The prayer of the martyred saints (6:9, 10) suggests that there were Israelites among them. They bore testimony to the word of God for a season, but power was not given them, as was the case with Moses and Elijah, to consume their enemies with fire; hence they were slain for the word of God and the testimony they held. Apparently there is no interference with the religious activities in Jerusalem until the middle of the tribulation when the daily sacrifice will be taken away and the abomination of desolation set up in the holy place. Daniel 12:11; Matthew 24:15.

That the beast comes out of the bottomless pit in the middle of this period is plain from the fact that power will be given him "to make war with the saints, and to overcome them" and *to continue forty and two months* (13:5, 7). This was before the image worship was instituted (13:15) and, undoubtedly, the two witnesses, now that their witness (testimony) was finished, are the first victims, for as 11:7 says, [he] *shall make war against them, and shall overcome them, and kill them.* ". . . they are reserved for the suffering of death, that by their blood they may extinguish Antichrist."[30]

". . . 'I will give to my two witnesses, and they shall predict a thousand two hundred and threescore days clothed in sackcloth.' That is, three years and six months: these make forty-two months. Therefore their preaching is three years and six months, and the kingdom of Antichrist as much again."[31]

"This is the beginning of Antichrist [12:7-9]; yet previously Elias must prophesy, and there must be times of peace. And afterwards, when the three years and six months are completed in the preaching of Elias, he also must be cast down from heaven, where up till that time he had had the power of ascending; and all the apostate angels, as well as Antichrist, must be roused up from hell."[32]

Why do they not prophesy during the second half of the tribulation?

The place of their witness is "in the street" of Jerusalem. Since the city is trodden underfoot of the Gentiles during the second half of the period, it will be altogether impossible for them to witness at that time.

Those that dwell in Judea are commanded to flee to the mountains when the abomination of desolation is set up in the holy place. Matthew 24:15. In Revelation 12:6, 14 the woman (Israel) is said to flee to a place of safety prepared of God, thus indicating that no witness is continued in Jerusalem.

The witnesses prophesy during half of the period, or for 1,260 days, thus showing that there is no interference with or cessation of their testimony during the entire period of their life, which would be impossible during the latter half of the seven years.

There is no indication in the succeeding chapters that any open witness continues on earth during the latter half. Moreover, the martyrs are slain during this time, not for witnessing to the word of God, but because they refuse to take the mark of the beast or worship his image. 15:2. Were the witnesses to prophesy the latter half, their death would be simultaneous with that of the beast. 19:20. This reduces the argument to an absurdity.

Verse 8. *And their dead bodies shall lie in the street of the great city, which spiritually is called Sodom and Egypt, where also our Lord was crucified.*

Their dead bodies. It is indeed remarkable that Moses and Elijah, who had the power to destroy their enemies by fire, should themselves be killed by the beast from the bottomless pit. This can only be possible—

because he was supernaturally empowered by the dragon (13:4);

because their testimony was finished;

by the permissive will of God.

[And may this not also indicate why "all the world wondered after the beast" who had such power? Revelation 13:3.—J. O. Y.]

The great city. The phrase occurs ten times in Revelation. 11:8; 14:8; 16:19; 17:18; 18:10, 16, 18, 19, 21; 21:10. Some authorities maintain that the reference is solely to Babylon (Rome). This plainly is not the case in the last reference (21:10), for it is designated "the holy Jerusalem" immediately following. Fortunately the term is followed by an earmark which shows what city is meant, viz., *where also our Lord was crucified.* To anyone who takes the words seriously there can be but one answer—Jerusalem. The word *also* emphasizes the fact that the witnesses were slain in the same city where Jesus was crucified. The Lord has His *great city* just as well as Satan. The Lord's great city is Jerusalem; that of Satan, Babylon. These two cities are each located at the Mediterranean (middle of the earth) and they will finally come to fateful conflict. The issue is apparent, for after the great city Babylon sinks forever into the yawning gulf of anguish and despair, the great city, the new Jerusalem, will descend out of heaven from God, having the glory of God. Some have declined to accept the view that the great city is Jerusalem on the ground that the epithet *great* is never applied to Jerusalem. However, it is so designated in other Scriptures. Nehemiah 7:4; Jeremiah 22:8; Lamentations 1:1. Besides, the title was applied to the city both in apocalyptic and in profane literature of that day.

Jerusalem will be completely under the control and domination of Antichrist and his evil associates. The temple will be defiled through the abomination of desolation standing in the holy place. The city will be laid desolate by the ravages of the Gentile hordes. For these reasons the derogatory synonyms are applied to it—Sodom and Egypt. Isaiah in his day already alluded to Jerusalem as Sodom (1:10), for her sins were like those of the doomed city—"How is the faithful city become an harlot! it was full of judgment; righteousness lodged in it; but now murderers" (Isaiah 1:21). No words could describe more truly the state of the *holy city* after she fell into the hands of the Gentiles. Like Egypt, where idolatry prevailed, so Jerusalem will be the seat of idol worship, for the abomination (the image of the Antichrist which all men will be required to worship) will stand in the holy place. Also like Egyptian days, Israel, God's chosen people, will be sorely oppressed.

Verse 9. *And they of the people and kindreds and tongues and nations shall see their dead bodies three days and an half, and shall not suffer their dead bodies to be put in graves.*

People and kindreds and tongues and nations. This is the fourth of six terms used (with slight variations) in the book to denote the sum total of humanity dwelling upon the earth. As noticed before, they never appear in the same order, signifying apparently the confusion and disorder prevailing in the world system at this time. Burial of the dead bodies is not permitted apparently in order to prolong the period of shame and ridicule heaped upon them by their hilarious spectators.

[*Shall see their dead bodies.* It is of some import to note in the Greek that the verb stands first in the sentence immediately following the conjunction, which lends emphasis to the thought of the verb. The earlier expositors no doubt found it difficult to interpret the *see*, except as it related to the dwellers at Jerusalem. However, within the fourth decade of the twentieth century the introduction of television makes the literal truth of the verb *see* entirely possible. One may understand the thought in this way, or else the preposition *ek*, out from, may have reference to the cosmopolitan character of the inhabitants of Jerusalem. In which case one would understand the syntax of the Greek to be the partitive use of the genitive case. Thus the sentence would read, *And they out of the peoples, and kindreds, and tongues, and nations* [which dwell in Jerusalem] *shall see their corpses.* . . . Either interpretation is sound exegesis. (There is some textual evidence for the present tense of the verb *see*. However, there is a classification of the present known to grammarians as the futuristic present, where a future act is referred to in the present for the graphic effect, so that the textual variant has no bearing on the interpretation.)—J. O. Y.]

Verse 10. *And they that dwell upon the earth shall rejoice over them, and make merry, and shall send gifts one to another; because these two prophets tormented them that dwelt on the earth.*

They that dwell upon the earth. This is the fourth of the thirteen occurrences of the earth dwellers. They consist of a distinct class who mind earthly things and who have hardened themselves against all spiritual impressions. There is no hint that any of them repented of their sins because of the witnessing of the two. The context shows that they are in complete agreement with the persecuting program of the beast (Antichrist).

Shall rejoice . . . make merry . . . send gifts. This is the only mention of rejoicing upon earth during the tribulation period. Notice that this rejoicing is over the death of God's two witnesses! Any who would rejoice over the cessation of divine witnesses undoubtedly belong to that group of which Paul wrote in II Thessalonians 2:10, 11, ". . . they received not the love of the truth, that they might be saved. And for this cause God shall send them strong delusion, that they should believe a [Greek: *the*] lie."

The death of the two witnesses is to the earth dwellers a veritable holiday, for they *make merry* and *send gifts one to another.* They congratulate themselves because the torment inflicted upon them by the two witnesses is now a thing of the past, but they are blind to the fact that a greater torment is awaiting them, for immediately following the words just quoted from II Thessalonians the apostle announces their doom: "That they all might be damned who believed not the truth, but had pleasure in unrighteousness" (II Thessalonians 2:12).

Verse 11. *And after three days and an half the spirit of life from God entered into them, and they stood upon their feet; and great fear fell upon them which saw them.*

Three days and an half. Apparently the time period, three days and a half, is mentioned to indicate that the bodies of the witnesses did "not see corruption."

Great fear fell. Their restoration to life was abundant proof to the merry-makers that a greater than the beast has undertaken in their behalf, for now great fear fell upon the bewildered spectators.

Verse 12. *And they heard a great voice from heaven saying unto them, Come up hither. And they ascended up to heaven in a cloud; and their enemies beheld them.*

A great voice. The loud voice is probably that of Christ because the words uttered are identical with those of 4:1. It may be that these same words of welcome will be heard by the dead in Christ when He descends from heaven with a shout. I Thessalonians 4:16.

Note again that this is not depicting the church age. Only the wicked are mentioned as having joy on earth during the entire tribulation period. Chapters 6—18. The wicked will see the righteous ascend to heaven in a cloud, while the rapture will occur in a moment, in the twinkling of an eye, and undoubtedly (like Enoch in type) believers will not be "found," for God "took" them. [So this can hardly be a type of the rapture.—J. O. Y.]

Verse 13. *And the same hour was there a great earthquake, and the tenth part of the city fell, and in the earthquake were slain of men seven thousand: and the remnant were affrighted, and gave glory to the God of heaven.*

A great earthquake. Earthquakes are mentioned on five different occasions, each of which occurs in connection with either the sixth or seventh series of judgments. The first (6:12), the second (11:13), and the third (16:18) are said to be *great,* with *mighty* added in the last instance. Those occurring in the seventh of each series are preceded by voices and thunders and lightnings. Thus they appear to be the climax in each series of judgments. They are the ominous mutterings of mother earth at the ill behavior of her children. When mankind did their worst, the earth quaked and the rocks were rent. Matthew 27:51, 54.[33]

The remnant were affrighted (lit., *became fearful*). The expression occurs five times in the New Testament. It is said before of the women when they entered the sepulcher (Luke 24:5), of the disciples when Jesus stood in their midst (Luke 24:37), of Cornelius when the angel appeared unto him (Acts 10:4), of those accompanying Saul when they heard the voice from heaven (Acts 22:9), of Felix when Paul reasoned with him (Acts 24:25).

By the remnant is meant those that were not slain by the earthquake. From the context it is impossible to determine whether they were moved with reverential fear or whether it was merely fright that is common to man when the earth quakes. The next clause, however, *gave glory to the God of heaven,* would seem to indicate that the fear led to their salvation. This view is supported by a few other passages. An angel is said to preach the everlasting Gospel; his message is, "Fear God, and give glory to him; for the hour of his judgment is come: and worship him . . ." (Revelation 14:6, 7). Later (16:9), when the fourth vial is poured out, it is said, "men . . . repented not to give . . . [God] glory." This passage implies that repentance must necessarily precede giving glory to God. In the Revelation 11 passage there is the positive declaration that the remnant gave glory to God. Note that it is not an utterance to that effect by the remnant as though they were proclaiming the words, "Glory to God," in which case there might be insincerity or mere formality, but the inspired writer testifies that they *gave glory to . . . God.* It therefore must have been a true expression of the heart and acceptable to Him who received it.

Observe also that in the Revelation 14 passage it is implied that to fear God and give glory to Him is receiving salvation since the angel is said to have preached the Gospel in those words. It is again evident that this is no longer in the church age, for not only is the Gospel message different but the motive for receiving it, *for the hour of his judgment is come,* is different as well. It is, however, entirely in harmony with the prophetic message of Isaiah, ". . . when thy judgments are in the earth, the inhabitants of the world will learn righteousness" (Isaiah 26:9).

Men seven thousand. It is very probable that the inhabitants of the city are Israelites who did not make their escape before the arrival of the beast.

The God of heaven. The phrase occurs 20 times in the Old Testament, yet only here and in 16:11 in the New Testament. The first mention is in Genesis 24:3, 7, where Abraham made his servant swear by the God of heaven that he would go to the land of his fathers to secure a bride for Isaac.

Later God dwelt among the children of Israel, between the cherubim, first of the tabernacle (Exodus 25:22; 1 Samuel 4:4), then of the temple (I Chronicles 13:6; II Kings 19:15). When Israel forsook the Lord, His presence and glory departed from the temple. Ezekiel 11:23, 24. After the plunder of the temple by Nebuchadnezzar and the captivity of Israel frequent mention is made of the *God of heaven.* He is then an absentee God. The title occurs nine times in Ezra and four times in Nehemiah. For a brief period God dwelt (tabernacled) among men in the person of Jesus Christ. He was Emmanuel—God with us. But as long as the time of the Gentiles (nations) continues (from Nebuchadnezzar to Armageddon), He continues as the God of heaven. To the child of God He is the *Father* in heaven, it is true, but not present upon the earth. Much less will He be here in person during the tribulation period. On the other hand, Satan the antigod will make his dwelling place here for a brief period. Not until after the Lord has reigned a thousand years and put all His enemies under His feet will God Himself return to the earth. But this final return of God Himself to the earth is as certain as the sure word of prophecy. Revelation 21:3.

Verse 14. *The second woe is past; and, behold, the third woe cometh quickly.*

In 8:13, at the close of the fourth trumpet, mention is made of three woes that are to come upon the inhabitants of the earth. The reference is to the three trumpets that were yet to sound. Consequently, the fifth trumpet was the first woe (9:1-12); the sixth, the second woe (9:13—11:14). The seventh trumpet, that is, the third woe, begins with the following verse and, as 10:7 stated, in it the mystery of God is finished. The words apparently point forward to the declaration in chapter 21:6a, "It is done."

The Seventh Trumpet (11:15-19)

Verse 15. *And the seventh angel sounded; and there were great voices in heaven, saying, The kingdoms of this world are become the kingdoms of our Lord, and of his Christ; and he shall reign for ever and ever.*

Keep in mind what was said in 10:7 regarding this passage, "In the days of the seventh angel, when he shall sound, the mystery of God is finished [Greek]." As stated before, this implies that the period covered by the seventh trumpet will take history to the end of the revelation of God's wrath (16:17), and of the revelation of His glory (21:6). In each instance there is the final declaration, "It is done."

Great voices. This is the tenth of the 21 occurrences of *loud* [Greek] *voices.* Note, here is the plural, *voices*—the only passage where this is the case. However, it does not denote that they come from the largest number, for not all the occupants of heaven are included, as the following verse shows. In 7:12, where many millions are engaged in praise, the singular is used. Neither does it signify different kinds of voices, for in 14:2a, where these occur, the singular occurs also. Since the present trumpet sounds for days, the plural probably suggests the continuation of the voices.

It is possible that the loud voices come from those of the great multitude mentioned in 7:9, 10. The elders follow; so this is all of the glorified groups as in 19:1 and 20:4. A careful examination of the language employed appears to identify 12:10; 19:1, 2; 20:4b as one group; the voices of those who refused to take mark of beast (15:2-4), including voices of 144,000 (14:2, 3), as another. These two glorified groups are apart from the elders. A few points may be added. Apparently the group consists either of angels, the cherubim, or the great multitude clothed with white robes. That they are not angels appears clear. Angels are mentioned only twice in Revelation as joining in acclamations of praise. In the first instance they respond to the adoration of the first glorified group, the elders (5:8-12); in the second instance they respond to the second glorified group, the white-robed multitude (7:9-12). This order of mention may readily be accounted for by the fact that the understanding of angels is inferior to that of the redeemed in things pertaining to redemption and the entire prophetic program. Cf. Ephesians 3:8-10 and I Peter 1:10-12.

The adorations pertain principally to redemption from or triumph over sin and evil. These the angels cannot appreciate or comprehend as can the redeemed.

Their praises apparently are secondary and in response to the happiness of the redeemed.

The present instance has to do with the coming kingdom. Their relation to it is quite inferior to those who have been delivered from sin and who now learn that the glorious triumph of the kingdom is at hand.

That they are not cherubim appears from what has already been said concerning angels, the cherubim being a form of angelic beings. Their religious expression consists of the worship of God for what He is, rather than of praises for His redemptive work. 4:8, 9. The cherubim are intermediaries between a holy God and sinful creatures. Their activities pertain particularly to the worship of God or to the execution of His judgment upon sin. The present announcement does not partake of either of these.

It may be concluded, therefore, that the loud voices come from the group arrayed in white robes. Observe that in 19:2, as here, the adoration of "much people" (Greek: great multitude) precedes that of the elders.

They are first because they are martyrs of Babylon (Rome), which is the persecuting power. When Rome is overcome, they are the first to break forth in praise. They include the white-robed of chapter 6, which according to 19:2 are martyrs of Babylon (Rome). In 19:2 they are first again in their praises after Babylon goes up in smoke.

Note, however, that when the reign is about to be introduced, the church (those wearing crowns) is mentioned first. This primacy is given to the church because the church will be over Israel. They will judge Israel.

The kingdoms of this world. Most authorities agree that the reading here should be in the singular, viz., *The kingdom of this world is become the kingdom of our Lord, and of his Christ.* However, the plural commends itself strongly. This fully accords not only with the dictum of Old Testament prophets (Ezekiel 21:26, 27; Daniel 2:35, 44; 7:14; Zechariah 14:9), but also with events related in chapters 19 and 20 of Revelation. The passage is proleptic, for the succeeding chapters clearly show that the kingdom of Christ has not yet actually come. The occasion of the announcement is undoubtedly the divine approval of the two witnesses in contrast with the dread and discomfiture of their enemies. To the glorified martyrs the ascension to heaven of the two witnesses was a harbinger of the final triumph of good over evil. The rule of the world was about to pass from the rulers of this world into the hands of Him "whose right it is" to rule. The change of sovereignty will not come by a gradual merging of the kingdom of this world into that of our Lord and His Christ, but (as the following chapters show) by a series of judgments issuing in a final crisis in which the sovereignty of world rulers energized by satanic power will vanish like chaff of the summer threshing floor while the kingdom of God will fill the whole earth. In the words of Scripture: "In the days of these kings [those ruling in the end time] shall the God of heaven set up a kingdom, which shall never be destroyed: and the kingdom shall not be left to other people, but it shall break in pieces and consume all these kingdoms, and it shall stand for ever" (Daniel 2:44). And again, ". . . the government shall be upon his shoulder: and his name shall be called Wonderful, Counsellor, The mighty God,

The everlasting Father, The Prince of Peace. Of the increase of his government and peace there shall be no end, upon the throne of David, and upon his kingdom, to order it, and to establish it with judgment and with justice from henceforth even for ever. The zeal of the Lord of hosts will perform this" (Isaiah 9:6, 7). Evidently the Lord is not yet seated on the throne of David, for the increase of His government and of peace is not in evidence today. Neither will human statecraft nor social evolution ever attain to the high objective mentioned, but "the zeal of the Lord of hosts will perform this."

Our Lord, and of his Christ. The phrase evidently alludes to Psalm 2:2: "The kings of the earth set themselves, and the rulers take counsel together, against the Lord, and against his anointed." *Christ* is from the Greek verbal adjective *Christos* and means anointed. Peter (Acts 4:26) quoted the passage as applying to the combined opposition of the (Jewish) rulers and officials of the Roman government to Christ and culminating in His crucifixion and death. However, the entire psalm will have its complete and final fulfillment at Armageddon, at which time the Anointed will be not the Vanquished but the Victor over all the kings of earth and (apostate) rulers who will have set themselves against Him, for He will ". . . break them with a rod of iron; . . . dash them in pieces like a potter's vessel" (Psalm 2:9). In anticipation of that final triumph and His possession of the kingdom, the psalm fittingly calls Him the *anointed one.* It is then that His request of the Lord will be granted: "Ask of me [God the Father], and I shall give thee [the Son] the heathen for thine inheritance, and the uttermost parts of the earth for thy possession" (Psalm 2:8).

Verses 16, 17. And the four and twenty elders, which sat before God on their seats [Greek: *thrones*], *fell upon their faces, and worshipped God, saying, We give thee thanks, O Lord God Almighty, which art, and wast, and art to come; because thou hast taken to thee thy great power, and hast reigned.*

The four and twenty elders . . . on their seats [Greek: *thrones*]. This is the eighth of the ten occurrences of the group of elders. Twice before mention has been made of one of them. 5:5; 7:13. Here they are seen seated on thrones. Four times (4:10; 5:8; 11:16; 19:4) they fall down and worship.

We give thee thanks. Giving of thanks is mentioned three times: once by the cherubim (4:9); once by the angels (7:12); and once by the elders (11:17). The elders address their thanksgiving to the Lord God, who is not only the Almighty but also the Eternal. (It should be said that the phrase, "and art to come," is omitted by most authorities.) The occasion of their thanksgiving is that He has taken His great power and has reigned. Observe again the prolepsis in this case, for the following chapters show that the beast (Antichrist) has power over all kindreds and tongues and nations for forty-two months (13:5, 7), and that the Lord will not reign until after the beast is destroyed (19:20; 20:6).

Verse 18. And the nations were angry, and thy wrath is come, and the time of the dead, that they should be judged, and that thou shouldest give reward unto thy servants the prophets, and to the saints, and them that fear thy name, small and great; and shouldest destroy them which destroy the earth.

While these words do not consist of thanksgiving, they nevertheless appear to be a continuation of those of the enthroned elders given in the preceding verse, as indicated by the pronouns of direct address, *thy* and *thou*. Like the former, they are proleptic in character, for none of the things enumerated take place during the middle of the tribulation period, as the chapters which immediately follow will show. The passage may be considered as containing seven particulars.

The nations were angry. This is fulfilled in 19:19, at which time "the beast, and the kings of the earth, and their armies, gathered together to make war against him [Christ] that sat on the horse, and against his army." There is an allusion to this event in 16:14, 16: "the spirits of devils, working miracles, which go forth unto the kings of the earth and of the whole world, to gather them to the battle of that great day of God Almighty. . . . And he gathered them together into a place called in the Hebrew tongue Armageddon." There is another apparent allusion here to Psalm 2:1, 2.

And thy wrath is come. These words find their fulfillment in 19:15: "And out of his mouth goeth a sharp sword, that with it he should smite the nations: and he shall rule them with a rod of iron: and he treadeth the winepress of the fierceness and wrath of Almighty God." Reference is made to this event in 6:16, 17, where the kings of the earth say to the mountains and rocks, "Fall on us, and hide us from the face of him that sitteth on the throne, and from the wrath of the Lamb: for the great day of his wrath is come. . . ." Out of the numerous passages pointing forward to the "day of God's wrath," observe a further quotation from Psalm 2:4, 5: "He that sitteth in the heavens shall laugh: the Lord shall have them [the kings of the earth] in derision. Then shall he speak unto them in his wrath, and vex them in his sore displeasure."

Attention should here be called to the fact that the Greek word for wrath (*orge*) is not applied to God's judgments until the very close of the tribulation period (16:19) with reference to the doom of great Babylon, the fulfillment of which does not take place until chapter 18. Wherever the word *wrath* does occur in preceding chapters (6:16, 17; 11:18; 14:10 [*indignation*]; 16:19), the statements are proleptic. Even the vial judgments are called the vials of the anger (*thumos*) of God. 16:1. Much confusion has come into prophetic writings because a proper distinction has not been made between the wrath (*orge*) and the anger (*thumos*) of God. Wrath is always used in the other books of the New Testament with reference to the coming wrath. Cf. Matthew 3:7; Luke 3:7; Romans 2:5, 8; 5:9; I Thessalonians 1:10; 5:9. Anger is never so used.

And the time of the dead, that they should be judged. The reference is to the wicked dead who will be judged at the great white throne (20:12) after the thousand years. Identical words for "the dead" and "judged" are used there as here.

The above three statements pertain to the wicked: their evil character and conduct, God's attitude toward them, God's final retribution upon them. Next observe three concerning the reward for the righteous.

That thou shouldest give reward unto thy servants the prophets. The reference is undoubtedly to the same group as in 10:7, namely, the Old Testament prophets. They are probably to be understood as representing Old Testament believers.

And to the saints. The title is applied 49 times to saints of the church period and about a dozen times (texts differ) in reference to believers of the tribulation period. It is impossible to determine who is intended by this group. The reference might be taken to include believers of the church age, or believers of the tribulation period (this is probable since the church group is making the announcement), or believers both of the church age and of the tribulation period.

And them that fear thy name. The command to fear is of rare occurrence in the church age. Here it is a part of the everlasting Gospel. 14:6, 7. The challenge occurs: "Who shall not fear thee, O Lord" (15:4)? The allusion is apparently to believers of the tribulation period.

Since it is likely that the third reference is to tribulation believers and the first to the Old Testament believers, there is a probability, at least, that by *the saints* is. meant the believers of the church age. Perhaps it is best, however, to attempt no lines of distinction and think of the three groups merely as including all believers of the Old and New Testament periods.

And shouldest destroy them which destroy the earth. There is a return here to judgment pertaining to the wicked. Why this statement does not immediately follow the first three in the series is somewhat problematic. Since the point of emphasis is God's dealing with the wicked, it is perhaps placed here to denote a climax of judgment. There is an allusion to Jeremiah's prophecy against Babylon, "Behold, I am against thee, O destroying mountain, saith the Lord, which destroyest all the earth" (51:25). The reference is to the judgment upon Rome (mystery Babylon), not only the political but also the religious successor of the former Babylon; for no sooner does she go up in smoke (Revelation 18:18) than a great voice of much people proclaims, "Alleluia . . . for he hath judged the great whore, which did corrupt the earth with her fornication" (Revelation 19:1, 2).

Verse 19. *And the temple of God was opened in heaven, and there was seen in his temple the ark of his testament: and there were lightnings, and voices, and thunderings, and an earthquake, and great hail.*

The temple of God. Observe that the chapter opens with the mention of the temple of God on earth (in Jerusalem) and closes with the statement that the temple of God was opened in heaven. As in the case of the two witnesses, heaven's gates stand ajar for those whom earth rejects and of whom she is not worthy.

The ark of his testament. Israel is dispersed and the temple defiled by the abomination of desolation standing in the holy place, yet the archetype in heaven remains and in it appears the ark of His covenant, denoting that "he is faithful that promised." Not only does this have reference to the past, but there is also an allusion to the further revelation contained in the following chapter. The appearance of the ark denotes His "[return] . . . with mercies" to Israel and His intervention in her behalf in the dark days of the second half of the tribulation. God provides for her in a miraculous manner in her flight from the enemy, and bids her "hide . . . for a little moment, until the indignation be overpast" (Isaiah 26:20).

There were lightnings, and voices, and thunderings, and an earthquake, and great hail. With each occurrence this refrain grows in intensity. It marks the close of events of tremendous importance and serves as a harbinger and monitor of greater things yet to come. Cf. 4:5; 8:5; 16:18-21. This is the signal closing in broad outline of the trumpet judgments. It is a matter of interest to observe that in the fulfillment the order of statement will be reversed. The last item presented relates to Israel, yet this will be first in order of fulfillment. Afterward will come the angry nations and the wrath. This will be followed by thanksgiving, and finally the kingdom of our Lord and His Christ.

The Episode of the Two Wonders and the War of Angels (12:1-17)

Verse 1. *And there appeared a great wonder in heaven; a woman clothed with the sun, and the moon under her feet, and upon her head a crown of twelve stars.*

A great wonder [Greek: *sign*]. The Greek word for wonder (*teras*), contrary to expectation, does not occur in Revelation. Moreover, it never stands alone, and in its 16 occurrences in the New Testament it is always associated with the word for "sign," *semeion;* and when thus associated they are always in the plural number (eleven times signs and wonders, five times wonders and signs).

This is the first of the seven occurrences of *semeion.* 12:1, 3; 13:13, 14; 15:1; 16:14; 19:20. A sign is a visible and familiar token by which the thing signified may be apprehended. This sign is declared to be a *great* sign, hence it may well serve to engage careful attention.

A woman clothed with the sun. In the Old Testament, Israel is repeatedly represented under the symbol of a woman and the Lord is referred to as her husband. Cf. Isaiah 54:5; Jeremiah 31:32; Ezekiel 16:32; Hosea 2:16. After her rejection she is called the desolate wife, a woman forsaken, a widow (Isaiah 54:3, 4, 6; Lamentations 1:1), adulteress (Hosea 3:1), and harlot (Jeremiah 3:6-10).

The woman in this text of Revelation can represent none other than Israel, as all the facts and evidence abundantly prove.

This is the second of four women mentioned prominently in Revelation. The woman Jezebel who knew the depths of Satan (2:20) is the archadulteress of the church period. The *woman clothed with the sun . . . and upon her head a crown of twelve stars* of the tribulation period is Israel restored. The woman arrayed (clothed) in purple and scarlet color and decked with gold and precious stones and pearls is the great whore of the tribulation period. 17:4. The woman arrayed (clothed) in fine linen clean and white is the bride, the Lamb's wife of the kingdom age.

It is insufficient to say (with commentators generally) that the *woman* is the great sign. In one aspect at least she is not a symbol but a woman in the plain literal sense. It is particularly her clothing that constitutes the sign—*a woman clothed with the sun, and the moon under her feet, and upon her head a crown of twelve stars.* Plainly the allusion is to Genesis 37:9, 10, for this is the only parallel passage in all the Scriptures and moreover the resemblance is very striking in the terms employed and the implications are undoubtedly to be regarded as identical in each case. The words of the passage are those of Joseph the rejected brother: "Behold, I have dreamed a dream more; and, behold, the sun and the moon and the eleven stars made obeisance to me. And he told it to his father, and to his brethren: and his father rebuked him, and said unto him, What is this dream that thou hast dreamed? Shall I and thy mother and thy brethren . . . bow down ourselves to thee to the earth?"

As in the case of teaching by parables, details must not be stressed, but only the point intended by the parable as a whole. Here the point intended is the ultimate bowing of all Israel (including his own father, mother, and brethren) to the once rejected son. The symbolism is of course proleptic. The sun and the stars evidently bear a double sense, for they also apparently allude to the coming glory of Israel foretold in such passages as Isaiah 60:1, 2, 3, 20: "Arise, shine; for thy light is come, and the glory of the Lord is risen upon thee. . . . The Lord shall arise upon thee, and his glory shall be seen upon thee. And the Gentiles [nations] shall come to thy light, and kings to the brightness of thy rising. . . . Thy sun shall no more go down; neither shall thy moon withdraw itself: for the Lord shall be thine everlasting light, and the days of thy mourning shall be ended." *The moon under her feet* may be compared to the apostate church during the tribulation period, for the church, like the moon, shines by reflected light. To change to the figure of Romans 11, now, as the wild olive tree, she has been cut off and Israel is about to be graffed in again.

Verse 2. *And she being with child cried, travailing in birth, and pained to be delivered.*

Being with child. The Bible in numerous passages compares the sufferings of Israel to those of a woman in travail (lit., birth pangs). The Lord in His Olivet discourse speaks of the first part of the tribulation as "the beginnings of sorrows [birth pangs]" (Mark 13:8). The latter half of the tribulation period is more particularly "the time of Jacob's trouble" (Jeremiah 30:7). The following verses will show the source of her affliction and suffering. Verse 2 has no reference to the mother of Jesus or to the Christ child, as is evident by several other pertinent passages from the prophets noted in connection with verses 4, 5.

Verses 3, 4a. *And there appeared another wonder in heaven; and behold a great red dragon, having seven heads and ten horns, and seven crowns upon his heads. And his tail drew the third part of the stars of heaven, and did cast them to the earth.*

Another wonder [sign] . . . *a great red dragon.* Again, in this passage the *sign* is not merely in that a dragon appears, but more particularly in that he is described as a *red dragon.* This denotes his murderous purpose. While he was a murderer "from the beginning," he is this with an emphasis in the "time of the end," as the following chapters abundantly testify. His immediate mention after the preceding sign—the woman clothed with the sun—is significant, for his evil designs are more especially directed against her, for he doubtless knows that God's future purpose "to restore all things" will never be realized without the repentance and restoration of Israel. If he destroys the woman, therefore, not God, but he will be triumphant at the last.

Seven heads and ten horns, and seven crowns upon his heads. These must be taken as earmarks of the sign. Plainly they point to the dragon's relation to Rome, the last world power. This is apparent from the following chapter (13:1), where likewise seven heads, ten horns and crowns are mentioned in connection with the reappearance of the Roman Empire. Here the crowns are upon the seven heads; in the latter instance, upon the horns, and since the horns are ten, so also is the number of the crowns. (See chapter 13 for exposition.)

The Greek text (as also Luther) rightly ends a sentence (verse 4) with the words, "and did cast them to the earth," for up to this point the sequence is in the order of time with respect to the dragon mentioned in verse 3. From verse 9 it is learned that the dragon too was cast out of heaven. It appears that when he was cast out, the stars, being subordinate to him, were cast out under the spell of his power. The stars of the present verse are represented as "angels" in verse 9. Cf. 1:20; 9:1, 11.

Verse 4b. *And the dragon stood before the woman which was ready to be delivered, for to devour her child as soon as it was born.*

This passage goes back to the time of the birth of Christ. While Jesus was born of Mary, the later Scriptures bestow no special favor upon physical affinity with Jesus. For a while at least even His brethren did not believe in Him. John 7:5. When one would confer special blessing upon His mother, His reply was, "Nay rather [Greek], blessed are they that hear the word of God, and keep it" (Luke 11:28). These words of Jesus ought surely to serve as a corrective of Mariolatry. It is significant that Jesus never referred to Mary as mother, but simply as woman (John 2:4; 19:26), and when others informed Him that she had come desiring to see Him, His reply was, "My mother and my brethren are these which hear the word of God, and do it" (Luke 8:19-21). It is significant too that Mary is not even mentioned by name after the baptism of the Holy Ghost, and when reference is made to His incarnation, the general term used is, "made of a woman" (Galatians 4:4). In the interpretation of this passage, therefore, one is not to think of Mary but of the general fact that He was the seed of the woman, that is, born of woman. The reference is to Herod whom the dragon instigated to destroy the *child whenever* [Greek] *it was born.* It is one of the strange anomalies of history that Herod, an Edomite (descendant of Esau), should be king of Palestine when Jesus was born. No wonder the angel gave the warning, "Herod will seek the young child to destroy him" (Matthew 2:13). While the woman (verse 1) symbolizes Israel of (Greek: *from*) whom as concerning the flesh Christ came (Romans 9:5), He after all was born of a particular woman, viz., Mary.

Verse 5. *And she brought forth a man child, who was to rule all nations with a rod of iron: and her child was caught up unto God, and to his throne.*

She brought forth a man child [Greek: *a son, a male*]. The reference here is unmistakably to the birth of Christ in Bethlehem of Judea. The Greek says, "she brought forth a son, a male." It is significant that nowhere in Scripture is any mention made of travail (birth pangs) in connection with the birth of Christ. Luke, the physician, alone gives details of the Christ child, but he makes no mention of birth pangs disturbing the quietness in the stable at Bethlehem, nor of a midwife with her kindly ministries, nor of an attending physician. It was indeed a silent night, holy night as far as the record goes—there was not even a baby's "low cry."

Who was to rule all nations with a rod of iron. This second clause plainly alludes to Psalm 2:9, "Thou shalt break them [the nations] with a rod of iron," and establishes the fact that the man-child is Christ. It should be remembered that a shepherd carries a rod (for correction) as well as a staff (for protection). At the Battle of Armageddon (19:15) mention is again made of His ruling the nations with a rod of iron, at which time the prophecy of the second psalm comes into fulfillment.

Caught up unto God, and to his throne. Clearly the reference is to the ascension of Christ. Objection has been taken to this view on the ground that the original word for *caught up* denotes a violent snatching away from danger. Cf. Jude 23; Acts 23:10. That the word is not restricted to such a usage is plain from its use in Acts 8:39, where the Spirit of the Lord caught away Philip, and again in II Corinthians 12:2, 4, where Paul is said to have been caught up into Paradise. In fact, the word may have the direct opposite sense, as is the case where the sheep in a place of safety is caught by the wolf (John 10:12), and again in the same chapter in the declaration, "[No one is able to] *pluck* them out of my hand" (verse 28).

Again, since the same word is used in connection with the rapture of the church, some have concluded that that event occurs at this time, namely, in the middle of the tribulation period. It has been observed, however, that the church (as represented by the elders) is already in heaven (chapters 4, 5) before the opening of the seals, that is, before the tribulation has begun. Again, the elders are seen in heaven in chapters 7 and 11.

But there are other reasons why such a view is untenable: The church cannot consistently be thought of as a bride and also as a son, a male; the man-child is caught up unto God and His (God's) throne. Now this position is true of Christ and of Him alone. He Himself declares, "I . . . am set down with my Father in his throne" (Revelation 3:21). The elders sit on thrones, but it is solely the prerogative of Christ to be caught up to God and His throne, which, as other passages declare, is to be seated at the right hand of God. Of the church it is said that at the rapture she will be "caught up . . . to meet the Lord [Jesus] in the air" and ever to be with the Lord. When the time comes for Him to reign, He will grant her to sit with Him (Christ) on His throne. Revelation 3:21.[34]

Verse 6. And the woman fled into the wilderness, where she hath a place prepared of God, that they should feed her there a thousand two hundred and threescore days.

This verse follows in order of time verse 4a: "and his [the dragon's] tail drew the third part of the stars of heaven, and did cast them to the earth," for the fleeing of the woman was the result of his (the dragon's) being cast to the earth as is seen by examining verses 13, 14. It might appear from verse 4 as though only the stars (which are symbols of angels—verse 9) were cast out, and that by Satan, but verse 9 shows that the dragon and his angels were all cast to the earth.

This verse reveals the fact of the woman's flight; verses 7-9, 13 give the cause of her flight.

A place prepared. This expression occurs elsewhere only in John 14:2, 3, where the reference is to the many mansions in the Father's house. Here it pertains to a place of refuge for the persecuted woman.

See verse 14 for further comments.

Verse 7. *And there was war in heaven: Michael and his angels fought against the dragon; and the dragon fought and his angels.*

Heaven. It does not necessarily follow that *heaven* here denotes the place where God dwells, for "there shall in no wise enter into it any thing that defileth . . . or maketh a lie" (21:27).

Satan is "the prince of the power of the air" (Ephesians 2:2). "Air" is the first heaven. Reference is made to "the birds of heaven [Greek]" (Matthew 6:26; 8:20; 13:32; Revelation 19:17). The stars are the second heaven. Matthew 24:29; Mark 13:25; Hebrews 11:12. Paul was carried into the third heaven (II Corinthians 12:2), i.e., where God dwells. It is probable therefore that what is intended here is that the war occurs in the first heaven, the place where the devil engages his power at the present time (of spiritual wickedness in the heavenlies—Ephesians 6:12).

War . . . Michael . . . against the dragon. The war between Michael and the dragon is in fulfillment of Daniel 12:1, where it is said: "At that time [season] shall Michael stand up, the great prince which standeth for the children of thy people." "Thy people," that is, Daniel's people, are Israel. Daniel 9:20. The passage continues: "And there shall be a time of trouble [Greek: tribulation], such as never was since there was a nation even to that same time: and at that time thy people shall be delivered." This points unmistakably to the fact that the woman of Revelation 12 is Israel and that her fleeing to the wilderness constitutes the deliverance spoken of by Daniel.

Verse 8. *And prevailed not; neither was their place found any more in heaven.*

The same expression occurs in Revelation 20:11, where it is said concerning the earth and the heaven, *and there was found no place for them.* The implication is that they once had their place established, which certainly would not be true of Satan and his angels, that is, they never had a place as such, in heaven where God dwells. They prevailed not, but Michael and his angels did as the next verse reveals. (Verse 8 is the 202nd or the last verse of the first half of the book, there being 404 verses altogether.) It is not without interest to observe that even now Satan *prevailed not; neither was . . . [there] place found any more in heaven* for him. At the close of the book he has no more *place* in earth, but his will be the place of torment forever and ever.

Verse 9. *And the great dragon was cast out, that old serpent, called the Devil, and Satan, which deceiveth the whole world: he was cast out into the earth, and his angels were cast out with him.*

The great dragon. A dragon is a monster serpent. He is a great red dragon (verse 3) because of his powerful and bloody career. He is the old serpent, because in his first appearance in Holy Writ he chose to incarnate himself in serpent form since he, like a serpent, is wily, subtle, treacherous. Devil and Satan are the only real names of the archenemy; the former is the Greek, the latter Hebrew. In the Old Testament (Hebrew) the name *Satan* is applied to him and in the Greek (Septuagint) *Devil (diabolos)* occurs. In the English Old Testament the title *Devil* does not occur and Satan is used only sparingly, viz., in I Chronicles

21:1, in chapters 1 and 2 of Job, (14 times), once in the Psalms (109:6), and three times in Zechariah, the third chapter. Devil is usually defined as slanderer and Satan as adversary, but they were originally regarded as identical in meaning, as is seen in the uniform translation of the Hebrew *Satan* by the Greek *Devil*.

The whole world. The Greek word for world (*oikoumene*) denotes the inhabited earth, that is, the part wherein men dwell.

He was cast out into [to] the earth. This is the only place in the Bible where mention is made of the actual casting down of Satan from heaven to the earth. The Bible nowhere states that when Satan sinned he was cast out of heaven. This is pure assumption and not revelation. On the other hand, the Bible plainly says that he was in the Garden of Eden and hence on earth when he sinned.[35] (See Ezekiel 28:13-18.)

[It should be of some interest to notice the Greek word for *earth, ge*. It is frequently translated *land* as in contrast to sea or in contrast to heaven. One could note a distinction between this word and the word for *world, cosmos. Ge* is a more restricted term. In other words, when Satan is cast out of heaven he is confined to the earth. If the battle took place in the heaven of the atmosphere, as Smith points out in the discussion above, this use of the word *earth* is certainly well chosen.— J. O. Y.]

Verse 10. *And I heard a loud voice saying in heaven, Now is come salvation, and strength, and the kingdom of our God, and the power of his Christ: for the accuser of our brethren is cast down, which accused them before our God day and night.*

I heard a loud voice saying. Who are these in heaven that say with a loud voice? First, negatively: they are not angels because angels never include "salvation" in their heavenly utterances (cf. 5:12; 7:12), for while they desire to look into the things pertaining to salvation (I Peter 1:10-12), they have no experience of it themselves; again, angels never refer to others as *brethren*, either of their own number or of any other group; the informing angel later declares: "I am *thy* fellowservant, and [the fellowservant] of *thy brethren*" (19:10; 21:9); they are not the elders, for these never say with a loud voice (4:10, 11; 5:9; 11:17); moreover, the latter group are clearly distinguished (cf. 7:13; 11:16; 19:4).

Second, positively: they are the robe wearers mentioned in 6:11; 7:13; they are the only saved group that cry with a loud voice; like the white-robed group, they begin their acclamation with the word "salvation" (7:10; 19:1); the *brethren* are undoubtedly those referred to in 6:11; they acclaim the coming of the kingdom as do the group already identified as the robe wearers (11:15); "his Christ" (or anointed), a characteristic phrase of the previous passage and alluding to Psalm 2:2, occurs here.

The saying of the group in heaven is obviously proleptic, as the chapters next following clearly testify. However, the casting out of Satan from the air, over which he held the power as prince (Ephesians 2:2), is to them a harbinger that the final triumph is about to come.

Before our God. This is to be understood as in His sight or notice, as when Satan addresses or accuses the Lord (Job 1) or God (Revelation 12:10). This does not necessarily mean bodily presence. Compare 14:10, where the image worshipers are said to be tormented with fire and brimstone before (*enopion*) the holy angels and before (*enopion*) the Lamb. Surely they are not in heaven where the holy angels and the Lamb are while thus in torment. The devil can accuse before God, just as Abram and the rich man could speak together, and Christ preached to spirits in prison—not Christ in prison preached to spirits.

Day and night. The phrase signifies continuously and occurs five times (4:8; 7:15; 12:10; 14:11; 20:10) and always in this order. It occurs elsewhere in the New Testament three times in this order and in the reverse order nine times.[36]

In this text the phrase relates to evil activities—there are only two other such instances recorded in the New Testament (Mark 5:5; Acts 9:24)—an omen suggesting the final triumph of truth and right.

Observe, on the other hand, while the cherubic voices rest not day and night saying "Holy, holy, holy, Lord God Almighty," of those who receive the mark of the beast it is said, "they have no rest day nor night," and "the smoke of their torment ascendeth up for ever and ever." In its last mention unceasing continuity of torment is the awful portion of the infernal trinity. In regard to the doom of the instigators and promoters of the climax of evil in the last days it is declared in unmistakable terms: "And the devil that deceived them was cast into the lake of fire and brimstone, where the beast and the false prophet are, and [they] [the verb is plural] shall be tormented day and night for ever and ever" (20:10).

Verse 11. *And they overcame him by the blood of the Lamb, and by the word of their testimony; and they loved not their lives unto the death.*

They overcame him. The overcomers are the brethren of the preceding verse. Brethren denotes closer relationship than fellow servants. Recall that there are three and only three groups of redeemed ones in heaven that will have a part in the first resurrection (20:4): the elders—those seated on thrones, the robe wearers—those slain for the word of God and the testimony which they held, and those who would not receive the mark of the beast. The brethren here clearly belong to the second group, for they are slain for the *word of their testimony.* They could not belong to the third group because the mark of the beast has not yet been inflicted upon anyone. Since the prayers of the robe wearers were not to be answered until both their fellow servants and their brethren should be killed, and since they will be answered when Babylon (i.e., Rome who imposes the mark of the beast) will have been destroyed (19:2), one can conclude that since the brethren belong to the second group, the fellow servants are those who will refuse to take the mark and who by dying as martyrs [*get*] *the victory over the beast* (15:2). The brethren therefore are martyrs who suffer death at a later period but for the same cause as those mentioned in 6:9 ff., but previous to those who refuse to take the mark of the beast. *They overcame him,* that is, the devil, by trusting in the atoning merits of the blood and holding to the word of their testimony, i.e., they publicly declared their faith even in the face of death.

Loved not their lives unto the death. The Greek has *soul* instead of *life,* that is, they loved not their *souls* unto death (the Greek omits the article, as in 2:10, "Be thou faithful unto death"). In this they follow not only the teaching but also the example of Jesus, for He declared, "the good shepherd giveth his soul for the sheep" (John 10:11), and again, "I lay down my soul for the sheep" (John 10:15). And in teaching His disciples He expressed a great fundamental principle: "whosoever will save his life [Greek: soul] shall lose it: and whosoever will lose his life [soul] for my sake shall find it" (Matthew 16:25). So here by losing their soul they find it; hence they overcome or are the real victors.

Verse 12. *Therefore rejoice, ye heavens, and ye that dwell in them. Woe to the inhabiters of the earth and of the sea! for the devil is come down unto you, having great wrath, because he knoweth that he hath but a short time.*

Ye heavens. This is the only place in Revelation where the plural *heavens* occurs. There may be an allusion here to the fact that Satan has now been dispossessed of occupancy of the entire heavenly spheres which he had held as prince of the power of the air. The use of both the plural and the singular in the Lord's Prayer is not without signification. The address is first, "Our Father who art in the heavens [plural]," while in a succeeding petition the singular occurs, "Thy will be done on earth as it is done in heaven," that is, in the third heaven where His will is perfectly in effect.

It is unthinkable that the wicked deceiver and liar should have been in heaven where God dwells, for nothing that maketh a lie shall enter the celestial city.

Ye that dwell in them. The word *dwell* is noteworthy, for it is *tabernacle* in the original, which signifies, to dwell temporarily, as it is said of Jesus, "[He] tabernacled among us" (John 1:14), that is, He was among men for a limited period only. The word is never applied to angels; neither is *euphraino, rejoice.* Apparently those that tabernacle in the heavens are those who have gone to be with the Lord in the rapture, including the group of martyrs who have died during the tribulation period, all of whom, as chapter 20 indicates, will belong to the first resurrection and will live and reign with Christ a thousand years. Their abode in the heavens will therefore be temporary, for when Christ appears they also will appear with Him in glory.

Woe to the inhabiters of the earth. In contrast with the rejoicing of those tabernacling in the heavens is the woe (ou-aye) of the earth dwellers. The word *inhabiters* here used signifies *to settle* or *dwell permanently.* Those to whom it is applied of course will sooner or later change their place of residence, but they are of the class who say, "The earth is good enough for me," and "who mind earthly things" in contrast with those who are strangers and pilgrims on the earth. This woe is probably synchronous or identical with the fifth trumpet (8:13), at which time the star falls from heaven to earth (9:1).

Sea and earth are here used as in 10:2, the one referring to the portion covered by water, the other the dry land which God in the beginning called *earth* and the waters He called *seas* even though the seas are a part of the earth. We use the terms similarly today.

For the devil is come down. The cause for the woe is plainly expressed. [The statement is introduced by the causal Greek conjunction *hoti,* which means *because.—*J. O. Y.] This shows that the cause of woes to the inhabiters of the earth (8:13), as seen in chapter 9, is that the devil had come down previously. (See

9:1, 2, the star having fallen [in the past] as here indicated.) In other words, 9:1 follows 12:12 in order of time. [Or as one finds at times in predictive Scripture the statement is made at one point and later the details are added, e.g., Genesis 1, 2.—J. O. Y.]

Having great wrath. The Greek word, however, is anger, which denotes rather the temporary outburst of wrath from within.

He hath but a short time. The anger is great, and much in evidence because he knows that he has only a short time. The Greek word for *time* is *season*. It is short because the entire tribulation period continues just seven years. Jesus mentioned that those days are to be shortened because of the elect, else no flesh would be saved. And Paul testifies: ". . . a remnant shall be saved: for he will finish the work, and cut it short in righteousness: because a short work will the Lord make upon the earth" (Romans 9:27b, 28). The dragon is doubtless conscious of his inability to triumph over Him who has so completely vanquished him in His resurrection from the dead. Apparently the dragon proceeds with this program of making war against the Lamb, in supposition that his deputies, the beast and the false prophet (who come on the scene in the next chapters), at the head of, and buttressed by, the combined powers of all nations, will be able to overcome Christ.

Verse 13. *And when the dragon saw that he was cast unto the earth, he persecuted the woman which brought forth the man child.*

Foiled in his purpose to destroy the man-child (in the days of Herod the king), the dragon now determines to destroy the woman (Israel) who brought forth the Christ-Messiah. [All of the Scriptures bear testimony to the fact of Christ's physical connections with Israel.—J. O. Y.]

Verse 14. *And to the woman were given two wings of a great eagle, that she might fly into the wilderness, into her place, where she is nourished for a time, and times, and half a time, from the face of the serpent.*

Here is resumed the thought of verse 6 above, the intervening verses having dealt with the cause of the woman's flight (verses 7-9), namely, the casting out of Satan, the reaction in heaven following his ejection from heaven.

Two wings of a great eagle. The figure of the eagle's wings is doubtless taken from two passages in the Old Testament in connection with Israel's flight into the wilderness: "Ye have seen what I did unto the Egyptians, and how I bare you on eagles' wings" (Exodus 19:4); "As an eagle stirreth up her nest, fluttereth over her young, spreadeth abroad her wings, taketh them, beareth them on her wings: so the Lord . . . did lead him" (Deuteronomy 32:11, 12). As Israel, through God's providence and care, escaped the pursuing enemy, so Israel, under God's protection and care, will be preserved in the future from being destroyed by the archenemy.

(Matthew 24:16 shows that the flight will be from Judea; hence the reference is to Israel. There will be those among Israel who are with child and who will give suck in those days. It will be woe to them because they will be overtaken by the pursuer.)

Into her place. God has prepared a place for her (cf. verse 6) in the wilderness to which the woman flees. Jesus evidently speaks of the same occasion in

Matthew 24:16; Mark 13:14, when He says: "Then let them which be in Judaea flee [same word as *fled*—verse 6 above] into the mountains." The word translated *wilderness* is the ordinary word for *desert*. The Gospels speak of the same, as "mountains." This involves no contradiction, for Jesus was Himself in the wilderness (desert) and He was during that time in "an exceeding high mountain." The time referred to in the Olivet discourses in the Gospels corresponds with this in Revelation 12, for both occur in the great tribulation.[37]

Nourished for a time, and times, and half a time. The word *nourish* is the same as *feed* in verse 6. As in the sojourn in the wilderness in the days of Moses, Israel undoubtedly will be nourished in a miraculous way in the future. The time note, "a time, and times, and half a time," is identical in duration with 1,260 days or 3½ prophetic years. The same language is used twice in Daniel. 7:25; 12:7. Allowing *time* to represent a year (as it is in the Hebrew of Daniel 11:13, "at the end of times, even years"), a time and a half would be equivalent to 1½ years. This would make *times* equal to two years; in other words, the phrase would be equal to 1 year, 2 years, and ½ a year, or 3½ years.

Verse 15. *And the serpent cast out of his mouth water as a flood after the woman, that he might cause her to be carried away of the flood.*

The flood may refer to literal waters. From Zechariah 14:5 one may note the reference to the flight of Israel in latter days as the context shows. The valley of Azal "reaches up to the city gates, so as to enable the fleeing citizens to betake themselves immediately to it on leaving the city."[38] It is possible that Satan will release a flood of waters from the huge city reservoir in Mt. Zion in order to overwhelm the fleeing Israelites and that they will be preserved miraculously by the opening of the earth at the divine command.

Of [by] the flood (lit., river-borne). The word *flood* is *river* and should be thus translated. The language is apparently figurative and alludes to such passages as the following:

"When the enemy shall come in like a flood [Hebrew: river], the Spirit of the Lord shall lift up a standard against him" (Isaiah 59:19).

"When thou passest through the waters, I will be with thee; and through the rivers, they shall not overflow thee: when thou walkest through the fire, thou shalt not be burned; neither shall the flame kindle upon thee" (Isaiah 43:2).

These passages are spoken directly to Israel and, as the context shows, in each case they are prophetic in character and point to the time under consideration in this text in Revelation.

The river may be a symbol for an expeditionary force commissioned by order of the "mouth" of Satan for the purpose of destroying the fugitives from Judea. [Though there is nothing in the text to suggest this.—J. O. Y.]

Verse 16. *And the earth helped the woman, and the earth opened her mouth, and swallowed up the flood which the dragon cast out of his mouth.*

The earth helped. There appears to be an allusion here to the time when "the earth opened her mouth, and swallowed . . . up . . . all the men that appertained unto Korah, and all their goods" (Numbers 16:32). *If* the flood (river) of the preceding verse represents a regiment of men commissioned by Satan to destroy

Israel, the Lord could easily perform a similar miracle at that time for the purpose of consuming them.

It should be added, however, that the preceding verse might be intended to be taken more literally. For instance, in these days of reservoirs and artificial lakes, it would be possible, while Israel is passing through some valley, for the dragon to release a flood of water from some elevated spot upon the fleeing Israelites and then, instead of the earth swallowing a regiment of men, she would open to engulf the river in order to prevent the waters from sweeping the fugitives to destruction. [This to the editor is certainly more in harmony with the context as well as the principle of interpretation accepted by Smith in his introduction.—J. O. Y.]

Verse 17. *And the dragon was wroth with the woman, and went to make war with the remnant of her seed, which keep the commandments of God, and have the testimony of Jesus Christ.*

The dragon was wroth. The dragon is angry with the woman because he failed to accomplish his purpose of destroying her. He now determines to make war with the rest of her seed.

To make war. Two varying modes of expression pertaining to armed conflict should be noted: to make war—the verb *make* followed by the noun *war;* the simple verb—to war. The former denotes prolonged conflict and occurs here and in 11:7; 13:7, and 19:19; the latter, denoting single combat—the act of fighting, occurs in 2:16; 12:7 (twice); 13:4; 17:14; 19:11.

Remnant of her seed. Some have understood that *remnant* is used here in a technical sense, namely, that by them is meant the faithful portion of Israel as in Romans 9:27 and 11:5. This, however, is an error, for the word *loipoi* never refers to the faithful remnant of Israel—not here, neither elsewhere in Revelation, nor in any passage in the New Testament. The passages in Romans are *leimma* and *kataleimma* respectively and they occur only in the two verses named above. On the other hand, we find that *loipoi* is used of those who were not faithful, but blinded. Romans 11:7.

The rest or *remnant,* applying to groups of individuals, is used in Revelation in the following passages: 2:24; 3:2; 9:20; 12:17; 19:21; 20:5, and always in a general sense, as an examination of the passages will plainly indicate.

In answer to the question, Who then are intended by the remnant (lit., the rest) in this passage? it should be clearly understood first who are included under the symbolic name "the woman." This, as noted before, is definitely stated in Matthew 24, where Jesus says, "Then let them which be in Judaea flee into the mountains." Consequently, by *the rest* one is to understand those Israelites who do not live in Judea.

Note the important statement, *the rest of her seed.* This implies clearly that by "the woman" fleeing we are to understand Israelites who dwell in Judea at the time and (as the verse continues) *which keep the commandments of God,* those fleeing too are believing Israelites who dwell in the land. The Scriptures plainly declare that when Zion travails she brings forth children, that is, spiritual children —those who have come to believe in Christ and are now His children.

It may be safely concluded that the *fleeing ones* (not the rest) constitute the remnant (or at least a portion of it) since they are preserved through the tribulation, a point that is always implied in the term "the remnant." On the other hand, the rest of the woman's seed become the objects of the dragon's pursuit and his purpose is to destroy all which keep the commandments of God and have the testimony of Jesus Christ. Among the list of his victims will be—Moses and Elias, the 144,000 Israelites previously mentioned, besides multitudes of others as the succeeding chapters reveal.

[This discussion is an effort to point up the distinction between *leimma, kataleimma,* and *loipoi* of the Greek.—J. O. Y.]

The Episode of the Beast Out of the Sea (13:1-10)

Verse 1. *And I stood upon the sand of the sea, and saw a beast rise up out of the sea, having seven heads and ten horns, and upon his horns ten crowns, and upon his heads the name of blasphemy.*

I stood. Probably the weight of testimony favors the reading, *"and he* [i.e., Satan] *stood upon the sand of the sea."* The thought then would seem to be that Satan, foiled in his purpose to destroy the woman, quits his pursuit (southward) and turns westward. Upon arriving at the Mediterranean, he calls the beast out of the sea; whereupon he gives him power and authority mentioned in the verses that follow. However plausible this may appear to be, it is manifestly thinking above what is written, for there is no word in the text indicating that Satan will have the power to call forth the beast. Moreover, in Daniel, chapter 7, the parallel passage, where four beasts come out of the sea, they apparently come forth entirely independent of creature agency.

The difference of the reading is simply the omission of the letter *n* in the change suggested. It would have been an easy matter for a scribe to drop the letter in order to conform to the interpretation he favored. Nearly all the cursives agree with the received text; besides, what has the greater weight, the internal evidence, points in the same direction. For instance, the eastern coast of the Mediterranean is some 1500 miles distant from Rome, where the beast makes his first appearance. Also opposed to such a view is the fact that the seer on other occasions always takes his stand at a point of observation most favorable for his purpose. 4:1; 17:3; 21:10.

A beast. A beast (cf. Daniel 7:17) may mean either a world kingdom (Daniel 7:23) or the king (emperor) ruling at a given time.

The sea. Some have understood the *sea* to be figurative and signify "the mass of humanity" on the ground of 17:15 where "waters" are interpreted as meaning "peoples, and multitudes, and nations, and tongues." There are, however, fatal objections to such a view. John is not in the habit of deferring explanations of figurative language. He does so at the first mention. In Daniel 7:2 the sea is called the *great* sea, a designation occurring 14 times in the Old Testament and invariably applied elsewhere to the Mediterranean. There is no point to the argument that in this case the adjective "great" does not occur, hence the Mediterranean is not intended, for in its last mention in Daniel 7 (verse 3) "sea" occurs without a qualifying word. If *sea* is figurative, *sand* would likewise have to be taken as figurative in this case—the mere statement is sufficient to refute the idea, unless it could be shown that certain people then as now were spoken of occasionally as having *sand*.

Having seven heads and ten horns. The expression occurs again in 17:3, 7, thus serving as one of the frequent marks of identity of this beast. It also is applied to the dragon (12:3) for the purpose of showing his intimate relation to the Roman Empire. The ten horns had already been referred to in Daniel's vision of the fourth world empire. Daniel 7:7.

The seven heads (an apparent monstrosity) are not mentioned by Daniel. However, he speaks of the fourth beast as being "dreadful and terrible" (Daniel 7:7, 19); so likely he saw the beast in like form, but since he received no interpretation of these, he described it merely in general terms.

Naturally a beast has only one head at a given time. The seven heads therefore may be considered as successive. This point is clear from a statement in 17:9, 10: "The seven heads are seven mountains. . . . And they [a correction for "there"] are seven kings: five are fallen [they have died], and one is [that is one was living when John wrote], and the other is not yet come." Note carefully:

The heads are said to be kings (emperors).

They are not contemporaneous but successive.

The last mentioned has "not yet come."

The ten horns are ten kings. Daniel 7:24; Revelation 17:12. These live and rule at the same time. Moreover, they live at the very end of the age because they will make war against the Lamb and the Lamb shall overcome them, for He is Lord of lords and King of kings—a plain allusion to Armageddon. Revelation 19:15, 16. Note also that they are said to agree and give their kingdom to the beast, which shows that they are living at the same time. It is self-evident therefore that the seventh, to whom these give their power and strength, "is not yet come."

And upon his horns ten crowns. In an earlier chapter (12:3) the crowns were on the heads because the dragon's relation to the imperial power in the time of Jesus' birth was about to be introduced, for then it was vested in the heads (emperors). In the present instance, however, the crowns are upon the ten horns, or subordinate kings, thus showing that when the beast rises the ruling power is vested in ten kings. The inference is that when Rome first comes into power in the end time, it will consist of a confederacy of ten kings who will rule conjointly. This clearly indicates that this passage points to a time previous to the middle of the tribulation period, for when that time comes the ten kings will give their power and strength (authority) to the beast. 17:13.

Upon his heads the name of blasphemy. The heads are emperors in succession. Five of these had fallen when John wrote; one (Domitian) was then ruling; another (Antichrist) is yet to come. It is a matter of history that the early emperors of Rome not only blasphemed God but deified themselves; they accepted worship. Temples were erected to them. In respect to the one that is yet to come, he will far outstrip his predecessors in their haughty assumptions and blasphemous attitudes.

Verse 2. *And the beast which I saw was like unto a leopard, and his feet were as the feet of a bear, and his mouth as the mouth of a lion: and the dragon gave him his power, and his seat, and great authority.*

The beast. In the preceding verse the reference is plainly to Rome. Here are the names of three beasts named in Daniel 7:4-6 as symbols of world kingdoms which preceded Rome and they occur in inverse order from that in their previous mention. Rome is said to be "like" the preceding empires in that she will embody within herself the leading characteristics of the former. She will advance with the velocity of the Grecian beast, the tenacity of the Medo-Persian, and the voracity of the former Babylonian. The inverse order occurs presumably because the seer looks backward in course of time. Introversion in chronological sequence occurs on a number of occasions in the Biblical record. Two examples are: "Thou wilt perform the truth to Jacob, and the mercy to Abraham" (Micah 7:20); "Then will I remember my covenant with Jacob, and also my covenant with Isaac, and also my covenant with Abraham will I remember" (Leviticus 26:42).

The dragon. In the last mention of the dragon, he "went to make war with the remnant of her [the woman's] seed" (Revelation 12:17). Here is his first gesture in that direction. While he remains hidden from the scene, he gives *his power, and his seat [throne], and great authority* to the beast. This bestowal of power and authority actually takes place after the things mentioned in the following verse.

Verse 3. *And I saw one of his heads as it were wounded to death; and his deadly wound was healed: and all the world wondered after the beast.*

And I saw. This is a new vision, thus calling special attention to what follows. Not only does this suggest the importance of what follows; it also implies the high significance of the preceding vision, as is always the case when a vision is brief in compass. In proof of the great importance of the preceding vision, note that what follows in the great drama as described up to and including chapter 19 is largely in consequence of the appearance of the beast out of the sea.

One of his [i.e., of the beast's] *heads.* A beast has a head and only one at a given time. The reference is to a head (or emperor) that is "not yet come."

As it were wounded to death. The force of the phrase is weakened and the real sense veiled in the translation as given. The Greek consists of two words, *hos esphagmenon.* One need not go far to ascertain their real import, for the precise term is predicated of the Lamb in 5:6 and is there translated *as it had been slain* (lit., *as having been slain*). There John saw a Lamb as it had been slain; here he sees one of the heads (the final Roman emperor) as it had been slain. Since the words in the former instance signify the death of Christ by violence, so truly will the final Roman emperor meet a violent death. In each instance the marks or insignia of violent death are apparent.

And his deadly wound was healed (lit., *the wound of his death was healed*). Here direct mention is made of his death, which thus establishes the truth of the former comment.

The healing of the beast synchronizes and is identical with his coming out of the bottomless pit. Revelation 11:7. The coming out of the sea must therefore refer to a time previous to his being healed. This no doubt is the reason why *beast* here is without the article, while in the former passage it appears. *The* beast naturally assumes his previous mention or existence—in this case the latter. The word occurs 36 times in Revelation and always has the article except in the present instance. It might appear as though 13:11 is an exception, but *another* beast is here in view.

By healing is meant restoration to life. This is plain from verse 14, where reference is made to the beast that had the "wound by a sword, and did live." The word "live" here denotes life after death. It is used similarly of Christ—1:18, "I am he that liveth, and was dead." And again, "The first and the last, which was dead, and is alive" (2:8). Thus we see that the death and resurrection of the beast are a parody on Jesus' death and resurrection.

And all the world [Greek: earth] *wondered after the beast*. Note that it does not say they wondered after the *head*. The inference is that when the head died the beast died, for a beast cannot live without a head. Note, too, that nothing is said about the body apart from the head. The reason is—in autocracy all authority is vested in the head or emperor. Even though the head appears to be a travesty on Christ as the head of the church, how utterly the symbolism breaks down when it comes to the body! In the one case, there is a love relation—"[he] loved the church, and gave himself for it." In the other, the body is a nonentity. Its claims and needs are entirely ignored in an absolute monarchy of "I am the State!" This is indeed a crucial passage and of unusual importance. Two questions naturally present themselves: Why does the whole earth wonder after the beast? Why this change of name from one of the heads to *beast* at this juncture?

The answer to the first question is seen in part from the parallel passage in 17:8: "The beast that thou sawest was, and is not; and shall ascend out of the bottomless pit . . . and they that dwell on the earth shall wonder . . . when they behold the beast that was, and is not, and yet is" (the more approved reading is, "and yet shall be"). Suffice it to say that here is to be found the key as to how the slain body was resuscitated. A beast that "was, and is not," by which is meant an emperor who had died when John wrote, will ascend out of the bottomless pit (the abode of the spirits of the wicked dead), and enter, and resuscitate the dead body, whereupon the dragon . . . [gives] him his power, and his seat [throne], and great authority, including the additional diabolical energies and activities subsequently mentioned, and more particularly in chapter 17, the last of which is his assembling of the armies of the earth to make war against the Lamb.

Thus the risen *head*, or emperor, will have the body of the one wounded to death but the spirit or animating principle of a beast that had *fallen* (that is, met a violent death) when John wrote. This emperor was apparently Nero.

In reply to the second question as to the change of title from "head" to that of "beast," one may observe that at this juncture, that is, by means of his death and resurrection, not only the autocratic but the beastly characteristics come clearly into view. Doubtless at this time the Roman emperor assumes the role of Antichrist and as "man of sin" is now revealed through "signs and lying wonders." II Thessalonians 2:3-9. Note again that the restoration to life is a travesty on the resurrection of Christ. Just as the early spread and the perpetuity of the Christian faith are grounded upon the resurrection of Christ, so the all but universal worship and homage accorded the beast in the last half of the tribulation period can only be accounted for by the resurrection of the fallen emperor of Rome.

Verse 4. *And they worshipped the dragon which gave power* [Greek: *authority*] *unto the beast: and they worshipped the beast, saying, Who is like unto the beast? who is able to make war with him?*

They worshipped. The antecedent of *they* is *all the earth,* by which is meant, as noted above, all its inhabitants. This statement, however, is qualified in verse 8 below, where the worshipers are restricted to those whose names are not written in the book of life.

The worship accorded the dragon appears to be a parody on divine worship in which the act of homage and reverence is directed to God, the ultimate source of all good. It is significant that in this book, while praises repeatedly ascend unto the Lamb, divine worship, in the eight occurrences in which the object of worship is expressed, is invariably directed to God. 4:10; 5:14; 7:11; 11:16; 14:7; 19:4. Thus in the first mention of worship of evil dignitaries it is directed to him who is the source of all evil, namely, the dragon (note, "worship devils," 9:20, should be "worship demons"—see the comment there). Observe, too, that here is the worship by force. All of the earth worship the dragon because of the power and authority vested in him and now delegated to the beast. Many of the nations of this day are obsessed with the idea that "might makes right" and are thus unwittingly moving onward as precursors of the worshipers of the dragon as here described.

They worshipped the beast. It is striking to note the repeated mention of this degrading act, occurring as it does in a total of nine passages—the last mention in chapter 20:4.

Who is like unto the beast? The challenge of these deluded worshipers appears to be in defiance of the erstwhile challenge of God's people after their miraculous deliverance from their pursuing enemy—"Who is like unto thee, O Lord, among the gods" (Exodus 15:11)? The challenge is answered in deeds, not words; not immediately, but at Armageddon, where the beast worshipers are slain by the sword of Him that sat upon the horse and served as the menu at the "table" of the Lord, and when the beast himself will be cast into the lake of fire. (See Revelation 19:11 ff.)

Verse 5. *And there was given unto him a mouth speaking great things and blasphemies; and power was given unto him to continue forty and two months.*

There was given unto him. The passive form, "it was given to him," occurs six times in this chapter—four times of the first beast, verses 5 (twice), 7 (twice); twice of the second beast, verses 14, 15 (and power was given). The giver is the dragon or Satan. This is clear from verses 2 and 4, where mention is made (both before and after his death and resurrection) of authority given to the beast by him. It must be thus understood in 7b and hence is implied in the intervening passages.

The bestowal of the gifts is mentioned six times in connection with the first beast. Verses 2, 4, 5 (twice), 7 (twice).

The gifts bestowed are likewise six:

(1) power. Verse 2.
(2) a throne. Verse 2.
(3) authority. Verses 2, 4, 5, 7.

(4) a mouth. Verse 6.

(5) to make war with saints. Verse 7a.

(6) to overcome them. Verse 7b.

It will be observed that the bestowal of authority is mentioned in a climactic order:

authority (merely). Verses 2, 4.

authority to continue 42 months. Verse 5.

authority over all kindreds and tongues and nations. Verse 7.

A mouth speaking great things. This is another earmark identifying this beast with the fourth beast of Daniel. Daniel 7:8, 11, 25. Some have understood this beast as referring to the fourth kingdom solely, and not to king as head of the kingdom. However, this view is plainly erroneous from the fact that a kingdom has no mouth, neither does a kingdom "speak great words against the most High" (Daniel 7:25). An image will be made of the beast. How could an image be made of a kingdom? The beast is associated with the dragon and the false prophet. Clearly the latter two are persons and the mutual relations show clearly that the beast who is mentioned between the dragon and the false prophet is a person likewise. Later the beast with the false prophet will be cast alive into the lake of fire. A kingdom is never spoken of as being cast as such into the lake of fire.

Blasphemies. Compare verse 1—"Upon his heads the name of blasphemy." The seven heads, or emperors represented by them, were all guilty of blasphemy in this that they not only claimed to be divine but they spoke reproachfully of the true God.

Power [Greek: *authority*] *was given unto him.* The beast was energized (authorized) by Satan—a travesty of God giving His power and authority to Christ.

To continue. The word *continue* here means simply to do or to perform.

Forty and two months. His ministry of authority continued for three and a half years as did that of Christ—another travesty of the divine arrangement, this time with respect to the duration of public service.

This is the last occurrence of this important time. Note the various forms, all of which express equal duration:

forty-two months. 11:2; 13:5.

one thousand two hundred and sixty days. 11:3; 12:6.

time, times, and half a time. 12:14.

The latter occurs twice in Daniel (7:25; 12:7), thus indicating that the two seers speak of the same things occurring at the same time.

Verse 6. And he opened his mouth in blasphemy against God, to blaspheme his name, and his tabernacle, and them that dwell in heaven (cf. Daniel 7:25—of the little horn [verse 8]—"he shall speak great words against the most High").

He opened his mouth. It is increasingly apparent that the reference is to a person, not a kingdom merely. A kingdom cannot open its mouth, for it has none.

Against God. There are not only the horrors of the blasphemies of Antichrist but their extent as well should be observed.

He is not content to be anti-*Christ* only, but energized as he is by Satan he is anti-*God.*

To blaspheme his name. He blasphemes the name of God—a probable allusion to II Thessalonians 2:4, where he is spoken of as both opposing God and exalting himself above everything that is called God or worshiped.

His tabernacle. He blasphemes His tabernacle, that is, His dwelling place. This is later identified with the "new Jerusalem, coming down from God out of heaven," for after its descent John "heard a great voice out of heaven saying. Behold, the tabernacle of God is with men." Since the new Jerusalem is apparently the same as the holy Jerusalem, the city foursquare described in 21:10 ff., nothing in all the Scriptures reveals the infamous character of any of God's fallen creatures as does this reviling of the city of indescribable beauty by the "firstborn of Satan." The noun *tabernacle* occurs only three times in Revelation. 13:6; 15:5; 21:3. In the second passage the reference is to "the true tabernacle, which the Lord pitched, and not man" (Hebrews 8:2), of which the earthly tabernacle was an example and shadow (Hebrews 8:5), and is spoken of as "the tabernacle of the testimony in heaven" because "the ark of the testimony" was in it, whereas the tabernacle here spoken of contains no ark.

Them that dwell in heaven. He blasphemes them that dwell in heaven (lit., them that tabernacle). The original word for *dwell* is the verbal form of *tabernacle* and denotes to dwell temporally as in a tent. The verb occurs four times. 7:15; 12:12; 13:6; 21:3. See also its only other use in the New Testament by the same apostle (John 1:14), where it is said the Word (Jesus) "dwelt [i.e., tabernacled] among us," in allusion to His brief career on earth. The same thought of transitoriness is expressed in II Corinthians 5:1, where the "earthly house of this tabernacle" is contrasted with the "house . . . eternal in the heavens." (The use of the word in Revelation 21:1 has been urged as not being in agreement with the idea of transitoriness, but the thought there appears to be with reference to the new earth which indeed has to do with the time element.)

The question naturally presents itself, "Who are these that tabernacle in heaven?" Note, first, that they are not angels, for angels are never spoken of as tabernacling in heaven, neither is there any hint in the Bible that they will ever quit their abode in heaven and come to dwell on the earth. The passage must therefore allude in the redeemed consisting of the church group and those who have come out of the great tribulation. These, it will be learned, will appear with Christ at His second coming; hence they are spoken of as tabernacling in heaven here and in 12:12. The word *tabernacle* stands in contrast with the earth dwellers. The word "dwell" used in that relation denotes to dwell permanently, to settle.

Verse 7. And it was given unto him to make war with the saints, and to over-come them: and power was given him over all kindreds, and tongues, and nations.

It was given unto him. This is the last of six statements pertaining to the bestowal of infernal gifts by the dragon upon the beast.

To make war with the saints. There is a direct allusion here to 12:17: "the dragon was wroth with the woman, and went to make war with the . . . [rest] of her seed." (See also Daniel 7:21; cf. Daniel 7:25—"he . . . shall wear out the saints of the most High.") He now fulfills his purpose, not directly, but through the beast whom he energizes with his power. It is certain therefore that among his victims will be the woman's seed, that is, Israel *not* of Judea and hence not those fleeing to the mountains. Matthew 24:16; Revelation 13:14.

To overcome them. The implication is that the saints died as martyrs at the hands of the beast. In 11:7 this is directly stated with reference to the two witnesses—"the beast . . . shall overcome them, and kill them."

Power [authority] was given him over all kindreds, and tongues, and nations. The external evidence (manuscripts, versions, and church fathers) is overwhelming that *peoples* should be inserted after kindreds. The internal evidence is all in favor of the inclusion since in the seven occurrences of the similar phrase denoting universality, only this one is limited to three terms. This is one of the numerous instances in which the relation of Satan and the beast is a travesty of God and Christ. The passage reminds one of Matthew 28:18, "All power [Greek: *authority*] is given unto me." This is the third mention of the conferment of power, and is (verse 5) in an ascending scale of emphasis.

This verse furnishes a most important key to the proper understanding of events occurring during the tribulation period. Since authority is given him over *all kindreds, and tongues, and nations* upon his ascent from the sea, any passage pertaining to rivalry of kings or conflict among kings in the "time of the end" (such as Daniel 7:8, 24; 11:40-44) must refer to a time preceding this universal dictatorship and therefore to the first half of the tribulation.

Verse 8. *And all that dwell upon the earth shall worship him, whose names are not written in the book of life of the Lamb slain from the foundation of the world.*

That dwell upon the earth. This is the seventh mention of the earth dwellers. Satan is both the prince of this world, the political head (John 12:31; 14:30; 16:11), and the god of this world, the religious head (II Corinthians 4:4). How entirely Satan has conferred his prerogatives and potentialities upon the beast is evidenced by the fact that all the earth dwellers are under his jurisdiction. He is their political head. They worship him. He is their religious head. Note, however, that power is given him over all the earth (kindreds, tongues, and nations) and yet the earth dwellers (a distinct class) are the only ones who are said to worship him.

That the earth dwellers do not include all those living upon earth is apparent because they are distinguished from the peoples and kindreds and tongues and nations. 11:9a, 10a; 14:6. It is clear that the children of Israel who flee to the desert will be miraculously protected and nourished during this period. Thus they certainly do not worship the beast.

Whose names are not written in the book of life. Thus the earth dwellers are further characterized. Their doom is certain, for the Word expressly declares in a later passage, "Whosoever was not found written in the book of life was cast into the lake of fire" (Revelation 20:15). The phrase, *the book of life,* occurs seven times in Revelation (3:5; 13:8; 17:8; 20:12, 15; 21:27; 22:19) and only elsewhere in Philippians 4:3. It is alluded to in Luke 10:20.

Of the Lamb slain (cf. 21:27—the Lamb's book of life = the book of life of the Lamb). The book of life is the book of the Lamb, moreover of the Lamb *slain,* thus signifying that only the names of those who have been redeemed by His blood will be found written in the book of life.

From the foundation of the world. This important phrase occurs again in 17:8. It is mentioned seven times in the New Testament. Attention is here given to two of the seven passages which clearly show that the formula refers to the opening chapters of the Bible. Hebrews 4:3—"The works were finished from the foundation of the world." The allusion here is to Genesis 2:1. Luke 11:50, 51a— "That the blood of all the prophets, which was shed from the foundation of the world, may be required of this generation; from the blood of Abel unto the blood of Zacharias, which perished between the altar and the temple." (The shedding of Abel's blood is referred to in the first book of the Bible—Genesis 4:10; that of Zacharias, according to the Hebrew arrangement of the Old Testament, in the last book—II Chronicles 24:20, 21.) No sooner were the works finished (Genesis 2 gives the details of the work of the fifth and sixth days) than came the temptation and fall of man and with it the promise of a Redeemer. Genesis 3:15. Thus "the Lamb slain from the foundation of the world." Not only in promise but also in type He is "the Lamb slain," for the coats of skins (note the plural) imply the shedding of blood. It may be concluded that God gave some word of instruction to Adam and Eve to the effect that "without shedding of blood [there] is no remission" of sins, for "by faith Abel offered unto God a more excellent sacrifice than Cain" (Hebrews 11:4). "Faith cometh by hearing . . . the word of God" (Romans 10:17). Abel, it may be assumed, heard and believed the word and therefore brought of the firstborn (Hebrew) of his flock. It is unthinkable that Abel, without a special revelation of God's will, would have conceived the idea.

Verse 9. *If any man have an ear, let him hear.*

This clause, with slight variations, occurs eight times in the first three Gospels. Matthew 11:15; 13:9, 43; Mark 4:9, 23; 7:16; Luke 8:8; 14:35. It occurs nowhere else in Scripture except in Revelation, where it also is used eight times, the other seven occurring in the messages to the seven churches. The variations, though slight, are significant. In the Gospels it is uniformly the plural, *ears;* here the singular, *ear*—the latter suggesting the high importance of the things mentioned.

In the Gospels, the appeal to hear invariably follows the message given. In the messages to the first three churches, the appeal precedes the promise to the overcomer, to which it relates. In the last four, it follows the promise and, since it closes the message, proves beyond question that it refers to what goes before. In the present instance, the appeal evidently goes with the warning following and thus corresponds with the order of statement as given in the messages to the first three churches. 2:7, 11, 17. This suggests the unusual importance of the succeeding verse. A unique difference occurs between this appeal and those to the churches in that the exhortation, "let him hear what the Spirit saith unto the churches," is not included. On the surface it would appear that the exhortation is all the more urgent. The omission signifies that the church is no longer on earth at this time. This is why the voice of the Comforter is not heard speaking to the living in all the chapters embracing the tribulation period. 6—18. Only once is His voice heard and that in connection with "the dead which die in the Lord." (14:13).

Now the important message follows the call to hear.

Verse 10. *He that leadeth into captivity shall go into captivity: he that killeth with the sword must be killed with the sword. Here is the patience and the faith of the saints.*

Authorities differ as to the preferred reading of the text, but the meaning is clear in the light of the context. There is apparently an allusion to such passages as Jeremiah 15:2 and 43:11.

Following the declaration and description of the beast's purpose to make war and to overcome the saints, the substance of a universal law which applies both to the oppressor and to the oppressed is given. It is variously expressed as: the law of retaliation, of retribution, of reprisal in the Latin phrase, *lex talionis,* payment in one's own coin (Haman will eventually hang on the gallows of his own making), and in such Scripture passages as "Whoso sheddeth man's blood, by man shall his blood be shed" (Genesis 9:6); "An eye for an eye, and a tooth for a tooth" (Matthew 5:38); "all they that take the sword shall perish with the sword" (Matthew 26:52); "avenge not yourselves, but rather give place unto wrath: for it is written, Vengeance is mine; I will repay, saith the Lord" (Romans 12:19); "Be not deceived; God is not mocked: for whatsoever a man soweth, that shall he also reap" (Galatians 6:7).

This law applies with unfailing force in times of persecution as here described. Saints in such times must not retaliate but rather heed their Master's injunction, "When they persecute you in this city, flee ye into another" (Matthew 10:23). If imprisonment is imposed upon them, they should take their sentence without complaint, for "it shall turn to . . . [them] for a testimony" (Luke 21:13). If they become subjects for martyrdom, they are to exercise patience and faith as becometh saints in view of the Lord's promise: "He that shall endure unto the end, the same shall be saved" (Matthew 24:13). Two great Bible scholars have spoken well on this point: "Apparently John means this as a warning to Christians not to resist force with force, but to accept captivity as he had done, as a means of grace,"[39] and H. B. Swete: "If a Christian is condemned to exile as St. John had been, he is to regard exile as his allotted portion, and to go readily; if he is sentenced to death, he is not to lift his hand against the tyrant; to do so will be to deserve his punishment."[40]

The law applies with equal force to the oppressor. It has ever been true that aggressor nations and all who have aspired to world dominion have been short-lived. The last world dominion will be no exception. The beast will continue a short space of forty-two months. Of this last persecuting power an angelic messenger in a later passage (16:6) declares: "For they have shed the blood of saints and prophets, and thou hast given them blood to drink; for they are worthy." Again the angel which announces the doom of Babylon (Rome) reiterates the same law of retribution: "Babylon the great is fallen, is fallen. . . . For all nations have drunk of the wine of the wrath of her fornication" (18:2, 3). A further word indicates, moreover, that the Lord is liberal with His reprisals: "Reward her even as she rewarded you, and double unto her double according to her works: in the cup which she hath filled fill to her double" (18:6).

The Episode of the Beast Out of the Earth (13:11-18)

Verse 11. *And I beheld another beast coming up out of the earth; and he had two horns like a lamb, and he spake as a dragon.*

"The antichrist has an acolyte [*akoloutheo*] represented under the image of a second beast having *horns like a lamb*, and called, later on, *the false prophet*."[41]

I beheld another beast. This beast is a correlative of the one just considered, for the word *another* manifestly alludes to the former. [The Greek word *allo* indicates one of similar nature.—J. O. Y.] However, the relations subsist not only in similarity but in contrast as well, for whereas the former comes out of the sea, this one comes out of the land. According to previous observations, when earth and sea are used conjointly, they are to be understood in their plain literal sense. By earth is understood "dry land" as in their first joint occurrence. Genesis 1:10.

It has already been shown that "sea" in Daniel 7:1, 2, to which Revelation 13:1 clearly alludes, is called the "great" sea, which term in all its occurrences denotes the Mediterranean. Rome on various occasions has laid claim to the Mediterranean Sea as "our sea." Since the great sea forms the western boundary of the land of Palestine, it is most probable that by *earth* is meant the land of Palestine.

It is noteworthy too that Mediterranean means the middle of the earth and that the land of Canaan, as well as its capital, is frequently referred to as being in in the midst (middle) of the earth. Italy, moreover, is approximately in the middle of the Mediterranean, as Jerusalem is in the middle of Palestine. Rome, the capital of Italy, is the world's great metropolis; Jerusalem, the Lord's. That these two world centers (the one dominated by Satan, the other by the Lord from heaven) will eventually come into mortal conflict is inevitable.

Two horns like a lamb. By this is probably meant a male lamb, thus denoting strength. However, his real character is seen in the further description.

He spake as a dragon. In the verses which follow he is shown as the great actor during the second half of the tribulation period. Eight times in the brief compass of five verses (12-16) he is said to "do." The original word is *poieo*. It is a more inclusive word than the English word "do." Various words—exercise, cause, do, make—are used to translate it. Like the first beast, he is energized by Satan; hence he both speaks and acts under the impact of that energy.

Verse 12. *And he exerciseth all the power of the first beast before him, and causeth the earth and them which dwell therein to worship the first beast, whose deadly wound was healed.*

All the power. The Greek word *exousia* actually indicates authority. The authority of the second beast is bestowed directly from the dragon and not mediately through the first beast. Here again is a parody on the Holy Trinity. Although both the Son and the Holy Spirit are divine, yet in their ministries to man they each were endued directly with authority and power by the Father.

First beast before him. The phrase *before him* is elsewhere translated "in his presence" (I Corinthians 1:29) or "in his sight" (Romans 3:20; Hebrews 4:13). What is meant is that he exercises (Greek: *poieo*) his authority in the presence of the first beast. [Greek, *enopion*, would clearly support this conclusion.—J. O. Y.]

Earth and them which dwell therein. The word *earth* (Greek: *ge*) is translated *world* in verse 3—in either case the inhabitants of the earth are intended. Here again, as in 11:9, 10, and verses 7 and 8 above, the earth dwellers (they *which dwell therein*) and the inhabitants of the earth are distinguished as two separate classes. Observe that the second beast causes (*poieo*) or makes both classes to worship the first beast. This is clearly an advance on verse 8. However, the language must be understood as that it is merely the *purpose* of the second beast to make worship of the first beast universal. That he will not accomplish this is evidenced not only by the fact that those of Israel who escape into the wilderness are excluded but we also know that many of the natives (possibly because the days are shortened) will live to worship the Lord in Jerusalem. Isaiah 2:4; Micah 4:3; Zechariah 8:20-23. Note in Revelation 18:4 that even in Babylon the Lord will have some people at the very close of the tribulation period whom He calls "my people."

Whose deadly wound. For *deadly wound* read—*the wound of his death.* The reference is to verse 3 above.

Verse 13. *And he doeth great wonders, so that he maketh fire come down from heaven on the earth in the sight of men.*

He doeth great wonders. He does (*poieo*) great signs (Greek). This appears as a travesty of the work of the Holy Spirit, for signs and wonders were frequently wrought after His coming. Acts 2:43; 4:16, 22, 30; 5:12.

Fire . . . from heaven. He makes (*poieo*) fire to come down from heaven. This may be a challenge to duplicate Elijah's performance of miracles. II Kings 1:10, 12; cf. Revelation 11:5. Since, however, the purpose is to *deceive,* the implication is that this sign was an imitation of the fire from heaven which appeared at the coming of the Holy Spirit [certainly not genuinely miraculous, for true miracles are mean to confirm, not deceive.—J. O. Y.]

In the sight of. This is from the same Greek word as "before" in the preceding verse. The fire came from heaven to earth in the presence of men.

Verse 14. *And deceiveth them that dwell on the earth by the means of those miracles which he had power to do in the sight of the beast; saying to them that dwell on the earth, that they should make an image to the beast, which had the wound by a sword, and did live.*

And deceiveth them . . . by . . . miracles. The deception is limited to the distinct class, the earth dwellers, and undoubtedly these all succumbed to the delusion. However, the purpose of the beast was apparently to deceive all men, for he makes fire to come down in their presence (as above), no restriction being made here to a particular class. The word for miracle is *sign,* the same as for "wonders" in verse 13.

Which he had power to do. For the words, *he had power to do in the sight of the beast,* read *it was given him to do in the presence of the beast* (Greek). These words seem to indicate clearly that the enabling of the second beast to do (*poieo*) came not from the first beast but from the dragon.

Saying. The word *saying* is important because it shows that the second beast is more than an actor; he is a speaker as well. The title applied to him in later passages (16:13; 19:20; 20:10), *the false prophet,* is therefore quite appropriate.

Make an image. It is noteworthy that the false prophet addresses the order to make (*poieo*) an image to the beast to the earth dwellers in particular. That they did so is not stated in so many words, but the following verses show plainly that they responded readily to his mandate. Reference to the image occurs ten times in six different chapters. 13:14, 15 (three times); 14:9, 11; 15:2; 16:2; 19:20; 20:4. As usual upon first mention, the word is anarthrous (without the article "the"). The important part the image is to play in the brief period yet remaining is seen by the frequent references later.

To the beast, which had the wound by a sword. Observe *an image to the beast,* that is, in his honor, and for his benefit, not merely an image *of* the beast. There is no mistaking who is meant by the beast, for again *the wound* alludes to verse 3 above, namely, to the first beast. The wound is inflicted by a sword.

And did live. These words are the equivalent, and hence an inspired interpretation, of "was healed" (verses 3, 12). It has already been noted that the phrase applied to the beast, "as it were wounded to death" (Greek: *hos esphagmenon*), is the exact equivalent of "as it had been slain" in reference to the death of Christ (Revelation 5:6), and so the words "did live" used in reference to the first beast are the exact equivalent of those spoken of Christ—"and is alive" (Revelation 2:8) in reference to the resurrection of Christ. Just as truly as the words applied to Christ speak of His death (by violence) and of His resurrection, so the precise language applied to the Antichrist can only signify his death (by violence) and his resurrection.

Verse 15. And he had power to give life unto the image of the beast, that the image of the beast should both speak, and cause that as many as would not worship the image of the beast should be killed.

And he had power to give life. For *and he had power . . .* read—*and it was given to him to give spirit unto the image of the beast* (Greek). The word for *life* is *pneuma* in the Greek. Out of a total of 385 occurrences in the New Testament, this is the only place where it is translated *life. Pneuma* means literally *wind* and is so translated in John's Gospel (3:8)—"the wind bloweth where it listeth." It is almost universally translated by spirit or ghost (in passages where the Holy Ghost is meant). The rendering "spirit" may refer either to the spirit of man or to the Holy Spirit.

What should be clear is that the false prophet did not give *life* to the beast. To give life is solely the prerogative of the Godhead. Like the magicians of old (Exodus 7:11, 22, *et al.*), he doubtless will perform feats of magical art and thus deceive many through this sleight of hand performance. Irenaeus, one of the earliest of the church fathers, spoke well on this point: "Let no one imagine that he performs these wonders by divine power, but by the working of magic. And we must not be surprised if, since the demons and apostate spirits are at his service, he through their means performs wonders, by which he leads the inhabitants of the earth astray."[42] For the word *life* we should substitute *breath* or *wind* (air). [That robots have been developed is common knowledge.—J. O. Y.]

The image of the beast. Observe the phrase, *image of the beast,* occurring as it does twice in this verse. This should settle the question once for all that by the first beast an individual is intended, for how could an image of an empire be possible? And again, how could an empire be killed by a sword and live again, after a brief period, with increased powers sufficient to command and secure all but universal homage and worship?

And cause that as many as would not worship . . . should be killed. He causes *(poieo).* It appears strange that some otherwise careful expositors understand this language as though what the beast, with his armor-bearer (as Irenaeus designates the second beast), purposes to do, he will actually accomplish, in executing all who will not worship the beast. Were this the case, all flesh would perish—those who refuse to worship the beast, and those who worship the beast; for, as has already been observed in unmistakable language, all who worship the image will be tormented forever and ever. 14:10, 11. No one can consistently hold the view that the nations of the earth will finally enjoy a period of peace on the earth if all the saints are martyred during the tribulation period and all the wicked are doomed to eternal torment. Bear in mind the words of our Lord, who spoke clearly on this point: "Except those days should be shortened, there should no flesh be saved" (Matthew 24:22). In the light of these words, the present context must be interpreted.

Verse 16. *And he causeth all, both small and great, rich and poor, free and bond, to receive a mark in their right hand, or in their foreheads.*

Six classes are enumerated, which is in accord with the prominence given to this number in this passage. Verses 12-18. The three pairs suggest association with the evil trinity, as well as extremes in social relationships, implying universal application of the terms submitted in the proposed decree. While the three pairs are of frequent occurrence in the Scripture, it is only here that they are brought together in a single sentence.

It will be observed that the couplets vary in the order of rank, the first—"small and great"—going from the lower to the higher, while in the two pairs following, the more honorable are mentioned first. Probably this implies that the false prophet begins his program with the little ones, who are more susceptible to his deceptions, and that if he gets them the big folks will follow.

A mark. Thayer, the Greek lexicographer, is undoubtedly right when he defines *charagma* as the mark stamped on the forehead or the right hand as the badge of the followers of Antichrist.[43] The word occurs eight times. 13:16, 17; 14:9, 11; 15:2; 16:2; 19:20; 20:4. The brand signifies ownership and was commonly used as a means of identification, on slaves as well as animals.

Right hand, or . . . foreheads. The mark on the *right hand* or on the *forehead* may be intended to enable one to distinguish between those who are engaged in intellectual pursuits and those who labor with their hands.

Verse 17. *And that no man might buy or sell, save he that had the mark, or the name of the beast, or the number of his name.*

The use of a mark or brand in civic, social, and industrial circles is becoming quite prominent. While this trend may be a forerunner of the mark of the beast, it is erroneous to conclude that these are what is meant by the mark of the beast. The beast and the false prophet must make their appearance before the mark of the beast is imposed and that will not be until after the middle of the tribulation period. When once the mark of the beast is imposed upon men, only those receiving the mark can either buy or sell. Since such restrictions are not yet in vogue, it is evident that the time for the mark of the beast has not yet arrived.

Or the name . . . or the number. The first *or* is omitted by many authorities. If it is retained, it should be translated *either.* Then the passage would read: *save he that had the mark—either the name of the beast or the number of his name.* The thought is that either the name of the beast or his number will be required as a brand or mark upon all.

Verse 18. *Here is wisdom. Let him that hath understanding count the number of the beast: for it is the number of a man; and his number is Six hundred threescore and six.*

Here is wisdom. There is apparently an allusion to Daniel 12:10: "None of the wicked shall understand; but the wise shall understand." The Daniel passage pertains to the precise period which is under consideration, namely, to "the time of the end." Moreover, the reference in each case is to the latter half of this period as the time notes indicate. Cf. Daniel 12:7; Revelation 12:14 and 13:5.

A similar but somewhat lengthened expression occurs in 17:9: "Here is the mind which hath wisdom." The thought is that wisdom is required for understanding what follows in each case. The Greek uses the definite article *the,* signifying that a special kind of wisdom is intended, undoubtedly the wisdom which God gives. James 1:5; 3:17; I Corinthians 2:13. As is often the case, the Book of Daniel furnishes several pertinent parallel passages. Daniel 1:17; 2:18, 20, 21, 23, 30.

Five times in Revelation clauses begin with the Greek word *hode* (here). Besides the present verse see 17:9. In these instances the reference is to what follows; in the remaining passages—13:10 and 14:12 (twice)—to what precedes.

Let him . . . count. Any who have insinuated that the undertaking of such a task is mere folly or presumption and that all attempts to do so are at best a mere guess should remember that the verb *count* is in the imperative. It is a command. It signifies "to calculate by the use of figures," that is, arithmetical figures. The word occurs only once elsewhere in the New Testament, in which case one building a tower is spoken of as first counting the cost. Luke 14:28. The allusion appears to be to the ancient custom of giving to letters of the alphabet a numerical value.

The beast. That this is the first beast is plain from the fact that the second beast gave orders to the earth dwellers to make an image to the beast which had the wound by a sword and did live. Verse 14; cf. verse 3. In verse 15 it is called the image *of* the beast. This beast is called "one of his heads" (verse 3) and is consequently one of the "seven heads" (verse 1) or one of the seven imperial heads, or emperors of Rome.

The number of a man. The number of the beast is said to be the number of a man. The beast is therefore not a kingdom merely, but a man—a human being.

Six hundred threescore and six. The number 666 is unique. Since the number 6 represents evil throughout the Scriptures, the three 6's may well represent the infernal trinity of the chapter, viz., the dragon, the beast, and the false prophet.

It is significant that six Roman numerals make up this total: I+V+X+L +C+D = 666. This alludes to the possibility of a Roman being the Antichrist. All the numerals from 1 to 36 total 666. *Beast* in the evil sense occurs exactly 36 times (6 x 6) in Revelation.

Some texts, including the received text, in place of the number 666 have three letters of the numerical value 666. They are χξς. The first and last letters are the same as those which begin and end the Greek word for Christ. The middle letter resembles in form a crooked serpent. This may show the serpentine character of the Antichrist, for thus Satan would seek to obliterate Christ. Anyone receiving the number of the beast would thereby bear testimony to his allegiance to the infernal trinity.

The question still remains. Can the individual be identified? The custom of using letters of the alphabet as numbers dates back to pre-Christian days. Numerous examples could be cited from Jewish literature. Not only is this usage found in the Hebrew writings, but in the Greek as well. Besides their ordinary use as a means of calculation, names of individuals were occasionally hidden under the numerical value of the letters composing them.

The numerical values were applied in this manner: the first ten letters of the alphabet increased by units, i.e., a-1; b-2; c-3, etc. After the tenth and up to the nineteenth inclusive they increased by tens, i.e., 20, 30, 40. From the twentieth on the increase is by one hundred, i.e., 200, 300.

This order holds throughout in the Hebrew. In the Greek alphabet, due to the fact that from very ancient times a letter was dropped between what are now the fifth and sixth letters and between the fifteen and sixteenth, two must be added in these places. A third letter was early discarded, but as this came after the last in the present alphabet, it does not affect the enumeration of values.

Revelation 17:9-11 and 19:19, 20 are almost indispensable to a full understanding of the problem in this chapter. However, suffice it to say that the beast now being considered is the one spoken of in chapter 17 as having "fallen," and is one of the five who had met with a violent death before John wrote, and yet he is said to be the last of the seven imperial heads of Rome. Now if it can be determined who are the five Roman emperors intended, it undoubtedly will be clear as to which of these will have the name totaling 666; at any rate, if perchance only one of them answers to the details. The name Nero Caesar does not occur in Revelation; in fact, nowhere in the New Testament except in the postscript to II Timothy in the Authorized Version, where it occurs in the Hebrew form *Kaisar Neron*. Had John used the name, he doubtless would have written it with the Hebrew endings as he does the other proper names, viz., Abaddon, Apollyon, and Armageddon, in which the second last letter is a long o. Using only the consonants as the Hebrew does, the numerical values of the Hebrew composing *Kaisar Neron* are: (K) = 100;   (S) = 60;   (R) = 200;   (N) = 50; (R) = 200;   (O) = 6;   (N) = 50.   As Nero alone totals 666, he must be the emperor intended. [At least one must admit a most striking coincidence has been cited.–J. O. Y.]

The Episode of the Lamb with the 144,000 on Mt. Zion (14:1-5)

Verse 1. *And I looked, and, lo, a Lamb stood on the mount Sion, and with him an hundred forty and four thousand, having his Father's name written in their foreheads.*

And I looked, and, lo, or *and I saw, and, behold.* This is the eighth time the strengthened form of this phrase occurs in which the seer not only announces his observation of a distinct vision but requests his auditor to see for himself.

A Lamb stood on the mount Sion. The Mount Zion upon which John sees the Lamb and the 144,000 standing (14:1) cannot be the earthly Mount Zion as Bengel, Hengstenberg, and others have correctly shown because those who are standing there, hear and learn the song sounding from heaven, which is sung before the throne and the four living creatures and the elders (14:3). The Mount Zion in this instance, as in Hebrews 12:22, belongs to the heavenly Jerusalem. The article before *mount Sion* clearly specifies a definite *Sion.* (Compare with this Galatians 4:26.)

It will be noticed that in every other case where *Sion* occurs in the New Testament (Matthew 21:5; John 12:15; Romans 9:33; 11:26; I Peter 2:6) it is without the article and without the qualifying word *mount.* It therefore may be assumed that *Sion* alone according to New Testament usage refers to the earthly city; *mount Sion* to the heavenly.

Some have taken Revelation 14:1 to be proleptic, and point forward to the 144,000 standing on the earthly Jerusalem. Since, however, "all Israel shall be saved" when "they . . . look upon . . . [him] whom they have pierced" at His second coming (Zechariah 12:10; Romans 11:26) and "a nation be born at once" (Isaiah 66:8), the Scriptures give no support to the view which holds that a select few of Israel will be marked with such a distinction after the return of the Lord. Were such the case, it would appear that those who fled from Judea and who were miraculously nourished in the wilderness for 1,260 days (Matthew 24:16; Revelation 12:6, 14) would share in this honor. Moreover, the *usus loquendi* (use of words) is also against such an interpretation, for John frequently speaks of earth dwellers (lit., sitters) but rarely of earth standers and never in the sense here implied. On the other hand, the word *stand* is regularly applied to groups or individuals in heaven or before the throne. Cf. 5:6; 6:17; 7:9, 11; 8:2; 15:2; 20:12.

These *hundred forty and four thousand* are apparently the same company as those mentioned in 7:1-8. Were this not the case, it would be an exception to the usual careful distinction made by the sacred writer by the use of "another." For instance, note "another beast," "another angel," "another sign," "another voice"; hence we should have here "another" 144,000. Observe, too, that mention is made of a seal or mark of identification *upon* [Greek] *their foreheads.* Cf. 7:3.

Having his Father's name written in their foreheads. Most of the manuscripts and all the early church fathers who quote the passage read, *Having his name [that of the Lamb] and the Father's name upon their foreheads.* Why this change in the seal from that of "God" in chapter 7 to both that of the Son (Lamb) and the Father? It is highly probable that when the former sealing took place early in the tribulation period, the one hundred and forty and four thousand of the tribes of Israel had not yet received Christ as their Saviour. Since, however, they returned to their land in recognition of the promise made to the fathers and foreseeing their faith, God graciously set His mark upon them, thus safeguarding them and apparently making them immune to the ravages of the trumpet judgments that followed in chapters 8 and 9. Thus the goodness of God doubtless led them to repentance and faith in the Lord Jesus Christ; whereupon, having become sons, they were sealed with the name of the Father and with the name of the Son.

Verse 2. *And I heard a voice from heaven, as the voice of many waters, and as the voice of a great thunder: and I heard the voice of harpers harping with their harps.*

A voice from heaven. The voice from heaven appears to be that of the 144,000 mentioned in the preceding verse. Their mention in the following verse corroborates this view.

Voice of many waters . . . a great thunder. The resemblance of the voice to the voice of many waters and a great thunder suggests majesty, sublimity, and enormity such as would naturally proceed from a multitude of the redeemed.

The description given marks this company as belonging to a third great group of glorified ones who are seen in heaven before the coming of Christ in glory. Chapter 19:11 ff. They apparently are identical with the second group mentioned in 19:6. The first group are the throne sitters (4:4); the second, the robe wearers (7:9, 13).

Harpers harping. The harps appear to identify the group as consisting of or belonging to those of 15:2.

Verse 3. *And they sung as it were a new song before the throne, and before the four beasts, and the elders: and no man could learn that song but the hundred and forty and four thousand, which were redeemed from the earth.*

A new song. Note that *a new song* is anarthrous (without the definite article). This points to the conclusion that this song is not the same as that sung by the elders. 5:8, 9. [Standard Greek grammars point out that the absence of the article emphasizes characteristic.—J. O. Y.]

Before the throne . . . beasts . . . elders. Since they sing *before* (lit., in the presence of) *the throne,* they cannot at the same time stand on the earthly Sion. They sing *before . . . the elders;* hence they constitute a different group. If they are on the earth, so would the elders have to be.

No man [Greek: *no one*] *could learn that song.* This includes the elders, which corroborates the above statement that their new song is different from the elders' new song.

Which were redeemed from the earth. They were *redeemed from the earth.* In 28 out of its 31 uses in the New Testament the original word for *redeem* is translated *buy.* However, in 5:9, here, and in verse 4 below it is correctly rendered "redeem." As 5:9 shows, the redemption is "to God." Since this implies change of ownership, it also, as is frequently the case elsewhere, includes removal. (Cf. Thayer.) Since this is directly stated concerning the one hundred and forty-four thousand, it is another proof that they are not standing on the earthly Sion.

Verse 4. *These are they which were not defiled with women; for they are virgins. These are they which follow the Lamb whithersoever he goeth. These were redeemed from among men, being the firstfruits unto God and to the Lamb. These . . . these . . . these.* The threefold repetition of *these,* together with its emphatic position, is meant to express the high honor of which they are worthy. The point is not in that they were superior saints, but in that they maintained their virtue and steadfastness in the midst of a corrupt social environment and in that they were obedient unto death in the evil day.

Not defiled with women; for they are virgins. These kept themselves undefiled in their social relations. From passages such as 9:21; 17:2; 19:2 the enormity of the sin of social vice during this period is emphasized. Elsewhere the use of *virgin* is applied to, or includes, men. Matthew 25:1; II Corinthians 11:2. Since these are Israelites, there is doubtless an allusion to passages in the Old Testament in which Israel is referred to as "the virgin daughter of Zion" (II Kings 19:21; Isaiah 37:22; Lamentations 2:13), and "virgin of Israel" (Jeremiah 18:13; 31:4, 21; Amos 5:2).

These are they which follow the Lamb whithersoever he goeth. Note that *Lamb* is the sacrificial name applied to Christ. The Lamb went to the cross; so these were obedient not only in daily walk and conduct but, like Him, "obedient unto death."

In the coming evil day and in the midnight of that day, when sin has its deepest dye and when virtue is at a premium, it is said of the 144,000, *These are they which were not defiled with women. . . . These are they which follow the Lamb whithersoever he goeth.* [Like saints from Moses to Paul, they stood for truth in times of deepest gloom.—J. O. Y.]

The firstfruits unto God and to the Lamb. The meaning of first fruits is to be found in its use in the Old Testament Scriptures in which the first ripe fruits were offered to God in token that the whole harvest belonged to Him. The first fruits consisted of a small portion of the harvest that followed.

This sense of the word also is apparent from its use in the New Testament Scriptures. The first converts of a country are referred to as the first fruits of the great harvest of Christians to follow. Romans 16:5; I Corinthians 16:15. The apostle declares, "if the firstfruit be holy, the lump [the greater mass] is also holy" (Romans 11:16). Christ is the first fruits of the resurrection harvest of all men. I Corinthians 15:20, 23. Similarly the 144,000 Israelites are the first fruits unto God and the Lamb of a greater harvest to follow.

Who is this greater company of the glorified that is yet to come? The reference can neither be to the church nor to the white-robed martyrs because their glorification has already taken place. It cannot be to the great body of Gentiles who will yet turn to the Lord, because Israel in the future will remain a distinct people from the nations and will be a blessing to them, "for out of Zion shall go forth the law, and the word of the Lord from Jerusalem" (Isaiah 2:3). "Yea, many people and strong nations shall come to seek the Lord of hosts in Jerusalem, and to pray before the Lord" (Zechariah 8:22).

This suggests the only simple and Scriptural answer. The one hundred and forty-four thousand *out of* (Greek) all the tribes of the children of Israel (7:4) are *the firstfruits* of "all Israel" which will yet be saved. Cf. Romans 11:26; Zechariah 12:9, 10; 13:1. It is when Jesus comes again after the tribulation that Israel will "look upon . . . [him] whom they have pierced," whereupon they will repent of their unbelief and sin; wherefore "all Israel shall be saved."

Verse 5. *And in their mouth was found no guile: for they are without fault before the throne of God.*

No guile. Most of the manuscripts and fathers have *lie* in the place of *guile.* Obviously, however, as Alford remarks, "the apostle has before him the words of Psalm 15:1 ff. so strikingly similar"[44] in which the original words for *guile* and *without fault* are found. It is probable that an error crept early into the text and was copied by the authorities who use the proposed reading.

The usage of words is also against the change because Peter's language (and he quotes verbatim from Isaiah 53:9) in I Peter 2:22, "neither was guile found in his mouth," has the original word *dolos* just as it is in our text. Nowhere in the Scriptures do we find a passage that would support the reading, "in their mouth was found no lie." The internal testimony is therefore against the revised reading. It is well to stay with the received text.

Without fault. The original for *without fault, amomos,* occurs seven times and is translated in six different ways: "without blame" (Ephesians 1:4); "without blemish" (Ephesians 5:27; I Peter 1:19); "unblameable" (Colossians 1:22); "without spot" (Hebrews 9:14); "faultless" (Jude 24); and *without fault* (Revelation 14:5). In two instances the reference is to the perfection of Christ. Hebrews 9:14; I Peter 1:19. The remaining passages refer to believers, either as being "without blemish" in Him, or in His presence. It should be said that the words, "before him" (Ephesians 1:4) and "in his sight" (Colossians 1:22), are identical in the Greek with "before his presence" (Jude 24).

Before [in the presence of] *the throne of God.* Evidently there has been a good deal of tampering with the text in the opening verses of this chapter. Most authorities drop this phrase entirely. Among those retaining the words is the Latin Vulgate. The internal evidence also favors their retention since nowhere is found such an isolated statement pertaining to saints as their omission, viz., "they are without blemish." It is only when in a glorified state that such a declaration is becoming or consistent regarding believers; hence the words are to be regarded as genuine and as furnishing conclusive proof that they are in heaven, since the throne of God is never spoken of as being on the earthly Sion.

The Angel Announcing the Everlasting Gospel (14:6, 7)

The rest of the chapter presents a sevenfold division consisting of the appearance of six angels including a vision of the Son of man between two groups of three angels each.

Verse 6. *And I saw another angel fly in the midst of heaven, having the everlasting gospel to preach unto them that dwell on the earth, and to every nation, and kindred, and tongue, and people.*

Another angel. Another is significant because had there been no previous mention of an angel flying in midheaven (Greek) the word *another* would be superfluous. The reference is obviously to 8:13, where the same language occurs. In commenting on that verse it was noted that the Revised Version reads *eagle* for *angel* in accordance with the Westcott-Hort edition of the Greek New Testament. On this point Dr. Nestle (who, however, wrote too early to anticipate the failure and fate of the Westcott-Hort canons of criticism) says: "The reading ἀγγέλου [angel] in viii. 13 . . . seems to me to be corroborated by ἄλλον ἄγγελον πετόμενον [another angel flying] in xvi.6."[45]

Everlasting gospel. The original omits the definite article; hence read everlasting gospel [stressing character.—J. O. Y.]. The inference may be that the substance of this Gospel is different in nature and content from that preached by the apostles, especially from what Paul calls "the gospel of the grace of God" (Acts 20:24). It is called an *everlasting gospel.* It will be recalled that on three different occasions (6:9; 11:7; 12:11) mention has been made of such as were slain because of the witness they bore on earth to "the word of God." Now since the beast and the false prophet have launched their program of destruction on the earth and human testimony is no longer possible, the God of the heavens deputizes three heavenly messengers to continue the witness in mid-air. Moreover, since Satan and his cohorts have so recently been ejected from heaven by Michael the archangel, there is not the slightest hint that there will be any successful attempt to interrupt their world-wide ministrations.

Unto them that dwell on the earth. The universality of this ministry is disclosed in that the message from midheaven is given to *them that dwell on the earth, and to every nation, and kindred, and tongue, and people.* Note that here, as in 11:9; 13:7, earth dwellers are mentioned as a distinct group from the other four terms which elsewhere (5:9; 7:9; 10:11; 17:15) are given as including all of earth's inhabitants. It is noteworthy that this distinct group, who apparently "mind earthly things" and devote themselves to sensual gratification, is mentioned first in connection with this final proclamation of good news by the heavenly messenger.

There is probably an allusion here to the words of Christ in Matthew 24:14, "This gospel of the kingdom shall be preached in all the world for a witness unto all nations; and then shall the end come." However, the witness of Moses and Elias during the first half of the tribulation period, as well as that of the 144,000, may also be included in the prediction of the Olivet discourse. Since the words tell of a proclamation of the Gospel of the kingdom as a sign of the end of the age, they must necessarily have their fulfillment in the period now being considered. The church has failed in this world-wide witness, but the Lord's Word will not fail. The world-wide witness will be accomplished during the tribulation period by heavenly messengers.

Verse 7. Saying with a loud voice, Fear God, and give glory to him; for the hour of his judgment is come: and worship him that made heaven, and earth, and the sea, and the fountains of waters.

Loud voice. The *loud voice* denotes solicitude and urgency. It is peculiarly appropriate to the implications of the message.

Fear God, and give glory to him. The nature and content of the heavenly

message call for special attention. The message undoubtedly is to serve as an anti-
dote to that given by the false prophet as well as to the entire program of the infernal trinity. In that message are the implications: "Fear the beast, give glory to
him, and worship him." Here it is, *Fear God, and give glory to him . . . and worship him.* But it is what follows that should cause men to make the wise decision.
Fear God, and give glory to him because He *made heaven, and earth, and the sea,
and the fountains of waters.* These are His credentials and the ground for the
urgent appeal.

What does the beast have to offer to solicit the homage and respect of mortal
man? What has he done to merit worship and glory from creatures made in the
image of God and endowed with the possibility of awakening in His likeness?
Nothing whatever! His authority and power are not his own and they have been
bestowed upon him by a defeated and fallen fiend; he killed God's two witnesses;
he has "a mouth speaking great things and blasphemies. . . . And he . . . [opens]
his mouth in blasphemy against God, to blaspheme his name, and his tabernacle,
and them that dwell in heaven."

With the rival candidates for the universal homage and worship of mankind
thus clearly portrayed, including their character and deeds, one should expect the
gates of salvation to be crowded with penitent seekers. Contrariwise, nothing in
Holy Writ so graphically portrays to what depths the sons of Adam may fall as do
the chapters of the immediate context. The incentives to wise choice and right
conduct on the part of God's auditors (which here constitute the entire human
race) are not yet exhausted, for in addition to this divine proclamation and invitation for men to fear God and give glory to Him, there follow two other celestial
messengers pronouncing doom upon the disobedient.

Why is there no call to repentance and faith in the Lord Jesus Christ in the
angel's message?

It is because God's dealing with man during "the end of the age" (6-18) is
unlike that of the church period. This is shown clearly by the change of vocabulary so strikingly different in the periods mentioned. The great and fundamental
words, such as grace, truth, faith, hope, love, joy, peace, mercy, etc., are either
entirely wanting during the tribulation period or else they are used in a different
or opposite sense. For instance, "joy" is used only of God's enemies (11:10), or
of the glorified in heaven (12:11); "peace" is mentioned only in the passage: the
red horse rider will "take peace from the earth" (6:4). In no instance during this
period is a command given to repent, and where the word occurs it is used negatively—men "repented not" (9:20, 21; 16:9, 11). Similarly no one is commanded
to exercise faith or to believe, and faith is ascribed only to martyrs. 13:10; 14:12.

It will be observed that the command to *Fear God, and give glory to him* is
given because the hour of His judgment is come. The ground for worshiping Him
lies in the fact that God made all things. Apparently the auditors were for the
most part unsaved men, yet it appears that their immediate salvation was not the
object of the angel's message. It was rather that they might refrain from taking
the mark of the beast and the worship of his image and thus escape the doom of
those who did. On the other hand, by fearing God, by giving Him glory, and by

worshiping Him they could be kept from the worship of the beast and probably be spared until greater inducements contingent upon events yet to come would lead them to genuine repentance and to a saving faith.

The Angel Announcing the Doom of Babylon (14:8)

Verse 8. *And there followed another angel, saying, Babylon is fallen, is fallen, that great city, because she made all nations drink of the wine of the wrath of her fornication.*

Another angel. This angel followed the one mentioned in verse 6; therefore he also flew in midheaven.

Babylon is fallen, is fallen. The repetition is for emphasis and denotes the utter ruin of the city. The words are a quotation from Isaiah 21:9 and occur again in 18:2. The expression is anticipatory as is evident from the fact that the city does not fall until the seventh vial is poured out (16:19), the details of which are given in chapter 18.

It has become increasingly clear even to opposite schools of thought that by Babylon in Revelation, Rome is intended. The testimony of the early church fathers is so convincing and decisive in this, that anyone familiar with it knows that they take this as an established fact. Just as Jerusalem "spiritually is called Sodom" (11:8), so Rome spiritually is called Babylon. And Rome is this in a two-fold sense, for she is both the religious and the political successor of the former Babylon.

That great city. (Greek: *the city, the great.*) Babylon is so designated seven times (14:8; 17:18; 18:10, 16, 18, 19, 21) and three times "Babylon the great" (16:19; 17:5; 18:2). She is the world's metropolis (mother city—17:5).

Because she made all nations drink. Why will Babylon fall? *Because all nations have drunk* [*so the Greek*] *of the wine of the wrath of her fornication.* Since various readings occur, note the following: Some texts read *who* instead of *for.* However, in 18:3 the precise language occurs—see there the first clause; hence not only is the evidence that *because* is to be retained, but the translation should likewise be uniform. It appears as if some scribe, partly because he observed that Babylon is not destroyed at this time and partly because he desired to express the guilt of Babylon in a more direct way, changed *have drunk* into *made . . . drink* and *because* into *who.* The language is proleptic (as is so frequently the case) and hence points forward to 18:3 ff. Where the fall of Babylon actually takes place, of course, it is true that the nations drank of the cup through her entice-ment, but they were not compelled to do so, i.e., they were not *made* to drink it. [It needs to be shown, however, that the word *drink* in Greek is causative in idea. —J. O. Y.]

Another variation occurs, namely, the omission of the phrase, *of the wrath,* and this apparently on internal grounds. For instance, it is claimed that wrath would not induce one to drink of the wine; hence some authorities omit the phrase, *who made all nations drink of the wine of the wrath of her fornication.* But this supposed correction removes no difficulty, neither is it pertinent from the fact that, as in the former case, the exact language of the text reappears in 18:3. The suggestion by Drs. Swete[46] and Charles[47] simplifies the purge. *The wine of the wrath* brings together two phrases which occur separately elsewhere, viz., "the wine of the wrath of God" (14:10) and "the wine of her fornication" (17:2). [The phrases from 14:10 and 17:2 translated from Greek by J. B. S.—J. O. Y.] The thought then is, the woman entices the nations with her "golden cup . . . full of abominations and filthiness of her fornication" (17:4), the nations drink the cup and are "made drunk with the wine of her fornication," on which account the wrath of God comes upon them. The passage may be paraphrased, therefore, as follows: "All nations have drunk of the wine [of Babylon] for which act of fornication the wrath [of God] came upon her."

The message of the angel is for the purpose of bringing comfort and hope to the faithful among the nations by announcing the impending doom on Babylon (Rome), the persecuting power. "The hour of . . . judgment is come"—it will not be long.

The Angel Announcing the Doom of the Beast Worshipers (14:9-13)

Verse 9. *And the third angel followed them, saying with a loud voice, If any man worship the beast and his image, and receive his mark in his forehead, or in his hand.*

Angel followed them. The last word suggests that the angels followed each other in short order—the third followed *them,* the other two. It is probable that the messages were given in close succession so that one had barely finished before the other began.

If any one [Greek] *worship the beast . . . and receive his mark.* This follows hard upon the iniquitous mandate of the beast (13:16, 17) to which it alludes. While the word *mercy* is not mentioned, yet it is clear that in wrath the Lord remembers mercy. Mercy lies in making known the consequences of refusing to heed the solemn warning, which means nothing less than consignment to the most terrible doom anywhere described in Holy Writ.

Verse 10. *The same shall drink of the wine of the wrath of God, which is poured out without mixture into the cup of his indignation; and he shall be tormented with fire and brimstone in the presence of the holy angels, and in the presence of the Lamb.*

The same [Greek: he himself] *shall drink of the wine of the wrath* [anger] *of God, which is poured out without mixture into the cup of his indignation* [wrath]. Observe that compliance with the order of the political head, and yielding to the enticement of the religious head (the woman with the golden cup—17:4) will bring upon each the wrath of God. Cf. 16:19. However, in this instance the wrath has this added note, *without mixture.* There is not a drop of mercy in it! Hence it makes the beast's devotee liable to the "hottest place in hell."

Tormented with fire and brimstone. It may not be possible to reconcile God's punishment of the wicked with His love and mercy. However, the words of the text and all similar statements appearing in the further references yet to come belong to "the words of the book of this prophecy." Let no one, therefore, take away these words, for the last warning near the close says with amazing directness, "If any man shall take away from the words of the book of this prophecy, God shall take away his part out of the book of life." If for no other reason, this act of elimination alone would make the guilty one a candidate for the very place he seeks to escape by his act, for it is written: "Whosoever was not found written in the book of life was cast into the lake of fire" (20:15).

Anyone disposed to discredit the Biblical teaching on the eternal destiny of the wicked should be reminded that Jesus and His beloved disciple said more in regard to this doctrine than all the remaining contributors to the New Testament record. The word "hell" occurs twelve times in the New Testament. Jesus mentioned it (*gehenna*) eleven times, James once. The word "fire" (pertaining to hell) occurs nineteen times (two other uses, Matthew 3:11; Luke 3:17, are in dispute): twelve are by Jesus, one by Jude, and six by John in Revelation. Various adjuncts occur with fire to express reality, severity, and ceaseless continuity, e.g., lake of fire, furnace of fire, fire and brimstone, hell fire, unquenchable fire, everlasting punishment, everlasting destruction, everlasting fire. Out of twenty-five occurrences as above, nineteen are by Jesus, four by John, one by Paul, and one by Jude. Eternal torment is spoken of as the portion of three parties: beast worshipers (14:11); the great whore (19:2); and the devil, the beast, and the false prophet (20:10).

In the presence of the holy angels, and in the presence of the Lamb. The Greek word (*enopion*) is here to be understood in the sense, *in the sight of*, as is frequently the case. Anyone receiving the mark of the beast or worshiping his image will be tormented in the sight of angels and the Lamb. This doubtless implies that while in torment the wicked will see angels whose kindly ministries they had spurned and Jesus who is here designated the Lamb because they rejected His atoning sacrifice. Their sight of their would-be benefactors intensifies their torment. This was undoubtedly the case with the rich man when he saw Lazarus far off, and comforted in the bosom of Abraham. Luke 16:19-31. In either case the couplet—

"For of all sad words of tongue or pen,
The saddest are these: 'It might have been!' "
will have a terrible significance.

The destiny of the image worshipers is fixed and unalterable, for they, in yielding to the behests of the beast, denied Christ before men; now He also denies them "before the angels of God" (Luke 12:8).

There is apparently here also an allusion to the angels flying in midheaven who have just concluded their messages of good news and timely warnings. The beast worshipers consequently are doubly worthy of stripes for refusing the name of the Father and the Son and instead taking the mark of the beast, and for rejecting the messages of the angels flying through mid-air. Now as they are in the sight of both Jesus and the angels, they have the eternal ages in which to lament the folly of their fateful choice.

Verse 11. *And the smoke of their torment ascendeth up for ever and ever: and they have no rest day nor night, who worship the beast and his image, and whosoever receiveth the mark of his name.*

The smoke of their torment ascendeth up for ever and ever. The torment is of those who worship the beast, and of those receiving his mark. The smoke ascends from the torment. The verb is in the present tense; there is no break and no cessation in the ascending of the smoke and consequently not of the torment. There can be no torment where there is no conscious living existence; therefore conscious living existence must be forever and ever. Forever and ever expresses the duration of God's existence. If His existence is without end, so is that of the wicked because the same term is employed to express the duration of both. This is the strongest term in the Scriptures denoting ceaseless continuity. It is used of the ascriptions of praise that ascend both to God and Christ; of the duration of His reign; of the torment of the beast worshipers, of the great whore, of the devil, the beast, and the false prophet; and of the future reign of His servants. Hence the absurdity of the view that being cast into the lake of fire implies cessation of existence.

They have no rest day nor night. No rest implies unbroken continuance of torment. There is no letup of its severity. The phrase, *day nor night,* expresses the same thought and is added for emphasis. How similar the doom of the evil trinity who concocted and executed this infamous ordeal of death and destruction is seen in their final sentence. Cf. Revelation 20:10.

Verse 12. *Here is the patience of the saints: here are they that keep the commandments of God, and the faith of Jesus.*

Here is the patience of the saints. As in 13:10b, an abbreviated form of the present passage, reference is made to what is mentioned before. In both passages there is apparently an allusion to Matthew 24:13, "He that shall endure unto the end, the same shall be saved," for two reasons: the passage in Matthew synchronizes with this, for it tells of the sign of the end of the age (Greek), which is identical with the tribulation period; the Greek word for patience is the same as that for endure, the one being the nominal, the other the verbal form.

They that keep the commandments of God. The words imply that despite the threat of the beast and the false prophet, there will be those who, heeding the message and warning of the angels flying through midheaven, will refuse to worship the beast and to receive his mark and die as martyrs. They keep the commandments of God and faith in Jesus even though it means death. Observe, however, that while these martyrs are slain because they refuse to take the mark of the beast and to worship his image, others are slain when the beast makes war against the saints and overcomes them. 13:7. Consequently, these belong to the last of the three glorified groups (see Appendices), the former to the second group, i.e., to those slain for the witness they held.

A little reflection will show that there will be many of the nations who will not receive the mark of the beast, for when Jesus comes in His glory "many nations" will come and worship the Lord at Jerusalem. None of these will have received the mark of the beast because it is expressly stated that all such will be tormented forever and ever. At least three reasons may be given why those of the (living) nations have not received the mark of the beast nor worshiped his image. Because the days are shortened. Matthew 24:22. Less than half of the tribulation period remains for the beast to carry out his program. Undoubtedly some among those unsaved at the time, while they are subservient to the authority of the beast, nevertheless are determined to refuse his mark. The vial judgments interfere directly with the program of the beast, for the first vial is poured out on the men who have the mark of the beast, while the fourth is poured out upon his throne. 16:2, 10.

Verse 13. *And I heard a voice from heaven saying unto me, Write, Blessed are the dead which die in the Lord from henceforth: Yea, saith the Spirit, that they may rest from their labours; and their works do follow them.*

I heard a voice. This is the fifth of the seven voices from heaven. 10:4, 8; 11:12; 14:2, 13; 18:4; 21:3. The unique significance of a voice from heaven is seen in the fact that the ordinary means of communication (through angel agency) is foregone and presumably the voice comes from one of the Holy Trinity, and probably—as it appears from this instance—from the Holy Spirit.

From heaven. The language implies that the Spirit no longer is an abiding Comforter on the earth, and consequently that the church has been removed from earth to heaven. Observe also that during the church period (chapters 2 and 3) whenever the Spirit spoke it was uniformly "unto the churches" in the formula, "He that hath an ear, let him hear what the Spirit saith unto the churches." No sound reason can be given for the omission of the phrase, "unto the churches," were she still on earth at such a time, for at no time would she need the voice of the Comforter so much as now were she in the midst of those terrible days. It is interesting to note that the voice of the Spirit is heard from heaven in the very heart of this unit of structure.

Write. The command to write is here given for the tenth time. Two more (19:9; 21:5) are to follow. This command also is always associated with matters of unusual importance. The seer may have lingered in contemplation over what has just occurred and needs to be reminded to proceed with his recording. Or it may be to make a point, as one in the process of dictation, when he wishes to emphasize an idea, remarks, "Now get this down as I say."

Blessed are the dead which die in the Lord. This is the second of the seven beatitudes recorded in the book. On another occasion (22:7) the command to write is followed by a beatitude. The blessedness of those dying (as martyrs) in the Lord is in marked contrast with the wretchedness of those dying with the mark of the beast upon them.

From henceforth. These words pertain especially to those who die as martyrs for refusing to submit to the dictates of the beast. The words *from henceforth* have the sense *from now on.* It is always true that those who die in the Lord are blessed, but it will be especially true of those who die as martyrs for their faith and obedience during the great tribulation.

Yea, saith the Spirit. This seems to indicate that the Spirit was the speaker in the words just uttered and now emphasizes His message with His "yea" in introducing further evidences of their blessedness.

That they may rest from their labours; and their works do follow them. That may well have the sense of *because*—they are blessed because they now rest from their labors. This again is in marked contrast to those dying with the mark of the beast, for of them it is said, "they have no rest day nor night" (verse 11). Before the beast worshipers die they will suffer with a noisome and grievous sore. 16:2.

Their works follow *with* them, that is, accompany them, is the sense of the original. As one by one these noble martyrs, who "keep the commandments of God, and the faith of Jesus" unto death, make their appearance in the glory, heaven delights to receive them.

The Harvest of the Earth (14:14-20)

Verse 14. *And I looked, and behold a white cloud, and upon the cloud one sat like unto the Son of man, having on his head a golden crown, and in his hand a sharp sickle.*

And I looked [= I saw] *and behold.* Because of the vast significance of the occasion (a distinct and separate vision appears to the seer) this formula is used. This is its tenth occurrence.

A white cloud. White denotes purity. It is a sharp contrast to the filthiness and corruption of earth and more particularly of the great whore, the false bride. The cloud may be the "sign" of the Son of man which heralds His coming. Matthew 24:30.

Upon the cloud one sat like unto the Son of man. One should be capitalized. No article appears before Son; hence the Greek says, *Son of man.* The One sitting is Jesus, who appears as man, that is, in bodily form like a man, although glorified, as man's body will be in the day of redemption. Philippians 3:20, 21.

The title *Son of man* occurs here and in 1:13, where it is also without the article, *like unto Son of man.* The title as applied to Christ is used in two senses: in reference to the humanity of Christ, and in reference to His capacity as judge. Note that the Father has committed all judgment to the Son because He is the Son of man. John 5:22, 27. The term is applied to Jesus in the Gospels 84 times, 21 of which refer to His second coming. It is highly significant that it is never used after the Gospels except once in Acts 7:56 in Stephen's vision, and only once in all the epistles (Hebrews 2:6) and that in a quotation from Psalm 8:4. The term is never used in respect to His personal relation to the church as the body of Christ. Its use here plainly denotes His appearing as judge.

A golden crown . . . a sharp sickle. The *crown of gold* indicates His glorified and highly exalted state; His royal authority. The sickle alludes to His appearing in the "time of harvest," as a Reaper. The *sharp sickle* denotes severity and judgment. Cf. 2:12; 19:15. The allusion is obviously not in respect to His coming for the church (I Thessalonians 4:13-18) but to His coming as judge at the end of the tribulation period.

Verse 15. *And another angel came out of the temple, crying with a loud voice to him that sat on the cloud, Thrust in thy sickle, and reap: for the time is come for thee to reap; for the harvest of the earth is ripe.*

Another angel. The thought is not that the Son of man is to be regarded as an angel since He is never spoken of as angel, but the angel is another in addition to the three previously mentioned in this chapter. Verses 6, 8, 9.

The temple. The angel comes out of the temple, showing again that God's judgments proceed from His holiness. Since *temple* is not accompanied by a descriptive or qualifying word (as in verse 17), some have taken this to be the earthly temple. However, from other Scriptures it is clear that the abomination of desolation at this time stands in the holy place. This at once precludes the idea that the angel proceeds out of the temple on earth.

Loud voice. This is the fourteenth mention of a loud voice. It would be a matter of interest and fruitful meditation to read consecutively the 21 occasions of the loud voices.

Thrust in thy sickle, and reap. This order of an angel to the Son of man is a remarkable occurrence. It is important to observe this high and sacred performance which is entrusted to an angel. No service is too sacred or lofty for a creature provided he has been divinely endued and commissioned for its performance. Cf. 8:3; 10:1-4.

For the time is come for thee to reap. The reason follows: *for the harvest of the earth is ripe.* It is a matter of surprise and regret to observe how many commentators have failed to notice the meaning of the word *ripe.* One of these dismisses the passage categorically with the trite comment, "ripe for glory." The use of *sharp sickle* in this connection itself should have dissuaded anyone from such an interpretation, for *sharp* (cf. 2:12; 19:15) implies judgment. However, the use of the word in the original should settle its meaning once for all for those whose attention has been called to it. It occurs 16 times in the New Testament and always in a bad or uninviting sense.

The word *ripe* is usually translated wither, e.g., of the fig tree which *withered* away (Matthew 21:19, 20); of the man with the *withered* hand (Mark 3:1, 3); of the branch which was cut off and *withered* (John 15:6); of the seed which sprang up and *withered* away because it lacked moisture (Luke 8:6). It is also translated *dried up* in a few instances: "the fig tree *dried up* from the roots" (Mark 11:20); "the water thereof [of the Euphrates] was *dried up*" (Revelation 16:12).

It should also be said that in more than 50 uses of the word in the Old Testament it is used in this bad, derogatory sense. Cf. Isaiah 40:23, 24; Amos 4:7.

It should be said too that in all the uses of the original Greek word, whether in the Old or New Testament, this is the only place where it is translated *is ripe.* Consistency therefore requires that it be translated here, "the harvest of the earth is withered," the thought being that the inhabitants of the earth are ready for judgment.

Verse 16. And he that sat on the cloud thrust in his sickle on the earth; and the earth was reaped.

This is simply the execution of the command by the angel directed to the Son of man. He will doubtless proceed according to His own explanation in the parable recorded in Matthew 13, that is, He will send forth His angels to execute the harvesting. [The passive form of the verb, *was reaped*, might add to this conclusion.—J. O. Y.]

Verse 17. And another angel came out of the temple which is in heaven, he also having a sharp sickle.

Another angel. The fifth angel now makes his appearance. He too has a *sharp* sickle which, as always, denotes severity in judgment.

Temple which is in heaven. The clause, *which is is heaven,* is not added as though the previous angel had come out of the temple on earth. Indeed the only time the earthly temple is mentioned is in chapter 11:1, 2. Rather, it is inserted by way of contrast to the terrible things which were to come upon the earth. The judgment of blood issues by order from within *the temple which is in heaven,* emphasizing the fact that it is not vindictive but vindicative—God's holiness requires Him to execute the frightful catastrophe in order to vindicate His own holiness and His abhorrence for sin, now that the iniquity of man has come to the full.

Verse 18. And another angel came out from the altar, which had power over fire; and cried with a loud cry to him that had the sharp sickle, saying, Thrust in thy sharp sickle, and gather the clusters of the vine of the earth; for her grapes are fully ripe.

The altar. The altar is that of burnt offering as in 6:9; 8:3a, 5, and again in 16:7. The judgment about to be inflicted is evidently in response to the prayers of the saints under the altar. (Cf. references just given.) This angel, like the one of verse 15 above, does not execute the judgment himself but, like the former, serves as an intermediary in giving the order: *Thrust in thy sharp sickle.*

The vine of the earth. The *vine of the earth* is probably so called in contrast with Israel, the vine of God's planting. Psalm 80:8, 14, 15; Isaiah 5:2-7; Jeremiah 2:21; Ezekiel 17:5-8; Hosea 10:1. By the vine of the earth is to be understood the aggregate of evil men from among all nations who will assemble in the land for the express purpose of destroying not only the vine which the Lord planted but the Lord which planted the vine.

Fully ripe. The iniquity of the nations is full and the time has come for the clock of judgment to strike.

Verse 19. And the angel thrust in his sickle into the earth, and gathered the vine of the earth, and cast it into the great winepress of the wrath of God.

Winepress of the wrath of God. The allusion is plainly to the assembled nations in the valley of Jehoshaphat at which time the Lord will be revealed from heaven to smite the nations with the rod of His mouth, elsewhere designated as the Battle of Armageddon the actual fulfillment of which is recorded in Revelation 19:15. Cf. Isaiah 63:3; Jeremiah 25:30, 31; Joel 3:13b-16a.

Verse 20. And the winepress was trodden without the city, and blood came out of the winepress, even unto the horse bridles, by the space of a thousand and six hundred furlongs.

The city is undoubtedly Jerusalem, for so the prophets declare, e.g., Joel 3:16; Zechariah 14:2, 3.

The symbolism is apparent.

The winevat represents the valley of Jehoshaphat.

The grapes represent the individuals composing the nations.

The grape juice represents the blood of the slain.

> (This probably includes that of horses, etc. Ezekiel 39:18-20; Revelation 19:17, 18.)

The treader represents the Lord. (Note again Isaiah 63:3.)

A *thousand and six hundred furlongs*. The 1600 furlongs are most likely to be understood as a lineal distance of 200 miles. Since the closing scene of the battle appears to be at Bozrah, the chief city of Edom, the southern extremity probably begins there and from there extends to the northern limits of Palestine, which would approximate the distance of 200 miles. A noted seismologist notes that a fault in the crust of the earth runs from below Jerusalem in a northerly direction through the Mount of Olives, and that sooner or later an earthquake may be expected in that area. The prophet Isaiah predicts, moreover, that when the Lord comes He will arise to shake terribly the earth. 2:21. It will be no difficult matter for Him at that time to change and arrange the contour of that region in such a manner that the fulfillment of the prophecy here described will be assured. It is probable that the twenty-ninth Psalm depicts a prophetic preview of this terrible shaking of the earth in its sevenfold reiteration of the voice of the Lord which, in tones of thunder, proceeds from the north, breaking the cedars of Lebanon, makes Lebanon and Sirion (Mt. Hermon—Deuteronomy 3:9) to skip like a young unicorn, divides the flames of fire, and finally after a distance of 200 miles shakes the wilderness of Kadesh (in the vicinity of Bozrah).

The reader should note that in chapter 14 there is a cycle of prophecy describing events and activities which will take place from probably the early part of the last half (3½ years) of the tribulation period until the coming of the Lord in judgment "immediately after the tribulation of those days" (Matthew 24:29, 30).

The Vial Judgments (Chapters 15, 16)

The Prelude (15:1—16:1)

Verse 1. *And I saw another sign in heaven, great and marvellous, seven angels having the seven last plagues; for in them is filled up the wrath of God.*

Another is in reference to two signs already mentioned (12:1, 3), where it was noted that *wonder* should be translated *sign*.

Great and marvellous. The two adjectives occur only in conjunction here and in verse 3 below in the entire New Testament. Clearly, they designate the significance of what is to follow.

Seven angels having the seven last plagues. The definite article does not occur; hence they are probably not identical with any of the seven angel groups mentioned before. 1:20; 8:2. Reference is made to them seven times in the plural form (15:1, 6, 7, 8; 16:1; 17:1; 21:9) and seven times in the singular (16:3, 4, 8, 10, 12, 17; 17:7). By the clause, *having the seven last plagues*, is meant that the infliction of these last plagues was entrusted to them. Since these are called the seven *last* plagues, the question naturally arises, How many plagues are there? All the judgments mentioned under the seals, trumpets, and vials are in reality *plagues*. This appears clear from the following considerations:

Judgments are also called plagues. 16:7; 18:8; 19:2.

The judgments under the seals, trumpets, and vials are similar to the plagues of the Old Testament Scriptures.

The similarity between the vial judgments which are called the *last* plagues and those mentioned under the seals and trumpets is evident.

The word *plagues* is used in connection with judgments on various occasions. Fire, smoke, and brimstone (9:18) are referred to as plagues. 9:20. The two witnesses are spoken of as having smitten the earth with plagues. 11:6. Infliction of death by a sword is in reality a plague, for this is the Greek original for "wound" (13:3b, 12, 14). The judgments of Revelation are spoken of in a summary way as plagues. 22:18.

Is filled up (lit., *is finished*). The word is the same as in 10:7. Note carefully that when the last vial has been poured out (16:17), "there came a great voice out of the temple of heaven, from the throne, saying, It is done." The plagues will end with the seventh vial.

The wrath of God. Unfortunately the translators have confused the importance of the distinction between the original words *anger* (*thumos*) and *wrath* (*orge*). The word here is *thumos*, i.e., *anger*. The word for wrath is the inward emotion, while anger denotes an outburst of the inner feeling. Wrath abides (John 3:36), while anger is a temporary ebullition or impulse. Wrath is an attitude, like holding a grudge; hence the exhortation, "Let not the sun go down upon your wrath." Anger is an act, like the slaying of Abel by Cain.

It is significant that the judgments of the tribulation period are spoken of both in the Old and New Testament as the result of God's anger, while the final outpouring of His displeasure is referred to as wrath. The judgments inflicted by the pouring out of the vials are uniformly spoken of as expressions of the anger of God and it is not until after the seventh vial has been poured out that great Babylon comes in remembrance before God, to give her the cup of the wine of the anger (Greek) of His wrath. 16:19.

Verse 2. *And I saw as it were a sea of glass mingled with fire: and them that had gotten the victory over the beast, and over his image, and over his mark, and over the number of his name, stand on the sea of glass, having the harps of God.*

Sea of glass. It is probable that the sea of glass is identical with that mentioned in 4:6 even though "as it were" (Greek: *hos*) takes the place of the definite article. (See the clause below where the article occurs and *hos* is omitted.) The variation may be accounted for by the qualifying phrase, *mingled with fire*, which takes the place of "clear as crystal" in the previous mention. The presence of *fire* denotes judgment, while "clear as crystal" suggests purity and holiness. The former vision took place before the time of judgment had come. These judgments issue forth from a holy God. In accordance with this reaction of a holy God upon sin "when it is finished," the sea of glass clear as crystal becomes a sea of glass *mingled with fire*. It is fitting that the symbol comes as a preface to the climax and final judgments in the outpouring of the vials of God's anger.

Them that had gotten the victory. This is a participial phrase consisting of the definite article followed by a participle; hence, literally, *those having overcome the beast.* The Greek syntax is the participle followed by ek, from or out of. This is the only instance of this preposition following the verb *overcome.* The intent is, *those having come off as victors in their conflict with the beast.*

Image, . . . mark, . . . number of his name. These plainly identify this beast with the first beast of chapter 13, repeatedly mentioned in the closing verses of that chapter and identified as the Antichrist. Like the martyrs of 12:11, they overcame by not loving their lives unto the death. They refused to worship the beast, to receive his mark or the number of his name. They overcame by refusing to yield to his demands and consequently died as martyrs. They follow in the train of their Master and by dying achieve an immortal victory.

As to their place among the glorified group as summarized in 20:4, they with the 144,000 of chapter 14 clearly belong to the third and last, for they "had not worshipped the beast, neither his image, neither had received his mark upon their foreheads, or in their hands."

Having the harps of God. Observe that the martyrs of chapters 14 and 15 are distinguished from the former groups of chapters 7, 11, and 12 by their harping with their harps and those from these by their being "slain for the word of God, and for the testimony which they held," and the first, the church group, from the two latter by their being seated on thrones, that judgment was given unto them, and by no mention of them having been slain.

Verse 3. *And they sing the song of Moses the servant of God, and the song of the Lamb, saying, Great and marvellous are thy works, Lord God Almighty; just and true are thy ways, thou King of saints.*

Song of Moses. The song of Moses has usually been taken to be that recorded in Exodus 15. Upon examination it will be observed that this song is nowhere called the Song of Moses. "Then sang Moses and the children of Israel this song unto the Lord, and spake, saying, I will sing unto the Lord, for he hath triumphed gloriously: the horse and his rider hath he thrown into the sea" (verse 1). This song would appear to be entirely inappropriate. The song intended is more likely the one in Deuteronomy 32. It is recorded that Moses wrote it and taught it (Deuteronomy 31:22) and "spake in the ears of all the congregation of Israel the words of this song" (Deuteronomy 31:30).

The reading of this song in the latter days will likely be one of the means God has to bring Israel back to Himself. The song itself states this in its closing sentence, and not only Israel but their *land* as well. 32:43.

In his commentary on Isaiah (Chapter I) Delitzsch in reference to "Moses' dying song" remarks: "This song is a compendious outline or draft, and also the common key to all prophecy. . . . In every age, therefore, this song has presented to Israel a mirror of its existence, condition, and future fate. And it was the task of the prophets to hold up this mirror to the people of their own times."[48]

Note the content of the Song of Moses (Deuteronomy 32): God's stability (He is our Rock) and faithfulness in contrast with the instability and fickleness of Israel (1-6); God's gracious provision and tender care for Israel (7-14) in contrast with their ingratitude and apostasy (15-18); "when the Lord saw it, he abhorred them. . . . And he said, I will hide my face from them"—corresponding to Hosea 1:9, "not my people"—"a very froward [perverse] generation, children in whom is no faith" (19, 20); God moves Israel to jealousy with those who are not a people (21; cf. Romans 11:11); Israel's dispersion and affliction with its climax in "the day of their calamity" (22-35) (this, the time of Jacob's trouble, and the tribulation, the great one, specify the same event); Israel's extremity is God's opportunity; He has compassion upon His servants "when he seeth that their power is gone"—"I wound, and I heal" (36-39); Israel's enemies are now God's enemies, as expressed in these words: "I will render vengeance to *mine* enemies, and will reward them that hate me" (verse 41).

> " I will make mine arrows drunk with blood,
> And my sword shall devour flesh
> With the blood of the slain
> And with the head of the princes of the enemy" (verse 42).

This translation of Deuteronomy 32:42 places the lines according to the poetry of the original Hebrew. Line three supplements line one; and line four, line two. Note the important change in the translation of the last line, a rendering which was decided upon before observing that the Bible Commentary, Gesenius, Bullinger, and others have substantially the same. The reference is plainly to Armageddon including the slaying of the Antichrist. Cf. Revelation 19:17-21. The song closes (verse 43) with God's favor upon His land and His people. The nations are bidden to rejoice. The "healing" of Israel apparently precedes that of the nations (cf. verse 39) as also the Scriptures elsewhere abundantly testify. Thus God makes good the words of His covenant with Abraham. Genesis 12:2, 3.

In comparing the so-called Song of Moses as recorded in Exodus 15:1-19 with the one just considered, the reader will observe that the former is occupied almost exclusively with the triumph of Israel over Pharaoh at the crossing of the Red Sea, while Deuteronomy 32 is a comprehensive survey of the entire history of Israel from the beginning to the end when she will be a blessing to all the nations of the world. This song is indeed a "key of all prophecy."[49]

Note again that this song shall testify against Israel as a witness when many evils and troubles are fallen upon them. Deuteronomy 31:21. Moreover, Moses declared, "I know . . . evil will befall you in the latter days" (verse 29) (cf. Deuteronomy 4:30, "when thou art in tribulation, and all these things are come upon thee, even in the latter days").

It is certain therefore that those Israelites who bear witness to the Word of God during "the time of Jacob's trouble" will not fail to include the Song of Moses in their testimony. Undoubtedly this new and last reminder, especially the closing of the song, coming as it does just before the outpouring of the last plagues, will be one of the most effective means of preparing the sons of Israel for the acceptance of their Messiah, when shortly they will "look upon . . . [him] whom they have pierced."

And the song of the Lamb. It does not say, "They sang the song of Moses and the Lamb," as it is frequently quoted. *Song* is repeated. In each case it is preceded by the definite article and connected by the conjunction *and*. Two songs are therefore implied.

The Song of the Lamb might pertain to a psalm such as the twenty-second, which so vividly expresses His lamblike character and sacrifice. It is significant that this same psalm which begins, "My God, my God, why hast thou forsaken me?" (words which the Lord uttered on the cross as the Lamb slain) also gives the issue and triumph of that sacrifice, "All the ends of the world [earth] shall remember and turn unto the Lord: and all the kindreds of the nations shall worship before thee" (verse 27). The psalm closes with "It is done" (Hebrew). The following words may be taken as a chorus to the two songs. However, it may be more appropriate to consider them as the song of the Lamb.

Great and marvellous are thy works. If the sign presaging the outpouring of the vials is marvelous, equally so are the works of the Lord God Almighty. The glorified saints know as much about the latter (soon to be) as the seven angels know of the former.

Just and true. The ways of God, whatever they may be to accomplish His purposes, are *just and true.*

King of saints. Manuscript evidence is in favor of the reading, *King of nations.* So is the internal evidence, for nowhere in the Scriptures is either the Father or the Son designated as *King of saints.* Note also "all nations" in the verse following which gives support to the title, *King of nations.*

Verse 4. Who shall not fear thee, O Lord, and glorify thy name? for thou only art holy: for all nations shall come and worship before thee; for thy judgments are made manifest.

Fear thee, O Lord. The opening words may refer to the message of the first angel flying in midheaven: "Fear God, and give glory to him" (14:7). However, there appears a distinct reference to Jeremiah 10:7: "Who would not fear thee, O King of nations?" Reverence and glory are due only to a holy God. Cf. Psalm 30:4; 97:12. The reason is plain—men become like the gods whom they worship; so the psalmist declares with respect to the gods of the heathen: *They that make them are like unto them.* Psalms 115:5; 135:16, 17, 18a.

All nations shall come and worship before thee. This glorious prospect is declared repeatedly in the Scriptures. Psalms 66:4; 72:11; 86:9; Isaiah 66:23; Zephaniah 2:11; Zechariah 14:16, 17. It is particularly heartening that such an announcement comes when the severest of all plagues are about to be released upon the inhabitants of earth. By what means or from what source will come the fulfillment of this glorious triumph? The next clause gives the answer: *for thy judgments are made manifest.* Not by a gradual correction of the *status quo* nor by the connivings of the human mind will the kingdom come; not by missionary effort, social betterment, the ballot box, peace conference tables, etc., but as the Old Testament prophet already in his day declared, "When thy judgments are in the earth, the inhabitants of the world will learn righteousness" (Isaiah 26:9). As many as 20 passages of Scripture can be found which show that the final glory will be preceded by tribulation or judgments.

Verse 5. And after that I looked, and, behold, the temple of the tabernacle of the testimony in heaven was opened.

I looked. A new vision introduces factors and movements which lead directly to the outpouring of the vials. Whenever the seer requests the attention by calling upon the reader to behold for his own interest or benefit, something of unusual importance is about to be introduced.

The temple. The word for temple in Revelation is always *naos,* that is, the sacred enclosure consisting of the holy place and the most holy, hence known as *the sanctuary.*

The tabernacle of the testimony. It is so called because it contained, in the most holy place, the ark of the testimony with the two tables of stone upon which were written the Ten Commandments. Exodus 32:15. The phrase, *tabernacle of testimony (skene matyrion),* occurs in Acts 7:44 and frequently in the Old Testament. Exodus 38:21; Numbers 1:50, 53 (twice); 10:11; 17:7, 8; 18:2.

Was opened. By this apparently is meant the veil is lifted, which indeed is a matter of the highest importance. In considering the details of the heavenly sanctuary, one should keep in mind that the imagery accords with the tabernacle in the wilderness rather than with either of the temples of later construction. Only regarding the former was it said, "See . . . that thou make all things according to the pattern shewed to thee in the mount"—an injunction repeated seven times.

Verse 6. And the seven angels came out of the temple, having the seven plagues, clothed in pure and white linen, and having their breasts girded with golden girdles.

The seven angels came out of the temple. Observe that the seven angels come out of the sanctuary, indicating again that the judgments of God are not vindictive but vindicative. Even though the vials of God's anger are poured out upon men who are hopelessly hardened in sin, yet their infliction proceeds from His holy character which requires Him to punish the obstinate and impenitent rather than from His justice which would incline Him to do so. [Though the distinction may be hard to draw at times.—J. O. Y.]

Clothed in pure and white linen. Since they are clothed like the glorified church, they may be the angels of the seven churches. Revelation 19:8, 14. The clothing of the angels should not be interpreted as identical with that of the bride (19:8, 14) since the words in the original language are radically different, the former being *hussinos;* the latter, *linon.* Neither are there sufficient grounds to read *lithon* (stone) for *linon.* Nor is the clothing of the high priest in mind. If it were, the plural form would be used instead of the singular; besides, the ministry of these angels is almost diametrically in contrast with that of the high priest.

Breasts girded with golden girdles. As in the case of the Son of man (1:13), the statement suggests that in wrath God remembers mercy. This investment of the angels accords with the fact that they proceed from the sanctuary.

Verse 7. And one of the four beasts gave unto the seven angels seven golden vials full of the wrath of God, who liveth for ever and ever.

One of the four beasts. By this is to be understood a living creature or cherub. At their first mention it was seen that they guard the holiness of the divine presence and that this function accompanies them in all their appearances upon the sacred page. It is but fitting therefore that one of these be divinely appointed to deliver the vials of anger to the seven angels. By this gesture they express their accord with the divine purpose to administer the climax of terrestrial torments upon the obdurate and impenitent.

Wrath of God. Note that the Greek for wrath is *thumos,* not *orge.* Therefore, read *anger of God*. As stated before, wrath is reserved unto the day of wrath at the close of the tribulation period.

For ever and ever. This is the eleventh occurrence of the term *for ever and ever.* This declaration respecting the eternal God suggests that He who in the beginning pronounced suffering and death in case of sin and disobedience still lives to execute the penalty upon the guilty.

Verse 8. *And the temple was filled with smoke from the glory of God, and from his power; and no man was able to enter into the temple, till the seven plagues of the seven angels were fulfilled.*

The temple was filled with smoke. The smoke filling the temple suggests the emanation of God's displeasure accompanying the outpouring of the vials of anger in judgment upon the wicked. The smoke proceeds from the glory and power of God, making it impossible for any *one* (Greek) to enter into the temple until the administration of the seven plagues is finished. Similar manifestations have occurred even when individuals alone were concerned in God's corrective measures. Psalm 18:6-8; Isaiah 6:3, 4.

16:1. *And I heard a great voice out of the temple saying to the seven angels, Go your ways, and pour out the vials of the wrath of God upon the earth.*

A great voice. This is the *great* chapter of the Bible. The word occurs eleven times: a great voice (verses 1, 17); great heat (verse 9); great river (verse 12); great day (verse 14); great earthquake (verse 18—twice); great city (verse 19a); great Babylon (verse 19b); great hail (verse 21a); great plague (verse 21b). All these great things relate themselves to the seven last plagues.

Out of the temple. While a cherub gives the vials to the seven angels, apparently God Himself gives the order to pour them out upon the earth. While the order is given to all the angels at one time, they pour them out consecutively.

Notice the marked similarity between the objects affected by the vial and the trumpet judgments. While there are variations in each case, there are certain similarities: first, the earth; second, the sea; third, rivers and fountains of waters; fourth, the sun; fifth, darkness; sixth, the Euphrates; seventh, voices, thunders, lightnings, earthquakes.

There is also a distinct difference in the first four of each, for while in the trumpet judgments only one third was affected, in the vial judgments there is no such reservation; hence the afflictions apparently will be universal. The exception occurs in the first, for some have been assured protection and support during the last 1,260 days. Chapter 12. (See also Isaiah 26:20, 21.)

The First Vial (16:2)

Verse 2. *And the first went, and poured out his vial upon the earth; and there fell a noisome and grievous sore upon the men which had the mark of the beast, and upon them which worshipped his image.*

Poured out his vial upon the earth. The first vial is poured out upon the *earth.* Compare with this the first trumpet. 8:7. While in each case the earth is the object of the plague, the result is very different. In the trumpet one-third part of the trees and all green grass was burnt up. Here a noisome and grievous sore falls upon the men who yielded to the mandate of the beast. An important point on interpretation is to be noticed in the former instance, for while only one-third part of the trees were burnt up, *all* of the green grass was burnt up. The point is that likewise while the sore fell only upon the devotees of image worship, it is possible that the whole earth suffers in some other way not distinctly mentioned.

This plague corresponds with the sixth plague of Egypt. It is interesting to note that the word translated *boil* in the Greek translation of the Old Testament is translated *sore* in the Greek of the New Testament.

Another important point on interpretation is seen in the fact that the pouring out of the first vial must have been some considerable time after the first beast (Revelation 13) came into power, which was at the beginning of the last half of the tribulation period. 13:5. The beast made war with the saints and overcame them (11:7; 13:7) before the appearance of the second beast. 13:11. Some time must have elapsed for the second beast to perform the miracles accredited to him previous to the making of the image. 13:12-14. The making and setting up of the image consumed some time for completion. Some time must have passed between the publication of the edict and the slaying of the 144,000. 13:15—14:3. Then followed the proclamations of the three angels flying through midheaven, the last of whom gave the message of warning regarding the worship of the beast or receiving his mark. 14:6-10. It would appear that the reception of the mark of the beast and the worship of his image had become widespread when the first vial was poured out.

From these considerations one may conclude that the outpouring of the vials does not take place till near the close of the tribulation period and that from all appearances they followed one another in close succession.

The men which had the mark of the beast. Since the judgment of the first vial is said to fall upon a particular class of men, i.e., *upon those which had the mark of the beast, and upon them which worshipped his image,* the implication is that there were those living who had not been or would not be brought under his power. Evidently he had not yet succeeded in inflicting his death-dealing edict in all parts of the inhabited world. Since the requirement was either to impose the mark or to kill each individual, and the days remaining, between the issuing of the edict and the time of the first vial, were already shortened to probably less than two years, it might well be the case that a considerable number of the people still living were not accosted by the emissaries of the beast.

The Second Vial (16:3)

Verse 3. *And the second angel poured out his vial upon the sea; and it became as the blood of a dead man: and every living soul died in the sea.*

Poured out his vial upon the sea. With this compare the second trumpet, when one third of the sea became blood and a third part of the creatures in the sea which had souls (Greek) died. 8:9. These plagues have their correspondence to the first plague in Egypt (Exodus 7:20, 21), at which time the Nile River was turned into blood and the fish that were in the river died.

The Third Vial (16:4-7)

Verse 4. *And the third angel poured out his vial upon the rivers and fountains of waters; and they became blood.*

The rivers and fountains of waters, that is, those waters which are intended to slake the thirst of man, are now affected, just as they were under the third trumpet. Waters are doubtless to be taken in a literal sense as is shown by the use of the term in 14:7.

Verses 5-7. *And I heard the angel of the waters say, Thou art righteous, O Lord, which art, and wast, and shalt be, because thou hast judged thus. For they have shed the blood of saints and prophets, and thou hast given them blood to drink; for they are worthy. And I heard another out of the altar say, Even so, Lord God Almighty, true and righteous are thy judgments.*

Angel of the waters. In the Book of Revelation a greater variety of ministries are assigned to angels than in all the rest of the Bible put together. Compare the ministry of the angel of the waters with the four angels of the winds (7:1-3), to whom it was given to hurt the earth and the sea, and with the angel which had authority over the fire (14:18).

The pronouncement by the angel of the waters, in the midst of the outpouring of God's anger, is apparently for the same purpose as was that of those who had gotten the victory over the beast in singing the Song of Moses and the Song of the Lamb; of the seven angels coming out of the temple having their breasts girded with golden girdles; and of one of the living creatures in delivering the seven golden vials to the seven angels—namely, to vindicate the Eternal God in the infliction of His righteous judgments upon the wicked in retribution for their murderous acts upon His saints. Such is the implication of the angel's declaration: *Thou art righteous, O Lord, which art, and wast, and shalt be, because thou hast judged thus.*

Which art, and wast, and shalt be. This is the fifth and last occurrence (with slight variation) of the formula denoting the eternal, independent existence of God.

They have shed the blood of saints . . . they are worthy. The reference is to martyrdom during the tribulation period, of which these who are given blood to drink are guilty. The sufferers are the victims of the inexorable law of retribution, variously expressed as the law of such for such, of eye for eye, the law of retaliation, *lex talionis*, reaping what you sow, being paid in one's own coin, falling in the ditch you dig for another, hanging on Haman's gallows.

Shedding of blood during this period is first mentioned in 6:9, 10. That group is identical with or included in the great multitude of martyrs described in 7:9-14. The next martyrs mentioned are the two witnesses who prophesied in 11:3-7. The order of words, *saints and prophets*, may be accounted for by the fact that the "slain" with no official title come first in the list of martyrs.

Omitting the expression, *which art, and wast, and shalt be*, the declaration of the angel falls in the following order:

Their shedding of blood proves they are worthy.

Because they are worthy the Lord judged them, that is, gave them blood to drink.

His giving them blood to drink proves that He is righteous. Remember, they are worthy (but what a worth!). [The fact is, they are blameworthy.—J. O. Y.]

Another out of the altar. Some authorities omit the words, *another out of,* and thus make *altar* the object of the verb. The internal evidence is, however, in favor of retaining them. Some living personality would have to be understood, because an altar cannot utter words. There seems to be a direct allusion to 14:18, where mention is made of an angel coming *ek* (out from) the altar. The altar here, as in the former instance, is evidently the altar of burnt offering. There is doubtless an allusion to the prayers of the martyrs (6:9, 10) under this same altar. The judgment of the third vial is still in answer to those prayers. They were asked to "rest . . . for a little season, until their fellowservants also and their brethren, that should be killed as they were, should be fulfilled." It will not be long until their testimony that their prayers have been fully answered will be heard. 19:1, 2. It may, therefore, be assumed that the voice is either from an angel at the altar representing the martyrs or else the combined voice of the slain.

True and righteous are thy judgments. It is fitting that this voice from the brazen altar should add the words, *Even so, Lord God Almighty, true and righteous are thy judgments,* to those already heard to justify the ways of God to man.

The Fourth Vial (16:8, 9)

Verses 8, 9. *And the fourth angel poured out his vial upon the sun; and power was given unto him to scorch men with fire. And men were scorched with great heat, and blasphemed the name of God, which hath power over these plagues: and they repented not to give him glory.*

Poured out his vial upon the sun. The correspondence with the plague of a fourth trumpet is seen in that on both occasions the sun is affected. (If anyone is disposed to think that the judgments under the trumpets are not plagues, let him observe that the word *smite* in the clause, "the sun was smitten," is the verbal form of the noun *plague*.) However, the contrasts in the two plagues are more conspicuous than the agreements. In the former instance, the moon and stars were likewise affected, while here it was only the sun. Only the third part was affected there, while here is no such limitation. The effect of the former was that light was lessened; here heat was intensified.

Power was given unto him. There is no word for *power* in the Greek, but the thought is implied. By *him* is to be understood the sun, not the angel. This is plain from a later clause where it is stated that *God has power over these plagues.* The thought then is, God gave power to it (the sun) to scorch men with fire.

To scorch men with fire. The Greek has the definite article, *to scorch the men with fire.* The reference seems to be to the men mentioned in verse 2. If this is the case (and the verses following appear to support the view), then this plague, like the first, is intended more especially for the image worshipers.

And men were scorched with great heat. The literal rendering of the first clause is, *and the men were scorched with a great scorching.* Note as before the use of the definite article before *men.* Again the reference is probably to the beast worshipers. This should not be construed to mean that the beast had succeeded in imposing the mark upon all the living, but the territory covered by the plagues was undoubtedly coextensive with that under the control of the beast. (The clause contains an example of what is known as "cognate accusative," the verb and its object having a kindred meaning. The expression emphasizes intensity.)

And blasphemed the name of God. Neither the erstwhile goodness of God nor His severity induced the men to fear God nor to turn from their evil ways. Contrariwise, they blasphemed His name and *repented not to give him glory.* Like Pharaoh, they hardened their hearts in the midst of the most terrible suffering mortal flesh can endure. However, one need not marvel at their impenitence and obduracy in the light of the proclamation of the third angel flying in midheaven: "If any man . . . receive his mark [the mark of the beast] . . . the smoke of their torment ascendeth up for ever and ever." [Which seems to seal their fate.—J. O. Y.]

The Fifth Vial (16:10, 11)

Verses 10, 11. *And the fifth angel poured out his vial upon the seat of the beast; and his kingdom was full of darkness; and they gnawed their tongues for pain, and blasphemed the God of heaven because of their pains and their sores, and repented not of their deeds.*

The seat of the beast. The Greek reads, *the throne of the beast.* The reference is to the first beast of chapter 13, or the Antichrist. Cf. II Thessalonians 2:4. This judgment undoubtedly serves as a decided check on the program of the beast. While the edict declared that all those who refuse to worship the beast should be killed (13:15), this must not be construed to mean that all men everywhere either worshiped him or were martyred. If that were the case, there would be no nations nor Israelites left to own Christ as King at His coming.

His kingdom was full of darkness. The similarity again appears in the corresponding trumpet judgment in that darkness accompanied both. Compare with these the ninth plague of Egypt when the land was covered with darkness which could be felt. Exodus 10:21.

They gnawed their tongues for pain. No description of mortals in agony approaches that endured by the doomed more nearly than this. Cf. Luke 16:19-31.

And blasphemed the God of heaven. In the previous judgment (verse 9), "[they] blasphemed the name of God"; here the blasphemy is directed against *the God of heaven.* Sin grows as it goes. The Bible gives repeated notice of this. Genesis 4:3-9; Psalm 1:1; 19:12, 13.

Because of their pains and their sores. This shows clearly they were suffering from their pains and from their sores (inflicted at the outpouring of the first vial) at the same time; consequently, the men here are the same as those mentioned in verse 2. This also supports the view that the vials were poured out in close succession.

And repented not of their deeds. This is the fifth and last mention of refusal to repent. The first has reference to Thyatira (2:21), which represents the papal church. She was warned that if she did not repent she would be cast into great tribulation. (Note also 9:20, 21; 16:9.)

The Sixth Vial (16:12)

Verse 12. *And the sixth angel poured out his vial upon the great river Euphrates; and the water thereof was dried up, that the way of the kings of the east might be prepared.*

The great river Euphrates. Special attention is attached to the Euphrates from the fact that it is one of the four rivers which flowed through the Garden of Eden. Genesis 2:14. It also forms the eastern boundary of the land "which . . . [the Lord] did swear to give . . . to Abraham, to Isaac, and to Jacob . . . for an heritage" (Genesis 15:18; Exodus 6:8); and to their seed after them. Deuteronomy 1:7; 11:24; Joshua 1:4.

It is remarkable to what extent preparation for the fulfillment of the prediction concerning the drying up of the great river already has been accomplished.

During the greater part of the year the people of Hillah (the village now representing Babylon at its lowest extremity) dig deep into wells into the dry river bed for their drinking water. About the village are a few date gardens which have suffered from drought during recent years.

". . . by far the larger portion of the region between the rivers [Euphrates and Tigris] is at present an arid, howling wilderness, strewed in the most part with broken pottery . . . and bearing nothing but the camel thorn, the wild caper, the colocynth-apple, wormwood, and the other weeds of the desert."[50]

A few parallel passages may be consulted with interest: "And the Lord shall utterly destroy the tongue of the Egyptian sea; and with his mighty wind shall he shake his hand over the river [Euphrates—so Delitzsch, Alexander, etc.], and shall smite it in the seven streams, and make men go over dryshod" (Isaiah 11:15). "And he shall pass through the sea with affliction, and shall smite the waves in the sea [Egyptian=Red], and all the deeps of the river [Euphrates] shall dry up: and the pride of Assyria [in the east] shall be brought down, and the sceptre of Egypt [west] shall depart away" (Zechariah 10:11).

The kings of the east. Surely this pertains to nations east of the Euphrates River, and since Japan is the farthest east, it would undoubtedly be included among the kings of the sunrising. It should be observed that *of the east* should read *from the east*, or *sunrising*. [Japan has, as all are fully aware, the self-styled designation, "The Land of the Rising Sun."—J. O. Y.] As in the case of the seal and trumpet judgments, between the sixth and the seventh of the series there is an episodical passage. This episode apparently is inserted to show that immediately after the events associated with the outpouring of the sixth vial, not only the kings from the east but the kings of the whole earth will be gathering "to the battle of that great day of God Almighty." [One is forced to think of Red China.—J. O. Y.]

(It is significant that Gog, the king of the north parts, and his accompanying hosts [Ezekiel 38:3, 15] are not mentioned here. Their not being mentioned is undoubtedly due to the fact that they had been destroyed previously (presumably seven years, i.e., at the beginning of the tribulation period). This explains the utter silence of the mention of the northern army.)

The Episode of the Unclean Spirits (16:13-16)

Verse 13. *And I saw three unclean spirits like frogs come out of the mouth of the dragon, and out of the mouth of the beast, and out of the mouth of the false prophet.*

Three unclean spirits. The demonic spirits (verse 14) incarnated themselves in forms resembling frogs. Compare these with those resembling horses (9:7) and with the infernal cavalry (9:17).

They issue from the mouths of the infernal trinity: the dragon, the beast, and the false prophet. The evil trinity is brought together in close conjunction and named in the order of rank and authority. They thus serve as an excellent guide for correct interpretation elsewhere, especially in chapter 13, concerning which considerable confusion has prevailed as to the identity of the two beasts. For convenience they are arranged in parallel columns.

Chapter		
13:4a dragon	13:4b beast	13:11 another beast
	:12 first beast	
16:13 dragon	16:13 beast	16:13 false prophet
19:	19:20 beast	19:20 false prophet
20:2 dragon	20:10 beast	20:10 false prophet
Devil		

[This to Dr. Smith seemed to be ample proof that the three composed what he called the "infernal trinity," and were a travesty on the Eternal Trinity. The devil from Biblical history is seen to be in constant effort to thwart or to counterfeit the work of the God of heaven.—J. O. Y.]

Verse 14. *For they are the spirits of devils, working miracles, which go forth unto the kings of the earth and of the whole world, to gather them to the battle of that great day of God Almighty.*

Working miracles. The Antichrist (II Thessalonians 2:9) and the false prophet (Revelation 13:13-15) have already been spoken of as working miracles during this period. Now they are followed by three demonic spirits who go forth deluding and inducing the kings of the entire habitable world to the great decisive battle of the ages, a battle not between rival kings of the earth but between all the kings of the earth and the Lamb that was slain on Calvary!

To the battle. Some have spoken of this engagement as one of a series of conflicts succeeding each other in rapid succession on the ground that it is referred to as a *battle.* While there are apparently shifting scenes in this last conflict, the point cannot be sustained because the original word for battle is *polemos,* which is always translated *war* when the reference is to this occasion, both in the nominal and verbal form. 17:14; 19:11, 19. The word for battle is *mache.* (See James 4:1 where both words occur, and hence are to be distinguished.)

God Almighty. This is the eighth out of the nine occurrences of the word *Almighty.* The word is mentioned only once elsewhere in the New Testament. II Corinthians 6:18. The occasion of its mention in each instance calls for the actual presence of the Almighty, and the reader will note this point in the passages with interest and profit.

Verse 15. *Behold, I come as a thief. Blessed is he that watcheth, and keepeth his garments, lest he walk naked, and they see his shame.*

I come as a thief. The expression, *come as a thief,* occurs seven times in the New Testament under various circumstances and relations. Note Matthew 24:43 and Luke 12:39 in which by way of simile the coming of Christ is likened to the coming of a thief to such as do not "watch." The Apostle Paul refers to "the day of the Lord" coming as a thief in the night to them that say, "Peace and safety." This will be accompanied by sudden destruction. He assures those who are children of the day that that day will not overtake them as a thief, "for God hath not appointed us to wrath" (I Thessalonians 5:2, 4, 9). The Apostle Peter likewise describes "the day of the Lord" as coming "as a thief in the night" in referring to the closing period of time when all things will be dissolved. II Peter 3:10. In the message to the church at Sardis comes the warning, "If therefore thou shalt not watch, I will come on thee as a thief." The inference is, as in the words of Jesus on Mt. Olivet, that He will not come as a thief to those who "watch" or are "ready."

In Revelation 16:15 the direct unqualified statement, *Behold, I come as a thief,* has reference, doubtless, to His coming in His revelation from heaven at the close of the tribulation, described in detail in 19:11 ff. Since He evidently comes only once as a thief, any former statements pertaining to His coming in this manner must be understood in reference to this final coming when indeed He will come as a thief "to kill, and to destroy" (John 10:10). Cf. II Thessalonians 1:7-9.

Blessed is he that watcheth, and keepeth his garments. This is the third beatitude. Commentators generally explain this keeping of garments as signifying the garments of salvation. The rest of the verse then is taken in a figurative sense: *lest he walk naked,* signifying spiritual nudity; *and they see his shame,* the manifestation of immoral or shameful character. But whatever grounds there may be for understanding the passage in a figurative sense, why should the literal sense receive no consideration by the commentators?

To take the garments as a symbol of salvation appears untenable from the fact that nowhere in Scripture is the believer exhorted to keep his own salvation. Consequently, it appears that literal garments are intended. There seems to be abundant reason for exhortations such as these since abbreviated garments and even nudism are being advocated by Christian professors even now. What may not be expected in warmer climates during the days of the tribulation?

This verse shows also that there will be some saved people on the earth at that time who have not died as martyrs, but who will have watched and will have kept their garments.

They see his shame. The *they* probably refers to the assembled nations. One who does not properly cover the body will become an easy victim in that day.

Verse 16. *And he gathered them together into a place called in the Hebrew tongue Armageddon.*

He gathered them. He undoubtedly refers to God Almighty. Verse 14. What strange synergism! In verse 14 the demonic spirits are said to gather the kings of the earth; here God Almighty is said to gather them. Note also that in verse 12 the water of the Euphrates River was dried up (apparently under the providence of God) to prepare the way of the kings of the east, ostensibly that they might conveniently reach their objective—the same battlefield.

Armageddon. Armageddon is literally the Mount of Megiddo overlooking the plain of Megiddo west of the mount and apparently including the plain of Esdraelon. This valley which has been the site of numerous great conflicts in past ages is adjacent to the valley of Jehoshaphat near Megiddo and the scene of this last and greatest of all conflicts. It is known as the valley of decision, signifying that here will be the great decision as to whether Satan or God Almighty will be the final and sole ruler on the earth. More details of this conflict will be given in the exposition of chapter 19 where the actual fulfillment is described.

The Seventh Vial (16:17-21)

Verse 17. *And the seventh angel poured out his vial into the air; and there came a great voice out of the temple of heaven, from the throne, saying, It is done.*

Poured out his vial into the air. Why should this the last vial, the last of the plagues of judgment, be poured out into the air? The question seems the more perplexing since the prince of the power of the air has been cast down upon the earth. Revelation 12:9. However, in these days of universal air-mindedness [and space-mindedness—J. O. Y.] a new answer seems to be forthcoming to this question which has kept commentators of former days guessing. True, Satan has been cast down out of the air, at the time indicated, but men of the earth have taken possession of it. It is generally conceded and is officially declared by responsible army officers that the nation having the greatest supply of planes [now missiles and satellites—J. O. Y.] is the nation that will win the war. The Scriptures declare that the northern army in the latter days will "ascend and come like a storm, . . . like a cloud to cover the land [of Israel]" (Ezekiel 38: 9, 16). The allusion to air travel seems to be beyond question, for how else could an army cover the land like a storm or cloud? While this war is apparently not identical with Armageddon (at least not in its first phase and objective) (Ezekiel 38:11, 12), it will ultimately be a part of that final conflict. Ezekiel 39:4, 17-20. The pouring out of the seventh vial into the air is probably a gesture pointing to the utter demolition of man's greatest final weapon in human warfare, when once the wrath of God is poured out in the great day of God Almighty.

A great voice . . . from the throne. The voice from heaven no longer comes through an intermediary but direct from the throne, that is, from God Himself. He proclaims the final word, *gegonen—it is done!* Here is the fulfillment of the proleptic statement in 10:7, "But in the days of the voice of the seventh angel, when he shall begin to sound, the mystery of God should be finished." The judgments which were to come upon the earth are concluded with those under the seventh vial. It is significant that the same words are repeated on a later occasion, and that they likewise come from Him that sits on the throne. 21:5a, 6a. This proclamation signifies that with the seventh vial His purpose in sending judgments upon sinful man has come to an end. The later announcement signifies that His entire program in behalf of the human family including His purpose in revelation has been brought to a final conclusion. In each case the proclamation is followed by details pertaining to things previously mentioned in a general way, chief among which is Babylon (Rome), the great whore, in the one text, and the holy Jerusalem, the bride, the Lamb's wife, in the other. It will be noticed too that in each case after the word of finality a few supplementary items intervene before the detailed description is given.

Verse 18. *And there were voices, and thunders, and lightnings; and there was a great earthquake, such as was not since men were upon the earth, so mighty an earthquake, and so great.*

The reader will recall that a similar refrain occurs at the close of the seals (8:5) and trumpets (11:19). The implication is that in each series of judgments the very close of the tribulation period is in focus and that the refrain of lightning and thunder in each case is intended as an omen of the approaching storm which is about to break upon the wickedness of man, ripe for judgment. With reference to the unprecedented severity of the earthquake, it is but to be expected that as man increases in wickedness, so the plagues will increase in destructive force.

Verse 19. *And the great city was divided into three parts, and the cities of the nations fell: and great Babylon came in remembrance before God, to give unto her the cup of the wine of the fierceness of his wrath.*

The great city. Two great cities have been cited (11:8), Jerusalem and Babylon (Rome), the former the city of God, the latter the headquarters of Satan. Here apparently Jerusalem is intended because she is distinguished from the cities of the nations, which would not be the case if Rome were meant; great Babylon is none other than Rome; if *the great city* were Rome, it would be absurd to refer to great Babylon as another city as is implied by the conjunction *and.*

Three parts. Compare 11:13 where a great earthquake caused the tenth part of the city (Jerusalem) to fall. The cause of this fall was apparently due to the great earthquake mentioned in the preceding verse and so the fall of the cities of the nations. Isaiah may have spoken of this earthquake when he declared that God would rise to shake terribly the earth. Isaiah 2:21.

Great Babylon came in remembrance. The details of the judgment upon Babylon are given in chapters 17 and 18. Babylon made the inhabitants of the earth drunk with the wine of her fornication; now God makes Babylon drunk with the *wine of the fierceness of his wrath.* Wine is used as a symbol of the stupefying effect of the sin of the great harlot. The time has now come for her to drink the cup of God's wrath.

Fierceness. This is an unfortunate translation, for it appears to convey a bestial characteristic of God. It is the same word (*thumos*) as that translated *wrath* (15:1, 7 and 16:1) and which should be translated *anger.* Now that *orge*—the proper word for *wrath*—occurs and is so translated, the former was translated fierceness. To avoid this confusion, all that is required is to translate *thumos* by *anger,* and *orge* by *wrath.* Therefore the phrase is *anger of wrath* and this is its first occurrence in the New Testament. As noted before (6:16, 17), *wrath* is the word used in all the Scriptures to express the inward emotion of displeasure or disapproval, while anger expresses the outburst of that emotion. The phrase, "anger of wrath," occurs some 39 times in the Old Testament. It is the basic term. The phrase, "anger of wrath," signifies anger proceeding from wrath. It is practically equivalent to another phrase, *wrath is kindled,* or *waxed hot,* and occurs mostly in the active sense. It should be thought of as "wrath kindled," literally wrath *angered.* This term occurs about 50 times in the Old Testament and in each case it signifies that the inward emotion expressed itself in an active manner upon the object of displeasure. By way of contrast it is interesting to observe that the phrase, "slow of wrath," which in the original occurs fourteen times, is four times translated long-suffering. Exodus 34:6; Numbers 14:18; Psalm 86:15; Jeremiah 15:15. At long last, the long-suffering of God is exhausted and wrath pours itself out in anger, first upon religious Babylon (chapter 18), and then upon political Babylon, including all the nations of the world who are her subjects and allies in making war against the Lamb (chapter 19).

Verse 20. *And every island fled away, and the mountains were not found.*

This verse serves clearly as an earmark to show that this time is parallel with 6:14, viz., at the close of the tribulation and just at the eve of the coming of the "Lamb" in wrath. 6:16. Here the cataclysmic phenomena are seen in their reverse order. In the former instance the statement is, "every mountain and island were moved out of their places." Introversions like these are frequent in Biblical literature.

Such mighty convulsions of nature should not be taken as an evidence that the present order of things in the universe has come to an end. The description given in Psalm 46, which speaks of the earth being changed (Hebrew) and the mountains carried into the midst of the sea and "The . . . [nations] raged, the kingdoms were moved: he uttered his voice, the earth melted," is even more spectacular, but after the commotion had ceased, the spectator is invited to "behold the works of the Lord, what desolations he hath made in the earth." This is followed with the glad tidings: "He maketh wars to cease unto the end of the earth; he breaketh the bow, and cutteth the spear in sunder; he burneth the chariot in the fire." All of which shows that these cosmic changes occur in conjunction with the battle of Armageddon when "he ariseth to shake terribly the earth" (Isaiah 2:19).

It is also evident that greater changes will take place at the appearance of a great white throne after "the thousand years . . . [are] finished." John saw the heaven and earth flee away "and there was found no place for them" (20:11).

Verse 21. *And there fell upon men a great hail out of heaven, every stone about the weight of a talent: and men blasphemed God because of the plague of the hail; for the plague thereof was exceeding great.*

Great hail. Note the point of resemblance between this "plague" of the seventh vial and that of the seventh plague in Egypt (Exodus 9:22 ff.), at which time "the Lord rained hail upon the land . . . and brake every tree of the field." Compare also the seventh trumpet, at which time there was great hail. 11:19.

While the hailstones in Egypt apparently were more numerous, these undoubtedly are more destructive since the weight of a talent is estimated at about 114 pounds. To be smitten by one of these would necessarily mean death to man and beast alike.

Men blasphemed God. Note again the ascending degree of evil on the part of the impenitent and obdurate. They "blasphemed the name of God" (verse 9). They "blasphemed the God of heaven" (verse 11), whom they may well have conceived as being an absentee God. They *blasphemed God.* There was no mistaking that surely "this is the finger of God." Wickedness plainly reached its zenith. One need not be surprised at this hardheartedness, for it was observed that all who worshiped the beast were absolutely and irrevocably abandoned by God and doomed to perdition. 14:9-11. The judgments of the Lord served their purpose. Now that the guilty are no more moved to penitence but rather to irrevocable obduracy, the time has come to "destroy them which destroy the earth."

3. BABYLON, THE GREAT (17:1—19:6)

The Mystery of the Woman and the Scarlet-colored Beast (17:1-18)

Verse 1. *And there came one of the seven angels which had the seven vials, and talked with me, saying unto me, Come hither; I will shew unto thee the judgment of the great whore that sitteth upon many waters.*

One of the seven angels. Observe that the angel here mentioned is one of those having the seven vials. Since the present chapter deals with details concerning "great Babylon" which "came in remembrance before God" following the outpouring of the seventh vial, it is most probable that the angel mentioned in connection with the seventh vial is the one intended here.

Come hither; I will shew unto thee. Similar words occur in 21:9 where apparently the same angel speaks.

The great whore. Babylon is called the great whore. In its seven occurrences in previous books of the New Testament (Matthew 21:31, 32; Luke 15:30; I Corinthians 6:15, 16; Hebrews 11:31; James 2:25) the word *whore* is uniformly translated *harlot.* (See also verse 5 below.) The true church is the bride of Christ. Babylon is designated a harlot because of her unfaithfulness to Christ the bridegroom, through her friendship and unholy alliance with the kings and the inhabitants of the earth. (Compare James 4:4.) A like terminology is used in the Old Testament. The Lord speaks of Himself as a husband to Israel (Isaiah 54:5; Jeremiah 31:32) and of Israel as being His wife. Compare also Isaiah 1:26 (Greek), where Jerusalem is called the mother city. When Israel became unfaithful through her alliance with other nations and worshiped other gods, she, too, was called a harlot.

There are three places in the Old Testament where this sin is frequently mentioned (Ezekiel 16, 23 times; Ezekiel 23, 25 times, making a total of 48, and the Book of Hosea, 28 times, or a total of 76 times). The word is always used in connection with unfaithfulness on the part of God's people, and is never applied to the nations who knew not God. Four different Hebrew words are used. Nearly all of them, however, are derived from the same stem.

That sitteth upon many waters. The harlot [*sits*] *upon many waters.* The word *waters* is used here in a metaphorical sense as is evident from the fact that in verse 15 they are declared to signify "peoples, and multitudes, and nations, and tongues." It also should be plain that where waters were mentioned in previous Scriptures (e.g., 8:10; 14:7) they were to be taken literally, for if that were not the case, the interpretation of the symbol would have been given at its first occurrence. The Lord is not in the habit of keeping the reader guessing at symbols and then at a later time explaining what the symbol means.

Verse 2. *With whom the kings of the earth have committed fornication, and the inhabitants of the earth have been made drunk with the wine of her fornication.*

In 14:8, where her first mention occurs by way of anticipation, Babylon

240

appears to have taken the initiative in this inordinate alliance with the world system. She is doomed because she made all nations drink of the wine of the wrath of her fornication. As long as the church keeps herself "unspotted from the world" and follows her appointed path of separation, the world will not seek her alliance. The symbol interpreted suggests that fellowship with the world has a stupefying effect on the believer's spiritual life even as the drinking of wine has on the physical life of a man.

Verse 3. *So he carried me away in the spirit into the wilderness: and I saw a woman sit upon a scarlet coloured beast, full of names of blasphemy, having seven heads and ten horns.*

In the spirit. John was said to be (come to be) in the spirit on two previous occasions. 1:10; 4:2. However, in this case he is *carried* or *borne away in* (the) *spirit*. The same is the case in 21:10. The reference does not appear to be to the Holy Spirit, seeing that he is carried by the angel, but to a state of spiritual ecstasy. (Compare the similar experience of Ezekiel in 3:12, 14; 8:3; 11:1, 24; 43:5 of his prophecy.)

Into the wilderness. The article is absent in the Greek, thus signifying that the reference is not to that wilderness mentioned in 12:6, 14.

And I saw a woman. The woman is the same as the harlot of verse 1. So by showing the woman, he shows the harlot. The judgment of the harlot must necessarily be deferred as further study will show.

A scarlet coloured beast. The woman sits upon a *scarlet coloured beast . . . having seven heads and ten horns.* The *seven heads and ten horns* at once identifies this beast with the one of chapter 13:1—hence with Rome. The woman or harlot represents a religious system. For convenience the interpretation given in verse 18 of this chapter may be anticipated: "The woman which thou sawest is that great city, which reigneth over the kings of the earth." This plainly identifies the woman. She was reigning over the kings of the earth when John was writing. She can be none other than Rome. It is true that when John wrote, religious—or what now may be thought of as papal—Rome did not reign over the kings of the earth, but pagan or Rome political did. However, the vision he had of the woman sitting on the beast refers to a time when the woman did or will rule over the kings of the earth. Her sitting on the beast shows that she had the controlling power over the beast. The reference therefore must be to a time antecedent to chapter 13, for there the beast had power over all nations and worship was accorded him by all save those whose names were written in the Lamb's book of life. For the time was (corresponding to the Thyatiran period) when no emperor could take office unless he was crowned by the pope. One (Henry IV) undertook to defy the power of the pope, whereupon the latter excommunicated and anathematized him. This led the king to penance (not repentance) and soon he made his way to the pope's castle seeking absolution. It was in the month of January when he, barefooted in the snow and in the garb of a penitent, made his appearance at the castle. The pope refused to admit him and forced him to wait outside the castle for three days before he absolved him from guilt. Truly the woman was riding the beast in those days. (That was in January, 1077.)

As already noticed, the seven heads denote seven successive emperors, for a beast has only one head at a given time. (Cf. verse 10.) Also, the ten horns denote ten kings reigning at the same time. (This point will be apparent from verse 13.)

Names of blasphemy. Here the names of blasphemy are on the beast, whereas in 13:1 they are on the heads. Since the heads represent emperors and the emperors are subject to the woman, the religious head, the political power does not express itself in a profane manner even though by nature it has a tendency to do so.

Verse 4. And the woman was arrayed in purple and scarlet colour, and decked with gold and precious stones and pearls, having a golden cup in her hand full of abominations and filthiness of her fornication.

Arrayed. Here is the height of adornment and at the same time the depth of corruption. The more the church loses her sense of inward values which "in the sight of God [are] of great price," the more she seeks to atone for this loss by adorning the outward man. It has always been so. Witness the daughters of Zion —21 pieces in a full dress, while at the same time the Lord refers to the "filth of the daughters" of Zion. Isaiah 3:18-26.

A golden cup. With the golden cup in her hand she simulates nobility and glory as though she were a true bride, but inside the cup is the nectar she affords, abominations and filthiness of her fornication, a potation fitted to provoke the vomit of fiends at the first draught. Note, too, the identity of this verse with 18:16. The adornment of the woman is similar to that of the great city.

Verse 5. And upon her forehead was a name written, MYSTERY, BABYLON THE GREAT, THE MOTHER OF HARLOTS AND ABOMINATIONS OF THE EARTH.

Mystery. This word is not a part of the name. Her name is given simply as "Babylon the great" both before (16:19) (Greek) and after (18:2; cf. also 14:8) this mention. Seven times she is referred to as the great city. Since there is no indefinite article in the Greek, we should read, *upon her forehead was a name written, mystery, Babylon the great,* by which is meant that this name is not to be taken literally but that it is a mystery or secret. This at once should correct the view that Babylon on the Euphrates is intended. But there are other reasons why that Babylon is not in mind here. At every turn it will be evident that what is said cannot be true of old Babylon as she appears today or will appear in the future. With respect to her present state, Fredericks Simpich remarks in an article in *The National Geographic Magazine* of December, 1938, entitled "Change Comes to Bible Lands": "Babylon, once a world center of power and glow, is now a pile of dust and broken walls. Now the trains for Basra whistle past on the track in the foreground, but there seems little to stop for. The Bible prophecies of its utter ruin have all become true."[51] With reference to the early fulfillment of the prophecy concerning Babylon, Delitzsch writes, "At the time of Strabo (born 60 B.C.), Babylon was a perfect desert. . . . Not an Arab pitches his tent there . . . this was simply the natural consequence of the great field of ruins, upon which there was nothing but the most scanty vegetation. But all kinds of beasts of the desert and waste places make their home there instead. . . . The animals mentioned, both quadrupeds . . . and birds . . . are really found there, on the soil of ancient Babylon . . . the ruins are still regarded as a rendezvous for ghosts."[52] With these testimonies in mind one can readily see that what is said concerning Babylon in Revelation has no reference to the Babylon on the Euphrates.

The mother of harlots. Babylon is called *the mother of harlots.* It is a well-known historic fact that what are known as the leading Protestant denominations are so called because they separated themselves from and protested against Roman Catholicism on account of her unscriptural and idolatrous practices. Many affiliated with these denominations, including prominent leaders, have now so far departed from the faith that they have outstripped the mother in their departure. By Babylon therefore we must include not only the mother but those of her daughters also who have denied the faith and in many instances the very Lord who bought them.

Verse 6. *And I saw the woman drunken with the blood of the saints, and with the blood of the martyrs of Jesus: and when I saw her, I wondered with great admiration.*

Drunken with the blood of the saints. That the woman (Babylon the great) can have no reference to the old Babylon is certain with added clarity. It is a noteworthy fact that this passage appears to lay the blame only on the woman (Rome religious or papal) and not also on the beast (Rome pagan or political). The reason may be in part that the world as such is blinded because of sin and hence does not comprehend the things of the Spirit. It should be recognized, too, that many of the persecutions come upon God's people because they have been unfaithful to Him. However, it is a matter of history that the woman (religious Rome or Roman Catholicism) has been responsible for much of the blood shed through the Christian centuries. It is a sad fact that some of her daughters (Protestant bodies), as Professor Moorehead remarks, "have stained their hands in the blood of some of the noblest and purest of God's children."[53] What Madame Roland said of liberty may with equal truthfulness be said of religion: viz., "O religion! how many crimes are committed in thy name!"

I wondered with great admiration. The seer *wondered with a great wonder* (Greek). This again is an example of the use of cognate words for the sake of emphasis. Cf. "they rejoiced with exceeding great joy" (Matthew 2:10); "his great love wherewith he loved us" (Ephesians 2:4).

Verse 7. *And the angel said unto me, Wherefore didst thou marvel? I will tell thee the mystery of the woman, and of the beast that carrieth her, which hath the seven heads and ten horns.*

Wherefore didst thou marvel? As above, the word *marvel* is the word *wonder.*

[The Greek text *Dia ti* idiomatically means *Why;* although literally it is, *On account of what,* or *Because of why.* Therefore several additional questions come to one's mind. Was the seer expected to understand the mystery without explanation? Did he wonder at the gaudy array? Did he wonder at the harlot's abomination and filthiness? Did he wonder at the stupidity of the kings and inhabitants of the earth to be enticed by the harlot? Did he wonder at the awfulness of being drunk *with the blood of the saints, and with the blood of the martyrs of Jesus?* The whole scene seems to the seer enigmatic, as he gazes upon it.—J. O. Y.]

I will tell thee. The angel now gives his word that he will explain the mystery of the woman, and of the beast. He does this in an inverted order, telling first about the beast (8-14) and then about the woman (15-18). This should be given careful attention, for much confusion has prevailed regarding the meaning of these verses.

Verse 8. *The beast that thou sawest was, and is not; and shall ascend out of the bottomless pit, and go into perdition: and they that dwell on the earth shall wonder, whose names were not written in the book of life from the foundation of the world, when they behold the beast that was, and is not, and yet is.*

The beast that thou sawest was, and is not. By *the beast that . . . was, and is not* is meant that the beast referred to had a real existence in the past but at the time John was writing was no longer alive. For examples of this usage of *is not* see Genesis 42:13, 32, 36; Job 27:19.

And shall ascend out of the bottomless pit. The beast is identified with the one of 11:7. Since the verb is in the future tense, it shows also that the time referred to is antecedent to the death of the two witnesses who are killed by the beast in the middle of the tribulation period. 11:3-12.

And go into perdition. The clause is repeated in verse 11. The fulfillment is given in 19:20 in the words, "And the beast was taken, and with him the false prophet. . . . These both were cast alive into a lake of fire burning with brimstone."

They that dwell on the earth. Since the passage now being considered and 13:8 are the only ones in which the earth dwellers are described as those *whose names were not written in the book of life from the foundation of the world,* both references describe the same group at the same time.

Shall wonder. Observe too that the present *wonder* follows immediately upon the ascension of the beast from the pit and that on the former occasion (13:3) the world wondered after the beast because the wound of his death was healed and he "did live." All of which confirms the view already given that the healing of the beast and his ascending from the abyss are necessarily factors of the same occasion.

That was, and is not, and yet is. The object of their wonder is now described as the beast *that was, and is not, and shall be present.* The manuscript evidence is practically unanimous for the changed reading of the last clause. The internal evidence is likewise decidedly in favor of the change, since the reading of the received text involves a contradiction, for how can it be said of the same thing that it "is not, and yet is"? The reading of the received text, which apparently was taken from that of Erasmus, differs only from that prevailing in the manuscripts, versions, and church fathers in the prefix of the last word (a single syllable) being made a suffix of the one preceding. Moreover, by so doing, the grammatical usage of the preceding word is contrary to every other instance where it occurs.

If *Kaiper* (and yet) is retained, its usage would be contrary to every other occurrence, for it would be conjoined with a verb, whereas elsewhere it is always used with a participle.

The expression, "was, and is not; and shall ascend . . . [from] the bottomless pit," is apparently to be considered as equivalent to "was, and is not; and shall be present" (or shall come). That is to say, *shall ascend* is equal to *shall be present* or *shall come*. Further, although Luther follows Erasmus, in the closing words he evidently anticipates the true sense when he translates "er wird wieder kommen," i.e., "he will come again," thus implying that he was here before. The following verses accord with the same conclusion.

Verse 9. *And here is the mind which hath wisdom. The seven heads are seven mountains, on which the woman sitteth.*

The mind which hath wisdom. In 13:18 a similar challenge for the would-be interpreter is seen. In attempting to give the sense of the following words every reliable expositor of the Word can only feel the need of asking for wisdom "of God, that giveth to all men liberally." One mark of wisdom is to believe and accept as final every interpretation given by God Himself, and not, as some have done, seek to reinterpret God's own interpretations.

The seven heads are seven mountains, on which the woman sitteth. The woman sits or is located upon seven mountains. This shows plainly that she does not sit on the Euphrates River, for there is no hint either in history or in revelation that that Babylon was located on seven hills. Neither can the allusion be to Jerusalem because that city in no sense fits into the prophetic picture of this chapter. Many names and descriptions are applied to Jerusalem in the Bible, but nowhere is she referred to as a city on seven hills. The city intended is undoubtedly Rome on the following evidence: as many as a dozen of the old Latin (Roman) authors speak of Rome as the city on seven hills; Roman coins (still preserved) bear the imprint of Rome as built on seven hills; Victorinus, the first commentator on Revelation, in his notes on the present verse, says, "That is, the city of Rome."

It must be kept in mind that the angel here tells the mystery of the beast. Verses 7, 8. The *seven heads* (of the beast) have here a geographical connotation. The seat of his authority is at Rome, the city of seven hills upon which also the woman sits.

Verse 10. *And there are seven kings: five are fallen, and one is, and the other is not yet come; and when he cometh, he must continue a short space.*

There are seven kings. The word *there* does not occur in the original and hence should be omitted as do Luther and the Revised Version. Note that the error does not occur in the text but in the translation. Unfortunately the insertion gives the clause an indefinite sense which is not warranted by the original.

The point at issue is that the seven heads of the beast have a double symbolic sense: a geographical—they refer to the seven hills of Rome; a political—*and there are seven kings.* The seven heads of the beast signify seven kings, and since a beast has only one head at a given time it is clear that the seven kings rule successively, not simultaneously. This much is implied also from the fact that Rome was an imperial power and that universal dominion was vested in one imperial head, namely, the emperor ruling at a given time. The seven heads therefore refer to seven particular emperors of Rome. These points become increasingly plain.

Five are fallen. The word *fallen* implies that these died an unnatural death as by violence. Cf. Judges 3:25; II Samuel 1:19, 25; 3:38. The thought then is that when John wrote five of the kings or emperors had died a violent death. It is true that of the twelve Caesars, all but one—Domitian, the one then reigning—had died when John wrote. However, three of these —Galba, Otho, and Vitellius—met violent deaths within the years 68 and 69, and Augustus, Vespasian, and Titus died natural deaths. For these reasons the six mentioned do not enter into the prophetic picture. Additional reasons might also disqualify them from consideration; for example, these kings did not blaspheme (13:1) nor deify themselves as did the rest. While some of his subjects apparently worshiped Augustus, Tertullian expressly states that Augustus refused the title "Lord."[54]

One is. By this is meant the emperor ruling when John wrote (cf. verse 8—"is not"), namely, Domitian, who therefore is the sixth.

The other is not yet come. The following words, "and whenever he cometh" (Greek), indicate that the *time* of the seventh is indefinite and uncertain, the allusion being to the final Antichrist, for he it is who in the end time makes war against the Lamb.

A short space. The short time he continues is identical with 13:5—"[authority] was given unto him to continue forty and two months." This statement also identifies him with the final Antichrist.

Verse 11. *And the beast that was, and is not, even he is the eighth, and is of the seven, and goeth into perdition.*

The beast that was, and is not. The thought is that the beast of verse 8, one of the five who had "fallen" when John wrote, is also (this is the sense of *kai* translated *even*) an eighth. The Greek is emphatic—he himself is also an eighth. As a further matter of Greek syntax, the absence of the article would show that this is not the eighth in a series, of which the kings before mentioned may form the first seven, but the sense is—the eighth is unique and distinct. He is so in that he is a composite of the spirit of the fifth and the body of the seventh.

He is the eighth, and is of the seven. The Greek word for eighth (*ogdoos*) is masculine, showing conclusively that an individual is intended and not a kingdom as some erroneously have held. [The Greek word *Basileia* (kingdom) is a feminine noun.—J. O. Y.]

The eighth is of (*ek*), that is, one from or out of the seven. He must therefore be one of the seven Roman emperors—this at once disposes of the view that Judas is intended. Note that he could not be identical with the seventh, for then he could not rightfully be called an eighth. The seventh is not yet come, whereas of this one it is said, he *was, and is not.* He could not be the sixth, for of him it is said he *is;* of this one, he *was, and is not.* Since the beast is one who was and is not, he must be one of the five who had fallen when John wrote. Since of these only Nero has the number of the name—666—he alone can be intended by the eighth. And since the facts show that the beast who is slain (13:3) and lives again (13:14) makes war against the Lamb (17:14; 19:19), and that likewise the beast who ascends out of the bottomless pit is the one who makes war against the Lamb (verses 8, 14), these two in some way must constitute an eighth as a distinct unit or personality. The only solution for the problem is that the eighth consists of the body of the seventh made alive by the spirit of the fifth, that is, by the spirit of

Nero who thus alone meets all the requirements of the final Antichrist. Of all mortals, he possibly heads the list in demonical wickedness. He was a blasphemer. He murdered his own mother in cold blood, his wife, and the two apostles—Peter and Paul—whose dead bodies he pitched with oil so that they served as torches in his garden. He burned the city of Rome—a feat he will repeat (chapter 18) when he reappears (cf. verse 16 below)—but accused the Christians of the dastardly act, which was followed by cruel martyrdom of many of the faithful. Finally he ended his wicked career by his own hand. Truly he goeth into perdition.

Verse 12. *And the ten horns which thou sawest are ten kings, which have received no kingdom as yet; but receive power as kings one hour with the beast.*

The points involved here appear to be as follows: the ten horns are ten kings of the Roman Empire when it again comes into power in the last days (Daniel 7:23, 24); another little horn will arise "after them," which is none other than the seventh beast spoken of in Revelation 17 (cf. Daniel 7:8, 24); the beast will "subdue" three of the ten kings (Daniel 7:24), whereupon the other seven will accept his overlordship and his power will then be supreme. For the brief space of an hour (cf. 18:10, 17, 19) the ten kings receive authority from the beast to reign as kings.

Verse 13. *These have one mind, and shall give their power and strength unto the beast.*

The ten kings are of one mind, for they agree to give their power and authority to the beast. The purpose of surrendering their newly acquired honors is apparently a piece of military strategy in view of the fateful conflict mentioned in the verse following. Unity of command is looked upon as a chief desideratum in major military operations. When comes the final decisive battle between the forces of good and evil, not only will the evil forces pool their powers by surrendering them to the beast, but on the side of righteousness, He who comes from Edom, with dyed garments from Bozrah, expressly declares, "I have trodden the winepress alone."

Verse 14. *These shall make war with the Lamb, and the Lamb shall overcome them: for he is Lord of lords, and King of kings: and they that are with him are called, and chosen, and faithful.*

These. By this is meant both the beast and the kings as is evident from 19:19. The present verse is but an anticipation and foreview of Armageddon as described in 19:11 ff.

War with the Lamb. Observe that the Lamb again comes prominently into view. Throughout the book praises are accorded to the Lamb by various groups— by the redeemed (5:9, 10), by an innumerable company of angels (5:11, 12), by every creature (5:13, 14), by a great multitude (7:9, 10), and by those refusing to take the mark of the beast (15:2, 3). It is the Lamb who releases the judgments upon the wicked nations, for it is He who opens the sealed book and introduces those judgments. 5:5; 6:1.

The assemblage, not only of the ten kings under the beast, but of all nations of the earth, is to be accounted for as the reaction of the kings of the earth both with respect to the praises accorded to the Lamb and with respect to the devastating and destructive judgments He has brought upon the nations. It is highly significant therefore that this virulent antagonism of the kings is described as culminating in a *war with the Lamb*. The title expresses our Lord's atoning work. The praises accorded the Lamb are introduced and perpetuated by those who have been redeemed by His blood out of every kindred and tongue and tribe and nation. The judgments have come upon those who have "[denied] the Lord that bought them."

The purpose of the assembled nations is then apparently twofold: retaliation for the sore judgments He has brought upon them; determination to dethrone and destroy Him and to exalt and enthrone the beast in His stead.

Lord of lords, and King of kings. The title, *Lord of lords, and King of kings*, occurs again in 19:16 but in reverse order. The repetition of this term is an indication that the two passages relate themselves to the same event.

They that are with him are called, and chosen, and faithful. The passage apparently anticipates that of 19:14, "And the armies which were in heaven followed him upon white horses, clothed in fine linen, white and clean." (Observe the close conjunction of this passage with the title just noted.) The armies "clothed in fine linen, white and clean" are identical with the bride, the Lamb's wife (cf. 19:7 with 21:9), the glorified church. The adjectives are each applied to her: called (Romans 1:6, 7; 8:28; I Corinthians 1:2, 24; Jude 1); chosen (Romans 16:13; I Corinthians 1:27; Ephesians 1:4; I Peter 2:9); faithful (Ephesians 1:1; Colossians 1:2; I Timothy 1:12; I Peter 5:12; Revelation 2:10).

Verse 15. *And he saith unto me, The waters which thou sawest, where the whore sitteth, are peoples, and multitudes, and nations, and tongues.*

This is an explanation of verse 1. It is one of the more than forty symbols which are interpreted in the book itself. Since this is the first instance in which the word *waters* is interpreted as being a symbol, it is inferred that previous uses of the word are to be taken in their plain literal sense. At least it would be expected that if a symbol had been intended in earlier uses of the word, the word would have been interpreted as such when first so used.

It may readily be seen why water is used in a symbolic sense when it is remembered that nearly every country in the world has a seacoast. The four words employed in explanation of the symbol indicate the world-wide influence of the great whore, papal Rome.

Verse 16. *And the ten horns which thou sawest upon the beast, these shall hate the whore, and shall make her desolate and naked, and shall eat her flesh, and burn her with fire.*

Horns . . . upon the beast. The manuscript evidence is overwhelmingly in favor of the reading, *and* the beast, instead of *upon* the beast. The internal evidence likewise supports the reading *and*, for the kings, seeing they have given their authority to the beast, would not be in a position to proceed with the action designated without his authority and consent.

The whore. The whore (woman), as explained before, is religious Rome. Note the future tenses of the verbs. The destruction of the woman (Babylon, Rome) is fulfilled and described in detail in chapter 18.

Verse 17. For God hath put in their hearts to fulfil his will, and to agree, and give their kingdom unto the beast, until the words of God shall be fulfilled.

For God hath put in their hearts to fulfil his will. Numerous examples occur in the Scriptures of wicked men whom the Lord used to fulfill His purposes: Pharaoh (Exodus 9:16), Nebuchadnezzar (Daniel 4:17), Cyrus (Isaiah 44:28; Ezra 1:1; 7:27). Compare "Surely the wrath of man shall praise thee" (Psalm 76:10).

The more literal translation would be, *to do his mind.* Compare "to do one mind" (verse 13 above). The more free rendering would be, *to carry out his purpose,* and *to carry out one purpose.*

To . . . give their kingdom unto the beast. This is the purpose intended and is the equivalent of the words in verse 13, "[to] give their power and . . . [authority] unto the beast."

Until the words of God shall be fulfilled. The clause is more correctly rendered, *until the words of God are finished.* The allusion apparently is to the final destruction of the world powers at Armageddon. The unanimity of purpose centered in the beast will make certain the gathering of all the wicked in the final assemblage and doom of the nations.

Verse 18. And the woman which thou sawest is that great city, which reigneth over the kings of the earth.

The woman of chapter 17 is *that great city* of chapter 18. (See verses 10, 16, 18 of the latter chapter.) The name of the city (a mystery—17:5) is Babylon, which is the city on seven hills, namely, Rome. She it was who was reigning over the kings of the earth when John wrote. The woman was sitting where the emperor reigned. Rome was both the religious and the political center of the world. [According to this prediction, she will be again!—J. O. Y.]

The Fall of Babylon (18:1-8)

Verses 1, 2. And after these things I saw another angel come down from heaven, having great power; and the earth was lightened with his glory. And he cried mightily with a strong voice, saying, Babylon the great is fallen, is fallen, and is become the habitation of devils, and the hold of every foul spirit, and a cage of every unclean and hateful bird.

Another angel. Consistency requires that the word *angel* be taken in a literal sense throughout the book, for in no case does the word signify either man or Christ, as some hold. If there is any case above another in which Christ is meant, it would apparently be the present instance, for not only has this one great power (Greek: *authority*) and comes down from heaven, but the earth was lightened with (*ek,* out of, as a source of) his glory. The same language is employed in 21:23: "The city had no need of the sun, neither of the moon, to shine in it: for the glory of God did lighten it." The word *another* implies that an angel had been previously mentioned. And such is the case, for in 17:1 one of the seven angels which had the seven vials is mentioned. It would be derogatory to the deity of Christ to speak of Him as another angel, when the one previously mentioned is a mere creature. Besides, as stated before, if an angel of a different kind were intended, the word heteros would be required as denoting distinction, but this word does not occur in Revelation. No grandeur or glory is too magnificent for an angel if he is divinely endued and commissioned for a high and holy purpose. An angel may even be deputized to give command to the Son of man. Revelation 14:15.

That the mission of the angel was of a high and sacred nature is apparent from the message he brings. In 14:8 another angel appeared with a similar mission and message. No one questions that by the former an angel in the literal sense is intended from the fact that he is mentioned as one of three flying through midheaven. [No further question need be asked about this one.—J. O. Y.]

Babylon the great is fallen. The solemn announcement of the doom of Babylon is proleptic, for (verse 8) her judgment has not yet taken place. Babylon of this chapter is identical with that of chapter 17 from the fact that as many as a dozen parallel passages occur. Since Babylon of the preceding chapter refers to Rome, the destruction of ancient Babylon on the Euphrates which occurred centuries before the Book of Revelation was written is not intended. But it is her religious antitype, the city situated on seven mountains, heir of and successor to the vice and corruption of the former city.

And is become the habitation of devils. The mention of the vile and demoniac occupants of the doomed city appears to allude to Isaiah 13:21, 22. Such is Rome to be at the last.

Verse 3. *For all nations have drunk of the wine of the wrath of her fornication, and the kings of the earth have committed fornication with her, and the merchants of the earth are waxed rich through the abundance of her delicacies.*

All nations . . . and the kings. It should be remembered that nations and kings are political systems, whereas the pronoun *her* has reference to the Roman religious system. If and when a religious system dominates and controls the political affairs of nations and kings as does Rome during the first half of the tribulation period, she not only loses all sense of sanctity through such illicit relationship but nations and kings likewise sink into the lowest depths of moral corruption. The swift judgment of God alone can put an end to "man's inhumanity to man." *All nations* are identified by the context with "the inhabitants of the earth" (17:2b) and *the kings of the earth* with 17:2a.

[Verse 3 reveals the cause of the fall of Babylon the great. No religious system has had a world-wide hold on nations and kings like Roman Catholicism. Nor has any dealt in similar merchandising.—J. O. Y.]

Verse 4. *And I heard another voice from heaven, saying, Come out of her my people, that ye be not partakers of her sins, and that ye receive not of he plagues.*

Come out of her. A call of similar import came to the former Babylon. Jeremiah 51:45. It is these parallels which have led many to conclude that referenc is had only to that ancient city and her doom. However, points of similarity d not necessarily prove identity. For example, scores of points of similarity exist ii the anatomy of certain animals, but this does not prove that a horse is a cow Besides the evidence already given, more will appear that the Babylon here de scribed is not that of the Euphrates valley.

However great the sins of Rome may have been and will yet be, it must be admitted that Protestantism at the last presents a dark picture also. It is assumed, moreover, that Laodicea presents a true description of Christendom at the close of the church age. Revelation 3:14-22.

The words *come out of* are uniform with those in 7:14 except that in this passage the Greek word *come* has the prefix *ek,* and signifies not only *come* but *come out,* literally *come out, out of,* or *come out from.* Not to respond to the appeal would make one a partaker of the sins of the doomed and of the plagues awaiting them.

Her plagues. The use of the term *plague* is worthy of note. As noted before, the word occurs in connection with the last series of judgments, namely, the vials (chapter 16), which are designated "the seven last plagues" (15:1). It is significant that after the last plague, the seventh vial, it is said, "great Babylon came in remembrance before God, to give unto her the cup of the wine of the fierceness of his wrath" (16:19). All of which proves beyond a shadow of a doubt that the present verse is synchronous with 16:19.

Verse 5. *For her sins have reached unto heaven, and God hath remembered her iniquities.*

This verse gives further reasons why judgment awaits Babylon and why the appeal to come out of her. The first clause alludes to Jeremiah 51:9: "for her judgment reacheth unto heaven, and is lifted up even to the skies." In noting these similarities between the language employed in connection with the Babylon of chapters 18 and 19 and those of Isaiah and particularly Jeremiah 51, perhaps it would be nearer to the point to say that the former passages were only partly fulfilled in Old Testament times and that the complete and final fulfillment will only come in connection with the later Babylon (Rome).

Her sins have reached unto heaven. The language employed here is simply a graphic description of the enormity of the sins—passing that of any other recorded in the Scriptures. Of Babel (i.e., Babylon) at the first, the order was, "Go to, let us build us a city and a tower, whose top may reach unto heaven" (Genesis 11:4). Here, when Babylon was "finished," *her sins have reached unto heaven—*a far worse spectacle.

[Here, then, is the call to escape because God's justice will surely fall.— J. O. Y.]

Verse 6. *Reward her even as she rewarded you, and double unto her double according to her works: in the cup which she hath filled fill to her double.*

Double unto her double according to her works. The woman (Rome religious) here faces the inevitable law of retribution technically designated *lex talionis,* literally, law of retaliation. In 17:16 it is stated that the ten horns (i.e., ten kings) and the beast shall destroy the whore. "For God hath put in their hearts to fulfil his will." These therefore are addressed in this passage: *Render to her as also she rendered to you and double to her double, according to her works. In the cup which she has mixed, mix to her double* [a simpler translation].

Similar instances of synergism, i.e., the collaboration of God and man in the execution of His will, occur in the Scriptures: the use of Moses' rod and the word of the Lord in the destruction, of the Egyptians (Exodus 14:26, 27); Aaron and Hur lifting up Moses' hands in the destruction of the Amalekites (Exodus 17:12, 13); the military maneuvers of Deborah and Barak and the divine ordering of the stars in their courses fighting against Sisera (Judges 4, 5); Gideon's three hundred breaking the pitchers and the Lord setting every man's sword against his fellow (Judges 7).

In the Mosaic code the *lex talionis* was "eye for eye, tooth for tooth, hand for hand, foot for foot, burning for burning, wound for wound, stripe for stripe, or same for same," but here, because of superior light and greater guilt, retributive judgment is double in severity.

Verse 7. *How much she hath glorified herself, and lived deliciously, so much torment and sorrow give her: for she saith in her heart, I sit a queen, and am no widow, and shall see no sorrow.*

Here is another instance of the law of retaliation (*lex talionis*). The words in contrast are probably to be taken in introversion, i.e., for self-glorification there will be sorrow; for luxurious living, torment.

She hath glorified herself. Her self-glorification is seen in that she says in her heart, *I sit a queen, and am no widow, and shall see no sorrow.* What a contrast when compared with John's description of her, viz., "the great whore that sitteth upon many waters" (17:1). "I saw a woman sit upon a scarlet coloured beast, full of names of blasphemy. . . . And the woman was arrayed in purple and scarlet colour, and decked with gold and precious stones and pearls, having a golden cup in her hand full of abominations and filthiness of her fornication" (17:3, 4). This is her real character.

I . . . am no widow. The words, *I . . . am no widow,* allude to Isaiah 47:8. In reality she is a widow because the Lord has forsaken her. She claims she is no widow because her lovers are the kings of the earth. 17:2; 18:3. She is like the church at Laodicea, which declares, "I am rich, and increased with goods," and knows not that she is "wretched, and miserable, and poor, and blind, and naked." Like those in the church who repented not of their fornication (2:21), she will be cast into great tribulation. Indeed she knows the depths of Satan. 2:24.

Verse 8. *Therefore shall her plagues come in one day, death, and mourning, and famine; and she shall be utterly burned with fire: for strong is the Lord God who judgeth her.*

Therefore. The two Greek words *dia touto* literally mean *on account of this.* The reference appears to be to the blatant boast just uttered.

In one day. The phrase is placed before the verb for the sake of emphasis. Judgment may appear to have tarried long, but when evil and guilt have reached such height it will be speedily executed. Other examples of swift judgment occur in the Scriptures. When "Belshazzar the king made a great feast to a thousand of his lords . . . brought the golden vessels that were taken out of the temple of the house of God . . . they drank wine, and praised the gods of gold, and of silver, of brass, of iron, of wood, and of stone. . . . In the same hour came forth fingers of a man's hand. . . . In that night was Belshazzar the king of the Chaldeans slain" (Daniel 5:1, 3-5, 30).

The rich fool soliloquized boastfully, "Soul, thou hast much goods laid up for many years; take thine ease, eat, drink, and be merry. But God said unto him, Thou fool, this night thy soul shall be required of thee . . ." (Luke 12:19, 20).

Death, and mourning, and famine. The words, *death, and mourning, and famine,* appear to be given in the reverse order of their experience, for only famine is really a plague, while mourning naturally follows famine, and death necessarily comes last.

Burned with fire. That the burning of the city actually occurs at this juncture is shown by the fact of the lamentations following.

The Three Lamentations of Men (18:9-19)

Verses 9, 10. *And the kings of the earth, who have committed fornication and lived deliciously with her, shall bewail her, and lament for her, when they shall see the smoke of her burning, standing afar off for the fear of her torment, saying, Alas, alas that great city Babylon, that mighty city! for in one hour is thy judgment come.*

The kings of the earth. The first to lament are the kings of the earth, referred to previously in 1:5; 6:15; 16:14; 17:2, 18; 18:3. These include *all* kings of the earth.

Bewail her, and lament for her . . . Alas, alas. There are two kinds of lamentation and they are each twofold. The kings bewail her (lit., *wail for her)* and lament (lit., *beat their beasts)* and say, *Alas, alas* (Greek: *ouai,* pronounced oo-aye, and elsewhere, 41 times, translated woe). The lament, *ouai, ouai,* is far more pathetic and heart-rending than the English, *Alas, alas.* The Greek word for alas *ouai* is onomatopoeic; that is, the word is formed from the sound produced. The repetition of its utterance would strike the ear as that of a bitter wail indeed. (Compare the threefold utterance in 8:13.)

Standing afar off for the fear of her torment. The kings were afraid they might be drawn into the vortex of her doom. Similar caution is expressed in the wail of the merchants (verse 15) and of the shipmasters (verse 17b).

That great city Babylon. Certainly this is none other than the one previously mentioned (14:8; 16:19; 17:5; 18:2), namely, Rome. In the Greek this reads, *the city the great Babylon.* The double use of the definite article *the,* the qualifying adjective *great,* and the announcement of her *fall* (which has now taken place) are alone sufficient to prove this identity.

Verses 11-17a. *And the merchants of the earth shall weep and mourn over her; for no man buyeth their merchandise any more: the merchandise of gold, and silver, and precious stones, and of pearls, and fine linen, and purple, and silk, and scarlet, and all thyine wood, and all manner vessels of ivory, and all manner vessels of most precious wood, and of brass, and iron, and marble, and cinnamon, and odours, and ointments, and frankincense, and wine, and oil, and fine flour, and wheat, and beasts, and sheep, and horses, and chariots, and slaves, and souls of men. And the fruits that thy soul lusted after are departed from thee, and all things which were dainty and goodly are departed from thee, and thou shalt find them no more at all. The merchants of these things, which were made rich by her, shall stand afar off for the fear of her torment, weeping and wailing, and saying, Alas, alas that great city, that was clothed in fine linen, and purple, and scarlet, and decked with gold, and precious stones, and pearls! For in one hour so great riches is come to nought.*

The merchants of the earth. The second lamentation comes from the merchants. It is said in verse 3 that "the merchants of the earth are waxed rich through the abundance of her delicacies." Verses 12 and 13 list these delicacies. Note they are merchandise of:

Costly ornaments: *gold, and silver, and precious stones, and of pearls* (verse 12a).

Costly clothes: *fine linen, and purple, and silk, and scarlet* (verse 12b).

Costly furnishings: *and all thyine wood, and all manner vessels of ivory, and all manner vessels of most precious wood, and of brass, and iron, and marble* (verse 12c).

Costly perfumes: *and cinnamon, and odours, and ointments, and frankincense* (verse 13a).

Costly foods: *and wine, and oil, and fine flour, and wheat, and beasts, and sheep* (verse 13b).

Costly conveyances: *and horses, and chariots* (verse 13c).

Costly chattel: *and slaves* (Greek: *bodies), and souls of men* (verse 13d).

The abundance of her delicacies. This could not describe the riches of Babylon on the Euphrates just previous to her destruction, but it accords with the description of the seven-hilled city (Rome, chapter 17). "The woman was arrayed in purple and scarlet colour, and decked with gold and precious stones and pearls, having a golden cup in her hand" (17:4).

(There are 27 and's in the description recorded in verses 12 and 13. This passage contains more and's than any other passage in Scripture and possibly more than any other passage of equal length in standard literature.)

And slaves, and souls of men. The inclusion of bodies and souls of men in this merchandising appears the most tragic because presumably they are bartered as though they were mere chattel.

The fruits . . . are departed from thee . . . and thou shalt find them no more at all. The utter destitution of the city is apparent because all things desirable and dainty have been destroyed. The sad and solemn refrain, *no more at all,* occurs here for the first time and seven times in all as the further description of the desolation continues.

The merchants . . . shall stand afar . . . weeping and wailing . . . Alas, alas. See verse 10 for exposition.

The prominence of the merchants is seen in that they are declared to be "the great men of the earth" (verse 23).

That great city, that was clothed in fine linen, and purple, and scarlet, and decked with gold, and precious stones, and pearls! That the woman of chapter 17:4 is identical with the great city here named is readily seen by comparing the two passages.

For in one hour so great riches is come to nought. This sentence readily belongs to verse 16 because it concludes the lamentation of the merchants. Here is given the reason for the lament. (Compare verses 10b and 19b.)

Verses 17b-19. *And every shipmaster, and all the company in ships, and sailors, and as many as trade by sea, stood afar off, and cried when they saw the smoke of her burning, saying, What city is like unto this great city! And they cast dust on their heads, and cried, weeping and wailing, saying, Alas, alas that great city, wherein were made rich all that had ships in the sea by reason of her costliness! for in one hour is she made desolate.*

The third group to lament are the shipmasters. Here is plain proof again that the later Babylon, Rome, is intended because the Euphrates upon which the former Babylon was built will be dried up. 16:12. Besides, the fact is that for many centuries the waters of the River Euphrates dry up during the summer so that people living in that area have to dig deep into the bed of the river to get sufficient supply of water for their use. (See the exposition on 16:12.)

The smoke of her burning. Note the previous mention of the fate of the city. 17:16; 18:8, 9. The latter part of the verse could not refer to the Babylon on the Euphrates because few inhabitants are there and no trade by ships for many centuries has been carried on.

Ships in the sea. Again Rome is intended and not Babylon, which was not situated on the sea as is Rome. Moreover, Rome will undoubtedly come into great prominence during the days ahead and will be the mother city of the world just prior to her destruction in the latter days as previous chapters abundantly indicate.

[Let it be said once more, "The higher one rises, the further one falls," and "Pride goeth before destruction, and an haughty spirit before a fall" (Proverbs 16:18). One needs in his imagination to see the awful contrast described in these verses. A once great city, prosperous, gorgeous to behold, glittering in the sun, influential around the world, suddenly comes to utter ruin in a single hour. Against the sky are billows of smoke. Intense heat keeps the onlookers at a distance. Nothing can be rescued. All must perish. A complete desolation is wrought. One would wish that all living now and then would turn to the God of heaven in penitence and plead His mercy to escape the "anger of his wrath."–J. O. Y.]

The Final Dirge of the Angel (18:20-24)

Verse 20. *Rejoice over her, thou heaven, and ye holy apostles and prophets; for God hath avenged you on her.*

Ye holy apostles and prophets. The appeal is addressed to the glorified mentioned in 19:1 ff., where they respond. Heaven is addressed first as the place of the glorified. The glorified group or groups might refer to the church only, as far as the language is concerned. The same language is used in Ephesians 3:5 in respect to revelation that has now come to the holy apostles and prophets. However, the passage may be translated, *ye saints, and ye apostles, and ye prophets,* as does the Revised Version. Most frequently the two terms, *apostles and proph-*

ets, are associated with the church group. I Corinthians 12:28, 29; Ephesians 2:20; 3:5; 4:11. The term *saints* would then fittingly apply to those slain during the tribulation. It is so applied in Revelation 13:10 and 14:12. [Although *saints* is frequently used in Paul's epistles when he addresses the believers in a given locality.—J. O. Y.] The translation of the Revised Version fits into the picture as described in 19:1-6.

For God hath avenged you on her. The literal translation of this clause is, *for God has judged your judgment upon her,* which gives the cause of His judgment upon Babylon. The sense is, *He has judged your case against her.* In other words, Babylon has slain you; now Babylon shall be slain.

Verse 21. *And a mighty angel took up a stone like a great millstone, and cast it into the sea, saying, Thus with violence shall that great city Babylon be thrown down, and shall be found no more at all.*

A mighty angel. This is the third mention of a mighty angel. (See 5:2 and 10:1.) The occasion calls for such a one.

Stone like a great millstone. A great millstone as an instrument of destruction goes back to Jeremiah 51:63, 64. A notable change, however, is to be observed because the former was cast into the Euphrates, this into the sea—presumably the Mediterranean as in verses 17 and 19 above.

No more at all. The doleful refrain, *no more at all* (Greek: *ou me* . . . etc.), occurs here for the second time. (See verse 14 above.)

Verses 22, 23. *And the voice of harpers, and musicians, and of pipers, and trumpeters, shall be heard no more at all in thee; and no craftsman, of whatsoever craft he be, shall be found any more in thee; and the sound* [Greek: voice] *of a millstone shall be heard no more at all in thee; and the light of a candle shall shine no more at all in thee; and the voice of the bridegroom and of the bride shall be heard no more at all in thee: for thy merchants were the great men of the earth; for by thy sorceries were all nations deceived.*

And the voice. It will be observed that the seven things heard proceed from voices, or sounds of *harpers, and musicians, and of pipers, and trumpeters,* . . . *of a millstone,* . . . *of the bridegroom and of the bride.* Besides, mention is made of the *craftsman, of whatsoever craft* [Greek: *technician of whatsoever technique*] . . . *and the light of a candle.* Instead of this diverse performance, whether by night or by day, there is now perpetual silence in this world metropolis.

No more at all is the doleful dirge of destiny.

For thy merchants . . . for by thy sorceries. The cause for the dreadful doom of the city is given in these two clauses: *for* [because] *thy merchants were the great men of the earth; for* [because] *by thy sorceries were all nations deceived.* The city was the sole purchaser of the 27 kinds of merchandise the merchants had for sale. When it was destroyed, they wept and mourned, "for no man buyeth their merchandise any more" (verses 11, 12). It is said, too, the merchants were made rich by her. Verse 15. That the merchants were the great men of the earth is also seen in that, whereas only two verses (9 lines) are given to tell about the kings of the earth and three verses (13 lines) about the shipmasters, six verses (32 lines) are given concerning the merchants.

The result of this godless trafficking with the merchants had a corrupting influence upon the city. In turn, because of her sorceries, she deceived all nations.

Because of these things judgment fell on the city. Dr. Swete has well spoken on this point: "Babylon has been submerged by her very greatness, for her greatness has been used to bewitch and mislead the world, and not to raise and purify it. . . . Traders who could make Rome their market rose to the first rank, became merchant princes (verses 3, 15), while Rome on her part acquired a world-wide influence which she used for evil; through their traffic with her all nations had learnt to adopt her false standards of life and worship."[55]

Verse 24. *And in her was found the blood of prophets, and of saints, and of all that were slain upon the earth.*

The sentence is a continuation of the preceding and gives another reason why the city was destroyed. Compare 17:6, "I saw the woman [that great city—17:18] drunken with the blood of the saints, and with the blood of the martyrs of Jesus." It is plain that the reference could not be to Babylon on the Euphrates because she perished long before there were any martyrs of Jesus. The passage plainly reveals that the reference is to Rome religious as the persecuting power, not Rome political.

[Some objection might be raised on the basis of the inclusion of the *prophets*. It needs to be remembered that in the New Testament reference is made to prophets then living. Furthermore, Babylon on the Euphrates was hardly responsible for much prophet blood. It is true that not all the martyrs died within the precincts of Rome itself, yet the edict for their execution issued from the imperial city. In that sense it could be said, *In her was found the blood of prophets, and of saints, and of all that were slain upon the earth.* A little thought will make clear that the time reference is to the era of the church, with especial emphasis on the close of the age, as the author so admirably sought to point out.—J. O. Y.]

The Four Alleluias of the Saints (19:1-6)

Verse 1. *And after these things I heard a great voice of much people in heaven, saying, Alleluia; Salvation, and glory, and honour, and power, unto the Lord our God.*

After these things. Since the rejoicing in heaven is in response to the appeal of 18:20, the great voice of much people must be after the things mentioned in the preceding chapter.

Much people. The *much people* in heaven are identical with the "great multitude" which John beheld in 7:9-12. Their identity is unmistakable.

The Greek words for *much people (ochlos polus)* are the same as for *great multitude.* 7:9.

Great voice (phone megala)—loud voice. 7:10.

Saying (lego)—saying. 7:10.

The four words of praise, *salvation (soteria), glory (doxa), honour (time), power (dunamis),* are taken from a series in 7:10, 12 in order of their occurrence.

Alleluia. The spelling accords with the Greek form *allelouia* and occurs only four times (verses 1, 3, 4, 6), in the English Bible. The word "Hallelujah" follows the Hebrew plural. The Old Testament uniformly and correctly renders the Hebrew original, *Praise ye the Lord.* It occurs 24 times and in the later psalms only.

Verse 2. *For true and righteous are his judgments: for he hath judged the great whore, which did corrupt the earth with her fornication, and hath avenged the blood of his servants at her hand.*

For. The Greek word *hoti* evidently has the sense of because in both clauses. The "great multitude" or "much people" shout "Hallelujah" or "Praise ye the Lord" because His judgments are *true,* i.e., faithful according to promise; and *righteous,* i.e., in rendering just judgment; and because He has judged, i.e., executed the penalty upon, the great whore which corrupted the earth with her fornication.

Evidently the judgment upon the great whore is referred to under the seventh trumpet (11:18) in the last clause, "that thou . . . shouldest destroy them which destroy the earth." With this judgment "the mystery of God . . . [is] finished" (10:7) because what further judgments come upon the earth are not mysteries. They have been revealed by the prophets both of the Old and New Testament Scriptures; moreover, they will be executed by the Lord Himself.

He . . . hath avenged the blood of his servants at her hand. Here is divine retribution. The blood shed by the hand of the great whore has now been required of her. The original law of retribution—"whoso sheddeth man's blood, by man shall his blood be shed"—still holds at the last, and the great whore could not escape it.

Another most important observation, and one which has been all but overlooked by commentators, is that here is not only a response to the appeal of 18:20 but also the answer to the prayer of the souls under the altar (6:10)—"How long, O Lord, holy and true, dost thou not judge and avenge our blood on them that dwell on the earth?" While there have been apparent allusions to this prayer and occasional responses to it in connection with the trumpet judgments (8:3 ff.) and the vial judgments (16:7), the great whore, the chief source and cause of the ever-increasing abominations upon the earth, has survived until the closing days of the tribulation period. *Judge* and *avenge* are the very words employed in the prayer of 6:10 and in the passage now under consideration. In other words, the prayer of the souls under the altar was answered when "the Lord our God" *judged the great whore* and *avenged the blood of his servants at her hand.*

Observe, too, that whereas in 6:10 the earth dwellers were responsible for the death of the souls under the altar, in 19:2 the great whore is said to have shed their blood. Cf. 18:24. This makes it clear therefore that the persecuting power in the beginning of the tribulation will not be Rome political but Rome religious, for the great whore can refer to the latter only. It should be carefully kept in mind that wherever mention is made of the earth dwellers during the entire tribulation period the reference is to the Roman religious system (6:10; 8:13; 11:10—twice; 12:12; 13:8, 12, 14—twice; 14:6; 17:2, 8), and even during the church age we find where the word is used (2:13—twice; 3:10) it refers to a group that apparently mind earthly things [though they boast a religious profession—J. O. Y.].

So then the "much people" (verse 1) are identical with the "great multitude" of chapter 7 and also with the souls under the altar who pray, "How long . . . [wilt] thou not judge and avenge our blood?"

There is a true dictum which says, "Things which are equal to the same thing are equal to each other." And so in this case, for the groups are earmarked as being clothed in white robes. Cf. 6:11 with 7:9, 14. Others who "came out of great tribulation" are included in the great multitude of chapter 7, but they both belong to the same martyr group who open and close their testimony with the shout of *Alleluia*.

Verse 3. *And again they said, Alleluia. And her smoke rose up for ever and ever.*

Here are the extremes of destiny: the one tormented, the other comforted. If the great whore should call for mercy, perhaps Abraham will remind her as he did the rich man, "Remember that thou in thy lifetime receivedst thy good things, and likewise . . . [the martyr group] evil things: but now . . . [they are] comforted, and thou art tormented." The smoke ascends from their torment. 14:11.

Verse 4. *And the four and twenty elders and the four beasts fell down and worshipped God that sat on the throne, saying, Amen; Alleluia.*

Four and twenty elders. As explained before, the twenty-four elders represent the church glorified. Chapters 4 and 5. Since the church group is mentioned before the robe wearers (chapters 6 and 7), the question may be raised, Why are the latter mentioned first in this chapter? The answer undoubtedly is, the robe wearers were martyrs slain by the great whore Rome and hence were the ones to whom the appeal of 18:20 was more especially directed. It has been noted that the Revised Version translates 18:20, "ye saints, and ye apostles, and ye prophets," and that the word *saints* is the one applied to martyrs of the tribulation period. 13:10; 14:12. In addition, many saints of the church age have been slain by Rome as her history abundantly testifies. That these are included here is plain from the language of 18:24, "And in her was found the blood of prophets, and of saints, and of *all* that were slain upon the earth."

Here is the last mention of both the beasts and the elders. They are mentioned together nine times. Both fall down here and in 5:8. In 5:14 the beasts say "Amen" and the elders fall down and worship. Here both groups appear to worship God and say *Amen* and *Alleluia;* however, it might be possible that as in 5:14 the "Amen" belongs to the beasts and the "Alleluia" to the elders and this the more likely because the beasts are not a saved group and hence to say "Alleluia," which means "Praise the Lord," would not seem applicable to them.

Verse 5. *And a voice came out of the throne, saying, Praise our God, all ye his servants, and ye that fear him, both small and great.*

A voice. A nameless voice comes out of the throne. That it is not the voice of Christ is evidenced by the fact that God is still alone on the throne, as He is throughout the entire tribulation period. In the preceding verse the proof of this lies in the literal rendering, "the [one] sitting on the throne."

All ye his servants. All servants are now commanded, "Praise our God." The question rises, Who are these servants?

They do not include the church group because these sit on thrones not only during the tribulation period, as is frequently mentioned concerning them, but also during the kingdom age. Matthew 19:28; Luke 22:30.

They include the robe wearers of chapters 6 and 7 because they speak of their fellow servants which should yet be killed (6:11), thus showing that they themselves were servants. Again it is said of them in 7:15, "they . . . serve him day and night in his temple." The "much people" of verse 1 are referred to as servants in verse 2. They include others "both small and great." Cf. 11:18. The following verse reveals a third group, which apparently are a part of the *small and great*, for they respond in the praises mentioned.

Verse 6. *And I heard as it were the voice of a great multitude, and as the voice of many waters, and as the voice of mighty thunderings, saying, Alleluia: for the Lord God omnipotent reigneth.*

Great multitude. Great multitude is the same as "much people" (verse 1) and "great multitude" (7:9), hence the robe wearers. 6:11; 7:9, 13.

The voice of many waters . . . of mighty thunderings. These are the same as a "voice of many waters, and . . . of a great thunder" (14:2). This same group are "harpers harping with their harps" (14:2b), hence identical with those who got "the victory over the beast, . . . having the harps of God" (15:2).

The 144,000 of 14:3 having their Father's name written on their foreheads are undoubtedly the same as the 144,000 Israelites having the seal of God in their foreheads. 7:2, 3. The two groups constituting *all* the servants of God are the robe wearers and the harpers. The combined voices of two groups say, *Alleluia: for the Lord God omnipotent reigneth.* Thus John heard the combined voices of the largest chorus, the greatest multitude proclaiming the greatest theme!

It will be observed that the throne sitters (the church) are not in this chorus. The reasons appear in the verses following.

4. THE MARRIAGE OF THE LAMB (19:7-10)

Verse 7. *Let us be glad and rejoice, and give honour to him: for the marriage of the Lamb is come, and his wife hath made herself ready.*

Let us be glad and rejoice. These appear to be the words of "all . . . his servants"—i.e., the two groups of verse 6. The same words (Greek: *chairo* and *agalliao*) occur in the same order in Matthew 5:12, where they are translated, "rejoice, and be exceeding glad," and in I Peter 4:13, "be glad . . . with exceeding joy."

And give honour to him. The literal rendering of this clause is, *and give glory to him.* In the preceding verses, praises ascended to God from three groups and were repeated by two of them because He had judged the great whore and avenged the blood shed by her hand. Now there is great rejoicing by all His servants because the marriage of the Lamb has come and His wife has made herself ready. It is clear why the church was not included in "all . . . his servants," the fact being that "his wife" is identical with the group represented by the elders, i.e., the church.

[In Smith's notes reference was made to three groups joining in the alleluias of praise. The first he indicated as robe wearers and identified them with those in chapters 6 and 7; the second as throne sitters, chapters 4 and 5; the third, *all . . . his servants,* as including the first, but not the second. Each group renders praise to God in this greatest of all alleluia choruses!

It is of some interest to note that three groups lament the fall of Babylon (chapter 18) and three groups give praise to God for His power and justice (chapter 19:1-7). The theme of the rejoicing is the righteousness and power of God. This is theodicy of the purest kind.—J. O. Y.]

Verse 8. *And to her was granted that she should be arrayed in fine linen, clean and white: for the fine linen is the righteousness of saints.*

Arrayed in fine linen. There is a marked contrast between the array of the bride, the Lamb's wife, and that of the great whore. The one is arrayed in *fine linen, clean and white;* the other "in purple and scarlet colour, and decked with gold and precious stones and pearls," and in her hand was a golden cup "full of abominations and filthiness of her fornication." On the contrary, the *fine linen, clean and white, . . . is the righteousness of saints.* Sin is referred to as spiritual nudity, whereas righteousness and salvation are spoken of as a garment.

The glorified are evidently not arrayed in material garments and yet they are referred to as being arrayed or covered. Man before the fall is said to have been naked in the sense that he wore no material garments. However, since he was created in the image of God, of whom it is said He "[covereth himself] with light as with a garment" (Psalm 104:2), man undoubtedly was enveloped with a similar covering. In his glorified state he will "awake with . . . [His] likeness" (Psalm 17:15), hence it is said he will "shine as the brightness of the firmament; and . . . as the stars for ever and ever" (Daniel 12:3); they will "shine forth as the

261

sun in the kingdom of their Father" (Matthew 13:43). The Apostle Paul says the resurrection bodies will differ in glory, as does that of the sun, the moon, and the stars, even as one star differs from another in glory (I Corinthians 15:40, 41); and again he writes that the body of our humiliation will be changed into the body of His glory (Philippians 3:21), which is described as "his face did shine as the sun, and his raiment was white as the light" (Matthew 17:2).

Verse 9. *And he saith unto me, Write, Blessed are they which are called unto the marriage supper of the Lamb. And he saith unto me, These are the true sayings of God.*

Write. This is the second instance of three in which John seems to have been so greatly absorbed with the scene just revealed that the informing angel had to give him a special order to write. Cf. 14:13 and 21:5.

They which are called. It is a singular, high, and never to be repeated honor to be called to the marriage supper of the Lamb. But it is a greater honor still to be the bride which calls. This honor have all those who constitute the church, the body of Christ.

This is the fourth beatitude. The invited guests are undoubtedly those who expressed joy and gladness (verse 7), and constitute the robe wearers of chapters 6 and 7 and the harpers of chapters 14 and 15.

The promise to "sup with him," made to those who open the door for Christ to come in (Revelation 3:20), is here fulfilled. Since this promise was made to a church group, it is evident by *the Lamb's wife* that the church is intended. John himself is a member of that body and, as is probable, the message just received appeared to him "too good to be true," so that the angel had to add the confirmatory words: *These are the true words* [Greek] *of God.*[56]

Verse 10. *And I fell at his feet to worship him. And he said unto me, See thou do it not: I am thy fellowservant, and of thy brethren that have the testimony of Jesus: worship God: for the testimony of Jesus is the spirit of prophecy.*

I fell at his feet to worship him. John seems to have been overawed with the implications of the message concerning the marriage supper of the Lamb, for now he assumes the messenger must be superhuman and worthy of worship. The angel retorts, *See thou do it not,* and gives for his reason the fact that he is of equal rank with John and with his brethren who bear testimony concerning Jesus. The angel declares categorically, *Worship God.* He alone is worthy.

5. THE BATTLE OF ARMAGEDDON (19:11-21)

Verse 11. *And I saw heaven opened, and behold a white horse; and he that sat upon him was called Faithful and True, and in righteousness he doth judge and make war.*

Many centuries ago Isaiah the prophet broke forth with the passionate appeal, "Oh that thou wouldest rend the heavens, that thou wouldest come down . . . to make thy name known to thine adversaries, that the nations may tremble at thy presence" (64:1, 2)! At long last the prophet's request finds its answer in a spectacular fashion.

I saw heaven opened. In 4:1 a door is opened in heaven at which time John heard the voice of a trumpet saying, "Come up hither."

It appears therefore that in the former passage a door is opened into heaven to receive the church; here heaven opens so that the church may accompany the Lord in triumph!

A white horse. Some hold the view that the white horse and his rider mentioned in 6:2 is the same as the one mentioned here. Upon examination, however, it appears that the only similarity between the two is the color of the horses. Note the following contrasts:

This rider comes from heaven; the former, from the earth. This one has five names indicating his deity; the former is unnamed. This one has on his head many crowns (Greek: *diadems*); the former has no crown in his own right, but a crown (Greek: *stephanos*) is given him. A number of other descriptive terms are here mentioned, all indicating the deity of this rider in unmistakable terms, none of which are ascribed to the former. If the former were Christ, as is plainly the case here, that would have been the rightful place to give the descriptions as they occur here. Since they are not mentioned, all the indications are that the one in 6:2 is a deceiver and Antichrist.

Called Faithful and True. The descriptive terms *faithful* and *true* have been previously (1:5; 3:7) applied to Christ.

In righteousness he doth judge and make war. This expression accords with what Isaiah says of the coming Messiah: "he shall not judge after the sight of his eyes" (11:3); "but with righteousness shall he judge the poor" (11:4).

Verse 12. *His eyes were as a flame of fire, and on his head were many crowns; and he had a name written, that no man knew, but he himself.*

Eyes . . . as a flame of fire. The descriptive term, *His eyes were as a flame of fire,* was already applied to Him (1:14) and again occurs (2:18) in the presentation of Himself to the church at Thyatira. The implication of this is that He is about to execute judgment upon His enemies.

On his head were many crowns. The many diadems upon His head are expressive of His royal majesty and sovereignty.

A name written, that no man knew, but he himself. This name is perhaps the same as He will write upon the overcomer. 2:17; 3:12. Commentators, however, must admit that they know nothing about the name in either case.

263

Verse 13. *And he was clothed with a vesture dipped in blood: and his name is called The Word of God.*

A vesture dipped in blood. The vesture is spoken of as being bloodstained before the treading down (verse 15) has taken place. Similar phraseology is employed in Isaiah 63:2, 3, to which this prophecy alludes, viz., "Wherefore art thou red in thine apparel, and thy garments like him that treadeth in the winefat? I have trodden the winepress alone; and of the people there was none with me: for I will tread them in mine anger, and trample them in my fury; and their blood shall be sprinkled upon my garments, and I will stain all my raiment."

The Word of God. The name, *Word of God,* applied here to the Lord, and only elsewhere in the New Testament in the writings of John the apostle (John 1:1 —three times, 14; I John 1:1; 5:7), is a pertinent testimony to the Johannine authorship of Revelation.

Verse 14. *And the armies which were in heaven followed him upon white horses, clothed in fine linen, white and clean.*

The armies which follow Him out of heaven constitute the bride, the Lamb's wife. This is seen in that they are clothed in fine linen, clean and white, as is His wife. Verse 8. Earmarks like this are always inserted for the purpose of identification, and since the fine linen is (or represents) the righteousness of the saints, the armies of heaven are not angels but redeemed and glorified human beings.

Verse 15. *And out of his mouth goeth a sharp sword, that with it he should smite the nations: and he shall rule them with a rod of iron: and he treadeth the winepress of the fierceness and wrath of Almighty God.*

A sharp sword. The mention of a sharp sword going out of His mouth occurs first in the description of the Son of man (1:16), then once each in His presentation and exhortation to the church in Pergamos (2:12, 16). The latter are warnings to the church that unless they repented they would meet the same judgment as the nations. In the former instances the purpose of the judgment may have been remedial. In Revelation 19, the context shows, it is altogether punitive.

And he shall rule. The next clause is emphatic, viz., *He himself* [Greek: *autos*] *shall rule them with a rod of iron.* The Greek for *rule them* means literally *to shepherdize.* A shepherd uses the rod for correction, but to rule with a rod of iron denotes severity, and, in the light of the context, the word probably means to destroy.

And he treadeth. Again the intensive pronoun is used, for the literal rendering of the next clause is, *He himself* [Greek: *autos*] *treads the winepress of the anger of the wrath of Almighty God.* The intensive pronoun suggests that He will not delegate the shepherdizing of the nations nor the treading of the winepress to another.

The winepress. In Hebrew the word is *gath.* The trough in which the grapes are trodden is full; the fats (vats—Hebrew: *qereb*), the reservoir into which the juice flowed, overflow. Joel 3:13. In 14:19 it is called "the great winepress of the wrath of God." It "was trodden without the city [of Jerusalem] and blood came out of the winepress, even unto the horse bridles, by the space of a thousand and six hundred furlongs [200 miles]" (14:20).

The place without the city is "the valley of Jehoshaphat" (Joel 3:12). It is also called "the valley of decision" (Joel 3:14) because there will be fought the greatest decisive battle of all time. The contending parties will be on either side: the kings of the earth and of the whole world (16:14) under the beast and his armies, of which there will be multitudes, on the one side (Joel 3:14); on the other, the Lord, not as lion but as the Lamb. There is no "noise of battle" as far as the record goes, which says simply, "and the Lamb shall overcome them" (17:14).

The fierceness and wrath. The anger (Greek: *thumos*) *of his wrath* (Greek: *orge*). That this is the correct reading is proved not only by manuscript testimony, but by internal evidence as well. Such is the reading of 16:19, which refers to the same event; besides, *and* in no case, either in the Old or New Testament, connects the two nouns. The meaning is that the wrath (*orge*) of God will pour itself out in anger (*thumos*) upon enemies in this great final conflict.[57]

Verse 16. *And he hath on his vesture and on his thigh a name written, KING OF KINGS, AND LORD OF LORDS.*

A name written. Counting the double name as two, as in verse 11, there are in six verses, six names or titles ascribed to the white horse rider, viz., *Faithful, True, the Name no man knew, the Word of God, King of kings,* and *Lord of lords.* The last two appear in inverse order in 17:14.

It is as King of kings and Lord of lords that He "treads the winepress of the anger [Greek] of the wrath of Almighty God." The Treader bears His own testimony: "I have trodden the winepress alone; and of the people there was none with me: for I will tread them in mine anger [Hebrew: *anger*], and trample them in my fury; and their blood shall be sprinkled upon my garments, and I will stain all my raiment" (Isaiah 63:3).

Verse 17. *And I saw an angel standing in the sun; and he cried with a loud voice, saying to all the fowls that fly in the midst of heaven, Come and gather yourselves together unto the supper of the great God.*

An angel standing in the sun. Faith believes what is written even if the mind cannot comprehend. The miracle of seeing an angel standing in the sun may not be so incomprehensible when one recalls the prediction, "The sun shall be turned into darkness . . . before the great and the terrible day of the Lord come" (Joel 2:31; cf. Acts 2:20). The present vision introduces the events pertaining to that day, as parallel passages plainly indicate.

Cried with a loud voice. The cry with a loud voice as heretofore (6:10; 7:2, 10; 10:3; 14:15; 18:2) denotes both importance and urgency.

To all the fowls. The summons to the fowls that fly in the midst of heaven is similar to that in Ezekiel 39:17, "Speak unto every feathered fowl," and apparently both refer to the same occasion.

Come and gather yourselves. The message, *Come and gather yourselves together unto the supper of the great God,* is similar to that in Ezekiel: "Assemble yourselves, and come; gather yourselves on every side to my sacrifice that I do sacrifice for you. . . ."

The supper of the great God. Here must be reference to the "carcase" (*ptoma*) of Matthew 24:28 and the "plague" (*ptosis*) of Zechariah 14:12.

Verse 18. *That ye may eat the flesh of kings, and the flesh of captains, and the flesh of mighty men, and the flesh of horses, and of them that sit on them, and the flesh of all men, both free and bond, both small and great.*

Here is another marked parallel to the sequel in Ezekiel 39:18, 19: "Ye shall eat the flesh of the mighty, and drink the blood of the princes of the earth, of rams, of lambs, and of goats, of bullocks, all of them fatlings of Bashan. And ye shall eat fat till ye be full, and drink blood till ye be drunken, of my sacrifice which I have sacrificed for you." (See verse 21 for further marks of identity with Ezekiel's testimony.)

Verse 19. *And I saw the beast, and the kings of the earth, and their armies, gathered together to make war against him that sat on the horse, and against his army.*

The beast. The beast is identical with the one mentioned in 11:7—the beast "that ascendeth out of the bottomless pit shall make war against them [the two witnesses], and shall overcome them, and kill them." He is also the same as the first beast of chapter 13, the number of whose name is 666, mentioned again in chapter 17 as the one that was and is not and yet shall be, namely, the Antichrist.

Gathered together. The gathering together of the kings of the earth and their armies has already been mentioned, including their place of gathering, viz., Armageddon. 16:13-16.

The purpose of their gathering is to engage in battle against Him that sat on the horse (called "Faithful and True, . . . [who] in righteousness . . . doth judge and make war"—verse 11) and against His army. However, "[He treads] the winepress alone" and thus His army, which is none other than His bride, is exempt from any engagement.

It is sometimes said there is no evidence that the church descends out of heaven to the earth. However, it is plainly declared that she (the armies, clothed in fine linen) follows Him as He descends; moreover, it would not be said that the kings gather to make war against His army if they were not with Him on the earth.

There are other passages which speak of Christ coming with His saints, e.g., "the coming of our Lord Jesus Christ with all his saints" (I Thessalonians 3:13).

"When Christ, who is our life, shall appear, then shall ye also appear with him in glory" (Colossians 3:4).

"Behold, the Lord cometh with ten thousands of his saints" (Jude 14).

Verse 20. *And the beast was taken, and with him the false prophet that wrought miracles before him, with which he deceived them that had received the mark of the beast, and them that worshipped his image. These both were cast alive into a lake of fire burning with brimstone.*

The beast. The beast is the same as of verse 19.

The false prophet. The false prophet is identical with the second beast of chapter 13:11 ff., as the following descriptive words plainly indicate.

These both were cast alive. As far as the record goes, the beast and the false prophet are the first to be consigned to the lake of fire. Others, like the rich man (Luke 16:19 ff.), have already been cast into *Hades* (Greek), but all such will be taken out of their habitation and judged at the great white throne judgment.

20:12-15. Not only will they be in the place of torment a thousand years longer than the rest of the (wicked) dead, but the mention that they are cast there *alive* would seem to indicate that their suffering will be more intense than that of the rest of the doomed.

Verse 21. *And the remnant were slain with the sword of him that sat upon the horse, which sword proceeded out of his mouth: and all the fowls were filled with their flesh.*

The reference is to the white horse rider, viz., the King of kings and Lord of lords (verses 11-16 above), by whom were slain the remnant, i.e., the kings of the earth and their armies (verse 19).

In the latter part of the verse—*all the fowls were filled with their flesh*—there is a further allusion to Ezekiel 39 (see especially verses 17, 20).

6. THE MILLENNIUM (20:1-15)

The Binding of Satan (20:1-3)

Verse 1. *And I saw an angel come down from heaven, having the key of the bottomless pit and a great chain in his hand.*

An angel come down from heaven. In two previous visions (10:1 and 18:1) mention is made of an angel coming down from heaven. In each case details of outstanding importance are added concerning the distinct mission of each angel.

Having the key of the bottomless pit. This is equal to saying that the angel has the authority to open or shut the bottomless pit. Compare 1:18, where mention is made of the Son of man having the keys of hell and of death. In that case, being divine, the Son of man has the authority in His own right, whereas the authority of the angel was given to him.

And a great chain in his hand. The great chain in the hand of the angel, like the key, is doubtless meant to be understood in a figurative sense, that is, he had the authority to bind (verse 2) and to loose (verses 3, 7). [It needs to be borne in mind, however, that Revelation 20 is not the only place in the Scripture where spirit beings are said to be bound with chains. The Apostle Peter writes, "For if God spared not the angels that sinned, but cast them down to hell, and delivered them into chains of darkness, to be reserved unto judgment . . ." (II Peter 2:4). So also Jude writes, "And the angels which kept not their first estate, but left their own habitation, he hath reserved in everlasting chains under darkness unto the judgment of the great day" (Jude 6).

These references in Peter and Jude each use a different word for *chain*. The Revelation passage finds common ground with Mark 5:3, where the demon-possessed man is said to have been bound with chains; with Acts 12:7, where the angel of the Lord released Peter from prison and his chains fell off; with Acts 28:20, where Paul declared to the Jews of Rome that he was bound with a chain for the hope of Israel; and with II Timothy 1:16, where Paul pays tribute to Onesiphorus who was not ashamed of Paul's chain. It is abundantly clear that the Greek word *halysis*, used in the above four references, is a literal chain. We can safely assume that the word in Revelation 20 can also be a literal chain.

It has been argued that spirit beings cannot be bound with literal chains. On this objection let it be noted that spirit beings are real beings; therefore real chains can bind real beings. Certainly the spirit world is not symbolic! Why is it not logical and reasonable to consider the chain of Revelation 20 as literal a chain as necessary to bind a literal spirit being—the old serpent?—J. O. Y.]

Verse 2. *And he laid hold on the dragon, that old serpent, which is the Devil, and Satan, and bound him a thousand years.*

[The author had some extensive notes on the place of the devil in the Christian era which can be condensed as follows: Ephesians 2:2 identifies him as the "prince of the power of the air." Revelation 12 records the heavenly battle in which Michael casts out the devil and his angels. Revelation 13 reveals the "infernal

268

trinity" in the persons of the dragon, the beast, and the false prophet (the second beast). In Revelation 19 one finds the beast and the false prophet cast into the lake of fire, leaving only the devil. He alone is now to be dealt with.—J. O. Y.]

And he laid hold on the dragon. Since Michael was the angel who cast Satan to the earth (Revelation 12), he is likely the angel who laid hold on the dragon at this time.

That old serpent. He is called the old serpent because it was he who deceived our first parents. *Devil* means slanderer and *Satan* (a Hebrew word) means adversary.

And bound him. Satan will be bound after the beast and the false prophet have been cast into the lake of fire. Revelation 19:20. Since these two do not make their appearance until the middle of the tribulation period (chapter 13), and they are not cast into the lake of fire until after the coming of Christ, and His smiting of the nations (19:1-15), the binding of Satan must take place not at the beginning of the church age, but after the second coming of Christ.

The Apostle Peter did not believe Satan was bound when he wrote, "your adversary the devil, as a roaring lion, walketh about, seeking whom he may devour" (I Peter 5:8).

Perhaps the strongest uninspired testimony that Satan is not bound during the church age is that of Menno Simons who wrote in the first half of the sixteenth century: ". . . it is evident that the old master, satan, the arch enemy of God and souls, is always about us, as a roaring lion, and seeks whom he may devour, as Peter says. He assails us in divers ways; now with the unclean, wicked nature of our depraved flesh, and anon with some enchanting, false doctrine and fair words; and again, by persecution, cross, and fears; then with liberty and worldly life of the flesh; now with riches and abundance, then again with defects, wants, and poverty. In short, he shoots his fiery darts constantly; they fly by day and by night, in secret and in public. He that does not zealously abide in the fear of God cannot withstand the manifold assaults of his temptations."[58]

A thousand years. The angel bound him (Satan) a thousand years. The present writer believes the numerical term, *a thousand years,* is to be understood literally because twenty-one cardinal numbers are mentioned in this book, all of which are doubtless to be understood in their literal sense. They are 1, 2, 3, 3½, 4, 5, 6, 7, 10, 12, 24, 42, 144, 1,000, 1,260, 1,600, 7,000, 12,000, 144,000, 100,000,-000, and 200,000,000.

If 1,000 is a symbol, what about 7,000 (11:13), 12,000 (7:5), or 144,000 (7:4)? Are these symbols also? If 1,000 years is a symbolic term, what about 5 months (9:10), 42 months (11:2), and 1,260 days (11:3)? To ask these questions is to show the absurdity of regarding the numbers as figurative, for on what ground could one consistently hold that one, 1,000, is figurative, and the others, including where multiples of 1,000 are used, are literal?

Finally, it is the Lord who gave these words, *a thousand years,* to John for His servants. 1:1. Since He chose these words to denote the period of time, then it must be safe and wise for men to use the same language as a vehicle of truth in telling others how long Satan will be bound. One ought seriously to consider the implications of his theology if he hesitates to give the message of God to men in the words He gave to John for His servants. Revelation 1:1.

Verse 3. *And cast him into the bottomless pit, and shut him up, and set a seal upon him, that he should deceive the nations no more, till the thousand years should be fulfilled* [Greek: *finished*]: *and after that he must be loosed a little season.*

And cast him into the bottomless pit. As mentioned above, the angel is probably Michael, for he it is that will cast him upon the earth during the middle of the tribulation period. 12:7-9.

On *the bottomless pit,* see 9:1, 2.

The threefold dealing with Satan—throwing him into the bottomless pit, closing it, and sealing it over him—should make it plain that this has not happened yet, for he could not thus be confined and at the same time go about in the world as a roaring lion, seeking whom he may devour.

That he should deceive the nations no more, till. . . . The purpose of the binding is not that he should be prevented from deceiving Christians, but the nations. The custody of Satan, however, was to continue only until the thousand years are finished. The use of the Greek word *achri* (until) implies that when the thousand years are ended, Satan's confinement in the pit would cease. That this is the sense of the word *achri* is proved by the following clause: *after these things* [Greek] *he must be loosed a little time* [Greek]. Moreover, in verse 8 below it is expressly stated that he will go out to deceive the nations after his release. Here are all the essential elements of a time period, viz., Satan was cast into the bottomless pit before the one thousand years; this is a *terminus a quo* (end from which); then we have the Greek word *achri* (until), denoting duration, and finally the loosing of Satan after the thousand years, i.e., a *terminus ad quem* (end to which). A prominent commentator, recognizing these facts, remarks: "if for one moment we might indulge in a play of the imagination, we might readily picture to ourselves that the binding and incarceration of Satan were to last but a few days. . . ."[59]

The mention of nations here shows conclusively that after the battle of Armageddon there will still be nations left upon the earth. The implication is that those assembled to make war against the Lord and His army consisted of men of war only. The same is implied in Zechariah 14:16: ". . . every one that is left of all the nations which came against Jerusalem shall even go up from year to year to worship the King, the Lord of hosts, and to keep the feast of tabernacles." (Cf. Revelation 21:24.)

The Reign with Christ (20:4-6)

Verse 4. *And I saw thrones, and they sat upon them, and judgment was given unto them: and I saw the souls of them that were beheaded for the witness of Jesus, and for the word of God, and which had not worshipped the beast, neither his image, neither had received his mark upon their foreheads, or in their hands; and they lived and reigned with Christ a thousand years.*

And I saw thrones, and they sat upon them. The reference is to the enthroned elders (4:4-8; 5:8-10; 19:4), representing the church.

And judgment was given unto them. These words accord with the same conclusion. For example, it was to the apostles (representing the church) that Jesus said, ". . . in the regeneration when the Son of man shall sit in the throne of his glory, ye also shall sit upon twelve thrones, judging the twelve tribes of Israel" (Matthew 19:28). Again, a few days later, after instituting the Lord's Supper, He said, "And I appoint unto you a kingdom, as my Father hath appointed unto me; that ye may eat and drink at my table in my kingdom, and sit on thrones judging the twelve tribes of Israel" (Luke 22:29, 30). Let those who hold the view that the church and the kingdom are identical and that Israel and the church are identical test the consistency of their view by substituting "church" for "kingdom" and for "Israel." According to the axiom that two things that are equal to the same thing are equal to each other, the kingdom would equal the church; Israel equal the church; therefore the kingdom equal Israel. [A preposterous conclusion, if language has any meaning!—J. O. Y.]

In writing to the church at Corinth the apostle declared, "Do ye not know that the saints shall judge the world?" And again, "Know ye not that we shall judge angels" (I Corinthians 6:2, 3)?

Observe, too, that in addressing the "seven churches which are in Asia," John declares He "hath made us kings and priests" (1:6; cf. 5:10). From these passages it is plain that the first group consists of those who sit on thrones, to whom judgment was given, referring to chapters 4 and 5 and representing the church.

Judgment was given to the first group only, that is, to those sitting on thrones, designated kings and priests, consequently the glorified church. Had the latter two groups been included in the exercise of judgment, the phrase, *judgment was given unto them,* would no doubt have been placed at the end of verse 4. That this high distinction belongs to the church alone is implied in the passages already quoted. Matthew 19:28; Luke 22:29, 30; I Corinthians 6:2, 3a.

And I saw the souls of them that were beheaded because of [Greek] *the witness* [*testimony*] *of Jesus, and because of* [Greek] *the word of God.* The language identifies this group at once with the martyrs of 6:9, "that were slain because of [Greek] the word of God, and because of [Greek] the testimony which they held."

Since verse 4 gives a summary of all those constituting the first resurrection, and only three groups are mentioned as composing it, this second group includes *all those* slain because of the Word of God and because of the testimony which they held. Besides those of 6:9 there are two additional groups who, by the earmarks accompanying their description, undoubtedly are thus included.

The two witnesses were killed by the beast when they had finished their testimony. 11:3, 7. The word *testimony* is the earmark of identification.

In 12:11 mention is made of those who overcame him (Satan, immediately after he was cast out of heaven—verse 9) "because of [Greek] the word of their testimony; and they loved not their lives [Greek: souls] unto the death." (The Greek omits the article before *death.*)

Other marks of identification occur: in 6:9 and 12:11 the martyrs are referred to as souls, as in Revelation 20; in 6:11 it is said "white robes were given unto . . . them" (nothing, however, is said about the number of those slain); in chapter 7 mention is made of a great multitude "clothed with white robes" (verse 9); in verses 13 and 14 of the same chapter the white robed are again mentioned as coming out of "[the] great tribulation." These, therefore, are evidently the same group as those of chapter 6:9-11 and hence are included in the second group of 19:4.

The word *behead* means to kill with an ax. Since this was the method of slaying employed by Rome, those slain because of "the word of God" mentioned in 6:9 were doubtless slain by her. And that religious Rome is intended appears certain from the fact that no sooner is she destroyed than the martyrs in heaven exclaim, "Alleluia . . . for he hath judged the great whore . . . and hath avenged the blood of his servants at her hand" (19:1, 2).

And which had not worshipped the beast, neither his image, neither had received his mark upon their foreheads, or in their hands. The Greek word for *which* is *hostis* (an indefinite relative pronoun), *hos* equals *who, tis* is *anyone*, that is, *anyone who;* in the plural, as here (see Thayer), it signifies *all those who.* This shows conclusively that a group distinct from the two previously mentioned is intended. The words, *had not worshipped the beast . . . hands,* are taken wholly from 13:16, 17 and thus distinguish this group absolutely from the two former groups. This glorified group is therefore the same as those "that had gotten the victory over the beast, and over his image, and over his mark, and over the number of his name . . ." (15:2). Their victory over the beast consisted in this that they refused to take his mark and hence they were slain and went "to be with Christ, which is far better."

In the consideration of the three glorified groups (19:1-6) it was observed that those spoken of "as the voice of many waters, and as the voice of mighty thunderings" (verse 6b) are the same as those in 14:2 of whom John said, "I heard a voice from heaven, as the voice of many waters, and as the voice of a great thunder." Those of 16:6b, therefore, belong to the third group of 20:4c.

They lived and reigned with Christ a thousand years. The meaning is, they came to life again. The reference is to the three groups above mentioned. John in his Gospel uses the word in a similar sense, e.g., "though he were dead, yet shall he live" (11:25); again, "because I live, ye shall live also" (14:19). The three groups in a glorified state are: (1) the throne sitters (chapters 4 and 5), (2) the robe wearers (chapters 6 and 7), and (3) the "Conscientious Objectors" (chapters 14 and 15). These were noted in conjunction in chapter 19:1-6 and are brought together in 20:4 in order to indicate plainly their joint participation in the future glory. The reign of the three groups is contemporaneous with the binding of Satan. In other words, the reign with Christ is of equal duration with the binding of Satan. The inconsistency and untenableness of the view that in this instance no period of time is intended, whereas in the former the binding of Satan in respect to the Christian has already continued for nearly two millenniums, should be quite apparent to anyone.

Verse 5. *But the rest of the dead lived not again until the thousand years were finished. This is the first resurrection.*

The rest of the dead. By the rest of the dead are meant the wicked dead.

They (like the rich man—Luke 16:23) will remain in *Hades* in conscious torment until the thousand years are finished. At that time *Hades* will give up its dead.

This is the first resurrection. The reference is to the three groups just mentioned. It is called the first resurrection and consists of the righteous in contrast with the last resurrection after the thousand years, consisting of the wicked. This resurrection is further distinguished by descriptive titles in earlier Scriptures, such as the following:

Of the many "that sleep in the dust," some shall awake "to everlasting life" (Daniel 12:2) in contrast with those that shall awake (evidently after the thousand years) "to shame and everlasting contempt" (Daniel 12:2b).

The Lord declares, ". . . when thou makest a feast, call the poor, the maimed, the lame, the blind: and thou shalt be blessed; for they cannot recompense thee: for thou shalt be recompensed at [signifying in the time of] the resurrection of the just" (Luke 14:13, 14).

"Marvel not at this: for the hour is coming, in the which all that are in the graves shall hear his voice, and shall come forth; they that have done good, unto the resurrection of life; and they that have done evil, unto the resurrection of damnation" (John 5:28, 29).

This passage is taken by some as proving that the resurrection of the righteous and the resurrection of the wicked will be simultaneous because both are spoken of as occurring the same hour. According to Scriptural usage, however, the word "hour" may designate a long period of time. Cf. John 4:23; I John 2:18.

In Daniel 12:2, where two classes are mentioned, the righteous are mentioned first. It is significant that this is always the case.

In his defense before Felix, the Apostle Paul declares, ". . . there shall be a resurrection of the dead, both of the just and unjust" (Acts 24:15). As stated before the order of mention is the same—first, that of the righteous, and second, that of the wicked.

In Hebrews 11:35 the reference appears to be to the faithful of the intertestament period (e.g., II Maccabees 6 and 7) who rather than deny their Lord suffered martyrdom that they might obtain a better resurrection, the resurrection of the righteous. From this study so far, three observations are clear:

where two classes are mentioned, the first always refers to the righteous;

where only one class is mentioned, the reference is always to the righteous;

and the resurrection of the wicked is never mentioned separately.

Now Revelation 20:5 refers to the righteous only and is designated *the first resurrection*. From these observations it is logical and consistent to conclude that in all the passages considered, those where only one class is mentioned (Luke 14:14 and Hebrews 11:35) and the first of those where two classes are mentioned (Daniel 12:2b; John 5:28, 29; Acts 24:15) consist of or belong to the first resurrection; and further, the second group of those where two classes are mentioned consists of those that live not "until the thousand years . . . [are] finished."

Verse 6. *Blessed and holy is he that hath part in the first resurrection: on such the second death hath no power, but they shall be priests of God and of Christ, and shall reign with him a thousand years.*

Blessed and holy is he. This is the fifth beatitude. *Blessed* and *holy* are epithets applied to the children of God here and now, some thirty and sixty times respectively (the word "saints" means holy ones). "[Without holiness] no man shall see the Lord." "He that is holy, let him be holy still." "The pure in heart . . . shall see God." Neither death, translation, nor "purgatorial" fires can purify the souls of men.

To have *part in the first resurrection* is in marked contrast with and is the only alternative to the "rest of the dead" who have "their part in the lake which burneth with fire and brimstone: which is the second death" (Revelation 21:8).

The second death. The second death is mentioned again in verse 14 and in 21:8.

And shall reign with him. Believers in the church age are never said to be reigning now except some self-styled kings at Corinth (I Corinthians 4:8) whom the apostle ridiculed with ludicrous irony, e.g., *ye* reigned as kings but *we* (Paul and Barnabas—the pronouns are emphatic) are fools for Christ's sake! It is "shall reign" in Romans 5:17; II Timothy 2:12. Even after the church is glorified (Revelation 5:10) they sing "we shall reign on the earth." (That is unquestionably the true reading. See comments there.)

Shall reign is identical with *shall be kings.* Believers are spoken of elsewhere as kings and priests (always in this order). 1:6; 5:10. Even now the church is a "royal [Greek: *kingly*] priesthood" (I Peter 2:9). She is this, however, only *de jure* (by right); during the one thousand years she will be so *de facto* (in reality). Believers are heirs of the kingdom now (James 2:5); when the kingdom comes, the saints will "possess" it. Daniel 7:22. The reign will be on the earth. Revelation 5:10; cf. Matthew 25:31 ff.; 24:29-31; I Thessalonians 4:13-17.

The Deception of the Nations (20:7-9)

Verse 7. *And when the thousand years are expired, Satan shall be loosed out of his prison.*

Expired. The Greek word for *expired* (*teleo*) is the same as that rendered "fulfilled" in verse 3 and "finished" in verse 5 and should have been uniformly rendered *finished.* (This variety of translation of the same Greek word is simply an illustration of the predilection of the translators for variety in order to avoid monotony, thus sacrificing in numerous instances sense for style.)

His prison. What is called prison here is the same as the bottomless pit. Verses 1 and 3. See also I Peter 3:19, where mention is made of the spirits in prison.

Verse 8. *And shall go out to deceive the nations which are in the four quarters of the earth, Gog and Magog, to gather them together to battle: the number of whom is as the sand of the sea.*

To deceive the nations. Those who live through and beyond the 1,000 years (no doubt for providential and equitable reasons) must be tempted by Satan as were the rest of humanity, and since the days of grace are past, they even as he will suffer "speedily" the vengeance of eternal fire.

See verse 3 as to why Satan was bound. His going out to deceive the nations immediately after his release appears to be implied in the fact that his release from prison and his determination to deceive the nations are expressed in the same sentence.

Evidently he will not have "learned a syllable" in his thousand-year school of experience since he will follow up his deception of the nations by gathering an innumerable host from the four corners of the earth to battle against the saints of the Most High.

Gog and Magog. Since Gog and Magog are mentioned here as Satan's cohorts in battle, some have erroneously concluded that this battle is identical with that described in Ezekiel 38 and 39. That such is not the case is evident from the following considerations:

Gog and Magog are here referred to as separate nations, whereas in the Ezekiel passage Gog is said to be of the land of Magog, Prince of Rosh (Hebrew), Meshech (Moscow), and Tubal (Tobolsk). Gesenius, the great Hebrew lexicographer, says Rosh refers to Russia, whereas Moscow and Tobolsk were the former capitals of Western and Eastern Russia respectively.

In the Ezekiel passage, the invading armies are said to come from the north parts (38:15); here they assemble from the four corners of the earth.

In Ezekiel, Gog is head of the hosts; here Satan gathers them together.

In Ezekiel the object of attack is to take a prey, to carry away silver and gold, to take away cattle and goods, to take a great spoil (38:13); here it is to make war against "the beloved city."

The former takes place *before* Armageddon (Ezekiel 39:17-20), *before* the restoration of Israel and *before* God sets His glory among the nations (Ezekiel 39:21 ff.). This battle will be after the thousand years are finished. (See verse 7 above.)

Ezekiel predicts, "in the latter [last] days" (38:16), a period of time either in reference to a time of tribulation preceding the kingdom (Numbers 24:14; Deuteronomy 4:30; 31:29; Jeremiah 30:24; Daniel 10:14) or to the kingdom age itself (Isaiah 2:2; Hosea 3:5; Micah 4:1). This (Revelation 20) will be not only after the tribulation and the kingdom age of a thousand years but after the little season that will follow the thousand years. (See verse 3 above.)

In Ezekiel some 18 details of judgment are given (38:19-22) as diverse as they well could be from the single act of God mentioned in Revelation 20:9, "fire came down from God . . . and devoured them."

The four quarters of the earth. It appears that Gog and Magog will be scattered as far as Israel, for when Israel will be gathered "the second time" (Isaiah 11:11, 12) they will come from "the four corners of the earth." With the rapid spread of communism in this day it is easy to understand how their numerous descendants after the thousand years will be found in all lands.

Because of their anti-Christian attitude the communists (of Russia) will doubtless be "left" when the Lord comes to take the church to Himself. Moreover, since they are not a part of the Roman Empire, the percentage of fatalities among them may not be as great during the tribulation period as that of the nations adjacent to Rome, the seat of Antichrist, thus accounting for the great number of their descendants after the 1,000 years. They will serve and worship the Lord and "the knowledge of the Lord [will cover the earth] as the waters cover the sea." Gog and Magog will doubtless be included among them; however, with their proclivity to unbelief, they apparently will fall an easy prey to the wiles of Satan after he is "loosed out of his prison" and [goes] out to deceive the nations.

A further proof that the 1,000 years constitute a period of time is implied in that a people not so much as mentioned before in the New Testament come so prominently into the prophetic limelight immediately after the thousand years. Consider, how could a people, by number as the sand of the sea, emerge into existence immediately after the "destruction from the Almighty" as recorded in Revelation 19:17-21? The prophet Isaiah, in describing the calamities of the tribulation, says there will be a "few men left" (24:6). The seer testifies that under the fourth seal authority was given to Death and Hades to kill "the fourth part of the earth" (i.e., its inhabitants) (Revelation 6:8); and under the sixth trumpet "the third part of men [were] killed, by . . . fire, . . . smoke, and . . . brimstone" (Revelation 9:18). Thus one half of men will perish under two plagues. Concerning the rest of the plagues no statistics are given; however, at Armageddon blood is said to come up to "the horse bridles, by the space of a thousand and six hundred furlongs" (14:20).

In addition to this enormous carnage of the wicked, note that the human family is reduced further by three righteous groups:

The throne sitters (chapters 4 and 5; 20:4a);

The robe wearers—"a great multitude, which no man could number" "which came out of [the] great tribulation" (chapters 6 and 7; 20:4b);

Conscientious objectors—"a voice from heaven, as the voice of many waters, and as the voice of a great thunder" who refuse to take the mark of the beast and of his image (14:1-4; 15:2-4; 20:4c).

It must be admitted therefore that by the removal "in the last days" of all the righteous and of the hosts of the wicked (as mentioned above) from the number of inhabitants of the earth, there will be comparatively speaking but "few men left," as Isaiah the prophet declares (chapter 24:6), at the close of the tribulation. And since the "little season," according to the previous usage of the term (verse 3 above), continues at most but half that time, how could the "few men left" during the "little season" multiply themselves into a multitude as numerous as the sand of the sea? To ask the question is enough to prove the untenability of the view that the thousand years do not signify a stated period of time.

The language of the passage likewise indicates the error of the view that the thousand years began either with the beginning of the church age or with the time of Augustine and end with the coming of the Lord. Those holding this view must admit there is a time period of a little season after the thousand years during which Gog and Magog, in number as the sand of the sea, will engage in battle under the leadership of Satan as described in verse 9 below.

For proof of the universal worship of God during the 1,000-year reign, which worship will include Gog and Magog, see Psalm 72:11, 17; Isaiah 2:2-4; 65:20,

22; 66:18, 19, 24; Ezekiel 36:38; Zechariah 8:4, 5, 20-23; 14:16-18b; Revelation 11:15; 15:4.

Verse 9. *And they went up on the breadth of the earth, and compassed the camp of the saints about, and the beloved city: and fire came down from God out of heaven, and devoured them.*

They went up. Since Jerusalem is located on Mt. Zion, the phrase *go up* to Jerusalem occurs some 20 times in the New Testament. Note also, "Jerusalem . . . whither the tribes go up . . . to give thanks unto the name of the Lord" (Psalm 122:3, 4).

The breadth of the earth. This agrees with verse 8 where Gog and Magog are referred to as being in the four quarters (corners) of the earth.

Compassed. The hordes of Gog and Magog *encircle* the camp of the saints, which comports with the former declaration that their number is great.

The beloved city. The phrase, *the beloved city,* is evidently to be understood as epexegetical or explanatory of the camp of the saints, the connecting *and* having the sense of *even* as in the phrase, "God and Father" (of frequent occurrence), in which "Father" and "God" refer to the same person. The name "beloved city" harks back to Psalm 78:68 and 87:2 where the endearing term plainly refers to Jerusalem. (Compare Isaiah 1:26: "Afterward thou shalt be called, The city of righteousness, the faithful city.") The promise of "grace" to Israel (Jeremiah 31:2; Zechariah 12:10) has truly been fulfilled, for in chapter 11:8, after the Gentiles (i.e., nations) have trodden down the city, it is designated "Sodom"; now it is *the beloved city.*

There could be no stronger nor more convincing evidence that there will be saints on the earth during the thousand-year reign, and that their chief city will be Jerusalem, than verses 8 and 9.

Their enemies who seek to destroy them are on earth. The number of saints must be great, else those seeking to destroy them would not assemble an army as the sand of the sea. The fire which destroys the invaders "[comes] down from God out of heaven," and when the smoke of their destruction has cleared away the saints are still there.

It is a sad and humiliating fact that the last act in the great drama of human history is, that a multitude "as the sand of the sea" "[gathered] . . . together to battle" at the instigation of Satan, and under his leadership, with the avowed purpose of bringing ruin to the metropolis of the kingdom of God on earth and of bringing to nought the saints dwelling therein, but it is heartening to learn that those who dig the fatal ditch will themselves fall therein and that the saints of the most high God shall not perish from the earth. [Surely "the Lord knoweth them that are his."—J. O. Y.]

The Doom of the Devil (20:10)

Verse 10. *And the devil that deceived them was cast into the lake of fire and brimstone, where the beast and the false prophet are, and shall be tormented day and night for ever and ever.*

The devil that deceived them. Satan's first act of deception occurred in the

Garden of Eden. It is a matter of interest to note that his first act is recorded in Genesis 3 (the third chapter from the beginning), whereas his last act on a world-wide scale is mentioned in Revelation 20 (the third chapter from the end).

It is a significant fact that the first prediction concerning Satan is the last to be fulfilled. In Genesis 3:15 his final doom is announced in the language, "it [referring to Christ, the seed of the woman] shall bruise thy [Satan's] head."

Shall be tormented . . . for ever and ever. The untenability of the view that to be cast into the lake of fire "will end it all" is seen in the fact that the beast and the false prophet were cast in before the thousand years, and when Satan was cast in after the thousand years, both the beast and the false prophet (the second beast of Revelation 13:11 ff.) were still there. The duration of their torment will be *for ever and ever* (Greek: "unto the ages of ages"), that is, as long as God lives (4:9, 10; 5:14; 10:6; 15:7), or ceaseless. Better to believe it here than to find it out hereafter.

The Final Judgment (20:11-15)

Verse 11. *And I saw a great white throne, and him that sat on it, from whose face the earth and the heaven fled away; and there was found no place for them.*

A great white throne. In 4:2 mention is made about *a* throne set in heaven; after that *the* throne (i.e., the one mentioned in 4:2) is mentioned 32 times. Here it is *a* throne again, i.e., a different throne from that mentioned before. The throne is further distinguished from the one in 4:2 in that it is designated a *white* throne. Moreover, it is a great throne, not merely in size but because of the great issues involved.

Him that sat on it. This phrase as before means *the* [one] *sitting thereon,* as always since 3:21 where Christ sits on His right hand.

The earth and the heaven fled away. The expression, *the earth and the heaven fled away,* is elsewhere (21:1) described as "the first heaven and the first earth were passed away." Similar expressions occur in Matthew 24:35; Mark 13:31; Luke 16:17; 21:33, and II Peter 3:10. That the language employed does not signify "the vanishing of the former heaven and earth into nothingness" is proved by the language of pertinent passages elsewhere. Cf. II Corinthians 5:17; James 1:10; Romans 8:19-23; II Peter 3:10, 13.

So the new heaven and new earth of Revelation 21:1 are not a new creation added to the sum total of existing things but a change "from the bondage of corruption" due to the sin of its inhabitants into a new heaven and earth "wherein dwelleth righteousness" (II Peter 3:10, 13).

It should occasion no difficulty to learn that when God brings about this change, no place is found for them in the range of human vision, and that hence the present (lower) heaven and earth fled away, later to appear as the new heaven and earth. Revelation 21:1.

Verse 12. *And I saw the dead, small and great, stand before God; and the books were opened: and another book was opened, which is the book of life: and the dead were judged out of those things which were written in the books, according to their works.*

I saw the dead. The dead here are the rest of the dead mentioned in verse 5 who live not again until the thousand years are finished; hence they include all the wicked dead previously referred to as the resurrection to "shame and everlasting contempt" (Daniel 12:2), the resurrection of "judgment" (Greek—John 5:29), the resurrection of the "unjust" (Acts 24:15).

Small and great. This is an inclusive term stressing the fact that none will be missing. The phrase occurs previously in 11:18; 13:16; 19:5, 18.

Stand before God. Those of the first resurrection are said to stand before the Son of man. The wicked dead necessarily must stand before God because they have not availed themselves of a Daysman to appear in their behalf, and to fall before Him is now too late.

And the books were opened. It required *books* to register the wicked; a single book suffices for inclusion of the righteous. This solemn declaration, however, accords with the saying of Jesus: ". . . wide is the gate, and broad is the way, that leadeth to destruction, and many there be which go in thereat: because strait is the gate, and narrow is the way, which leadeth unto life, and few there be that find it" (Matthew 7:13, 14).

The book of life. The book of life is apparently so called because in it are recorded the names of those who have part in the resurrection. Its presence here may be in order to silence any false claims by such who expected to meet God's favor because they had done many wonderful works. Matthew 7:22; cf. verse 13 below.

According to their works. God is fair and just in His judgments, for even the wicked are judged *according to their works.* The phrase, "[He will] render to every man according to his works" (or its equivalent), occurs as many as 42 times in the Scriptures—elsewhere in Revelation in 2:23; 18:6; 20:13, and 22:12.

Verse 13. And the sea gave up the dead which were in it; and death and hell delivered up the dead which were in them: and they were judged every man according to their works.

And the sea gave up the dead. Special reference is made to such as were drowned (and doubtless in many cases consumed) in the sea, probably because resurrection is spoken of as a coming out of the graves or as the graves opening. Since the resurrection of the just took place before the thousand years, the reference here is to that of the wicked who perished in the sea.

Death and hell delivered up. The Greek words for *death (thanatos)* and *hell (hades)* are mentioned together five times in the New Testament as follows: I Corinthians 15:55; Revelation 1:18; 6:8; 20:13, 14. These two terms include the wicked of all ages at the time this judgment is set.

The word *hades* occurs eleven times in the New Testament. It is translated "hell" ten times and once (I Corinthians 15:55) "grave." In order that it might be distinguished from the Greek word *gehenna*, the real hell of everlasting fire, the Greek word *hades* should have been transliterated into English, i.e., "hades."

[It would seem more logical to consider *death and hell* as inseparable companions, as indicated in Revelation 6:8, and so they are called upon together to give up the dead in their hold, the conjunction *and* being considered as connective.

The term *death* being a collective noun would call for the plural pronouns *they* and *their*. Thus the persons held by the companions *death and hell* are brought before the "great white throne" of God to stand trial for the deeds done in the body and to be assigned their rewards *every man according to their works*. It is therefore a gathering of all the wicked to receive individual retribution.—J. O. Y.]

According to their works. See verse 12.

Verse 14. *And death and hell were cast into the lake of fire. This is the second death.*

[It is therefore to be understood as the final state of the rebellious from which there is no resuscitation. The first death is physical and temporal; the second, spiritual and eternal.—J. O. Y.]

Verse 15. *And whosoever was not found written in the book of life was cast into the lake of fire.*

Whosoever was not found. The expression is similar to that made of Enoch (Hebrews 11:6), which implies that search was made, but no trace was found. Their claims for inclusion among those listed in the book of life are rejected because the Judge of all the earth [whose judgment is "according to truth" (Romans 2:2)—J. O. Y.] deemed them unworthy a place in the sacred register.

[A more literal translation of the verse would read, *And if anyone was not found inscribed in the book of life, he was cast into the lake of fire.* This would clearly indicate the complete equity of the Judge, a careful search being made. What impinging of the conscience these wicked dead will experience, as the neglected opportunities roll through the memory!—J. O. Y.]

The parties meeting this awful doom will experience the truth of the dictum, "The death of death through death brought death to death."

7. THE GREAT FINALE (21:1-8)

Verse 1. *And I saw a new heaven and a new earth: for the first heaven and the first earth were passed away; and there was no more sea.*

A new heaven and a new earth. The *new heaven* and *new earth* are mentioned elsewhere only by Isaiah (Isaiah 65:17; 66:22) and Peter (II Peter 3:13).

In the first passage Isaiah evidently refers to the eternal age, i.e., after the 1,000 years; however, in the verses following (18-25), he plainly alludes to the millennium. He says, ". . . the child shall die an hundred years old; but the sinner being an hundred years old shall be accursed" (Isaiah 65:20b). This cannot refer to conditions prevailing in the new heaven and new earth, for the voice out of heaven in Revelation 21:4 below declares, "there shall be no more death."

The same order of statement obtains in the prophet's later message, for in 66:22 he mentions the new heaven and the new earth, whereas in verse 23, he declares, ". . . that from one new moon to another, and from one sabbath to another, shall all flesh come to worship before me, saith the Lord"—words which cannot apply to the eternal age.

This introversion of prophetic passages, i.e., the mention of first fulfillment last and last fulfillment first, is no exception in the Old Testament Scriptures. A notable example occurs in the last two verses. Malachi 4:5 speaks of "the great and dreadful day of the Lord"; while in verse 6, ". . . he shall turn the heart of the fathers to the children. . . ." As it happens, the last prophecy of the Old Testament is the first to be fulfilled in the New. In Luke 1:17 occurs Gabriel's message to Zacharias: "And he shall . . . turn the hearts of the fathers to the children"; whereas "that great and notable day of the Lord" is mentioned first in Acts 2:20, which evidently still awaits fulfillment.

The description given by Peter in his second epistle (3:10, 11), pertaining to the breaking up of the present order of the cosmos, appears even more cataclysmic than that given by John, the seer. In no case, however, does the language employed in these parallel passages support the view that "the former heaven and earth have vanished into nothingness."

For the first heaven and the first earth were passed away. It is significant that the only other place in prophetic passages where the words, "heaven and earth shall pass away," occur, they pertain to the certainty of the imminency of the second coming of Christ and not to the final consummation of all things.

It must be admitted that if there is such a thing as the former heaven and earth vanishing into nothingness, the present passage is the strongest to support such a view. However, the exact opposite is the true interpretation. Cf. II Corinthians 5:17; Romans 8:20-22.

There was no more sea. The statement, *and there was no more sea,* shows that the reference is to the eternal age, for the *sea* is repeatedly mentioned as existing in passages pertaining to the kingdom age. Psalm 72:8; Isaiah 11:9; 60:5; Ezekiel 47:10, 20; 48:28; Zechariah 9:10; 14:8.

Verse 2. *And I John saw the holy city, new Jerusalem, coming down from God out of heaven, prepared as a bride adorned for her husband.*

The holy city. Jerusalem is called the holy city (Matthew 4:5; 27:53) and doubtless due to her rejection of the Messiah not again until Revelation 11:2, where the Gentiles tread down the city, after which she spiritually is called Sodom; now at the last she is again the holy city. In Revelation 3:12 the name *new Jerusalem* is already applied proleptically to the city in the promise to the overcomer and identified as the city "which cometh down out of heaven from my God."

The high significance of *new* is implied in that it calls for a separate and distinct vision from that of the preceding verse.

Prepared as a bride. The inclusion of the word *prepared* may hark back to Jesus' promise to prepare a place in His Father's house for His own. John 14:2, 3. The simile is *prepared as a bride* instead of simply "the bride, the Lamb's wife" as in verse 9 below, perhaps because the new Jerusalem here mentioned is not to be understood as the exact parallel of, but rather as more inclusive than, the holy Jerusalem of the latter verse.

By more inclusive is meant that it consists not merely of the church, but of Israel as well. It evidently includes all the redeemed of all ages, the eternal abode referred to in II Corinthians 5:1, where Paul writes, "We know that if our earthly house of this tabernacle were dissolved, we have a building of God, an house not made with hands, eternal in the heavens." It is the city "which hath foundations, whose builder and maker is God" (Hebrews 11:10). In both passages the reference is to God only and this accords with the thought that Jesus has now surrendered the kingdom to the Father that God may be all in all.

Verse 3. *And I heard a great voice out of heaven saying, Behold, the tabernacle of God is with men, and he will dwell with them, and they shall be his people, and God himself shall be with them, and be their God.*

A great voice. This is the last great (or loud) voice of the 21 in Revelation. As noted before, the qualifying word denotes both importance and urgency.

The tabernacle of God. In the previous mention of the tabernacle of God the reference is to the tabernacle in heaven (13:6; 15:5); this one is with men and on the new earth. The tabernacle of God is also in marked contrast with the tabernacle in the wilderness (so frequently mentioned in the Pentateuch) where God dwelt between the cherubim.

He will dwell with them. The word *dwell* is the verbal form of *tabernacle;* hence, He will *tabernacle* with them. The same word is used in 7:15, but followed there with the phrase, "shall tabernacle over [Greek] them."

It is a matter of absorbing interest to observe that parallel conceptions occur in the opening chapters of the Bible with those near the close. The Lord God is said to be walking in the garden and to be present amongst the trees of the garden. Genesis 3:8. "He placed [Hebrew: caused to dwell or stationed] at the east of the garden . . . Cherubims" (Genesis 3:24). After Cain had sinned, he is said to "[have gone] out from the presence of the Lord," all of which implies that God had His dwelling place (as was later the case—Exodus 25:22; I Samuel 4:4; II Samuel 6:2c) between the cherubim.

And they shall be his people, and God himself shall be . . . their God. This is a beautiful, meaningful, and oft-repeated expression of the final, unbroken, and complete reconciliation and fellowship between God and man in Holy Writ: "I . . . will be your God, and ye shall be my people" (or its equivalent) occurs nine times; "ye shall be my people, and I will be your God" occurs twelve times—a total of 21 times.

It has been argued that peoples (i.e., plural) is the correct reading because the Greek has the plural form *laoi*. But there are twice as many authorities in favor of the singular. (See Alford *in loco*.)[60] Attention should also be called to the fact that after the human race had been divided into families and tongues and countries (Genesis 10:5, 20, 31), the race is referred to as one people (singular— Genesis 11:6). So the argument has no validity.

Charles in resolving the problem comments as follows: ". . . λαός [*laos*] . . . seems to be the original reading";[61] and later on, ". . . λαοί [*laoi*] is a corruption . . . and λαός [*laos*] . . . is a right emendation of the text." He then cites the supporting evidence.[62]

The expression, *God himself*, is significant because this implies that here is the final consummation of all things, that is, ". . . the end [*telos*], when he [Christ] shall have delivered up the kingdom to God, even the Father; when he [Christ] shall have put down all rule and all authority and power. For he must reign, till he hath put all enemies under his feet. . . . And when all things shall be subdued unto him, then shall the Son also himself be subject unto him that put all things under him, that God may be all in all" (I Corinthians 15:24, 25, 28).

It will be noticed that the divine title *God* alone is mentioned five times in verses 2-4, now that redemption is completed and the new heaven and new earth have appeared. (Cf. Genesis 1:1—2:3, the making of the former heaven and earth, where God is used a total of 34 times in 34 verses.)

Verse 4. *And God shall wipe away all tears from their eyes; and there shall be no more death, neither sorrow, nor crying, neither shall there be any more pain: for the former things are passed away.*

God shall wipe away all tears. The Greek uses the singular, *every teardrop.* Cf. Revelation 7:17. Barring God's great redemptive program, this is doubtless the most condescending, compassionate, and affecting act of God. That Almighty God should stoop to wipe away every teardrop from the eyes of those who "[come] out of [the] great tribulation," as do those in Revelation 7:17, will be especially meaningful to them; but since the endearing words are repeated here, it is plain that they apply to all who have suffered for righteousness' sake.

No more death. The Bible records in the third chapter of Genesis that death, sorrow, crying, and pain came into the world; here in the second last chapter the promise is that they shall be no more, because *the former things* [consequent upon sin entering into the world] *are passed away.*

Verse 5. *And he that sat upon the throne said, Behold, I make all things new. And he said unto me, Write: for these words are true and faithful.*

He that sat upon the throne. The Greek says, *the* [*one*] *sitting upon the throne.* God is now alone on the throne. This comports with the previous statement that Jesus at this time (if time it may be called) has surrendered "the kingdom to . . . the Father . . . that God may be all in all."

All things new. The new heaven, the new earth, the new Jerusalem, all are included in this summary statement, *Behold, I make all things new.* It is significant that the verb *make* is used here and not "create," suggesting that that which was marred by sin was removed and that which was basic and eternal was beautified and glorified.

Write. As on two former occasions (14:13 and 19:9) where the seer appears to have been overwhelmed with awe by the marvelous import of a new revelation and for the moment apparently forgot the divine mandate: "What thou seest, write in a book" (1:11), so here the order is renewed: *Write: for these words are true and faithful.*

Verse 6. *And he said unto me, It is done. I am Alpha and Omega, the beginning and the end. I will give unto him that is athirst of the fountain of the water of life freely.*

And he said . . . It is done. The throne sitter announces the end of the temporal human drama. *It is done* signifies the ultimate end of God's revelation to man. None of the words following, to the close of the book, pertain to things after what is here revealed. Similar declarations occur elsewhere. (Cf. Genesis 2:1 and 2:19, 21, 22; Ezekiel 39:8 and 39:9-20; Revelation 16:17 and 16:18-21 and Revelation 17, 18, where summary statements are made and then details are outlined.)

I am Alpha and Omega. In the words, *I am Alpha and Omega, the beginning and the end* (the word *end* is *telos,* denoting a point in time, not a period of time), is contained the divine attestation that revelation of things to come has reached its utmost limit.

Details then follow, including three gracious promises to the faithful (verses 6, 7), the doom of the wicked (verse 8), followed by a glowing description pertaining to the bride, the Lamb's wife, and the city foursquare (21:9–22:5), followed by the epilogue (22:6-21).

I will give . . . the water of life freely. This promise and the first in verse 4 above are given in reverse order in 7:17b. [How gracious is God's promise! After such scenes of judgment and outpouring of wrath, His grace transcends to offer freely, without charge, the water of life to all who thirst.–J. O. Y.]

Verse 7. *He that overcometh shall inherit all things; and I will be his God, and he shall be my son.*

Many are the gracious promises pertaining to what the faithful will inherit, e.g., the earth (Matthew 5:5); everlasting life (Matthew 19:29); the kingdom (Matthew 25:34; I Corinthians 6:9, 10); the promises (I Peter 3:9); but only here *all things.* [Cf. I Corinthians 3:21-23.–J. O. Y.]

The third promise, *I will be his God, and he shall be my son,* clearly shows that God is the speaker and that there is no longer a Mediator between God and man. [And that Edenic fellowship has been completely restored.–J. O. Y.]

Verse 8. *But the fearful, and unbelieving, and the abominable, and murderers, and whoremongers, and sorcerers, and idolaters, and all liars, shall have their part in the lake which burneth with fire and brimstone: which is the second death.* These are still the words of God but in marked contrast with His "exceeding great and precious promises" to the faithful. Verses 6, 7. This is the first of three lists of the wicked recorded in these last two chapters. The remaining two occur in 21:27 and 22:15. For convenience and comparison they may be classified as follows:

(1) 21:8—fearful, unbelieving, abominable, murderers, whoremongers, sorcerers, idolaters, and all liars—eight groups.

(2) 21:27—all who defile, all who work abomination, and all who make a lie—three groups.

(3) 22:15—dogs (sorcerers, whoremongers, murderers, idolaters) and all who love a lie and (all who make a lie)—seven groups less five repetitions leaves two additional.

All who in 21:27 and 22:15 is the correct rendering. The original Greek word *pan* is "collective abstract neuter" and should be rendered in the masculine gender. John 3:6; 6:37, 39; 17:2; I John 5:4.

Those groups in parentheses in (3) are repetitions of (1) and (2).

There are in all $8 + 3 + 7 = 18$ classes listed in the three groups. Subtracting the 5 duplicates leaves 13 different classes.

Liars are foremost among the doomed: *all liars, all who act a lie, all who love a lie,* and *all who make a lie.* One may love a lie if another says it for him. One may make or act a lie without saying a word. Sorcerers, whoremongers, murderers, idolaters are mentioned twice. The first group have their part in the lake of fire; the second (21:27) will not enter the city foursquare; the third (22:15) are without (the city) foursquare.

Note that God alone is mentioned in connection with the new things of 21:1-6a. After the divine attention (21:6b) it is He who bestows three gracious promises (21:6c, 7) and closes with announcement of the doom upon the wicked (verse 8).

One must not err, however, by concluding that the Son has now retreated into a position of inferiority. God exists eternally as the triune God. Revelation has now arrived at the end of the day of redemption (21:1-6a) and one should not think of God as apart from the Son and the Spirit but as the triune God eternally existing in three persons, Father, Son, and Holy Ghost [though each had His singular role in the plan of the redemption of man.—J. O. Y.].

8. THE HOLY JERUSALEM (21:9—22:5)

Verse 9. *And there came unto me one of the seven angels which had the seven vials full of the seven last plagues, and talked with me, saying, Come hither, I will shew thee the bride, the Lamb's wife.*

One of the seven angels. The same angel in 17:1 bade John, "Come hither; I will shew unto thee the judgment of the great whore." In the two chapters, 17 and 18, are given the condition and the end of the great adulterous scarlet-clothed woman. What a contrast with the glorious description of the Lamb's wife, the holy Jerusalem, as revealed in Revelation 21:9 ff.!

The Lamb's wife. In 19:7 the church is called His (the Lamb's) wife in prospect. Here the church is recognized as the Lamb's wife because the marriage (19:9) is past.

Verse 10. *And he carried me away in the spirit to a great and high mountain, and shewed me that great city, the holy Jerusalem, descending out of heaven from God.*

Carried me away in the spirit. This phrase has its counterpart in 17:3, the purpose being to secure a suitable vantage point. Here it is a great and high mountain; on the former occasion, a wilderness. (Note not *the* wilderness; the Greek significantly omits the article.)

That great city. The great city here mentioned is in marked contrast with the great city of 17:5, 18; 18:10, 16, 19. That the city is great is evident from its dimensions given below (verse 16) and is implied in the many dwelling places (Greek) in the Father's house. John 14:2. The great city of chapter 17 is man's; this one, God's.

The holy Jerusalem. Apparently it is designated *holy Jerusalem* to contrast it with the unholy condition into which the earthly Jerusalem had fallen. (In 11:8 it is called, "the great city, which spiritually is called Sodom . . . where also our Lord was crucified.")

Descending out of heaven from God. The city descends out of heaven from God into which His bride enters when He comes to receive her unto Himself. Apparently after the thousand years are finished and the heaven and earth pass away, the city necessarily passes away also; however, only again to come from God out of heaven after the appearing of the new heaven and new earth. Verse 2 above.

Verse 11. *Having the glory of God: and her light was like unto a stone most precious, even like a jasper stone, clear as crystal.*

The glory of God. The order is holiness, glory, light, shine. Note: holy—glory (Isaiah 6:3; 63:15), glory—light (Revelation 18:1; 21:11), glory—shine (Ezekiel 43:2; Luke 2:9), light—shine (Matthew 5:16; John 1:5). Glory is really glow-ry, and it should be pronounced as a long o.

Her light. The Greek, *phoster*, means *luminary*, i.e., *light holder* or *light bearer*. The light really is the radiance of God's holiness. See below—verse 23, "the glory of God did lighten it, and the Lamb is the light thereof." The same Greek word (*phoster*) is applied to believers who, "in the midst of a crooked and perverse nation, . . . shine as lights [luminaries] in the world" (Philippians 2:15).

Verse 12. *And had a wall great and high, and had twelve gates, and at the gates twelve angels, and names written thereon, which are the names of the twelve tribes of the children of Israel.*

A wall great and high. In addition to *having the glory of God* (verse 11) two more descriptions are given concerning the city—a wall great and high, and twelve gates—the former denoting solidarity and security; the latter, a means of entrance or exit.

Twelve gates . . . twelve angels . . . twelve tribes. The number twelve is conspicuous in the "holy Jerusalem" section (21:9–22:5); viz., twelve gates (21:12a, 21); twelve angels (21:12b); twelve tribes (21:12c); twelve foundations (21:14a); twelve apostles (21:14b); twelve pearls (21:21); twelve manner of fruits (22:2) —a sevenfold description. The number appears also in multiple form in the mention of twelve thousand furlongs (21:16) and of 144 cubits (21:17).

The presence of an angel at each gate suggests that they serve as ministering spirits sent forth (Hebrews 1:14) as occasion requires their service from the "Jerusalem which is above" to the now "beloved" city on earth. 20:9.

The names of the twelve tribes of Israel inscribed on the gates of the heavenly city and the order of their placement on each side are probably the same as given in the description by Ezekiel (48:31-34) of the earthly city Jerusalem.

Verse 13. *On the east three gates; on the north three gates; on the south three gates; and on the west three gates.*

Assuming therefore that Ezekiel's arrangement of the twelve tribes was according to the pattern showed him of the heavenly city, that is, of the holy Jerusalem, the order of placement beginning as John does may be arranged as follows:

On the east, north to south: Joseph, Benjamin, Dan

On the north, west to east: Reuben, Judah, Levi

On the south, east to west: Simeon, Issachar, Zebulun

On the west, south to north: Gad, Asher, Naphtali

Ezekiel sees (43:2, 4) that the glory of the God of Israel will come into the house of the Lord by way of the gate "whoso prospect is toward the east." The marvel is that Dan, by whom idolatry was first introduced into Israel (Judges 18:30, 31) and whose name is probably omitted for this cause from the number who are sealed (Revelation 7:4-8), is now stationed on the "glory side" of the city along with Joseph and Benjamin, the sons of the beloved wife of Jacob. This is a remarkable example of the passage which declares, "where sin abounded, grace did much more abound" (Romans 5:20). One would think grace could go no further.

Since the holy Jerusalem is declared to be the bride, the Lamb's wife, that is, the church, the question naturally arises, Why then are the names of the twelve tribes inscribed in its gates? The answer seems to be that these names continually bear witness to the fact that "salvation is of the Jews" (John 4:22). Not only were the apostles Jews but Christ Himself was of Jewish ancestry.

The mention of Israel only in connection with the gates appears to indicate that even then the two, Israel and the church, were not constituted as a co-ordinated unit of believers because, were this the case, we should have twenty-four gates instead of twelve.

Verse 14. *And the wall of the city had twelve foundations, and in them the names of the twelve apostles of the Lamb.*

Twelve foundations. What has been said concerning twelve gates (and not twenty-four) applies likewise to the number of foundations; that is, if Jews and Gentiles were a united group, one would expect here not merely twelve but twenty-four foundations.

Again Old Testament saints are not included in the foundations because they are never spoken of as apostles, much less as apostles of the Lamb. The Lamb relationship of Christ is altogether a New Testament concept. Only the New Testament believers, that is, the church, are known as the body of Christ. "The twelve tribes" is an unheard-of terminology in reference to the church. Thus here is a decisive testimony that Israel and the church remain two distinct groups even through the millennial period. This comports with the passages in Matthew 19:28 and Luke 22:29, 30 that in the kingdom age the apostles (as representing the church) will sit upon twelve thrones judging the twelve tribes of Israel.

Further in this connection it is a matter of interest to observe that Abraham in his day "looked for a city which hath foundations, whose builder and maker is God" (Hebrews 11:10). It is significant, however, that the twelve foundations are declared to be not the twelve tribes of Israel, but the twelve apostles of the Lamb. Compare Ephesians 2:20 where the church is spoken of as being "built upon the foundation of the apostles and prophets" (evidently New Testament prophets are in mind as shown in Ephesians 3:5). It should be remembered also that due to the disobedience of Israel in her failure to keep the Sinaitic covenant (Exodus 19:5, 6), she forfeited her place of pre-eminence offered her on condition of obedience and for this reason the kingdom of God was taken from her (Matthew 21:43) and given to the church (Luke 22:29). And all this accords with the other testimony in the Revelation context that Israel and the church will remain distinct groups during the millennial age. (For the discussion on foundations see verse 19.)

Verse 15. *And he that talked with me had a golden reed to measure the city, and the gates thereof, and the wall thereof.*

He that talked with me. The one talking with John was identified in verse 9 above as "one of the seven angels which had the seven vials full of the seven last plagues."

A golden reed. The ordinary Jewish measuring reed was about ten feet long. This one moreover was of gold, corresponding with the city of pure gold, which the angel is about to measure. No details are given about his measuring the gates, but the measuring of the city is mentioned in verse 16; of the wall in verse 17.

Verse 16. *And the city lieth foursquare, and the length is as large as the breadth: and he measured the city with the reed, twelve thousand furlongs. The length and the breadth and the height of it are equal.*

Foursquare. Like the holy of holies both in the tabernacle and in the temple of Solomon, where God had His dwelling place, the holy Jerusalem is a perfect cube. It is a house of many dwelling places. John 14:2.

Twelve thousand furlongs. Twelve thousand furlongs are equal to fifteen hundred miles, and since the length and the breadth and the height are equal, each dimension is fifteen hundred miles. In view of the fact that warning has been given not to take from the words of this prophecy (22:19), it is well not to limit the Builder and Maker of the city foursquare by reducing it to dimensions far inferior to those indicated by divine inspiration, e.g., by making the superstructure pyramidal in form. This certainly would be contrary to what appears to be its prototype, the holy of holies both of the tabernacle in the wilderness and of the temple of Solomon, which were a cube in their dimensions.

Taking the measurements as being those of a perfect cube, then, its base of fifteen hundred miles long and wide would be as large as the combined area of all the states in the union of the United States of America except nine, viz., Montana, Utah, Nevada, Arizona, Washington, Oregon, California, Alaska, and Hawaii. Or, measuring from the Pacific coast, it would cover the United States as far east as the Mississippi River, with a line extending north through Chicago and continuing on the west coast of Lake Michigan up to the Canadian border.

With an infinitude of space at the Father's disposal, there certainly will be no need for the place He is preparing for the saved of all the ages to be in any way narrow and cramped for each individual. Its occupants will consist not only of all those who have believed in God and in Christ (John 14:1) but also of all infants who have died throughout all time, though they will not remain infants because all will be perfect. Thus space will be needed.

There is a probable allusion to the height of the city foursquare by the prophet Amos when he testifies concerning the divine Builder and Maker, ". . . he that buildeth his stories in the heaven . . ." (Amos 9:6). For the uses of the Hebrew word for stories (*ma-a-lah*) compare the following passages: Exodus 20:26; I Kings 10:19, 20; II Chronicles 9:18, 19; Ezekiel 40:22, 26, 31, 37, 49—where it is translated *steps;* II Kings 9:13; Nehemiah 3:15; 12:37; Ezekiel 40:6—these are in the feminine gender and translated *stairs;* Joshua 15:7; 18:17; Judges 1:36; II Kings 9:27; Nehemiah 12:37; Jeremiah 48:5; Ezekiel 40:31, 34, 37—the masculine form translated *the going up;* Numbers 34:4; II Samuel 15:30—*ascent;* Nehemiah 9:4—*stairs.*

An examination of the passages will show that they pertain chiefly to ascents in or entrances into a sacred edifice or enclosure.

Verse 17. *And he measured the wall thereof, an hundred and forty and four cubits, according to the measure of a man, that is, of the angel.*

And he measured. The one measuring is still the angel of verse 9 above.

An hundred and forty and four cubits. Reckoning the cubit as eighteen inches, the wall would be two hundred and sixteen feet high, the measure of the angel being the same in this instance as that used by man.

Verse 18. *And the building of the wall of it was of jasper: and the city was pure gold, like unto clear glass.*

The building. [The Greek word, *endomesis,* means *structure*—J. O. Y.] and thus signifies the materials of which the wall is composed. Thus the wall was of jasper; the city of pure gold, both clear as crystal. Verse 11.

Verses 19, 20. *And the foundations of the wall of the city were garnished with all manner of precious stones. The first foundation was jasper; the second, sapphire; the third, a chalcedony; the fourth, an emerald; the fifth, sardonyx; the sixth, sardius; the seventh, chrysolyte; the eighth, beryl; the ninth, a topaz; the tenth, a chrysoprasus; the eleventh, a jacinth; the twelfth, an amethyst.*

The foundations . . . were garnished. The thought is that each foundation constituted a mighty gem in the glorious structure of the wall of the city four-square.

The foundations of the wall were garnished with every precious stone (Greek). Such being the case, one may be certain that they include all the colors of the rainbow, the seven prismatic colors.

The word *garnished* (Greek: *kosmeo*), translated "adorned" in verse 2, is one of the words occurring both in the description of the new Jerusalem (verses 1-6a) and in that of the holy Jerusalem (21:9—22:5).

King, in his *Precious Stones and Gems,* quoted in *The Bible Commentary,*[63] gives the description of the respective gems as follows: jasper, dark green; sapphire, blue; chalcedony, greenish sort of emerald; emerald, bright green; sardonyx, red and white; sardius, bright red; chrysolyte, golden yellow; beryl, bluish green; topaz, yellowish green; chrysoprasus, apple-green; jacinth, blue; amethyst, violet and purple.

Beginning from the last color mentioned, a marked similarity can be seen with seven prismatic colors—violet, indigo, blue, green, yellow, orange, red. The first jasper is identical with the color of the wall above and there can be no doubt but that the colors blend harmoniously with the wall of jasper, the first mentioned, and consequently with that of the wall.

Mr. King apparently errs when he describes the first as dark green, since the jasper of the wall is described as being *clear as crystal.*

It is now clear why the foundations do not consist of twelve sections (three on a side) round about the city, each separately extending up to the wall of jasper, but of twelve courses or layers, each of which (i.e., one above the other) encircles the entire city.

According to the sectional view, each separate color would extend up to the wall of jasper. It will be seen at once that the matching of color with jasper in the wall above would be lost. Again, viewing the city from any direction, with foundations thus varying, would destroy the symmetry and beauty so apparent where colors blend as they do when round rises upon round to the wall above.

Attention should be called to the fact that a somewhat similar arrangement of precious stones is mentioned in connection with the breastplate of the high priest (Exodus 28:17-20) and with the king of Tyre (Ezekiel 28:13).

Verse 21. *And the twelve gates were twelve pearls: every several gate was of one pearl: and the street of the city was pure gold, as it were transparent glass.*

With this verse ends the description of the city foursquare. It may be summarized as follows: the city is of pure gold, clear as crystal (verses 11, 18); the wall of jasper (verse 18); the foundations of precious stones, portraying all the colors of the rainbow (verse 19); the gates of pearl (verse 21); and the street material of *pure gold, as it were transparent glass.*

The street. The word for *street, plateia,* appears to be used in a generic sense and hence pertains to the entire outlay of broadways amidst the many mansions.

Verse 22. *And I saw no temple therein: for the Lord God Almighty and the Lamb are the temple of it.*

No temple. There is no temple in the city because it is not a Jewish city. On the other hand, since the "holy Jerusalem" is the bride, the Lamb's wife, there is no temple in it because a temple never was a holy place of or for the church.

The word *temple* in this place is *naos.* This was God's dwelling place—the holy of holies of the Jews which they themselves dared not to enter. In contrast, every believer in the church is said to be the temple, the *naos,* of God (I Corinthians 3:16, 17—twice; II Corinthians 6:16—twice), or of the Holy Ghost (I Corinthians 6:19). What is most marvelous is that all the building grows or increases into a holy temple (Greek) in the Lord. Ephesians 2:21. Note the sacred relationship between the believer and the Holy Trinity—God, the Holy Ghost, and the Lord.

These facts plainly show that the "holy Jerusalem" (verse 10) is for the time being not the new Jerusalem (verse 2) of the eternal state, for in those ages of ages the Trinity will have achieved its redemptive purposes and, as in the beginning, the tabernacle of God will be with men, "and God himself shall be with them, and be their God," and the promise to every overcomer is, "I will be his God, and he shall be my son" (verse 7).

Verse 23. *And the city had no need of the sun, neither of the moon, to shine in it: for the glory of God did lighten it, and the Lamb is the light thereof.*

No . . . sun . . . moon, to shine in it. It does not say there will be no more a sun or moon in the sky. Since the city is lighted up by the glory of God and by the Lamb, it *had no need of the sun* [compare verse 7 above], *neither of the moon.*

Undoubtedly the prophet Isaiah was speaking of this day when he declared, "Moreover the light of the moon shall be as the light of the sun, and the light of the sun shall be sevenfold, as the light of seven days, in the day that the Lord bindeth up the breach of his people, and healeth the stroke of their wound" (Isaiah 30:26; cf. 60:19).

For the reasons stated in the preceding verse, it may be assumed that whenever God and the Lamb are mentioned together, the reference is not to the eternal state when Jesus will have delivered the kingdom to the Father, that God may be all in all. I Corinthians 15:24, 28.

Verse 24. *And the nations of them which are saved shall walk in the light of it: and the kings of the earth do bring their glory and honour into it.*

Nations. The fact that there are nations mentioned as being upon the earth plainly shows that this is not the new heaven and new earth but conditions on the earth during the millennial age. [It should be noted, however, that these are *the nations of them which are saved.*—J. O. Y.]

Kings of the earth. It is not meant that the kings of the earth actually enter the city foursquare. The latter part of the verse consequently should read, bring their glory *to* or *unto* it.

Verse 25. *And the gates of it shall not be shut at all by day: for there shall be no night there.*

Compare in this connection Isaiah 60:11, "Therefore thy gates shall be open continually; they shall not be shut day nor night."

Some speak of the latter part of the verse as being redundant. As opposed to such a view let it be noted that if this were omitted, then it would appear as though they were shut by day. The thought seems to be that there is no occasion for someone to forget opening them in the morning and thus they would be found closed the day following. However, the passage from Isaiah gives us the correct thought—"they shall not be shut day nor night."

Verse 26. *And they shall bring the glory and honour of the nations into it.*

The passage is a repetition of the last clause of verse 24 apparently for emphasis in view of the declaration of verse 25.

Verse 27. *And there shall in no wise enter into it any thing that defileth, neither whatsoever worketh abomination, or maketh a lie: but they which are written in the Lamb's book of life.*

There shall in no wise enter into it any thing that defileth. This statement implies, as Dr. Charles asserts, that "the unclean and the abominable and the liars are still on the earth, but, though the gates are open day and night, they cannot enter." It proves, too, that the new heaven and new earth have not yet displaced the "heaven and earth now existing because it is unthinkable and contrary to divine revelation that evil personages, whether men or demons, should so much as receive mention in relation to that glorious and eternal day."

The Lamb's book of life. The book of life has been mentioned before. (See 13:8.) It is here called the Lamb's book of life because only those who have been redeemed by the blood of the Lamb will have their names written in this book.

Worketh abomination . . . a lie. The point should be noted that one may be guilty of working or acting a lie without saying a single word. Such a one is as much guilty of lying as is one who lies by word of mouth.

The word *make* is in italics so that *lie* is the object of *work.* The Greek word is in the present tense. The meaning is therefore that the one who practices lying, that is, one who habitually lies, is barred from entrance into the city.

[It should be further noted that the Greek syntax of verse 27 would permit a translation as follows: *And in no case should enter into it anything profane, either the one doing abomination or falsehood.* The stress is laid upon the absolute purity of all who have access to the city and that the possibility for entrance lies in having one's name *inscribed in the book of the life of the Lamb.*—J. O. Y.]

[It is with deep regret that the editor had no opportunity to counsel with the author, for on occasion it seemed completely clear that if counsel had been possible, some apparent inconsistencies might have been resolved.

It would seem worthy to consider *the holy . . . [city], descending out of heaven from God,* as the eternal abode of *the Lamb's wife,* as Alford, Seiss, Swete,

Scroggie, Newell, Kuyper, Ottman, Sauer, and others do; thus the seer saw the bride in her new and eternal home. The Old Testament prophets predict that during the reign of Christ Jerusalem of Palestine will be His headquarters. Micah 4:1, 2; Isaiah 2:1-5; Zechariah 14:16 ff. The number of similarities between the *new* Jerusalem and the *holy* Jerusalem would seem to emphasize identity.

The distinction between Israel and the church on the basis of the twelve gates and twelve foundations does not seem to agree with the comments on 21:16, where emphasis is laid on "the saved of all the ages." Would it not seem that the *unity* of believers is stressed by the very fact that the gates were named after Israel and the foundations after the apostles? Cf. Romans 3:29, 30. Certainly nothing in the eternal state will mar the glory of the place or the happiness of the saints.

It needs to be pointed out also that other commentators before Smith had taken his view, e.g., Charles, Scott, and Talbot.

With regard to the "temple" of 21:22 it may be stated that in the eternal state God dwells, tabernacles, with His people. Consequently they have no need for a *naos*. Faith has become sight. Symbols have become realities. Face to face relation does away with any mediatorial vehicles. There is direct communication.

Furthermore, 21:24 does in no way suggest the entrance of any defilement in the words, "the nations of . . . [the saved] shall walk in the light of it." The Greek word *ethnos* has a wider meaning than Gentiles or unsaved. It may mean a *multitude* or *company*. So then, *the company of the saved shall walk in the light of it*. The word *nations* here is qualified by the adjectival phrase, *of the saved*. The glory and honor of the kings shall become a part of the *holy city*. Note: It will not necessarily be the kings; rather, their glory and honor. So also the honor and glory of the nations, not the ungodly nations themselves.

Finally the seer in 22:2, describing the tree of life, speaks of the *twelve manner of fruits . . . and the leaves of the tree . . . for the healing of the nations*. There are preventive medicines as well as corrective. Is it not conceivable that these leaves serve as a continual therapeutic for the *nations*, multitudes, who inhabit the eternal city so that the tragedy of Eden will never be repeated? Certainly the last clause of 22:5 would indicate the eternal state: *and they shall reign for ever and ever*.

It is with deep humility that these comments are made, for the editor has profound admiration for the labors of the late Dr. Smith. He found in him a trusted friend and counselor and one whose integrity urged him on in Bible exposition. Yet withal, to be honest with himself, it was necessary to point out what he felt Dr. Smith himself might have corrected had he had opportunity before the Lord called him home.—J. O. Y.]

22:1. *And he shewed me a pure river of water of life, clear as crystal, proceeding out of the throne of God and of the Lamb.*

Pure river of water of life. The *pure river of water of life* which proceeds out of the throne of God, like the light of the city foursquare, is clear as crystal and has its source at the throne of God.

This is a plain allusion to the river mentioned both by Ezekiel and by Zechariah. The former prophet, however, speaks of a river as proceeding from under the threshold of the house eastward (Ezekiel 47:1), and as issuing out of the sanctuary (Ezekiel 47:12) and again as going from Jerusalem, half of them toward the former sea (east sea) and half of them toward the hinder sea (western, that is, the Mediterranean, whereas the river mentioned by John proceeds *out of the throne of God and of the Lamb*). Evidently the river of the earthly tabernacle was the counterpart of the one issuing from the heavenly as was the case with the earthly tabernacle and temple. Seven times the earthly tabernacle is said to be after the pattern of the heavenly shown to Moses in the mount. This close and vital relationship between the earthly and heavenly is all the more apparent during the millennial age as will be observed below.

The throne of God and of the Lamb. The distinctions in the Godhead continue, indicating that here as in chapter 21:9 ff. the Scriptures speak of the kingdom age, not the eternal state.

Verse 2. And in the midst of the street of it, and on either side of the river, was there the tree of life, which bare twelve manner of fruits, and yielded her fruit every month: and the leaves of the tree were for the healing of the nations.

In the midst of the street of it. The river is spoken of as being in the midst of the street. [The pronoun *it* is a personal pronoun used in the genitive case, denoting possession, and is in the feminine gender. What one needs to discover is the antecedent of the pronoun. *River* is a masculine noun as is also *throne*. It would indicate then that the antecedent of *it* must be *city*, a feminine noun used in 21:23. Thus, whatever city is described in 21:23 is further described in 22:2.–J. O. Y.]

Tree of life. The expression, *tree of life*, is evidently used in a generic sense, denoting kind or variety. The sense is, this kind of tree was on either side of the river along the street. For the phrase, *either side of the river*, is *enteuthen . . . enteuthen*. They are used by the same author in his Gospel (John 19:18) and translated "on either side one," lit., one "on this side" and one "on that." Ezekiel, who describes the earthly counterpart, declares, "at the bank of the river were very many trees on the one side and on the other" (Ezekiel 47:7).

Here again evidence points to the fact that this is not the eternal or perfect state because according to Ezekiel the leaves of the trees are "for medicine" and the Revelation passage declares they are *for the healing of the nations.* When that which is perfect is come, medicine for and healing of nations will be forever a thing of the past. (Note editor's comment at the end of chapter 21.)

Verses 3-5. And there shall be no more curse: but the throne of God and of the Lamb shall be in it; and his servants shall serve him: and they shall see his face; and his name shall be in their foreheads. And there shall be no night there; and they need no candle, neither light of the sun; for the Lord God giveth them light: and they shall reign for ever and ever.

No more curse. After Adam's sin, God said, "cursed is the ground for thy sake" (Genesis 3:17). In the kingdom age there shall be no more curse. Again, "thorns . . . and thistles shall it bring forth" (Genesis 3:18)—these continue until this day. However, the prophet Isaiah, speaking of the future age, declares, "Instead of the thorn shall come up the fir tree, and instead of the brier shall come up the myrtle" (Isaiah 55:13).

Throne of God and of the Lamb. Since mention is made of *the throne of God and of the Lamb,* it is evident that Christ has not yet delivered up the kingdom to the Father, neither does the mutual occupancy of the throne by God and the Lamb comport with the statement, "then shall the Son also himself be subject unto him that put all things under him, that God may be all in all" (I Corinthians 15:28).

Servants shall serve him. Neither will they serve Him in the eternal age. Each glorified soul then will be to Him a servant without any mediation of the Lamb who will Himself be subject to God. Revelation 21:7.

They shall see his face. This comports with another testimony of the apostle when he declared, ". . . we know that, when he shall appear, we shall be like him; for we shall see him as he is" (I John 3:2). The "beatific vision" is the happy portion of the believer at Christ's second coming.

The name in the forehead serves as a mark of identification as in 7:3 and 14:1.

No night . . . no candle, neither light of the sun . . . they shall reign for ever and ever. See similar statements in Revelation 21:23, 25. The eternal reign is spoken of as yet to be realized in contrast with the limited reign of a thousand years. 20:6.

[There are several facts the author must have overlooked. If the future tense of *they shall reign* has reference to some future time, then *there shall be no night* (verse 5a), *they shall see his face* (verse 4a), *his servants shall serve him* (verse 3c), *the throne of God and of the Lamb shall be in it* (verse 3b), *there shall be no more curse* (verse 3a) are also referring to a future time. The Greek future tense may refer to a time future to the writer, and thus John saw these experiences as future. Another point to note is the linear action of the future tense. In this respect it is like the present, with the exception of the time element. Therefore the idea seems to be the ongoing experience of no night, etc., forever and ever.

. The service rendered in the phrase, *his servants shall serve him,* is a religious exercise in the meaning of the Greek *latreuo.* Worship of God is a religious service which His servants will render "throughout" all the aeons of eternity.

It would, therefore, seem proper, as well as possible, to consider this the picture of the eternal state when God will have made "all things new"; the two thrones, the reigning of the redeemed, having reference to the relation of God, Christ, and man in the final state, each in his own right and sharing with the other.

The carefulness which characterized Smith's work as a student of the Word makes it obvious that these points of grammar must have been unintentional oversights.—J. O. Y.]

With slight variations the words of A. T. Pierson[64] on verses 3 to 5 are adapted:

And there shall be no more curse—perfect restoration.

But the throne of God and of the Lamb shall be in it—perfect administration.

His servants shall serve him—perfect subordination.

And they shall see his face—perfect transformation.

And his name shall be in their foreheads—perfect identification.

And there shall be no night there; and they need no candle, neither light of the sun; for the Lord God giveth them light—perfect illumination.

And they shall reign for ever and ever—perfect exultation.
[This would appear to be the *perfect state!*—J. O. Y.]

FOOTNOTES, PART IV

1. Thayer, p. 581, col. a.
2. Tregelles, p. 10.
3. Victorinus, "Commentary on the Apocalypse of the Blessed John," from the fifth chapter, 8, 9, *The Ante-Nicene Fathers*, Vol. VII, p. 350, col. b.
4. See Appendix, p. 334, "Kings and Priests."
5. Swete, p. 85.
6. Alford, Vol. IV, pp. 612, 613.
7. Souter.
8. Swete, p. 86, col. a.
9. Thayer, p. 669, col. a.
10. Charles, Vol. I, p. 167.
11. Swete, p. 88, col. b.
12. Charles, Vol. I, pp. 169, 170.
13. Thayer, p. 609, col. a.
14. Charles, Vol. I, pp. 172-74.
15. Stuart, Vol. II, p. 161.
16. Thayer, p. 589, col. b.
17. Swete, p. 92, col. a.
18. Robertson, *Grammar*, p. 846.
19. Charles, Vol. I, p. 179.
20. *The Apocrypha*, "Ecclesiasticus," p. 108, col. b.
21. See Appendix, p. 339, "The Glorified Groups of the Tribulation."
22. Charles, Vol. I, pp. 226, 227.
23. *Ibid.*, p. 227 (note).
24. Some have found fault with the view that John's ascent to heaven is typical of the rapture of the church because those holding the view believe Christ will again return to earth. But note, so does John. Others hold that he is not a true type because *he* does not stay in heaven. The point to be borne in mind in evaluating either objection is that a type does not necessarily have to agree with the antitype. If it did, there could be no true human type of Christ. A type requires likeness merely in one point. Jonah, for example, was a type of Christ only in that he was three days and three nights in the belly of the whale as was Jesus three days and three nights in the heart of the earth. John, however, is a type of the rapture of the church not only because he is caught up after his vision of the churches was complete and before the tribulation began, but also in the attending circumstances—the open door, the sound of the trumpet, and the call,
25. See Appendix, p. 340, "The Holy City."
26. See Appendix, p. 342, "The Two Witnesses."
27. Seiss, Vol. II, pp. 232, 233.
28. Hippolytus, *The Ante-Nicene Fathers*, Vol. V. p. 248, col. b.
29. *Ibid.*, Frag. 39, p. 184.
30. Tertullian, "De Anima" Chap. L, *op. cit.*, Vol. III, p. 227, col. b, p. 228, col. a.
31. Victorinus, "Commentary on the Apocalypse," *op. cit.*, Vol. VII, p. 354, col. a.
32. *Ibid.*, p. 356, col. a.
33. The numbers employed in this chapter present some point of comparison. The 42 months (3½ years) and the 1,260 days cover the entire tribulation period—the latter referring to the first

half, during which time the two witnesses prophesy, and the former to the latter half, when the beast (Antichrist) will have authority *over all kindreds, and tongues, and nations.*

The three and one-half years of the ministry of the two witnesses are equal in duration to the ministry of Christ. So also, the three and one-half days between death and resurrection may be said to be approximately the period between the death and resurrection of Christ. Note also that in each case ascension to heaven was in a cloud.

The 7,000 whom the Lord had reserved for Himself in connection with days of Elijah in the olden time (I Kings 19:18) may be contrasted with the 7,000 slain by the earthquake.

34. See Appendix, p. 346, "The Man Child."

35. See Appendix, p. 349, "The Fall of Satan."

36. It is interesting to observe that of these, seven refer to Christian activity: four to prayer —Luke 2:37; I Thess. 3:10; I Tim. 5:5; II Tim. 1:3; one to warning—Acts 20:31; two to labor and travail—I Thess. 2:9; II Thess. 3:8. All but one of these seven relate to Paul's ministry— another key to the amazing achievements of the great apostle.

37. See Appendix, p. 351, "The Preservation of Israel."

38. Jamieson, Fausset, Brown, Vol. II, p. 881.

39. Robertson, *Word Pictures*, Vol. VI, p. 402.

40. Swete, p. 168, col. a.

41. Godet, p. 385.

42. Irenaeus, *The Ante-Nicene Fathers*, Vol. I, p. 557, col. b.

43. Thayer, p. 665.

44. Alford, Vol. IV, p. 686, col. b.

45. Nestle, p. 333.

46. Swete, pp. 184, 185.

47. Charles, Vol. II, pp. 14, 15.

48. Delitzsch, *Biblical Commentary on the Prophecies of Isaiah*, Vol. I, pp. 74, 75.

49. *Ibid.*

50. *The International Standard Bible Encyclopaedia*, Vol. II, Art. "Euphrates," p. 1039, col. a.

51. Simpich, p. 731.

52. Delitzsch, *op. cit.*, pp. 304-6.

53. Moorehead, Vol. II, p. 124.

54. Tertullian, "Apology," Chap. XXXIV, *The Ante-Nicene Fathers*, Vol. III. p. 43, col. b.

55. Swete, p. 241.

56. A number of plausible reasons might be given why the marriage supper of the Lamb did not take place immediately after the rapture of the church just previous to the tribulation period. However, since nothing is revealed on this interesting question, we content ourselves with the assertion that as long as the great whore continues to make her false claims that she is the true bride of Christ—which claims have been persisted in through the centuries and which will be accentuated to the highest pitch during the tribulation period—that long the marriage supper can not consistently take place. It is only after the false claimant is removed and silenced forever that the way is open for the true bride to make herself ready for the marriage.

57. By way of information to those interested in the use of the phrase "anger of wrath" or "wrath of the Lord" in the Old Testament:

"Anger (*haron*) of wrath (*aph*)" occurs 33 times; "anger (*hari*) of wrath (*aph*)," 6 times— a total of 39 times; "wrath (*aph*) of anger (*haron*)," never.

"Wrath (*aph*) of the Lord" occurs 4 times; "wrath (*aph*) of God," 3 times; "anger (*haron*) of the Lord (or God)," never.

In the New Testament "wrath (*orge*) of God" occurs in John 3:36; Rom. 1:18; Eph. 5:6; Col. 3:6, and 19:15 (the present verse)—5 times. "Wrath of the Lamb" occurs once—in Rev. 6:16. However, in five more passages either the pronoun "his" or "my" occurs with wrath: Heb. 3:11; 4:3; Rev. 6:17; 14:10 (indignation—wrath); 16:19, thus making a total of eleven.

"Anger (*thumos*) of God" occurs only in the New Testament and this in passages in which the wrath of God pours itself out in anger upon the obdurate and impenitent beast worshipers, viz., 14:10, 19; 15:1, 7; 16:1.

58. Simons, p. 241.
59. Kuyper, p. 292.
60. Alford, Vol. IV, p. 737.
61. Charles, Vol. II, p. 207.
62. *Ibid.*, pp. 377, 378.
63. *The Bible Commentary*, Vol. IV, p. 832.
64. Pierson, p. 102.

5

PART V
THE EPILOGUE
22:6-21

THE EPILOGUE

The Epilogue ((6-21)

Verse 6. *And he said unto me, These sayings are faithful and true: and the Lord God of the holy prophets sent his angel to shew unto his servants the things which must shortly be done.*

The language is practically identical with the first verse of the Prologue which reads: "A Revelation of Jesus Christ, which God gave unto him, to show unto his servants the things which must shortly come to pass; and he sent and signified it by his angel unto his servant John" (Smith's own translation). The correspondence is seen in five parallel statements.

1. The Revelation of Jesus Christ—These sayings [Greek: words] . . . faithful and true.

2. Which God gave—the Lord God of the holy prophets.

3. Sent and signified by his angel—sent his angel.

4. To show unto his servants—to show unto his servants.

5. Things which must shortly come to pass—things which must shortly be done [Greek: *come to pass*].

(For further parallels see comments on the Prologue.)

Verse 7. *Behold, I come quickly: blessed is he that keepeth the sayings of the prophecy of this book.*

Behold, I come quickly. This corresponds with the note of imminency in the latter part of Revelation 1:3, "for the time is at hand."

Blessed is he that keepeth the sayings of the prophecy of this book. This corresponds with the first portion of Revelation 1:3, "Blessed is he that readeth, and they that hear the words of this prophecy, and keep those things which are written therein." This is the sixth beatitude of Revelation.

Verses 8, 9. *And I John saw these things, and heard them. And when I had heard and seen, I fell down to worship before the feet of the angel which shewed me these things. Then saith he unto me, See thou do it not: for I am thy fellowservant, and of thy brethren the prophets, and of them which keep the sayings of this book: worship God.*

I . . . saw. Here is the last of the visions of John mentioned in this book. Also the last of his auditions. [It is a statement covering the entire book.—J. O. Y.]

I fell down to worship. John was so overawed by the total vision shown him by the informing angel that he again errs (as in 19:10) by falling down to worship him. Here, as on the former occasion, the angel disdains the proffered honor and retorts with the reprimand: *See [thou do it] not: for I am thy fellowservant, and of*

301

thy brethren the prophets, and of them which keep the sayings [Greek: *words*] *of this book: worship God.*

Verses 10, 11. *And he saith unto me, Seal not the sayings of the prophecy of this book: for the time is at hand. He that is unjust, let him be unjust still: and he which is filthy, let him be filthy still: and he that is righteous, let him be righteous still: and he that is holy, let him be holy still.*

[*Seal not the sayings.* Of the two ways of expressing prohibitions, the angel chooses the one meaning "don't begin." By this is suggested that at no time was the Revelation to have been a sealed book from the time of its recording. It is hoped that certainly in the last of the twentieth century Bible-believing scholars will pay closer attention to the *prophecy of this book,* for indeed, *the time is near.* Let none fall into the trap of which Peter warned in II Peter 3:3, 4, "Knowing this first, that there shall come in the last days scoffers, walking after their own lusts, and saying, Where is the promise of his coming? for since the fathers fell asleep, all things continue as they were from the beginning of the creation."—J. O .Y.]

He that is unjust. . . . These solemn words declare the fixity of destiny. There will be no purgatorial fires to cleanse from pollution of sin nor reincarnations in which to slough off moral degeneracy. "As the tree falls, so shall it lie." There will not only be fixity but also extremes of destiny—"one to darkness and the frozen tide, the other to the crystal sea."

Most momentous and solemn are these words of warning loudly proclaiming the heavenly mandate, "now is the accepted time . . . now is the day of salvation."

Verse 12. *And, behold, I come quickly; and my reward is with me, to give every man according as his work shall be.*

I come quickly. This is the second occurrence of the note of imminence in the concluding section. (Cf. verse 7.) It occurs again in verse 20 in climactic and intensified form: "Surely I come quickly." The solemn words of warning remind one of similar words by Jesus during His earthly career. Matthew 24:44.

Every man according as his work shall be. Whereas salvation is of grace, rewards are according to works. These or kindred words are repeated many times in the Scriptures. For the convenience of the reader, and in order that their wide distribution and manifold relationship may be distinctly recognized both in the Old and New Testaments, herewith are cited the Scripture references: in the Old Testament, II Samuel 3:39; 22:21, 25; I Kings 8:32, 39; II Chronicles 6:23, 30; 15:7; Ezra 9:13; Psalm 18:20, 24; 28:4; 62:12; Proverbs 24:12, 29; Job 34:11; Jeremiah 32:19; 50:29; 51:6; Isaiah 59:18; Jeremiah 17:10; 25:14; Lamentations 3:64; Ezekiel 7:3, 4, 8, 9, 27; 18:30; 24:14; 36:19; 39:24; Hosea 4:9; 12:2; Zechariah 1:6; in the New Testament, Matthew 16:27; Luke 23:41; I Corinthians 3:8; II Corinthians 5:10; 11:15; II Timothy 4:14; Hebrews 2:2; Revelation 2:23; 11:18; 18:6; 20:12, 13; 22:12. The reading of these passages cannot fail to solemnize the heart of the believer.

Verse 13. *I am Alpha and Omega, the beginning and the end, the first and the last.*

The compound titles are mutually explanatory and similar in concept. The following is a summary of their occurrences:

I am: Alpha and Omega	the beginning and the end(ing)—1:8	
I am: Alpha and Omega		the first and the last—1:11
I am:		the first and the last—1:17
		the first and the last—2:8
I am: Alpha and Omega	the beginning and the end—21:6	
I am: Alpha and Omega	the beginning and the end	the first and the last—22:13
4	3	4

Verse 14. *Blessed are they that do his commandments, that they may have right to the tree of life, and may enter in through the gates into the city.*

Blessed. This is the seventh and last beatitude. Because of their importance and for the benefit of the reader they are arranged here in consecutive order.

"Blessed is he that readeth, and they that hear the words of this prophecy, and keep those things which are written therein" (1:3).

"Blessed are the dead which die in the Lord from henceforth" (14:13).

"Blessed is he that watcheth, and keepeth his garments . . ." (16:15).

"Blessed are they which are called unto the marriage supper of the Lamb . . ." (19:9).

"Blessed and holy is he that hath part in the first resurrection . . ." (20:6).

"Blessed is he that keepeth the sayings of the prophecy of this book" (22:7).

"Blessed are they that do his commandments . . ." (22:14).

That do his commandments. The Revised Version here reads, "Blessed are they that wash their robes," instead of *do his commandments.* That the former is in error appears from the following considerations:

The external testimony: two eminent church fathers[1] quote the passage with the same thought as that in the Authorized Version.

The internal testimony: white robes are worn only by the second glorified group, designated "robe-wearers"—this garment being mentioned only in 6:11 and 7:9, 13, 14. Since these come "out of [the] great tribulation" (7:14) they are "tribulation saints." The saints referred to in Revelation 22:14 have the right to *enter in through the gates into the city.* The city referred to is the city foursquare, the dwelling place of the bride, the Lamb's wife. 21:9.

The church is not arrayed in *white robes* (*stolai*) but in *white raiment* (*himation*). Revelation 3:5; 4:4. Consequently the group referred to in this last of the beatitudes must be the church, not tribulation saints, which proves conclusively that the reading "wash their robes" is erroneous.

Verse 15. *For without are dogs, and sorcerers, and whoremongers, and murderers, and idolaters, and whosoever loveth and maketh a lie.*

Dogs. The term *dogs* alludes to persons of a low and base character. Isaiah 56:10; Philippians 3:2. For exposition see Revelation 21:8.

Verse 16. *I Jesus have sent mine angel to testify unto you these things in the churches. I am the root and the offspring of David, and the bright and morning star.*

I Jesus. The Revelation of Jesus Christ which God gave Him to show unto His servants and which was signified by His angel unto the church is now finished. *I Jesus* is found nowhere else in the Scriptures, emphasizing its importance.

The root and the offspring of David. . . . The second sentence alludes to Isaiah 11:1, "And there shall come forth a rod [that is, a *twig* or *shoot*] out of the stem [stock] of Jesse, and a Branch shall grow out of his roots." The reference is plainly to Jesus who according to the flesh was the offspring of David, the son of Jesse.

The bright and morning star. To the overcomer at Thyatira the promise is, "I will give him the morning star" (2:28). The term harks back to Numbers 24:17, ". . . there shall come a Star out of Jacob. . . ." In a physical sense it is applied to several of the planets but more particularly to Venus because of its superior luster. As morning stars they shine brightest if and when the moon has set in the west, that is, when neither sun nor moon is in the sky, at which time only, the slogan, "It is always darkest just before sunrise," is true to fact. [Perhaps the parallel is to be seen in the relation of the morning star to the daydawn. When Christ appears, the *new* day is about to dawn. In this manner He is the *morning star.*—J. O. Y.]

Verse 17. *And the Spirit and the bride say, Come. And let him that heareth say, Come. And let him that is athirst come. And whosoever will, let him take the water of life freely.*

The *Spirit*, as He who "[reproves] the world of sin, and of righteousness, and of judgment," says, Come.

The *bride*, that is, the church, through the ministry of the Word, says, Come. The individual believer who has responded to the call to service by letting his light shine before men that they may see his works is thereby extending the same invitation. And finally all who are desirous of responding to the gracious influence of this united testimony may take of the water of life freely. [The divine invitation is echoed by redeemed mankind.—J. O. Y.]

Verse 18. *For I testify unto every man that heareth the words of the prophecy of this book, If any man shall add unto these things, God shall add unto him the plagues that are written in this book.*

Our Lord declared, "The scripture cannot be broken." To the same effect is the testimony of Moses, "Ye shall not add unto the word . . . neither shall ye diminish ought from it" (Deuteronomy 4:2; 12:32); and of Solomon, though wisest of all men, "Add thou not unto his words, lest he reprove thee, and thou be found a liar" (Proverbs 30:6); and of John, the beloved disciple, in the words above.

One may add to the words of this prophecy by supplementing the words which man's wisdom teaches and thus be "left" when the Lord comes to receive His faithful ones to Himself, to suffer the plagues written in this book as described under the seals, trumpets, and vials.

Verse 19. *And if any man shall take away from the words of the book of this prophecy, God shall take away his part out of the book of life, and out of the holy city, and from the things which are written in this book.*

The implication is that there will be such as had their names written in the book of life and who were on the way which leads to the holy city and yet because of their extreme folly of taking away from the words of this prophecy they will be cast into the lake of fire, for such is the doom of those whose names are not found written in the book of life. 20:15.

Verse 20. *He which testifieth these things saith, Surely I come quickly. Amen. Even so, come, Lord Jesus.*

I come quickly. For the third time Jesus announces His soon return. Verses 7, 12. The Greek word *tachu* means *suddenly*. (Cf. Matthew 24:27.) The change of the living is said to be "in a moment, in the twinkling of an eye" (I Corinthians 15:52). It is said that the Bell Telephone Company has perfected a device for measuring the duration of the twinkle of an eye which they assert to be 11/100 of a second. Since the change occurs at the last trump (I Corinthians 15:52), evidently the dead will be raised at the first trump. I Thessalonians 4:16.

Even so, come. The Greek word *nai* is rendered *yea* 24 times; *even so* five times. *Come, Lord Jesus,* is the response of the seer eagerly awaiting the coming of the Lord. His longing has been deepened by all he has seen and heard. Each true believer after reading "the prophecy of this book" will join with John, *Even so, come, Lord Jesus.*

Verse 21. *The grace of our Lord Jesus Christ be with you all.*

It is interesting to observe that John uses the very words of Paul in his closing salutation. Paul uses it in all of his epistles in accordance with his declaration in II Thessalonians 3:17.

[How fitting a benediction to close the last revelation, and the revelation of the last events of the human drama! Endurance unto the end will be possible only by the supply of *the grace of our Lord Jesus.* This grace every believer draws upon and hopes for in *the Revelation of Jesus Christ.*—J. O. Y.]

FOOTNOTES, PART V

1. Cyprian, "The Treatises of Cyprian," Treatise XII, Second Book, Testimonies 22, *The Ante-Nicene Fathers,* Vol. V, p. 525, col. a; and Tertullian, "On Modesty," Chap. XIX, *op. cit.,* Vol. IV, p. 96, col. a.

APPENDICES

APPENDICES

1. WORD STUDY OF REVELATION 6—19

A few notes are appended after each word. In chapters 6—19 are the following words:

(1) God (60 times). Almighty God (6 times). As such He is the one from whom the judgments proceed.

(2) Lamb (17 times). As such He introduces and executes the judgments. It is the divine reaction upon men who reject His atoning work.

(3) Heaven (41 times). Judgments descend from heaven; martyrs ascend to heaven.

(4) Throne of God (15 times). The tribunal of justice from which all judgments proceed.

(5) Temple (15 times). The judgments issue from the holy place, showing that they are vindicative rather than vindictive.

(6) Voice (44 times). Heaven is silent now; then His voice will be heard "even to the ends of the earth" (Jeremiah 25:31).

(7) Angel (good) (51 times). Their ministry now is silent and unseen. Then they sound trumpets heralding oncoming judgments; fly through midheaven proclaiming messages of hope, warning, and doom; and pour out vials of wrath upon the impenitent and obdurate.

(8) Trumpets (14 times). These are judgment trumpets and have no connection with the trumpet that raises the dead in Christ for the meeting in the air.

(9) Great and loud (71 times). The great God does great things in this period. And it is a significant fact that chapter 16, where the vials are poured out, is the "great chapter" of the Bible, the word occurring there eleven times in its 21 verses.

(10) Earth (68 times). The theater upon which the judgments are enacted, in consequence of which many "learn righteousness."

(11) Anger (Greek: *thumos*) (10 times). Three to vials. Only eight times in the rest of the New Testament.

(12) Wrath (Greek: *orge*) (16 times). The Greek word always relates to His coming revelation from heaven.

(13) Judgment (13 times). Both nominal and verbal forms included here.

(14) Plague (13 times). As the plagues come upon the earth, heavenly voices exclaim, "True and righteous are thy judgments." Note that "judgment" and "plague" occur each 13 times.

(15) Beast (34 times; 36 in all). The personal Antichrist is revealed at this time.

(16) Dragon (12 times). Occurs only in Revelation. A personal name for the devil.

(17) Thunder (9 times). Remarkable that the son of thunder (Mark 3:17) alone uses this word once in the Gospel, nine times here.

(18) Lightning (3 times). Always with thunder in this book. The signal of approaching storm.

(19) Blasphemy (noun and verb) (8 times). Spoken of Antichrist and his followers.

(20) Fornication (noun and verb) (14 times). One of the outstanding sins of the apostate church and beast worshipers.

(21) War (noun and verb) (13 times). The Bible makes no distinction between a war and a battle (such as has been done by certain expositors). There is but one Greek word for both.

(22) Kill (21 times). Two Greek words are translated "kill" and "slay."

(23) Blood (17 times). Used chiefly in reference to martyrdom and judgments upon men.

(24) Fire (17 times). Mostly in connection with plagues and the final doom.

(25) Burn (7 times). Used in reference to plagues and the final doom.

(26) Brimstone (5 times). Used as above.

(27) Bottomless pit (5 times). The abode of evil spirits.

Important words either omitted entirely or used sparingly are as follows:

(1) Father. The word occurs only once and that of the glorified martyrs "having his Father's name written in their foreheads" (14:1). This is the more remarkable when we observe that in his other writings John uses this title 142 times.

(2) Holy Spirit. It occurs only once and that in his testimony regarding those who have died in the Lord. 14:13. Contrast this with the emphasis John gives elsewhere regarding the Spirit of truth and the Comforter and with the sevenfold occurrence in chapters 2 and 3. (Fifteen times in his Gospel; and four times Comforter.)

(3) Church. Not a single mention of the church occurs in these chapters. The word occurs 19 times in the first three chapters (apparently covering the church age) and once in the closing chapter (22:16) to show that the testimony of the book is to be given in the churches. The implication is that the church is no longer on earth in the time covered by these chapters.

(4) Grace. This is one of seven English mighty monosyllables of the New Testament. There is no mention of this word in these chapters. The word occurs 225 times in the Bible—69 times in the Old Testament and 156 times in the New. God is still the God of grace, but since men refused grace and the church period according to divine prediction ends in apostasy from within, He now uses another instrument to bring men to Himself, namely, the rod of affliction. The prophetic word is clear as to the result of this method of divine providence: (a) As to Israel: "In their affliction [Hebrews: tribulation] they will seek me early" (Hosea 5:15). (b) As to the nations: "When thy judgments are in the earth, the inhabitants of the world learn righteousness" (Isaiah 26:9).

(5) Mercy. There is no mention of this word. It occurs 288 times in the Old Testament; 70 times in its various forms in the New. Neither does compassion, a word closely akin to mercy, occur here. So terrible is the suffering that men tormented for five months seek death, but it flees from them; again it is said, "they gnawed their tongues for pain," yet not a syllable of mercy breaks from the courts of heaven. No divine testimony that in wrath He remembers mercy, nor that the Lord is "moved with compassion."

(6) Truth. No mention is made of this mighty monosyllable although it occurs 45 times in the other writings of John. It reminds one of the poetic lines, "Truth, crushed to earth shall rise again—the eternal years of God are hers," for it accords with the sure word of prophecy: "Truth shall spring out of the earth; and righteousness shall look down from heaven" (Psalm 85:11). Only in the kingdom age which follows the tribulation will earth be thus in tune with heaven.

(7) Faith. The word occurs twice—each time in connection with the threat

of martyrdom. The acid test of saints then on earth will be the maintenance of faith and patience in the face of death. 13:10; 14:12.

(8) Hope. No mention. The star of hope fails to rise in the world's dark night.

(9) Love. "The greatest of these" is mentioned only once and that in a negative form in reference to martyrs now glorified who "loved not their lives unto the death" (12:11). There is no mention of God's love for man, of any one loving God, or of love of man for man.

(10) Joy. The only occasion of rejoicing on earth mentioned in this section is after the beast has killed the two witnesses. 11:10. "The earth dwellers rejoice and make merry" when they see their dead bodies lie on the streets of Jerusalem.

(11) Peace. Once only is the word mentioned—in the beginning of the tribulation period (6:4) the red horse rider "[takes] peace from the earth."

(12) Believe. No mention. Contrast this with the frequent use by the apostle in his Gospel—100 times, and in his first epistle—10 times.

(13) Repent. Only used negatively here—four times it is said they "repented not." There is no exhortation to repent; contrast this with the eight occurrences in chapters 2 and 3.

(14) Pray. The various words for prayer occur 343 times elsewhere in the New Testament. In Revelation not once is either of these words applied to anyone on earth. Once in heaven glorified elders have golden vials, which are the prayers of saints (5:8), and martyrs cry with a loud voice for vengeance upon their enemies (6:10). This is plainly no prayer by members of the body of Christ. Once on earth the kings of the earth and the great men "say" to the mountains and rocks, "Fall on us, and hide us from the face of him that sitteth on the throne, and from the wrath of the Lamb" (6:15, 16).

(15) Comfort. Another of the words strangely absent here at a time when it would appear comfort is so sorely needed.

(16) Good. Two words are translated "good," occurring each 102 times in the New Testament. Neither occurs in these chapters. Seven times in Genesis 1 God pronounced His creation good. It would be a sad picture indeed if, as some would suggest, history on earth would end in a dark period such as here described.

2. COMPARISONS OF I THESSALONIANS 4:13-18; REVELATION 19:11-21; JOHN 14:1-3

In making the comparisons we limit the list of words to nouns, adjectives, and verbal forms. As a result we find:

There are 36 such words in I Thessalonians 4:13-18.

There are 94 such words in Revelation 19:11-21.

Only nine words are common to both and this only once each. These words are: others (= remnant in 19:21), have, God, say, word, Lord, alive, voice, heaven. (This is the order of their first occurrence as they appear in I Thessalonians 4, Greek.)

For convenience we present the words common to both passages in the order of their occurrence:

I Thessalonians 4:13-18		Revelation 19:11-21	
others	verse 13	heaven	verse 11
have	" 13	have	" 12
God	" 14	word	" 13
say	" 15	God	" 13
word	" 15	Lord	" 16
Lord	" 15	voice	" 17
alive	" 15	say	" 17
voice	" 16	alive	" 20
heaven	" 16	others	" 21

It will be noticed that the order of these words is very irregular. "Have" which comes second in each list is the only one common in the order of succession. Observe, too, that in each case the first word of one column comes last in the other. Again not in a single instance do two words occurring together in one column, up or down, appear together in the other. Hence it is impossible that one sentence or even one phrase can be alike in the two lists. And finally not one word in the two lists is used in the same relation or connection. Notice also the remarkable contrast in the two passages between the chief actors, God and the Lord. In the latter passage we read of the "winepress of the wine of the anger of the wrath of Almighty God" (Greek). Again, "the supper of the great God" consists of "the flesh of kings, and the flesh of captains, and the flesh of mighty men, and the flesh of horses, and of them that sit on them, and the flesh of all men, both free and bond, both small and great." No less terrible appears "the wrath of the Lamb." "His eyes . . . [are] as a flame of fire," "out of his mouth goeth a sharp sword, that with it he should smite the nations," and He it is that "treadeth the winepress of the fierceness and wrath of Almighty God."

How different the former passage where "the trump of God" and the "shout" of the Lord wake the sleepers in Jesus and welcome them, together with those that live and remain, to the meeting in the air. Note also the following contrasts:

I Thessalonians 4	Revelation 19
Only the righteous are in the picture.	Only the wicked.
The dead are raised to life.	The living go to death.
The saints ascend to meet the Lord.	Saints descend with the Lord.
They are the guests at the marriage supper of the Lamb.	They constitute the supper of the great God.
They are forever with the Lord.	The leaders (and later all their followers) are cast into the lake of fire.

It would be difficult if not impossible to find elsewhere any two important passages of Scripture that are so diverse in the words employed and so opposite in their implications. It appears as though this dissimilarity was providentially directed in order to safeguard the reader from error and confusion as to their interpretation.

We believe the comparison of the words of these two passages will convince all open-minded readers that they describe different events. We have dealt entirely with the words of Scripture. True interpretation must be based upon the written word, not on reason, speculation, or imagination. Our further study will, we trust, make it equally clear that the former event will take place previous to the tribulation period, the latter immediately after that period. It is the writer's firm conviction that unless the reader believes and accepts this distinction he will never arrive at a correct interpretation and understanding of our book.

Let us now compare two passages of Scripture which, by the words employed, clearly show that they refer to the same event. They are John 14:1-3 and (one of those just considered) I Thessalonians 4:13-18.

John 14:1-3		I Thessalonians 4:13-18	
trouble	verse 1	sorrow	verse 13
believe	" 1	believe	" 14
God, me	" 1	Jesus, God	" 14
told you	" 2	say to you	" 15
come again	" 3	coming of the Lord	" 15
receive you	" 3	caught up	" 17
to myself	" 3	to meet the Lord	" 17
be where I am	" 3	ever be with the Lord	" 17

Observe:
The words or phrases are almost an exact parallel.

They follow one another in both passages in exactly the same order. Only the righteous are dealt with in each case. There is not a single irregularity in the progression of words from first to last. Either column takes the believer from the troubles of earth to the glories of heaven.

It is but consistent to interpret each passage as dealing with the same event —the rapture of the church. And we may add that the words of John 14:1-3 have no more similarity to the passage in Revelation 19:11-21 than have the words of I Thessalonians 4:13-18.

3. Visions of the Apocalypse Listed

Believing a list of the things John saw will help to arouse interest in the study of the book, we herewith submit them in the order of their occurrence:

(1) I saw seven golden candlesticks and the Son of man. 1:12, 13.
(2) I saw, and, behold, a door opened in heaven. 4:1.
(3) I saw upon the thrones four and twenty elders sitting. 4:4.
(4) I saw in the right hand of Him that sat on the throne a book. 5:1.
(5) I saw a strong angel proclaiming with a loud voice. 5:2.
(6) I saw, and, behold, in the midst of the throne a Lamb standing. 5:6.
(7) I saw many angels round about the throne. 5:11.
(8) I saw the Lamb opened one of the seals. 6:1.
(9) I saw, and behold a white horse. 6:2.
(10) I saw, and behold a red horse. 6:4.
(11) I saw, and behold a black horse. 6:5.
(12) I saw, and behold a pale horse. 6:8.
(13) I saw under the altar the souls of them that were slain. 6:9.
(14) I beheld and, lo, there was a great earthquake. 6:12.
(15) I saw four angels standing on the four corners of the earth. 7:1.
(16) I saw another angel ascending from the east. 7:2.
(17) I saw, and, behold, a great multitude. 7:9.
(18) I saw the seven angels which stood before God. 8:2.
(19) I saw an angel flying through the midst of heaven. 8:13.
(20) I saw a star fallen (Greek) from heaven unto the earth. 9:1.
(21) I saw the horses in the vision. 9:17.
(22) I saw another mighty angel come down from heaven. 10:1.
(23) I saw a beast rise up out of the sea. 13:1.
(24) I saw one of his heads as it were wounded to death. 13:3.
(25) I saw another beast coming up out of the earth. 13:11.
(26) I saw, and, behold, the (Greek) Lamb standing. 14:1.
(27) I saw another angel flying through midheaven. 14:6.
(28) I saw, and behold a white cloud and the Son of man. 14:14.
(29) I saw another sign in heaven. 15:1.
(30) I saw as it were a sea of glass. 15:2.
(31) I saw, and, behold, the temple in heaven. 15:5.
(32) I saw three unclean spirits like frogs. 16:13.
(33) I saw a woman sit upon a scarlet colored beast. 17:3.
(34) I saw another angel come down from heaven. 18:1.
(35) I saw heaven opened, and behold a white horse. 19:11.
(36) I saw an angel standing in the sun. 19:17.
(37) I saw the beast and the kings of the earth. 19:19.
(38) I saw an angel come down from heaven. 20:1.
(39) I saw thrones and they sat upon them. 20:4.
(40) I saw a great white throne. 20:11.
(41) I saw the dead, small and great, stand before God. 20:12.

(42) I saw a new heaven and a new earth. 21:1.
(43) I John saw the holy city, new Jerusalem. 21:2.
(44) I John saw these things and heard them. 22:8. [Referring directly to the immediately preceding context as well as the entire book.—J. O. Y.] The phrase occurs again in 21:22, but it is negative and tells us what he did *not* see, while in 22:8 we have a summary statement, "I John saw these things," similar to that in the opening of the book, "All things that he [John] saw," 1:2, thus emphasizing the fact that the entire book consists of a series of visions.

4. THE SEVEN SPIRITS WHICH ARE BEFORE THE THRONE

There are two prevalent interpretations of these words: (1) They signify the Holy Spirit in His sevenfold perfections or energies. (2) They signify seven special angels, presumably seven archangels. In order to determine which of these views is correct we will consider each under three heads: the language employed, the context, the parallel passages.

1. *The Holy Spirit in His Sevenfold Perfections or Energies.*

a. The language employed. *The seven spirits.* The Greek, like the English, has the definite article, "the" seven spirits, which points to a previous mention. Those who hold the view that the reference is to the Holy Spirit base their conclusion on Isaiah 11:2. The language occurs elsewhere in 3:1; 4:5; 5:6. Neither of these passages (as we shall see) lends support to the view that the Holy Spirit is intended. The number seven is nowhere else employed to denote the perfection of either member of the Godhead; that is to say, we read nowhere of seven Gods, seven Christs, or seven Holy Spirits.

b. The context. The phrase occurs in conjunction with God the Father (which is and which was and which is to come) and with Jesus Christ. Since the combined mention of the Trinity occurs in various places in the Scripture, one might forthwith conclude that the "seven spirits" allude to the third person of the Godhead. The phrase occurs in the salutation addressed to the seven churches which are in Asia. This at once raises the question: Is it consistent or in accordance with Biblical usage that the Holy Spirit be included in a salutation addressed to a church? Without exception, the answer is in the negative, for in a total of sixteen occurrences of greetings previously mentioned by the apostles they invariably come alone from God the Father and from Jesus Christ. In no place is the Spirit included in a greeting to a church or to an individual. Why should this be the case? Undoubtedly, because the Spirit abides in the church as well as in the individual forever (Greek: *unto the age,* John 14:16). The argument that the association of the "seven spirits" with the Father and with Jesus Christ proves that the Holy Spirit is intended falls to the ground on two counts: (1) greetings never come "from" (which implies absenteeism) the Holy Spirit, and (2) the view involves a self-contradiction—greetings cannot consistently come from one that dwells within.

The "seven spirits" are said to be "before [lit., in the presence of] the throne." The expression denotes variously: inferiority, reconciliation, subservience, favor, or worship, on the part of those being or standing before the throne; and this, whether the position is before God or earthly kings. As to the former, it is said of: Abraham (Genesis 18:22; 19:27), Elijah (I Kings 17:1; 18:15), Elisha (II Kings 3:14; 5:16), Moses and Samuel (Jeremiah 15:1), Gabriel (Luke 1:19), elders (Revelation 4:10; 11:16), the great multitude (Revelation 7:9; 11:15), seven angels (Revelation 8:2), the dead, small and great (Revelation 20:12). As to the latter, it is used of: Joseph before Pharaoh (Genesis 41:46), Solomon's servants before Solomon (I Kings 10:8), Daniel and his three friends before Nebuchadnezzar (Daniel 1:5, 19; 2:2), and Esther before King Ahasuerus (Esther 5:1, 2).

The term is never used of one member of the Godhead standing before another with the singular exception that Jesus deigns to appear before the Father to confess those that confess Him. Matthew 10:32; Luke 12:8.

However, it is altogether contrary to the present office and ministry of the Holy Spirit to conceive of Him as being or standing before the throne. Consequently the seven spirits who occupy this position cannot signify the Holy Spirit.

c. Parallel passages. Isaiah 11:2 is the only important passage in favor of the view that by the "seven spirits" the Holy Spirit is meant. It reads as follows: "The spirit of wisdom and understanding, the spirit of counsel and might, the spirit of knowledge and of the fear of the Lord." The passage is not descriptive of the sevenfold perfections of the Holy Spirit. This is evident from the fact that some of the highest of His attributes are here omitted. He is elsewhere called: the Holy Spirit, the Spirit of truth, the Spirit of life, the Spirit of glory, and the eternal Spirit. In the opening clause we have a general and all-inclusive statement: "the spirit of the Lord shall rest upon him." That the title denotes the Holy Spirit in all His fullness is shown by the fact that He is thus distinctly designated 25 times in the Old Testament and four times in the New. Luke 4:18; Acts 5:9; 8:39; II Corinthians 3:18. This title consequently cannot be taken to represent one of seven perfections of the Spirit. The three couplets following this title consequently must be taken not as parallel with, but subordinate to, the initial clause. Hence, we are to understand that the Spirit of the Lord is: a Spirit of wisdom and understanding, a Spirit of counsel and might, a Spirit of knowledge and of the fear of the Lord. We note that Spirit is mentioned but once with each couplet, suggesting that we are to think of three relationships and not of six. It would indeed be contrary to all Biblical usage to express holy relationships in a sixfold manner, since the number six invariably denotes evil. Neither can we bring in the number seven here, for both the structure of the passage and the inner sense forbid such a conception. Upon examination we find an interrelationship apparent in the three couplets: (a) Wisdom and understanding are close synonyms. (b) Counsel and might—skill to advise and ability to execute. We see the association of these terms among the names of the Messiah: "Wonderful, Counsellor, The mighty God" (Isaiah 9:6). (c) Knowledge and fear of the Lord are likewise closely related in that "the fear of the Lord is the beginning of knowledge" (Proverbs 1:7).

The three couplets were probably intended to express various relationships of Christ: Wisdom and understanding are attributes inherent in, and related to, Him. It is significant that these two were manifest in Him in a remarkable manner in His childhood (Luke 2:40, 47), and before the Holy Spirit descended upon Him (Luke 3:22). Counsel and might express His relation to men and they were continually in evidence during His earthly ministry. Knowledge and fear of the Lord express more particularly Christ's relation to the Father as noted in His constant sense of God's presence, and His perennial piety.

From what has been said we observe that the spiritual qualities enumerated in the three subordinate phrases are not those of the Holy Spirit. In the phrase, "the spirit of wisdom," the thought is not that the Spirit is wise. By the phrase, "the spirit of fear," it is not meant that the Spirit is reverent. Wisdom, understanding, counsel, might, knowledge, and reverence are attributes or characteristics of Christ in consequence of the Holy Spirit resting upon Him. Similarly, the terms "spirit of judgment" and "the spirit of burning" (Isaiah 4:4) denote, not personal qualities, but effects of the Spirit. And so in relation to men it is said, "to one is given by the Spirit the word of wisdom; to another the word of knowledge" (I Corinthians 12:8). He is designated as the Spirit of wisdom and knowledge because He bestows these on men. Fear of the Lord is not an attribute of, but a bestowal by, the Holy Spirit; and since this is the case, the other qualities mentioned must have a similar significance. If it be considered strange that the Spirit bestowed these gifts upon Christ, we need but call attention to passages pertaining to events introductory to His earthly ministry:

At His baptism, the Holy Spirit descended upon Him (Luke 3:22),

Jesus, being full of the Spirit, returned from the Jordan (Luke 4:1),

Jesus returned in the power of the Spirit into Galilee (Luke 4:14),

His own testimony, "The Spirit of the Lord [the very title here employed] is upon me, because he hath anointed me to preach the gospel" (Luke 4:18).

Apparently the special qualities here enumerated were such bestowments or endowments by the Spirit upon the Messiah "in the days of his flesh" as will eminently qualify Him to fulfill His ministry on earth, to judge and rule the righteous, and to punish the wicked.

That Isaiah 11 is emphatically Messianic is seen in the sevenfold repetition of personal pronouns (his, him) applied to Him. Verses 2-5. That it is strongly eschatological is seen not only in His capacity of judge and ruler (verses 3, 4), but also in the blessing that is to come upon all creation including the outcasts of Israel and the dispersed of Judah from the four corners of the earth (verses 6-12).

2. *The Seven Spirits Identical with Seven Angels.*

We come now to consider the view that by the "seven spirits" we are to understand seven angels. As in the former discussion, we will test the view in a threefold manner: by the language employed, by the context, and by parallel passages.

a. The language employed. Since the Greek has the definite article, comments will be deferred on this point until the section "parallel passages." The identical phrase occurs elsewhere, in Revelation, three times. 3:1; 4:5; 5:6. Mention is also made of three groups of seven angels: (a) the angels of the seven churches (1:20), (b) seven angels appear having the seven trumpets (8:2, 6), (c) seven angels appear having the seven last plagues (15:1).

There is no question concerning likeness in nature of spirits and angels. In each case the idea is incorporeal creatures. Is there any Scriptural proof, however, that they are identical? If so, why should two different names be applied to them? The answer, which is plain and simple, is found in Hebrews 1:14. The apostle, speaking of angels, raises a question which can only be answered in the affirmative: "Are they [the angels] not all ministering spirits, sent forth to minister for them who shall be heirs of salvation?" Angels, therefore, are ministering spirits sent forth. The Greek word for angel signifies messenger, and a messenger means one sent with a message. Hence, as being before the throne they are spirits, but when entrusted or sent forth with a message they are angels. (We shall see below that the seven spirits are "sent forth into all the earth.")

b. The context. As noted before, the phrase occurs in conjunction with God the Father and Jesus Christ. The question naturally presents itself: Is it consistent or in accordance with Biblical usage that spirits (angels) be thus conjoined with members of the Godhead? The answer is in the affirmative as the following passages indicate: "The Son of man . . . shall come in his own glory, and in his Father's, and of the holy angels" (Luke 9:26),

"I charge thee before God, and the Lord Jesus Christ, and the elect angels" (I Timothy 5:21),

"The Lord himself shall descend from heaven with a shout, with the voice of the archangel, and with the trump of God" (I Thessalonians 4:16),

"I [Jesus] will confess his name before my Father, and before his angels" (Revelation 3:5).

It will also be noted that in the execution of judgments during the tribulation period (Revelation 6–18) the Lamb (Christ) opens the seals (chapter 6), angels sound the trumpets (chapters 8, 9), and the vials are expressly called the "vials of the wrath of God" (chapters 15, 16).

The words of Dr. Charles, probably one of the greatest apocalyptic scholars, have a peculiar fitness at this place.

"For whatever be the dignity possessed by the seven spirits, they were after all merely created beings in the opinion of the seer, and could not therefore be put by him on a level with God and Jesus Christ or represented as fitting objects for man's worship."[1] It will be noticed that Dr. Charles does not conceive of them as signifying the Holy Spirit, for He is not a created being.

Another question will naturally present itself: Why should the seven spirits be joined in the greeting to the seven churches?

The seven spirits are probably identical with the angels of the seven churches. If this be so, they would, with much propriety, send their salutation. The Apostle Peter writes that angels desire to look into the things pertaining to salvation, including the sufferings of Christ and the glories that shall follow. I Peter 1:10, 11. To them (angels), Paul declares, is made known by the church, the manifold wisdom of God. Ephesians 3:10. While the messages in chapters 2 and 3 are intended for the churches, they nevertheless are addressed to the angels. Because of the keen interest on the part of the angels in things pertaining to the churches, greetings from them appear to be in good order.

c. Parallel passages. The seven spirits which are before the throne may be identical with the seven archangels. Only two of these, Gabriel and Michael, are mentioned in the Scriptures, the former in Daniel 8:16; 9:21; Luke 1:19, 26, the latter in Daniel 10:13, 21; 12:1; Jude 9; Revelation 12:7. However, the implication is that there were more archangels than these, for Michael is spoken of as "one of the chief princes" (Daniel 10:13).

In Ezekiel 9 reference is made to six men and among them a man "clothed with linen." These were summoned to bring judgment upon the wicked men of Jerusalem. The man "clothed with linen" is undoubtedly the same as the one thus described in Daniel 10:5; 12:6, who appears to be Michael. In Daniel 12:1 the pronoun is plural and refers to God's people, Israel. The word "men" should present no difficulty, for both Gabriel and Michael are thus designated.

Isaiah makes mention of "the angel of his presence" (63:9) who delivers God's people when afflicted. The reference is doubtless to Michael, who, as we have seen, stands for the children of Daniel's people (Israel) in the time of affliction. Daniel 12:1. (Compare Genesis 24:7; Exodus 23:20; 32:34.)

The extra-Biblical Jewish writers make frequent mention of the archangels. In Tobit 12:15 we have the words, "I am Raphael, one of the seven angels, which stand and enter before the glory of the Lord." There is some variation among their names, the most approved probably being those cited in the Book of Enoch, chapter 20, namely, Uriel, Raphael, Raguel, Michael, Sariel, Gabriel, and Remeil.

We have already stated that only two archangels are named in the Scriptures (Gabriel and Michael). It is interesting to observe that Gabriel is prominently mentioned in connection with the birth of John the Baptist, the earliest historical incident pertaining to the New Testament era. Luke 1:19-25. He is also the angel who announced the conception and birth of Jesus as well as the name. Luke 1:26-35; Matthew 1:20, 21. Since Gabriel is apparently the informing or revealing angel (Daniel 8:16; 9:21, 22; 10:14, 21), he is probably the "archangel" mentioned in I Thessalonians 4:16. He gives us his own testimony: "I am Gabriel, that stand in the presence of God" (Luke 1:19), or we may translate "that stands before God." Thus Gabriel as well as Michael (see above, Isaiah 63:9) may be spoken of as an angel "of his presence."

While Gabriel is the great revealer, Michael is the great contender. He not only contended with the devil about the body of Moses (Jude 9) but it is he who in the future will cast Satan upon the earth. Revelation 12:7-9. He is expressly designated "archangel" in the former passage.

Some have erroneously held that certain passages where Michael and Gabriel are intended have reference to God. They fail to recognize that the word Michael signifies "who is like God" and Gabriel means "strength of God." It should be remembered that angels commissioned to represent God may manifest potentialities and resemblances ascribed to Him. Angels may even give orders to members of the Godhead, e.g., one of their number commands the Son of man to reap. Revelation 14:15. They may resemble God as when a mighty angel appears whose face was as the sun and his feet as pillars of fire. 10:1; cf. Daniel 10:5, 6.

There are other passages in the Revelation in which the words "the seven spirits" occur.

(1) These things saith he that hath the seven spirits of God, and the seven stars (3:1). In the phrase, "the seven stars," we have an allusion to 1:16. He (the Son of man) had in His hand seven stars. The allusion is also to 2:1: "He that holdeth the seven stars in his right hand." However, in 1:20 the symbol is explained: "The seven stars are the angels of the seven churches." By substituting the plain literal sense for the figurative, chapter 3:1 could then read, "He that hath the seven spirits of God and the seven angels." Since angels are spirits sent forth (Hebrews 1:14), the expressions "seven angels" and "seven spirits" are synonymous, referring to the same creatures in different relationships: as before the throne they are spirits, as sent forth they are angels. The word "and" therefore has the sense of even; thus, the sense of chapter 3:1 is: "the seven spirits of God, even the seven angels." This rendering of the Greek word for "and" (kai) is frequent in the New Testament, occurring over 100 times. A good example is: "God, even the Father," which occurs six times. Romans 15:6; I Corinthians 15:24; II Corinthians 1:3; I Thessalonians 3:13; II Thessalonians 2:16; James 3:9. Dr. Charles therefore rightly says, "Whether these seven spirits are to be identified with the seven archangels cannot be inferred with certainty, but this identification may be regarded as highly probable. . . ."[2] The same was already observed by the early Greek commentators of the apocalypse; e.g., Oecumenius of the tenth century, Andrew of Caesarea of the fifth century, and Aretas of Caesarea of the sixth century[3] express themselves in similar language. Since "hath" denotes control or possession, it is clear that the seven spirits cannot refer to the Holy Spirit. Nowhere in the Scriptures is there any warrant for the view that the Son of man has the Holy Spirit in His power. The conception that the Holy Spirit is mentioned in conjunction with the seven stars is alike contrary to revelation and good sense.

(2) "There were seven lamps of fire burning before the throne, which are the seven spirits of God" (4:5). The seven lamps of fire correspond with the seven stars. Both are fitting symbols of the glory and luminosity of angels. Compare the description of the angel of the Lord: "His countenance was like lightning, and his raiment white as snow" (Matthew 28:3).

(3) "And I beheld, and, lo, in the midst of the throne and of the four beasts [living creatures], and in the midst of the elders, stood a Lamb as it had been slain, having seven horns and seven eyes, which are the seven spirits of God sent forth into all the earth" (5:6). "Having" must be understood in the same sense as "have" or "hold" in 1:16; 2:1; that is, it denotes ownership or control. This is not a description of the Lamb (Christ), but the seven horns and seven eyes are characteristic and symbolic of the seven spirits of God sent forth into all the earth. The horns denote strength and the eyes understanding of the seven spirits, not of the Lamb.

"Sent forth" is the translation of precisely the same Greek word as that similarly translated in Hebrews 1:14: "Are they [the angels] not all ministering spirits, sent forth. . . ?" Since angels are spirits "sent forth," the seven spirits here sent forth are undoubtedly to be understood as referring to angels. It is highly significant therefore that at this point the fourfold repetition of "the seven spirits" (1:4; 3:1; 4:5; 5:6) ceases, and that at the next mention of a group of seven (8:2) we have the first occurrence of the term "the seven angels." Evidently the definite article in the latter passage refers back to the seven spirits. We conclude therefore that the seven personages "which are before his throne" (1:4) are spirits (angels), being "sent forth" or commissioned.

5. THE LORD'S DAY

We will again test each view in a threefold manner: by the language employed, by the context, and by parallel passages.

1. *The Christian Sabbath.*

a. The language employed. In support of this view it is contended, first, that the phrase is the one familiarly employed to denote the first day of the week. Second, that because of the nature of his vision, it was likely that the vision came to John on this day. Third, that the term was used in reference to the first day of the week by several of the early church fathers: Ignatius, The Teaching of the Twelve Apostles, Clement of Alexandria. Fourth, that the words here employed are never used elsewhere in reference to the future day of the Lord. Upon examination, however, it appears that these conclusions are based upon insufficient evidence.

On the contrary, the term "the Lord's day" has never been applied to the first day of the week, either in profane literature or in revelation. Moreover, it is necessary to account for the definite article, which occurs here in the original. "John was in the Spirit on the Lord's day."

The view either altogether ignores, or else, as some of its advocates admit, does not account for the presence of the article.

b. The context. The view that his being in the Spirit took place on our Sunday receives no support from the use of adjacent language either preceding or following the text. What warrant or precedent is there in Scripture for projecting the idea of a vision on Sunday (rather than any other day of the week); in connection with the coming of Christ in the clouds (verse 7); with the declaration of Christ's divine attributes (verse 8); with his being on the Isle of Patmos (verse 9); with hearing the voice as of a trumpet (verse 10); with his writing in the book (verse 11); with his turning to see the voice behind him (verse 12)? Plainly the view that John was in the Spirit on Sunday receives no support from the context. The idea appears to be altogether irrelevant.

c. Parallel passages. There is not a single instance on record either in the Scriptures or in the annals of history in which the term "the Lord's day" is applied to our Sunday. If such were the case, no explanation could be given why Justin Martyr[4] and Barnabas[5] used the terms, "Sunday" and ". . . the day also on which Jesus arose again from the dead," respectively [and thus clearly the first day of the week—J. O. Y.] [In fact, Tertullian[6] repudiates the use among Christians of the name Sunday for the first day of the week.—J.O.Y.] The former name came from a heathen source, while "the first day of the week" is the only one employed in the rest of the New Testament. The passages are: Matthew 28:1; Mark 16:2, 9; Luke 24:1; John 20:1, 19; Acts 20:7; I Corinthians 16:2.

It is noteworthy that the Apostle John uses the term twice in his Gospel. It is quite untenable that he would employ the term "the first day of the week" in his Gospel, and the term "the Lord's day" in the same sense in this context without a word of explanation, for we know that both were written near the close of his life, and some scholars even hold the view that the Gospel was written after the Revelation.

One does not find a parallel passage in the New Testament in which language bearing any semblance to the term "the Lord's day" is applied to the first day of the week. Moreover, the view completely ignores the definite article. Absence of the article where one might be expected may be accounted for in some other way, but an interpretation which ignores its presence stands self-condemned.

2. The Future Day of the Lord.

The second interpretation holds this to be the day of the Lord in which He executes justice.

a. The language employed. "On the Lord's day." We call attention to the Greek preposition en, translated on in this instance. The word occurs 157 times in Revelation. In about three out of four cases, the word is translated by in, the second most frequent translation being with, 25 times. Only one other time do we have the translation on, viz., "on the earth" (5:13). In each case, where the preposition is followed by the word "day" (2:13; 9:6; 10:7; 11:6; 18:8), as here, it is rendered by in. The testimony is therefore that it should be similarly translated here, viz., "in the Lord's day." This would comport with the view that the reference is to a time period—the future day of the Lord.

This view accounts for the use of the definite article "the." It holds that the reference is to the day of the Lord which is mentioned with slight variations 20 times in the Old Testament and four times in the New. Delitzsch, the great Old Testament commentator, called this expression, ". . . the watchword of prophecy from the time of Joel downward."[7] (See Isaiah 13:6.)

A parallel term, "the last days," occurs 14 times in the Old Testament and four times in the New; and as Delitzsch says, "always . . . in an eschatological sense."[8] Isaiah 2:2. Another synonymous term, "in that day," occurs still more frequently—over 100 times in the Old Testament and generally in an eschatological sense. It occurs 12 times in the New Testament in a similar sense. That the phrases, "the day of the Lord," "the last days," and "in that day," are identical in meaning is shown by the fact that they are frequently used interchangeably. (See, for example, Isaiah 2.) The chapter opens with "And it shall come to pass in the last days" (verse 2). Verse 11 declares, "the Lord alone shall be exalted in that day." Verse 12 then continues, "For the day of the Lord of hosts shall be upon every one that is proud and lofty."

Anyone familiar with the New Testament Scriptures is well aware of the fact that frequent mention is made of a coming day. Some twenty different terms relating to end time are found in over seventy different passages. Besides those already mentioned, note the following: a day, his day, the days, those days, days of the Son of man, day of the Lord, day of the Lord Jesus Christ, day of redemption, day of visitation, day of wrath.

Since the Book of Revelation consists of an orderly presentation of all things foretold by the prophets yet awaiting fulfillment, we should expect the mention of some synonym referring to the end time in this closing picture of things to come. The entire first chapter being introductory, and pointing forward to "things which must shortly come to pass," we should expect in this place some mention of the coming day.

Of all the numerous terms thus employed, that of "the day of the Lord" is the most significant and comprehensive. Instead, however, we find here only the approximate term, "the Lord's day," and no similar term occurs in all the succeeding chapters.

That the terms, "the day of the Lord" and "the Lord's day," as employed in our text are identical, we propose to show by the following considerations:

The Hebrew language has no word for Lord's. There was no way of saying "the Lord's day"; hence we have instead the expression, "the day of the Lord." The same is true of the Septuagint, which is the Greek translation of the Old Testament, for it likewise uses the expression, "day of the Lord." The Greek word *kuriake* (Lord's) is not found in the concordance of the Septuagint. In the New Testament, the same formula, "the day of the Lord," occurs four times, viz., Acts 2:20; I Thessalonians 5:2; II Thessalonians 2:2; and II Peter 3:10. The first is a quotation by Peter from the prophet Joel. Thus the formula was introduced in the New Testament, and Peter naturally used the same expression in his last epistle. Paul likely used this formula in his first writing—the two epistles to the Thessalonians. (It should be said that the formula, "the day of Christ," occurs in our translation in II Thessalonians 2:2, but that all the church fathers who quote the text have, "day of the Lord." The same is all but universally true of all the manuscripts. Thus the evidence is overwhelmingly in favor of the latter reading, and we may add, the internal evidence apparently requires this reading.)

The adjective form *(kuriake)* "Lord's" occurs only here and in I Corinthians 11:20 where Paul says, "this is not to eat the Lord's supper." (See below, "Parallel passages.") It was formerly supposed that Paul coined the word, but it has since been found in the koine (the language of the common people as it was spoken in the New Testament times). We shall see that Paul had a special reason for using the expression, "the Lord's supper," instead of the "supper of the Lord," and that John in our text had a similar reason for using the term, "the Lord's day," instead of "the day of the Lord."

Due to the comparative scarcity of adjectives in the Hebrew language, similar formulas frequently are employed in the original Hebrew text of the Old Testament. For instance: instead of saying royal statute, the Hebrew says statute of the king; instead of royal crown, crown of the kingdom; instead of royal seed, seed of the kingdom; and instead of royal diadem, diadem of the kingdom. Again, since there is no adjective for valiant, instead of a valiant man, the Hebrew says uniformly a man of valor, and due to the conception that valor is a living principle, we have frequently sons of valor.

Even in cases where the Hebrew supplies an adjective, a noun is frequently used instead. For example, while the adjective "holy" is used in some instances, we find that the nominal form is far more frequent. For instance, instead of a holy hill or mountain, we have mountain of holiness; for holy garments, garments of holiness; for holy city, city of holiness; for holy temple, temple of holiness; for holy place, place of holiness; for holy house, house of holiness.

An important point of interpretation is based upon the usage of these formulas. Note that the latter of two nouns receives the emphasis which denotes importance, distinction, or antithesis. Take any of the formulas: day of the Lord, man of valor, seed of the kingdom, mountain of holiness. The first noun (followed usually by *of*) is said to be in the construct state, the second in the absolute. The first is dependent; the second, being the more important word, is not. The first is pronounced hurriedly, and where the law of the language permits, the vowels are shortened. Moreover, the construct has no separate accent, but is pronounced hurriedly as though it were a part of the following word. It may usually be seen clearly why the words are arranged in the order they appear. For instance, "Lord" is more important than "day"; "valor" is more rare than "man"; "seed" is a common word, but "seed of the kingdom" has special significance, and for a similar reason, the word to be stressed is not "mountain," but "holiness." Therefore in the formula, "day of the Lord," "Lord" is the emphatic word. In the discussion of parallel passages it will be clear that in the New Testament formula, "the Lord's day," the emphasis falls on the same word, "Lord's," and not on day, thus showing that the Old Testament term, "the day of the Lord," and John's term, "the Lord's day," are identical in significance, and that, hence, the word "Lord" (or Lord's) in each case receives the emphasis.

Another important consideration is that instead of a Hebrew noun in the construct state, with the sign "of" following, we have on numerous occasions, the prefix "le," which signifies "to" or "for." (Cf. Isa. 2:12.) In the first mention, the literal rendering is a day for or to the Lord. The Lord has a day —a day which is in a special sense His day. Similarly we have an altar for or to the Lord; a feast to the Lord; an offering to the Lord; a people for the Lord; a house for the Lord; and in the Hebrew always a passover to the Lord. Thus we have proof positive in the Old Testament that the day of the Lord when it comes will be in a very particular sense the "Lord's" day.

The Hebrew has no word for "Lord's." It is significant that in our English translation, this possessive or adjectival form occurs some 115 times modifying more than fifty different nouns. For instance, the "Lord's house" appears 21 times, the "Lord's anointed" ten times, the "Lord's hand" six times, the "Lord's anger" five times, the "Lord's people," "tribute," "offering," and "passover," each four times. Moreover, the same original phrases are frequently rendered two ways in our translation, e.g., the Lord's house and the house of the Lord, the Lord's passover and the passover of the Lord, the Lord's anger and the anger of the Lord, the Lord's name and the name of the Lord, the Lord's anointed and the anointed of the Lord, the Lord's servant and the servant of the Lord, the Lord's people and the people of the Lord.

We observe therefore that there is no reason why the translators should not also have rendered the Hebrew original, "the Lord's day," as well as "the day of the Lord." If they had done this, the question of their identity would never have been raised. The real objection to the view that by "the Lord's day" we are to understand "the day of the Lord" is based apparently on a biased translation and not on sound interpretation.

b. The context. The entire context (including the verses preceding and those immediately following) supports the view that by the Lord's day, the future day of the Lord is intended. (a) The ascription of praise, verses 5b, 6 above, bears a close resemblance to the adoration of the elders in Revelation 5:9, 10. (b) The announcement of the Lord's second coming (verse 7) is in full agreement with the thought of the coming Lord's day. (c) The sounding of a trumpet accords precisely with events related to the second coming. There is the mention of a first and a last trumpet at the rapture of the church (I Thessalonians 4; I Corinthians 15); seven trumpets sound during the tribulation period; a trumpet sounds after the coming of the Lord (Matthew 24:31; Isaiah 27:13). In Revelation 4:1 we have this same voice "as . . . of a trumpet."

All these passages we have quoted are related to the coming day of the Lord; and as we observe, the Lord's day occurs at the very heart of these passages, while, on the other hand, Sunday has no organic relation with the events previous to or after these passages.

c. Parallel passages. These include over one hundred passages in the Old Testament which appear under such terms as: "the last day," "in that day," "the day of the Lord." That these passages are synonymous has already been shown by the fact that they are used interchangeably. Isaiah 2:1, 11, 12. Their identity is frequently observable in later Scriptures.

Such expressions as "the day of the Lord's wrath" (Zephaniah 1:18), "the day of the Lord's anger" (Zephaniah 2:2, 3), "the day of vengeance" (Proverbs 6:34; Isaiah 61:2; 63:4), "the time of the Lord's vengeance" (Jeremiah 51:6), and "the day of wrath" (Proverbs 11:4; Zephaniah 1:15, 18) point forward to the same period, namely, the end of time.

In the New Testament we have called attention to the fact that some twenty terms are employed in describing the future day of the Lord. Also it may be noted that the Book of Revelation purports to give a description of things which must come to pass up to and including the end. All the prophets have said, in their variations of terminology respecting the last days, still awaiting fulfillment, is but "The revelation of all the last things, which the Apocalypse of the New Testament embraces in one grand picture. . . ."9

We must limit our further discussion under this head to a few additional passages in the New Testament.

"When ye come together therefore into one place, this is not to eat the Lord's supper. For in eating every one taketh before other his own supper" (I Corinthians 11:20, 21b). Apart from the use in Revelation 1:10 this is the only use of the adjectival form "Lord's" (Greek: *kuriake*) in the New Testament. It is significant that the apostle in adjacent passages uses (in the Greek) the ordinary forms: cup of the Lord (I Corinthians 10:21; 11:27), table of the Lord (I Corinthians 10:21), body of the Lord (I Corinthians 11:27, 29), blood of the Lord (I Corinthians 11:27), and death of the Lord (I Corinthians 11:26).

The reason for the change of the form to the possessive, "Lord's," is undoubtedly to contrast the Lord's Supper with one's own supper. It should be plain that the emphasis is not on supper since the contrast is not based on this word. For instance, the apostle did not mean to distinguish between the Lord's "supper" and the Lord's "breakfast," but between the "Lord's" supper and "man's" supper. Thus "Lord's" is used for the sake of emphasis. According to the Greek usage, the emphasis in the phrase, "the Lord's day," corresponds precisely with the Hebrew usage in the phrase, "the day of the Lord," for according to the variant law of language, the emphasis in each usage falls on the words "Lord" and "Lord's." The terms are absolutely parallel in their implications.

"With me it is a very small thing that I should be judged by you or by man's day; indeed, I judge not even mine own self. For I know nothing against myself, yet am I not hereby justified; but he that judgeth me is the Lord. Therefore judge nothing before the time until the Lord come" (I Corinthians 4:3-5a).

The above is a literal rendering of the Greek text. Man's judgment as in the Authorized Version is an interpretation, not a translation. It is so rendered because man judges now. Man's day (corresponding to the time of the Gentiles, lit., nations) began with Nebuchadnezzar whom God chose as world ruler after Israel had rejected God from ruling over them. Man was on the judgment seat when Christ was condemned to die. The Apostle Paul refused to accept the verdict of man's day; consequently he peremptorily declared: "Judge nothing before the time," that is, until the Lord come. The apostle in this place contrasts man's judgment with the Lord's judgment; according to the Greek, man's day with the Lord's day. Although the Lord's day is not expressed, it is plainly implied, just as in our former passage the term "man's supper" was not expressed but implied. (See Alford, Meyer, Ellicott, and Stanley.)

It is significant that the same apostle in the same epistle uses the rare Greek word (*kuriakos*) Lord's and (*anthropinos*) man's. It is still man's day, and this day will continue as long as the Lord sits at the right hand of God. He will leave that place when He comes to meet His church in the air. From then on will be the Lord's day. He will have His day then as man has his now. It will continue until He will have delivered the kingdom unto God the Father, "when he shall have put down all rule and all authority and power. For he must reign, till he hath put all enemies under his feet" (I Corinthians 15:24, 25).

"As the lightning, that lighteneth out of the one part under heaven, shineth unto the other part under heaven; so shall also the Son of man be *in his day*" (Luke 17:24). The context shows that "his day" has reference to the coming of the Lord. In the same discourse, in speaking to His disciples regarding this future advent, He declared: "Watch therefore: for ye know not what hour your Lord doth come" (Matthew 24:42). The only fitting antecedent for "his" (the possessive pronoun) is "Lord's"; hence "in his day" is the equivalent of "in the Lord's day."

It has been well said that John thought in Hebrew but wrote in Greek; and this he did when he wrote, "the Lord's day," instead of the Hebrew form, "the day of the Lord," for only in this form does the Greek like the Hebrew place the emphasis on the word "Lord." Thus it has been conclusively shown that the Greek form, "the Lord's day," corresponds exactly with the Hebrew form, "the day of the Lord." [And consequently must refer to the time when these visions John had will become reality. This, of course, makes the Book of Revelation simply an unfolding of events during the time known by the Old Testament prophets as "the day of the Lord."—J. O. Y.]

6. DEATH AND HADES

The Greek word for hell is *hades*, the place of departed spirits, not the final hell (Greek: *gehenna*). The former word occurs eleven times in the New Testament, the latter twelve times. The Hebrew word for *hades* is *sheol*. The word occurs 65 times in the Old Testament and is translated "grave" 31 times, "hell" 31 times, and "pit" three times. Death and hell are mentioned alternately and in close proximity 18 times in the Old Testament—eleven times in the order "death and *sheol*," seven times "*sheol* and death." In the New Testament death and hell occur together five times and in each case in this order except in Revelation 1:18. However, even here, the weight of authority, including Irenaeus and Cyprian, favors the same order.

Death is a state or condition brought about by sin as numerous passages show, e.g., "the wages of sin is death" (Romans 6:23), and "sin, when it is finished, bringeth forth death" (James 1:15). *Sheol* or *hades* is a receptacle and abode of the dead. The righteous as well as the wicked were anticipating entrance into that solitary abode. Such was the testimony of: Jacob (Genesis 37:35; 42:38), Job (Job 7:9; 14:13; 17:13), David (Psalm 6:5; 16:10; 30:3), Hezekiah (Isaiah 38:10), and Jonah (Jonah 2:2). But while *sheol* was regarded by the righteous as a place of solitude and spiritual inertia (Psalm 30:9; 88:10-12; 115:17; Isaiah 38:18), men like Job and David were biding the time of ultimate release (Job 14:14; Psalm 16:10). On the other hand, the wicked are spoken of as going alive into *sheol* (Numbers 16:30, 33; Psalm 55:15), as burning in the lowest *sheol* (Deuteronomy 32:22), as being turned into *sheol* (Psalm 9:17), as being in agreement with *sheol* (Isaiah 28:15, 18), and as being cast into *sheol* (Ezekiel 31:16). While there is an apparent difference in the state of the righteous and of the wicked dead of the Old Testament, the story (not parable) of the rich man and Lazarus (Luke 16:19-31) presents a more complete comprehension of the spiritual condition of both classes. The Old Testament passages do not present the full revelation either of the blissful state of the righteous or of the misery of the wicked.

The story of the rich man and Lazarus as it pertains to the present purpose is briefly as follows: The rich man was in *hades*. Like all Old Testament saints, after their departure, Abraham was in *hades*, too. Between them was a great gulf fixed over which neither could pass. The gulf was wide, for the rich man sees Abraham "afar off" with Lazarus in his bosom. While the rich man was in torment in a flame, Lazarus was comforted in the bosom of Abraham. This shows that while the wicked dead of the Old Testament period were tormented, the righteous were in a state of bliss and happy fellowship. It also implies recognition between the wicked and the righteous, for the rich man recognized both Lazarus and Abraham. Abraham, moreover, knew things about the life of the rich man.

In the New Testament period great changes take place in regard to *hades*, and its occupants. What are these changes and how are they brought about?

Consider the following Scripture passages pertaining to the question: (a) Jesus Himself declared, "the Son of man [shall] be three days and three nights in the heart of the earth" (Matthew 12:40—the reference is to the period between His death and resurrection). (b) To the penitent thief He said, "Today shalt thou be with me in paradise" (Luke 23:43). This is the second of the sayings of Jesus on the cross and hence the words were spoken before the noon hour. Both Jesus and the thief died and were taken from the cross before sunset; hence they were together in paradise before the day closed. (c) Peter, in his sermon at Pentecost, called attention to the fulfillment of the prophecy of David in the words: "He [David] seeing this before spake of the resurrection of Christ, that his soul was not left in hell, neither his flesh did see corruption" (Acts 2:31). This not only shows that Jesus was in *hades*, but implies that He remained there until the time of His resurrection. Clearly, therefore, *hades* is regarded as the equivalent of the "heart of the earth" and of "paradise."

According to Paul, one having the righteousness which is from faith speaks on this wise, "Say not in thine heart, Who shall ascend into heaven? (that is, to bring Christ down from above:) or, Who shall descend into the deep? (that is, to bring up Christ again from the dead)" (Romans 10:6, 7). In other words, such a one believes that Christ has already come from heaven and that He had been in the bottomless pit. The same word "deep" (Greek: *abyss*) occurs in Luke 8:31— the demons besought Jesus that He would not command them to go out into the "deep." This followed another question, "art thou come hither to torment us before the time" (Matthew 8:29)? The point to note here is that the "deep" is the destined abode of demons or evil spirits.

In another place, Paul adapts the language of Psalm 68:18, "When he ascended up on high, he led captivity captive, and gave gifts unto men." On this he comments, "Now that he ascended, what is it but that he also descended first into the lower parts of the earth" (Ephesians 4:8, 9)? In other words, before He ascended, He descended into the lower parts, which is to be regarded as identical in meaning with "the heart of the earth" and hence with "paradise," "*hades*," and the "abyss."

Peter has an important passage relevant to our discussion: "By which [spirit] also he went and preached unto the spirits in prison; which sometime were disobedient, when once the longsuffering of God waited in the days of Noah" (I Peter 3:19, 20). The original word *sometime* is translated *in the old time*, verse 5, where the reference is to the time of Abraham and Sarah. It should be noted that the word *preach* here is *kerusso* which signifies *to announce* as a herald, and may mean evil as well as good tidings. Undoubtedly the former is intended; for the Lord has no Gospel of salvation for disobedient spirits. That the *prison* is identical with the "abyss or bottomless pit" is evident from the following considerations: (a) Both are the abode of evil spirits. (b) "The bottomless pit" mentioned in Revelation 20:3 is spoken of as a "prison" in verse 7. (c) In Revelation 1:18 the key of *hades* is mentioned, while in 9:1 we read about the key of the bottomless pit.

It is evident that the terms, "heart of the earth," "paradise," "*hades*," "the abyss," "lower parts of the earth," and the "prison" (as mentioned by Peter), are used interchangeably, and hence are synonymous expressions. It is further evident that the changes mentioned are closely associated with the death, resurrection, and ascension of Christ.

It is relevant to determine what the expression, "he led captivity captive," and related passages may mean. Since death precedes and is the gateway to *hades*, it was necessary for Jesus first to conquer death. He did this by dying. He passed into and through that dismal shade, not as a victim, but as a victor, for His was "the power of an endless life" (Hebrews 7:16). The Death of deaths then brought death to death. By dying, He abolished death. II Timothy 1:10. This means that He robbed death of its power. He partook of flesh and blood "that through death he might destroy [render inoperative, or deprive of power—the same word is translated 'abolish'] him that had the power of death, that is, the devil" (Hebrews 2:14). He laid down His life at the cross that He might take it up again at His resurrection. Thus "death is swallowed up in victory" (I Corinthians 15:54b); and the believer in Christ can exultingly exclaim, "O death, where is thy sting? O grave, where is thy victory" (I Corinthians 15:55)? for He "giveth us the victory through our Lord Jesus Christ" (I Corinthians 15:57b). The resurrection was the proof of Jesus' triumph over death and hades.

Jesus did more, according to Paul's testimony in Ephesians 4:8-11, than merely pass through hades as a victor. According to His own word, the penitent thief was with Him in paradise before the day of crucifixion had come to a close. Undoubtedly this is what Paul meant when he declared, "He . . . descended first into the lower parts of the earth." Remember, hades had two compartments with a great gulf intervening. Paradise apparently was the portion inhabited not only by Jesus and the penitent thief, but also by Abraham and Lazarus as well as all Old Testament saints. It appears, however, that paradise was a portion of the prison, hades, and that in this prison the righteous as well as the wicked were held captives. It is to the righteous captives (those in paradise) that the apostle refers when he says, "When he ascended up on high, he led captivity captive"—i.e., He took those who were in captivity in the paradise side of hades with Him (as a conqueror leads with him his captives); on high—i.e., to heaven. That paradise was no longer below as a portion of hades in the days of the apostle is evident from his own testimony when he speaks of himself in II Corinthians 12:2 as "one caught up to the third heaven," which experience he mentions again by way of repetition in verse 4 as having been "caught up into paradise," thus showing that paradise was now identical with the third heaven, by which is meant the heaven of the blessed where God dwells.

This, of course, does not mean that the "bodies" of the Old Testament saints have been glorified. Paradise possesses only the spirits of men, and these only—not their bodies—were led captive by Jesus at His ascension. Thus the words of Peter are to be understood: "For David [that is, his body] is not ascended into the heavens" (Acts 2:34).

7. The Ministry of Angels

The Hebrew word malak occurs 214 times. It is translated angel 112 times and in each case the reference is to literal angels. It is translated messenger 97 times, ambassador four times, and king once, all of which, with one exception (Malachi 3:1), refer to a human being. Moreover, the single exception is a prophecy concerning Christ's coming in the form of man. The Greek word anggelos occurs 186 times. It is translated angel 179 times; the remaining seven are translated messenger, three of which (Matthew 11:10; Mark 1:2; Luke 7:27) refer to John the Baptist, one each to messengers sent by John (Luke 7:24), by Jesus (Luke 9:52), by Rahab (James 2:25), and once the reference is to Paul's thorn in the flesh (II Corinthians 12:7).

Not once in the 102 occurrences in the Old Testament and seven in the New where a human being is in view did the translators render the original anggelos by the word angel. The translators of the KJV and RV render anggelos in Revelation as "angel." If these scholars thought that anggelos referred to a human being, they would have rendered it messenger here as they did elsewhere. The above should settle the question, thus proving that the word "angel" here denotes a celestial being and does not denote a human official.

Stars are used elsewhere as symbols of spirit beings. Stars are in the heavens and hence are appropriate symbols of heavenly beings. Likewise candlesticks are objects on earth symbolizing churches on earth. Compare the parallelism in Job 38:7, "When the morning stars sang together, and all the sons of God [i.e., angels] shouted for joy." In Isaiah 14:12, Satan is spoken of as the morning star. Jesus is the bright and morning star mentioned in Revelation 2:28 and 22:16. He is the day star of II Peter 1:19. The star of Revelation 9:1 is the angel of the bottomless pit. (Cf. 9:11.) The stars of Revelation 12:4 are identical with the angels of 12:7, 9.

Revelation is above all others a book of angels. The word occurs 76 times. It is but reasonable to believe that the word is used in the same sense throughout. Especially is this the case since there is no qualifying or distinguishing word such as *heteros* (i.e., another of a different kind).

In 3:1, the word *angel* occurs in the address to the church at Sardis. It occurs again (in the plural) in 3:5, where it plainly refers to heavenly messengers. It is altogether improbable that the word in 3:1 and in 3:5 would be used in such close proximity in a different sense without a word of explanation.

The word *angel*, especially in the sense of a human messenger, implies subordination, inferiority, and subservience. This is seen in the messengers sent by John, by Jesus, and by Rahab. On the other hand, the word *bishop* denotes an overseer, one vested with authority. Thus *messenger* and *bishop* express opposite relationships.

The letters to the churches are addressed to the angels. They are recipients, not bearers of the messages. On the other hand, no message is ever addressed to human messengers. They are bearers, not recipients of a message.

No mention is made of the messenger or messengers who delivered the letters to the several churches. If, as some suppose, messengers could have been sent by the churches to John to receive the messages, he would have "given," not "sent," them the messages ("send," 1:11). The following arrangement will enable the reader to compare the deliverance of the book to John and to the angels:

The Sender	The Bearer	The Receiver
1:1 He (Jesus) sent it	by an angel (messenger)	to John to seven churches, e.g.,
1:11 John sent it	unnamed	to angel of Ephesus, to angel of Smyrna, etc.

The concept that bishops are at the right hand of God in a sense different from believers in general is foreign to the teachings of Scripture. This, however, is said of the seven stars in 1:16; 2:1. In 3:1, the seven spirits of God and the seven stars are apparently parallel conceptions. The word *and* in this case has the sense of *even*, e.g., "God and Father" is equivalent to "God, even the Father."

It is contrary to the facts of historic testimony that at the time John wrote the book, only one bishop was in charge of a congregation. When Paul left Ephesus (Acts 20) there were still elders at that church, and it is entirely improbable that in so short a time there would now be only one bishop (corresponding to the angel) in the city. Moreover, in the writings of the earliest church fathers, we find still a plurality of bishops in each congregation.

Why should there be an angel of a church? The Scriptures frequently mention special missions and responsibilities of angels with respect to individuals and to nations. In the Old Testament angels appeared or ministered to Sarah (Genesis 16:7-11), Hagar (Genesis 21:17), Abraham (Genesis 22:11, 15; 24:7), Eliezer (Genesis 24:40), Jacob (Genesis 28:12; 31:11; 32:1; 48:16), Moses (Exodus 3:2), Balaam (Numbers 22:22-35), Gideon (Judges 6:11-22), Manoah's wife (Judges 13:3-9), Manoah (Judges 13:13-21), David (II Samuel 24:17), an unnamed prophet (I Kings 13:18), Elijah (I Kings 19:5, 7; II Kings 1:3, 15), Gad (I Chronicles 21:18), Ornan (I Chronicles 21:20), Shadrach, Meshach, Abednego, and Daniel (Daniel 3:28), Daniel (Daniel 6:22), Zechariah (Zechariah

1:9-19; 2:3; 4:1-5; 5:5-10; 6:4, 5), and Joshua the high priest (Zechariah 3:1-6).

In the New Testament angels appeared or ministered to Joseph (Matthew 1:20-24; 2:13, 19), Jesus (Matthew 4:11; Mark 1:13; Luke 22:43), the women (Matthew 28:5; Luke 24:23), Zacharias (Luke 1:11-19), Mary (Luke 1:26-35), the shepherds (Luke 2:9-13), Lazarus (Luke 16:22), Mary Magdalene (John 20:11, 12), the apostles (Acts 5:19), Philip (Acts 8:26), Cornelius (Acts 10:3, 7, 22; 11:13), Peter (Acts 12:7-11), and Paul (Acts 27:23).

Angels occasionally had missions to nations. An angel led the way in the journey of Israel to the promised land. Exodus 14:19; 23:20, 23; 32:34; 33:2. An angel appeared to Israel in the land. Judges 2:1-4; cf. 5:23. The angel of His presence saved Israel. Isaiah 63:9. What appear to be angelic beings (the Prince of Persia and the Prince of Grecia), with whom Michael and Gabriel contended, apparently held dominion over these countries. As Bishop Lightfoot remarks: "The 'princes' in the prophecy of Daniel present a very near if not an exact parallel to the angels of the Revelation. Here, as elsewhere, St. John seems to adapt the imagery of this earliest apocalyptic book."[10]

The Lord at times commissioned angels to execute judgments. An angel destroyed 70,000 Israelites. II Samuel 24:15, 17; I Chronicles 21:12-14. An angel smote 185,000 Assyrians. II Kings 19:35; II Chronicles 32:21. An angel smote Herod Agrippa I. Acts 12:23.

The following miscellaneous passages pertain to angelic ministries:

"The angel of the Lord encampeth round about them that fear him, and delivereth them" (Psalm 34:7).

"He shall give his angels charge over thee, to keep thee in all thy ways" (Psalm 91:11).

"Despise not one of these little ones; for I say unto you, That in heaven their angels do always behold the face of my Father which is in heaven" (Matthew 18:10).

"I say unto you, there is joy in the presence of the angels of God over one sinner that repenteth" (Luke 15:10).

"For this cause ought the woman to have authority [Greek] on her head because of the angels" (I Corinthians 11:10). The reference is to the veil, a sign that she is under authority to man.

[From this detailed study of the function of angels, their places in the Book of Revelation should become clear to any diligent student. They are shown to be ministering spirits sent forth to do the bidding of God and of Christ, whether that bidding has to do with the present order of affairs, or that order when the day of the Lord in the prophetic sense becomes a reality.—J. O. Y.]

8. As a Thief

A few Scriptures which illustrate the use of the term "as a thief" are grouped together in the following paragraphs:

Matthew 24:43; Luke 12:39—"But know this, that if the goodman of the house had known in what watch the thief would come, he would have watched, and would not have suffered his house to be broken up." Undoubtedly, as their context shows, these passages are given by the Lord in reference to His coming at the rapture. However, an important rule of Bible interpretation is that details of a parable are but a scaffolding for the conveyance of the truth and are not to be relied upon independently as a safe criterion in sound interpretation, and in no case must they be allowed to contradict plainly revealed truth elsewhere. What is known as the "point" in the parable is the importance of watchfulness, not the coming of the thief, because it is implied that if the goodman of the house had watched, the thief would have come in vain.

I Thessalonians 5:2-4—"For yourselves know perfectly that the day of the Lord so cometh as a thief in the night. For when they shall say, Peace and safety;

then sudden destruction cometh upon them, as travail upon a woman with child; and they shall not escape. But ye, brethren, are not in darkness, that that day should overtake you as a thief."

We make the following observations:

As we shall see, the Lord's coming *as a thief* is always related to the *day of the Lord* in nonfigurative or nonparabolic language.

That the day of the Lord is not identical with the meeting in the air (I Thessalonians 4:13-17) is evident from the fact that the Thessalonians knew perfectly the things pertaining to *the day of the Lord,* but on the contrary that apostle had "need" to write them regarding the rapture of the church in order that they might not be ignorant of that particular event.

The day of the Lord begins with the great tribulation when it is designated "a time of travail"—Jeremiah 30:6, 7; Matthew 24:8 ("sorrows" equals travail)— and described as such (Revelation 6-18); it is openly introduced in His triumph over His enemies when He is revealed from heaven (Revelation 19:11-21); and it continues unabated in triumph and glory for "a thousand years" (Revelation 20:1-6; cf. II Peter 3:8), and ends with the introduction of a new heaven and new earth.

When *they* (those who are *not* brethren, verses 1 and 4) will say *Peace and safety,* then sudden destruction will come, i.e., the tribulation will then begin, and *they* (as above) *shall not escape. Not* is emphatic here, for in the Greek we have a double negative: not, not, equivalent to *never, no never.*

They who shall *not escape* are evidently mentioned in contrast with those who watch and pray (Luke 21:36), for the latter will be accounted worthy to escape all these things that shall come to pass.

Observe, too, that in the Greek of verse 4 the pronouns are emphatic, i.e., "But ye, brethren, are not in darkness, that that day should overtake you as a thief." Here it is definitely stated that the day of the Lord does not overtake the brethren as a thief, but instead they will then "stand before the Son of man" (Luke 21:36, as above), implying that they have previously been caught up to meet the Lord in the air and thus they are ever *with the Lord.*

II Peter 3:10—"But the day of the Lord will come as a thief in the night; in the which the heavens shall pass away with a great noise, and the elements shall melt with fervent heat, the earth also and the works that are therein shall be burned up." Further comments are not necessary except to say that the day of the Lord, at which time He will come "as a thief," is plainly not synchronous or identical with His coming for the church. (Cf. I Thessalonians 4:13-17.)

Revelation 16:15—"Behold, I come as a thief. Blessed is he that watcheth, and keepeth his garments, lest he walk naked, and they see his shame." This coming plainly has reference to Revelation 19:11 ff. The announcement comes after the sixth vial is poured out, which occurs just previous to His coming "after the tribulation" (Matthew 24:29). That there will be some people saved and on the earth during the tribulation period our studies plainly reveal. See, for example, 18:4—"Come out of her [Babylon], my people."

Again we see that His coming as a thief has no reference to His coming for the church at the rapture. The threat that He would come upon them as a thief implies that those who fail to watch will pass into the great tribulation, since, as we have seen, His coming as a thief is at the close of that period. The masses will be so blinded and hardened then that they will be altogether neglectful and ignorant of prophetic truth; hence they will not know what hour the Lord will come upon them.

9. To Blot Out of the Book of Life

When Moses requested the Lord to blot his name out of His book which He had written, the Lord replied, "Whosoever hath sinned against me, him will I blot out of my book" (Exodus 32:33). That this "book" has no reference to the genealogical tables of the priests is seen in that the Lord calls it "my" book. That God was a bookkeeper already in Old Testament times is seen further from Nehemiah 13:14; Psalm 56:8; Isaiah 65:6. The first register of men is recorded in Exodus 32:32. There is here ". . . the assumption of the existence of a divine 'book of life' (Exodus 32:32, 33; Daniel 12:1; cf. Psalm 139:16). . . . The reference here is to persons who were entered in the book of God, on account of the good kernel of faith within them. . . ."11

In Psalm 69:25-28 we have a reference to Judas (cf. Acts 1:20) and others who were guilty of the death of Christ. In verse 28 occurs the expression, "Let them be blotted out of the book of the living, and not be written with the righteous." In other words, their names had been written in the book; now because of their sin, they were to be erased. (Cf. Deuteronomy 9:14; 25:19; 29:20.)

"Any one taking away from the words of the book of this prophecy, God shall take away his part out of the book of life," which is comparable to saying He would blot out his name from the book. The one taking away is by implication a believer. Whether we read "book of life" or "tree of life," as some texts do, the retribution would be alike in either case.

It will be a matter of interest to compare the positive side of the promise with similar words of our Lord during His earthly ministry. For convenience, we quote the passages in parallel form:

"Whosoever therefore will confess in me before men, in him will I confess also before my Father which is in heaven" (Matthew 10:32, Greek.)	"Whosoever shall confess in me before men, in him shall the Son of man also confess before the angels of God" (Luke 12:8, Greek).	"He that overcometh . . . I will confess his name before my Father, and before his angels" (Revelation 3:5).

The one confessing and the one overcoming share alike the divine favor. We are probably to infer that the two characteristics are inseparable, that is, the confessor is an overcomer.

The phrases in me and in him have not received due recognition among commentators, one reason being that the prepositions in do not appear in the translation. These express union with Christ in a mutual relationship. This truth is expressed in numerous passages, e.g., "He . . . dwelleth in me, and I in him" (John 6:56; 15:5); "ye in me, and I in you" (John 14:20). The same truth is repeatedly expressed in the epistles.

Christ is said to be in the believer in II Corinthians 13:5; Galatians 2:20; Ephesians 3:17; Colossians 1:27; and the believer "in Christ" (including "in him," "in whom") some thirty times in Ephesians alone.

To confess in him therefore signifies that by our lives we show to others that we belong to Him, and if so, He assures us that when we come to stand before Him, He will confess before the Father and the holy angels that He has made His dwelling in us.

In confirmation of the above interpretation, we quote from the following writers:

"The ἐν [in] . . . shows the ground or root of the confession, namely, a living union with Christ. He does not mean a mere outward confession of the mouth but a genuine and consistent confession of the whole life."12

"Confess in me"—"indicates a sense of unity with Christ, and of Christ with the man who takes an open stand for Him."13

"A peculiar but very significant expression. Lit., 'Confess in me.' The idea is that of confessing Christ out of a state of oneness with Him. 'Abide in me, and being in me, confess me.' It implies identification of the confessor with the confessed, and thus takes confession out of the category of mere formal or verbal acknowledgment. . . . The true confessor of Christ is one whose faith rests in Him.

Observe that this gives great force to the corresponding clause, in which Christ places Himself in a similar relation with those whom He confesses. 'I will confess *in him.*' It shall be as if I spoke abiding in Him."[14] Matthew 10:32.

10. FROM THAT HOUR

The question to be studied is, Can a passage of Scripture be found which tells about being kept *from the hour* and from which may be learned whether exemption from or security in the hour is intended? Fortunately there is one (though only one) such in the Bible. As strange as it may seem, no one (as far as the present writer's knowledge goes) has called attention to this invaluable aid in the correct interpretation of the passage. We refer to John 12:27: "Now is my soul troubled; and what shall I say? Father, save me from this hour: but for this cause came I unto this hour." It is true, we have here the word *save* instead of *keep*, but it is obviously used in the sense of being kept or delivered from or during an impending evil so as to escape it, as is the case in Romans 5:9: "We shall be saved from wrath through him," and in I Thessalonians 1:10: "Which delivered us from the wrath to come." The crucial question then is, What is meant by the words, "Save me from this hour"—exemption from it or security in or through it?

It is significant that Jesus is the speaker and John the writer just as is the case in the Revelation text, and that in each case mention is made of a coming hour of suffering. In all probability, therefore, the meaning of the phrase *from the hour* is similar in both instances.

That Jesus' suffering at this time was proleptic or anticipatory and that the "hour" spoken of was in reality still in the future is evident in that He Himself declares a few days later, "With desire I have desired to eat this passover with you before I suffer" (Luke 22:15), and later still, just previous to His arrest, "Behold, the hour is at hand [Greek: *near*], and the Son of man is betrayed into the hands of sinners" (Matthew 26:45). The phrase "is at hand" always denotes proximity and never total arrival. It is used similarly in reference to both time and space. As for space, see the following verse in reference to the near approach of Judas: "Behold, he is at hand that doth betray me" (Matthew 26:46).

The occasion of the utterance in the Gospel was during the first part of the Passover week at the coming of the Greeks who desired to see Jesus. Their coming brought the fateful hour immediately to His consciousness, for He well knew that "except a corn of wheat fall into the ground and die, it abideth alone." Only by dying can it bring forth much fruit. Jesus was apparently "troubled" in anticipation of the awful ordeal just ahead, including the suffering of the cross, the bearing of the sins of the world, and the hiding of the Father's face as foretold by the prophets.

It will be observed that there are two opposing sentiments and that they are conjoined by the strong adversative conjunction *but* (Greek: *alla*). The conjunction occurs hundreds of times in the New Testament and it is used most often where strong opposition is intended.

In the first portion (preceding *but*) Jesus is in a state of distress, dread, and perplexity, while in the latter He manifests purpose, poise, and determination. First His human frame shrinks and His human will revolts in contemplation of the awful ordeal just ahead; then His divine nature and will spring into action and supremacy. Whereupon He determines to fulfill the divine purpose concerning Him by being "obedient unto death, even the death of the cross." This much is implied in the words, "for this cause came I unto this hour."

We now call attention to the remarkable similarity between Jesus' manner and utterances on this occasion and those expressed in the garden but a few days later. So great are these resemblances that the former occasion may well be regarded as a prelude to Gethsemane. We do not find Him entering the garden in the attitude of resignation and composure as we see Him leave the scene. On the other hand, as the fateful hour draws nearer, the same conflicting emotions harass Him in the garden with increasing intensity. For convenience we herewith indicate a threefold parallelism between the utterances of Jesus on the two occasions:

His Troubled Soul

The Coming of the Greeks	In the Garden
(1) Now is my soul troubled. From the Greek of Psalm 42:6.	(1) My soul is exceeding sorrowful, even unto death. Matthew 26:38. The first portion is from Psalm 42:5a.

His Will (as human, initial, and tremulant)

(2) Save me from this hour.	(2) a. Take away this cup from me. Mark 14:36. b. Remove this cup from me. Luke 22:42.

The Father's Will

(3) But [alla] for this cause came I unto this hour.	(3) Not my will, but [alla] thine, be done. Luke 22:42.

His Will (as divine, final, and triumphant)

(4)	(4) The cup which my Father hath given me, shall I not drink it? John 18:11.

Jesus in the distress of His soul, first at the coming of the Greeks and later in the garden, had recourse to the same psalm. This unanimity of sentiment and likeness of direction for relief and comfort binds the two incidents into one.

Whatever Jesus meant when He said, "Remove this cup from me," He also meant in the previous declaration, "Save me from this hour." The sentiment expressed is a clear indication that Jesus was truly human as well as divine. Evidently He prayed for exemption from the dreadful hour because His human nature shrank at the terrible thought of bearing the sins of the world [better, becoming the sacrifice—J. O. Y.], and above all, of His being utterly forsaken of God as foretold by the psalmist (Psalm 22:1) and expressed in the woeful cry of the dying hour, "My God, my God, why hast thou forsaken me" (Matthew 27:46)?

It is Jesus' own testimony that His will was counter to that of the Father in His declaration, "Not my will, but [alla] thine, be done." It is significant that the three synoptists (though with interesting variations) cite this important declaration. Matthew 26:39; Mark 14:36; Luke 22:42. It is evident that the prayer was but a temporary and spasmodic outbreak of His human will from His behavior shortly after, for when His enemies were approaching to apprehend Him, He declared, "Rise, let us be going [i.e., to meet them]: behold, he is at hand that doth betray me" (Matthew 26:46). And again when His friends sought to rescue Him, His retort was, ". . . the cup which my Father hath given me, shall I not drink it" (John 18:11)?

It should be noted that cup and hour are used interchangeably: the "cup" in reference to the content or nature of the suffering, the "hour" to the duration. He prayed that "if it were possible, the hour might pass from him" and "take away this cup from me" (Mark 14:35, 36). Again compare two passages which were spoken in close succession just after the agony in the garden: ". . . behold, the hour is at hand" (Matthew 26:45), and ". . . the cup which my Father hath given me, shall I not drink it" (John 18:11)? Both these passages show that the hour of drinking of the cup (of suffering) was still in the future.

When Jesus prayed, "Father, save me from this hour," or its equivalent— from drinking the cup (of suffering), He did no more mean mere security during the suffering than when He prayed, "Remove this cup from me." On both occasions His request was that He might be spared the ordeal of the suffering incident to the hour and not that He might pass securely through it.

The "cause" for coming to the hour was, that like the corn of wheat, He might die and bring forth much fruit. Consequently, the former clause, "save me from this hour," to which the latter stands opposed, obviously expresses His desire for exemption *from* the hour, that is, the period of suffering which, by divine appointment, preceded His death.

We conclude, therefore, that since the words, "save me from this hour," express the desire of Jesus for exemption from the period of suffering, as scheduled in God's great purpose concerning Him, so the instance, "I . . . will keep thee from the hour of . . . [trial]," likewise means that He will exempt the church from the coming period of trial which is to try the earth dwellers.

There are numerous parallel passages teaching this same truth, i.e., the pretribulation rapture of the church, the most convincing and unmistakable being those appearing in Revelation. See Appendix 18, "The Tribulation," page 355.

In this connection, it appears important to make a few remarks regarding the use of the prepositions *ek* and *apo*, the former meaning either "from" or "out of," the latter most generally "from."

The two prepositions are frequently used interchangeably. Scores of examples occur in the New Testament. This interchange is met with most frequently in the parallel accounts of the Gospels.

John uses *ek* more than three times as often as *apo* and more than one half as often as all the rest of the New Testament writers put together.

Whereas *apo* is frequently translated "from," nevertheless *ek*, too, is translated "from" oftener than "out of." Sometimes "out of" would be improper. Anyone taking the pains to examine the uses of *ek* in Revelation will discover that the translation "from" would make good sense throughout, whereas "out of" would in some cases involve an absurdity. [Though it should be acknowledged that the primary sense of *ek* is "out of" as from within, while *apo* is "from" as a starting point; the basal case being involved.—J. O. Y.][15]

Some have argued that if Jesus meant to convey the idea that the church would be immune from the hour of trial, He would have used *apo* instead of *ek*. The contention is that He used *ek* in the sense that He would keep the church out of the hour, meaning He would keep her safe in or during the hour. Now if we apply the same reasoning to the use of *ek* in John 17:15, then the words, "I pray . . . that thou shouldest keep them out of [the evil one]," would really mean safe in the evil one, that is, safe in the devil. Thus the absurdity of such an interpretation at once becomes apparent. Consequently, the only proper translation of *ek* is "from" in this case; hence the translation given in our Bibles is correct, "I . . . will keep thee from the hour."

That *ek* is used in the sense of "from" by other writers is apparent by its use in Acts 15:29: "That ye abstain from meats offered to idols, and from blood, and from things strangled, and from fornication: from [ek] which if ye keep yourselves, ye shall do well." Surely the apostles who sent these words to the Gentile brethren did not mean they will do well if they will keep themselves safe *in* the things mentioned! [The interpretation Smith has sought to refute clearly has ignored the basic meanings of both preposition and case. The ablative case can never mean "in," when it is the case of separation.—J. O. Y.]

11. KINGS AND PRIESTS

[The matter of the reign of the Lord and/or of the saints has occasioned much discussion in the field of eschatology for generations. A careful Biblical study of the whole context of the idea is in order.—J. O. Y.]

Where this reign shall take place is clearly stated in the final clause of the song in Revelation 5:10, ". . . we shall reign on the earth."

Some have erroneously translated "over the earth." The phrase "on the earth" (epi tes ges) occurs 64 times in the New Testament, sixteen of which are found in this book. That the translation "over the earth" is an error can easily be ascertained by trying it out in other passages. For instance, let anyone test it in its first occurrences: Matthew 6:10, 19; 16:19, or in Revelation 3:10; 5:3; 6:10; 7:1; 8:13 of the sixteen occurrences in Revelation and he will readily discover that the suggested change in the rendering is untenable and in some cases absurd.

What is meant is that the sphere of the reign is upon the earth. Even where the word "over" is used in the translation, as in Luke 19:17, 19, it is evident that one individual could not be "over" ten cities at the same time. Assuming that the city foursquare or the house of many mansions is the abode of the glorified during the kingdom age, any glorified saint will be able to do his part in judging the world from his celestial abode, just as well as an earthly monarch can exercise dominion over lands far removed from his terrestrial abode.

From the transfiguration scene (wherein there is really a bird's-eye view of the coming kingdom—see Peter's testimony, II Peter 1:16-18) may be learned that the glorified may appear on earth for a distinct purpose and immediately again disappear. Undoubtedly in some such manner saints will reign upon the earth, exercising authority over ten cities or five cities according to their desert or capacity. Luke 19:17-19.

We may be certain that the testimony of the glorified elders is true. Observe, however, that even though they have been glorified, their reign is still in the future, for they testify not we reign, but we shall reign on the earth. It is significant that the reign of the saints is always spoken of as in the future in previous Scriptures, e.g., "They . . . shall reign in life by one" (Romans 5:17); "If we suffer, we shall . . . reign with him" (II Timothy 2:12). The same is true concerning the ministry of judging, e.g., "Do ye not know that the saints shall judge the world? . . . Know ye not that we shall judge angels" (I Corinthians 6:2, 3)? See also Matthew 19:28 and Luke 22:29, 30.

There is, however, one solitary exception as to the futurity of the reign of saints and that is the claim of certain members of the church at Corinth to the effect that they are reigning now. The apostle, however, meets their stilted arrogance with some of the keenest sarcasm in Holy Writ. He thus expostulates: "Now ye are full, now ye are rich, ye have reigned as kings without us: and I would to God ye did reign, that we also might reign with you. . . . We [the apostles] are made a spectacle unto the world, and to angels, and to men. We are fools for Christ's sake, but ye are wise in Christ; we are weak, but ye are strong; ye are honourable, but we are despised" (I Corinthians 4:8-10). On this retort of Paul, the Bible Commentary pointedly remarks: "Again the apostle fulminates in irony: peal upon peal of cathartic sarcasm. 'Already sated are ye! Already grown rich! Apart from us ye attained kingship!' We apostles did think that the Messianic fullness of joy and endowment of the inheritance and enthronement of the saints all belonged to another aeon: but your tumid assertions transcend our sober instructions!"[16] Anyone who thinks he is reigning now should meditate upon these words of the apostle.

It will be observed that these comments are based on the Authorized Version of Revelation 5:9, 10. The Revised Version reads quite differently as the following quotation will show: "Worthy art thou to take the book, and to open the seals thereof: for thou wast slain, and didst purchase unto God with thy blood men of every tribe, and tongue, and people, and nation, and madest them to be unto our God a kingdom and priests; and they reign upon the earth." It must be admitted (although it is not generally known) that the reading of the Revised Version of this passage has given occasion for acceptance by honest and conscientious Bible students of the view that the rapture of the church will not take place before, but either in the middle or at the close of the tribulation period. Possibly the strongest opponent of the pre-tribulation rapture view is Alexander Reese in his *The Approaching Advent of Christ*. He, however, stakes his whole contention ön the reading of the Revised Version of verses 9, 10, as his own words abundantly testify, for he says, "That the opinion should arise that the twenty-four elders represent the saints risen and raptured, is natural enough in view of the ancient readings of Revelation 5:9, 10. For there we read the following song of the elders: 'Thou art worthy to take the book, and to open the seals thereof: for thou wast slain, and hast redeemed *us* to God by thy blood out of every kindred, and tongue, and people, and nation;·and hast made *us* unto our God kings and priests: and *we* shall reign on the earth' " (italics his). On this he remarks: "Certainly these words seem conclusive that here we have the *redeemed*" (italics ours). He continues, "All this, however, is changed now. Both the Revised Version and American Revised Version and every independent translation that has since appeared, have radically altered the reading and translation. The Revised Version bids us read the song of the elders thus: 'They sing a new song, saying, Worthy art thou to take the book, and to open the seals thereof: for thou wast slain, and didst purchase unto God with thy blood men of every tribe, and tongue, and people, and nation, and madest them to be unto our God a kingdom and priests; and they reign upon the earth.' " He then remarks: "It is scarcely necessary to point out how the new translation has swept away completely whatever basis existed for making these twenty-four elders symbols of the heavenly redeemed. . . ."[17] It is unsafe to stake one's view on a single passage as does Dr. Reese when he admits that if the "old reading" were correct, "certainly these words seem conclusive that here we have the redeemed," for even if the new reading were correct, it would not disprove or even contradict the numerous other passages which show that the rapture occurs before the tribulation. Before doing so, an examination of the facts as to the correctness of the reading, the Authorized or the Revised Version, is in order.

The Text.

"The former reading ['Thou . . . hast redeemed us'] is attested by the (Sinaitic), (Vatican) [i.e., uncials], most of the cursives, the Vulgate, the Syriac, Memphitic, and Armenian versions, Hippolytus, Cyprian, Augustine, Fulgentius, Andreas, Haymo, Arethas, Primasius, and others. In some of these, however, τῷ θεῷ [to God] follows ἡμᾶς [us] instead of preceding it, while in others it is altogether wanting. This is simply due to the fact that τῷ θεῷ [to God] was omitted by one of the ancient scribes in copying, as several documents still attest, and that in restoring it to the text it was misplaced—having been inserted after instead of before ἡμᾶς [us]. This, however, does not militate in the least against the genuineness of ἡμᾶς [us]. The Revisers reading . . . is attested to only by A and the Ethiopic Version. . . . That 'us' is a proper reading is seen in the fact that the song in which it occurs was shared by 'the four-and-twenty elders,' who represent redeemed and glorified saints. . . ."[18]

"But in verse 9, ἡμᾶς [us] should certainly be read. There was an opinion, many years ago, that it rested on but slight authority. This arose through an error in a reprint of Griesbach's text; so that he was supposed to have excluded it. On this misprint interpretations were based. Now of all collated MSS. the *Codex Alexandrinus* alone omits ἡμᾶς [us]. . . ."[19]

What about the fact of the omission of *us* by A only? "Who hast redeemed us?" The Alexandrian manuscript drops the word between two columns. Nevertheless, Feihendorf, Westcott and Hort, and the Revisers follow suit with this authority only. No cursive, not Aleph (the Sinaiticus), the Vaticanus, no versions but the Ethiopic which is unreliable in such matters. Hoskier calls the omission of *us* in verse 9, "that huge blunder."[20]

Out of a total of some three hundred authorities on the text of Revelation 5:9, only one—the Alexandrian manuscript in custody at the British Museum—lends any occasion for the omission of *us* in verse 9. It is true that the Ethiopic Version does not contain the word, but this text is so corrupt or has such a loose paraphrase at this place that its text is worthless in such a matter. It would appear therefore that the chances that the Westcott-Hort Greek text is right in omitting *us* are as one is to three hundred. Of course no court of justice would decide favorably for its exclusion on such meager evidence. Yet this is exactly what Westcott and Hort have done. One cannot account for this irregularity unless the authors were blindly prejudiced in favor of the text which happened to be in the custody of their own native land.

Dr. Tregelles, also a member of the Revision Committee and next to Dr. Scrivener probably the most accomplished textual scholar on the committee, stoutly opposed the omission of *us* in his subsequent writings.

As is well known, however, the Revisers followed suit with the Westcott-Hort text by omitting *us*, and since the verb "redeemed" called for an object, they supplied the word "men," i.e., "and hast redeemed men out of every nation, etc."

It remained for Dr. Hoskier to give the deathblow to such a procedure. He is qualified to speak with authority on the matter, for he is the first man to collate all the authorities on the text of Revelation—both uncial and cursive manuscripts, church fathers, all existing versions, ancient commentaries, *et al.* His own testimony is, after he discovered that the Alexandrian manuscript stood alone, he determined to re-examine the original document in order to ascertain the exact state of the text in this place, when to his surprise he observed that the omission occurred between two columns. It is well known that in such cases omissions occur most frequently. No wonder therefore he refers to it as "that huge blunder." It is hoped the omission occurred inadvertently and not intentionally or on doctrinal grounds. The omission, however, was most unfortunate, for it gave men like Dr. Reese occasion to oppose the view that the elders represent the redeemed of the church in the glorified state before the opening of the seals, and hence before the tribulation begins. Chapter 6 ff. It is to be hoped that Dr. Reese informed himself of the correctness of the reading, "Thou . . . hast redeemed us," and if such is the case, that he testified from the heart that "Certainly these words [as in Authorized Version] seem conclusive that here we have the redeemed."[21]

The Commentators.

"Some critics and expositors have rejected ἡμᾶς (us), for the reason that it is omitted in the Codex Alexandrinus, and in the Ethiopic version; though the latter is not much more than a loose paraphrase. The Codex Sinaiticus, however, which was discovered in 1860, and which is of equal antiquity and authority with the Codex Alexandrinus, contains it. The Codex Basilianus, in the Vatican, contains it. The Latin, Coptic or Memphitic, and Armenian, which are of great value, contain it. And so do *all other mss. and versions.* And to discredit it, simply and only because it does not appear in that one single Codex of Alexandria, is most unreasonable and unjust to the weight of authority for its retention. Dr. Tregelles, on full examination, was firmly convinced of its right to a place in the text, before the Codex Sinaiticus appeared; and the presence of this ἡμᾶς in that ms. ought to settle the question of its genuineness forever. The evidences from the context, also argue powerfully for a construction which necessarily embraces it, whether expressed or not. We regard it as indubitably genuine."[22]

Dr. Kuyper, the great Dutch commentator, in commenting on the context of the "new song" attributes it to the elders, which would lend weight to the retaining of the first person pronoun.[23]

Note also Dr. Robert Cameron who, for many years, was the editorial mouthpiece through the "Watchword and Truth" of the mid and post tribulation rapture theory. His right-hand man in the support of this view was Dr. W. J. Erdman. Like Dr. Reese, Dr. Erdman made a statement to the effect that "if the reading of the received text was correct, the pre-tribulation view would rest on a firm foundation"; but basing his view on the recently published Revised Version, with its perverted rendering of 5:9, 10, he (like Reese) declared all this is changed now. However, Dr. Cameron learned of the fallacy of the Revised rendering, and he (be it said to his everlasting credit) had the grace and courage (before he laid down his pen) to reverse his opinion of this crucial text. His words are: "It is evident that the church is represented by elders and living creatures, for they sing, 'Thou hast redeemed us unto God by Thy blood.'" In a footnote he adds: "Since the discovery of the Sinaitic manuscript, there can be no doubt that 'us' is the correct reading. The preponderance of evidence is overwhelming in favor of its retention."[24]

The Church Fathers.

Hippolytus, 170-236—a disciple of Irenaeus, Irenaeus of Polycarp, Polycarp of John, the writer of Revelation. "And they sing a new song, saying, Thou art worthy to take the book, and to open the seals thereof: for thou wast slain, and hast redeemed us to God by thy blood."[25]

Cyprian, 200-258—"And they sang a new song, saying, Worthy art Thou, O Lord, to take the book, and to open its seals: for Thou wast slain, and hast redeemed us with Thy blood from every tribe, and tongue, and people, and nation; and Thou hast made us a kingdom unto our God, and hast made us priests and they shall reign upon the earth."[26]

Augustine, 354-430—"Thou art worthy to take the book, and to open the seals thereof: for Thou wast slain, and hast redeemed us to God by Thy blood out of every kindred, and tongue, and people, and nation."[27]

It will be observed that the only church fathers which quote this verse have "us" in their text. It is noteworthy that Augustine quotes *us*, for he lived after the days of Constantine, showing that the word remained in the text after at least two of the uncial manuscripts (the Vatican and Sinaitic), if not the Alexandrian likewise, had been copied.

It will be observed that both Hippolytus and Augustine do not quote the latter portion of the verse in full. This may be accounted for by the fact that the text had been tampered with in some quarters. This indeed had been the case with many portions of Scripture as several church fathers themselves declare. To this the great scholar and member of the Revision Committee, Dr. Scrivener, bears striking testimony: "It is no less true to fact than paradoxical in sound, that the worst corruptions to which the New Testament has ever been subjected, originated within one hundred years after it was composed; that Irenaeus [A.D. 150] and the African Fathers and the whole Western world with a portion of the Syrian Church, used far inferior manuscripts to those employed by Stunica, or Erasmus, or Stephanus, thirteen centuries later when moulding the Textus Receptus [Authorized Version]."[28]

The fear of persecution may account for the omission or change of the phrase, "we shall reign upon the earth," in the quotations of the first two fathers. On the other hand, Augustine may have omitted the phrase intentionally, for, according to his view, the reign of saints had already begun with the reign of Constantine.

The Testimony of Versions.

The Latin Vulgate, Fourth Century:
"And they were singing a new song, saying: Worthy art Thou, O Lord, to take the book and to loose the seals thereof, because Thou wast slain and hast redeemed us with Thy blood out of every tribe, and language, and people, and nation, and hast made us to our God a kingdom and priests, and we shall reign over the earth."

The Armenian (English by Fred. C. Conybeare), Fifth Century:
"And they were hymning a hymn new and saying, Worthy is the Lamb to take the book and to open the seals thereof, because Thou wast slain and hast bought us unto adoption with Thy blood out of all tribes, and tongues, and peoples, and Gentiles, and hast made us priests of our God, and we shall reign upon the earth." (See Hoskier's remark on this.)

Oecumenius, Seventh Century:
"And they sing a new song, saying, Worthy art Thou to take the book and open the seals thereof, because Thou wast slain and didst purchase us to God with Thy blood, from every tribe, and tongue, and people, and nation, and didst make them kings and priests unto our God, and they shall reign upon the earth."

Beatus, Eighth Century (in Pierpont Library, New York):
"Thou art worthy to take the book and to open the seals thereof, because Thou wast slain and hast redeemed us to God with Thy blood out of every tribe, and people, and language, and nation, and Thou hast made us to God a kingdom and priests, and we shall reign on the earth."

Coptic Version (in Pierpont Library, New York):
"And they sang a new song, saying, Thou art worthy to take the book and to open its seals: because Thou wast slain and Thou boughtest us for our God with Thy blood out of every tribe, and language, and people, and nation. Thou madest us a kingdom for our God and priests, and they will reign over the earth."

Beza, Sixteenth Century:
"And they sing a new song, saying, Worthy Thou art who dost take the book and dost open its seals, because Thou wast slain and didst redeem us to God through Thy blood from every tribe, and language, and people, and nation, and madest us kings and priests, and we shall reign over the earth."[29]

Following is the reading of Tischendorf's seventh edition of his Greek text published in 1859, previous to his discovery of the Sinaitic manuscript. The changed form appeared in his eighth edition published in 1872.

"And they sing a new song, saying, Worthy art Thou to take the book and to open the seals thereof, for Thou wast slain and hast redeemed us to God with Thy blood out of every kindred, and tongue, and people, and nation, and hast made us unto our God, kings and priests, and we shall reign upon the earth."

The text as it appears in his eighth edition published in 1872:
"And they sing a new song, saying: Worthy art Thou to take the book and to open the seals thereof, because Thou wast slain and hast redeemed to God with Thy blood out of every kindred, and tongue, and people, and nation, and hast made them to our God a kingdom and priests, and they shall reign upon the earth."

It will be observed that the former text of Tischendorf agrees exactly with the Authorized Version. The eighth edition is similar to that of the Alexandrian manuscript in that it omits *us* in verse 9, and puts the last two verbs into the third person. What Hoskier said of the Alexandrian text applies therefore equally to Tischendorf's eighth edition, so that we may say: The Armenian Version has *we shall reign*. This shows conclusively that Tischendorf's eighth edition is in error in verse 9 by omitting *us*. (The point apparently is that with Armenia being so far distant, there could have been no possibility of collusion.)

It may appear strange that Tischendorf should have departed from the reading of his own favorite text and adopted the reading of the Alexandrian manuscript at this place. However, this is but one of the 3,572 places in which Tischendorf departed from his previous edition. Concerning this vacillatory spirit of Tischendorf, Dr. Ellicott in his brochure on the "Revision" has pointedly remarked: "Which of this most inconstant critic's texts are we to select?" Surely not the last, in which an exaggerated preference for a single manuscript which he had the good fortune to discover has betrayed him into an almost childish infirmity of critical judgment."[30] Tischendorf was persuaded that the Sinaitic and the Vatican had a like ancestry, and besides he persuaded the scholar, Dr. Hort, the father not only of the Westcott-Hort edition but of the Revised Version as well, that the two uncials issued from the same workshop. It is claimed by Tischendorf and supported by Scrivener "that the scribe who wrote the latter [i.e., Vaticanus] is one of the four [D] to whose diligence we owe the former [Sinaiticus]."[31] And if it be asked, When and where did they come into existence? the evidence points to the time when Constantine called for fifty copies of the Sacred Scriptures, and the place was probably Alexandria, in Egypt. And since the Alexandrian manuscript had its origin there, the three uncials probably alike had their birth in the same "workshop." One of the rules of the Revisers was that when two of these manuscripts agreed, it was considered "as a strong presumptive evidence for the genuineness of a reading." It is now known that the agreements consisted frequently in the like corruptions of the text.

A word should be said about the Latin text by Beza. It follows the text preserved by the Waldenses which was based on the early Itala (as opposed to the Manuscripts A and B of the Vatican-Alexandrian) School. And finding its way early to the hills of the Vallenses, it escaped the corruptions of Rome and her allies in the north of Africa. This text found its way farther north and was the basis of Beza's text and that of Luther. It is said that "Beza was undoubtedly the best exegetical scholar on the Continent at the time the Authorized Version was made, and his influence upon it was, upon the whole, very beneficial."[32]

12. The Glorified Groups of the Tribulation

A right view of the varied glorified groups of the tribulation period goes a long way toward the proper understanding of this confessedly difficult portion of Scripture in order that the reader may have this benefit clearly before him it appears justifiable to assemble some of the information on the subject. There is surely some evidence that the great multitude clothed with white robes (7:9, 14) are identical with (or at least include) the souls slain for the Word of God in 6:9-11.

Chapter 7 consists of two episodes: the former, the sealing of the 144,000; the latter, of the white-robed multitude. The former has a prospective implication, for it points forward (verses 1-3) to the trumpet judgments described in the following two chapters (cf. 8:7-11; 9:4); the latter is retrospective and presumably points back to the slain under the seal judgments of chapter 6 and more particularly to the fifth seal where a toll is taken of the faithful souls slain for the Word of God. Here then may be an illustration of what has been called the law of recurrence in which, after making a brief statement of a fact, the same is referred to again for the sake of adding details.

Observe that those in chapter 6 were slain for (lit., because of) the Word of God and for (because of) the testimony which they held, whereas of the great multitude it is said that they came out of the great tribulation.

Tribulation as used in connection with God's people always implies martyrdom because of adherence to the faith. (Compare "ye shall have tribulation ten days: be thou faithful unto death"—2:10.)

Observe that *white robes* were given unto those slain for the Word of God.

If *white robes* are the special reward of martyrs of this period slain for the purpose stated, the white-robed multitude would likewise consist of martyrs for the same purpose and hence include those of chapter 6.

But what appears to establish this identity beyond question is the fact that nowhere else in all the Scriptures do we read of a group clothed in white robes. This statement moreover is based upon the original Scriptures. We have the mention of "white raiment" in connection with the church group (cf. chapter 3:5 and 4:4), but the original word for raiment is *himation* while the word for robe is *stole*. The former is the ordinary word for garment, while the latter denotes a long flowing robe reaching down to the foot.

It may be a matter of interest that the only case in Scripture where an individual is mentioned as wearing a white robe is where an angel appeared at the grave of our Lord. Mark 16:5.

Passing now to later passages note chapters 14 and 15. Here is a third group slain because they refused to take the mark of the beast and hence they got "the victory" over him. 15:2. Like the elders, they harp with their harps, but there is neither mention of white raiment nor of harps.

Observe in the next place that in 20:4 we have a summary statement of the glorified groups and that there three and only three groups are mentioned:

And I saw thrones, and they sat upon them, and judgment was given unto them. This constitutes the elders or church group seen in chapters 4 and 5.

And I saw the souls of them that were beheaded for the witness [i.e., testimony] *of Jesus, and for the word of God.* This is the group mentioned in chapters 6 and 7. (Note 6:9.)

And which had not worshipped the beast, neither his image, neither had received his mark upon their foreheads, or in their hands. This is the group mentioned in chapters 14 and 15. (Note 15:2.) For convenience let us think of the first group as the throne sitters; the second as the robe wearers; the third as the conscientious objectors of the tribulation period because they refused to take the mark of the beast.

Of these three groups it is said, *They lived and reigned with Christ a thousand years.* And again, *This is the first resurrection.* It would appear therefore as an established fact that there are three and only three glorified groups in heaven during the tribulation. It is up to the careful interpreter to try to place the various redeemed ones of these chapters into one or the other of these three groups.

13. THE HOLY CITY

The Choice.

Just previous to his departure, Moses, the servant of God, spoke by way of prediction of the place the Lord God would choose to put His name. He repeated the statement at least 21 times, not only for their encouragement but also to arouse their interest. All but one of these passages (Deuteronomy 31:11) are found in his great address. Deuteronomy 12—26.

In the historical books (principally I Kings and II Chronicles) mention is made of a city, and its name given. The earliest mention is by Solomon in his sermon of dedication. II Chronicles 6:6—"I have chosen Jerusalem, that my name might be there." The word "city" occurs 20 times in these two books and "Jerusalem" ten times. House (referring to the temple) occurs no less than 45 times. A characteristic passage is I Kings 8:44—"The city which thou hast chosen, and . . . the house that I [Solomon] have built."

The Purpose.

This is clearly stated in the phrase, "to put his name there." It occurs nine times in Deuteronomy. The same term and those of similar significance, as "for my name," "unto my name," occur as often as 70 times, referring either to the house (temple) or to the city.

Realization.

Both the choice and the purpose of God are realized when "the house of the Lord was finished." As to the choice, observe that in the two passages just quoted it is no longer "the place I will choose," as in the Deuteronomy passages, but "I have chosen Jerusalem," "the city which thou hast chosen." Both of these testimonies of the Lord occur in the sermon and prayer of dedication of Solomon which followed immediately after the completion of the temple.

That the purpose of God was realized is seen in the *name* of the house—it is called the house of the Lord and the house of God (II Chronicles 5:14); and in the divine manifestation twice repeated—after the placing of the ark into the most holy, and after the prayer of dedication. In each case "the glory of the Lord filled the house [of the Lord]." The psalmist speaks of the house of the Lord as the dwelling place of Thy name. Psalm 74:7.

The Sanctification.

After the dedication the Lord appeared unto Solomon saying, "Now have I chosen and sanctified this house, that my name may be there for ever: and mine eyes and mine heart shall be there perpetually" (II Chronicles 7:16; cf. I Kings 9:3). Sanctifying the house made it a holy place, and Jerusalem was a holy city because in it was the house which the Lord had sanctified. Isaiah and Jeremiah each speak of the city (Zion and Jerusalem) as being the place of the name of the Lord. Isaiah 18:7; 60:9; Jeremiah 3:17.

The Separation.

In his dedicatory prayer, Solomon anticipated the sin and consequent dispersion of Israel. I Kings 8:46, 47; II Chron. 6:36. Jeremiah in six passages tells of the defilement and desolation not only of the house "which is called by my name" (7:10, 11, 14, 30; 25:29; 32:34; 34:15) but of the city and the land as well. A characteristic passage says: "Then will I cause to cease from the cities of Judah, and from the streets of Jerusalem, the voice of mirth, and the voice of gladness, the voice of the bridegroom, and the voice of the bride: for the land shall be desolate" (Jeremiah 7:34). This state of desolation of the house, the city, and the land continues during the entire tribulation period, for the treading underfoot is to continue for 42 months. Revelation 11:2. Let us keep in mind in this connection that the name of the "holy city" is applied to Jerusalem during this time of desolation save only the two passages referring to the new Jerusalem yet to come.

The Restoration.

This likewise is anticipated in the prayer of Solomon, for he intercedes in behalf of Israel that God would hear and forgive them, deliver them from their captors, and restore them to their inheritance. I Kings 8:47, 49, 50. This accords with Peter's sermon (Acts 3:19-21) in addressing the men of Israel where he declares that the times of restitution (Greek: *restoration*) are conditioned upon the repentance and conversion of Israel.

That they will repent is declared in numerous passages of Scripture, but we will confine our remarks to three which make mention of "the name of the Lord."

"Surely the isles shall wait for me . . . to bring thy sons from far, their silver and their gold with them, unto the name of the Lord thy God, and to the Holy One of Israel, because he hath glorified thee" (Isaiah 60:9). This is spoken concerning those who turn from transgression in Jacob. "To bring thy sons from far" alludes to the regathering of Israel from many lands. And instead of saying unto Zion or Jerusalem, it says, "unto the name of the Lord thy God."

"At that time they shall call Jerusalem the throne of the Lord; and all the nations shall be gathered unto it, to the name of the Lord, to Jerusalem: neither shall they walk any more after the imagination of their evil heart" (Jeremiah 3:17).

Here the name of the Lord is given as the equivalent of Jerusalem.

The passage is just preceded with the appeal, "Return, thou backsliding Israel" (Jeremiah 3:12, 14).

Their regathering is implied, for they shall multiply and increase in the land (verse 16), and no more backslide (verse 17).

". . . the place of my throne, and the place of the soles of my feet, where I will dwell in the midst of the children of Israel for ever, and my holy name, shall the house of Israel no more defile . . ." (Ezekiel 43:7).

(1) The place of my throne is Jerusalem. (See preceding passage, Jeremiah 3:17 just considered.)

(2) The Lord's feet will then be in Jerusalem.

(3) He will dwell in the midst of Israel forever.

(4) My holy name (i.e., Jerusalem), the house of Israel shall no more defile.

The writer cannot comprehend how anyone who believes all the prophets have said can fail to understand that there must be a regathering and conversion of Israel and a return to their own land, nor how these Scriptures by a stretch of the imagination are fulfilled in the church.

The Consummation.

We have just observed that the glory of the Lord filled the house of the Lord in the days of Solomon. The prophet Ezekiel tells of the departure of the glory of the Lord from the temple because of Israel's sin and apostasy. 9:3; 10:4, 18; 11:22, 23. Now in Ezekiel 43:2, 4, 5 the glory of the Lord comes back by way of the east and fills the house and the earth shines with His glory.

After reciting the division of the land among the original twelve tribes of Israel (of which we have spoken elsewhere) the book closes with the significant statement: "The name of the city from that day shall be, The Lord is there." Nine passages in Deuteronomy already noticed end with the phrase, *to put his name there.* Twenty-five passages in all contain the words, *his name there.* The same words occur in the last sentence of Ezekiel, only instead of *his* occurs the noun to which it refers, viz., Lord, while the word for *there* occurs in a lengthened or demonstrative form, viz., *shammah.* This strengthened form appears for emphasis: the Lord's there, that is, where all these verses have declared He would be. The statement in the Hebrew is, *Jehovah Shammah.* [It may be added, where the Lord is is a holy place. Thus Jerusalem is indeed The Holy City.—J. O. Y.]

14. The Two Witnesses

Much discussion has surrounded the identity of those two witnesses. In reference to Elijah several passages of Scripture declare definitely that he is yet to come. Since there is some misunderstanding on this point, all the passages involved in the order of their occurrence will be quoted:

"Behold, I will send you Elijah the prophet before the coming of the great and dreadful day of the Lord" (Malachi 4:5).

"He [John the Baptist] shall go before him [Jesus] in the spirit and power of Elias" (Luke 1:17).

"And they [of the Pharisees] asked him [John the Baptist] . . . Art thou Elias? And he saith, I am not" (John 1:21).

"And if ye will receive it, this is Elias, which was for to come [Greek: which is to come]" (Matthew 11:14).

"And his disciples asked him, saying, Why then say the scribes that Elias must first come? And Jesus answered and said unto them, Elias truly shall first-come, and restore all things. But I say unto you, That Elias is come already, and they knew him not, but have done unto him whatsoever they listed" (Matthew 17:10-12; cf. Mark 9:11, 12).

With these passages now before us, let us deduce the conclusions in accordance with the import of the language employed. We will consider them in the order of their occurrence.

The coming of Elijah will be before the coming of the great and dreadful day of the Lord. The same day is described in Joel 2:31 as the great and terrible day of the Lord and quoted in Acts 2:20 with the translation, that great and notable day of the Lord. However, dreadful, terrible, and notable are all from the same Greek word; so there can be no mistaking of the identity of the passages. In Matthew 24:29 we read, "Immediately after the tribulation of those days shall the sun be darkened, and the moon shall not give her light, and the stars shall fall from heaven . . ." thus showing that the great and dreadful day of the Lord will come "immediately after the tribulation of those days." Since Elijah comes before the great and dreadful day of the Lord, he must be on earth sometime during the tribulation period.

In the second passage we observe some similarity between John the Baptist and Elijah. He was to go before Jesus in the spirit and power of Elijah. He would turn the hearts of the fathers to the children. (However, there is a notable omission of the clause in the prophecy concerning Elijah and the heart of the children to the fathers. Malachi 4:6.) Moreover, if John the Baptist were identical with Elijah, the sentence would mean, Elijah will go before Him in the spirit and power of Elijah, thus reducing the sentence to an absurdity.

In answer to the question, Art thou Elias? John replies with a direct negation: I am not. Neither was there a mistake in naming him, for the angel Gabriel had told Elisabeth, "Thou shalt call his name John." And when others called him Zacharias after the name of the father, the mother answered emphatically, "Not so; but he shall be called John" (Luke 1:60). And as to his father, no sooner had he written, "His name is John," than his mouth was opened and his tongue loosed and he spoke and glorified God. Luke 1:63, 64. With all this performance about his name, John knew very well that he was not Elijah.

The fourth passage appears to support the view still persistently held by some that John was the predicted Elijah. However, the translation (upon which the error is based) is faulty and is correctly rendered: "this is Elijah, that is to come" (Revised Version), or "that will come" (Luther). Jesus therefore plainly declares that the coming of Elijah is still future; hence John could be referred to as Elijah only in a metaphoric sense. He was Elijah in the sense that he came in the spirit and power of Elijah and that his ministry was similar to that of Elijah who is yet to come, for both prepare the way of the Lord by preaching repentance.

In the last passage two important points call for careful consideration:

The question of the disciples, "Why then say the scribes that Elias must first come?"

It will be noticed that the disciples asked the question immediately after the transfiguration. In order to comprehend the significance of their question it must be recognized that the transfiguration was really a bird's-eye view of exhibition in miniature of the coming kingdom. According to Mark's account, Peter, James, and John at that time saw the kingdom of God come with power. Mark 9:1, 2. Peter in his second epistle refers to the occasion as the "power and coming of our Lord Jesus Christ and declares he was one of the "eyewitnesses of his majesty" when he was with Him in the holy mountain. II Peter 1:16, 17. It was because they "thought that the kingdom of God should immediately appear" (cf. Luke

19:11) that they came to Jesus with the question, "Why then say the scribes that Elias must first come?" Especially note that Jesus says Elijah indeed comes and restores *all* things after *John had been put to death* (cf. Matthew 17:10-13; Mark 9:12, 13) so that John could not fulfil the prophecies about Elijah. It is also clear that according to the record of both Mark (6:14, 15) and Luke (9:7-9), John the Baptist and Elijah are not identical because they are clearly distinguished in these passages; note also the adversative "but." Jesus in His reply endorses the view of the scribes on this point in an emphatic manner: "Elias truly shall first come [that is, before the kingdom comes], and restore all things."

The second question is, What is intended by the words, "shall . . . restore all things"? A few passages from the Book of Acts apparently make the point clear. After His resurrection, Jesus again spoke to His apostles "of the things pertaining to the kingdom of God" (Acts 1:3). "When they [the apostles] therefore were come together, they asked of him, saying, Lord, wilt thou at this time restore again the kingdom to Israel?" His answer was, "It is not for you to know the times or the seasons, which the Father hath put in his own power" (Acts 1:6, 7). Just previous to His triumphal entry, Jesus found it necessary to speak a parable to His disciples because they thought the kingdom of God should immediately appear. Luke 19:11-27. In this parable, Jesus plainly taught them that He would first depart into a far country to receive for Himself a kingdom and then, having received the kingdom, He would return to reward His servants (verses 16-26) and to destroy His enemies (verse 27).

Jesus having left them (in His death) and having returned (at His resurrection), the disciples apparently assumed the probability that the time for the restoration of all things had now come, hence their question, "Wilt thou at this time restore again the kingdom to Israel?"

The answer to our question, however, does not come until after the day of Pentecost. Peter, one of the Twelve, now under the inspiration of the Holy Spirit, addresses the "men of Israel" (Acts 3:12) in these most significant words: "Repent ye therefore, and be converted, that your sins may be blotted out, when [Greek: in order that] the times of refreshing shall [may] come from the presence of the Lord; and he shall [might] send Jesus Christ, which before was preached unto you: whom the heaven must receive until the times of restitution [restoration] of all things . . ." (Acts 3:19-21). Observe in this passage:

a. The word *restitution* is correctly translated *restoration* in the Revised Version, and is the noun form of the word *restore*, occurring in the passages cited above. Matthew 17:11; Mark 9:12.

b. The repentance of Israel is the condition upon which their own sins are blotted out; only then will the seasons of refreshing come from the presence of the Lord, only then will Jesus Christ return, and, finally, only then will all things be restored. In other words, only through the repentance of Israel will the way be open for the full and final blessing upon all men and all things.

The notion that Enoch is one of the witnesses is found in several apocryphal books and apparently was borrowed from them by a few of the church fathers. On the other hand, Victorinus, the first commentator of Revelation, remarks that many believe that Elisha or Moses was with Elijah. Since Victorinus makes no mention whatever of anyone holding the view that Enoch is one of the witnesses, it appears that this view had been abandoned at the time of his writing (near the close of the third century). It is important to observe that Victorinus bears a testimony which has far greater weight than a personal opinion.

A few remarks should be made concerning the opinion held by certain writers. The chief argument, and what might appear a plausible one, is based on the assertion of Scripture, "it is appointed unto men once to die" (Hebrews 9:27). In respect to Enoch, emphasis is placed on the word *die*, i.e., it is appointed unto men once to *die*. Enoch did not die; so he, it is claimed (like Elijah), must yet reappear and die in order to sustain the declaration of this Scripture.

In respect to Moses, emphasis is placed on the word *once*, i.e., it is appointed unto men *once* to die. Moses has died once in the past. Were he to *appear* and die, it would violate the statement of this Scripture, for then he would die *twice*. Before replying to each point separately, observe that the passage of Scripture consists of a general statement. It is almost an axiom that "there are exceptions to all rules" and this is indeed the case in this instance, as will appear from the following particulars:

Regarding the contention for Enoch, the Scripture plainly declares that those who are alive and remain unto the coming of the Lord will *not* die. On the other hand, they will be changed "in a moment, in the twinkling of an eye" and be caught up together with the dead in Christ "to meet the Lord in the air." I Thessalonians 4:15-17; I Corinthians 15:51, 52. It is noteworthy that the same chapter (I Corinthians 15) which declares "in Adam all die," also contains the statement, "We shall not all [the living] sleep, but we shall all be changed." All believers, therefore, who are alive when Jesus comes will never die. One of the great sayings of Jesus apparently finds its fulfillment on this occasion: "I am the resurrection, and the life: he that believeth in me, though he were dead [Greek: die] yet shall he live: and whosoever liveth and believeth in me shall never die" (John 11:25, 26). That is to say, Jesus will be the resurrection to those who will have died when He comes, and the life to those then living, for they will never die. Observe, too, the relevant passage in Hebrews 11:5: "By faith Enoch was translated that he should not see death." Since faith comes by hearing the Word of God, it appears that God had informed him "before his translation" that he should not die. Enoch received this information "by faith"; so God "took him" and he did not see death. Observe, too, that this statement regarding Enoch was made over 3,000 years after his translation. Since "the gifts and calling of God are without repentance," we should not suspect a reversal of God's declaration respecting Enoch in the future. We conclude, therefore, that Enoch will not see death and thus will continue forever a true type of the believer who will be alive when Jesus comes and will never die. It should yet be stated, if Enoch were intended as the second witness, we should suspect earmarks pointing to him as in the case of Elijah. Why should the divine author attach the earmarks, turning water into blood and smiting the earth with plagues (which can only refer to Moses), and then intend that we are to believe He means Enoch? To speak bluntly, God does not do that way. If He meant Enoch, He would doubtless have used such earmarks as "These walk with God" and "Before their translation they had this testimony, that they pleased God." But there is not one syllable that points to Enoch and the only way is to take the hints given seriously and unhesitatingly accept them as pointing to Moses.

Coming now to the objection to Moses' being one of the witnesses on the ground that it is appointed unto men only *once* to die, we remark:

The force of this objection disappears when it is remembered that all the individuals raised from the dead in Old and New Testament times have died the second time. If God could and did make exceptions to the rule "once to die" in the past, He may consistently do so in the future.

Evidently, Moses' body did not return to dust "by Nebo's lonely mountain," for we read in Jude 9 that Michael contended with the devil, "the prince of the power of the air," concerning it. We are told (in extra-Biblical literature) that to Michael was given the custody of the body of Moses and that he escorted it to heaven. If this is the case, the contention probably took place when Michael undertook to convey it through the region of the air over which Satan is the prince. Later we find Moses and Elijah appearing with Christ on the Mount of Transfiguration, not as spirits merely, but like Him, in glorified bodies, else how could they have been recognized and distinguished by the apostles? And since

Elijah is coming again (as most agree) in bodily form, in all probability Moses, his companion in glory, will appear again also and in like form. Let the reader now turn to Revelation 11:5, 6 and observe again the earmarks placed there by the unerring hand of divine inspiration for the express purpose of revealing truth to the honest seeker. If this is done in faith, believing the things that are written, it can lead to but one conclusion, namely, that the first two, consuming enemies by fire and shutting up heaven that it rain not, point clearly to Elijah and the second two, turning water into blood and smiting the earth with plagues, point unmistakably to Moses.

15. THE MAN CHILD

Comments and remarks on relevant passages in respect to the woman mentioned in Revelation 12:2, 5 are apropos:

Verse 2—"And she being with child cried, travailing in birth, and pained to be delivered."

Verse 5—"And she brought forth a man child, who was to rule all nations with a rod of iron: and her child was caught up unto God, and to his throne."

The former passage is prospective and looks forward to Israel during the tribulation period, which is in particular "the time of Jacob's trouble" (Jeremiah 30:7), during which she will pass under the rod of affliction, resulting in her repentance and restoration. Her sufferings are the birth pangs incident to her repentance and conversion and allude to the spiritual children which she is about to bring forth.

The latter passage is retrospective and harks back to the birth of Christ and His ascension. This backward look occurs here apparently for the purpose of preparing the reader for the further revelation now to be made concerning the woman, including the renewal and culmination of Satan's avowed purpose to destroy her. Verse 4b.

Let us now carefully note certain Scripture passages shedding important light upon the foregoing verses. The testimony to the view above expressed, that the first passage pertains to the "affliction" of Israel during the great tribulation, and the second to the birth of Jesus the man-child in the days of Herod the king, is, as we shall see, both cumulative and conclusive.

Since the original words for *travail* (birth pangs) and *bring forth* are not always translated by the same English words, it will be a benefit to the reader if we render them by the same English word in each case.

Isaiah 66:7—"Before she travailed, she brought forth; before her pain came, she was delivered of a man child [Hebrew: male]." Observe the bringing forth, that is, the birth of the man-child precedes the travail or birth pangs.

The original word for man-child is male and is the same (both in the Hebrew and Greek) as that occurring in Genesis 1:27, in the clause, "male and female created he them."

The word translated *before* in its 56 occurrences always denotes anteriority and the precedence in time and may be a long period. (Compare Psalm 90:2; Isaiah 42:9; 48:5.) Such is the case in the present instance, for (as we shall see further) while the man-child was born at the beginning of the Christian era, the travail of Israel will not begin until the time of Jacob's trouble, that is, in the coming period of tribulation.

The passage in our chapter as noted above (verse 5) has two words in the original for man-child, viz., a *son*, a *male*, while in the verse we are considering in Isaiah only one "male" occurs. Note, however, that the prophet Isaiah, in two previous passages (7:14; 9:6), designates the child born, "son." The occurrence of the two words together in one verse incidentally proves their identity—the son of chapters 7 and 9 in Isaiah is the male child of chapter 66.

The usage of words just considered should correct two errors.

The view that since the word for male is in the neuter gender, Jesus was without sex. However, the proof is on the other side, for precisely the same word is used in numerous instances where it is set in contrast with the female sex, for example, Genesis 1:27 (as above); 5:2; 6:19, 20; Exodus 1:16, 17; Leviticus 1:3, 10.

The view that by man-child the church is meant, for neither the church nor any religious system is ever symbolized by a word denoting the male sex; for example, Israel is spoken of as the wife of Jehovah, the church as the bride of Christ, and apostate Israel as well as the apostate church as a harlot.

Isaiah 66:8—"Who hath heard such a thing? who hath seen such things? Shall the earth be made to bring forth in one day? or shall a nation be born at once? for as soon as Zion travailed, she brought forth her children."

The staggering questions are raised in view of the astounding declaration following: "as soon as Zion travailed, she brought forth her children."

Observe in the preceding verse that the birth was before the travail, consequently with no accompanying travail; here the travail immediately precedes the birth and is the occasion for it.

The birth before the travail was that of a child; that is, of children; that is, of a nation. The allusion is of course to Israel and to her spiritual birth occasioned by the awful affliction that will come upon her during the tribulation period. As the prophet Hosea remarks (5:15)—"In . . . [her] affliction [Greek: tribulation] . . . [she] will seek me early."

The birth without the travail when the child is born is therefore single, individual, literal, physical; that preceded by travail, corporate, national, figurative, spiritual.

It is significant that in every mention of the birth of Christ, not the slightest hint is given regarding birth pangs. To quote: "A virgin shall conceive, and . . . [bring forth] a son" (Isaiah 7:14). "Unto us a child is . . . [brought forth], unto us a son is given" (Isaiah 9:6). "She shall bring forth a son, and thou shalt call his name Jesus" (Matthew 1:21). "She . . . brought forth her firstborn son: and he called his name Jesus" (Matthew 1:25). "Thou shalt conceive in thy womb, and bring forth a son, and shalt call his name Jesus" (Luke 1:31). "And she brought forth her firstborn son" (Luke 2:7). And so in Revelation 12:5, "And she brought forth a man child."

Every syllable of this last sentence is taken from the preceding statements referring to the birth of Christ and this should settle it once for all that by the man-child Jesus is intended and none other.

On the other hand, the travail of Zion (Israel), at which time she brings forth "children," and then a "nation" is brought forth in a day can have no reference to the birth of Jesus in Bethlehem of Judea.

Micah 5:2, 3—"But thou, Bethlehem Ephratah, though thou be little among the thousands of Judah, yet out of thee shall he come forth unto me that is to be ruler in Israel; whose goings forth have been from of old, from everlasting. Therefore will he give them up, until the time that she which travaileth hath brought forth: then the remnant of his brethren shall return unto the children of Israel."

The chief priests and scribes rightly applied verse 2 to the birth of Christ in the lowly town of Bethlehem. Here, too, there is not the slightest hint of pangs in connection with His coming forth.

The initial word "therefore" (verse 3) occurs (in the original) seven times in Micah's prophecy. 1:8, 14; 2:3, 5; 3:6, 12; 5:3. They are the translation of the same Hebrew word except the first, which means literally "on this account." In each case there is a reference to the "incurable bias" to apostasy on the part of Israel. In the first instance we note the effect of Israel's sin upon the prophet: "I will wail and howl, I will go stripped and naked: I will make a wailing like the dragons, and mourning as the owls." In the remaining passages the details of

Israel's guilt are emphasized together with the judgments that were about to come upon her as a consequence. In its last occurrence we have the climax of judgment. One of their own number should come forth out of obscurity as ruler of Israel and "give them up."

What is meant by giving up? The import of these words may be inferred by the context, but there can be no doubt of their meaning in the light of a passage by Hosea, a prophet who uttered his message but a short period previous to that of Micah. We refer to Hosea 11:8, 9—"How shall I give thee up, Ephraim? how shall I deliver thee, Israel? how shall I make thee as Admah? how shall I set thee as Zeboim? mine heart is turned within me, my repentings are kindled together. I will not execute the fierceness of mine anger, I will not return to destroy Ephraim: for I am God, and not man. . . ." Nowhere in the Old Testament is there a stronger exhibition of God's love for His people. Observe, for example, a few verses preceding: "When Israel was a child, then I loved him, and called my son out of Egypt. . . . I taught Ephraim also to go, taking them by their arms. . . . I drew them with cords of a man, with bands of love" (Hosea 11:1-4). And this in spite of his glaring defection as emphasized so repeatedly in the prophetic message of Hosea. Ephraim stands for Israel as being the foremost in guilt. "Ephraim is joined to idols: let him alone" (4:17); "O Ephraim, thou committest whoredom" (5:3); "Ephraim is . . . broken in judgment" (5:11); "Ephraim, he hath mixed himself among the people; Ephraim is a cake not turned" (7:8); "Ephraim hath hired lovers" (8:9); "Ephraim hath made many altars to sin" (8:11). To "give up," therefore, signifies to deliver to destruction as was the case with the cities of the plain, Admah and Zeboim, which were destroyed with Sodom and Gomorrah. Deuteronomy 29:23. In the days of Hosea's prophecy, the "repentings" of God suffered Him not to "execute the fierceness of . . . [his] anger" (11:8, 9), but a generation later the prophet Micah declared, ". . . therefore will he give them up," not once and for all time, but "until the time that she which travaileth hath brought forth." *Then the remnant of his brethren shall return unto the children of Israel.* By this is meant that the people of Israel scattered abroad will return to those already in the land. This has not yet taken place, nor will it take place until "the Lord shall set his hand . . . the second time to recover the remnant of his people" from all the places whither He has driven them. In other words, Israel is still "given up" and will be until the bringing forth of her children. Our next passage will indicate, beyond a shadow of a doubt, the exact period of time in which Israel will travail with child.

Jeremiah 30:6, 7—"Ask ye now, and see whether a man [Hebrew: male] doth travail with child? wherefore do I see every man with his hands on his loins, as a woman in travail, and all faces are turned into paleness? Alas! for that day is great, so that none is like it: it is even the time of Jacob's trouble; but he shall be saved out of it."

The bringing forth here is plainly not that of a virgin giving birth to a male child. On the other hand, "every man" is in travail as a woman in childbirth. The imagery employed—"every man with his hands on his loins" and "all faces . . . turned into paleness"—is descriptive of the terrible agony that will befall Israel on this occasion as noted above.

The exact time of this affliction is indicated in unmistakable terms, for it is the time of Jacob's trouble, which is none other than that of the great tribulation. How may we be certain that there can be no allusion here to the birth of Jesus? Among other reasons, from the fact that Jesus Himself spoke of this time at the close of His ministry upon the occasion of His Olivet discourse: "For then shall be great tribulation, such as was not since the beginning of the world to this time, no, nor ever shall be" (Matthew 24:21; cf. Mark 13:19). Plainly there can be only one time that is different from every other time, yet this earmark is found in both passages. Our passage says that day is great, *so that none is like it.* Daniel speaks of the same time when he says, ". . . there shall be a time of trouble [tribulation], such as never was since there was a nation even to that same time: and at that time thy people shall be delivered . . ." (Daniel 12:1). Similarly Joel: "A day of darkness and of gloominess, a day of clouds and of thick darkness . . . there hath not been ever the like, neither shall be any more after it . . ." (Joel 2:2).

Micah 4:9b, 10—". . . pangs [travail] have taken thee as a woman in travail [bringing forth]. Be in pain [travail], and labour to bring forth, O daughter of Zion, like a woman in travail [bringing forth]: for now shalt thou go forth out of the city [Zion-Jerusalem], and thou shalt dwell in the field, and thou shalt go even to Babylon; there shalt thou be delivered; there the Lord shall redeem thee from the hand of thine enemies." This example of the past should suffice to show that travail accompanies spiritual deliverance. A remnant of Israel was delivered through Cyrus the king and it appears Israel as a nation never worshiped idols since.

Note that the deliverance of Daniel's people (Israel) (Daniel 12:1), their being saved out of it (Jeremiah 30:7), and "for the elect's sake" of the Olivet discourse are parallel expressions and such as that of Isaiah 66:8, "as soon as Zion travailed, she brought forth her children," and Micah 5:3, "then the remnant of his brethren shall return unto the children of Israel," are closely related and refer to the same time. "All these are the beginning of sorrows [Greek: birth pangs]" (Matthew 24:8).

Jesus is here speaking of the end of the world (Greek: consummation of the age) by which is meant the period of great tribulation. The beginning of birth pangs occurs therefore in the first half of the tribulation and hence, not at the birth of Christ. The passages already quoted from Matthew and Mark allude to the second half, for they are descriptive of the great tribulation that will be after the abomination of desolation is set in the holy place. Matthew 24:15, 21. The passages we have considered show clearly that the birth of Christ is never associated with birth pangs and, on the other hand, these are always related to the affliction of Israel in the last days in consequence of which she will seek the Lord, repent of her sins, whereupon He will pour out upon them the spirit of grace and supplication and proclaim the blissful reconciliation, "I . . . will be your God, and ye shall be my people."

16. THE FALL OF SATAN

To gather the full picture together one needs to turn first to Ezekiel 28:13-18:
"Thou hast been in Eden the garden of God; every precious stone was thy covering, the sardius, topaz, and the diamond, the beryl, the onyx, and the jasper, the sapphire, the emerald, and the carbuncle, and gold: the workmanship of thy tabrets and of thy pipes was prepared in thee in the day that thou wast created.

"Thou art the anointed cherub that covereth; and I have set thee so: thou wast upon the holy mountain of God; thou hast walked up and down in the midst of the stones of fire.

"Thou wast perfect in thy ways from the day that thou wast created, till iniquity was found in thee.

"By the multitude of thy merchandise they have filled the midst of thee with violence, and thou hast sinned: therefore I will cast thee as profane out of the mountain of God: and I will destroy thee, O covering cherub, from the midst of the stones of fire.

"Thine heart was lifted up because of thy beauty, thou hast corrupted thy wisdom by reason of thy brightness: I will cast thee to the ground, I will lay thee before kings, that they may behold thee.

"Thou hast defiled thy sanctuaries by the multitude of thine iniquities, by the iniquity of thy traffick; therefore will I bring forth a fire from the midst of thee, it shall devour thee, and I will bring thee to ashes upon the earth in the sight of all them that behold thee."

The chapter opens with a description of the king of Tyre with respect to his pride and riches which led him to assume the role of deity. Since the king was under the direct influence of his self-deification and pride superinduced by his abundance of wealth, the Lord speaks to him as though he were one and the same with Satan himself, even as He did later to Peter ("Get thee behind me, Satan . . . for thou savourest not the things that be of God, but those that be of men"—Matthew 16:23). That the Lord addresses Satan from verse 13 on in the Ezekiel passage and not any longer the king of Tyre is plain from the fact that He speaks of him as having been in Eden the garden of God, that he was the anointed cherub that covereth, that he was perfect in his ways from the day that he was created, *till iniquity was found in him*. Observe also that the cause of his fall was that his heart was lifted up because of his beauty and that he corrupted his wisdom by reason of his brightness. The word "brightness" is that which is used in connection with the effulgence and glory of God. Psalm 50:2; 80:1. In consequence of this iniquity his doom is announced: "I will cast thee to the ground [Hebrew: earth]"—apparently a direct prophecy of what occurs in Revelation 12. The description of his doom continues: "I will lay thee before kings, that they may behold thee. . . . I will bring thee to ashes upon the earth in the sight of all them that behold thee." This seems to allude to his final doom after the one thousand years. Plainly this description could not be applied to a human being but only to the glorious cherub who, after the creation of man, reappeared in the garden of Eden with the subtle purpose of destroying our first parents to whose care the Creator now entrusted the care of that beautiful spot on earth. We now turn to Isaiah 14:12-17.

"How art thou fallen from heaven, O Lucifer, son of the morning! how art thou cut down to the ground, which didst weaken the nations!

"For thou hast said in thine heart, I will ascend into heaven, I will exalt my throne above the stars of God: I will sit also upon the mount of the congregation, in the sides of the north:

"I will ascend above the heights of the clouds; I will be like the most High.

"Yet thou shalt be brought down to hell, to the sides of the pit.

"They that see thee shall narrowly look upon thee, and consider thee, saying, Is this the man that made the earth to tremble, that did shake kingdoms;

"That made the world as a wilderness, and destroyed the cities thereof; that opened not the house of his prisoners?"

Many have taken this passage as referring to the original fall of Lucifer (the shining one similar to the covering cherub in Ezekiel 28) from heaven. Careful attention to the context, however, shows that such a view is untenable.

Observe the statement, "How art thou cut down to the ground [Hebrew: earth], which didst weaken the nations!" Now we know that Satan had sinned before man was created, but here he is described as having fallen after he had weakened the nations, and apparently his fall was imposed upon him as a judgment for having weakened the nations.

Observe, too, that Lucifer was not in heaven at the time, for he says, "I will ascend into heaven." And again, "I will ascend above the heights of the clouds." Consequently he must have been below the clouds, namely, upon the earth, when he cherished his diabolical ambition to be like the Most High.

Verse 15 describes the judgment that awaits him: "Yet [or therefore] thou shalt be brought down to hell [Hebrew: *Sheol;* Greek: *Hades*], to the sides of the pit." In other words, instead of going up he will go down—down to *Sheol*. This is exactly what will befall Satan at the close of the tribulation period. He will be cast into the bottomless pit (Revelation 20:3)—not into hell but into *Sheol*, or the bottomless pit, which, as we have seen, are parallel terms. This shows too that Antichrist is not intended because he will not be cast into the bottomless pit but into the lake of fire. Revelation 19:20.

Note what follows: "They that see thee shall narrowly look [Hebrew: peep] upon thee, and consider thee, saying, Is this the man that made the earth to tremble, that did shake kingdoms; that made the world as a wilderness, and destroyed the cities thereof; that opened not the house of his prisoners?"

Again we see that this can have no reference to the original fall of Satan, for there were no kingdoms on the earth when he sinned, seeing that he had sinned before the first human pair were created. But how true today—the weakening of the nations and the shaking of the kingdoms.

No doubt some have concluded that the fall here described refers to the original fall from heaven since the verbs "fallen," "cut down," "weaken," "shake," etc., are in the past tense. This mode of expression is, however, very common in prophetic literature. Compare, for instance, chapter 53:4-6 by the same prophet: "He hath borne our griefs, and carried our sorrows. . . . He was wounded for our transgressions, he was bruised for our iniquities. . . . The Lord hath laid on him the iniquity of us all." These verbs are in the past tense and yet we know the reference is to the death of Christ. Strictly speaking, verbs in the Hebrew language have no tense (in the English sense), hence the time of action has to be determined by the context. And so in chapter 14 the prophet is referring to the future fall of Satan as described in Revelation 12. Undoubtedly Jesus was looking forward to the same event when He declared, "I beheld Satan as lightning fall from heaven." The report of the disciples that the devils are subject to them was to Him a token that the forces of righteousness will eventually triumph over the forces of evil. He is also the star John saw that had fallen from heaven, to whom was given the key of the bottomless pit from which will emerge the beast (Revelation 11:7), as well as demonic spirits (Revelation 9). It should be remembered that the episodes of chapter 12 antedate the events of chapter 9, for it would seem that the activity of evil spirits of chapter 9 can best be accounted for by the fact that the bottomless pit has been opened by Satan who has been cast out of heaven.

17. THE PRESERVATION OF ISRAEL

[The passage in Revelation 12:14 would suggest that all this is within the plan and purpose of God. He has not been taken off guard. A place has been prepared for Israel in the wilderness. One should have no more difficulty accepting this truth than he would accepting God's providential care of Israel during the time of the Exodus and wilderness wanderings.—J. O. Y.]

Several passages from the Old Testament which apparently pertain directly to the preservation of Israel and refer to the same time as Revelation 12 will be cited and commented upon.

"Come, my people, enter thou into thy chambers, and shut thy doors about thee: hide thyself as it were for a little moment, until the indignation be overpast. For, behold, the Lord cometh out of his place to punish the inhabitants of the earth for their iniquity: the earth also shall disclose her blood, and shall no more cover her slain" (Isaiah 26:20, 21).

"At that time shall Michael stand up, the great prince which standeth for the children of thy people: and there shall be a time of trouble, such as never was since there was a nation even to that same time: and at that time thy people shall be delivered, every one that shall be found written in the book" (Daniel 12:1).

Note: The time is plainly that of the great tribulation; at that time Michael shall stand up (just as in Revelation 12) for Daniel's people, who we are told are Israel (Daniel 9:20); those who are thus delivered have their name written in the book. In the Olivet discourse those "who are in Judaea" are requested to flee to the mountains. It appears that God will especially honor those who return to the promised land and apparently the faith that leads them to that land will eventually also lead them to accept Jesus as their Saviour during the days of the tribulation; thus they will have their names written in the book, and hence be delivered during that time by fleeing into the wilderness.

"Seek ye the Lord, all ye meek of the earth, which have wrought his judgment; seek righteousness, seek meekness: it may be ye shall be hid in the day of the Lord's anger" (Zephaniah 2:3).

Note Ezekiel 20:33 ff., where it speaks about Israel being brought into the wilderness and the Lord pleading with them there and purging out the rebels— another passage referring to the protection of the faithful in the time of the great tribulation (i.e., the day of the Lord's anger).

". . . behold, I will allure her [Israel], and bring her into the wilderness, and speak comfortably unto her [lit., speak to her heart]. And I will give her her vineyards from thence, and the valley of Achor for a door of hope: and she shall sing there, as in the days of her youth, and as in the day when she came up out of the land of Egypt. And it shall be at that day, saith the Lord, that thou shalt call me Ishi; and shalt call me no more Baali" (Hosea 2:14-16).

The passage shows that the portion of Israel whom the Lord brings into the wilderness and to whose heart He speaks has become fully reconciled to God. She now calls the Lord *Ishi*, which means *my husband*. Verse 23 of the same chapter declares, ". . . and I will have mercy upon her that had not obtained mercy; and I will say to them which were not my people, Thou art my people; and they shall say, Thou art my God." (The intervening verses should be carefully noted.)

The valley of Achor (trouble) was so called because the sin of Achan, "the troubler of Israel" (I Chronicles 2:7), occurred at this place. However, after the stoning of Achan the trouble of Israel at Achor was immediately followed by the conquest of Ai, which was but the "earnest" of the entire conquest of Canaan; thus the defection of Achan was overruled for the good of Israel and proved to be her door of hope. So when Israel in the future time of trouble passes through that same valley of Achor, it will be to them a door of hope as they wend their way to the place God has prepared for them.

Passing through the valley has ever been a means of grace to the true believer. If it is the valley of Baca (weeping), he makes of it a well of refreshing (Psalm 84:6); if perchance it be the valley of the shadow of death, he bears the triumphant testimony, "I will fear no evil: for thou art with me; thy rod and thy staff they comfort me" (Psalm 23:4).

The song they sing will doubtless be one of redemption and deliverance similar to that of Exodus 15 and may probably allude to that recorded in Isaiah 12.

"Thus saith the Lord, The people which were left of the sword found grace in the wilderness; even Israel, when I went to cause him to rest [lit., I will go and give him rest—Ellicott]" (Jeremiah 31:2). The context makes it clear that the reference is to Israel "in the latter days." While the word "grace" is not mentioned once in Revelation during the portion dealing with the tribulation period, it is nevertheless true that the fugitives of Israel will find "grace in the wilderness" as Jeremiah 31:2 abundantly declares.

A variety of opinions have been expressed as to the location of the place whither Israel is to flee. Some suppose it to be Pella to which the inhabitants of Jerusalem fled in the days of her destruction by the Roman armies in A.D. 70. Others have mentioned a circular valley a short distance south of Jerusalem. However, these are mere guesses or suppositions unsupported by any Biblical testimony.

Now we learn from Daniel 11:40 ff. that the willful king in his marauding expeditions during the first half of the time of the end enters the glorious land and overthrows many countries. Edom, Moab, and Ammon alone escape out of his hand. Regarding this passage Dr. Moorehead remarks: "Daniel . . . declares that 'the King,' the Antichrist, will be prevented from taking Edom, Moab, and Ammon. All other lands will fall under his victorious arms. These shall escape. May it be that it is to this rocky, almost inaccessible territory the saved remnant will flee?"[33]

The present writer inclines to this view and more particularly so because of the further hints of Scripture passages which appear to point directly to such a conclusion.

Balaam in his prophecy directed to Balak these remarks: ". . . come therefore, and I will advertise [= advise] thee what this people shall do to thy people in the latter days. . . . There shall come a Star out of Jacob, and a Sceptre shall rise out of Israel, and [He] shall smite the corners of Moab, and destroy all the children of Sheth. And Edom shall be a possession, Seir also shall be a possession for his enemies . . ." (Numbers 24:14, 17, 18).

The prophecy pertains to the relation of Israel to Moab in the latter days, thus showing plainly that it still awaits fulfillment.

Star and *Sceptre* are Messianic titles. The former refers to His relation to the church (Matthew 2:2; II Peter 1:19; Revelation 2:28; 22:16), the latter to His rule over Israel and the nations (Genesis 49:10). Only in the latter sense does He use the sceptre. "The sceptre shall not depart from Judah . . . until Shiloh come," but it (the sceptre) has never been committed to the church as an instrument of conquest or aggression.

Moab and Edom are His (the Lord's) enemies—there is no word or syllable in the original to warrant the occurrence of "for" (verse 18). While the sceptre is the Lord's, Israel as in olden times is apparently entrusted with its use for the subjugation of His (as well as their) enemies, for the prophecy is introduced with the express declaration, "I [Balaam] will . . . [advise] thee [Balak, king of Moab] what this people [Israel] shall do to thy people [Moab] in the latter days."

Moab therefore as well as Edom will become the possession of Israel by conquest in the same manner as Canaan was subdued in the time of Joshua, that is, under the direction and power of Him who is the "captain of the Lord's host."

The verse following declares: "Out of Jacob shall come he that shall have dominion." In point of time therefore the prophecy of Balaam appears to fit precisely into the period we are now considering—it refers to the latter days and apparently just preceding the coming of Him who shall have dominion.

"And he shall set up an ensign for the nations, and shall assemble the outcasts of Israel, and gather together the dispersed of Judah from the four corners of the earth. . . . They shall fly upon the shoulders of the Philistines toward the west; they shall spoil them of the east together: they shall lay their hand upon Edom and Moab; and the children of Ammon shall obey them" (Isaiah 11:12, 14).

We know that the gathering together of "the outcasts of Israel" has already begun. In 1940 the population of the Jews in Palestine amounted to 456,743. The larger part of these returned to the land promised to their fathers after the Balfour Declaration.

[In the first ten years of the reconstitution of Israel as a nation phenomenal progress has been made in the Land of Promise. It is known that not all Jews who returned stayed. However, Israel is a nation again! Students of prophecy intently watch developments in the tense Middle Eastern countries. Surely it would appear that "all that the prophets have spoken" will come to pass, because "the zeal of the Lord of hosts will perform this." The population statistics for Palestine in 1957 showed a total of 1,872,000.[34] Recent archaeological studies in the Negev show that Israel has real possibility for expansion. Nelson Glueck's *Rivers in the Desert* would remarkably support this view.—J. O. Y.]

Those fleeing to the wilderness do not include the 144,000, for these latter suffer martyrdom as chapter 14 reveals. All this goes to show that a considerable number of Israelites will have returned to Palestine previous to the return of the Lord after which all Israel will return to the land of their fathers.

Apparently the Philistines will be friendly toward Israel, for they shall fly upon their shoulders toward the west and "they shall spoil them of the east together," that is to say, "they shall lay their hand upon (i.e., subdue) Edom and Moab; and the children of Ammon shall obey them."

Since the Scripture speaks of a place prepared, we might infer that no conflict would be necessary for its occupancy, but when Israel was about to undertake their journey to the land of promise, while they were encouraged by the promise, "Behold, I send an Angel before thee, to keep thee in the way, and to bring thee into the place which I have prepared" (Exodus 23:20), they nevertheless were required to subdue the inhabitants of Canaan before they could secure its possession.

"Take counsel, execute judgment; make thy shadow as the night in the midst of the noonday; hide the outcasts; bewray [betray or expose] not him that wandereth. Let mine outcasts dwell with thee, Moab; be thou a covert to them from the face of the spoiler: for the extortioner is at an end, the spoiler ceaseth, the oppressors are consumed out of the land" (Isaiah 16:3, 4).

The outcasts apparently are those of Israel making request of Moab for a dwelling place within the borders and a covert (hiding place) from the face of the spoiler. The spoiler appears to be identical with the dragon which persecutes the woman and causes her to flee for refuge. The plea of Israel is accompanied with the prospect that the period of the spoiler or extortioner will soon be over and that oppressors will soon be cut off, so that the refuge they are seeking will not be of long duration.

As in previous passages the occasion appears to be just previous to the destruction of the spoiler and the establishment of God's kingdom on earth as the verse following clearly declares: "And in mercy shall the throne be established: and he shall sit upon it in truth in the tabernacle of David, judging, and seeking judgment, and hasting righteousness" (Isaiah 16:5).

The Scripture passages appear to fit into the very period being considered, namely, the latter portion of the tribulation period, just previous to the establishment of the kingdom. The manifest relation of Israel to Moab, Ammon, and Edom at this time appears to favor the view that these countries will serve as an asylum for Israel during the period of her flight from Judah.

Bear in mind that these nations have a close affinity to Israel since Moab and Ammon are the sons of Lot, and Edom (Esau) the brother of Jacob. While the first two had an incestuous origin, the latter sold his birthright and all of them were among the chief of the enemies of Israel.

Of Moab and Ammon it is said that the Lord turned their captivity in the latter days (Jeremiah 48:47; 49:6); so apparently they were restored to favor with God and thus grace triumphed over human infirmity. For Edom, however, the Biblical record has not one good word; and his epitaph reads, "he is not." And of Bozrah (the capital) she "shall become a desolation, a reproach, a waste, and a curse; and all the cities thereof shall be perpetual wastes" (Jeremiah 49:10, 13). Moreover, while of Moab and Ammon the Word declares, "They shall know that I am the Lord" (Ezekiel 25:7, 11), of Edom it is said, "I will lay my vengeance upon Edom by the hand of my people Israel: and they shall do in Edom according to mine anger and according to my fury; and they shall know my vengeance, saith the Lord God" (Ezekiel 25:14). Thus the descendants of Jacob will be used as God's instruments to execute vengeance upon the descendants of Esau in the latter days—a notable illustration of the lines:

> "From the same cradle,
> From the same mother's knee,

One to darkness and the frozen tide,
The other to the crystal sea."

18. The Tribulation

It is significant that in the first reference to this period this very term is employed. The passage reads, "And the Lord shall scatter you among the nations, and ye shall be left few in number among the heathen, whither the Lord shall lead you. And there ye shall serve gods, the work of men's hands, wood and stone, which neither see, nor hear, nor eat, nor smell. But . . . from thence thou shalt seek the Lord thy God, thou shalt find him, . . . [when] thou seek him with all thy heart and with all thy soul. When thou art in tribulation, and all these things are come upon thee, even in the latter days, . . . thou turn to the Lord thy God, and shalt be obedient unto his voice;

"(For the Lord thy God is a merciful God;) he will not forsake thee, neither destroy thee, nor forget the covenant of thy fathers which he sware unto them" (Deuteronomy 4:27-31). We have omitted the three *if*'s in verses 29 and 30. The Hebrew word *'im* meaning *if* does not occur here; hence its presence obscures the sense. In the case of the second *if*, substitute *when* (Hebrew: *ki'*, meaning when or for). "In the latter days" occurs 14 times in the Old Testament and should be uniformly translated "in the last days."

The term is used both in relation to Israel and to the nations, either in connection with the tribulation period or with the glorious days following. The Lord will not forget (or change) His covenant with Israel, for His gifts and callings are without repentance. Romans 11:29.

The next passages are taken from the Olivet discourse: "For nation shall rise against nation, and kingdom against kingdom: and there shall be famines, and pestilences, and earthquakes, in divers places. All these are the beginning of sorrows. Then shall they deliver you up to be afflicted [lit., to tribulation], and shall kill you: and ye shall be hated of all nations for my name's sake" (Matthew 24:7-9).

"Then shall be great tribulation, such as was not since the beginning of the world to this time, no, nor ever shall be" (Matthew 24:21).

"Immediately after the tribulation of those days shall the sun be darkened, and the moon shall not give her light, and the stars shall fall from heaven, and the powers of the heavens shall be shaken:

"And then shall appear the sign of the Son of man in heaven: and then shall all the tribes of the earth mourn, and they shall see the Son of man coming in the clouds of heaven with power and great glory" (Matthew 24:29, 30).

"But in those days, after that tribulation, the sun shall be darkened, and the moon shall not give her light, and the stars of heaven shall fall, and the powers that are in heaven shall be shaken. And then shall they see the Son of man coming in the clouds with great power and glory" (Mark 13:24-26).

In the first passage, verse 8 tells of the beginning of sorrows. *Sorrows* is translated *travail* in I Thessalonians 5:3, i.e., birth pangs, in allusion to the severe agonies already setting in at the beginning of the tribulation.

The *great tribulation* is described as being so terrible that no suffering ever was or ever shall be comparable with it. The language necessarily implies that there can be only one such period in the entire course of human history. Jeremiah, Daniel, and Joel use similar language respecting the time of suffering in the future; consequently, these prophets speak of the same period of tribulation as does Jesus in the Olivet discourse.

The tribulation spoken of cannot refer to any period of martyrdom or persecution in the past from the fact that we are expressly informed that *immediately after the tribulation of those days shall the sun be darkened, and the moon shall not give her light;* and as the verse following (cf. the passage from Mark) shows, *then . . . they shall see the Son of man coming in the clouds of heaven with power and great glory.* Neither of these things happened immediately after any tribulation of the past. The language makes it plain that the coming of the Son of man will be preceded by the greatest period of human suffering in the annals of history; hence it is vain to imagine that the kingdoms of this world will gradually emerge into the kingdom of God.

(We omit comments in this place on Romans 2:9 and II Thessalonians 1:6, where the word "tribulation" apparently is likewise used in an eschatological sense. We consider them when we take up the passages pertaining to the rapture of the church previous to the tribulation.)

The last passage under this head is Revelation 7:13, 14: "And one of the elders answered, saying unto me, What are these which are arrayed in white robes? and whence came they?

"And I said unto him, Sir, thou knowest. And he said to me, These are they which came out of great tribulation, and have washed their robes, and made them white in the blood of the Lamb."

The Greek has the definite article—*the* great tribulation, thus alluding to the past references to this period. Observe that whereas the church is said to be *kept out* of this period, the tribulation saints are said to *come out* of it. Those that *come out* are said to be a great multitude which no man can number of all nations, and kindreds, and people, and tongues. This shows that not only Israelites but men of all classes come out of the great tribulation and this accords with the notable declaration of Isaiah which says, "When thy judgments are in the earth, the inhabitants of the world will learn righteousness" (Isaiah 26:9).

The Time of Trouble.

The term occurs in the following passages:

"O Lord, be gracious unto us; we have waited for thee: be thou their arm every morning, our salvation also in the time of trouble" (Isaiah 33:2).

"Ask ye now, and see whether a man doth travail with child? wherefore do I see every man with his hands on his loins, as a woman in travail, and all faces are turned into paleness?

"Alas! for that day is great, so that none is like it: it is even the time of Jacob's trouble; but he shall be saved out of it" (Jeremiah 30:6, 7).

"And at that time shall Michael stand up, the great prince which standeth for the children of thy people: and there shall be a time of trouble, such as never was since there was a nation even to that same time" (Daniel 12:1).

The Hebrew word for trouble (*tzar* or *tzarah*) is the same as that rendered *tribulation* in Deuteronomy 4:30.

The word for time (*eth*) is translated season in Psalm 1:3; Proverbs 15:23; Jeremiah 5:24, etc. Compare also "the time of old age" (Psalm 71:9); "the time of the singing of birds" (Song of Solomon 2:12); "the time of harvest" (see below). The word therefore denotes a period and not merely a point in time. The phrase, *the time of trouble*, is therefore the equivalent of the period, or season of tribulation. In the first passage quoted above, the Lord is spoken of as "our salvation . . . in the time of trouble." Further studies will show that this is actually so, for (to cite but one example) in Revelation 7:3, 4, the servants of God are sealed in their foreheads, their number totaling a hundred and forty-four thousand of all the tribes of Israel.

As in the passage in Matthew 24:8; I Thessalonians 5:3, suffering of men is compared with that of women in childbirth.

"[There is] none . . . like it" corresponds with a similar phrase in Matthew 24:21; Mark 13:19, besides the three passages in the Old Testament, and must necessarily refer to the great tribulation yet to come.

It is designated the time of *Jacob's* trouble in Jeremiah 30:6, 7. The inclusion of Jacob in this instance undoubtedly harks back to Genesis 35:3, where the term "the day of my distress" (Hebrew: *tzarah*) occurs for the first time, the occasion being that of Jacob's purpose to build an altar unto God at Bethel where God appeared unto him and answered him in the day of his distress, when he had fled from the face of his brother Esau. Genesis 35:3, 7.

Some have advanced the argument: If Revelation 3:10 were meant to be understood that the church would be kept *from* the hour of tribulation (i.e., be raptured before that hour), the preposition *apo* not *ek* would have been used. The presence of *apo*, however, appears to prove the opposite; for in Jeremiah 30:7 *apo* is used (in the Septuagint translation) and yet it is designated the time of Jacob's trouble. The argument therefore, light as it is, falls to the ground.

Affliction.

The Hebrew words *tzar, tzarah* are the same as those rendered trouble or tribulation, so that affliction should be understood as identical with the former term. The same is true of the passage in the New Testament where the Greek is *thlipsis*. In the following passages it is plainly used in an eschatological sense:

"In all their affliction he was afflicted [lit., affliction was to him]" (Isaiah 63:9).

"I will go and return to my place, till they acknowledge their offence, and seek my face: in their affliction [tribulation] they will seek me early" (Hosea 5:15).

"For in those days shall be affliction [tribulation], such as was not from the beginning of the creation which God created unto this time, neither shall be" (Mark 13:19).

That the first passage relates to the end time is evident from the context. No passage of Scripture exhibits more impressively the mercy and long-suffering of the Lord. The purpose of the tribulation is not only punitive but also disciplinary and remedial.

The passage from Hosea foretells clearly what followed the rejection of Jesus by His own people, the Jews. He returned to heaven and will remain there until they seek the Lord, and this they will do as a result of the sufferings inflicted upon them during the tribulation. That many will turn "early" to the Lord is seen in the 144,000 Israelites sealed in their foreheads as recorded in Revelation 7.

The passage from Mark is parallel with that of Matthew 24:21 already noted.

The Time of Harvest.

"For thus saith the Lord of hosts, the God of Israel; The daughter of Babylon is like a threshingfloor, it is time to thresh her: yet a little while, and the time of her harvest shall come" (Jeremiah 51:33).

"Let both grow together until the harvest: and in the time of harvest I will say to the reapers, Gather ye together first the tares, and bind them in bundles to burn them: but gather the wheat into my barn. . . . The harvest is the end of the world; and the reapers are the angels. As therefore the tares are gathered and burned in the fire; so shall it be in the end of this world" (Matthew 13:30, 39b, 40).

"And another angel came out of the temple, crying with a loud voice to him that sat on the cloud, Thrust in thy sickle, and reap: for the time is come for thee to reap; for the harvest of the earth is ripe" (Revelation 14:15).

That chapters 50 and 51 of Jeremiah allude to the end-time tribulation is seen in that some thirty references are made to them in chapters 17 and 18 of Revelation, all of which yet await fulfillment.

The harvest spoken of is not a harvest of good things but a harvest of judgment as another passage in the same chapter says: "This is the time [or season] of the Lord's vengeance" (Jeremiah 51:6). To the same effect are the words of Joel: "Put ye in the sickle, for the harvest is ripe: come, get you down; for the press is full, the fats [vats] overflow; for their wickedness is great" (3:13).

The second passage is taken from Jesus' parable of the tares and wheat. In explanation Jesus declares:

The field is the world. The word for *world* is *kosmos* by which is meant not the earth (*ge*) but the world of men. The good seed (sown by the Son of man) are the children of the kingdom. The tares (sown by the devil) are the children of the wicked one. The harvest is the end (Greek: *sunteleia*) of the world (Greek: *aion*, i.e., age); the reapers are the angels.

(1) The harvest is spoken of as a season, i.e., a period of time. Verse 30.

(2) The word for *end* is not *telos*, which denotes a point in time, but *sunteleia*, i.e., "an ending up together." The two words are carefully distinguished in Matthew 24:3-14. See under "The time of the end" below.

The Son of man now makes an important comparison:

"As therefore the tares are gathered and burned in the fire; so shall it be in the end [*sunteleia*] of this world [*age*]. The Son of man shall send forth his angels, and they shall gather out of his kingdom all things that offend [stumbling blocks], and them which do iniquity [i.e., practice lawlessness]; and shall cast them into a furnace of fire: there shall be wailing and gnashing of teeth. Then shall the righteous shine forth as the sun in the kingdom of their Father" (Matthew 13:40-43).

That the account here given of the time of harvest can have no reference to the rapture of the church is evident from several considerations:

Here the wicked are first dealt with, i.e., they are taken out of the kingdom; then, that is, after the removal and destruction of the wicked, "the righteous [shall] shine forth as the sun in the kingdom of their Father" (Matthew 13:43), whereas in those passages where Jesus speaks to His own about His coming, He mentions only the righteous. For example,

"I will come again, and receive you unto myself; that where I am, there ye may be also" (John 14:3). "Then shall two be in the field; the one shall be taken, and the other left" (Matthew 24:40). The word for *take* is *paralambano*, the same as that translated "receive" in John 14:3, and that translated "take" in Matthew 17:1, "And after six days Jesus taketh Peter, James, and John"; and in Matthew 20:17, "And Jesus going up to Jerusalem took the twelve disciples apart in the way [that is, into close fellowship]." Some have erroneously taken this word for *take* as identical with verse 39 above in the passage, "the flood came, and took them all away" (Matthew 24:39), which, however, is *airo* and is used in John 15:2: "Every branch in me that beareth not fruit he taketh away."

The word for "left" (Matthew 24:40) is literally "to send from one's self." Thayer gives as the first definition "to bid go away or depart." While the word has some good uses, the same authority cites this passage and its parallel in Luke 17:34-36 (*aphiemi*) as standing opposed to *paralambano* and as signifying "to leave one by not taking him as a companion."

19. THE BEAST OUT OF THE EARTH

Who is the beast out of the earth?

He is one of three great world potentates appearing on earth at the beginning of the latter half of the tribulation period:

Satan is cast down from heaven (the air) to the earth. Revelation 12:9-12.

The beast rising out of the sea—he is the Antichrist, for as we have pointed out, it is *this* beast that makes war against the Lamb. 17:14; 19:19.

The beast out of the land.

It is not difficult to see that the trinity of personages here represented are a caricature or travesty upon the divine Trinity. However, the semblance is only in power and wisdom, for in character and moral status they are altogether in contrast with the holy Trinity. Force, intrigue, and deception are the weapons which they vainly ply to achieve their objective. As to rank and relationship there is a marked resemblance between the celestial and the infernal trinity.

As to Satan let Isaiah speak: "Thou hast said in thine heart, I will ascend into heaven, I will exalt my throne above the stars of God . . . I will ascend above the heights of the clouds; I will be like the most High" (Isaiah 14:13, 14). Satan, once "the anointed cherub that covereth" and "perfect in . . . [his] ways," by ambition fell. He, however, retains superhuman power and boasts the ownership of the kingdoms of this world. Matthew 4:8, 9. Jesus Himself designates him "the prince of this world" (John 12:31), and John the apostle declares, "the whole world lieth in the evil one" (I John 5:19, Greek).

In the arrangement of the evil trinity Satan is God. He is plainly anti-God.

As to the First Beast.

He, too, claims divine prerogatives, for "he . . . sitteth in the temple of God, shewing himself that he is God" (II Thessalonians 2:4). Moreover, "he . . . [opens] his mouth in blasphemy against God" (Revelation 13:6). However, both his authority and power are delegated to him by the dragon (verse 2), and the great words he spoke and the blasphemies he uttered were "given" to him by the dragon (verses 5, 6). His last act is to make war *against* the Lamb. He is therefore plainly the anti-Christ. Jesus in His Olivet discourse declared there shall be false Christs. Apparently these false Christs will culminate in the one Antichrist. He spoke of them as appearing in the beginning of the tribulation period (Matthew 24:5) and again in the latter half (Matthew 24:23, 24). The first prophecy will be fulfilled in Revelation 6:1, 2; the latter in the time we are now considering.

As to the Second Beast.

He is represented in symbol as a lamb having two horns, by which is probably meant a male lamb, thus denoting strength; however, his real character is seen in the further description, "he spake as a dragon." In the verses following we recognize him as the great actor during the second half of the tribulation period. Eight times in the brief compass of five verses (12-16) he is said to *do* things. The original word is *poieo*. It is more inclusive than our word *do*, as we note by the various words used in its translation—*exercise, cause* (three times), *do* (twice), *make* (twice). Like the former beast he is energized by Satan; hence he both speaks and acts under the impact of that energy.

The following verses clearly show that his acts are a travesty upon those of the Holy Spirit and that in the organism of the diabolical trinity he is the anti-Spirit.

He is the false prophet. He is so designated in 16:13; 19:20; 20:10. As in our chapter, the three evil personages of the satanic trinity are mentioned in close conjunction, and where the three occur in the order of rank as expressed in our chapter thus:

Chapter 13	16:13	19:20	20:10
the dragon	the dragon		devil
the first beast	the beast	the beast	beast
the second beast	the false prophet	the false prophet	false prophet

As will be the case of the false Christs who will finally head up in the one supreme spirit-antichrist, so the false prophets of the end time will finally culminate in *the* false prophet appearing on this occasion.

A few words should be said as to who the second beast is not. He is not the

Antichrist. We have already shown that this title belongs to the first beast, for he, the beast having seven heads and ten horns (13:1; 17:3), it is who makes war against the Lamb. 17:14; 19:19. The distinguishing marks of blasphemy, self-deification, and the demand for universal worship are clearly absent in the description following. On the other hand, he seeks not his own but the glory and honor of the first beast.

He is not (as some have supposed) the pope of Rome. This is plain from the fact that Rome (Babylon) will be destroyed in chapter 18, whereas the false prophet will still be alive and an associate of the first beast at the battle of Armageddon, for it is not till then that he with the first beast will be cast into the lake of fire. Revelation 19:20.

20. The Resurrection from the Dead

The erroneous view is widely prevalent even among religious leaders that "resurrection from the dead" is synonymous in meaning with "rising from death." The fact is, "resurrection from death" (*thanatos*) is not so much as mentioned in the Scriptures. Unless used in a figurative sense, death is a state or condition denoting the absence of life or nonexistence, whereas the dead (*nekroi*) are very much alive; even the wicked dead are said to "stand before God" (Revelation 20:12).

The dead (according to the Biblical usage of the term) are all those who have departed from this life into another mode and place of existence. Since the ascension of Christ the righteous are "with Christ" in paradise or the third heaven (II Corinthians 12:2, 4); the wicked in *hades* (Luke 16:23).

The resurrection of Christ was a resurrection from the dead as the following passage declares: "As they [Peter and John] spake unto the people, the priests, and the captain of the temple, and the Sadducees, came upon them, being grieved that they taught the people, and preached through Jesus the resurrection from the dead" (Acts 4:1, 2).

Had the apostles simply preached the resurrection *of* the dead, the Pharisees would not have joined the Sadducees in their opposition, for they "allow" there is a resurrection *of* the dead. Acts 24:15. What the Pharisees were grieved about was that the resurrection was unique in that it was *from* the dead, implying as it does that the rest of the dead were not raised. It is true that others were raised previously, but these were not raised by their own power and they evidently died afterward. Again mention is made that when Jesus yielded up the ghost, "graves were opened"; however, these came out of the graves after His resurrection, and undoubtedly returned to them.

The Apostle Peter in his first epistle gives a similar testimony, for he says, "[God] . . . hath begotten us again unto a lively hope by the resurrection of Jesus Christ from the dead," that is, from among the dead (persons) remaining in their graves. I Peter 1:3.

The testimony of Luke 20:35. "They which shall be accounted worthy to obtain that world [Greek: *age*], and the resurrection from the dead."

The passage shows that a certain worth or fitness is required in order to qualify for admittance into that age, by which undoubtedly the kingdom age is intended, for no particular fitness is required in having part in the final resurrection preceding the white throne judgment.

The passage is strikingly similar to Hebrews 11:35, where the same Greek word for obtain (*tungchano*) occurs and in place of *resurrection from the dead* as here we have there (as already noted above) *a better resurrection*. Consequently, we infer that the *resurrection from the dead* is identical with *a better resurrection*.

The testimony of Philippians 3:11. According to the most approved reading we should translate, ". . . if by any means I might attain unto the out-resurrection the one [—which is] from the dead."

The apostle counted his seven physical gains (verses 5-7) but loss that he might acquire seven spiritual gains: win Christ, be found in Him, having the righteousness which is of God by faith, know Him, (know) the power of His resurrection, the fellowship of His suffering, and lastly attain unto—have a share in—the out-resurrection the one [—which is] from the dead.

There would be no point in Paul's listing his own personal resurrection as the climax of his gains unless the reference were to a special and *better* resurrection. His testimony is a distinct proof that the resurrection *from the dead* is that of a privileged class only, viz., those of the "first resurrection," which live and reign with Christ a thousand years.

There are two lists of passages consisting of the verbs *anistemi* and *egeiro* in conjunction with the phrase *ek nekron* rendered "rise from the dead." *Anistemi ek nekron* occurs 12 times (9 of which refer to Christ); *egeiro ek nekron* 30 times (22 of which refer to Christ). The renderings are familiar: he is (Greek: *was*) risen from the dead, rose from the dead, was raised from the dead, etc.

We cannot consider this large group of passages pertaining to the rising from the dead. Suffice it to say that thought of the One rising from the dead (that is, from all the rest as to their bodies remaining in the graves) must have been a familiar conception in the days of the apostles.

In the later apostolic period (Acts 26:23) occurs the unique expression, "that Christ should suffer, and that he should be the first that should rise from the dead." A correct rendering, however, shows that this passage does not belong to the "from the dead" list. The literal translation reads: "that Christ should suffer and be first from the resurrection of the dead." The passage is precisely the same as Romans 1:4, where the literal rendering is really *from* or *by* the resurrection of the dead. (See Alford, *in loco*.)

While faithfulness to the original phraseology requires the rendering given in Acts 26:23, the thought expressed is nevertheless the same as that of Colossians 1:18 and Revelation 1:5 where *protokos ek nekron*, that is, the first born or begotten from the dead, occurs. Compare also I Corinthians 15:23, where the resurrection is spoken of under the symbolism of a harvest of which Christ is the first fruits. In these several passages reference is made to Christ's priority in the resurrection of all men.

"I will raise him up at the last day" (John 6:39, 40, 44, 54; 11:24). The righteous clearly are intended in these passages; consequently they belong to the first resurrection. Since John elsewhere speaks of the last hour (I John 2:18, Greek) as already existing, he probably uses the last day as referring to the close of the church age. All the passages considered as belonging to the first resurrection are such as belong to the church age; that is, to the first of the three groups of whom it is said, "This is the first resurrection" (Revelation 20:5b).

[In addition to these considerations the editor would like to add that his thesis for the Bachelor of Theology degree is entitled, *The New Testament Usage of Ek Nekron as Applied to the Doctrine of the Resurrection*. From examining every occurrence of the Greek phrase in context it became unmistakably clear that reference is *never* made to the wicked dead, but always either to Christ or to the righteous dead. No problem should arise, therefore, for the exegete if we conclude that Revelation 20 teaches a separate and distinct resurrection of the righteous dead and is designated as *the first resurrection*, while the wicked do not rise until *the thousand years are finished*. The above-mentioned thesis is cataloged in the library of Eastern Mennonite College as an unpublished thesis.—J. O. Y.]

21. ON NONCONFORMITY

It is only too true that the Christian Church (including her leaders) has departed far from the teaching of Scripture, including that of the Apostle Paul (Romans 12:2; I Timothy 2:9, 10) and Peter (I Peter 3:3, 4). "Be not conformed to this world," in the first passage, means "do not follow the fleeting fashions of this age." The original word for *conform* refers to the sight and sense; hence, fashion, dress, clothing, food, gesture, words, and actions. As to the passages in I Timothy and I Peter, the interpretation which has secured a wide acceptance is that the sense of these passages is not that outward adornment is prohibited but rather that it is permissible provided it be held secondary to the inward adornment; in other words, *some* outward adornment is allowed provided the inward adornment is prized more highly. Now the correctness of an interpretation may be tested by passages where the same crucial words occur. The determining factor here is as to what is intended by the negative (not—Greek: *ou* or *me*) when followed by the adversative (but—Greek: *alla*). Fortunately there are over four hundred passages in the New Testament where the negative is followed by *alla* and which, as here, are not modified by some such word as only or also.

For convenience we will take a few examples from the epistles of Peter:

"Ye were *not* redeemed with corruptible things, as silver and gold . . . *but* with the precious blood of Christ" (I Peter 1:18, 19).

"Being born again, *not* of corruptible seed, *but* of incorruptible, by the word of God, which liveth and abideth for ever" (1:23).

"*Not* the putting away of the filth of the flesh, *but* the answer of a good conscience toward God" (3:21).

"Feed the flock of God . . . *not* for filthy lucre, *but* of a ready mind" (5:2).

"*Neither* as being lords over God's heritage, *but* being ensamples to the flock" (5:3).

"For the prophecy came *not* in old time by the will of man: *but* holy men of God spake as they were moved by the Holy Ghost" (II Peter 1:21).

"God spared *not* the angels that sinned, *but* cast them down to hell" (2:4).

"The Lord is *not* slack concerning his promise . . . *but* is longsuffering to usward" (3:9a).

"*Not* willing that any should perish, *but* that all should come to repentance" (3:9b).

Now let us take I Peter 3:3, 4 and explain it according to the alleged interpretation: "Whose adorning let it be in part that outward adorning of plaiting the hair, and of wearing of gold, and the putting on of apparel, but let it be mostly the hidden man of the heart. . . ." Applying this interpretation to a few of the other examples we would have:

"Ye were redeemed in part with corruptible things, as silver and gold, but mostly by the blood of Christ."

"We were born again partly of corruptible seed, but chiefly . . . by the word of God."

"Feed the flock of God partly for filthy lucre, but principally with a ready mind."

Let the reader apply the interpretation to the remaining passages and if he desires to the several hundred remaining passages where the simple negative is followed by the simple adversative, and he will be convinced all the way of the absurdity of the proposed interpretation.

[This type of exegesis, while to some perhaps not the most convincing, illustrates the place of language syntax. Were Smith to have written a full discussion *On Nonconformity*, he would have shown the relation of Romans 12:1, 2 to the whole study. The Greek word *schema* used in compound in its verbal form in Romans 12:2 by all odds means outward appearance. It is contrasted with the inner experience of the metamorphosis of the mind. Certainly every spiritual-minded person can see the utter folly of adopting unregenerate men's attitudes and practices in bodily appearance. Basic ethical principles are never relative. It would greatly enhance the Christian cause if all professing godliness would practice it!—J. O. Y.]

22. "Son" Applied to Christ

It is noteworthy that "Son of God" never occurs in the Old Testament, even though it is so translated in Daniel 3:25. Literally it would read "a son of the gods." These are the words of Nebuchadnezzar, who knew nothing about the second person of the holy Trinity.

The bare title "Son" likewise does not occur in the Old Testament except in a prophetic sense. Psalm 2:7, 12; Isaiah 7:14; 9:6; Hosea 11:1. The order in time of fulfillment of these passages is as follows:

"A virgin shall conceive, and bear a son" (Isaiah 7:14) and "Unto us a child is born" (Isaiah 9:6) were fulfilled at the birth of Christ. Matthew 1:18-25; Luke 2:7.

Hosea 11:1, "I . . . called my son out of Egypt," was fulfilled when Joseph and Mary returned with the child, Jesus, to the land of Israel. Matthew 2:20, 21.

Psalm 2:7 was fulfilled at the resurrection of Christ. Acts 13:33; Romans 1:4. On this Delitzsch has well remarked: "Paul teaches us in Acts 13:33 (compare Romans 1:4) how the 'today' [this day] is to be understood. The 'today,' according to its proper fulfillment, is the day of Jesus' resurrection. Born from the dead to the life at the right hand of God, He entered on this day. . . ."[35]

Psalm 2:12—"Kiss the Son, lest he be angry, and ye perish from the way, when his wrath is kindled but [for] a little." To *kiss* signifies to do homage and pertains to one's proper attitude toward the Son at His appearing in view of the coming day of wrath.

That the proper application of the "Son of God" to our Lord was still future previous to His coming into the world is plain from the future form of the verbs associated with the titles applied to Him before His birth; e.g., "Thou shalt call his name Jesus" (Matthew 1:21; Luke 1:31). "They shall call his name Emmanuel" (Matthew 1:23). "He . . . shall be called the Son of the Highest" (Luke 1:32). "That holy thing which shall be born of thee shall be called the Son of God" (Luke 1:35).

Since our Lord was repeatedly called the Son of God previous to His resurrection, it would appear more consistent to say that He was first called the Son of God at His birth, and declared or proved to be the Son of God by His resurrection from the dead.

FOOTNOTES, APPENDICES

1. Charles, Vol. I, p. 12.
2. *Ibid.*, p. 13.
3. *Ibid.*, p. CLXXXVIII.
4. Justin Martyr, "First Apology," Chap. LXVII, *The Ante-Nicene Fathers*, Vol. I.
5. Barnabas, "Epistle XV," *op. cit.*, Vol. I.
6. Tertullian, "Ad Nationes," *op. cit.*, Vol. III.
7. Delitzsch, *Biblical Commentary on the Prophecies of Isaiah*, Vol. I, p. 298.
8. *Ibid.*, p. 113.
9. *Ibid.*, p. 424.
10. Lightfoot, p. 38.
11. Delitzsch, *op. cit.*, Vol. I, p. 154.
12. Lange, p. 197.
13. Robertson, *Word Pictures in the New Testament*, Vol. I, p. 83.
14. Vincent, Vol. I, p. 61.
15. Robertson, *Grammar*, pp. 574-80, 596-600.
16. *The Bible Commentary*, Vol. III, p. 271, col. a.
17. Reese, pp. 91, 92.

18. Whitney, Vol. II, pp. 303, 304.

19. Tregelles, *The Hope of Christ's Second Coming*, p. 77.

20. Hoskier, *Concerning the Genesis of the Versions*, Vol. I, p. 392.

21. Reese, p. 92.

22. Seiss, Vol. I, p. 249.

23. Kuyper, pp. 56-62.

24. *Watchword and Truth*, July, 1906 (unverified).

25. Hippolytus, "Fragments from Commentaries" (On Daniel) *The Ante-Nicene Fathers*, Vol. V, p. 181, col. b.

26. Cyprian, "The Treatises of Cyprian," *op. cit.*, Vol. V. 522, col. a.

27. Augustine, "A Treatise on the Merits and Forgiveness of Sins, and on the Baptism of Infants," Schaff, *Nicene and Post-Nicene Fathers*, Vol. V, p. 34, col. b.

28. Scrivener, p. 511.

29. Quotations from the several versions were not verified by the editor.

30. C. J. Ellicott, *Revision of the New Testament*, pp. 46, 47. Copied by Smith in his personal copy of Tischendorf's VIII Edition.

31. Scrivener, p. 113.

32. Schaff, *A Companion to the Greek Testament and the English Version*, p. 239 (footnote).

33. Moorehead, p. 94.

34. *World Almanac and Book of Facts for 1958*.

35. Delitzsch, *Biblical Commentary on the Psalms*, Vol. I, p. 91.

BIBLIOGRAPHY

BIBLIOGRAPHY

Alford, Henry. *The Greek New Testament*. Boston: Lee and Shepard, 1872, 4 vols.

Bible Commentary, The. Edited by F. C. Cook. New York: Charles Scribner's Sons, 1886, 10 vols.

Bullinger, E. W. *How to Enjoy the Bible: or, The "Word" and "the Words," How to Study Them*. London: Eyre and Spottiswoode, 1921.

Charles, R. H. *A Critical and Exegetical Commentary on the Revelation of St. John*. New York: Charles Scribner's Sons, 1920, 2 vols.

Delitzsch, Franz, D.D. *Biblical Commentary on the Prophecies of Isaiah*. Translated from the German by the Rev. James Martin, B.A. Edinburgh: T. & T. Clark, 1879, 2 vols.

Delitzsch, Franz, D.D. *Biblical Commentary on the Psalms*. Translated from the German by the Rev. Francis Bolton, B.A. Edinburgh: T. & T. Clark, 1895, 3 vols.

"Ecclesiasticus," *The Apocrypha*. Translated out of the Greek and Latin tongues, being the version set forth A.D. 1611 compared with the most ancient authorities and revised A.D. 1894. Oxford: At the University Press, 1913.

Glueck, Nelson. *Rivers in the Desert*. New York: Farrar, Straus and Cudahy, 1959.

Godet, F., D.D. *Studies on the New Testament*. London: Hodder and Stoughton (New York: George H. Doran Co.), n.d.

Gray, James M., D.D. *Synthetic Bible Studies*. New edition revised and enlarged. New York: Fleming H. Revell, c. 1906.

Hatch, Edwin. *Essays in Biblical Greek*. Oxford: The Clarendon Press, 1889.

International Standard Bible Encyclopaedia. James Orr, General Editor. Chicago: The Howard-Severance Co., 1915, 5 vols.

Jamieson, Robert, D.D., Rev. A. R. Fausset, A.M., Rev. David Brown, D.D. *A Commentary, Critical, Practical, and Explanatory on the Old and New Testaments*. New York: Fleming H. Revell Co., n.d., 6 vols.

Kuyper, Abraham. *The Revelation of St. John*. Translated from the Dutch by John Hendrik de Vries. Grand Rapids: William Eerdmans Publishing Co., 1935.

Lange, John Peter, D.D. *The Gospel According to Matthew*. Translated from the third German edition with additions, original and selected by Philip Schaff, DD. New York: Charles Scribner and Co., 1870.

Lightfoot, J. B., D.D. *The Christian Ministry*. New York: Thomas Whittaker, 1883.

Moorehead, William G. *Outline Studies in the New Testament*. New York: Fleming H. Revell, 1910.

Moulton, Richard G., M.A., Ph.D. *The Modern Reader's Bible*. New York: The Macmillan Co., 1918.

Nestle, Eberhard. *Introduction to the Textual Criticism of the Greek New Testament.* London: Williams and Norgate, 1901.

Newton, Benjamin Wills. *Thoughts on the Apocalypse.* London: Partridge and Oakey, 1853.

Pierson, A. T. *The Bible and Spiritual Criticism.* New York: The Baker and Taylor Co., 1905.

Ramsay, W. M. *The Letters to the Seven Churches.* London: Hodder and Stoughton, n.d.

Reese, The Rev. Alexander, *The Approaching Advent of Christ.* London: Marshall, Morgan and Scott, Ltd., n.d.

Roberts, Rev. Alexander, D.D., and James Donaldson, LL.D. *The Ante-Nicene Fathers.* 8 vols. Buffalo: The Christian Literature Co., 1886.

Barnabas, Epistle of (Epistle XV), Vol. I.

Clement of Alexandria, "The Stromata," Vol. II.

Clement of Alexandria, "Who Is the Rich Man That Shall Be Saved?" Vol. II.

Cyprian, "The Treatises of Cyprian," Vol. V.

"Epistle of Mathetes, a Disciple of the Apostles, to Diognetus," Vol. I.

Hippolytus, "Against the Heresy of One Noetus" (Sec. 6), Vol. V.

Hippolytus, "Fragments from Commentaries" (On Daniel), Vol. V.

Hippolytus, "On the Twelve Apostles," Vol. V.

Justin Martyr, "Dialogue with Trypho," Vol. I.

Justin Martyr, "First Apology" (Chap. LXVII), Vol. I.

"Martyrdom of Polycarp, The," Vol. I.

Origen, "De Principiis" (Bk. I, Chap. II, Sec. 10), Vol. IV.

Tertullian, "Ad Nationes," Vol. III.

Tertullian, "Apology," Vol. III.

Tertullian, "De Anima," Vol. III.

Tertullian, "On Modesty," Vol. IV.

Tertullian, "Prescription Against Heretics," Vol. III.

Victorinus, "Commentary on the Apocalypse of the Blessed John," Vol. VII.

Robertson, A. T. *A Grammar of the Greek New Testament in the Light of Historical Research.* Nashville: Broadman Press, 1934.

Robertson, A. T. *Word Pictures in the New Testament.* New York: Harper and Brothers, 1933, 6 vols.

Schaff, Philip, D.D. *A Companion to the Greek Testament and the English Version.* New York: Harper and Brothers, 1883.

Schaff, Philip, D.D., LL.D. *A Select Library of the Nicene and Post-Nicene Fathers of the Christian Church.* 14 vols. Buffalo: The Christian Literature Co., 1886.

Augustine, "A Treatise on the Merits and Forgiveness of Sins, and on the Baptism of Infants."

Scrivener, Frederick Henry Ambrose, M.A., D.C.L., LL.D. *A Plain Introduction to the Criticism of the New Testament.* Third edition. Cambridge: Deighton, Bell and Co., 1883.

Seiss, J. A., D.D. *The Apocalypse.* Tenth edition. New York: Charles C. Cook, 1909, 3 vols.

Simons, Menno. "A Fundamental Doctrine," *The Complete Works of Menno Simons.* Elkhart, Ind.: John F. Funk and Brother, 1871.

Simpich, Frederick. "Change Comes to Bible Lands," *The National Geographic Magazine,* Vol. LXXIV, Dec. 1938, pp. 695-750.

Souter, Alexander. *Novum Testamentum Graece.* Oxonii: E. Typographeo Clarendoniano, 1910.

Stier, Rudolf. *The Words of the Risen Saviour and Commentary on the Epistle of James.* Translated from the German by William B. Pope. Edinburgh: T. & T. Clark, 1866.

Stuart, Moses. *A Commentary on the Apocalypse*. New York: Van Nostrand and Terrant, 1851, 2 vols.

Swete, H. B. *The Apocalypse of St. John*. London: Macmillan, 1911.

Thayer, Joseph Henry, D.D. *A Greek-English Lexicon of the New Testament*. New York: The American Book Co., *c.* 1889.

Tregelles, S. P., LL.D. *The Book of Revelation*. London: Bagster & Son, 1859.

Trench, Richard Chenevix. *Commentary on the Epistles to the Seven Churches*. London: Macmillan, 1883.

Van Braght, Thieleman J. *The Martyrs' Mirror*. Translated from the Dutch by Joseph F. Sohm. Scottdale, Pa.: Mennonite Publishing House, 1938.

Vincent, Marvin R., D.D. *Word Studies in the New Testament*. 4 vols. New York: Charles Scribner's Sons, 1887.

Whitney, Rev. S. W., A.M. *The Revisers' Greek Text*. Boston: Silver, Burdett & Co., 1892, 2 vols.

World Almanac and Book of Facts for 1958, The. Edited by Harry Hansen. New York: New York World-Telegram.

Yoder, J. Otis. *The New Testament Usage of Ek Nekron as Applied to the Doctrine of the Resurrection*. Unpublished thesis, Eastern Mennonite College, Harrisonburg, Va.